Global Political Economy

Global Political Economy

Evolution and Dynamics

Third Edition

Robert O'Brien and Marc Williams

palgrave
macmillan

First edition 2004
Second edition 2007
Third edition 2010

Published by
PALGRAVE MACMILLAN

Palgrave Macmillan in the UK is an imprint of Macmillan Publishers Limited, registered in England, company number 785998, of Houndmills, Basingstoke, Hampshire RG21 6XS.

Palgrave Macmillan in the US is a division of St Martin's Press LLC, 175 Fifth Avenue, New York, NY 10010.

Palgrave Macmillan is the global academic imprint of the above companies and has companies and representatives throughout the world.

Palgrave® and Macmillan® are registered trademarks in the United States, the United Kingdom, Europe and other countries

ISBN 978–0–230–24120–6 hardback
ISBN 978–0–230–24121–3 paperback

This book is printed on paper suitable for recycling and made from fully managed and sustained forest sources. Logging, pulping and manufacturing processes are expected to conform to the environmental regulations of the country of origin.

A catalogue record for this book is available from the British Library.

A catalog record for this book is available from the Library of Congress.

10   9   8   7   6   5   4   3
19   18   17   16   15   14   13   12   11

Printed in Great Britain by the MPG Books Group, Bodmin and King's Lynn

To our daughters

Isabella and Louisa

The world is yours to explore and improve

Contents

List of Boxes, Tables, Figures and Maps   xiii

Preface to the Third Edition   xvi

List of Abbreviations   xviii

Introduction   1

PART I   THEORETICAL PERSPECTIVES

1   **Approaches to Global Political Economy**   9
     Locating the field   9
         Economics   10
         Political Science   11
         Political Economy   12
         International Relations   13
     Understanding the global political economy   14
         The economic nationalist perspective   17
         The liberal perspective   21
         The critical perspective   24

2   **Methods and Theorists**   30
     Methodological issues   30
         Case studies and large n studies   30
         Rational choice   32
         Institutionalism   34
         Constructivism   36
     Four theorists and today's debates   37
         Susan Strange – unorthodox realist   38
         Robert Keohane – liberal institutionalist   39
         Robert Cox – historical materialist   41
         John Ruggie – constructivist practioner   43
     Where are we now? Globalization and IPE   45
     Approach of the book   48

PART II EVOLUTION

3 Forging a World Economy 1400–1800   53
   Regions of the world economy   55
      The Middle East   57
      China   58
      India   60
      Africa   61
      Americas   61
      Europe   62
   European expansion   69
      Into the Americas   71
      Along Africa: the slave and triangular trade   74
      On the peripheries of Asia   78
   Conclusion   81

4 The Industrial Revolution, Pax Britannica and Imperialism   87
   The industrial revolution   88
      What was the industrial revolution?   88
      Why Britain? Why then?   92
      What did the others do?   94
   Pax Britannica   95
      The gold standard and capital flows   96
      Free trade   99
      Balance of power   102
   Renewed imperialism   106
   Conclusion   111

5 The 20th Century: World Wars and the Post-1945 Order   116
   War and economic disorder   116
      The world wars   117
      Inter-war economic failure   119
   The post-1945 order   125
      The United States and the Western economic system   126
      The struggle for development   131
      State transformation   133
      International organizations and governance   135
      The information revolution   138
   Conclusion   141

PART III   DYNAMICS

6   **International Trade**   147
   Definitions   147
   Theoretical perspectives: free trade and protectionism   150
   Major developments   157
     Growth and protectionism   157
     Changing institutional arrangements   163
   Key issues   169
     Developing country interests   (170)
     Regional trade agreements   177
     Legitimacy   180
   Conclusion   183

7   **Transnational Production**   184
   Definitions   186
   Theoretical perspectives: explaining the growth of TNCs   190
   Major developments   193
     The globalization of production   194
     Changing organizational principles   201
   Key issues   204
     Re-evaluating the benefits of FDI   204
     State–firm interactions   210
     Regulating capital   214
   Conclusion   216

8   **The Global Financial System**   217
   Definitions and background   217
   Theoretical perspectives: the Mundell–Fleming model   221
   Major developments   223
     The move to floating exchange rates   223
     Financial innovation   227
     The 1980s debt crisis   232
   Key issues   236
     Changes in regional and reserve currencies   238
     Financial crises and international regulatory mechanisms   243
     Global financial crisis   249
   Conclusion   253

9   **Global Division of Labour**   255
   Definitions   255
   Theoretical perspectives: Adam Smith and his critics   258
   Major developments   262

Changes in the production process   262
From the new international to the global division of labour   263
Key issues   267
Global restructuring: the rise of China and India   267
The struggle for workers' rights in a global economy   271
The division of labour and global stability   275
Conclusion   279

10   **Gender**   280
Definitions and background   280
Theoretical perspectives: GPE as if gender mattered   284
Major developments   288
Women in the world economy: employment trends and
prospects   288
Gender and global public policy   292
Key issues   298
The feminization of poverty   298
Globalization of reproductive work   300
Gender and global restructuring   303
Conclusion   306

11   **Economic Development**   307
Definitions   310
Theoretical perspectives on growth and development   315
Major developments   322
Development and national capitalism, 1947–81   323
Development, neoliberalism and beyond, 1982–2009   327
Key issues   331
The organization of development   331
Debt and debt relief   336
North–South conflict   339
Conclusion   342

12   **Global Environmental Change**   344
Definitions and background   345
Theoretical perspectives: IPE and environmental studies   348
IPE debates   348
Environmental studies debates   351
Major developments   355
Bringing the environment in   356
Mainstreaming environmentalism   361
Key issues   364
Sustainable development   364

Trade and environmental degradation 368
Climate change negotiations 370
Conclusion 372

13 **Ideas** 374
Definitions 374
Theoretical perspectives: ideas about ideas 375
Major developments 379
The information revolution and the information society 379
The rise and stall of the Washington Consensus 383
Key issues 387
Technological diffusion 387
Property rights and life (HIV/AIDS) 389
Ideas, interests and the global financial crisis 391
Conclusion 396

14 **Security** 398
Definitions: three views of security 398
Theoretical perspectives: integrating security and political
economy 402
Major developments 407
The Cold War security structure 408
The post-Cold War security structure 410
Key issues 414
Economic statecraft and security 415
Transnational crime 418
Disease, pandemics and security 420
Conclusion 422

15 **Governing the Global Political Economy** 424
Definitions 424
Theoretical perspectives: whither the state? 425
Major developments 428
Proliferation of governance levels 430
Proliferation of actors 434
The Global Compact 438
21st-century challenges 440
Development and growth 440
Equality and justice 443
Democracy and regulation 446
Conclusion 449

IPE?

16   Conclusion: Issues in Contemporary GPE Theory   **451**
    Understanding GPE: the eclectic framework revisited   452
    Trends in contemporary GPE theory   455
        Consolidation   455
        Integration   456
        Expansion   458
    Conclusion   460

Glossary   462

References   467

Index   503

List of Boxes, Tables, Figures and Maps

Boxes

2.1	Prisoner's Dilemma	34
3.1	The utility of money	65
3.2	Banks and financial instability	67
3.3	Ayutthaya vs Venice	80
4.1	The gold standard	98
4.2	Comparative advantage	100
4.3	Imperialism in the Congo	104
4.4	Global famines	110
5.1	Decolonization and violence	132
6.1	The costs of protectionism: a liberal perspective	153
6.2	Health risks and hormone-treated beef	162
6.3	Developing country coalitions in the WTO	171
6.4	The Cairns Group	173
6.5	The cotton initiative	174
6.6	Australia and Regional Trade Agreements	178
6.7	Democracy and the WTO	181
7.1	Global commodity chains	186
7.2	Vertical, horizontal and conglomerate TNCs	189
7.3	Government regulation, international capital and financial instability: the case of South Korea	198
7.4	Export processing zones: an ILO perspective	200
7.5	Wal-Mart, the TNC	205
8.1	Balance-of-payments confusion	220
8.2	The United States–China financial relationship	228
8.3	Microcredit: financial innovation for the poor	231
8.4	Debt and AIDS	236
8.5	Dollarization, randization and pulaization in Zimbabwe	240
8.6	Key facts about Chinese funding of US debt	242
8.7	Spread of turmoil in the US financial industry	251
9.1	Globalizing elites	265
10.1	Feminization as devalorization	281
10.2	Gender inequality facts	282
10.3	Measuring the global gender gap	282

10.4	The glass ceiling	291
10.5	Gender and the Millennium Development Goals (MDGs)	296
11.1	The Millennium Development Goals	308
11.2	Implementing the MDGs: targets to be achieved by 2015	309
11.3	Confucianism and economic development	322
11.4	Group of 77 membership, 2009	326
11.5	Structural adjustment: the case of Mexico	328
11.6	Multilateral debt relief initiative: country coverage, 2009	338
12.1	Technocentric and ecocentric approaches to sustainability	353
12.2	Advancing environmentalism: the United Nations Conference on the Human Environment (UNCHE)	357
12.3	Advancing environmentalism: the United Nations Conference on Environment and Development (UNCED)	358
12.4	Advancing environmentalism: the United Nations World Summit on Sustainable Development (WSSD)	359
12.5	Bhopal	360
12.6	The Summers memo	363
13.1	The uneven distribution of knowledge: patents and Nobel Prize winners	388
13.2	Bioprospectors and biopiracy	391
13.3	Twelve financial deregulation policies, 1998–2008	394
14.1	Food security	401
14.2	Defence procurement	405
14.3	The securitization of HIV/AIDs	422
15.1	The BRICs	427
15.2	The covert world	437
15.3	The Global Call to Action Against Poverty	446

Figures

8.1	Developing-country external debt as a percentage of GNP	237
8.2	Regional averages: external debt as a percentage of GNP	237
9.1	Gender inequality in economic activity	257

Tables

1.1	Interpretations of the Asian financial crisis	16
1.2	Comparing the perspectives	27
3.1	Summary of European expansionist activity	70
5.1	Decline in value of selected high-technology stocks, 2000–3	140
6.1	Tariff rates on industrial products for selected WTO members	149

6.2 Growth in the volume of world trade and production by
  major product groups, 2000–7 158
6.3 Value of world merchandise trade by region, 2007 160
6.4 GATT negotiating rounds 165
6.5 WTO Ministerial Conferences 168
6.6 World merchandise trade, 1948–2007 169
6.7 GDP composition by sector: agriculture, 2009 172
7.1 The 25 largest corporations by revenues 185
7.2 World FDI flows, 2005–8 187
7.3 Growth of global capital flows 197
7.4 Cross-border mergers and alliances, 2000–8 203
8.1 National expenditure on social services vs debt 235
9.1 Remittances from migrants 265
9.2 Remittance flows to developing countries, 2002–7 266
10.1 Male and female labour force participation rates (LFPR),
  2007 289
11.1 Social indicators of development for selected countries, 2005 312
11.2 HDI vs GNP ranking 314
11.3 Economic and welfare indicators for Asian NICs 319
11.4 Comparison of Latin American and East Asian economies,
  1965–80 321
11.5 IBRD lending by region, fiscal years 2000 and 2008 332
11.6 IBRD lending by theme, fiscal year 2008 333
11.7 IBRD lending by sector, fiscal year 2008 334
11.8 Ratio of external debt to GDP, 2001–5 337
12.1 A sample of environmental legislation in Australia 362
15.1 IMF voting rights vs population 433

Maps

3.1 Regions of the 15th-century world economy 56
3.2 European political economy 1400–1500 63
3.3 Transatlantic triangular trade 77
4.1 Pre- and post-scramble Africa 109

Preface to the Third Edition

The aim of the book is to provide the tools that will enable readers to understand and explain developments in the global political economy. As a result the main structure of the book remains unchanged from previous editions. This structure – a discussion of theoretical perspectives; a survey of the historical evolution of the world economy; and exploration of key frameworks and structures of the global political economy – has proved successful. Nevertheless, we recognize the importance of contemporary events and therefore all of the chapters have been revised to take account of significant changes in the global political economy since the second edition was published in 2007. The global financial and economic crises (2008–9) have transformed the landscape of the global political economy and this edition takes account of the impact of these crises on the structures and processes of the global economy.

This edition is different from the previous editions in a number of ways. First, the original theoretical chapter has been expanded into two chapters and these have been grouped then under a new section, 'Theoretical Perspectives'. Chapter 1 now includes a new section, 'Locating the Field', meant to orient readers to the field and its relationship to other academic fields of study. In addition, we have expanded the methods content from a box to a section and added one person to our key figures section to reflect the growing theoretical diversity of some parts of the field. Second, while writing the previous books we were conscious of a glaring omission – consideration of the security dimensions of global political economy (GPE). This version rectifies that problem by including a chapter on security. Third, we have also updated the book to take account of issues that were in the background in the early part of this century, but have recently become more prominent. These issues include the politics of food, patterns of consumption and new forms of financial crisis. Finally, each chapter has been revised to take account of new events and scholarship.

It has been a pleasure to continue working together to produce this third edition of our textbook. Our joint efforts are aided by many others. We would like to thank the anonymous reviewers of this and previous editions. We have greatly benefited from their comments and suggestions, although we may not have responded in all the ways that they might have hoped. We also owe an ongoing debt to present and former colleagues and students at the universities of Sussex, New South Wales and McMaster. Numerous instructors and students at other universities have also provided helpful feedback. Finally, thanks also go to our supportive publisher Steven Kennedy for timely and pertinent advice. Although we greatly appreciate everyone's help, the errors remain ours alone.

ROBERT O'BRIEN
MARC WILLIAMS

List of Abbreviations

AEZ	Agri-Export Zone
AFL-CIO	American Federation of Labor and Congress of Industrial Organizations
APEC	Asia-Pacific Economic Cooperation
ASEAN	Association of Southeast Asian Nations
BIS	Bank for International Settlements
BST	Bovine Somatropin
CEDAW	Convention on the Elimination of All Forms of Discrimination Against Women
COMECON	Council for Mutual Economic Assistance
CP	Commercial Paper
CTM	Confederation of Mexican Workers
DSU	Dispute Settlement Understanding
ECB	European Central Bank
ECPAT	End Child Prostitution in Asian Tourism
ECSC	European Coal and Steel Community
EEC	European Economic Community
EFTA	European Free Trade Association
EOI	Export Oriented Industrialization
EPZ	Export Processing Zone
ERM	Exchange Rate Mechanism
EU	European Union
FDI	Foreign Direct Investment
FSF	Financial Stability Forum
FZLN	Zapatista Front of National Liberation
G-5	Group of 5
G-7	Group of 7
G-8	Group of 8
G-20	Group of 20
G-77	Group of 77
G-90	Group of 90
GATS	General Agreement on Trade in Services
GATT	General Agreement on Tariffs and Trade
GDP	Gross Domestic Product
GNP	Gross National Product
GPE	Global Political Economy
HDI	Human Development Index

HIPC	Heavily Indebted Poor Countries
IBRD	International Bank for Reconstruction and Development
ICFTU	International Confederation of Free Trade Unions
ICSID	International Centre for the Settlement of Investment Disputes
IDA	International Development Association
IEOs	International Economic Organizations
IFC	International Finance Corporation
ILO	International Labour Organization
IMF	International Monetary Fund
IMS	International Monetary System
IPE	International Political Economy
IPRs	Intellectual Property Rights
IR	International Relations
ISI	Import Substitution Industrialization
ITO	International Trade Organization
JIT	Just-In-Time
KMP	Peasant Movement of the Philippines
KRRS	Karnataka State Farmers' Association
MAD	Mutual Assured Destruction
MAI	Multilateral Agreement on Investment
MDGs	Millennium Development Goals
MDRI	Multilateral Debt Relief Initiative
MEA	Multilateral Environmental Agreement
MERCOSUR	Common Market of the South
MFA	Multi-Fibre Agreement
MFN	Most Favoured Nation
MIC	Methyl Isocyanate
MIGA	Multilateral Investment Guarantee Agency
MNC	Multinational Corporation
MNE	Multinational Enterprise
MST	Landless Workers' Movement
MTN	Multilateral Trade Negotiations
NAFTA	North American Free Trade Agreement
NAM	Non-Aligned Movement
NATO	North Atlantic Treaty Organization
NGOs	Non-Governmental Organizations
NICs	Newly Industrializing Countries
NIEO	New International Economic Order
NTBs	Non-Tariff Barriers
ODA	Official Development Assistance
OECD	Organisation for Economic Co-operation and Development

OLI	Ownership, Location and Internalization
OPEC	Organization of Petroleum Exporting Countries
PGA	Peoples' Global Action
PPMs	Process and Production Methods
R&D	Research and Development
S&D	Special and Differential Treatment
SAPs	Structural Adjustment Programmes
SPS	Sanitary and Phytosanitary Measures
TBT	Technical Barriers to Trade
TNC	Transnational Corporation
TNE	Transnational Enterprise
TPRM	Trade Policy Review Mechanism
TRIMs	Trade-Related Investment Measures
TRIPs	Trade-Related Intellectual Property Rights
UN	United Nations
UNCED	United Nations Conference on Environment and Development
UNCHE	United Nations Conference on the Human Environment
UNCTAD	United Nations Conference on Trade and Development
UNDP	United Nations Development Programme
UNEP	United Nations Environment Programme
UNGA	United Nations General Assembly
UNHCR	United Nations High Commissioner for Refugees
UNICEF	United Nations Children's Fund
VERs	Voluntary Export Restraints
WHO	World Health Organization
WTO	World Trade Organization

Introduction

During 2008 a simmering financial crisis in the United States bubbled to the surface and rapidly spread through the US housing, banking, investment and credit markets. Major financial firms disappeared while many others tottered on the brink of collapse. The US government was forced to spend billions of dollars to support the financial sector as the country plunged into recession. The credit crisis spread internationally, bankrupting Iceland and forcing the United Kingdom into a severe economic downturn. The effects of US financial woes were felt much further afield than Europe. The crisis reduced economic output in most countries and posed a severe threat to developing states as their sources of aid, credit and export markets dried up. A global economy that had previously appeared stable and prosperous had very quickly transformed into a fragile and dangerous place.

The global financial crisis subsequently led to a global economic crisis. The implications for all of the issues – trade, production, finance, labour, gender, development, environment, ideas, security and governance – discussed in Part III of the book have been profound. We will briefly recap some of the consequences of the global economic crisis here. The international trading system has experienced the largest contraction since the 1930s (WTO, 2009a); the crisis has turned 'global companies into national champions' (Pisani-Ferry and Santos, 2009, p. 10); the global financial crisis has raised serious questions about regulation, the global financial architecture and the fragility of the global financial system (UNCTAD, 2009a); falling economic growth has led to rising unemployment and a worsening jobs crisis (ILO, 2009a); women's vulnerability was heightened as a result of the crisis (World Bank, 2009a); in the developing world, 'Major advances in the fight against extreme poverty from 1990 to 2005 ... are likely to have stalled' (United Nations, 2009a, p. 4); in terms of the environment, the financial crisis has sparked debate on whether it will, for example, have a negative impact on efforts to halt climate change (*Guardian*, 2008); in the realm of ideas as national governments rolled out stimulus packages it brought a challenge to neoliberal ideas long dominant in policy-making circles (Harvey, 2009); security has been undermined as the crisis has exacerbated conflict (Bakrania and Lucas, 2009); and it has already led to a change in global governance with the rise to prominence of the G-20 (Helleiner and Pagliari, 2009).

This book is not about the financial crisis, but it does provide the tools to understand the origins and implications of such a crisis. Our text introduces

1

readers to the origins, evolution and operation of the global political economy which spawned the financial crisis. By studying the global political economy we can gain a better understanding of the events that shape our world.

When using the term 'global political economy' we are referring to the environment from the last quarter of the 20th century until today. This is an era where states, corporations and citizens struggle to order their environment in a world characterized by intensified globalization. We reserve the term 'global' to describe the complex political economy of this period, while for previous eras we speak of the world economy or international political economy. However, many people prefer the term 'international political economy' to refer to this subject matter. As a result, we will still use the term 'IPE' to refer to the academic field of study surrounding the interaction of economic and political phenomena across state borders.

International Political Economy (IPE) emerged as a subject of study in Western universities in the mid-1970s. From its tentative beginnings as one course within a degree programme, IPE has developed into a distinct subfield of International Relations. In some universities it has outgrown political science departments to take on a larger interdisciplinary flavour. Similar to its 'parent' disciplines, IPE remains a field in which different theoretical traditions present the student with competing descriptions of 'reality' and conflicting explanatory frameworks. A review of the teaching and study of IPE in the 1990s identified both continuities and change in the issues considered important by scholars (Denemark and O'Brien, 1997). Some issues such as the impact of transnational corporations, international finance and international trade have remained central to the core issues covered in IPE courses. The centrality given to issues such as Third World development and the North–South conflict have varied over the past three decades. Meanwhile, issues such as East–West relations, energy and the impact of producer cartels have vanished to be replaced by a focus on environmental concerns and gender. In terms of a broad overview of the international political economy, analysis has shifted from a concern with interdependence to an obsession with globalization.

The aim of this textbook is to provide an accessible introduction to the study of IPE. In pursuit of this aim, it follows two strategies that distinguish it from many other IPE textbooks. First, it adopts an historical approach to the study of IPE and offers students, the interested public and scholars a broad overview of how the modern global political economy has come into being. Instead of beginning with an analysis of contemporary global political and economic structures, the book seeks to provide an easily accessible but brief history that draws out important factors in the creation of our present situation. For example, every major IPE text discusses post-war monetary relations, but few take the time to explain the origins of monetary systems and the various forms of money. In our teaching we have found that the best way for students to appreciate the nuances of the present international monetary system is to consider the development of money and credit in its historical context. Second, the book seeks to move beyond the repetition of the three dominant theoretical perspectives (mercantilism, liberalism, Marxism) on IPE as a framework of analysis. It seeks to reflect both the developments in IPE scholarship in the past 30 years and the main debates between orthodox and heterodox scholars through attention to a broad range of themes, issues and perspectives in IPE. Unorthodox or heterodox approaches to IPE have become much more developed since the first wave of IPE texts in the 1980s by Joan Spero (1981), Robert Gilpin (1987), Susan Strange (1988), Stephen Gill and David Law (1988). Ecological, feminist, neo-Gramscian and post-structural approaches now compete with traditional perspectives and shed new light on old problems. Central to our strategy is a framework that integrates material and ideational aspects of IPE.

Plan of the Book

The text is divided into three parts. Part I locates the field and examines key theoretical approaches and methodologies (Chapters 1 and 2). The complexities of the global political economy cannot be properly understood through a study of the 'facts' without any recourse to theories of IPE. Because the meaning and impact of economic and political change are controversial and contested, Chapter 1 provides an introduction to the main competing perspectives in IPE. It begins by locating the field among a range of disciplines – economics, political science, political economy and international relations. The second part of the chapter introduces the traditional IPE debate between economic nationalism, liberalism and critical perspectives (primarily Marxism). We provide an overview of these schools of thought by focusing on the key actors, dynamics and views on conflict and cooperation. Chapter 2 introduces readers to some of the varied methods used by scholars in the field. It provides an overview of case studies, rational choice, institutionalism and constructivism. The second part of the chapter outlines how the field has developed since the 1970s by considering the careers and work of four prominent IPE scholars (Susan Strange, Robert Keohane, Robert Cox and John Ruggie) and the issues around which existing scholarship clusters. The chapter concludes by outlining the book's own theoretical approach.

Part II (Chapters 3–5) considers the evolution and eventual domination of a European-based world economy. Chapter 3 provides an overview of key historical processes that led to the transformation of regional economies and the beginnings of the creation of the contemporary global economic system. It is organized into two main sections. The first contrasts various regional political economies – the Middle East, China, India, Africa, the Americas and Europe in the early 15th century. The second section of Chapter 3 charts the expansion of a European-centred international political economy into other areas of the world, namely Africa, the Americas and Asia. It stresses the variety of patterns of interaction including slavery, genocide, war and trade. The chapter assesses the varied pattern of European–non-European interaction. Chapter 4 examines the domestic and international basis of British power in the mid-19th century, the development of the Pax Britannica as a structure of international governance and the rise of imperialism in the 19th century.

Chapter 5 turns its attention to the 20th century, beginning with an assessment of the impact of the two world wars on the international political economy. It then moves on to an overview by examining the key post-war developments of the global political economy. Attention is drawn to the five following trends: the role of the United States as a major power and the creation of a Western system; the process of decolonization and the pursuit of development; the changes in the structure of the state; the growth in international organizations in both the inter- and non-governmental sectors; and the rapid pace of technological innovation and how this is both changing the form of economic activity and serving as a source of power. Finally, the chapter concludes by raising the issue of globalization.

Part III (Chapters 6–15) focuses on the recent dynamics of the global political economy. In one sense the global political economy can be treated as a single whole, as we do in Part II of this book, but in another sense it is also composed of various structures or frameworks each with its own set of actors, processes, institutions and rules. Of course, many actors participate in more than one framework and there are linkages between them. Nevertheless, in common with standard texts in economics and political economy we have classified the diverse practices in the world economy into certain key frameworks. We do not claim that any single framework is dominant, but we do suggest that the ten frameworks (trade, production, finance, labour, gender, development, environment, ideas, security and governance) analysed in this book constitute critical spheres of activity in the world economy.

The argument in each chapter in Part III, with the exception of Chapter 16, is divided into four sections – definitions, theoretical perspectives, major developments and key issues. The section on definitions provides an introduction to some of the key terms and concepts used in analysis of the particular framework. The aim here is not to proffer definitive definitions but rather to discuss some of the key issues pertinent to an understanding of the framework. The theoretical perspectives section is important in raising key issues related to the normative elements of the global political economy framework. It shows the importance of knowledge in the construction of frameworks or structures in the global political economy. In our analysis, knowledge and knowledge claims are co-constitutive parts of the framework. That is, knowledge is internal and integral to the structure rather than an external set of considerations. What counts as knowledge is not secondary but rather a central feature of the political economy framework. The beliefs that actors hold about cause–effect relations will influence the actions they will take. Within the world economy, states, firms, international organizations and social movement actors have conflicting views about the issues under scrutiny. In keeping with the historical focus of this book, the section on major developments provides an overview of key changes within the particular framework in the period since 1945. Finally, in each chapter we focus on three current issues. There are other equally important issues that cannot be addressed in each chapter, but we have chosen ones that combine topicality with relevance to the evolution of the global political economy and contrasting IPE perspectives

The final chapter (16) reviews the theoretical ground covered in the text and examines the state of theory in IPE today. It identifies three trends: consolidation, integration and fragmentation. We hope that after readers have completed this chapter and the book they will have a working understanding of the global political economy.

Globalization

Writing at the beginning of the 21st century it is impossible to ignore the phenomenon of globalization. An intense debate currently exists between proponents and opponents of what may be termed 'globalization studies'. The book enters the globalization debate through a number of its concerns. One of the central issues of contention in the controversy over globalization is that of historical evidence. In delineating the scope, nature, depth and breadth of change in the global economy this book contributes to this debate. Moreover, in so far as globalization is a process of historical change rather than a specific condition, the evidence here contributes to an assessment of this process. Second, in charting the evolution of the modern state the book confronts a central issue in the globalization debate. We reveal the historical development of the modern state, and consequently challenge arguments that present essentialized portraits of the state.

Our analysis in Part III is informed by the evolving nature of globalization. We believe that the intensification of globalization since the early 1970s has changed the world political economy from an international to a global undertaking. While there are some who suggest that talk of globalization is overblown (Hirst and Thompson, 1996), we are of the view that the decreasing significance of time and space as barriers to human interaction is having a profound impact upon the organization of production, the exchange of products and services, the circulation of finance, the gendered division of labour, the possibilities for development, the ecology of the planet, the transmission and power of ideas, the pursuit of security, the mobilization of political forces and forms of national and international governance. The spread of economic relations worldwide has had a significant impact upon how people live their lives and how governance is practised. Our book explores these issues in further detail in the following chapters.

Part I

Theoretical Perspectives

Chapter 1

Approaches to Global Political Economy

In its present form, the field of Global Political Economy (GPE) is a relatively new undertaking at Western universities. This chapter introduces readers to the field. The first section begins the task by locating GPE in relationship to a number of key disciplines, especially political science and economics. The second section helps readers to begin the task of understanding the global political economy by considering three of the main theoretical traditions that have inspired scholars in the field – economic nationalism, liberalism and critical theories. The following chapter deepens our theoretical understanding by exploring the issue of method in GPE and considering the work and careers of four influential theorists.

Locating the field

To situate the study of global political economy among other subjects it is useful to make some preliminary comments about the organization of knowledge in the social sciences. Although Western knowledge and universities are separated into distinct subjects, fields and departments, this was not always the case. Before 1900, intellectuals often worked on a number of different fields that would not fit into today's compartments. Thus, Adam Smith, who is often seen as the founder of liberal economics in the late 1700s, was a professor of Moral Philosophy rather than an economist. As knowledge has grown fields have become more specialized. Those interested in the culture of other societies drift into anthropology departments, those interested in the operations of society into sociology, people concerned with the study of power and politics into political science departments and those focused upon the economy into economics departments. Each field has developed its own theoretical and methodological approaches to answering a particular set of questions. The same subject can be examined in different disciplines from a variety of perspectives.

The specialization of knowledge in the social sciences corresponded with the solidification of nation-states in Western Europe. Social sciences disciplines increasingly became national disciplines. People would study the French society or the US economy in isolation from other societies or economies. In some respects this made sense. National states were becoming more developed and their regulatory activity was having an increasingly significant impact upon the people within the hardening borders. However, this methodological nationalism meant that the connections between societies and their relationship to the outside world were neglected.

Global political economy tries to bridge some of these historic divides. It crosses the boundaries between the study of politics and economics, as well as the national and the international. Depending upon the approach, it will also draw upon other fields such as geography or history. We'll briefly examine some of the neighbouring fields to develop our understanding of global political economy's place.

Economics

The word 'economics' comes from the Greek *economia*. In its original use it meant the management of the household. Over the centuries, study of the economy has varied greatly. Today the discipline is dominated by a particular approach to the economy which is 'neoclassical' economics.

The central problem for neoclassical economists is how to allocate scarce resources. Human desires are seen as unlimited, while the resources to fulfil them are finite. The problem then becomes how to allocate those resources most efficiently. The solution to this problem is to be found in the efficient operation of markets. Markets are places where informed individuals can make mutually advantageous exchanges. Consumers became very important in this approach. Well-informed individuals acting upon their own economic self interest will send signals about what should be produced. Left alone, the sum of these individual choices will result in the most efficient allocation of resources.

Neoclassical economists sought to fashion their subject into a science and separate it from the study of politics and philosophy. Whereas political decisions might be influenced by emotions, economic decisions are based upon rationality. Politics and politicians are often seen to block the operation of the free market and prevent it from operating efficiently. In an attempt to make the discipline of economics more scientific, many modern economics departments have turned increasingly to using mathematical models to analyse the economy and advance arguments in favour of particular policy options.

Neoclassical economics tends to view governments and government intervention in the economy as inefficient. Governments are needed to provide some basic public goods such as police forces, armies and institutions which ensure that a free market is able to function. However, they should be confined to as small a role as practically possible.

Although neoclassical economics dominates many economics departments, there are other approaches to the field (Stilwell, 2002). Keynesian economics sees government as being crucial to a well-functioning economy. Keynesians believe the government should provide a wider range of public goods (such as health care) and that government spending is needed to move economies out of recession or depression. Their view is that when businesses fail to invest for economic growth, governments must step in. Institutional economics is another variant; it argues that markets are not 'natural' but are the result of a series of institutions such as the legal structure, the financial system and social values. These economists argue that the discipline should focus on the real world rather than abstract models of a free market that never actually exists. Both Keynesian and institutional economics have a much more expansive and positive view about the role of government. There are other approaches to economics such as Marxist, feminist and ecological perspectives, but these tend not to de taught in economics departments.

While neoclassical economics purports to be based on how a free market really works, some have suggested that the study of economics actually changes how people think and behave. Neoclassical economists and their students may tend to behave the way their models say people behave more than people who have not been immersed in these theories. One study comparing economics students with those in maths, law, science and business found that economics students trained in the use of mathematical models were far more likely to resolve a conflict between profit maximization and worker welfare in favour of profit maximization than their colleagues in other departments (Rubinstein, 2006).

The field of economics brings many useful ideas and concepts to the study of global political economy. Key theories of comparative advantage, supply and demand and the operation of markets both can explain particular events and have informed the action of decision-makers. In terms of the perspectives outlined in the next section, liberal theory draws very heavily on the field of economics.

Political Science

The use of power and politics is the subject of Political Science. However, there is a wide variety in what is actually studied and how it is studied in the various sub-fields. For example, Political Theory examines key political and philosophical texts about how societies should be governed. Comparative politics considers how different countries are governed and tries to learn general lessons from the varying political institutions or cultures. German, US or British politics examine the political systems of those countries. For example, US politics can examine the operation of the US Congress, the Presidency, voting patterns, the influence of lobbying and pressure groups on public policy. Public Administration studies the state bureaucracy and the implementation of particular policies.

Despite these varieties in the field, many political science studies share a number of common characteristics. First, they are concerned with power or the ability of one set of actors to have their preferences implemented. This is a different world from the economists who see decision-making as being the result of well-informed, equal and free individuals expressing their rational preferences. In the world of politics, decision-making is influenced by argument, ideology, institutional features and the threat of violence. Second, many political studies focus upon institutions, most notably the state or the machinery of government. Whereas neoclassical economists are obsessed with the operation of the market, political scientists often cannot tear their vision away from the operation of the state.

As a result of this perspective political science brings a number of elements to the study of global political economy: the focus on power, the state and the welfare of particular communities (as opposed to all communities).

Political Economy

If economics has become increasingly abstract and detached from the economy as it actually operates and political science tends to ignore the economy by focusing on political institutions, then the answer must be to integrate these two fields into the study of Political Economy. Unfortunately, the term 'political economy' has meant a number of different things to different people over time. Prior to the rise of neoclassical economics political economy referred to the work of scholars such as Adam Smith, David Ricardo and Karl Marx. However, the neoclassical turn stripped the political from the economic. Some scholars that did not share this desire continued to examine how politics structure the economy and how the economy influenced politics. For this strand of thinking politics and economics are inseparable.

However, *The Oxford Handbook of Political Economy* takes a very different approach to the subject matter. Rather than view the field as the interrelationships between economics and politics, it defines the subject matter as consisting of 'the methodology of economics applied to the analysis of political behaviour and institutions' (Weingast and Wittman, 2006, p. 3). In this approach the unit of analysis is the individual and that individual follows a rational decision-making behaviour to maximize his/her goals. Game theory or mathematical models are used to inform the analysis, while statistical tools or experiments are used to demonstrate the validity of particular propositions.

So, within the mainstream political economy can mean an attempt to integrate politics and economics along the line of institutional economics *or* it can mean the application of neoclassical economics assumptions and methods into the study of politics. Outside these understandings another version of political economy survived the shift to neoclassical economics. A Marxist political economy tradition flourished but was ignored by many Western academics. Indeed, the association of political economy with Marxism was one of the reasons for the continued neglect of political economy in university economics departments. Some of these Marxist studies, such as Paul Baran and Paul Sweezy's *Monopoly Capital* (1966), provided important insights into the dynamics of political economy.

International Relations

The field of international relations is often located in political science departments. Its origins as a distinct area of study date back to the aftermath of the First World War. European leaders and publics were shocked at the length and lethality of that conflict. As part of their efforts to prevent the outbreak of another disastrous war, efforts were made to increase understanding about the causes of war and the operations of the international system. The field of international relations was given this task. As a result, the field has tended to focus on issues of war and peace, the foreign policy of various states and the operation of international organizations.

Whereas many of the other fields have stressed the importance of developments internal to the state, International Relations is focused on interactions between states. The focus is on how the international system operates rather than the internal workings of particular states. There is some examination of the making of foreign policy, but the emphasis is on its interaction with the foreign policy of other states.

The dominant theoretical approach in international relations has been realism. This theory stresses the lack of any overreaching power in the international system (anarchy) and the continuous competition for power between states. More liberal approaches have focused on the possibilities of states to cooperate, the role of international organizations and law to foster cooperation and the significance of regional integration, free trade and democracy to foster peaceful relations between states.

In the 1970s as US power seemed to be decreasing and economic issues were becoming more significant, some scholars turned their attention to international economic issues. The early 1970s witnessed a major change in the international monetary system as fixed rates were abandoned, the price of energy rapidly escalated during the oil crisis and inflation and unemployment plagued Western countries. Efforts to include 'economic' issues alongside the traditional security concerns of international relations were the beginning of the study of international political economy.

Over the last twenty years the field of international relations has moved in many different directions. International or global political economy has carved out a place in the study of international relations. While realist and liberal approaches are still important, other theoretical orientations have proliferated. Feminist approaches stressing the role of gender, Marxist approaches emphasizing class, constructivist and post-structural approaches emphasizing the role of language and culture, and post-colonial approaches focusing on the legacy of imperialism have broadened the subject matter and methods of the field.

Global political economy studies can, and do, draw upon a range of fields other than economics, political science and international relations. Some authors, such as ourselves, may have an historical bent and draw upon the work of historians to explain today's developments. For example, Chapter 3 draws upon the work of Janet Abu-Loughod and her analysis of early world economies in the 1400s. Geography is increasingly relevant for GPE as insights from geographers about the importance of space and scale are absorbed. For example, geographic approaches can be used to explain the factors that determine the geographic location of foreign direct investment and production (Dicken, 2007) or how workers use local advantages to frustrate the ambitions of global companies (Herod, 2001). Sociological studies can assist in our understanding of particular groups in the global economy. For example, studies on transnational classes or globalizing elites (Sklair, 2001) highlight how particular groups benefit from and drive economic globalization. As the GPE has become more institutionalized, legal studies are of increasing significance. Legal analysis of the World Trade Organization helps scholars understand the powers and limits of that organization's dispute settlement mechanism (Jackson, 2006). More recently insights from cultural studies and the humanities, which emphasize the constructed nature of our reality and the important role of discourse in shaping that reality, have been developed.

In summary, global political economy, as presented in this text, crosses the fields of economics, political science, political economy, international relations and it draws upon work in geography, history, sociology, law and cultural studies. Now that we have provided you with its location in the social sciences, let us turn our attention to three theoretical traditions in the field.

Understanding the global political economy

During 1996 and into 1997 a small number of investors and currency traders began to have doubts about whether Thailand's economy would be able to continue its record of remarkable growth. Fearing a reduction in economic prosperity and profit, some of these investors began to withdraw their money and investments. The outflow of money forced the Thai central bank to devalue its currency, the baht. This began a process which was later called the 1997 Asian financial crisis. By the time the crisis had run its course several Asian countries experienced economic depression, the government of Indonesia was overthrown, countries previously labelled economic miracles (for example, South Korea) were forced to seek loans from the International Monetary Fund (IMF) and the viability of the international financial system was called into question.

Although the 1997 Asian financial crisis was clearly a significant development in the global political economy it was not immediately apparent what caused the events, what were its most significant aspects or what lessons might be drawn from the crisis to prevent a similar event from occurring. Indeed, a number of different stories can be told about the crisis (see Table 1.1). One story, which we'll call the liberal story, would locate the causes of the crisis primarily in the financial policies followed by Asian states (McLeod and Garnaut, 1998). This view suggests that resources were directed to inefficient uses because of corrupt business practices and political influence over financial institutions. The term 'crony capitalism' was developed to capture this inappropriate model of political economy. The lesson to be drawn from the crisis is that financial markets will eventually punish economic activity which violates or ignores liberal economic principles. The solution is for developing countries to have more transparent financial practices and follow a more liberal economic model.

A second story would stress the significance of state power in creating and exploiting the crisis (Weiss, 1999). In this view the problem arose because developing countries liberalized their economies prematurely and allowed large amounts of money to flow into and out of their countries too quickly. This undermined the East Asian model of political economy and caused a crisis. This approach would stress how the United States used the Asian crisis as an opportunity to force some states to restructure along lines that benefited American business. During the crisis Asian states attempted to counter American initiatives at the IMF and to continue to resist the undermining of their particular form of capitalism (Higgott, 1998). The lessons from the crisis are that states need to be careful about liberalizing their economic activity and must pay attention to guarding their national interest.

A third story (critical) would focus on the role of US private business interests and the US government in creating the conditions for a financial collapse. It would suggest that the US government pressured developing states into liberalizing their economies because this suited the interests of the US Treasury and leading financial firms on Wall Street (Wade and Veneroso, 1998). Once the crisis took place, the same interests pressed the IMF to demand that Asian economies restructure in a way that would open markets for US firms. This story would probably also stress the high degree of suffering caused by the financial collapse and the fact that its costs were very unevenly distributed. For example, the collapse of the Indonesian economy pushed millions further into poverty, but left wealthy financial interests in

Table 1.1   Interpretations of the Asian financial crisis

	Liberal	**State power**	**Critical**
Causes	Crony capitalism, lack of transparency	Over-rapid liberalization, reduced state capacity to regulate	Predatory liberalism, power of financial interests, systemic flaws
Key issue(s)	Corruption, lack of liberal economic practices	Clash of Anglo-American vs Asian models	Human suffering caused by financial collapse
Lessons	Increase transparency and good practice in developing countries	Limit financial speculation through state policies	Reform international financial system, defend national system

developed countries relatively untouched. In this view the international financial system facilitates the rapid movement of money between countries and contributes to the reoccurrence of financial crisis in many parts of the world (Walton, 2002). Action needs to be taken to curb financial specula-tion, such as a tax on large short-term foreign exchange transactions. States should also consider restricting the ability of investors to move their funds abroad rapidly.

This brief example of the Asian financial crisis demonstrates that the same event can be analysed in several different ways. Indeed, most major develop-ments are interpreted through competing explanations. Facts do not exist independently of explanatory frameworks. Facts are pieces of information that are thought to correspond to reality and be true, but the way in which they are perceived and judged is influenced by theory. In order to make sense of the world and to enable us to take constructive action, humans develop theories to help determine which facts are most important and what signifi-cant relationships there are between different events. Theories are used for a variety of purposes: they can prioritize information and allow individuals to turn their attention to the most important issues; they can be used to make predictions about the future so that action can be taken to prepare for upcoming events; they can be used to plan action or mobilize support for particular action. Every person utilizes theory to run their life even if they do not engage in explicit theorizing.

Actors in the global political economy and those studying it use a variety of theories and use them for a variety of purposes. Some people are interested in prediction. For example, they would like to be able to predict what type of monetary system would lead to stable economic growth, or to predict the likelihood of war between democratic states. Others believe that prediction is nearly impossible because so many factors come together to influence events. These people are more likely to use theory in an attempt to understand the world rather than to predict what will happen next.

In this book we use and describe a number of theories in order to better understand the world around us. The development of IPE is often constructed around a debate between three contending schools of thought, paradigms or approaches. Some commentators refer to contending paradigms, others to different schools of thought and yet others to competing approaches but it does not really matter for our purposes whether they are seen as paradigms, schools of thought or approaches. The central point is that three main contending perspectives have been used to explain developments in the global political economy. Although analysts distinguish between these three approaches there is a wide variety of thought within each approach and much work in IPE draws on more than one of them. In addition, there are a number of approaches outside these three, such as environmentalism, feminism and post-structuralism, which contribute to the study of IPE. These will be introduced later in the text. Before addressing the current state of theory, however, we will next introduce the key propositions of the three perspectives and highlight the major differences between them.

The economic nationalist perspective

One school of thought brings together analysts who focus on the role of the state and the importance of power in shaping outcomes in the international political economy. These theories stress the importance of the interest of the nation or the state in understanding activity in international relations. This grouping is variously termed mercantilist, neomercantilist, statist, state-based theory, power politics or economic nationalist. We use the term 'economic nationalism' to refer to this perspective because at the centre of such analyses is the protection of the national unit. The underlying economic argumentation may alter, for example, but the objective of economic intercourse remains the same. The origin of this school of thought can be traced back to the emergence and expansion of the nation-state in Europe in the 15th century. Mercantilism was a doctrine of political economy that governed the actions of many states until the liberal revolution in Britain in the mid-19th century. Mercantilists believed that there was only a limited amount of wealth in the world and that each state must secure its interests by blocking the economic interests of other states. This is known as a zero-sum game. One state's gain is another state's loss. From the 15th until the 19th centuries European states strove to establish overseas empires that would be as self-sufficient as possible. Trade between neighbouring colonies of rival empires was discouraged.

Two famous advocates of mercantilist theory were Alexander Hamilton (1791/1991) and Fredrick List (1885/1991). Alexander Hamilton was a founding father of the United States. Writing in the 1790s he urged Americans to protect their manufacturers from foreign competition so that they could industrialize and increase their power. Almost a hundred years later, Fredrick List argued that Germany should industrialize behind trade barriers so that it could catch up with the economic might of Great Britain. He believed that only the economically strong advocated free-trade policies because others would lose out in the ensuing competition.

One central question for students of the contemporary global economy relates to the persistence of mercantilist thought. It could be assumed that an economic perspective based upon unrivalled state power is of limited relevance in a world characterized by globalization. While this may be correct, contemporary economic nationalist thought should not be dismissed as some atavistic throwback to an earlier era. It reflects, on the one hand, an acknowledgement that states remain at the centre of power within the global political economy and, on the other, that there is an intimate connection between power and wealth. Economic nationalist thinking, whether it is termed neomercantilism or statism, remains important in both analysis and practice in the contemporary global economy. For example, states may protect strategic industries against foreign rivals or attempt to export more than they import for long periods of time. Japan has been accused of being a mercantilist state because in comparison to other advanced industrialized countries its economy is relatively closed.

Key actors.   Economic nationalist or mercantilist theories view the state as the main actor in the global political economy. A major assumption of economic nationalists is the primacy of the political over other aspects of social life. Statist writers begin from a focus on the group (the state or nation) rather than the individual. Economic nationalist thought begins from two major assumptions. The first is that the inter-state system is anarchical and that it is therefore the duty of each state to protect its own interests. At the core of the various historical versions of economic nationalism is the belief that an economic community persists and acts for the good of all its members. The second assumption concerns the primacy of the state in political life. As the state is the central instrument through which people can fulfil their goals it follows that the state remains the pre-eminent actor in the domestic and international domains. Economic policy should be used to build a more powerful state.

From this perspective the state is prior to the market and market relations are shaped by political power. Economic nationalist thought is both descriptive and predictive. Descriptively economic nationalists maintain that production, consumption, exchange and investment are all governed by political power. Markets are not 'natural'; they can only exist within a social context. For mercantilists political needs and purposes are seen largely as being achieved through the form of the state. It remains at the core of social life. But economic nationalists move beyond description and also provide policy advice. Given their analysis of the dynamics of political economy such advice is geared towards supporting and maintaining state power.

Economic nationalists recognize the importance of market-based actors such as firms, but subordinate their importance to that of the state. Within this perspective the economic power of transnational corporations is acknowledged, but the overall power of such firms remains limited. In the end firms are subject to the dictates of states. In so far as firms have become important economic actors this is only because states have abandoned regulation or lessened controls on the movement of capital.

Key dynamics.   From an economic nationalist perspective international political economy (IPE) is constituted through the actions of rational states. If international relations are conceived as a struggle for power, international political economy is a struggle for power *and* wealth. The determination of a state's fate resides in its ability to ensure that its citizens reap advantages from international production and exchange. Market relations are important indicators of power and wealth but the market is governed by the activities of states. Economic activity is subordinate to political goals and objectives. Furthermore, economic actors are subject to political authority. The consequence of the salience of the state is that international economic relations are international political relations. The global economy in this view is subordinate to the international political system.

IPE scholars working in this perspective argue that the nature of the global economy reflects the interests of the most powerful states. For example, Krasner (1976) has suggested that systems of free trade are most likely when a single power dominates the international system. This dominant, or hegemonic, power is needed to provide leadership and absorb the short-term costs of maintaining a free-trade regime. Analysts such as Robert Gilpin (1981) have argued that changes in the distribution of power between states increase the chances of conflict in the international system. Because of this view, considerable time can be devoted to contemplating the rise and fall of great powers (Gilpin, 1987; Kennedy, 1987).

In the heated debate over globalization both defensive and sceptical economic nationalist perspectives can be heard. The defensive posture arises from a fear that globalization may prevent state actors from fulfilling their goals. This, of course, is merely the continuation of the long-held suspicion of economic exchange held by economic nationalist thinkers.

Unlike proponents of free trade, economic nationalists believe that the gains from trade are unequally distributed and favour those with greater economic and political power. Thus defensive economic nationalists can recognize globalization as a threat and seek to counter its impacts. On the other hand, sceptical economic nationalists reject many of the current liberal arguments about globalization. They contend that globalization is largely a myth and that the power of the state remains undiminished. Since economic actors are subordinate to political power these analysts argue that the policy environment conducive to globalization has been created by states. It therefore follows that states can alter this environment by changing their policies. Moreover, it can be claimed that since states remain powerful actors and the only legitimate centres of authority in the modern world nothing significant has occurred in the global political economy.

Conflict and cooperation.   Within international relations theory, realism, with its focus on the primacy of the state, the anarchical nature of international relations and the inevitability of conflict, provides the foundation for economic nationalist thought. If realism is the perspective in international politics, economic nationalism is its equivalent doctrine in political economy. Both share a commitment to the state and to the role of power in social life. Power-based theories such as economic nationalism and realism view the world as anarchic, lacking any central authority. Relations between states are thus characterized by unending conflict and the pursuit of power.

International economic relations are therefore perceived in zero-sum terms, that is, the gain of one party necessitates a loss for another party. The system structure is perceived in conflictual terms. While economic nationalists believe that market relations can be positive, they think that such activity can also be negative. Since participating in markets is potentially negative, economic nationalists argue in favour of state control of key economic activities or for state assistance to central economic sectors. The continued salience of economic nationalist perspectives is easily visible today in production, consumption, trade and investment. In terms of production, economic nationalist sentiment is visible in arguments concerning the continued production of some good or service within particular national borders. This can be seen in terms of security concerns; that is, a state should not be reliant on the import of a specific good otherwise in times of conflict this good may be unavailable. Some countries, such as France, protect their agricultural sector, while the United States defends defence technology. It can also be seen in terms of the preservation of the cultural values of the nation. For example, many economic nationalists believe that it is vital to maintain the production of certain cultural products such as film and music within national borders. In relation to consumption, economic nationalist arguments have been made against cultural imperialism, that is, in favour of the view that the import of some products pollutes the nation through the introduction of foreign values. Whereas a liberal would argue that the sovereignty of the consumer is paramount, economic nationalists maintain that the values of the nation are more important. From the foregoing it is easy to see how, in the sphere of exchange, economic nationalists support protection of domestic industries. Furthermore, economic nationalist thought is behind arguments that seek to restrict foreign investment, and supports the 'rights' of local investors over foreigners.

The liberal perspective

In contrast to the economic nationalist theories, liberals focus either upon the individual or a wide range of actors from the state to the corporation to interest groups. They do not see the state as a unitary actor, but as influenced by numerous factors. Rather than stress the inevitability of conflict, liberals search out the conditions for cooperation. They tend to play down the role of force and coercion in human affairs and emphasize the ability of individuals to choose between attractive courses of action. Liberals see the world system as one of interdependence rather than anarchy. States and peoples can cooperate for mutual benefit in the liberal view. Rather than a zero-sum game where one's gains are the other's losses, liberals see a positive-sum game where the pie grows bigger and everyone gains. Liberal theories of political economy emerged in 18th- and 19th-century Britain in the wake of the industrial revolution. Political economists such as Adam Smith (1776/1983) and David Ricardo (1817/1992) preached the virtues of government non-interference in the economy and free trade.

Today's global economy is governed largely according to liberal principles. For example, the trade regime is based upon the goal of free trade: money flows into and out of most countries without great difficulty and all forms of economic activity are increasingly liberalized. There is a wide variety of liberal thought. It ranges from those who see the state fading away in an emerging borderless world (Ohmae, 1990) that will be dominated by private business to liberal institutionalists (Keohane and Nye, 1977) who stress the continuing importance of the state, but see it enmeshed in webs of interdependence and international organization. The book by Landes (1998), mentioned in Chapter 3, takes a particular type of liberal approach. It argues that those with liberal values have been most successful in the global economy and implies that these values were freely chosen by people in Europe and the West. However, he parts ways with those liberals who argue that individual choice is more significant than cultural institutions.

Key actors. Within the liberal perspective there are a number of key actors. For liberals the starting point of analysis is the individual. Liberal economic theory, of which neoclassical economic theory is a variant, begins from the analysis of individual wants and preferences and has constructed a powerful explanatory framework on this basis. In the context of analysis of the global economy, liberal theorists focus on the behaviour of individuals, firms and states. Unlike in economic nationalism, the key economic actor is the individual rather than the state. Individuals in pursuit of self-interest will maximize the benefits of economic exchange for society. Within liberal theory the firm plays an important role. Unlike mercantilists who view the firm with a degree of suspicion, liberals see the firm as a source of economic wealth. The state is viewed with hostility by many liberals since it brings politics into the realm of economics. Liberals believe that if individuals are left freely to engage in production, exchange and consumption all will benefit and that the insertion of state control distorts benefits and adds costs to participants in the market. From a liberal perspective the transnational corporation is a positive force. Transnational corporations (TNCs) bring advantages to both home and host countries. From the perspective of the home country the TNC represents an optimal mix of technology, managerial skill and capital. For host countries TNCs boost their economies through the transfer of capital, technology and access to markets.

Key dynamics.   For liberal theorists the market lies at the centre of economic life. Economic progress results from the interaction of diverse individuals pursuing their own ends. While liberals acknowledge that market relations are not always optimal, they tend to argue that intervention in the market is most likely to produce suboptimal outcomes. There is, of course, a broad spectrum of liberal thought: for example, John Maynard Keynes (1936), whose economic theories laid the foundation for interventionist, welfare governments in the immediate post-World War II period, and Friedrich Hayek, whose free-market philosophy guided the neoliberal revolution of the 1980s are both economic liberals. They both subscribe to a belief in the positive role of markets and the ability of the market to lead to prosperity. Liberals differ over the importance of market imperfections and the policies that ought to be implemented to deal with market failure.

For liberal theorists IPE is constituted by a search for wealth. On the whole open markets will enhance growth and wealth, and firms will disseminate material wealth across the globe. Economic failure in this perspective is often the result of government intervention. Many liberal theorists have been at the forefront of the debate on globalization. For what can be termed 'hyper-liberals', globalization is not only a reality (indeed an inevitability!), it is a positive force for good. Globalization breaks down artificial (for which read political) barriers and by unleashing the force of production it can contribute to enhanced happiness for humankind. Thus, hyper-liberals welcome globalization. Keynesian-influenced liberals or those of a reformist stance perceive certain problems with the unfettered operation of the free market and, therefore, are sensitive to some unwanted consequences of globalization. They support globalization but emphasize the need for attention to market reform.

Conflict and cooperation. Liberal theorists view international relations and the international political economy as essentially cooperative. Indeed, they believe that market relations will lead to positive outcomes for all. In other words, economic relations are positive-sum. A standard liberal theory that exemplifies this belief is the theory of comparative advantage, which shows that, even in a situation where one country enjoys a superiority in the production of all goods and services over a second country, trade between the two countries will benefit both countries.

One persistent liberal belief has been that economic nationalist policies lead to conflict. Unlike Marxist writers who denounce the growth of global capitalism as a cause of war, liberal theorists view increased international interaction as a source of prosperity and peace. The liberal belief in the connection between protectionist policies and conflict and the reverse argument, namely that capitalism favours peace, are central to liberal critiques of the international economic order. The German philosopher Immanuel Kant (1795/1991) foresaw an era of perpetual peace when systems of free trade, a coalition of republican states and the fear of destructive warfare would bring about an era of calm and prosperity. Near the end of the First World War, US president Woodrow Wilson (1918/1986) advocated liberal principles of free trade, self-determination and the use of international organizations to settle disputes between states.

The framers of international economic institutions after the Second World War were supporters of this view. It was argued that the war had its origins in the economic nationalist policies of the 1930s. As a consequence of the Great Depression, governments resorted to a series of protectionist measures that eroded confidence in international cooperation. As a result of economic nationalist policies the basis of collective security was shattered and an atmosphere conducive to dictators was created. The shift from economic competition to military conflict was in this view inevitable. Hence, there was the need to design institutions after the war to foster international economic cooperation and to include within those institutions mechanisms to prevent states from resorting to competitively nationalist policies.

Within the study of international relations, liberal theories of world politics and liberal theories of political economy share assumptions concerning the pluralist nature of the international system and the feasibility of cooperation. Theories of interdependence developed in the 1960s to explain the connection between increased economic exchange and interconnectedness and the long peace among Western nations after 1945. They echo classical liberal political economy. These theories emphasized the economic and political benefits of economic interchange. Interdependence was proffered as both a description of events and a prescription for the solution of conflict.

In the 1980s and 1990s liberals continued to argue that international cooperation was both possible and desirable. In contrast to economic nationalists or realists, liberals argued that international agreements or regimes would maintain international economic order even if hegemonic states declined (Keohane, 1984). With the end of the Cold War and the rapid spread of liberal economic models to many states in the 1990s, it appeared that the liberal faith in cooperation and progress was justified. Some even went so far as to claim that history had ended because the liberal democratic model had triumphed over other forms of social organization (Fukuyama, 1992).

The critical perspective

Another set of theories emerged in the 19th century in reaction to liberal thought. These theories move away from the individual and states to consider other units of analysis. They are sometimes called critical theories because they question the way the world is organized and sometimes they are labelled as radical because they challenge established forms of organization. The three most common variants of critical thought in IPE are Marxist, feminist and environmentalist theories. Post-structuralist approaches have also recently been applied to IPE. This chapter concentrates on Marxist theories, while environmental theories will be highlighted in Chapter 12, feminist theories in Chapter 10 and post-structuralist theories in Chapter 13.

Marxist theories focus upon class and the interest of workers rather than state interests. Writing during the English industrial revolution, Karl Marx took issue with the idea of a harmony of interests that the liberals advocated. Marx and his co-author, Engels, discerned an ongoing conflict between workers and capitalists that would only be resolved when the workers seized power (Marx and Engels, 1848/1977). In contrast, feminist theories look at gender relations between women and men. They seek to uncover how our ideas about what men and women are supposed to be shape the ways in which society is organized. An 18th-century early feminist writer, Mary Wollstonecraft (1792/1992), criticized male liberal theorists for ignoring the role and interests of women in their political theories. Green theories have taken the environment and the planet as the objects to be highlighted. They examine how people shape and are shaped by the environment. Neo-Gramscian theories, which evolve out of Marxism, stress the role of transnational classes and ideology in their efforts to understand the global economy. We use the term 'critical' as a label for these theories because they are united by a critical attitude to prevailing social arrangements. In this section we focus on Marxism since it is the oldest of the theories grouped under the critical perspectives heading.

These critical theories stress the nature of oppression within and across societies and the struggle for justice waged by or on behalf of workers, women and the environment. Frank's (1998) study, *ReOrient*, is close to this form of analysis because he stresses European exploitation of others' resources in the 'Rise of the West'. However, he differs from traditional Marxists who have seen Western civilization as being at the forefront of human development because it was the birthplace of capitalism. Frank disputes both the claim that capitalism originated in Europe and that European developments are more significant to world history than developments in Asia. For radical analysts, the world appears as a layer cake with one group sitting on top of another, across state boundaries.

Key actors.   Marxist writers begin with a focus on class as the main 'actor' in the global political economy. They reject the individualism of liberal theory and embrace the collectivist approach of economic nationalist perspectives. However, Marxist theory rejects statism and focuses instead on the significance of class. This focus arises from the Marxist account of capitalist relations which are predicated on exploitation. The Marxist concept of class has been open to various interpretations and critiques. We define class simply as arising from one's position in the structure of production. Marx defined class in relation to the structure of production which creates owners of the means of production (the bourgeoisie) and the labourers who sell their labour power to the bourgeoisie (the workers).

Within Marxist writing the firm is an instrument of exploitation. Transnational corporations contribute to the exploitation and oppression of the working class. The centralization and concentration of capital visible in the form of TNCs is a key feature of imperialism whereby dominance is expressed in the global political economy. In this perspective the state is the representative of class interests rather than the expression of the harmony of communal interests posited by mercantilists.

Key dynamics.   Dominance and exploitation among and within societies provide the main dynamic for Marxist theories of international political economy. Unlike liberals Marxists view market relations as inherently exploitative. Under capitalism workers are denied a fair remuneration because capitalists pay workers less than their labour is worth. Marxists view international economic relations as inherently unstable and conflictual because of three tendencies of capitalism. First, the tendency for the rate of profit to fall sees capitalists engaged in fierce competition with each other and it will tend to drive down the wages of workers. Second, capitalism leads to uneven development as some centres increase their wealth and growth at the expense of others. Uneven development sows the seeds of conflict between countries. Third, Marxists argue that capitalism leads to overproduction or underconsumption, giving rise to fluctuations in the business cycle and undermining social stability.

A revision of Marxist thought called 'dependency' theory has been used to explain the persisting poverty of many states. Dependency theory suggests that poor countries faced immense obstacles to development because they were vulnerable to economic exploitation from developed states (Dos Santos, 1970). The links between the rich and the poor were thought to make the poor poorer and the rich richer. Underdevelopment of some parts of the world was caused by development in other parts of the world. This school of thought informed developing countries' attempts to create a New International Economic Order (NIEO) in the 1970s (Cox, 1979). This approach was undermined in the 1980s as many developing states adopted liberal economic policies in the wake of the debt crisis.

Radical theorists have tended, for a variety of reasons, to oppose globalization. It has been argued, for example, that globalization is a myth or merely imperialism in modern clothes. According to this argument, globalization represents an ideological intervention into political economy. It ostensibly describes changes in the world but in reality it is a set of prescriptions in support of free markets and an instrument to increase the power of capital over labour, the West over other states, and an instrument designed to further the interests of the leading capitalist power, the United States. In this sense globalization has to be resisted since it too maintains and increases exploitative relations. At the heart of the radical argument is the view that globalization is not distinctive. That is, discussion of globalization is merely the contemporary version of imperialism. To discuss political economy in terms of globalization may mask real power relations.

In the 1980s and 1990s, Marxist IPE was reinvigorated by the work of scholars drawing inspiration from Antonio Gramsci. Writers such as Robert Cox (1996a) and Stephen Gill (1993) focused on the role of social forces and ideology in liberalizing and globalizing economic relations. They argued that globalization based on neoclassical liberal economic principles was a political project which transformed national states into instruments of global liberalization and economic management. Part of this project involved convincing people that neoliberal policies were actually in their best interest. In this view, the hegemony of a particular world order requires an ideological dominance which secures the broad consent of those ruled in an unequal and unjust manner.

Conflict and cooperation.   Critical writers tend to perceive international economic relations as a zero-sum game. The structure of global capitalism is fundamentally conflictual. Two forms of conflict are prevalent in the global

Table 1.2 Comparing the perspectives

Aspect	Economic nationalist	Liberal	Critical
Historical origins	15th century	19th century	19th century
Major figures	Hamilton, List, Krasner, Gilpin, Strange	Smith, Ricardo, Kant, Wilson, Keynes, Hayek, Keohane, Nye	Marx, Lenin, Frank, Cox
Variants	Mercantilism, realism	Free trade, interdependence	Marxism, feminism, environmentalism
Level	State-centric; atomistic	Pluralist atomistic	Global structure
Human nature	Aggressive	Cooperative	Malleable
Units	States	Firms, states, NGOs, IGOs	Class, gender, planet, global capitalism
View of the state	Unitary actor	Pluralist state: diverse interest	Representative of class interest groups
View of TNCs	Beneficial/ harmful	Beneficial	Exploitative
Behavioural dynamic	State as rational actor	Individual as rational actor but outcomes not always optimal	Dominance and exploitation within and between societies
Market relations	Potentially negative	Positive	Exploitative
System structure	Anarchy/ conflictual	Cooperative/ interdependence	Hierarchy/ conflictual
Game metaphor	Zero-sum	Positive-sum	Zero-sum
Hegemony	Importance of a dominant state	Post-hegemonic cooperation	Hegemony in state and society
International institutions	Not very significant	Important	Serve interests of wealthy (states, firms and classes)

economy. Within states capitalists and workers have competing interests and the state is the scene of a class struggle as the workers and bourgeoisie clash. According to Marxists this conflict is objective and arises from the law of motion of capital. In the international arena the clash between workers and capitalists is often obscured by nationalism and the intervention of the state. Through the mechanism of imperialism dominant states oppress weaker ones and this sets up an international struggle between imperialists and their victims.

International conflict is inevitable because of the drive for profit. Different capitalists seek the protection of their state and this leads to war. Marxist theories of imperialism have in different ways accounted for the tendency of capitalist states to go to war. The most well known of these theories, Lenin's theory of imperialism, combined two different explanations of capitalist development. One part of his theory focused on underconsumption in domestic markets. Because of underconsumption capitalists were compelled into overseas adventures since they could not maintain their rates of profit on the basis of domestic demand. Another part of his theory focused on the growth of finance capital and the merger between finance and industrial capital to form monopoly capital that sought to gain profit through overseas lending. He argued that conflict and war are a necessary end result of this competition.

At the turn of the 21st century conflict between social forces was also seen to take place on a global scale. Elites attempting to constitutionalize neoliberal principles in institutions such as the World Trade Organization and the International Monetary Fund met with opposition from social movements trying to safeguard environmental regulation, raise labour standards, improve gender equity and lobby for economic justice (O'Brien *et al.*, 2000). Critical analysts depict a global conflict which takes place within, above and across states (Gill, 2003).

Contending perspectives: a summary.   The question arises as to why there are so many theories and what the relationship is between various theories. There are several reasons for the existence of multiple theories. Two of the reasons are described by Robert Cox (1986, p. 207): 'Theory is always *for* someone and *for* some purpose.' Each theory has a different goal in mind. For example, economic nationalist theories are concerned with the security of the state, liberal theories with building wealth or cooperation and critical theories with pursuing economic, gender or environmental equity. While they are all trying to understand the world, they are looking at different aspects of human existence. A second and related reason is that a particular theory usually advances the causes or interests of a particular group. Richer, more satisfied people and states tend to favour liberal theories which do not threaten their interests, while those disadvantaged by the system are more likely to espouse critical theories. A third explanation is that it is impossible to prove a theory right or wrong. Evidence is often disputed and interpreted in different ways. Moreover, unlike the laws of nature, people are able to reflect upon their behaviour and change their form of organization and interaction. People may act according to mercantilist theories in some eras or situations and along liberal principles in others.

Table 1.2 presents a summary of the perspectives. In the discussion so far our intention has been to highlight the existence of various interpretations. But what is the relationship between various theories? Are they in conflict or can they be made compatible? At their core, theories about international political economy are incompatible because they have different basic assumptions about the units of analysis, the nature of the system and the motivation of actors. Yet, each theory can point to some evidence to support its existence and each seems to be useful in explaining some aspect of the global political economy. Some theorists (Strange, 1988) have suggested that people take an eclectic approach to theory – picking and choosing as they wish. This can have some advantages, but risks incoherence as one jumps from perspective to perspective. Readers should consider some systemized form of integration where various theories may be used under particular circumstances or in a hierarchy. For example, one could have a general power politics approach while conceding that the system is also characterized by class and gender exploitation and that there are times when cooperation can be more beneficial than conflict. Alternatively, some theories may be more applicable in selected time periods.

In the following chapter we turn our attention to issues of method and survey the work of some leading figures in the field.

Chapter 2

Methods and Theorists

This chapter moves away from an analysis of broad theoretical perspectives to consider the issue of methods and particular theorists. Although there has been a long history of vigorous debate surrounding theories in IPE, recent years have seen increasing discussion around methodological issues. This chapter outlines some prominent methods and touches on the controversy sparked by different methodological approaches. The second part of the chapter surveys the work of four leading theorists. The survey is designed to give readers a sense of how particular scholars develop research programmes and undertake very different theoretical projects.

Methodological issues

An interested observer of global political economy who has first familiarized themselves with some of the basic approaches to the field (as described in Chapter 1) must then decide how they will study the events and processes that interest them. They must decide what method is most suitable for their investigation. However, the question of method is complicated by three issues. The first is that different methods demand different skills and training. The second is that methods themselves embody particular theoretical assumptions and may be more value-laden than they initially appear. The third issue is that adherents of particular methods may dismiss the arguments of people using different methods because they do not accept their research as valid (due to faulty methods). In this section of the chapter we briefly examine four methods: case studies, rational choice, institutionalism and constructivism.

Case studies and large n studies

One of the most common approaches to studying global political economy is to use case studies. A case study is a detailed investigation of a particular event or issue. The event is studied to determine why a particular thing happened the way it did. A detailed analysis is designed to reveal causal factors that can either be applied to similar situations or serve as a starting point for theory building.

There are a number of different types of case studies and each has its particular use (Odell, 2001). Descriptive case studies describe a particular event, but do not provide analysis or engage in theoretical debates. They are very useful as evidence for other types of studies. They can provide the raw material or data for other scholars and students. Other cases are chosen because they may help evaluate the plausibility of a particular theory. A 'least likely' case study is one where a particular theory is unlikely to seem applicable. If the theory actually holds in that unlikely case, the theory is considerably bolstered. Alternatively, a 'most likely case study' examines a case that is very likely to support a theory. If it can be show that the theory does not hold in such a supportive case, great doubt is shed on whether the theory will apply in any case. Comparative case studies are undertaken in the hope that different cases will shed light on when particular theories hold and when they do not. Comparing and contrasting cases can often shed more light than a single case.

'Large n studies' is a name given to statistical investigations which use a data base to find common features or causes across a large number of cases. For example, there might be a hypothesis that free trade makes countries wealthy. One could investigate a particular case to see if the proposition held true in that instance, but scholars (and public officials) are likely to be interested in whether or not it holds true as a general rule across a wide variety of cases. Can it be shown that under most circumstances free trade brings wealth and thus should be a policy that most countries should follow? Rather than do a case study of every country in the world it makes more sense to examine the data from a large number of countries. Countries could be evaluated according to the degree to which they engage in free trade and their wealth per capita could then be compared. The study would then show whether there was any relationship between the wealth of a country and its openness to trade. If a relationship was found there could then be a debate about whether free trade created the wealth or wealthy countries prefer free trade or whether some other factor generated both wealth and free trade.

Case studies and multi-country statistical studies both have their advantages and disadvantages (Odell, 2001). The advantages of case studies are that they are useful for generating theories, concepts, typologies and hypotheses. They provide rich empirical material for investigation. They help us understand how particular things happen. In areas where no statistical data is available, the case study is often the only possible method of studying a phenomenon. The biggest disadvantage to the case study is that one can never be certain about how representative the case is. Does it represent a general trend or is it the exception to the rule? Does it have any applicability to other cases or is it unique? Large n studies help us determine whether a particular proposition is generally applicable or limited to a small number of cases.

Rational choice

The rational choice approach to understanding politics was pioneered in the study of US politics, especially the operation of its legislature. The method then spread to the analysis of comparative politics, international relations and global political economy. It explains outcomes as the result of the choices of individual actors (either an individual person or a group considered to be acting as an individual, such as a state). Within this framework actors are assumed to be utility maximizers (they attempt to maximize their gains and minimize their losses). Individuals try to improve their situation by calculating costs and benefits before choosing the best path of action.

Rational choice theories have generated significant insights into political behaviour, especially concerning how the aggregation of individual choices can lead to surprising outcomes (Geddes, 2003, pp. 193–7). One insight is that systems of majority rule do not always result in implementing the policy preferences of a majority of citizens. Although a political system may be a relatively fair and competitive democracy, majority preferences may be ignored. Smaller, wealthier interest groups are more likely to have the resources and motivation to influence public policy than poorer unorganized sectors of the population. In addition, if the benefits of a public policy are highly concentrated, but the costs are spread widely throughout the population, those reaping the benefit are highly motivated to lobby while the many individuals paying a very small cost are unlikely to put much effort into opposing the policy. This type of logic is often used to explain trade protectionism where an industry can reap profits from tariff protection, but individuals citizens pay such a low cost that they do not mobilize to defend their interests.

Rational choice theories have also highlighted the problem of collective action in the areas of public goods and common pool resources. Public goods have two characteristics: i) they can be enjoyed by more than one person without any reduction in the good and ii) people cannot be excluded from their consumption. Clean air and water are examples of public goods. The problem with such goods is that it may not be rational for any individual to do the work required to provide a public good because it will be consumed by others with only a small benefit returning to the initiator. Thus, a corporate polluter may gain economic benefits from dirty production, but any individual will be reluctant to bear the cost of cleaning up the mess. Common pool resources refer to environments, such as oceans or air, which are shared by a large group of people, but not owned by anyone. Here the incentives are for each person to make maximum use of the resource to everyone's detriment. This phenomenon can be seen in the overgrazing of common sheep pastures and the overfishing of ocean stocks. Rational choice theory shows how what is rational for the individual leads to poor outcomes for the group, or society.

An offshoot of rational choice is game theory. Whereas rational choice looks at the strategic behaviour of individuals, game theory examines decision-making of actors who are heavily influenced by the possible behaviour of other parties. These actors calculate their own interest in the light of what they believe others will do. It concerns the strategic interaction of a number of actors. Theorists have constructed a number of scenarios or games such as Prisoner's Dilemma, Chicken and Stag Hunt. The rules of the games differ, forcing players to behave in particular ways. For example, Prisoner's Dilemma discourages players from cooperating, which leads to a poor overall outcome. In contrast, in the stag hunt players that can manage to cooperate will be rewarded with such large benefits that there is a great incentive to maintain cooperation (see Box 2.1).

How can these abstract games contribute to understanding global political economy (Carlson, 2000)? Prisoner's Dilemma can help explain why countries keep protectionist measures in place even though free trade would benefit them more. A country (country A) may be concerned that if it opens up the domestic market to foreign producers, other countries may keep trade barriers resulting in an economic loss for country A. While all countries may be better off under free trade any individual country can gain from keeping trade barriers. So, if country A keeps its trade barriers, it will gain if other countries reduce their barriers because it can export to them. On the other hand, if other countries do not reduce their barriers and country A keeps its barriers, A protects its own market. The problem of one country seeking the benefits of free trade, but not liberalizing its own trade is one of free riding. It wants the benefits of the system, but will not itself participate in bearing any costs. Since the same logic applies to all the countries, there is very little incentive for countries to reduce their trade barriers even though everyone would be better off if they did.

The Prisoner's Dilemma does not mean free trade is impossible. Games can change over time as rules are changed. For example, there is a tendency for actors to change their behaviour if they play the same game a number of times. They learn the costs of cooperation and non-cooperation. Alternatively, the game can be changed if the rules are altered. The players might create an institution such as the World Trade Organization (WTO), which reduces the ability of countries to cheat or free ride and takes away the cost of cooperating. The WTO encourages all countries to adopt free trade and provides information to its members about who does not abide by the rules. This gives member states increased confidence that other countries will not free ride. It changes the calculations that each state makes so that cooperation seems like a much more rewarding policy.

Box 2.1   Prisoner's Dilemma

A simple Prisoner's Dilemma illustrates how some environments can lead rational actors to choose decisions that lead to poor outcomes. Imagine that police arrive at the scene of a robbery and they also discover a dead body. They arrest two suspects (Person A and Person B) who have stolen articles in their possession. At the police station the suspects are put into separate rooms and interrogated. The prisoners are given the following options. If both suspects keep silent each will be convicted of robbery and given a one-year sentence. If one person confesses and identifies the other as the killer, the informer will be freed and the killer will go to prison for life. If both confess and identify the other as the killer they will both be sentenced to a term of ten years for manslaughter. Both prisoners are assured that the other prisoner will not know of their decision until the trial. What is the most likely outcome of this scenario? The game can be shown in the table opposite.

The best joint strategy for both prisoners is to stay silent and get a relatively light sentence of one year. However, each prisoner knows that if the other informs and they stay silent they will stay in prison for the rest of their life. They also know that the other player has a large incentive to inform because they could earn their freedom. Thus, the best individual strategy is to inform on the other. Prisoner A knows that if B stays silent and A informs, A will win freedom. On the other hand, if B chooses to inform, A also needs to have informed or A will go to

→

Institutionalism

As a methodology institutionalism focuses on the importance of formal and informal institutions in producing political outcomes. It shares an affinity with institutional economics mentioned in the previous chapter because both focus upon the rules and institutions which shape human behaviour. At the core of institutionalism is an emphasis on the importance of rules. While rational choice methods highlight individuals pursuing self-interest, institutionalists focus upon the broader rules of the game. The global economy is conceived not as the result of the actions of diverse individuals but as the outcome of the interaction of simple and complex institutions which shape individual decisions (Spruyt, 2000). In IPE institutionalism is most familiar in the writings of liberal scholars who emphasize the powerfully constraining and beneficial impact of institutions.

One area where institutionalism has been prominent is in discussion about the varieties of capitalism (Hall and Soskice, 2001). What accounts for

➜

	Prisoner A stays silent	Prisoner A informs on B
Prisoner B stays silent	Robbery conviction – 1 year each	Prisoner A – freedom for informing Prisoner B – life for murder
Prisoner B informs on A	Prisoner A – life for murder Prisoner B – freedom for informing	Prisoner A – 10 years for manslaughter Prisoner B – 10 years for manslaughter

prison for life. Prisoner A's best option, no matter what B does, arises when A informs. Both A and B follow a similar logic of informing and end up with a prison sentence of ten years, which is far longer than the one year if they had both stayed silent. The dilemma is that if each player responds to their individual incentives they end up being much worse off than if they had adopted a coordinated strategy (staying silent).

When one changes the rules of the game the outcome can also change. For example, if both Prisoner A and B were members of the mafia they would have a large incentive of stay silent, fearing reprisals from other members of the criminal organization.

different forms of capitalism and will these grow or shrink over time? Do different parts of the world exhibit distinct forms of capitalism which will evolve along divergent paths or are countries bound to converge around a particular superior form of capitalism? Institutionalists have pointed to distinct forms of political, social and economic arrangements to explain continuing variation between countries. Some have stressed the role that finance has played in different systems. An Anglo-American market where firms raise money on the stock market has been contrasted with a German model where banks have more direct relationships with corporations or a Japanese model which linked manufacturing and finance in large conglomerates. Neo-corporatist work contrasts models where labour was included in government decision-making to models where labour was excluded or suppressed. Countries have also been examined with regard to the nature of their welfare regimes (Esping-Anderson, 1990).

As the varieties of capitalism literature illustrates, many instituionalists come from a comparative politics background. They tend towards using case studies and stressing the differences between political economies and the distinctive role that institutions play in shaping behaviour.

Constructivism

Constructivism begins from the premise that there is an intimate and reciprocal connection between human subjects and the social world (Palan, 2000). Whereas rational choice analysis takes values and beliefs for granted, constructivists see beliefs and values as something that have to be explained and as crucial in shaping and determining 'reality'. Whereas institutionalists focus on rules as the driving forces in constraining and shaping behaviour in a context where identity is essentially fixed, constructivism posits that norms and values go beyond shaping actors' interests – they in themselves constitute identities and hence interests. From this perspective the global political economy is a set of material conditions and practices, a set of normative statements about the world and an academic discipline. It is not reducible to one of these but is always constructed as the interaction of these three 'structures'. This is also true for any 'issue' in IPE. For example, to understand development we have to look at development in relation to material privation, the values attached to economic growth and prosperity (as well as negative values attributed to poverty) and the ways in which development is studied and analysed.

A constructivist approach to IPE encourages analysts to look in different places for explanations than rational choice or institutionalism. They call into question the preferences that are assumed in rational choice approaches (Abdelal, 2009). Constructivists ask: 'What are actors' preferences, how have they been created and how might they change?' They direct attention to the role of ideas, norms, identities and social understanding in guiding behaviour. How is it that at one point in time the pressing economic issue is thought to be inflation, while at other times it is unemployment? Why do some people and institutions preach the value of the market as a decision-maker and others stress political institutions? What is the impact of the dominance of one idea over another and how do such things come about?

There are two complicated and divisive issues surrounding debates about method. The first has to do with the dominance of particular methods and the second has to do with the relationship between method and theory. Some scholars fear that a narrow set of methods is beginning to dominate the field and marginalize other methods, scholars and research. Rational choice and the use of statistical methods have become extremely popular in many US universities and leading journals. Scholars using case study and constructivist methods can feel that their work is taken less seriously because they use different standards of evidence.

A second issue is that while some scholars view methods as value neutral, others believe that methods are infused with particular theoretical and value assumptions. Adherents of the different theoretical perspectives can, in principle, use any methodology, but it has tended to be the case that economic nationalists and liberals favour rational choice or institutionalism while critical theorists favour variants of constructivism. Many rational choice studies share the basic assumptions of neoclassical economists about rational utility maximizing actors and therefore seem closely aligned with liberal assumptions. Constructivist approaches stress the shifting nature of social reality so they tend to be less conservative than approaches which take existing meaning as given, such as rational choice perspectives. Constructivist approaches are more likely to be used by analysts seeking to critique or change the existing system.

Methods like rational choice and constructivism do indeed contain theoretical assumptions. Some may even argue that they are theories rather than methods. However, our perspective is that they are better viewed as methods that can be used with a variety of theories. For example, although rational choice methods draw upon many liberal assumptions, they can be used by people of a very different theoretical bent. During the 1980s a branch of Marxism – Analytical Marxism – used rational choice methodology (see Elster, 1985). In a similar way, although constructivism points one to look at how reality is made through people's ideas and understandings, one could take a realist, liberal or Marxist view of what influences a particular construction.

Concerns about the dominance of particular methods or the value-laden assumptions inherent in various methods means that what might otherwise be a dry discussion about how to conduct research can often be a much more lively and animated debate about the nature of knowledge and political orientations.

Four theorists and today's debates

This section provides an overview of the body of work of four IPE theorists in the last quarter of the 20th century. The review is undertaken for three reasons. First, it illustrates how the field has evolved over recent years. Second, attention to each scholar's work demonstrates how they combine or mix insights from different intellectual traditions and that the student of IPE need not be imprisoned in any particular approach. Finally, it reveals how misleading labels can be when applied to particular pieces of work or collections of work which are more nuanced than a label might suggest. These particular scholars were chosen because they have long academic and publishing records, have been prominent in different areas of the field and have interesting career and intellectual trajectories. There are, of course, many important scholars, but these four give a sense of the variety in the field. For each scholar we discuss their career path, theoretical orientation, major works and issues and contributions to the field.

Susan Strange – unorthodox realist

Susan Strange (2002) admitted that she never meant to become a professor, but ended up in the role after stints in journalism (with the *Observer* and *The Economist*) and working at a British foreign affairs research institute (Chatham House). She eventually established herself teaching in the International Relations Department of the London School of Economics. In later years she moved to Warwick University and contributed to the growth of its IPE programme.

Strange's theoretical approach is difficult to characterize neatly (Tooze and May, 2002). It contains a strong element of power politics or economic nationalism in that she focuses upon the exercise of power and pays considerable attention to key state policies in structuring the global economy. She takes a realist approach in advising students to focus upon the role of interests and to constantly ask the question 'Who benefits?'. Yet, her work is also unorthodox because Strange urged observers to take account of the growing role of markets, corporations and technological innovations in changing the environment in which the state operates. In a series of exchanges with American IPE scholars Susan Strange continuously went against the mainstream by variously arguing that the study of regimes was faddish and mistaken (1982), that US hegemony was not declining in the 1980s (1987) and that globalization was transforming the nature of state authority (1996).

Strange's early work concentrated on international monetary affairs such as Britain's policy for the pound sterling. In writing about the field of IPE she constantly argued that it should be an interdisciplinary area that brought together international relations and international economics. She argued against international relations specialists whom she saw as fixated on the state and questions of war and peace, as well as international economists who ignored questions of power.

Strange viewed IPE as a method of understanding the world that focused upon the relationship between markets and authority. Her broad approach is set out in a 1988 textbook called *States and Markets*. The text argues that in addition to relational power (A forces B to do A's will) power resides in structures. Structural power is the ability to shape the rules of the game in a particular area. Those who create the operating framework for everyone's activities exercise power by eliminating some possibilities and making some outcomes more likely than others. Strange maintained that there were four key structures of power (security, production, finance, knowledge) and numerous secondary structures (transport, trade, energy, welfare). Strange reasoned that since the United States exercised considerable structural power in the key structures, talk of US decline was mistaken.

In the 1990s Strange increasingly turned her attention to non-state actors. In a major collaboration with a business school professor (Stopford and Strange, 1991) she argued that traditional notions of diplomacy being an inter-state practice had to be expanded to include state–firm and firm–firm interactions. In a following book, Strange (1996) identified other actors such as business associations, bureaucrats and even mafias that were operating transnationally and undermining the authority of states.

Strange conducted most of her empirical research in the area of finance and credit. She argued that the creation and control of credit was a significant source of power in the global economy. True to her realist roots she traced the liberalization and globalization of finance to particular decisions or non-decisions of the most powerful states. Finance was globalized because it suited the interests of the most powerful states (principally the United States and the United Kingdom). However, Strange also worried that the failure of states to exercise proper regulatory control over financial flows was turning the system into a form of 'casino capitalism' (1986). She questioned the stability of a liberal global financial system that outgrew government control. Her fear was that a widespread financial collapse would lead to a closing of the global economy (1998).

Susan Strange played a prominent role in founding and supporting the study of IPE as an interdisciplinary field in Britain. Her pioneering studies in the field of finance inspired a new generation to examine the power relations flowing around credit issues. Strange's insistence that IPE be an open field of intellectual enquiry influenced the development of the field in Britain by bringing in work from a number of different disciplines. Her stinging criticism of US intellectual trends provided room for British scholars and students to ask different types of questions and use different methodologies from their US counterparts. She left a rich legacy of scholarship, enquiry and institutions in her wake.

Robert Keohane – liberal institutionalist

Robert Keohane was born into an academic family and began a US teaching career after graduating from Harvard in 1966 (Keohane, 1989a). His academic career has taken him to Stanford, Brandeis, Harvard, Duke and Princeton universities. His research has had a major role in influencing the study of IPE and IR in the United States and beyond.

Keohane is a central figure in what has become known as the liberal institutionalist approach to IPE and world politics (1989b). This approach suggests that institutions or sets of rules and norms can have a significant effect upon state behaviour if they have mutual interests. Institutions include formal international organizations, international regimes or conventions and custom. Liberal institutionalism was developed as a critique of realist/power politics/economic nationalist approaches to international relations and IPE. The emphasis is on how institutions can help states overcome barriers to cooperation. Although Keohane himself prefers to be known simply as an institutionalist (2002, p. 3), the adjective 'liberal' is still useful because it refers to some of the liberal attributes that underlie his approach. These include a focus on the individual and a belief that properly designed international institutions can go some way to creating a more humane global system.

Keohane's first major work was written with Joseph Nye and tried to integrate realist (power politics) and liberal thought by focusing on bargaining in situations of interdependence. In *Power and Interdependence* Keohane and Nye (1977) argued that there were certain times and issue areas when the assumptions of realist or power politics approaches did not hold sway. They labelled these situations as 'complex interdependence' and argued that under certain circumstances states could use international institutions to bolster cooperation. They also argued that in such situations cross-border links between officials could lead to outcomes different from those that power politics approaches would have predicted.

In 1984 Keohane published a book called *After Hegemony*. It sought to explain why, contrary to realist assumptions, states continued to cooperate and participate in international agreements even after the major power which sponsored the agreements entered a period of relative decline. This was a significant issue because many analysts were worried about the decline of US power relative to other states and feared that this would make the international political economy increasingly unstable. Keohane focused on post-1945 arrangements in the issue areas of money, trade and oil. He argued that the benefits of arrangements in these issue areas, or regimes, continued independent of the rise or decline of the power of particular states. Regimes exist because they facilitate negotiations between states and allow states to overcome barriers to collective action such as uncertainty. Keohane's work helped to spark increasing attention to the issue of regime creation and maintenance. Indeed, regime theory became a mainstay of US IPE scholarship.

Another important aspect of *After Hegemony* was Keohane's use of economic theory to explain the activity of states. Drawing inspiration from economic theories that claimed to explain the activity of corporations, Keohane analysed state behaviour in terms of market failure, transaction costs and uncertainty. Market failure refers to a situation where transactions do not take place because the market is arranged in such a way as to make otherwise rational activity irrational. In the case of IPE states might not agree to cooperate because they are unsure of the motives of other states. Regimes help to resolve this market failure by providing information about other states' behaviour and an element of predictability in inter-state interactions. States cooperated in international regimes because these regimes solved particular problems such as lack of information and uncertainty about other states' intentions and behaviour. Keohane's use of economic models and theories of rational choice coincided and blended well with the importation of economic models in other areas of US political science. The success of his book and persuasiveness of his argument helped to bolster rational choice methodology in US IPE.

In the 1990s Keohane (2002) turned his attention to two issues raised in his earlier work – domestic politics and the problem of state compliance with international regimes. The issue of domestic politics concerned how state-based theories of international interaction might be integrated with under-standings of nationally based politics. How do domestic politics affect international relations? The issue of compliance moves on from considering the origins and maintenance of regimes to thinking about why and how states obey international rules. This path leads towards more study of the role of international law in influencing state behaviour.

Robert Keohane has been one of the most influential US writers in the field of IPE and IR. His work has advanced understanding of the conditions under which states are able to cooperate through international regimes.

Robert Cox – historical materialist

For Canadian-born Robert Cox academic life was a second career after spending 25 years in the international civil service at the International Labour Organization (ILO). At the ILO Cox served as a staff officer to the director general, chief of the Programme and Planning division and as direc-tor of the International Institute for Labour Studies. After leaving the ILO, Cox took a teaching position at Columbia University in New York before settling at Toronto's York University in 1977.

Robert Cox describes his approach to IPE and IR as historical materialist (2002a, pp. 27–9). The historical part involves recognizing that each histor-ical era has a particular sensibility and set of institutions and understandings. This contrasts with approaches which claim there are universal laws of human behaviour which apply across time. The materialist part places the organization of production and the social relations around production at the centre of analysis. In other words, class and class conflict play an important part in understanding political economy. Cox takes a particular approach to historical materialism which mixes theoretical insights from Marx with those of scholars such as Vico, Sorel, Weber, Gramsci and Polanyi. The result is that many liberals and economic nationalists label Cox a Marxist, while many Marxists argue that he has deviated from the Marxist path

(Schechter, 2002). Thus, the labels one picks up depend heavily upon who is doing the labelling.

As the title of a collection of Cox's essays indicates, his primary interest has been *Approaches to World Order* (1996a). However, the specific focus moved from international organizations to social forces to civilizations. Cox's early work focused upon international organizations, especially the ILO. In the 1970s he and Harold Jacobson (1974) worked on decision-making in international organizations. They tried to understand what factors were most influential in shaping the programmes of international organizations.

Cox's experience at the ILO and his study of international organizations prompted him to think about the nature of power and dominance in the global economy. He (1983) theorized that powerful states exercise a form of hegemony that goes far beyond military strength. Hegemonic states such as Britain in the 19th century or the United States in the 20th century drew their power from a particular form of production and social relations. Hegemony requires dominance in the economic, political, social and ideological realms. A hegemonic power is able to convince others that their interests are the same as those of the dominant power. As a result, hegemonic states try to express their interests as universal norms and use international organizations to influence other states.

Central to Cox's work has been the idea that 'production generates the capacity to exercise power, but power determines the manner in which production takes place' (1987, p. 1). The ability to produce things generates resources and objects that can be used to influence events, but the production of things takes place under the shadow of coercion. For example, the industrial revolution boosted British productivity and allowed it to exercise an international role in the 19th century. However, the organization of production was accomplished by the use of force, whether it was in the case of slavery in the cotton industry or forcing people out of the countryside into factories in Britain.

Cox also argued that it was a mistake to focus on the state and ignore the role of social forces (1986). Social forces are groups of people who occupy a particular place in the global economy by virtue of their role in the organization of production. Some social forces such as the people who own or work in an internationally competitive industry advocate free trade while other social forces will oppose free trade as a threat to their interests.

In the theoretical realm Cox (1986) was significant for highlighting the differences between critical theory and problem-solving theory. Problem-solving theory looks at the world as it is and concentrates on how issues can be addressed in the existing system. Critical theory stands back from the existing order and asks how that order came about and under what conditions it could be changed to a different form of order. Critical theorists seek to contribute to a better social order. They thus embrace emancipatory strategies. Problem-solving theory is about managing the system and critical theory is about changing the system. Most radical analyses which call for major changes in the global political economy fit into this critical category.

Cox's later work shifted to new areas of investigation. He acknowledged two weaknesses in his earlier work – the neglect of gender and of environmental issues (2002a). Attempts to theorize world order need to take account of how men and women are differentially incorporated into the global economy and of people's relationship to the environment. The key questions that drew his attention in later years were 'How can a global system function in a non-hegemonic or pluralist manner? How can people who have different understandings of how the world operates and how it should operate create a system for humane global governance?' The two areas he chose to explore were civil society and civilizational interchange (2002a).

Cox's most significant impact in the study of IPE has been to raise critical questions about the system of international order and to contemplate how one might get to a more egalitarian and sustainable system. This has led him to disagree with the normative and practical implications of economic liberalism, the fatality of economic nationalism and the dogma of fundamentalist Marxism.

John Ruggie – constructivist practitioner

John Ruggie emigrated to Canada from Austria in the 1950s. He studied politics and history at McMaster University in Southern Ontario before earning a Political Science PhD at the University of California, Berkeley. He subsequently taught at the University of California, Berkeley and San Diego, Columbia University's School of International and Public Affairs and Harvard's Kennedy School of Government. Since the late 1990s Ruggie has also worked with the United Nations at very senior levels.

Ruggie wrote a series of important articles on a variety of topics in International Relations and International Political Economy from the 1980s to the 1990s. The work most relevant to IPE highlights the operations of international regimes and the social construction of world order. In 1982 his article (Ruggie, 1982) on international regimes and embedded liberalism argued that the international arrangements in trade and money were limited by the domestic normative preferences of key states. The United States and the United Kingdom both wanted domestic full employment so they created international rules which would support such strategies. The international system reflected the social desires or social purpose of the actors that created them. The international liberal system was embedded in a series of national deals and priorities that prevented the system from moving in a purely liberal direction. In contrast to approaches which predicted the nature of international order from the power capabilities of various states, Ruggie argued that one must go further to determine what the identity of particular states were. In his view a US-centred hegemony would look very different from a Russian- or a British-centred hegemony.

In examining international regimes, agreements and organizations Ruggie also argued that analysts need to examine actors' understandings of institutions, as well as the institutions themselves. Behaviour needs to be interpreted. For example, the norm of an international trade agreement might be that countries do not raise tariffs on manufactured goods. In one particular year several countries might raise tariffs on cars. Evaluating the health of this agreement through an examination of the actors' behaviour would lead to the conclusion that the agreement is broken or very weak. However, actors themselves may have a different understanding of each other's behaviour and view the agreement in a more positive light. It may be that in that particular year a recession forced governments into temporary protectionist measures and this was understood by all concerned as a temporary reaction. An interpretive or constructivist account would discern that the regime was still intact while a rationalist approach would consider the regime to have been weakened.

A thread running through Ruggie's work is his concern with social constructivism in the field of international organization and IPE (1998). Ideas about appropriate behaviour, rules governing behaviour, the institutions that embody particular ideas and norms all play a significant part in shaping the global political economy in his view.

In the late 1990s Ruggie took on a policy role working for the United Nations as Assistant Secretary-General for Strategic Planning. In that post he helped establish and oversee the UN Global Compact and worked on the UN General Assembly's proposal and ratification of the Millennium Development Goals (more on both of these later in the book). In 2005 Ruggie took up the post of Secretary-General's Special Representative for Business and Human Rights, where his task is to propose measures to strengthen the human rights performance of the business sector around the world.

This policy role fits very well with Ruggie's scholarly work, which stresses the idea of social construction. The Global Compact is a set of principles for businesses in the fields of environmental and human rights. The Millennium Development Goals (MDGs) set out targets for improving development indicators such as education and health. Both initiatives are meant to highlight key priorities in the hope that this will shift the behaviour of key actors. In the case of the Global Compact the hope is that peer pressure and information will encourage business to behave ethically. For the MDGs the goal is to encourage states to direct more resources and aid towards meeting the basic needs of citizens.

John Ruggie's work advanced understanding about the intersubjective nature of regimes and opened the door for constructivism as an approach to understanding global order. In the policy field his work has advanced projects which attempt to shift the norms and practices of actors in the fields of global business ethics and development.

Where are we now? Globalization and IPE

In trying to capture the field of IPE today it is helpful to think about two key features. One is the ongoing debate about methodology outlined above. The second, to which we devote more attention given the focus of this text, is the way in which debates about globalization have impacted on research priorities.

In this respect there are clear echoes of the problems addressed by Strange, Keohane, Cox and Ruggie. As we have argued above (and will in the remainder of this book), international political economy as an approach to explaining developments in the global political economy has to be understood in relation to a changing historical context. It is possible to conceive of IPE in Western universities as marked by three major debates – interdependence, declining American hegemony and globalization. Recent and current research in IPE is informed by the contemporary debate on globalization, and within this debate four issues have informed scholarship. These themes are the changing role of the state, regionalism, inequality and governance.

Research on the state arises from the central question of the contemporary relevance of the state in an age of globalization. Two distinct but interrelated clusters of scholarship have emerged. The first focuses on the ways in which the authority of the state has been disrupted or enhanced by the processes of globalization. The empirical focus is on the impact of changes in the production and finance structures on state authority, legitimacy and autonomy. No consensus exists in the literature and a vigorous debate continues with three identifiable research streams. Some authors argue that globalization is forcing the state into retreat (Strange, 1996); others contend that the state is changing but in ways that signal complex transformation rather than a decline in its role (Cerny, 2000); and another group of scholars provide evidence to support their claim that state structures remain resilient in the face of a changing global economy (Garrett, 2000; Gritsch, 2005; Weiss, 2003). More material for debate in this area has been added by the global financial crisis of 2008–9 and the various state responses to that crisis.

The second cluster of the state debate emerges from the earlier studies of Keohane on the determinants of the conditions under which states cooperate. Recently two issues have come to the fore in this scholarship. First, the question of how domestic politics might be integrated into our understanding of international affairs (Milner, 1997) and, second, the legalization of international relations (Goldstein *et al.*, 2000).

Research on regionalism was stimulated by the emergence in the late 1980s of the so-called new regionalism. Expansion and transformation of existing regional organizations such as the Association of South-east Asian Nations (ASEAN) and the European Union (EU) and the emergence of new regional groupings, for example, the Asia-Pacific Economic Cooperation (APEC) and the North American Free Trade Agreement (NAFTA) led to a reawakening of interest in regionalism and the construction of a new agenda in the study of regionalism (Hurrell, 1995). Research on regional integration was transformed in two significant ways. First, one of the main normative goals has been discarded. Studies of both old and new regionalism are concerned with the transformation of political community, but whereas in the 1960s and early 1970s scholars' interest was particularly concerned with the role of regional organizations in fostering cooperative and peaceful relations among states, current research is less concerned with the peace dividend. Instead, contemporary research is concerned with the shift of authority from national to regional levels, the distributional impact of regional groupings and the relationship between regionalism and globalization (Coleman and Underhill, 1998; Gamble and Payne, 1996). Second, the scope of research has broadened to focus on the role of non-state actors such as transnational corporations and social movements rather than the previous concentration on inter-state activity (O'Brien, 1995).

The problem of national and global inequality while central to critical perspectives in IPE was until recently of limited concern to other more orthodox approaches. Globalization has brought to the fore concerns with the politics of change and global restructuring, thus highlighting the issue of inequality (Hurrell and Woods, 1995). Scholars from the economic nationalist (Banuri, Khan and Mahmood, 1997; Hines, 2000) and critical perspectives (Amin, 1997; Hoogvelt, 1997) have developed research agendas to document the ways in which processes of global restructuring lead to increased marginalization and social exclusion. This in turn has stimulated research by liberal IPE scholars (Bourguignon and Morrison, 1992; Burtless *et al.*, 1998; Krugman and Venables, 1995; Stewart and Berry, 1999). Two issues have been at the forefront of this scholarship. The first issue concerns the implications of transformations in the global political economy for public and private actors in the developing world. The central question concerns the benefits and costs of globalization for developing countries and for the poor in developing countries. Feminist scholars with a focus on gender issues provide an important contribution to this stream of analysis (Afshar and Barrientos, 1999; Dickenson and Shaeffer, 2001; Marchand and Runyan, 2000). The second major issue is that of the role of global economic institutions in the management of globalization. Here attention has focused on the adjustment policies, liberalization strategies and the normative function of major global economic organizations (Mihevc, 1995; Stewart, 1995; Stiglitz, 2002; Williams, 1994).

The fourth major theme in contemporary empirical research focuses on the problems of (global) governance (Hewson and Sinclair, 1999; Nye and Donahue, 2000). At issue are the various ways in which states, firms, social movements and individuals are coping with transformations in the global economy. One strand of research is concerned with the politics of resistance and investigates the diverse ways in which labour unions, NGOs and civil society groups articulate resistance against practices of change and (global) restructuring (Khagram, Riker and Sikkink, 2002). A second strand of research concentrates on assessing the extent to which non-state actors, including firms and non-governmental organizations (NGOs), intersect with national, regional and global governance structures. In response to recent civic action and protest against international organizations and globalization, work on civic associations, NGOs and social movements is increasing (O'Brien *et al.*, 2000). This work expands upon the neo-Gramscian IPE approaches by shifting the focus from elite groups to non-elites. It has been greatly strengthened by the empirical studies and theoretical challenges of feminist and environmentalist scholars incorporating gender and the environment. Another research trajectory focuses on the role of the corporation in the international political economy. This can take the form of studies investigating the role that corporations have played in influencing state and international organization policies. For example, leading US and European pharmaceutical, information technology and entertainment companies have been very successful in protecting their patent rights through changes to international trade law (Sell, 1999). Other studies have looked at the activity of corporations which are trying to set up their own forms of authority through market mechanisms (Cutler, Haufler and Porter, 1999). For example, bond-rating agencies evaluate the creditworthiness of states and firms, giving an authoritative verdict on how much they should pay in order to borrow money (Sinclair, 1994). These two strands of research are linked but the literature on the firm gives more attention to the nature of rule-making by private actors, while the NGO literature is often concerned with how citizen groups try to shape economic relations in a more equitable manner.

It will become apparent in the following chapters that IPE remains a contested field, with no single theoretical tradition in a position of unrivalled dominance. However, certain kinds of explanation are more powerful than other forms. Below we set out the key features of our theoretical approach. In the final chapter we return to consider this synthesis and the issue of contemporary theorizing in IPE.

Approach of the book

We have seen that IPE is often conceived as a debate between three contending schools of thought. We have also seen that different scholars pursue particular research agendas and that methodological issues can loom large in designing and reporting research findings. Scholars (and practitioners) of IPE tend to base their analysis on sets of assumptions common to a specific paradigm. As argued above, all IPE analyses are written from a particular theoretical perspective. Theoretical assumptions guide choices about which theories and events should be highlighted and which will not make it into the study. Our purpose in this book is to provide readers with the theoretical tools and empirical knowledge needed to develop their own understanding of how the global political economy works. This is a challenging task as this chapter has already demonstrated. We do this on the basis of a framework of analysis indebted to insights of the three IPE perspectives, but not fully ascribing to the assumptions and propositions of any one of these perspectives. We will return to the three main approaches when they are helpful for understanding particular developments. For example, liberal theories help us understand some of the elements of British policy in the 19th century and the thinking behind multilateral trade institutions in the 20th century. However, in assembling the material for the book we have been guided by an approach that reflects our view about how international or global political economy should be understood. It reflects our synthesis of elements of the three contending paradigms.

The framework of analysis outlined below and developed in the remainder of the book is intended to provide a guide to understanding international political economy. The aim of the framework is to allow students to organize and simplify in a systematic manner the evidence necessary to explain contemporary developments in the global political economy. The framework is an organizing device and not a theory or a new perspective. It seeks to integrate key concepts and theoretical insights from different approaches into an overarching, multidimensional approach. As detailed below, our framework integrates six key elements: historical change, structure-agency dynamics, integration of cognitive structures, political-economic processes, institutionalism and the salience of domestic structures.

First, our approach is historicist in that it is sensitive to historical change. The nature of political economy, its major institutions and ideas about how it operates change over time (Cox, 1996a, pp. 49–59). This book places historical development at the centre of its explanatory framework, and recognizes history as both the context or framework within which meaning is located, and an ideological concept which is evident in various perspectives on political economy. Theories about how the world works arise in particular historical contexts and need to be linked to those contexts. A historical sensitivity is also important to understanding the path-dependent nature of the evolution of the global political economy. Some states and groups of people have become locked into particular development patterns because of events that took place many years ago. For example, many developing countries export low-value commodities because their economies were oriented to this task during the age of imperialism.

The role of historical practices in development raises a second point, which is the relationship between structure and agency. Put simply this is the question of whether overarching structures such as the organization of production or the institution of patriarchy determine the action of agents (states, firms, people) or whether agents engage in free choice and construct their own environments (Wendt, 1987). We view the relationship as dynamic and do not privilege either systemic or unit level variables. There are dangers in reifying structures on one hand and in reducing complex events to individual action on the other. In rejecting structural determinism and methodological individualism we seek to understand the ways in which structures constrain action and agency impacts on structural constraints. The existence of a structure of patriarchy does not, for example, determine that all males will exploit women.

Third, we recognize the salience of ideas or cognitive structures as significant elements in the GPE and examine the role of ideas in structuring outcomes (Finnemore and Sikkink, 1998). Norms, values, ideologies and ideas are constitutive elements of the global political economy. This means that they help to make the world the way it is rather than only reflecting how we think about the world. While ideas are linked to material developments and interests, they are not derived solely from the material structures of the global economy. On the contrary, ideas shape, mould, facilitate and constrain the activities of economic agents. For example, if it is believed that inflation is the economic problem most destructive of stability, harmony and progress this becomes an economic 'fact' and redistributivist policies are subsumed to the dictates of the fight against inflation. Fighting inflation ceases to be perceived as a policy choice and instead is taken to be a central and natural feature of economic governance. Another example would be the ideas supporting patriarchy. It might be assumed that women are naturally docile and dextrous, thus making them the ideal choice for particular types of employment. The importance of ideas, intellectual schemes and ideologies will therefore be investigated rather than taken as given. Certain claims to the contrary notwithstanding, political economy is not value-free and arguments over economic theories cannot be dismissed as rhetoric.

Fourth, we stress the inseparability of economics and politics, and therefore reject the separation of the economic from the political at the core of liberal and mercantilist approaches. Whereas liberalism separates the economic from the political and mercantilism subsumes the economic to the political we insist that the economic constitutes the political and the political constitutes the economic. One of the ways that this becomes apparent in the text is that we link events in the field of economic development with the deployment of organized violence and the ramifications of warfare.

Fifth, we view institutions as constantly undergoing change. Perspectives that take the institutional context as a given are deficient. Recently economics and political science literatures have recognized the importance of social institutions in structuring market behaviour. We begin from the recognition that formal and informal institutions play significant roles in structuring outcomes in the international system. We therefore investigate the impact of institutions and emphasize the contribution of formal organizations to the evolution of the global economy. Two of the significant institutions we examine in the text are the changing nature of the state and the organization of international or world order. For example, the states discussed in the third chapter have mercantilist and imperialist characteristics while the industrial revolution sees the emergence of a liberal British state. Following the Second World War, many Third World countries were characterized by developmental states and Western countries adopted some form of the Keynesian state.

Finally, our view of the global political economy is sensitive to the relationship between changes in domestic social orders and structures of international order and global political economy (Cox, 1986; Skidmore, 1997). Social and class conflict in key states can bolster or undermine the principles and institutions upon which a particular world order rests. A leading explanation for the success of European expansionist activity in the 16th and 17th centuries was the greater relative autonomy that merchants enjoyed in Europe compared to empires in other parts of the world. Another example is the role that mobilized populations played in thwarting the attempts to build a stable liberal international system between 1918 and 1939. Changes in citizen expectations about government behaviour made it impossible to impose the economic medicine that liberal theory demanded.

Keeping the main approaches and our own blend of important characteristics in mind, we now turn our attention to the evolution and dynamics of the global political economy.

Part II

Evolution

Chapter 3

Forging a World Economy 1400–1800

Why do we inhabit a world where there are such great inequalities of wealth and life chances between regions? Why do some countries seem to be caught in a trap of producing products whose value declines over time, such as sugar or coffee? What accounts for the racial hierarchies in countries such as the United States and South Africa? Why do some societies and countries seem suspicious of the foreign and economic policies of Western states, corporations and civic associations? The answers to these questions are partially rooted in the origins of the global economy. Indeed, a full understanding of today's global economy requires a familiarity with patterns that were initiated hundreds of years ago.

Croce's argument that 'however remote in time events thus recounted may seem to be, the history in reality refers to present needs and present situation wherein those events vibrate' (Croce, 1941, p. 19) implies that history is constantly rewritten in light of existing debates and sensibilities. New histories often tell us as much about the times in which they were written as they do about the historical events themselves. An interesting example of this can be seen in the last decade of the 20th century when several prominent scholars engaged in a debate about the 'Rise of the West'. They tried to explain why political and economic power was concentrated in the hands of several Western states (Western Europe and the United States). On one side of the debate were those who congratulated today's winners in the global economy by arguing that the rich were wealthy because they had the most virtuous social, economic and political institutions. We can call this the cultural approach. The rich are rich because they have a culture that supports success. A prominent exponent of this view is Harvard historian David Landes in his book *The Wealth and Poverty of Nations* (1998). The other side of the debate argued that Western success was accidental and temporary, built upon force and expropriation as much as any positive cultural attributes. We can call this the global historical approach because it stresses the role of other civilizations and refutes the historical claims of the culturalists. Such an approach challenges the notion that history has ended because Western states have discovered the ultimate model for structuring economic, social and political relations. A prominent illustration of this approach is John M. Hobson's *The Eastern Origins of Western Civilization* (2004).

The debate between cultural and global historical explanations about the 'Rise of the West' became heated because it concerned the present and the future as much as it did the past. Participants claimed that they had discovered the secrets to why some are rich and others are poor. Such knowledge can be used by others to restructure their societies in hopes of similar success. The practical implications are immense. The culturalists see the cause of poverty as the behaviour of the poor, while the global historicist side sees it as a result of the relationship between the poor and the rich. The policy implications of the first view are that the poor are themselves primarily responsible for improving their position, while the implication of the second view is that the system of political and economic relations must be changed to create greater equity. The first message offers comfort to those already enjoying economic success, while the second urges mobilization and change. This second section of the book joins the debate about the history and structure of the emerging global economy.

How far back in history should we go to get a better understanding of today's patterns of inequalities and wealth generation? In his best-selling book, *Guns, Germs, and Steel*, Jared Diamond (1997) argued that we need to go back 11,000 years to find the ultimate causes of differences in economic development between people and regions. In his view environmental and geographic factors such as differences in plant and animal species, rates of migration and diffusion within and between continents, and total area/population size of continents privileged the peoples of Europe and Asia over people in other parts of the world. The ability to produce food and domesticate animals allowed for the creation of civilizations which overwhelmed societies with less complicated divisions of labour.

Our investigations will begin in the late 1400s when Spanish adventurers forcefully integrated sections of the Americas into an intercontinental economy that already linked parts of Europe, Africa and Asia. This chapter focuses on the period when the major regional economies in Asia, Africa, Europe and the Americas were brought into increased contact through the persistence of European expansionism. It is the beginning of the first truly worldwide or global economy. This will be accomplished in two steps. First, we will provide a brief overview of the major economic areas before the Spanish conquest of the 1500s. This will give us an understanding of the diversity of political economy arrangements around the world and will lay the groundwork for understanding the varying pattern of European–non-European interaction in subsequent centuries. Second, we will look at the pattern of European engagement with other parts of the world from the 1490s until the early 1800s. The conclusion analyses the historical record in terms of the key frameworks used in Part II of the book (trade, production, finance, labour, gender, development, environment, security, ideas and governance).

The chapter has two major arguments. First, the regional political economies that were connecting during this period varied greatly in terms of social, political and economic organization. Second, this heterogeneity created a variety of interactions from free exchange to open warfare and slavery. A third point, explored in following chapters, is that these interactions would have long-lasting effects.

Regions of the world economy

This section provides a snapshot of several areas of the world prior to European contact with the Americas which created the first truly worldwide political economy. In the year 1400 there was little hint that the residents of Europe would have such an influence upon the majority of people who lived in other regions. As the Portuguese, Spanish, Dutch, English and French steadily moved outward from their own continent they encountered a variety of people and social organizations. Rather than expanding into a vacuum, the Europeans interacted with established civilizations, economic systems and military forces.

There are several points to keep in mind. First, with few exceptions economic activity was on a local level. Agricultural production was the norm and this was usually centred upon a market town with an agricultural hinterland of about 30 kilometres (Schwartz, 1994, p. 13). Second, despite the predominance of this local activity, intercontinental trade routes moving luxury goods had existed for thousands of years. Third, at the heart of these trade routes lay very different civilizations with distinct political economies. Indeed, some approaches to international relations and global history take different civilizations as their starting point (Braudel, 1994; Cox, 1996b).

Janet Abu-Lughod (1989) has provided an interesting account of the world system before Europeans began their transatlantic voyages. Her research reveals a system of trade and economic exchange reaching from China to Europe. The system was composed of eight overlapping regions. Economic activity was concentrated within these regions, but they were linked to neighbouring regions allowing products to move from eastern Asia to western Europe. Map 3.1 reproduces Abu-Lughod's diagram showing the regions, but it also adds four additional regions that will be discussed below under 'Africa' and 'Americas'. Moving from west to east on the Eurasian continent, the first area is the region which brought together northern and southern Europe. The second region sits above the Mediterranean, crossing the divide between Christian southern Europe and the Islamic centres of Egypt. This Mediterranean region overlapped with three central regions. Region 3 covered the overland trade routes which stretched across central Asia to China and were maintained by the Mongols. Region 4 included the territory around the Tigris and Euphrates rivers (modern-day Iraq) down to

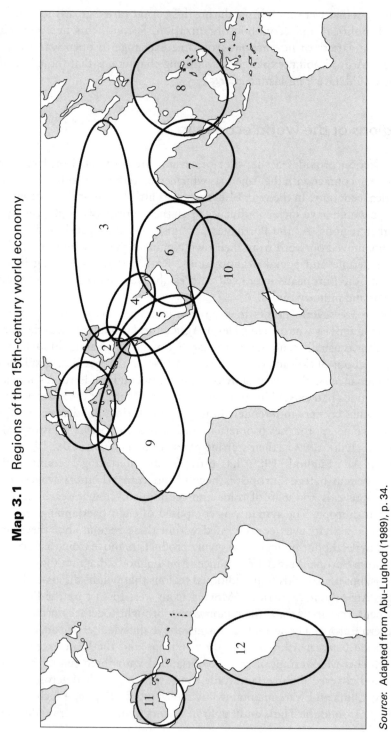

Map 3.1   Regions of the 15th-century world economy

Source: Adapted from Abu-Lughod (1989), p. 34.

the Persian Gulf. Region 5 also joined the Mediterranean and the Indian Ocean, but through Egypt and the Red Sea. Products making their way into the Indian Ocean were then transported across Region 6, which covered the Arabian Sea, linking Arabia with the western coast of India. Region 7 linked India with South-east Asia, while Region 8 finished the route by taking in China and South-east Asia. This meant that there were three routes for products to move from China to Europe. The northern route moved goods overland from China via central Asia through the Mediterranean into the European region. Alternatively, products could move by sea through South-east Asia, the Indian Ocean and then into the Mediterranean either through the Persian Gulf or the Red Sea.

Abu-Lughod's work omits African trading regions, so we have added two regions which cover certain areas of sub-Saharan Africa. One region brought goods from sub-Saharan Africa into northern Africa and the Mediterranean/European world (Region 9). The other brought African goods into the Middle East and Asia via the Indian Ocean (Region 10). Our map also includes two regions in the Americas which were not joined to the African–European–Asian system. These are Region 11, which belonged to the Aztec empire, and Region 12, ruled by the Incas.

Although it would take years to travel around this circuit of trade in the 1400s and the volumes of trade were minuscule by today's standards, economic activity was increasing across the system. Let's turn our attention to each of these regions to get a brief idea of their nature. We are particularly interested in the types of economic activity and political relations that characterized each region.

The Middle East

In Abu-Lughod's diagram of 14th-century regions, the Middle East acts as the key gateway between the Mediterranean/European and the Eastern worlds. Indeed, the desire to get around this gateway was one of the key motivations driving European merchants into the Atlantic Ocean, around Africa and across to the Americas. By the time of Christopher Columbus' voyage across the Atlantic, there had already been a 700-year history of bloody and lucrative interchange between European Christendom and Middle Eastern Islam. Islamic and Christian clashes took place from the south of France, through modern-day Egypt, Israel and Turkey, to the gates of Vienna. Yet, this rivalry was balanced by many instances of cooperation with alliances and economic interchange between Europeans and Middle Easterners. For example, the Genovese sold Christian and pagan slaves to the Mamlukes in Egypt who then trained them as soldiers to be used against the Crusaders while the Venetians financed an Ottoman fleet to battle the Portuguese in the Red Sea.

For almost 1,000 years Islamic warriors waged successful military campaigns against European forces. Behind those Middle Eastern armies stood a dynamic economy, extensive trade networks, bustling cities and great centres of learning. In retrospect we can see that the 15th century was a period of transition in the Middle East. While the religion of Islam was dominant, forms of political authority were the object of intense rivalry. Although ultimate political authority eventually came to rest in the hands of the Sultan of the Ottoman Empire, this occurred only after a period of conflict with and between Turkish tribes, Mongols, Persians and Mamlukes. The competition between rival sources of political power characteristic of Europe was not absent in the Middle East. However, by the early 1500s one empire, the Ottoman, held the upper hand. It proceeded to extend its rule eastwards and westwards towards Europe. On land and at sea the Europeans had great difficulty matching the might of Islamic forces in the 15th century. It would not be until the second siege of Vienna in 1683 that European militaries would start to win consistent victories.

The Mamlukes, followed by the Ottomans, presided over a thriving trading economy. In the 14th century, Cairo had a population of approximately half a million, which was only exceeded by one or two cities in China (Abu-Lughod, 1989, p. 212). The Mamlukes developed a structured and prosperous trading relationship with the Venetians. Through force of arms they prevented Europeans from seizing Egyptian territory that would have granted direct access to the wealth of India and China via the Red Sea. Venetians docked in Alexandria to wait for access to spices, dyes, pepper, silk, cotton and porcelains from Malaysia, India and China.

Outside of the Mediterranean, Arab traders pursued economic activity along the coast of eastern Africa, the western coast of India and into South-east Asia. Zanzibar, off the coast of eastern Africa, was occupied by Arab traders as early as the 8th century. The cultural remnants of this early commercial activity can be seen in the Muslim populations of countries such as Malaysia and Indonesia (the largest Muslim country in the world).

China

Of all the great civilizations of the 15th century, China was the largest and most powerful. It produced products that were greatly desired by the elite in other regions of the world. Chief among these products were ceramics and silk. China contained the world's largest cities, advanced technology and impressive military forces. Indeed, the wonders of China were so great that when the Italian Marco Polo returned from his travels to that land, his observations were often dismissed as being fanciful.

During the 14th and 15th centuries China was also undergoing dramatic changes. In 1370 the Chinese had finally succeeded in driving out Mongol rulers and re-established a Chinese emperor. This line of rulers was called the Ming dynasty (1368–1644). Initially, the Mings launched several long-range trading voyages as far as the eastern coast of Africa. Their ships were five times as large as later Portuguese ships and they contained far more cargo space and cannons. They would have been capable of crossing the Pacific Ocean if they had attempted the task (McNeill, 1982, pp. 44–5). Indeed, had the voyages continued it is possible that the Chinese might have sailed around Africa and reached Portugal, as well as 'discovered' the Americas. However, expeditions to the west (1405–33) were eventually halted by the Ming emperors and the sea-going fleet decommissioned. For the next several hundred years, the Chinese were less engaged with the outside world and fell behind relative to the expanding Europeans.

There are several possible explanations for why the naval excursions were ended. One has to do with court politics. The leader of the expeditions (Zheng He) was both a Muslim and a eunuch and eventually lost the support of the emperors. Another explanation is that although the voyages brought back interesting goods, there was little that the Chinese found that they actually needed. Unlike the Europeans, who were desperate for spices and silks, the Chinese did not find anything so attractive that it would justify the expense of further exploration. Finally, the centre of gravity in China shifted towards the north and internal development. The Mings moved the capital from Nanjing northwards to Beijing and became more concerned with land rather than sea threats. In addition, new locks on the Grand Canal joined the Yangtze and Yellow river valleys, securing year-round rice transport in internal waters. This greatly reduced the importance of any maritime threats to Chinese stability and hence the need for a powerful navy (McNeill, 1982, p. 47).

In terms of political structures, the Ming Chinese emperor was the sole source of law. His views might be restrained by appeal to precedent and scholarly discussions or debates, but his power was absolute (Mote, 1999, p. 637). China was governed by a single political authority, unlike the rival states that fought continuously in Europe. The court sat in Beijing and governors of provinces reported to the bureaucracy and the court in the capital city. The emperor was supported by a well-trained bureaucracy that was selected through a process of examination. Confucian scholar-officials played the major role in running the bureaucracy and advising the emperor. Increasingly during the Ming dynasty, eunuchs played a key role in running the court and providing services to the emperor. In some cases, such as the admiral Cheng Ho, they accomplished great feats. In other cases they advanced their interests over that of the empire and cut the emperor off from developments in his realm.

India

Like China, India also possessed an ancient civilization, considerable economic wealth and military might. However, India was a more diverse and decentralized political economy than China. The northern section of India had experienced a series of invasions from Persian, Mongol, Turkish and Afghan tribes. In the 15th century, the northern region, known as the Delhi Sultanate, was ruled by descendants of invading Islamic forces, but they were constantly under attack from new waves of invaders. The Sultanate was ravaged by the Mongol descendant Timur (Tamerlane) in 1388 and Delhi was sacked in 1398. Internal cohesion was difficult to maintain. One hundred and twenty-five years later a descendant of Timur (Barbur) invaded India and set up the Mughal (Mongol) dynasty. Many of India's architectural wonders, such as the Taj Mahal, date from the Mughal era.

Other parts of India were ruled by independent kingdoms. The southern region was dominated by the Hindu kingdom of Vijayanagar from 1336 to 1565. It was often engaged in conflict with its neighbour, the Bahmani empire. The eastern province of Bengal was usually controlled by independent rulers and the western coastal area of Gujarat also enjoyed independence. There were numerous other smaller kingdoms during this period.

Ports in coastal areas of India enjoyed a great deal of autonomy from the inland empires and economic activity was conducted by a wide range of social and economic groups. In Kerala external trade was conducted by Jews and Christians who had been resident since the 6th century. In other parts of India, Jains, Buddhists, Muslims and Hindus were involved in trade (Bouchon and Lombard, 1987). On the western coast of India, the state of Gujarat dominated trade moving from the Middle East to the east coast of India. On the east coast, Bengal played a major part in moving goods on to South-east Asia. However, these coastal areas were relatively peripheral to the land-based empire. For example, it is reported that when the Mughal emperor Akbar visited the recently conquered Indian ports of Cambay and Surat in the late 1500s, it was the first time that he had ever seen the ocean (Risso, 1995).

Reflecting on the experiences of the Middle East, China and India it is noteworthy that while these civilizations engaged in maritime activity, it was difficult for maritime interests to influence political power. The large land-based empires engaged in seaborne trade and established wide-ranging activity crossing the Mediterranean, Red Sea, Persian Gulf, Indian Ocean and around the seas to China. However, the Ottomans, Chinese and Mughals were primarily concerned with events within their existing empires and concentrated most of their effort in land-based expansion and defence. This was a very different pattern from the maritime-dependent Portuguese, Spanish, Dutch and British empires.

Africa

To Abu-Lughod's diagram of trading networks outside of the Americas we added two ellipses to cover interaction with sub-Saharan Africa. One ellipse covers land on either side of the Sahara desert and the difficult trade across that arid sea. In western Africa gold mines supplied European demand for currency while pepper was shipped north for consumption in food seasoning. This trade eventually encouraged the Portuguese to sail around the desert to establish direct trading contacts. The second ellipse integrates the trade of eastern Africa with that of the Indian Ocean. In eastern Africa trading posts exported slaves, ivory, iron, rhinoceros horn, turtle shell, amber and leopard skins to India and beyond. Both of these networks had existed for thousands of years.

Africa contained a large variety of political groups (Shillington, 1995). Northern African states were integrated into the Islamic empire. In Ethiopia, a Christian kingdom was founded in the 4th century which maintained its independence until the late 1930s. In the Shona state of Great Zimbabwe, 10-metre high stone enclosures surrounded the king's residence. Around the great lakes area of Central Africa, the Luba and Lunda empires concentrated on fishing and hunting. They purchased iron and salt from the north and copper from the south, which was made into rings, bracelets and necklaces. In summary, the large continent contained a number of different political economies linked together through trade.

Americas

Although the existence of the Americas came as a surprise to Europeans, many areas were marked by advanced civilizations. Advanced civilization, in terms of intensive agricultural activity and large cities with complicated architecture, took place in two regions of the Americas. One region was the Incan empire in the Andes in Peru and Bolivia which stretched from Ecuador to Chile. The other was in Mesoamerica – Mexico and Guatemala. This was the home of the Maya who were starting to decline and the Aztecs who were in the process of creating a large empire.

The Spanish encountered a well-developed empire when they began contact with the population of Mexico. The Aztecs ruled Mexico and were the successor to a series of civilizations which included the Olmec, Teotihuacan and Toltecs. Although there were differences between these civilizations some continuities are noticeable (Davies, 1982). Similar to old-world civilizations, the Americans demonstrated an ability to build and maintain cities, erect large monuments and support sophisticated forms of art. The Aztec capital, Tenochtitlan, dazzled the Spanish invaders because of its large population and elaborate beauty. Its population was over ten times that of leading Spanish cities of the same era. Unlike the Europeans and Asians, the Americans faced greater transportation difficulties. Lacking beasts of burden most goods were carried by foot. Water transport was also limited due to the presence of mountain ranges (Andes) or inland empires. This meant that more energy had to be expended on transportation than in other parts of the world.

Exchange of goods was primarily in the form of tribute rather than trade. Goods were traded, but the empires tended to accumulate things by demanding them as tribute from weaker states. Dominated cities provided goods for the elite of the empire. Under the Aztecs, political relations were characterized by the use of force. There was severe punishment for disobeying the king and the Aztecs engaged in the practice of human sacrifice to appease the gods. The Aztec civilization exploited conquered peoples to amass wealth. Thus, when the Spaniard Cortes began his conquest of Mexico he found willing local allies eager to throw off Aztec oppression.

Europe

The political economy of the area now known as Western Europe underwent significant changes during the 13th to 15th centuries which placed a series of European states in a much stronger position in relation to outside powers. The two most significant changes were: increased economic activity and integration across Europe, and the consolidation of European political authority into rival states. We'll examine the increased economic activity by considering new trading patterns and the role of money and finance. Under consolidation of rival states, we'll review both the emergence of nation-states and the consequences of changing forms of European warfare. The combination of these changes set the stage for European expansion.

New patterns of trade.   The 14th and 15th centuries saw the western European economy build bridges between its southern and northern centres. In the south a handful of small Italian cities (Venice, Amalfi, Pisa and Genoa) began to develop their commercial roles, while in northern Europe economic activity developed in the Low Countries of present-day Belgium and the Netherlands and in the North and Baltic seas. Gradually, economic activity began to link together these two poles of European commerce (see Map 3.2).

The Italian cities amassed wealth by tapping into the lucrative trade in the Mediterranean. They gathered silk from China, ivory from Africa and spices from India, Africa and South-east Asia. Spices were in high demand amongst the European elites because they masked the taste of rotten food in an era before refrigeration. Key spices included ginger, saffron, mace, cinnamon, sugar, cloves and nutmeg. The favourite spice, however, was pepper. Some years, a million pounds of pepper would pass through Venice. In return for

Map 3.2   European political economy 1400–1500

such goods the Italians were required to either pay in gold and silver, or ship goods to other regions in the Mediterranean. These products included timber, grain, linen, cloth, salt and slaves from the European interior (Braudel, 1994, p. 107).

Although the Italians were developing their commercial and financial skills, the rise of the Italian cities depended upon war just as much as upon trading skills. It was the Crusades which launched the trading fortunes of Christendom and Venice. The men of northern Europe spent large sums of money in Italy as they paid for their passage to the Holy Land. Christian states in the Middle East opened an additional gateway to secure pepper, spices, silk and drugs. For the struggling Italian city-states the main battle was not between Christian and Muslims, but with their fellow Italians. Venice and Genoa engaged in a long and difficult commercial rivalry across the Mediterranean.

Simultaneously, a commercial network was developing in northern Europe with the Belgian city of Bruges emerging as a second Venice. Bruges participated in a series of Flemish fairs by 1200, exploited its English contacts and welcomed Genovese ships in 1277. Its population grew from

35,000 in 1340 to 100,000 by 1500 (Braudel, 1994, p. 99). Its textile industry thrived and, by 1309, Bruges had set up its own stock market, the Bourse.
Outside of Belgium, northern economic activity was facilitated by the
seaborne commercial triumph of the 'Hansa' (a group of merchants), which
operated in the Baltic, North Sea, English Channel and Irish Sea. In 1356 the
Hanseatic League, an alliance of trading ports, was created. The products of
the north and east (wood, wax, fur, rye and wheat) were sent west for salt,
cloth and wine. In contrast to the Italian luxury trade, most northern products were bulky items such as Polish grain, herring, salt, wine, wood, or
Swedish iron. Raw wool was the most valued product, much of it finding its
way into the manufacturing of textiles in Flemish industry or into Italy.
There were some northern luxury products, however. These included fine
Flemish cloth, furs, amber for jewellery, beeswax for candles and honey.

Although this economic activity increased wealth in many parts of
Europe, there was an imbalance in trade. Money drained from the north of
Europe to the south and eventually to the east of the Mediterranean and
beyond. High-priced and desirable goods came into Europe from China,
India, the Middle East and Africa. In return the Europeans had some large
bulk goods to offer, but this was often not sufficient. Luxury goods that
could not be offset with trade had to be purchased with silver or gold.
However, there was a limit as to how much silver or gold Europeans were
able to mine. Eventually this would leave Europeans with three choices: they
could find new sources of silver and gold; they could try and seize the goods
they wanted by force; or they could develop more desirable goods for trade
purposes. As we shall see in later chapters, all of these strategies were
pursued with varying degrees of success. Their biggest breakthrough was
seizing American silver to buy Asian products.

Money and finance.   Now that we have raised the issue of finance and
money, it is appropriate to take a detour to consider the growth of financial
innovation in Europe. New forms of money, credit and the control of money
developed in this period and were crucial to the growing wealth and military
power in Europe and beyond. For people today, living in the age of electronic
banking and credit cards, it is easy to take the presence of money and credit
for granted. Yet, these institutions have not always existed as they do today.
Moreover, the existence of an accepted form of money which is easily inter-
changeable and the instrument of credit is essential for anything more than a
primitive economy (see Box 3.1).

Although various forms of money have been in existence for approximately 4,000 years (iron, tobacco, cattle, shells, beads, whiskey, stones), it is
only in the last century or so that the value of money has been readily
accepted by the public without intense scrutiny (Galbraith, 1996). There has
often been doubt about how much value was stored in the commodities used

Box 3.1   The utility of money

Consider a fanciful, but useful example from an era before money existed. In this context, money can be defined simply as an object that is commonly offered or received for the purchase or sale of goods or services. When there is no money, economic activity must take place on the basis of barter. One product is exchanged for another product rather than for money. For example, your neighbours might give you some firewood if you baked some bread for them. Now, imagine a gathering of four people seeking to exchange products in a society that does not have money. One is a farmer who has brought several bushels of wheat, another is a shepherd bringing some wool from his sheep, a third has brought a horse for exchange and the fourth is a blacksmith with some simple tools such as knives. One problem arises when people try to exchange products of unequal value. Suppose that the person with the horse would like to barter for a single knife. The trade may not take place because the tool-maker can't make change for a horse. Another problem could arise if one person does not want the product of another. For example, the shepherd may want the farmer's wheat, but the farmer may not want the shepherd's wool. The shepherd might have to trade his wool for a knife and then trade the knife for the wheat. Alternatively, he may not be able to barter for a product that the farmer wants and the economic exchange is frustrated. The problem is only solved if all of these people value a single commodity. They could sell their own products for that commodity and use it to purchase other people's goods. That valued commodity is called money.

as money. In the case of metal coins, there has always been the risk that the issuing authority would debase the currency. Debasement occurred when the person minting the coins diluted the gold or silver with other metals and passed it off as a pure product. For example, rather than issuing a gold coin which contained 100 per cent gold, a ruler might be tempted to claim that it was 100 per cent gold but put in 15 per cent copper. The hope was that the coin would still purchase the same amount of goods as the original gold coin, but cost less to make because there was a smaller gold content. Eventually, users of the coin would discover the change and would demand more of it to pay for the same amount of goods. The amount of goods the coin could buy would decrease over time as it became debased. A modern form of debasement is inflation, where money loses its value as prices for goods rise.

Another difficulty in the age of multiple coins was the problem of exchanging money from various jurisdictions. How could one be sure of the value of a foreign coin? Even more serious was the possibility of counterfeit coins. When people from diverse jurisdictions met at trading centres they would often prefer to be paid in coins that had a better reputation for keeping their value than others. The result was that traders would take the valued ones and keep them for private use while the debased ones were passed on. This habit of hoarding good currency led to Thomas Gresham's famous observation in 1558 that bad money always drives out good. The problem of creating a stable international monetary system, which facilitates the exchange of foreign currencies and trade, continues to this day. We will explore some of its dimensions in Chapter 8.

A key advance in financial history was the development of banking and provision of credit. Today we tend to encounter three types of banks. Most people will be aware of deposit banks, also sometimes called commercial or clearing banks. They take deposits and give loans to individuals and corporations. Examples include Citibank, Barclays or Deutsche Bank. These banks project a serious image and rely upon their reputation for sound finance to attract and keep customers. Investment or merchant banks are a second type of bank. They make deals between rich individuals or companies to finance business investments and corporate takeovers. They tend to be more aggressive than deposit banks. Finally, countries also have a third type of bank – the central bank. This is the bank of the country. It is run by the government and is tasked with printing and distributing money and controlling the supply of money within a country (see Box 3.2).

The creation of credit greatly facilitated the growth of European economic activity. Credit notes allowed a person to buy now and pay later. This facilitated economic growth as some people and enterprises were able to conduct business that otherwise would not have taken place. A modern example of such activity is the house mortgage. Very few people would be able to buy a house if they were required to pay for it in cash. However, by taking a loan and paying it off over a long time period, many people can own houses. A similar mechanism was needed to finance long-distance trade.

Another significant development in this area was the beginning of companies with partners or shareholders rather than a single owner. For example, in Italy there was an arrangement called the *commenda*. When launching a trading voyage one merchant would supply two-thirds of the capital while another would supply one-third and manage the enterprise abroad. Both would share the profits. This allowed young adventurous merchants to trade with other merchants' capital. As trade was conducted over greater distances and time periods there was more demand for pooling investment in the form of the corporation. Large infrastructure projects such as canal-building and, later, railroads contributed to the rise of shareholding companies and eventually the creation of stock exchanges (Kindleberger, 1993, pp. 190–8).

The development of accepted forms of money, credit and banks was a

Box 3.2   Banks and financial instability

Although banks and credit allow people to undertake more economic activity, they also pose a financial risk. People, companies or states can take on too much debt and have difficulty repaying the loan. In the case of the banking industry there is always risk that customers panic and cause the collapse of a bank. Banks lend money out of their deposits via currency or notes of credit. However, there is a problem if all depositors come to the bank at once to ask for their money back. The bank will be unable to pay because the money has been distributed to other customers in the form of loans which cannot be instantly recalled. If there is a hint that a bank may be in financial trouble, depositors will rush to withdraw their money, thereby guaranteeing the bank's collapse. A bank must be able to retain the confidence of its depositors if it is to survive. In national banking systems the central bank often acts as a lender of last resort. The lender of last resort guarantees a proportion of depositors' money in the hope that this will prevent a run on the bank. There is no official lender of last resort in the international system.

precondition for financing European economic, political and military expansion from the 1400s until today.

Rise of sovereign territorial states.   A key development in Europe during the 15th to 17th centuries was the transition from feudal forms of organization to new political structures to the eventual emergence of sovereign territorial states. The push for political formations such as city-states, leagues and sovereign states came from merchants in cities seeking greater economic freedom to capitalize on growing long-distance trade (Spruyt, 1994). In Italy, the wealth of the luxury trade with the East allowed particular cities to develop resources great enough to guarantee their economic and military independence. In France, merchants allied with the king to undercut the power of the nobility and free up commerce. This led to the creation of the centralized state. In Germany the king sided with the nobles, forcing cities such as Lubeck and Bremen to band together in the Hanseatic League.

Over time, the state form of organization proved to be more successful than the league or city-state. The state differed from other forms of medieval political organization because it was both sovereign and territorial. Sovereignty meant that there was no higher form of political authority than the states. The king or the parliament was the ultimate legal authority, concentrating law-making and use of violence in their hands. This contrasts with the feudal system where sovereignty was diffuse and authority was shared or contested amongst various actors such as the church, the empire, cities and lords. It also contrasted with leagues of cities where decision-making was difficult to achieve and more difficult to enforce.

The state was also territorial which means that its authority was confined to a particular geographic area. Unlike universalistic organizations such as the church, which claimed authority over all Christians, states limited their jurisdiction to confined borders. The French king claimed authority over people living in France, but recognized the authority of the English king over people living in England. France and England might dispute the specific borders of each country or even try to conquer each other, but there was no question that they recognized each sovereign's right to govern his or her own people as they wished.

The emergence of the sovereign territorial state had several important consequences. First, it proved to be more efficient at mobilizing economic resources than other forms of organizations. A single power with a given territory was gradually able to create national markets for commerce. This involved the destruction of the numerous barriers to economic activity that had grown up in the feudal era. Prominent among these barriers were varying customary laws, dangerous travel conditions, tolls on roads or waterways, a multitude of currencies and diverse weights and measures. By standardizing coinage, weights and measures, developing common laws protecting private property and ensuring safe and easier transit, states were able to increase economic activity and bring resources into their own treasuries.

A second important consequence was the competition created by a system of sovereign states. European states engaged in deadly economic and military competition with each other for hundreds of years. At times this weakened their position with the rest of the world, as in the aftermath of the First and Second World Wars. However, this state rivalry and the inability of any single European state to create a lasting empire over Europe (with the brief exception of Napoleon) injected a certain dynamic into European relations. Innovation in one European state would often be copied in others seeking to keep up in the competitive battle. City-states and states turned to the external world to gain an advantage over their European rivals. For example, as Venice grew stronger, Genoa supported Portuguese and Spanish attempts to break Venetian power by sailing around Africa or across the Atlantic. Although Columbus sailed from Spain he was originally from Genoa and had approached the Portuguese for support.

As Charles Tilly (1999) points out, wars drove European state formation. Conflict between European political authorities and their need for capital to finance ever more destructive wars contributed to the rise of nation-states. Nation-states proved to be more efficient at raising revenue and mobilizing military forces than either the city-states of Italy or leagues of cities such as the Baltic-based Hanseatic League. The centralization of violence within a state's control was so significant that the sociologist Max Weber concentrated on this feature when he defined a state as 'a human community that (successfully) claims the monopoly of the legitimate use of physical force within a given territory' (Gerth and Mills, 1958, p. 78).

This competitive European state system often had negative implications for people outside of Europe. Where they were strong enough, Europeans used other parts of the world either as a battleground for their struggles or as venues to mobilize resources that they could use to further their rivalry. European strength depended upon their ability to reap the benefits from increased trade, financial innovation and military developments.

In summary, the early 1400s witnessed numerous thriving and dynamic civilizations. China, India and the Ottoman Empire stood out as powerful land-based powers. Regional economies in Asia, Africa, Europe and the Americas varied in terms of political structures and economic activity. There was little indication at the time that Europeans would become as influential as they did in later centuries. Indeed, Europeans desired foreign products much more than other parts of the world desired European goods. Europe appeared economically weak. In political terms Europe was composed of fragmented and warring political authorities. European technology and military forces were on a par with those of some other areas, but did not overshadow the military might of other civilizations. Despite these seemingly inauspicious indicators, the age of European expansion began in the 15th century.

European expansion

In the middle of the 1400s Portugal, and then Spain, began a process of European exploration, expansion and conquest that would continue in various forms and guises for over 500 years. In time, the Portuguese and Spanish were surpassed by the Dutch, French and English states. Europeans launched a three-pronged attack on the political, economic and cultural foundations of the societies they encountered (Abernethy, 2000). Where they could exercise power over other groups, Europeans established new political structures ruling over local peoples in the form of colonies. They restructured local economies, transferring new forms of production oriented to satisfying European demands and tastes. They also transformed local cultures by introducing Christianity, notions of European racial superiority and, eventually, Western political ideologies such as nationalism, liberalism and Marxism. This section sketches out the reasons for this expansion and the varying patterns of interaction established between Europeans and Americans, Africans and Asians, from the Italian Renaissance until the industrial revolution.

Table 3.1 Summary of European expansionist activity

European power	Most active years	Countries/regions	Local interaction	Economic activity
Portugal	Mid-1400s to late 1600s	Brazil, West and Southern Africa, coastal ports in India and China	Conquest, trade, coastal ports	Fish, spices, sugar, slaving, intra-Asian trade
Spain	Late 1400s to late 1700s	North Africa, Americas, Philippines	Conquest	Silver and gold extraction
Holland	Early 1600s to late 1700s	Indonesia, North America	Trade, port seizure, conquest	Spices, intra-Asian trade, slaving
Great Britain	Early 1700s to mid-1900s	North America and Caribbean, Africa, Middle East, South and South-east Asia, Australia, New Zealand	Conquest, settler colonies, trade	Fish, furs, raw materials, sugar, cotton, slaving, drugs
France	1600s to mid-1900s	North America, Caribbean, North and West Africa, India, South-east Asia, Oceania	Conquest, trade	Spices, furs, sugar, slaving
Belgium	Late 1800s to 1960s	Congo	Conquest	Rubber extraction
Germany	Late 1800s to 1940s	South, West and East Africa	Conquest	Minor economic interests
Italy	Late 1800s to 1940s	Libya, Ethiopia	Conquest	Minor economic interests
United States	Early 1800s to ?	North and Central America, Caribbean, Hawaii, Philippines, Vietnam, Middle East	Conquest, occupation, trade	Natural resources

The causes of European expansion have generated considerable academic and political debate. This chapter highlights several important factors: greed, fear, knowledge and biological good fortune. The greed was for valued products from outside Europe. Fear was created by the competition from other European powers and the Islamic forces of Egypt blocking trade routes to the Far East. Knowledge was contained in the crucial technologies enabling the development of the sea-going cannon-carrying sailing ship. The biological good fortune of the Europeans lay in their possession of a stock of threatening diseases and productive domesticated animals.

The waves of European expansion are summarized in Table 3.1. It lists the major expansionist powers, their period of greatest activity, the regions they operated in, the types of local activity they conducted and the major economic sectors that they dominated. The first four countries are prominent in this chapter while the next countries are featured in following chapters.

Into the Americas

We begin our survey of European expansion in the Americas because this is the area of the world where Europeans had an early and dramatic success in subjugating the peoples and environment of another continent. In the 15th century the sailors of Portugal and Spain sailed west into the Atlantic Ocean in an effort to secure the luxuries of the East. As will be discussed below, the Portuguese sailed down the African coast and eventually into Asia. The Spanish headed west across the Atlantic hoping to reach China. Rather than reaching China they encountered the Americas and quickly went about plundering its wealth. The resulting collision of European and American civilizations can be compared to an avalanche. A combination of European disease, livestock and force of arms swept American civilization before it, creating waves of destruction.

A key factor in explaining this swift collapse of American civilization is the role played by the introduction of European diseases. Diseases such as smallpox, measles and, to a lesser extent, malaria ravaged aboriginal populations causing up to 100 million deaths in less than 100 years. It has been estimated that the pre-Spanish conquest population of Central America and Mexico of 25 million declined to 1.5 million by 1650. Similarly, the population of Peru may have declined from 5 million to 300,000 in the 1780s (Wolf, 1982, p. 134).

Prior to the Spanish arrival, Americans were a very healthy group of people. Their migration to the American continent via the frozen Bering Strait and subsequent isolation from other parts of the world meant that the humans living there developed free of the numerous deadly pathogens breeding on the Euro-Afro-Asian land mass. The peoples of the Old World had created crowded civilizations, engaged in extensive agriculture and domesticated large numbers of animals. Each of these steps resulted in the creation and spread of new forms of disease. For example, living in dirty cities close to human garbage bred cholera and dysentery; close human contact with cows, sheep and chickens led to the spread of animal diseases into the human population in the form of tuberculosis and smallpox (Nikiforuk, 1996).

When the Spanish arrived in the Americas they unknowingly unleashed their pathogens upon a vulnerable American population. Smallpox was the most devastating disease, exterminating villages and tribes. The spread of disease was facilitated by bringing large numbers of native inhabitants together as slaves for the mines. Living in unhealthy conditions, they were made even more vulnerable to illness. Smallpox spread across the continent, preceding the arrival of Europeans into the American interior. The continent seemed empty to many European settlers as they spread across the Americas, partly because so much of the population had already been killed.

Europe's ecological imperialism was not confined to disease. Another element in the success of the European invaders was the livestock they introduced into the Americas. Horses provided power for agricultural development and military advantage over the native population; pigs, rabbits and cattle provided for food and changed the environment to pasture land; bees provided settlers with honey. All of these animals were strangers to the Americas and provided their owners with a significant advantage in surviving in a new environment. Europeans came to the Americas not only as individual warriors, settlers or traders, but also as 'part of a grunting, lowing, neighing, crowing, chirping, snarling, buzzing, self-replicating avalanche' (Crosby, 1996, p. 194). That avalanche buried the majority of the native population and set the groundwork for the creation of a 'new' world.

The Euro-American political economy.   European political-economic strategy in what they termed the 'new world' was both mercantilist and imperialist. Europe's relations with the Americas were imperialist in that they subjugated local economies to the power of the European states and reoriented economic activity to serve only the interests of those states. Leading European states used the Americas as a resource for their empires. Many local economies and polities were destroyed and refashioned to serve the Spanish, Portuguese, French and English crowns. With regard to relations between European states, commercial activity was mercantilist. Economic activity was designed to increase the wealth and power of particular states and economic barriers were created to keep out contact with other states. For example, efforts were made to prevent Spanish and Portuguese or English and French colonies from trading with each other. Economic activity was viewed as a zero-sum game. Each country tried to be as self-sufficient as possible and to deny their rivals the opportunity of creating wealth. The

British and French crowns licensed private individuals to raid the fleets of opposing nations. The Spanish viewed such activity as piracy.

The Spanish initially came to the Americas seeking a route to China and India. In their first encounters with native Americans, it was gold which caught their eye. Although gold continued to be a source of fascination for the Spanish and other Europeans, it was silver which accounted for the majority of the wealth confiscated from the Americas. Spanish silver did not flow only to Europe: large quantities also were shipped across the Pacific Ocean. Silver was shipped from Acapulco in Mexico to the Spanish-controlled Philippines where it was exchanged for Chinese goods, especially textiles (silk). In 1797 more Spanish bullion went from Acapulco to Manila than was transferred across the Atlantic Ocean. Between 1570 and 1780 it is estimated that 4,000–5,000 tons of silver went to the Far East to pay for goods (Wolf, 1982, p. 154). The Americas had been forcibly entered into the world economy and Europeans were consuming the benefits of the integration.

The effort to mine silver led to a transformation of the American economy. The Spanish needed labour for their mines, and supplies to maintain the mining industry. Labour was provided by native American and African slaves. Silver-processing was exceedingly dangerous as it involved the use of mercury and resulted in mercury poisoning. The mines were at high altitude, and work was conducted under physically draining conditions. Desperate for relief, the native working population increasingly turned to a substance previously confined to Inca religious ceremonies – coca leaf. Chewing the leaves dulled the workers' pain and the Spanish were happy to democratize coca consumption to keep the silver flowing (Pomeranz and Topik, 1999, pp. 156–8).

Mining also shifted the local economy away from pre-Hispanic agriculture to the silver veins of the Sierra Madre and Volibian mountains. It created a demand for food and supplies. Drawing upon their feudal heritage the Spanish introduced a system of large landholdings called 'haciendas'. These were landed estates worked by labourers settled upon them and directly dependent upon the estate owners. The highly unequal pattern of land ownership and resulting political influence of a landholding elite frustrated economic and political transition for hundreds of years.

After the Spanish conquest, the surviving native American communities played a vital but unequal role in what is now Latin America. Spain and Portugal focused upon resource extraction and never engaged in large-scale emigration to the Americas. In contrast to what became the United States and Canada, the Spanish relied upon local labour and integrated native Americans into their society in a hierarchical manner. The former native nobility often supervised local communities but were deprived of power. Locals were converted to Christianity, although Christianity itself was forced to accommodate local forms of worship and myths. In general, native Americans were integrated into the Spanish system as reservoirs of labour and sources of cheap agricultural and craft products. They were often subject to Spanish tribute or taxes and were forced to hire themselves out to pay their forced debts.

Spanish settlement in the Americas, similar to European settlement in other territories, created a racial division of labour that would last for centuries. In the Spanish case, relatively few Europeans emigrated to the Americas. Europeans and their descendants dominated the elite levels of society, with the children of Spanish/native American unions taking a secondary role. At the bottom of the society were native Americans, excluded from the political system, but providing essential labour. In the north of America the pattern was different as native Americans were excluded from society and Africans were imported for the intensive labour role.

Spain was not the only European state to carry out economic activity in the Americas before the industrial revolution. Two years after the Spanish contact with the Americas, Portugal and Spain signed a treaty which granted Spain all the lands 370 leagues west of the Cape Verde Islands and Portugal all lands east. Portugal took Brazil and the South Atlantic, which led to Asia, while Spain took the rest of the Americas. In Brazil, the Portuguese concentrated on the production of sugar on large plantations as an export crop. This activity spread to the Caribbean, where it was copied by the Dutch, French and English who became rivals. This will be dealt with in greater detail in the following section on relations with Africa.

In the north of America, a number of states were engaged in economic activity. The Portuguese were attracted by the fish off the banks of Newfoundland and New England. They were followed by French and English fleets. As Portuguese and Spanish maritime power decreased around 1600, the French, British and Dutch were able to establish permanent settlements along the eastern seaboard and pursue a four-legged form of gold – the beaver. The demand for beaver to make expensive and fashionable hats for the European upper classes drove Europeans further into the American continent. As a result of the beaver trade, native American groups within the interior became involved in hunting the increasingly scarce mammal. Over time, native Americans moved from being partners in the fur trade to subordinate producers (Wolf, 1982, p. 194). As Canada and the United States became settler colonies for an overflow of Europeans in the 18th and 19th centuries, an even worse fate awaited aboriginal inhabitants. Some groups were eliminated through genocidal warfare, others were made economically dependent and herded onto reserves.

Along Africa: the slave and triangular trade

In contrast to the Americas, Europeans did not enjoy a pathogen advantage in their relations with Africa. In fact, the presence of malaria on the African continent dictated a very different relationship. Europeans were confined to the coasts of sub-Saharan Africa, depending upon Africans being willing to engage in trade. Attempts to proceed further into the continent (with the exception of southern Africa, which had a more moderate climate) met with disease and death for most Europeans. Large-scale colonization of Africa would not occur for another 400 years, until the development of improved rifle technology and the anti-malarial drug quinine.

Europe's maritime engagement with sub-Saharan Africa began with the Portuguese. The initial desire to sail along the African coast came from the hope that they could secure gold without having to rely on the trans-Saharan trade, which brought the commodity up from Senegal. In addition to gold, the Portuguese sought pepper, ivory, dyewoods, beeswax, leather and timber, as well as some slaves from Africa. In return they exchanged textiles, wheat, brass utensils and glass beads. In later years they brought Brazilian tobacco. Slaves purchased from African traders were originally sent back to Portugal. Since slavery marked the prime economic interaction between Europe and Africa in the period under discussion, it is useful to focus upon this activity.

Slavery was not a new institution to either the Europeans or the Africans. In African tradition, slaves were usually acquired as a result of unpaid debts, the judicial process or war. They were not used as the basis for economic activity. In Europe, the Roman and Greek Empires rested upon slave power. During the Crusades, Europeans and Muslims enslaved each other. In the 13th century Venetians and Genovese imported Turkish and Mongol slaves. Slaves were used to grow sugar cane in Cyprus and Sicily and to work in mines. In the 14th century Europe imported Slavs and Greeks. In Scotland miners and saltpan workers were still enslaved in the 17th and 18th centuries.

The beginning of the slave trade was thus not unusual for either of the parties. The transatlantic slave trade took the form of a joint European–African operation. Europeans financed, organized and drew the primary benefits from the trade. The capture, delivery, control and maintenance before the voyage was primarily an African affair. Europeans took over for ocean transport and beyond. Although some Europeans seized Africans directly as slaves, they usually exchanged metal, firearms, textiles, rum and tobacco for their human cargo.

As Europeans began to mine for silver and gold and introduce new crops into the Americas, the nature and size of the slave trade changed dramatically. Slaves were required for mining silver and gold. Portugal introduced sugar from the Mediterranean into Brazil and it later spread to the Caribbean. American tobacco was exported to Europe, while cotton plantations were introduced from Asia. All of these products required a large workforce for their harvesting.

A number of forms of labour were harnessed to this activity. To state the obvious, this was backbreaking work that few people would freely choose. The Europeans first enslaved the local native American population. Their numbers were limited, however. Many died from disease while others escaped to form rebel communities. The Europeans also tried indentured labour from their home countries. Impoverished Europeans would agree to work for a number of years as labourers in return for their eventual freedom and an opportunity for a new life in the Americas. However, many European labourers died before their term was up and it became an increasingly unattractive option.

The solution for plantation and mine owners was to move labour in large numbers from Africa to the Americas in the form of slaves. Many Africans would die in the plantations, but they were replaced by more slaves. Why did Africa become the source of slave labour? As mentioned earlier, there was already trade in slaves before the introduction of plantation economies into the Americas, which provided a precedent. Furthermore, Africans transported across the Atlantic were at a greater disadvantage than native American slaves. It was virtually impossible for Africans to return home, while many Americans were able to flee to neighbouring areas. Those Africans that survived transport to the Americas faced years of hard labour before dying in poverty. Their descendants could expect much the same fate. When slavery was finally abolished Africans would remain on the bottom of the socio-economic scale, stigmatized by poverty and racism for generations.

Similar to many historical events, there is some dispute about the number of Africans that were forcibly moved from their homes to slavery in the Americas. It is estimated that between 1450 and 1900 somewhere between 9 and 13 million Africans were transported to the Americas (Iliffe, 1995, p. 131). The trade began relatively slowly with some 275,000–370,000 being sent from 1451 to 1600. Almost 2 million were sent in the following 100 years and about 6 million between 1700 and 1800 as the plantation economies grew. An additional 3 million were transported in the 19th century. Mortality rates from the brutal methods of transportation were high – as much as 14 per cent on Dutch ships. Exact figures are difficult to establish, but one estimate is that for every 100 Angolans taken as slaves in the 18th century, ten died during initial capture, 22 died on the way to the coast, ten in coastal holding areas, six died on the voyage and three in the Americas before starting work (Iliffe, 1995, p. 135).

This horrendous economic activity was one side in what was called the triangular trade (see Map 3.3). Europeans manufactured various goods such as textiles, guns, beads and semi-precious stones and exchanged them for slaves in Africa. The slaves were transported across the Atlantic, where they worked on plantations and in mines. The products of their labour – silver, cotton, sugar – were then exported at great profit to Europe and beyond.

Map 3.3   Transatlantic triangular trade

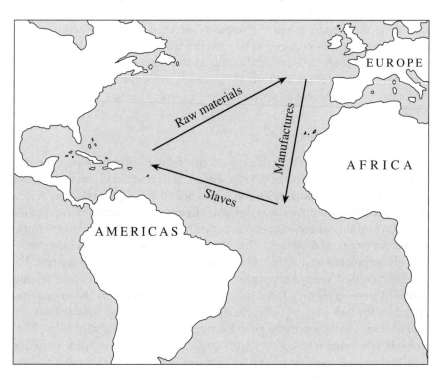

English cities such as Bristol and Liverpool became major slaving ports until Britain ended its participation in 1807. Large fortunes were created on the backs of slave labour.

The triangular trade allowed Europeans to export more products to Africa and use cheap labour to produce commodities in the Americas. The growing slave plantations and American colonies also served as a market for European manufactured goods. In a controversial book Eric Williams (1944) suggested that the profits from the slave trade fuelled the industrial revolution in Britain. While Williams may have underestimated the importance of the European market to the industrial revolution, the triangular trade certainly did contribute to the European economic take-off in the 1800s (Wolf, 1982, pp. 199–200).

On a personal level and in terms of specific communities, the consequences of the transatlantic slave trade were horrific. Individuals suffered immense deprivation, families and communities were shattered and millions died. The effects upon African civilization were more mixed. In western Africa groups along the coast were able to use trade with the Europeans to strengthen their hands against interior rivals. For example, the Asante were able to build an empire in the 18th and 19th centuries by using Dutch weapons to enlarge their territory and acquire more slaves. In the Niger Delta it transformed society into slave-accumulating organizations and subjugated people further inland. In the Congo it had the opposite effect, devastating the polity and creating rival groups engaged in slavery and war. In general, Africa suffered from the slave trade as its political economy was rearranged and millions were transported to another continent. However, Africans continued to resist European encroachment and would do so for many years.

On the peripheries of Asia

Voyages to America and Africa grew out of the European search for new trade routes to Asia. In the 1490s Vasco da Gama finally sailed around Africa and reached India, with the assistance of an Arab navigator. A new route to the wealth of Asia was opened. However, the pattern of interaction with Asian political economies was far different from European experience in the Americas and Africa. The Asian empires were often larger, more densely populated and more productive than the European countries. For several hundred years Europeans were confined to seaports and trading posts. In some cases they faced military defeat and in others they were frustrated by the lack of goods of sufficient quality to trade with Asians.

The Portuguese were the first Europeans to sail around Africa. They immediately came into contact with an expanding Muslim trade network. The Portuguese could not hope to compete with Asians in a head-to-head struggle so they attempted to control strategic pressure points, such as Goa, Hormuz and Malacca. Their attempt to expand into China was defeated in battle in 1521. The pattern of seizing coastal ports to gain a foothold in lucrative Asian trade was repeated by the Dutch and the British.

The Europeans were confined to working the sea lanes between trading outposts in Asia. The Portuguese, then the Dutch and the English moved cargo between Asian ports and back to Europe, amassing wealth for their own countries, but making limited progress into the Asian heartland. Although mercantilist economic theory posited a world where European states would trade with their colonies on a North–South basis, the economic realities dictated a much more profitable trade for Europeans in facilitating economic relations between different parts of the non-European world.

The success that the Europeans did enjoy was due to the gun-bearing sailing ship. Around 1400 AD the Europeans combined the square rig of their designs with the lateen rig of the Arabs. They then equipped this with cannon. After 1500, cannons were installed below decks and the galleon made its appearance – half warship, half merchantship. It overwhelmed Arab and Asian naval opposition in direct confrontations, but could do little to subdue large land empires or stop the local trade conducted by smaller vessels.

Early Portuguese and Dutch economic activity in South-east Asia relied heavily upon a relatively egalitarian gendered division of labour between European traders and native businesswomen (Pomeranz and Topik, 1999, pp. 28–31). The European merchants encountered existing commercial networks that were often run by local women. Local women had well-established business connections and a familiarity with the economy that proved invaluable to the Europeans. The business opportunities provided by these women, combined with the extreme difficulty of attracting European women to the colonies, led to widespread intermarriage between Portuguese/Dutch merchants and Asian businesswomen. In many cases local women were able to continue amassing wealth as their sickly European partners succumbed to tropical diseases. This state of affairs lasted for about 200 years until the 19th century. As technical innovations took hold, such as the Suez Canal, telegraph and vaccinations, it became more possible to pursue a 'European' lifestyle in Asia. This resulted in European men bringing European wives to the colonies, causing the marginalization of native women and increasing differentiation between Europeans and non-Europeans. As Europeans became more entrenched and powerful, their need and tolerance for local cultures decreased.

The British followed the Portuguese and Dutch into the Indian Ocean and eventually gained direct control over a large Asian land-based power – India. Colonization of India proved to be a financial windfall for the British which enabled them to build a much larger empire. As British schoolchildren were taught, the sun never set on the Empire because it spanned the globe.

The British began very modestly in India. The British East India Company initially accepted the sovereignty of local Indian rulers. However, in 1757 the company intervened in a local power struggle in Bengal and ended up taking power in the territory. At about this time the Muslim-dominated Mughal empire entered a stage of crisis. This allowed the English to defeat local Indian forces in battle at Hyderabad in 1789 and Mysore in 1799.

British participation in Indian trade created large private fortunes which were brought back to England. With each new success the Indian economy was reorganized to pay for English warfare and conquest. Indian agriculture was switched to export crops that would benefit Britain such as cotton, sugar, tobacco, jute, indigo and opium. The English also imposed new patterns of tax and introduced English law. English machine-produced cottons were introduced after 1814, destroying the high-quality Indian textile industry. A new army was created with English officers and Indian troops. The British forces succeeded in suppressing an 1857 revolt against the Company's rule in India, but the British government was so concerned that it relieved the East India Company from ruling India and took direct control.

Although the British had succeeded in subjugating India, they were unable to make much progress with China. The Chinese were not very interested in trade with red-haired barbarians. The English were confined to the trading

---

Box 3.3   Ayutthaya vs Venice

Ayutthaya is located in Thailand just outside of Bangkok. Its historical significance is that it was the capital of Thailand for over 400 years (1351–1767) and was one of the wealthiest cities in South-east Asia (Gamier, 2005). This wealth facilitated the building of an impressive city marked by beautiful temples. A city surrounded by rivers, Ayutthaya served as a crossroads for Chinese, Malay, Indonesian, Indian and even Persian goods. European merchants also set up trade posts in the city. It acted as a key centre of exchange linking eastern and southern Asian trade.

Despite its significance, far fewer people have heard of Ayutthaya than the European city of Venice. This is partially because Venice is still a thriving city which attracts tourists from around the world, while Ayutthaya is less of a tourist destination and no longer a major international centre. However, another explanation lies in the fact that histories of the global economy usually emphasize Western locations and developments while ignoring significant developments in other parts of the world. A view of the world which places Europe and her offspring settler colonies (United States, Canada, Australia, New Zealand) at the centre of world history without understanding the role of other countries and peoples is criticized for being Eurocentric.

---

port of Canton and sought silks, porcelain and medicines. In exchange for these products the English had to pay in silver, since they possessed no goods that the Chinese wanted. The situation became more serious as the English developed a taste for tea. Tea-drinking had begun in England in 1664, introduced by the Dutch. By 1783 consumption was 6 million pounds a year, later rising to 15 million pounds (Wolf, 1982, p. 255). All of this consumption had to be paid for in silver, which originated in the Americas. China became the tomb of American silver.

England desperately needed to find a commodity that it could exchange for desired Chinese goods. They could not export silver to China indefinitely. British harvesting of sandalwood devastated the forests of Fiji between 1804 and 1810 and Hawaii between 1811 and the 1830s, but this was not sufficient to pay for Chinese products (Pomeranz and Topik, 1999, p. 161). The answer to British problems was to export drugs grown in India. The drug of choice was opium, which is highly addictive and is known in other forms as heroin. In 1773 the East India Company established a monopoly over the opium trade and smuggled it into China. US traders also became involved, shipping opium from Turkey to New York to China. The Chinese declared the trade illegal, but this did not stop British and American entre-preneurs. By 1828 the British had been able to reverse the flow of silver so that more left China than entered it. Not content with smuggling drugs, British and US merchants pushed for the right to sell them openly to China. The Chinese market was finally opened as a result of British victory over the Chinese in the Opium Wars (1839–42). British gunboats were the crucial ingredient in persuading the Chinese to open their border to drugs. The European drug strategy was a success for their trade balances, but a disaster for China. It shifted the economic balance in favour of Europe and created millions of opium addicts in China. The present-day export of cocaine from Colombia to the United States, which has sparked a 'drug war' in the United States and Latin America, pales in comparison to this historical episode.

It was in this era that we see the beginnings of the modern corporation in the form of the Dutch and British East India Companies (Pomeranz and Topik, 1999, pp. 163–6). These companies were different from other forms of business such as family firms or temporary companies in several ways. First, they were impersonal in the sense that partners in the company did not have to all know each other. Second, the owners of the companies did not directly control the companies. Directors were elected to run the companies and owners or investors either accepted their decisions or sold their share of ownership. Third, the companies were designed to be permanent. They would survive change in owners and were founded for an unlimited time period. Earlier ventures were usually created for a limited time such as the completion of a single voyage or for a series of voyages. The expectation of the East India Companies was that they would engage in commercial activity for as long as it was financially viable.

This new type of economic organization was needed because the commercial activity undertaken demanded large amounts of capital over a long time period. Return voyages from Europe to Asia could take up to three years. Capital invested would often need to be spread over several voyages due to the possibility that any single trip would not be successful. Another significant reason for huge capital expenditures is that much of the commercial activity was combined with expensive military action. In this mercantilist era, European intercontinental trade was typified by the seizure of territory, building of forts and provision of armed vessels. This greatly increased the cost of commercial activity, but was essential if merchants were to ward off their European rivals and cling to their footholds on the Asian mainland.

Conclusion

The early era of forging a world economy from the 1400s until the mid-1800s was not a savoury process. Coercion was often more in evidence than cooperation. European expansion decimated civilizations with disease, enslaved millions of Americans and Africans, worked millions of others to death, reoriented local economies to serve European elite interests and trafficked in drugs to undermine other civilizations. The period saw great transformation in key frameworks of political economy as Europeans increasingly collided with other centres of wealth and power. In this section we will review these changes using the frameworks that serve as separate chapters in the second part of the book (trade, production, finance, labour, gender, development, environment, ideas, security and governance).

It has been said that *trade* is an activity as old as human civilization and this chapter has outlined various trading systems in existence over the period 1400–1800. Apart from forms of local exchange, international trade (that is, cross-border trade) is a significant feature of this period. We showed the importance of long-distance trade and intercontinental trade routes to a number of societies. No simple or single imperative accounts for this trade, although trade was mainly stimulated by the desire to attain goods not produced domestically. This differs from the current international trading system where developed states import goods that are also produced locally. The trade discussed above varied from the exotic to the tragic; from the sale of spices and metals to the sale of human beings. This chapter shows both some of the continuities in the history of international trade and some of the contingent features of trade. Among the continuities are the search for exotica and mass consumption goods. On the other hand, the chapter alerts us to the fact that goods considered moral in one epoch may not be perceived as such at another period in history. For example, while slavery and the trade in slaves still exists it is universally condemned as a practice.

The push and pull of markets played a key role in driving European expansion. European lust for luxury goods from the East motivated states and merchants to find new sources of supply. It was European inability to produce particular products such as silk and spices which drove them out of their regional shell. When they could not take what they wanted by force (which was most of the time), Europeans engaged in trade. However, in several locations trade which originally was conducted upon the basis of relative equality eventually had disastrous effects upon local economies. The fur trade in the north of America eventually undermined the independence of native Americans while the slave trade devastated large parts of Africa as it evolved from a minor activity to a large-scale operation.

During the four centuries covered in this chapter *production* remained primarily agricultural and was largely designed for local use. Although there were no great advances in the technology of production, there were significant changes in who produced what and for whom. European conquest of the Americas radically altered the production structure of two continents. Native economies were either destroyed or reorganized to supply raw materials (metals, crops, furs) to European states. In the southern United States, Latin America and the Caribbean the patterns of production relations consisted of a small wealthy landholding class and a large disempowered and sometimes enslaved labouring class working in agriculture or mining. In the northern United States and parts of Canada settler colonies were set up with a more equal distribution of land and an industrial base was slowly nurtured. In Africa, the capture and export of slaves grew from a relatively minor practice to a large economic activity which destabilized some societies and brought resources to others.

Long-distance trade led to and was facilitated by *financial* innovation. An important element in European expansion was the development of financial instruments to fund exploration, trade and war. The development of banking and provision of credit was a key advance. Money had to be lent over long periods of time so that risky but highly profitable trade could take place. Economic activity over great distances and long time periods also encouraged the development of impersonal and long-standing corporations. Giant economic actors such as the British and Dutch East India Companies were required to engage in intercontinental trade. They were also needed because economic activity often required military security from foreign rivals and local populations. As a result, these companies employed military forces to protect and extend their interests.

The reorientation of production in various continents led to the emergence of a division of *labour* which increasingly grouped the export sector of countries into particular tasks. Europeans took on the roles of producing manufactured goods, shipping goods between continents and running plantations and mines on several continents. Africans were incorporated into the division of labour as providers of slaves. Native Americans were either exterminated, marginalized on reserves or poor land, or integrated into subordinated labour relations. In Asia, large land empires ensured more balanced relations with the European adventurers and traders. Indian, South-east Asian and Chinese producers continued to make highly desirable products and insisted upon fair compensation for their goods.

Gender relations were central to the interaction between Europeans and non-European societies. In cases where the two communities were of equal strength, European men often relied on women from other cultures for assistance. An example given above was of business arrangements between Portuguese men and Indonesian businesswomen. However, in areas where Europeans exercised power over other peoples a more unequal and fiercely contested set of gender relations emerged (Mies, 1998, pp. 90–110). Europeans worked to undermine the place of women in Asia and Africa and the Americas, seeing independent women as a sign of a 'backward' society. In plantation societies Europeans engaged in a struggle with female slaves to increase or decrease their birth rate according to the economic demands of the owners.

In this era we can see the origins of some of today's *development* dilemmas. The economies of what are now Latin America and the Caribbean were forcefully integrated into the world economy in the role of natural resource producers. European and Asian crops (for example, cotton, sugar cane) were introduced and the economy was organized to benefit Western capitalists. This resulted in two developments: certain areas were locked into producing products whose value would decrease over time, and wealth was transferred from the producers of the products (often native Americans or slaves) to the owners of the mines and plantations (European landholders, capitalists and settlers). In Africa the slave trade allowed some tribes to increase their power relative to African rivals, but it destroyed other societies and weakened the continent as a whole. In Asia, European impact was far less significant until the 19th century. Indeed, it is likely that the transfer of European silver (taken from the Americas) to pay for goods stimulated Asian industry.

During this period the natural *environment* in the Americas went through massive change. European introduction of crops and animals shifted the existing balance between people and nature to a new dynamic which saw the increasing subjugation of nature to human economic activity.

Ideas played an important part in the period between 1400 and 1800 as a world economy was in the process of formation. At the simplest level the knowledge structure provides the technology and know-how of societies and civilizations. We have shown how different societies, empires and civilizations had developed various levels of technological sophistication at the beginning of this period and how the technological bases of these societies changed over the course of these four centuries. There is no need to recap on this history here except to reinforce the point that during this period Europe rose from a subordinate position to a potentially dominant one.

The knowledge structure also provides what can be termed 'world views', that is the meta-structure determining the reception of knowledge and structuring perception of human–environment relations. Once again this period provides an example of the wide diversity in human thought and behaviour. It also shows how some world views proved more adaptable to changing environmental conditions while others failed to cope with advances in technology.

The third aspect relating to the role of knowledge pertains to ideas about the relationship between humans. The organization of society, of economics and politics rests on ideas about social relations. From the Incas, to the Chinese, to Africans, to Europeans, different systems were developed during this period. And yet at the end of this period we stand on the verge of the global dominance of just one of these systems of thought. The analysis above has attempted to provide some answers to the rise of Europe while acknowledging that no definitive answer can be given. It has shown in all three areas of the knowledge structure identified – technical, rational and social – that the world in 1400 exhibited greater diversity than our world at the beginning of the 21st century. It also has demonstrated that working on very different principles peoples were able to develop functioning polities and economies. By the end of this period the ideational structure of one group of people was becoming dominant. This chapter has argued that this is not because these ideas were, in themselves, superior but that in combination with other themes examined they contributed to the transformation of Europe in a manner that resulted in European dominance and expansion as other societies experienced conquest, decay and decline.

The *security* structure was crucial to influencing the international economy in this period. Some historians (Parker, 1996) have argued that European military superiority was the key variable in explaining the success of European endeavours, but this is debatable. Spanish military technology was not much more advanced than that of the native Americans. In Asia, the Indian and Chinese military were for centuries more than capable of resisting European arms. It is true that Western naval technology proved crucial for securing coastal ports, but Western land forces would have to await the invention of better rifle, artillery and machine-gun technology in the 19th century before gaining a decisive edge over non-Europeans.

The relative equality in arms suggests that European military success was often dependent upon the cooperation of local collaborators (Thompson, 2000, p. 79). Americans, Africans and Asians were in competition with other Americans, Africans and Asians just as European states were struggling against each other. Alliances between locals and Europeans against other locals or other Europeans were common. For example, the Spanish Conquistador Cortes relied upon local tribes to help defeat the Aztecs. Europeans needed Africans to supply slaves to their coastal stations. The British allied with Indians who opposed Mughal rule to gradually take over the whole country. European success depended upon local cooperation.

The growth of the international economy cannot be separated from developments in domestic and international *governance* arrangements, including the use of organized violence. In terms of domestic governance arrangements, the most significant political development was the rise of the modern state in Europe. As the reigning monarchs of Europe fought each other they needed to finance their wars. The discovery that the centralized state was more efficient at raising revenue for the purposes of conducting military campaigns contributed to the demise of city-states and the various leagues of states. Competition spurred innovation within states and resulted in other areas feeling the impact of European struggles.

The emergence of a new form of political organization was intimately linked with developments in the market. First, the territorial state was effective in the removal of barriers to economic activity across space and place. A multiplicity of political authorities had resulted in an often insurmountable range of barriers to commerce – for example, customs duties and tolls. The creation of a single political authority (similar to the creation of a common market or free-trade area today) breaks down barriers within the same territorial space. Second, the emergence of the state not only abolished various barriers to commerce but also encouraged trade through legislation. The development of law, common currencies and various methods of standardization – for example, of weights and measures – facilitated economic exchange and the development of the market.

The pattern of European interaction and the rules that governed interaction across civilizations varied greatly according to the ability of other groups to resist European dominance. In the case of the Americas, Europeans imposed their own form of political economy as they overwhelmed local groups. In Africa, Europeans were prevented from moving in much beyond the coastal regions, but their thirst for slaves reshaped African societies. In most parts of Asia, Europeans were confined to coastal trading cities by larger and more powerful Asian empires. Some European advance was made in India after 200 years, but China resisted European power well into the 19th century. European expansionism also resulted in widely diverse patterns of cultural transformation in the societies they encountered (Curtin, 2000). In some cases, such as southern Africa, new racial hierarchies were introduced through migration, while in others cases, such as Mexico, European and native cultures fused into a new entity.

Interactions brought about by European expansion had great implications for Europe, as well as for those it encountered. 'Discovery' of the Americas caused Europeans to re-evaluate their place in the cosmos and reconsider their relationship to other peoples. Did these other peoples have similar rights to Europeans? Were they equal in the eyes of God? While European actions often seemed to answer these questions in the negative, a more egalitarian view of non-Europeans would eventually emerge in the late 20th century. In commercial terms new products flooded into Europe, changing social and political organizations. One example was the introduction of the potato, which allowed millions of poorer Europeans to have a richer diet. More significantly, the flow of American silver allowed Europe to engage in greater trade with Asian centres.

Entering the 19th century, Europe had increased its wealth and power relative to other parts of the world. It had wrought destruction upon the Americas, weakened Africa, but was held at a distance in much of Asia. It would await the industrial revolution before European expansion could make further inroads. We begin with this development in the following chapter.

Chapter 4

The Industrial Revolution, Pax Britannica and Imperialism

In the long and painful process of forging a global political economy there are three events that stand out above all others. The first is the European conquest of the Americas and the integration of that hemisphere into a worldwide economy. The second is the industrial revolution which transformed economic, political and social relations in Europe and echoed around the world. The third is the information revolution whose effects are only now starting to become more clear. This chapter concentrates on the second key event, the industrial revolution and its consequences. We begin by recounting the origins of the industrial revolution in Britain and the factors which facilitated it. The second section focuses upon the international system that was created as a result of the advantages the revolution gave to Great Britain and other Western powers (Pax Britannica). The third section examines one of the consequences of the increased power flowing from the industrial revolution – the era of renewed imperialism.

There are several points we can take from this historical overview of the 19th century. First, both wealth and power flowed to the elites of states which were able to harness innovation in production technologies. The industrial revolution increased British power and wealth to such an extent that some scholars describe the mid-1800s as a period of British hegemony or Pax Britannica. The German and US lead in the second industrial revolution at the end of the 19th century propelled them into prominent roles in the early 20th century. Technological innovation and the ability to adapt to new methods of production are important.

Second, the liberal market of the 19th century was created at some human cost. Within Britain people were herded into cities and factories. Vulnerable women and children were the initial factory labour forces until a 'free' labour market eventually dragged in male workers. In the international arena, the wealth generated by the British textile industry relied upon US slave labour to produce the input of raw cotton. Progress had its costs and they were distributed very unevenly.

Third, although the benefits of free trade were loudly proclaimed, the practice was much more limited. Bolstered by the productivity increases of the industrial revolution, Britain led the way in pursuing free trade unilaterally. Some countries followed the example in order to secure key technologies.

However, once other countries felt themselves in direct competition with Britain, they often erected protectionist barriers. Britain was eventually surpassed in the second industrial revolution by two highly protectionist countries – the United States and Germany.

A fourth point is that the international order required particular domestic arrangements to function smoothly. Two of the important mechanisms of the 19th-century system relied upon the exclusion of public opinion from policy-making. The gold standard required automatic social and economic adjustment to trade flows. The balance of power necessitated strategic decisions based upon calculation of interest to the exclusion of ideology or affinity. These practices were possible because the mass of the people were excluded from political participation. However, as democratization continued in the 19th century and a rising tide of nationalism spread across all European states, it was much more difficult to control policy options.

A final point is that the developments in European industrial innovation shifted the balance of power between Europeans and non-Europeans, sparking a renewed bout of expansionism and competition. Large parts of Africa and Asia which had previously resisted European expansion succumbed to the force of European arms and industrial might. Once again, economies were reoriented to serve foreign interests, often with disastrous consequences for local populations.

The industrial revolution

What was the industrial revolution?

To simplify a complex phenomenon, the industrial revolution involved the application of machinery to production, the introduction of new energy sources to power the machines and the reorganization of the labour force into factories. The first industrial revolution began in Britain and lasted about 100 years from the mid-1700s until the 1870s. Changes began in the textile industry with cotton and were followed by the steel industry, especially in the form of railroads. In the 1870s a second industrial revolution focusing upon new products and technologies swept the Western world, led by Germany and the United States. Elsewhere, the results were much more varied. A few states such as Japan, Russia and Canada successfully mimicked the British example, while many other states are still attempting to industrialize their societies at the beginning of the 21st century.

Let us begin by looking at the British textile industry in the 1700s. At this time the British were engaged in serious competition with Dutch and Indian textile producers. While they were able to combat Dutch production because of cheaper products and labour costs, they were unable to compete with

Indian products. Indian textiles were both cheaper and of a better quality than those produced in England. The solution to this competitive problem was the protection of the domestic market by forbidding the British East India Company to import Indian textiles into the UK.

The British wanted to improve their productivity, but ran into a serious technical barrier. The key problem was the lack of synchronization between spinning and weaving. It took a long time to use a spinning wheel to spin the cotton into thread and a relatively short time to weave it into a garment. The pace of weaving was dependent upon the speed at which cotton could be spun. A series of inventions in the late 1700s remedied these problems. The invention of the spinning jenny allowed a spinner to spin several threads of yarn simultaneously. The water-frame drew out fibres on rollers and wound them on upright spindles. The 'mule' combined the features of the water-frame and jenny. By 1790 steam power was applied to the mule, massively increasing the amount of cotton that could be processed in a specific time.

The application of steam-powered machinery to the production of textiles increased productivity and led to the creation of the factory system. The dramatic improvement can be illustrated if we compare how British production increased in relationship to its Indian rivals. An Indian hand-spinner in the 1700s took about 50,000 hours to process 100 pounds of cotton suitable for weaving. In England, Crompton's mule cut the time to 2,000 hours, power-assisted mules of 1795 cut it to 300 hours, and by 1825 it was down to 135 hours (Wolf, 1982, p. 273). Being able to produce the same product in 1/370th of the time it took competitors had devastating consequences for those not experiencing the industrial revolution. The British could make far more products in the same time period and sell them for much lower prices than their rivals.

The introduction of mechanized production meant that the labour force had to gather in a single place to work with the machines. This resulted in the development of the factory system. The factory system concentrated a large number of workers engaged in different technical operations on one site. It took over from the putting-out system in which small household establishments processed raw materials. Under the putting-out system, producers would have to distribute material to be assembled or processed to individual households and await the finished product. This was not an ideal system from the owner's perspective because they had little control over work intensity, the duration of labour, embezzlement, pilfering or quality, which all resulted in delays in processing and delivery. It was more advantageous for workers, who would sometimes spend most of the week engaged in other activities and then work very hard for a couple of days to fulfil their quota.

The cotton factories of the industrial revolution were essentially spinning mills. Weaving kept pace by a multiplication of hand looms and manual weavers. From 1805 the working day was lengthened by introducing artificial light with gas lighting. Factory work was extremely unpopular with the British population. They exhibited a general unwillingness to work in factories. Although factory wages were sometimes higher than those in other unskilled industries, male workers were originally reluctant to enter the workforce because they lost independence. As a result, the bulk of the factory workforce came from the more exploitable sector of the population – women and children. It is estimated that in 1838 only 23 per cent of textile workers were adult men (Hobsbawm, 1987, p. 68). As the factory system progressed, more men entered the workforce and women were gradually confined to the domestic sphere. Early unions were often male-dominated and saw women workers as competition. Many men who lost control over their work by being reduced to factory automatons reasserted control through domestic violence at home or against women in the workplace (Stearns, 1993, p. 62). The difficult working conditions in factories sparked waves of resistance, ranging from the activity of Luddites destroying machines to the formation of trade unions and the growth of Democratic and Chartist movements.

The growth of cotton and other types of factories had a number of effects on British society. In some locations it led to the creation of great metropolitan areas. For example, the population of Manchester expanded from 24,000 people in 1773 to over 250,000 people by 1851 (Wolf, 1982, p. 276). According to Hobsbawm (1987, p. 65) the industrial revolution ushered in a new economic relationship between people, a new system of production, a new rhythm of life, a new society and a new historical era. This new system had three primary elements. First, the industrial population was divided into capitalist employers, who owned the factories and materials, and workers, who owned nothing but their labour which they sold for wages. Second, production was organized in the factory with specialized machines and specialized labour. Third, the entire economy became dominated by capitalists pursuing profit.

There was a crucial international dimension to the industrial revolution in terms of both demand and supply. In terms of supply, the cotton came from outside of Europe. In the late 1700s most came from the Caribbean, but by 1807 more than 60 per cent came from the United States. Between 1815 and 1860 cotton proved vital to US economic health as it accounted for more than half of the total value of US exports (Wolf, 1982, p. 279). The production of this vital input to the industrial revolution was undertaken through the use of slave labour and the removal of native Americans from their land as the plantations moved further west in the United States. On the demand side, Western states created foreign markets for their products. For example, once British manufacturers held the competitive advantage they were able to destroy the Indian textile industry by exporting machine-made cloth and yarn at prices far lower than those of their handicraft rivals. By 1840 the

Indian industry was destroyed and India was reduced to providing raw cotton as a British export to China.

The second phase of the industrial revolution was characterized by developments in iron and coal power. Its most visible aspect was the tremendous growth in railroad-building. The first railroad connected the coalfields of Durham, England with the coast. After Britain, the United States became the centre of railroad growth (Wolf, 1982, p. 292). Railroading sponsored the second phase of the industrial revolution, shifting production away from cotton to iron and steel. England turned to coal as the energy source for this economic activity. Railroad construction rose from 45,000 miles in 1840 to 228,000 miles in 1880. British iron production reached 2.5 million tons in the 1850s. Exports of railroad iron and steel tripled between 1845 and 1875, while exports of machinery increased ten times (Wolf, 1982, pp. 291–3). Railroads became the shock troops of industrialization from Argentina to the Punjab. They opened up vast new areas to further economic activity and tied parts of the world closer together.

A revolution in transport was also part of the industrial revolution. In the last quarter of the 19th century overland freight rates declined 90 per cent due to the railroads. Shipping also made dramatic strides. In 1853 iron-hulled ships were introduced, while steel hulls made an appearance in 1864. Sailing ships were eclipsed by steamships, which had greater tonnage and speed. A clipper ship with 1,000 tons cargo capacity took 120–130 days to go from London to the south coast of China. In 1865 a steamship with 3,000 tons could undertake the journey in 77 days (Wolf, 1982, p. 293). Steamships conquered the Atlantic in the 1840s and 1850s, and Asian seas by the 1890s. Alongside the triumph of steamships came the building of canals across Egypt and Panama. The Suez Canal in Egypt was completed in 1869 and cut the sailing time to Asia from England in half. Unfortunately for Egypt, it also resulted in their bankruptcy and virtual rule from Britain. Approximately 50 years later, US companies would overcome even greater obstacles (primarily malaria) to finish the Panama Canal in 1915 through the use of Jamaican and Chinese labour. From this time on, the United States actively intervened in the operation of Central American states to ensure the safety of 'its' canal.

The advent of the railroad also saw the rediscovery of a particular form of business enterprise – the corporation. As outlined in the previous chapter, today's transnational corporations were foreshadowed by the British and Dutch East India Companies. Although the early phase of the industrial revolution was conducted by family businesses, a more permanent and long-term organization such as the corporation was needed for the railway expansion. This was because the sums of money needed for investment were very large and the time-frame for realizing profits was long term (Pomeranz and Topik, 1999, p. 164).

Why Britain? Why then?

The industrial revolution catapulted Britain into becoming a world power and decisively tilted the balance between Asia and Europe. The question arises as to why it occurred in Britain and why it happened at this time. Although there is a great debate on the subject, most analysts highlight three factors: the growth in European knowledge and technology, the rise of the liberal state and Britain's unique role in the international economy. We will deal with these in turn.

David Landes (1998, pp. 200–9) puts a great deal of emphasis on the development of a culture of knowledge in Europe and Britain. He stresses the European scientific revolution and the Enlightenment, which sought to move understanding beyond religious interpretation. Europe developed three key characteristics. First, there was a growing autonomy of intellectual enquiry. Scientists were gradually able to break free of the church and state to pursue their discoveries according to scientific principles rather than theocratic dogma. Second, a language of proof was developed in the scientific method. This required that knowledge be backed up by verifiable experiments. Finally, there was a routinization of research which turned the pursuit of invention into a regular practice.

Technical expertise was not the preserve of Europeans or the British, it was shared by other civilizations. In order to prosper, technological changes had to be supported by a political and economic structure. The industrial revolution required tremendous changes in many aspects of people's lives. What type of environment facilitated such changes? In Britain it was the advent of the liberal state.

The liberal state facilitated the industrial revolution by giving more power to markets and rewarding or punishing behaviour which assisted or retarded the efforts of the emerging industrial capitalists. The liberal state and economy were created through the use of force (Polanyi, 1957). People were forced out of home production and into factories so that cotton mills would have a workforce. This was called creating a free labour market. The political power of agricultural labour and landholders was curbed so that the rising merchant class would be free to import and export products and hire and fire labour.

An example of the type of change that was required was the 1834 Reform of the Poor Law Act. This law repealed the previous system of poor relief which had stipulated that individual parishes were responsible for their own poor people. Under the new system the poor were encouraged to move to cities to work in the new industrial system rather than face even more horrendous conditions in poorhouses. A national police force was also assembled to deal with the violence caused by forcing people into new forms of labour. A liberal state is not necessarily a less active state.

The creation of the liberal state while supported by a particular class alliance was informed and inspired by liberal ideology. An ideology is a world view which advocates a particular way of organizing social, political and economic life. Nineteenth-century Britain saw the blossoming of liberal ideology. On the economic side, liberalism promoted the ability of economic agents to engage in activity with limited interference from state authorities. Adam Smith (1776/1983), the Scottish philosopher, is even today well known for expounding the doctrine of *laissez-faire – laissez-passer*. The English translation (from French) is 'let it be, let it pass'. This refers to letting goods pass between points without hindrance such as tolls, taxes or other state interference. On the political side, liberalism was known for advancing the civil rights of individuals against the powers of the state. Theorists such as John Stuart Mill (1859/1980) pushed for responsible and representative government which respected individuals' civil and political rights. Although such rights were articulated in universal terms, in practice they excluded the majority of Britain's population by being limited to property-owning men. As Mary Wollstonecraft (1792/1992) had pointed out in the previous century, the emerging liberal system was seriously flawed because it did not extend rights to women.

The horrors of the industrial revolution caused a reaction on the part of those forced to bear the cost. This period saw the formation of trade unions and democratic movements. In the ideological realm, Karl Marx emerged as the dominant theorist of class relations. His writings urged the working class to unite and overthrow the capitalist class. The publication of the *Communist Manifesto* served to inspire millions of people around the world struggling for a more equal society. Marx and Engels (1848/1977, p. 224) described an expanding worldwide system in which, 'The need of a constantly expanding market for its products chases the bourgeoisie over the whole surface of the globe. It must nestle everywhere, settle everywhere, establish connections everywhere.' This captured the dynamic of the industrial revolution, but also resonates with global activity in the early 21st century. Marx envisioned a new form of society (communism) that would be based upon the common ownership of production which would distribute the fruits of people's labour evenly throughout society.

In addition to benefiting from a scientific base and a liberal state, Britain was located in a favourable international position. Due to its naval supremacy it was able to import cotton easily from the American hemisphere and to transport slaves across the Atlantic. Once textile production picked up, it was able to access foreign markets. This was important because many people in Britain were too poor to afford the volume of products being produced. The navy also acted as a source of demand for the emerging iron industry because of its need for weapons.

Following upon the heels of the industrial revolution and the transformation of transportation technology the world economy experienced tremendous growth. For example, whereas international trade increased in value by 30 per cent from £300 million to £400 million between 1800 and 1830 it jumped five times to £2,000 million between 1840 and 1870. Whereas in the early 1840s Britain accumulated £160 million in credits abroad, this rose to £250 million in the 1850s and exploded to £1,000 million by 1873 (Hobsbawm, 1987, p. 139). People joined the increasing international flow of goods and capital. Whereas over 1 million Europeans emigrated to the United States between 1800 and 1840, over 7 million emigrated between 1840 and 1870.

While we can identify various factors that contributed to the industrial revolution taking place in Britain in the 19th century, it is more difficult determining if this is the only mix that would have led to such a dramatic increase in productivity. Scientific knowledge was necessary for the application of machinery to production, but other societies had such expertise. It is harder to say whether a particular place in the international economy was a prerequisite for the industrial revolution. Increasing demand and supply in a national market may have been sufficient, allowing a more national economy to experience these changes. A liberal state facilitated the required social transformation, but less market-oriented states could also transfer resources. The spread of industrialization to several different types of societies at different times suggests that the British were the first to hit upon one of potentially several different mixes of factors which catapulted humanity into a new era.

John M. Hobson (2004, pp. 190–218) has gone as far as to argue that in a longer historical perspective Britain was simply one stop on a long and multi-country technological innovation path. Britain successfully adapted Chinese technologies with some local knowledge and was able to hold the technological lead for a brief period in the 19th century. Its place in the history of the global economy depends very much upon one's historical and geographic perspective.

What did the others do?

The surge of industrial activity in Great Britain caused considerable concern in other states. British industry was becoming more productive and competitive while the British state was becoming more powerful. European rivals and the newly emergent United States struggled to catch up. The race to catch up created a wide series of policy mixes from industrial sabotage, to brief periods of free trade, to protectionist policies to defend industry.

In the early part of the industrial revolution France was Britain's most serious rival. The French monarch tried to modernize his own economy by importing British technicians to update industrial techniques. The commercial rivalry was overshadowed as France plunged into revolution and confrontations generated by the Napoleonic Wars. The two countries which surpassed British accomplishments and led the way into the second industrial revolution of chemicals and electricity were Germany and the United States. Both followed protectionist paths towards industrialization. German theorist Fredrick List (1885/1991) was critical of the British notion that free trade was the best method to advance economic growth. He argued that if Germany was to catch up with Britain it must protect its fledgling industries or risk being confined to primary products. List's writings echoed the mercantilist views of an earlier era and foreshadowed protective policies such as strategic trade theory in the 1980s.

The United States used British capital to finance its industrialization. The US civil war gave a boost to northern arms manufactures that contributed to further industrialization in the 1870s and 1880s. Increasing immigration and westward expansion fed continued economic growth behind high tariff barriers. By the early 1900s the United States was leading in many industries and introducing new forms of production such as mass production of the automobile.

Japan was the only Asian state able to respond rapidly to the challenge of Western industrialization. Following the abolition of feudalism, and the political reform known as the Meiji Restoration (1868), the Japanese government began a process of state-led industrialization (Stearns, 1993, pp. 113–29). Government-led companies began the initial investment in railroads, mines, shipping and textiles. Private enterprise followed government action. For example, Mitsubishi, which was run by former samurai warriors, launched itself into the shipping industry. Japanese industrialization relied even more heavily on female labour than European industrialization and the working conditions for most Japanese workers were worse for a longer period of time than for their European counterparts. The success of its efforts were proved when, much to the shock of Europe, Japan defeated Russia in the Russo-Japanese war of 1905. Japan's industrial prowess was felt by much of the rest of Asia in the Second World War.

Pax Britannica

The rise of British industrial and military power led to a particular form of international system that is sometimes called the Pax Britannica. This translates into the British peace and is an allusion to the famous Pax Romana, which was the relative peace and order characteristic of the Roman Empire at its height. The term is clearly an exaggeration because there were many areas where British power was limited and there were many violent wars. However, it does focus attention on an emerging European-centred international system which reached further than previous attempts at international order. The period is significant because it was generally based upon liberal principles that are similar to the guiding principles of today's dominant powers and institutions. Three of the international arrangements that Britain tried to make the basis of the international system were: the gold standard, free trade and the balance of power.

The gold standard and capital flows

Economic activity such as the exchange of goods and services is facilitated by a recognized form of money. Just as sound money helps move a local or national economy past the shortcomings of barter, a sound international monetary system will assist the exchange of goods and services across borders. In the international sphere there is no international money and no international central bank. The international monetary system (IMS) is the mechanism for exchanging one currency for another. This is necessary because in order to import a product you need to pay the exporter in a currency that they can use. If they are not intending to buy one of your products, they will probably want to be paid in their own currency. The international monetary system helps to determine on what terms and by what methods others will accept your currency.

It is useful to outline some of the key elements of the IMS before explaining the 19th-century arrangement. A monetary system must address three issues (Cooper, 1987, p. 4). The first is the role of exchange rates. Will they be fixed in relation to other currencies or will they float, with their value changing in response to the market? A second issue is the nature of reserve assets. This refers to the commodity or form of money that the central bank will hold on hand to meet demands for payment of currency. A bank's reserves could be composed of gold or foreign currencies. The final issue is the control of capital movement. Does a state allow money to flow freely in and out of its borders or are there restrictions as to how much can be moved over a particular period? In Chapter 7 we will see systems that vary from the gold standard in each of these areas.

A major problem for countries participating in an international monetary system is the balance of payments. The balance of payments is the total of the value of goods and capital flowing in and out of a country. Crudely, do you sell enough to pay for what you buy abroad? If you are buying more than you are selling you have a balance of payments deficit: you run the risk of running out of money. There are several steps that can be taken in this situation. You can reduce imports or increase exports. In economies that are heavily influenced by state policy, it is possible to increase or decrease the amount of imports by command. In more open economies one can either deflate the economy, devalue the currency or increase the competitiveness of local products. Increasing the competitiveness of domestic products is the most attractive strategy: better products will sell more easily, increasing revenues. However, this may take time or may be difficult to achieve. A second possibility is that the economy may be deliberately deflated or slowed down. If the economy slows, imports will decrease and the balance of payments should improve. The third option is to devalue or lower the value of your currency in relationship to that of your trading partners. This should make the cost of your products cheaper to foreigners and lead to an increase in sales. Both of these policies have costs. Deflation puts people out of work. Devaluation lowers real wages by making imports more expensive. It also risks inflation or price rises as foreign products become more expensive.

The era of British economic prominence in the 19th century is noted for its particular solution to the problems of exchanging currencies and balance of payments. It was called the gold standard. Although the British were on a gold standard from the end of the Napoleonic Wars to 1914, the heyday of the international gold standard was 1875–1914. The gold standard was never completely respected, but many states adhered to its principles in a consistent manner. In order for the gold standard to work three factors had to hold true. First, countries were required to fix their currencies in relation to gold. This meant that they had to declare that their currency was worth a particular amount of gold and then be willing to exchange it for gold. The second requirement was to allow the relatively free movement of gold across state boundaries. The third requirement was that currencies would be able to change value in relationship to each other while staying fixed to gold. An example of the operation of the gold standard is provided in Box 4.1.

This system required two prerequisites if it was to function smoothly. The first was an international system of credit which circulated funds between countries to finance economic activity in different parts of the world (Germain, 1997). Wealth from the centre of the world economy would have to be circulated or reinvested in other countries if a large number of states were going to be able to engage in international economic activity. In the 19th century this role of credit provision was played by London. Private banks channelled the wealth produced by the industrial revolution into foreign investments. After 1815 London became the financial centre of the world, as its banks were able to draw in British money and invest it where the profit was greatest in Britain or abroad. In 1873 deposits in London banks were £120 million compared to £40 million in New York, £13 million in Paris and £8 million in Germany (Hobsbawm, 1987, p. 152).

A second important element was that the national state and society must be willing to accept automatic deflation. This required a politically inert population where the lower classes were shut out of decision-making. In Britain this was accomplished by only allowing a minority of the population to vote. This kind of system often exposed class divisions. In general, political and economic elites favoured the gold standard because it came close to automatically maintaining balance of payments equilibrium. However, the working class resisted the mechanisms because they bore the cost of deflation and unemployment.

The presence of London as a financial anchor and the creation of the gold

Box 4.1   The gold standard

Imagine two countries who are members of the gold standard and their trade is in balance. Let us choose England and France. Remember that their currencies are fixed to gold, but can freely move in relationship to each other. The values are not historically accurate, but serve to illustrate the principle. Their situation is illustrated in Stage 1 below.

Now consider a change in their trading relationship. The British begin to import more from France than they export to it. This might be because the drinking of French wine becomes more fashionable in Britain. This change in trade increases the British demand for French francs (FFs) because they are required to pay for more French imports. However, the French don't have as strong a demand for British pounds sterling (£s) because they have not increased their consumption of British goods. The French must be encouraged to sell their FFs for £s by offering a greater rate of exchange. It thus costs more £s to buy FFs on the market. The hypothetical result is that the British must now give £15 for FF10. This is illustrated in Stage 2.

If this state of affairs were to last for too long, the eventual result would be a gold drain from Britain. An entrepreneurial French citizen could use their FF10 to buy £15. This could then be exchanged in Britain for 1.5 oz of gold. The gold could then be brought back to France and exchanged for FF15. The money-changer would make a profit of FF5 minus the cost of exchanging money and transporting the gold. If this was done on a large enough level, the profits could be great. This is an early version of a common practice in today's global financial markets – making a profit from the changing value of a currency's foreign exchange rate.

→

standard facilitated the movement of money from one country to another (Germain, 1997, pp. 44–58). Indeed, the 19th century saw the beginning of very large capital flows through the international system. In the 1800s, French money poured into Russia, German capital moved into the Americas and Africa. As previously mentioned British money helped the United States industrialize. Japan also benefited from British loans and modernized, quickly becoming a world power.

There were differing views as to the political impact of such capital flows. Lenin (1917/1969), the Communist theorist and revolutionary, saw these flows as leading to imperialism and eventually war. Karl Polanyi (1957) saw the interest of capitalist investors or *haute finance* as contributing to peace amongst the major powers. The wealthiest investors who had a stake in the

→

The next part of the process contained the element that would bring the system back into balance. In each country the supply of money was determined by central banks based upon the ratio of gold they held. When gold started to flow out, the bank would have to call money in or reduce the amount it loaned out by raising interest rates. This in turn, slowed growth and reduced imports. In our example, as the British had less money to spend, they would reduce their import of French wine, reduce the need for French francs, restore the exchange rate and stop the outflow of gold. In France the inflow of gold would have the opposite effect, expanding their money supply, increasing imports and depreciating the currency.

The result would be Stage 4, which is the same as Stage 1. This equilibrium would hold only for a brief moment in time as tastes and competition quickly moved the flows of trade and gold again. The model becomes more complicated as other countries are added. The two key points are that the gold standard tended towards re-establishing balance and it provided the security for people to exchange currencies, knowing that they were backed by gold.

	French currency		*British currency*
Stage 1:	1 oz gold = 10FF	trades for	£10 = 1 oz gold
Stage 2:	1 oz gold = 10FF	trades for	£15 = 1.5 oz gold
Stage 3:	10FF exchanged for £15 exchanged for 1.5 oz exchanged for 15FF		
Stage 4:	1 oz gold = 10FF	trades for	£10 = 1 oz gold

prosperity of many different countries would lobby their national governments for the cause of peace. Although bankers appeared to have limitless power, when the clouds of war gathered in the early 1900s they had a minor political role compared to mass nationalism.

Free trade

The 19th-century international system was notable for the appearance of the doctrine and practice of free trade. This doctrine is even more prominent today. The key date in the 19th century was 1846, the year Britain repealed the Corn Laws. The Corn Laws had protected British aristocrats and farmers from imported corn. At the time, corn was used to make bread. The dispute pitted industrialists and many workers against landowners and farmers. The industrialists wanted cheap corn so that the cost of bread would be lowered and they could reduce or limit their workers' wages. This would give their products a competitive advantage in international markets over products from countries where food, and therefore wages, were more expensive. British workers also supported the repeal of the Corn Laws because they wanted to pay less for bread. The farmers and landowners feared that foreign competition would lower or eliminate their profits.

Box 4.2   Comparative advantage

Stage 1: No trade
In the first stage, two countries (the United States and the United Kingdom) produce two products, but do not engage in trade. Each country employs 100 workers in the steel industry and 100 workers in the textile industry. The Americans have newer plants, so they are more productive. Thus, 100 US workers make 900 units of steel while 100 British workers only make 400 units of steel. One hundred US weavers make 300 units of cloth while 100 British weavers make only 200 units of cloth.

Country	Resources	Products
United States	100 steel workers	900 units steel (1:9)
United Kingdom	100 steel workers	400 units steel (1:4)
Total		1300 units steel
United States	100 weavers	300 units cloth (1:3)
United Kingdom	100 weavers	200 units cloth (1:2)
Total		500 units cloth

United States makes steel and cloth more efficiently.

Stage 2: Specialization
In preparation for trade relations, each country shifts resources to specialize in products in which they are comparatively stronger. While the United States makes both products more efficiently it has a greater advantage in steel (9 units per worker vs 4 units per worker) than cloth (3 units per worker vs 2 units per worker). The United States will shift workers into its strongest product while the United Kingdom will shift workers into the product that it is most competitive in, compared to the United States. The United Kingdom will move more resources than the United States because it needs to make a greater adjustment due to its relative inefficiency. The United States shifts ten workers out of cloth to steel; the United Kingdom shifts 20 workers out of steel to cloth.

→

David Ricardo, a stock-trader and member of parliament, articulated the liberal theory of comparative advantage which made the intellectual case for free trade. It remains in force today and is the bedrock of those arguing for economic integration and free trade. Prior to Ricardo, many liberals believed that you should engage in trade if you had an absolute advantage in a product. If you made the best cloth or wine, you would gain from a system that allowed for the freer trade of goods. Ricardo's (1817/1992) theory was more revolutionary. He suggested that by specializing in the

➜

Country	Resources	Products
United States	110 steel workers	990 units steel (1:9)
United Kingdom	80 steel workers	320 units steel (1:4)
Total		1310 units steel
United States	90 weavers	270 units cloth (1:3)
United Kingdom	120 weavers	240 units cloth (1:2)
Total		510 units cloth

Stage 3: Trade
However, the United States still needs 30 units of cloth and United Kingdom needs 80 units of steel. So:

The United States can trade 80 units of steel for 30 of cloth from the United Kingdom.

Stage 4: Results after trade

United States	990 units of steel produced – 80 units traded
	= 910 units of steel, **an increase of 10 units of steel**
	270 units of cloth produced + 30 units imported
	= 300 units of cloth. Same as pre-trade number
United Kingdom	320 units of steel produced + 80 units traded
	= 400 units of steel. Same as pre-trade number
	240 units of cloth produced – 30 units exported
	= 210 units of cloth, **an increase of 10 units of cloth**

Even though the United States had an absolute advantage (it could produce both products more efficiently) both countries were still able to gain from trade after specializing in their areas of comparative advantage. Both countries are wealthier after specializing in the products in which they have a comparative advantage.

product that you make best and engaging in free trade you can benefit even if other people make the products better than you do. Under this theory even countries that are economically weak will benefit from a free-trade system because their resources will be used more efficiently. Free trade was a universal good.

For many people at the time, and even today, the notion of comparative advantage is counter-intuitive. How is it possible that one can benefit from trade with a country that is more efficient? Box 4.2 illustrates how Ricardo's theory operates.

Although the British state signed on to the free-trade economic policy, the wider international acceptance of the doctrine was mixed. The golden era lasted for about 25 years from 1846 to the 1870s. Some European states initially participated, but the United States did not. Once lagging states had acquired some basic ingredients of the industrial revolution, protectionist policies were seen by most countries as the key to matching and surpassing Britain's economic power. Renewed moves to free trade would have to await the post-1945 US-led trading system which is examined in Chapter 6.

The last third of the 19th century combined a number of apparently contradictory trends. As the world fragmented into rival imperialisms, capital and human mobility were at record levels. Britain lost its productive advantage, but maintained its commitment to economic liberalism because of the strength of its financial industry. Germany and the United States, which were becoming more advanced in production, remained protectionist rather than embracing free trade as the British did at the height of the industrial revolution.

In the recent debate about globalization some scholars have pointed to this era as evidence that today's openness is not unique. For example, Hirst and Thompson (1996) argue that the high rates of migration, trade and investment just before the First World War indicate a very open system. While there was indeed a great deal of activity, it often took place in the context of empire and at much slower speeds than in the 21st century.

Balance of power

The 100 years from the end of the Napoleonic Wars in 1815 until the outbreak of the First World War in 1914 passed without a major war involving all the European powers. There were localized wars, such as the Crimean War, which pitted Britain, France and Turkey against Russia, and the Franco-Prussian War, but not the kind of systemic conflict such as raged in the early 19th and 20th centuries. Under the balance-of-power system, violence was not ruled out. Force could be used to contain rivals or in the case of the popular revolutions of 1848 to support particular regimes against democratic movements. The key was to prevent conflict from degenerating into a system-wide war. This relatively peaceful era contributed to an international system that favoured a growth in international trade and finance.

We are interested in why the leading European military states were able to prevent a general war. The security arrangements or structure at this time are known as the balance of power. It had three characteristics. The first characteristic was that there was a general agreement on what was called the Concert of Europe. This was an arrangement between the major European powers following the turmoil of the Napoleonic Wars. It provided for communication and consultation between the powers to ensure that no single state grew too strong. A second characteristic was that states would shift alliances and allegiances to balance the growing power of any particular state. If any state seemed to be getting too powerful, a coalition would emerge to contain that state. This led a British statesman (Castlereagh) to famously declare that there are 'No permanent alliances, just permanent interests'.

The third characteristic of this system was that consideration of other states' ideology and domestic public opinion had to be excluded from the decision-making process. If alliances and military action were designed for keeping a balance of power, cooperation with any form or nature of state would be pursued if this kept the balance. Maintenance of the balance might require constitutional democracies to cooperate with absolute monarchies against other constitutional democracies. Public opinion would also be excluded because it might be necessary to ally with a state that had recently been an enemy. The general public might not support sudden shifts in diplomacy so their views would have to be ignored. This was not a difficult task since none of the states in question would qualify as democracies by today's standards.

The primary balancing role in this environment went to Britain. It had two considerable weapons that it could launch against the growing power of rival states. The first was the British navy which enjoyed supremacy over the waters of the world. During the mid-19th century the Royal Navy was as powerful as the next three or four navies combined (Kennedy, 1987, p. 154). The navy could be used to interfere with opponents' supplies, support allies or raid coastal waters. The second advantage was Britain's wealth which could be funnelled to allies on the continent. The British government was able to provide financing to other states to keep armies in the field against Britain's rivals.

While this system appeared stable and lasted for 100 years, it went through a series of changes, becoming rigid in the first decade of the 20th century (Craig and George, 1983, pp. 28–48). As the century progressed, states continued to build their overseas empires, and engaged in imperialist rivalry. The industrialization of Germany threatened British dominance as the two countries engaged in naval and imperial competition. The system of

Box 4.3   Imperialism in the Congo

One of the most horrific events in the new wave of imperialism was Belgian King Leopold II's exploitation of the Congo. Belgium's activity in the Congo was somewhat unique because a vast area of land became the personal property of a king rather than of the state. It was horrific because millions of Africans died, and brutal methods such as severing people's hands were used to force local people into labour.

Through clever diplomacy during the Berlin Conference of 1884–5 King Leopold II was able to establish a personal protectorate over large areas of central Africa (Pakenham, 1991, pp. 239–55). This area became known as the Congo Free State. It was more than 70 times the size of Belgium itself and about one 13th of the whole of Africa. The King was tasked with developing the Congo for the benefit of its people, but used the territory to amass a large personal fortune and to finance monuments and buildings in Brussels.

The King of the Belgians became very rich and millions of Africans died because of the international desire for a new, modern commodity – rubber (Hochschild, 1999, pp. 158–66). The demand for rubber increased dramatically in the 1890s as the technology to refine rubber into a host of products was perfected. Rubber was needed for tyres, hoses, tubes and electrical wiring covers. Demand for rubber could be met most efficiently by planting and cultivating rubber trees in Latin America and Asia. However, this required considerable care and years before a harvest would be ready. The Congo contained wild rubber trees which could be harvested immediately to meet the spiralling demand. This was the source of Leopold's wealth.

→

flexible and shifting alliances gradually hardened as Europe became divided into two camps. The Triple Entente of France, Britain and Russia confronted the Triple Alliance of Germany, Austria and Italy. Formal treaties were bolstered with secret treaties pledging one state to come to the aid of another. States committed themselves to disastrous policies without understanding the severe consequences. The assassination in August 1914 of the Archduke of Serbia sparked a series of events that gradually drew European states, the United States and the British Commonwealth into a long and bloody war. Ignoring the example of the US civil war, which previewed industrial warfare, leaders foolishly predicted speedy victory.

Peace and wealth for whom?   The notion of a Pax Britannica helps us understand some aspects of an evolving global political economy but

➡

In order to harvest wild rubber, workers had to venture into the forest and engage in the difficult and dangerous practice of draining sap from rubber vines. African males were pressed into this labour by rubber agents who took their families hostage until a certain amount of rubber was harvested. Another common practice in this 'rubber terror' was to chop off the hands of Africans who failed to meet their quotas or who resisted European demands for more rubber. Although it is difficult to establish the numbers of lives lost because of the rubber trade, one credible estimate is that up to 10 million people died through a combination of murder, starvation, exhaustion, disease and a plummeting birth rate (Hochschild, 1999, pp. 225–33).

The horror of this Western atrocity comes down to us in English literature through Joseph Conrad's (1902/1999) novel *The Heart of Darkness*. Conrad worked for four months on a steamship travelling the Congo river. The terrible events he saw in the Congo caused him to write a novel about the voyage of a man up a river to find a European who crossed the line into brutal insanity. The same story was later adapted as the movie *Apocalypse Now*.

A final interesting note about the sad history of Belgian intervention in the Congo was that it gave rise to the first international human rights campaign of the 20th century (Hochschild, 1999). In 1903 the Congo Reform Association was formed to lobby against the human rights abuses in that country. It campaigned in Europe and the United States until 1913, when it was determined that the Belgian government, which had taken over running the Congo from the King, had instituted sufficient reforms.

---

obscures others. One problem is that it tends to focus on inter-European affairs and fails to consider a crucial aspect of the industrial revolution, which was a new wave of European imperialism sweeping over the African continent and parts of Asia. Second, it overstates the degree to which liberal principles governed the system and downplays the flaws that led to its demise. These shortcomings are so serious that the next section is devoted to considering the new imperialism and the breakdown of the liberal system.

An additional problem with the Pax Britannica approach is that it ignores the very large-scale violence taking place in several parts of the world that was linked to the growth of the international market. In the United States, tensions between the export-oriented, commodity-producing south and the protectionist north erupted in the US civil war. This was the most violent and costly war in American history. In China the social dislocation from the

Opium Wars provided the background for a Christian-influenced rebellion against the Emperor (Waley-Cohen, 1999, p. 159). It is estimated that 10–20 million Chinese died during the Taiping Rebellion and the ensuing conflicts (Pomeranz and Topik, 1999, p. 169). In the Congo, the King of Belgium carved out his own private empire (see Box 4.3). Approximately 10 million Africans died in the effort to harvest rubber for export (Hochschild, 1999). These are forgotten lives in a Western-centred view emerging with the Pax Britannica. One needs to ask: peace and wealth for whom?

Renewed imperialism

Is it a coincidence that the era of unprecedented economic growth known as the industrial revolution was quickly followed by an era of unprecedented imperial expansion? Was this 'new imperialism' an inevitable consequence of capitalism or the result of political rivalry between European states? We'll first review the events surrounding the new imperialism and then consider some alternative explanations.

As described in Chapter 3, European expansionism began in the 1400s and proceeded with varying speeds and intensities in different parts of the world. In the first half of the 1800s European powers relinquished formal control in the Americas, but created new colonies in southern Africa, Algeria, India and southern Vietnam. In the Americas, Spanish colonies were able to assert their independence, but remained economically vulnerable to Europe and later the United States. European expansion accelerated in the last quarter of the century. Between 1878 and 1913 Europeans extended their control over an additional one-sixth of the earth's surface (Abernethy, 2000, p. 81). Moving from coastal settlements, Europeans expanded into the interior of the African and Asian continents. No longer satisfied with economic exchange, European traders and states insisted upon formal political control in the form of new colonies. China was not colonized, but Western powers carved out spheres of influence in the country.

This era of expanding Western powers brought four significant developments (Abernethy, 2000, pp. 84–7). First, traditional European powers enlarged their empires. Holland expanded its reach in what is today known as Indonesia. Portugal pushed out from its coastal areas in southern Africa to take over Angola and Mozambique. France established colonies in northern and western Africa, as well as in Madagascar, Indochina and islands of the Pacific. Britain expanded its hold over India and attempted to dominate a portion of African territory stretching from Egypt to southern Africa. Spain was an exception to this trend as a series of wars of independence deprived it of its Latin American colonies.

Second, three new European states entered the colonial movement.

Following their own unification as nation-states Italy, Belgium and Germany rushed to seize colonies in Africa. The Italians were the least successful, suffering defeat at the hands of the Ethiopians in 1896, but managing to conquer Libya. Belgium carved out an immense territory in the Congo. Germany, riding the power derived from the second industrial revolution seized territory in southern, western and eastern Africa.

Third, two Western states outside the European core completed continental expansions, subduing native populations and creating large states. In the Americas, the United States rolled over native Americans and Mexicans as it completed its drive to the Pacific Ocean. It then engaged upon a policy of expanding overseas by seizing the Spanish colonies of Puerto Rico and the Philippines and invading Cuba. Control of the Hawaiian Islands was also taken from their native inhabitants. This expansion had its counterpart in Asia as Russia extended eastwards, dominating large stretches of land in its drive to the Pacific Ocean.

Finally, an Asian state was able to adapt to the industrial revolution, and began its process of empire-building. In the 1890s Japan seized Taiwan and it took control of Korea in 1905. Japanese interests in Manchuria continued to grow and its imperial ambitions were later pursued in the 1930s, leading to war with the United States.

The most dramatic bout of this expansionism was called the 'scramble for Africa'. This was literally a race between European powers to divide the African content among themselves. Over a period of approximately 35 years the African continent was transformed from being relatively independent, with Europeans confined along its edges, to being completely under foreign control, with the sole exception of Ethiopia (see Map 4.1). When the scramble was over, 10 million square miles, 110 million people and 30 colonies were added to European possessions (Pakenham, 1991, p. xxiii).

The subjugation of Africa was marked by what Pakenham (1991) calls the four Cs: Commerce, Christianity, Civilization and Conquest. Europeans first engaged with Africa because of commerce. During the scramble immense fortunes were made. Consider the case of Cecil Rhodes, the diamond and gold magnate. His actions resulted in the accumulation of vast wealth, the subjugation of an African nation (the Ndebele) and the creation of a country by him and named after him (Rhodesia). In addition, his name lives on through the establishment of the Rhodes Scholarship at Oxford University. Christianity also played a role as missionaries flocked to Africa. They moved deeper into the interior, converting natives in the hope that this might save their souls and spare them from the Arab slave trade. European troops soon followed as one group or another of missionaries had to be saved from the local inhabitants. European explorers, settlers and traders justified their activity in terms of civilizing Africans. It was claimed that they were bringing the virtues of advanced civilization to Africa.

As Africans resisted, it increasingly became necessary to use military force or conquest to establish European goals. There were some African successes in resisting European imperialism. For example, the Zulus defeated a British force at Isandlwana in 1879. For almost 20 years (1880s and 1890s) Samori Touré led African resistance to French colonialism in western Africa. In 1896, 100,000 Ethiopian soldiers maintained the independence of their state by defeating an Italian force of 15,000 at the battle of Adowa. However, the overall trend was one of European imperial armies and their African conscripts inflicting large-scale defeats and harsh reprisals on African forces. Examples include the Battle of Omdurman (1898), where a British-led force killed 10,000 Sudanese warriors at a cost of 26 British soldiers. The Germans dealt with rebellion by the Hereros in south-western Africa by exiling a tribe of 20,000 to die in the desert in 1904. With the exception of Ethiopia, all of Africa fell to European arms.

Many different explanations have been advanced to help us understand the imperialism of the late 19th century. Some of the theories stress developments in European countries while others focus on developments outside Europe; some see the imperial drives as motivated by economic factors while others stress the role of military competition.

The two most prominent explanations centre on Europe and financial factors. A liberal, John Hobson (1902) argued that imperialism was caused by underconsumption in Western states. The mass of the population were kept poor and could not buy the goods being produced. Economic interests such as the finance industry, arms exporters and shipping pushed government into expanding overseas so that these interests could continue to make a profit. Hobson's solution to this situation was a redistribution of income within Western states. This would allow people to buy the goods being produced and would end the need for imperialism in other parts of the world. For Hobson, the design of the Western economic system promoted imperialism, but this could be reversed by changing public policy.

Lenin's (1917/1969) famous analysis of imperialism was informed by Marxism. Similarly to Hobson, he thought that imperialism was caused by the economic system in Western states. Industrialists and bankers combined their interests in pursuing overseas markets. Lenin saw this as the highest and last form of capitalism. Unlike Hobson, he argued that this imperialist impulse was an inevitable feature of capitalism and could only be ended by revolution in the colonized world and in the imperial metropole. He contributed his part to this development by leading the Russian Revolution and creating the Soviet Union in 1917.

Another European-focused explanation argues that the imperialist upsurge was the result of military and strategic competition between European states. The scramble for colonies was the result of European competition between Britain, France, Germany, Italy, Portugal, Belgium and

Map 4.1 Pre- and post-scramble Africa

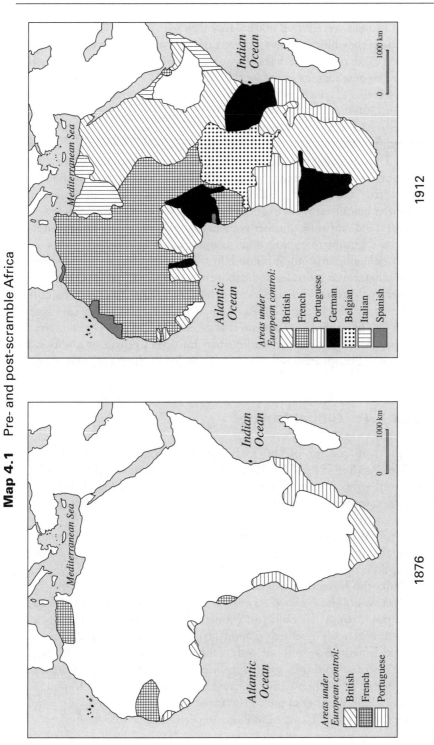

1876

1912

Source: Adapted from Pakenham (1991), pp. 19, 670.

Spain. Colonies were seized not because they were economically profitable, but because they blocked the ambitions of rival states or served as a symbol of power and prestige. Africa was carved up as the great power game extended to new regions of the world.

Racism also played a significant role in facilitating renewed imperialism (Hobson, 2004, pp. 219–42). European imperialists convinced themselves that they had a moral obligation to civilize other parts of the world. Inhabitants of other countries were not capable of handling their own affairs. This civilizing mission involved seizing other people's land to make them more productive, converting non-Christians so that they would recognize the 'true' God, and replacing local political and educational structures so that the colonized would benefit from improved institutions. It was this frame of mind and view of other peoples that allowed many European individuals and groups to exploit other peoples while believing that they were actually behaving in a moral fashion. In some cases, such as the handling of famine relief, racist attitudes had lethal consequences (Box 4.4).

Other analysts have tried to locate relevant explanations in the colonized societies instead of Europe. For example, Ronald Robinson (1972) suggests that the fate of imperial adventures was determined, to a large extent, by the nature of local collaborators rather than European power or abilities. He argues that European powers relied upon local elites (collaborators or

---

Box 4.4   Global famines

In the last quarter of the 19th century three large-scale famines (1876–9, 1889–91, 1896–1902) devastated much of what is today referred to as the developing world (Davis, 2001). It is likely that changes in the temperature of ocean currents (El Niño) disrupted rainfall patterns in many tropical countries. The lack of rain generated crop failures. At the same time government policy was unwilling or unable to mitigate famine conditions. The result was the death of between 30 and 50 million people. India, China and Brazil were particularly badly hit. In India the British rulers refused to intervene, believing that the free market would resolve food shortages. There was little sympathy for the local population. The ability of people in England to pay higher prices for grain actually resulted in food being exported from India to the United Kingdom as millions of Indians died from starvation. In most famine-struck countries grain surpluses were available, but were not distributed to the population because they could not afford to pay for them. While weather conditions created shortages it was poverty and state inaction which caused millions to perish in horrible agony.

mediators) to manage relations with the local population. When these elites were weakened or in danger from local forces, Europeans had to expand their participation into outright rule. When the Europeans ran out of local collaborators, a process of decolonization began.

The upsurge in imperialism in the late 19th century was such a widespread phenomenon that a combination of factors and theories is necessary to gain a full understanding. We can begin by agreeing with Geoffrey Barraclough (1967, pp. 43–64) that the process of industrialization enabled Western states (and Japan) to dominate areas of the world that had previously been beyond their reach. Scientific advance gave some states, societies and businesses the means to dominate other states, societies and businesses. Racist ideologies provided the political and moral justifications for intervention in other societies. However, to explain why a certain imperial power expanded in a particular area, one needs to assess the factors in Europe, in the target states, and the ties that bound the two areas together (Doyle, 1996).

Conclusion

Looking back at the 19th-century international system from today, we see elements that are strikingly similar to those in our own time. Some parts of the international economy were characterized by large-scale flows of capital, goods and people across state boundaries. Several advanced countries were experiencing a revolution in production which increased inequality within and between countries. Liberal economic principles dominated in some states while others sought to develop through more mercantilist policies. Several Western states possessed the military capability of using force to intervene or dominate affairs in other continents.

The differences are also notable. In our present era, the formal political control which characterized the imperial activities of Western states has largely disappeared. Information technologies have accelerated the speed of economic activities and created new channels of communication within firms and between peoples. Rules for international activity have been formalized into international law and a host of international organizations facilitate coordination between states, firms and citizens. Finally, a series of global issues such as human rights, economic justice and environmental sustainability have created new transnational coalitions.

The 19th century is known as the century of free *trade*, although our analysis shows that this is an overstatement since the practice was often not observed by many states. Nevertheless, from the mid-19th century the dominant power, Great Britain, led the way in promoting and supporting free trade. The British did so not seeking reciprocity but on a unilateral basis. But many countries feeling unable to compete with British economic dominance erected protectionist barriers. However, the practice of free trade only tells part of the story. Equally crucial in the emergence of a global economy was the ideology of free trade. It was during the 19th century that this pervasive modern economic ideology was born.

There were important changes in the *production* structure in this period. The most important was the industrial revolution and the attendant developments in its wake. These included the development of industrial capitalism and the export of capital from Europe to northern America, southern America and Asia. Capitalism emerged as a dominant economic, political and social system in the mid-19th century in the aftermath of the industrial revolution. The new power of industrial production, with its division of labour and emphasis on new technological improvements, initiated fundamental changes in the relations between individuals and communities. The developments in production were harnessed by national elites to supplement their power domestically in intra-state struggles and to enhance the power of their state in international competition. The industrial revolution also provided the material resources which allowed Western states to extend their dominance over other parts of the world.

Finance played an important part in the construction of an international economy in the 19th century. It was important in the industrialization of all countries that managed to make the transition to self-sustaining economic growth. For example, the United States used British capital to build its railroads. The export of capital is seen by many as a key instrument in the development of imperialism. During this period financial flows increased and the geographic spread of finance expanded. The interests of financiers and industrialists frequently came into conflict but in the latter half of the century, in many centres, alliances developed between financial capital and industrial capital. Another major innovation in the development of market capitalism was the advent of the joint-stock corporation. The shift from the family business as the main form of private enterprise to the modern corporation was attendant on the growth of the railways since the sums of money needed for investment were very large and the time-frame for realizing profits was long term.

The industrial revolution fed an increasing differentiation in the division of *labour*. Within industrializing states the wealth accumulated by the new industrial classes stood in sharp contrast with the living conditions of the new industrial proletariat. The transformation of the workforce from a primarily agricultural one to an industrial one and the changes in the gender division of labour were crucial features of economic, social and political change. The exploitation of the working classes and the conflict between capital and labour became the subject of political agitation and the domain of novelists and poets. At times it was feared by some social critics (and hoped for by others) that capitalist exploitation of the workforce would destroy the social and moral fabric of society.

The industrial revolution also sharpened the international division of labour between countries. Western states, led by Britain and then the United States and Germany, raced ahead, producing manufactured goods. Other parts of the world were increasingly incorporated into European colonial empires as the producers of raw materials for industrialized countries. For some countries this role continues today.

Countries industrialized in a manner that had distinct *gender* patterns. Initial factory work was usually performed by the most vulnerable elements of the population – women and children. They did not share in the vast sums of wealth being created, but were a crucial element of the increased productivity that gave power to others. The exploitation of gender relations for colonial benefits outlined in the previous chapter spread with the renewed imperialism of the late 19th century.

The states that were able to industrialize in the 19th century became the developed countries of the 20th century while those that were unable to industrialize faced major *development* challenges in the 20th and 21st centuries. The only Asian state able to take Western technology and successfully industrialize was Japan. Today, Japan is a leading advanced economy. The fate of non-industrializers was to fall behind their Western competitors. After keeping Western states at bay for hundreds of years, India became a British colony, while China was forced to grant spheres of influence to a series of Western powers. Today the information revolution may be playing a similar role in creating inequalities between different parts of the world.

The process of industrialization polluted the *environment* of the cities and countryside in Europe and Japan. A similar pattern occurred wherever industrialization took place. Globally, the process of industrialization changed the earth's ability to regulate the atmosphere because of the amount of carbon released into the air. The Kyoto Protocol is the legacy of the pollutants created by the industrial revolution.

Ideas and knowledge were essential to the evolution of the world economy in the 19th century. We can see three different ways in which ideas were critical to that evolution. First, in a technical sense the industrial revolution was based on scientific and technological innovation. The series of events we refer to as the industrial revolution is thus inconceivable without reference to the development of scientific and technological expertise. In short, the industrial revolution involved the application of scientific and technological developments to production, the introduction of new energy sources to power the machines, and this in turn was linked to the reorganization of the labour force into factories.

However, underlying the specific inventions and technological breakthroughs were ideas about science, technology and religion. In other words, the specific inventions depended on developments in underlying world views. At this second level of the impact of ideas, we can highlight the role of the Enlightenment, which ushered in new ways of thinking about the natural and social worlds. The spirit of enquiry unleashed by the Enlightenment was critical to fostering change in the international economy. This was mainly through freeing intellectual enquiry from the theocratic straightjacket in which it had been encased. This growing autonomy of the mind to pursue intellectual enquiry ushered in a new way of scientific thinking and the development of modern scientific method with its emphasis on independent proof and verification.

A third set of ideas about the social world and social relations also helped to transform the international economy. Three ideologies – liberalism, nationalism and racism – were especially important in this process. Liberal ideology and the rise of the liberal state underpinned an international economic system committed at least in principle to liberal economic values. At the domestic level, liberal ideas supported the growth of capitalism and the development of laissez-faire policies. At the heart of 19th-century liberalism was the belief in progress. Nationalism was responsible both for redrawing the map of Europe and for stimulating the economic growth of countries determined to catch up with the leading states. On the one hand, nationalism helped to maintain domestic stability as populations identified themselves with their (emerging) states, but, on the other, it also led to a backlash against liberal economic ideology as some states resorted to economic nationalist policies in their drive for industrialization. Racist ideology was also crucial in shaping 19th-century developments as racist ideas permeated European imperial expansion. European imperialism was based on myths of European superiority and, whether articulated in terms of the white man's burden to civilize inferior races or as the right of Europeans to rule lesser races, this racial ideology helped mould and shape relations between European states at the centre of the world economy and peoples on the periphery.

In the area of *security*, the 19th century has often been seen as a period of relative peace because the balance of power prevented any pan-European war for almost 100 years. However, this view reflects a Eurocentric bias. Violence in the international system was rampant for many non-European peoples subject to various forms of European imperialism. Many of Africa's population were subject to violence as European countries scrambled to take over the continent. China was shaken by the Tai Ping rebellion in the wake of the Opium Wars, while famine relief in India was hindered by British authorities. The United States itself was torn apart by civil war in a conflict pitting the industrial and protectionist north against the agricultural free-trading southern states.

In terms of national *governance*, this period saw the rise of the nation-state and the development of a liberal state. The liberal state presided over capital accumulation through its regulation of capital and labour. It was through the instrumentality of the liberal state that rights and responsibilities were assigned. The liberal state was essential to the growth of domestic capitalism and the emergence of an international economy through the role it played in increasing the power of markets and the formulation of policies designed to reward or punish behaviour which assisted or retarded the efforts of the emerging industrial capitalists.

The liberal state and Pax Britannica rested on a specific domestic political settlement in which the majority of the population was disenfranchized and played no role in policy-making. As the century progressed working people began to agitate for increased access to political participation. One of the main differences between the 19th-century and 20th-century international economic systems resides in the role played by the working class (and peasantry) in political decision-making. With the advent of the universal franchise, greater attention was given by governments to the needs of workers. Of course, as detailed above, there were gains and the domestic settlement in 1914 was different from that of 1815. Nevertheless, for most of this period governments represented elites and could ignore the demands of most of the population. Importantly, this period saw increased conflict between the interests of rural landowners and industrialists. As the century progressed these conflicts tended to be resolved in favour of the industrial bourgeoisie. One way in which working-class agitation was quelled was through the rise of nationalism. Although socialist parties emerged committed to class struggle in which national borders were supposed to be transcended, the nationalist myth proved more potent as an organizing device.

The following chapter outlines how we moved from the wreckage of the 19th-century system to a 21st-century global political economy which shares some of its predecessor's characteristics, but has many new dimensions.

Chapter 5

The 20th Century: World Wars and the Post-1945 Order

The 19th-century liberal and imperialist order came to an end with the onset of the First World War in 1914. Over 30 years passed between the end of the 19th-century system in 1914 and the beginning of a new world order in 1945. These three decades were marked by the two world wars and an inter-war economic collapse. The wars and economic turmoil had a profound impact on the nature of the post-1945 system in which we now live.

This chapter examines the impact of the turmoil from 1914 to 1945 on the post-war system and the nature of that system itself. The two world wars dramatically weakened Western Europe on the world stage and led to the creation of new forms of state in Europe and other continents. The economic turbulence of the inter-war years encouraged the United States to play a prominent role in the post-1945 era and contributed to the creation of a series of international organizations to monitor the global economy.

The era which stretches from 1945 until today has been marked by several developments. The first has been the dominant role played by the United States and the triumph of a Western-centred political economy over the Soviet Union. A second development has been the political independence of former Western colonies and the struggle for development by most of the non-Western world. A third change has been the transformation of the role of the state in the developing and developed world to a more liberal and competitive entity. A fourth transformation has been the growth of international organizations in governing global affairs. A final noticeable change has been the advent of a revolution in information technologies and its impact upon social, political economic and military organization.

War and economic disorder

This section examines the impact of two world wars and years of economic dislocation on the international political economy. The painful lessons learned from these years were significant factors shaping the design of the post-1945 system.

The world wars

The First and Second world wars were massive shocks to the international economy, forcing a retreat from liberal and imperial policies. The First World War disrupted trade and finance patterns, leaving European states much weaker in 1918 than they had been before the war. The pattern of international trade suffered two effects. First, there was a change in the direction of trade as countries switched trading partners. Second, there was a change in the composition of exports as domestic production was switched from the export sector to war production. Denied access to European goods, many countries turned to domestic production or alternative suppliers. This allowed some areas of the world such as Latin America to accelerate their own industrialization. Following the war, the task of European reconstruction was thus made more difficult since old markets were no longer open.

Capital movements were also affected as the pre-war pattern of the export of capital to primary commodity-producing areas was reversed with capital directed to Europe to aid in the war effort. Moreover, the international gold standard was abandoned and international financial dealings became a destabilizing element. Some short-term investment was temporarily not recoverable and some previously attractive investments were no longer available. The war turned a number of debtor nations into creditors and some creditor nations into debtors. For example, the United States, which had started the war as a debtor nation, had a healthy surplus of over £1,000 million by 1922 as a direct result of its role in financing the war in Europe. On the other hand, Germany entered the war as a creditor and emerged as a debtor. The major European belligerents (Britain, France and Germany) ended the war with a vastly reduced stock of foreign investments.

The appalling destruction of the First World War discredited the balance of power, secret treaties and power politics as tools of organizing the international system. After exacting revenge against Germany for beginning the war, the victorious powers attempted to create a security system which relied upon international law and international organizations. For various reasons this system proved inadequate to maintain peace and the world was plunged into another war 20 years later. The economic roots of this failure are outlined below; this section considers the political framework that proved woefully inadequate.

Following the lead of US President Woodrow Wilson, the victorious allies outlined a more liberal system of peace and security which rested on free economic relations and international organization. President Wilson (1918/1986) outlined this liberal strategy in his famous Fourteen Points speech to the US Congress in January 1918. Wilson's Fourteen Points set the agenda for the inter-war international order. He called for the end of secret treaties and for free trade, arms reduction, national self-determination and an international organization for settling disputes between states.

At the centre of this system was an international organization called the League of Nations (Bennett and Oliver, 2002, pp. 27–45). Most states belonged to the League, although ironically, the United States did not join. The US Senate responded to isolationist pressure and refused to give the President permission to join the League. This weakened the institution, depriving it of the financial and military resources of the most powerful state in the international system.

The League's primary task was to keep the peace. The League had a system of negotiation, arbitration and adjudication to encourage states to resolve their conflicts peacefully. Member states agreed to respect each other's territorial integrity. In addition, they professed belief in a system of collective security. Any attack on a member state was to be considered an attack on the international community as a whole. The League had the ability (on paper) to institute immediate economic and political sanctions upon any aggressor state. They could also raise military forces from member states to repel the aggressor's military action.

A series of crises in the 1930s demonstrated the League's shortcomings in preventing and containing war. Its first major failure was in September 1931 when Japan invaded China and occupied Manchuria. Although Japan was criticized for its aggression, the League was unable to reverse its occupation. In 1935 the fascist Italian government launched an invasion of Ethiopia. Ethiopia had already successfully fended off European imperialism during the 'Great Scramble'. Although Ethiopia appealed to the League for help and fought the invaders, it was conquered by Italian forces. League sanctions were half-hearted and temporary. Following failure against Japan and Italy, the League proved unable to halt Hitler's annexation of Austria and Czechoslovakia. It similarly proved incapable of preventing the outbreak of the Second World War as Japan renewed its invasion of China and Germany attacked Poland.

The most devastating criticism of this form of international order was provided by E. H. Carr (1939) on the eve of the outbreak of the Second World War. Carr argued that the liberal notion of harmony of interest was utopian. Peace was not a shared interest when some states were dissatisfied with the status quo and could benefit from war. Similarly, the notion of collective security is misleading because states that did not feel threatened by an aggressive act would not use force to repel it. Carr advanced a realist critique of the liberal naiveté of the dangers of aggressive states. However, he also warned that realism without some dose of utopianism was power without a purpose.

The Second World War produced greater change for the world economy than its predecessor. One result was that it fundamentally altered the balance of global economic power and effectively marked the shift of power from Europe to the United States. The war finally put an end to the Depression in the United States as the country increased production for its war machine. Both the size of productive plant and the physical output of goods increased by more than 50 per cent. At the end of the war the United States accounted for more than a half of the world's manufacturing output. Another important factor in the rise of the United States was its dominance of international finance. The United States lent enormous sums to the Allies during the course of the conflict. At the end of the war the Allied powers were thus heavily indebted to the United States.

A second development was the creation or elaboration of welfare states in Western Europe. Within Europe, leftist groups such as the communists and labour parties emerged with massive electoral support because of their opposition to fascism. Conservative and business parties were placed on the defensive as large numbers of people demanded a redistribution of resources following the defeat of Germany, Italy and their collaborators in other states. The result was that European states were forced to put a priority on building domestic economies and introducing legislation which distributed benefits more broadly than before the war.

A third impact of the war was large-scale destruction to property and infrastructure especially in Europe and Asia. Physical destruction and consequent social and administrative chaos resulted in a loss of production and export capacity. Key economic actors such as Germany and Japan ended the war unable to play the role they had performed in the pre-war economy. Moreover, they became a burden on the victorious coalition. The scale of devastation was such that it posed a serious problem for post-war reorganization. The destruction of physical plant and the shortage of capital devastated large regions. The gap between former great powers and the United States increased because the American continent had been spared the ravages of war.

A fourth impact was the shift in relative power between Europe and the societies in its colonies. Similarly to 1918, European states emerged economically drained from world war. Japanese wartime victories in Asia highlighted the vulnerability of European colonial armies. The end of the Second World War also marked the beginning of the end for most of Europe's colonies.

Inter-war economic failure

The inter-war period of international economic relations was marked by change, uncertainty, erratic growth and depression. Leading states were unable to re-establish a stable international economic order. In Western states the era was divided into three phases. The first phase lasted from the end of the war until the mid-1920s. Domestically, states struggled to revive their economies. Internationally, the value of currencies floated freely against each other and states attempted to liberalize economic relations between themselves. In some countries, such as Germany, this was the period of the great inflation. The second phase was characterized by a return to the gold standard and rising unemployment in many states. This period stretched from the mid-1920s until the early 1930s. The third phase occurred from 1932 until the outbreak of the Second World War and was marked by retreat from the international economy to regional economies as states attempted to deal with economic problems on a unilateral basis.

Following the First World War, elites in the victorious countries were eager to re-establish a liberal trading and financial system. Their failure to acknowledge the changed reality of the international political economy led to financial disaster and eventually war. There were several problems with the attempt to re-establish open economic relations. First, in creating rigid and punitive international monetary and credit systems, leading states failed to recognize the economic damage caused by the war and the heavy burden of war reparations on the system. This weakened already damaged economies. Second, international economic arrangements did not take into account the views and interests of the mass societies mobilized by the First World War. As a result, there was a popular backlash against liberal policies and a movement to state-led development. Finally, the largest power in the system was not fully committed to making the sacrifices needed to maintain an open international economy. The lack of US support weakened the system as it headed into crisis. We will consider these problems in turn.

Rigid monetary and financial systems.   There are two aspects of the international monetary and financial system that proved to be very problematic. The first was the decision to re-establish the gold standard at pre-war levels and the second was the system of war reparations from Germany to France in compensation for the First World War.

States were eager to move back to the security of the gold standard which would give people confidence in the value of their currency and facilitate international trade. A problem emerged when states were so committed to the gold standard that they disregarded the harm it caused to their national economies. Several states fixed their currency to gold in ways that damaged their national economies. For example, Britain fixed its currency to gold at the same rate as it was before the war even though the economy was weaker. This meant that the British currency was overvalued and its exports were expensive for other states. This reduced employment as British exporters lost business and jobs. In Germany, the government eventually succeeded in curbing runaway inflation, but restricted the money supply until the economy ground to a halt, causing a massive increase in unemployment. The fixation with monetary stability and unwillingness to adjust the value of currencies and money supply to boost economic growth prevented governments from responding positively to recession and depression.

The punitive side of the international economic system can be seen in the Treaty of Versailles, which ended the First World War. It stipulated that Germany make reparation payments to the victorious countries because it was guilty of starting the war. This, in turn, created some of the conditions for the financial crisis of 1931 and the collapse of the liberal international economic order. This political decision was taken without serious reflection on its impact on the international economy. The reparations issue became an important one in immediate post-war European economic and political relations.

International financial crisis broke out in 1931. In May of 1931, Austria's largest bank (the Creditanstalt) was discovered to be insolvent, partly as a result of depreciation of its assets and partly because of the withdrawal of foreign funds. Because the German and Austrian financial systems were relatively close, the crisis spread to Germany. Britain wanted to aid Germany, but needed US financial assistance to do so. The United States would only help if the French also contributed. The French government would only help Germany if it granted further political concessions to France. The German government, already under pressure from the National Socialist Party (Nazis) for being too weak, was unable to accommodate the French government. Rather than face the possibility that their currency would collapse, the German government instituted capital controls (prevented people from selling German currency) and began to close their economy to the outside world. The events in Germany put pressure on other states and eventually both Britain and the United States left the gold standard and concentrated on improving their domestic economies. By 1932 major states had retreated into economic relations with states that used a common currency. Thus, Germany traded with its neighbours in central Europe in the mark zone, Britain concentrated its trade with the Empire in the sterling area, the Americans operated in the dollar zone and French worked in the franc zone.

As states restricted economic relations with each other the world tumbled into recession. Kindleberger (1986) suggests that the world depression of the 1930s was widespread, deep and long because Britain and the United States failed to undertake several key tasks of international economic management. In addition to failing to keep an open market for goods through free-trade policies, the states were unable to provide credit to countries in need. There was no lender of last resort. When financial crisis hit the international system, there was no lender who could step in with capital to stabilize the system. Domestically, the lender of last resort is the central bank. Britain played this role in the international system of the 19th century, but the isolationist United States refused to play a similar role in the inter-war system.

Popular mobilization and new forms of state.   The inter-war period is a good example of how a particular form of international order rests upon the balance of social forces between and across states (Cox, 1986). Karl Polanyi (1957) used the phrase 'double movement' to describe the dynamic at work in the early 20th century. The first part of this movement was the attempt to create a liberal market system. This involved the creation of a labour market where people sold their labour for wages with little welfare protection, some degree of free trade and adherence to the gold standard. The second part of the double movement was the political reaction to the suffering caused by this liberal market. Social groups mobilized and put pressure on governments to protect them from the ravages of the market.

What was the problem with the liberal market? The main problem was the assumption that people were a commodity adjusting to the supply and demand of the market in the same way that commodities such as land or capital might adjust. People were viewed as 'labour' and policies assumed that they would freely participate in lowering their wages and income according to the economic models. However, the adjustments demanded by the market were so great and so brutal that people refused to accept lower standards of living and demanded governments take action to protect them.

Several alternatives emerged to the 19th-century economic liberal state that limited economic and political participation by the majority of its citizens (Cox, 1987, pp. 164–209). During the First World War, a major challenger emerged in the form of communism. Taking advantage of Russia's disastrous performance in the war, the Bolsheviks were able to seize power in Russia. They began a process of seizing the means of production (factories, farms) and turning them into state-run economic enterprises. Russia became a command economy where products were produced according to a series of government plans which set targets and dictated what should be produced. The free market of supply and demand was extinguished. The communist form of organization was popular among many of the workers who had been excluded from the benefits of capitalist production. Later in the century, communism was taken up by many peasant-based societies in the developing world, such as China, Vietnam and Cuba.

A second alternative to the liberal system was fascism. Fascism came to power after 1930 when the market system was in crisis (Polanyi, 1957, pp. 237–48). The fascist solution to the difficulties of re-establishing liberal economies was to keep a market economy, but to eliminate all democratic institutions in the industrial and political realms. Fascist strongmen offered their services to conservative forces threatened by the rise of socialism and communism. Capitalists were protected from leftists in the parliament and in the streets in return for handing the political realm over to fascist parties. This appeal was particularly powerful in states such as Germany and Italy, where fascism used unsolved national issues to gain power.

Because of the horror of war and genocide unleashed by fascism in the 1930s and 1940s, it is possible to overlook just how successful Nazism was in dealing with economic challenges. Contrary to liberal prescriptions, the Nazis instituted strict exchange controls and signed bilateral trading arrangements to create a restricted trading zone. Also contrary to liberal opinion at the time, the Nazis undertook massive spending on public works and armaments. Between and 1933 and 1938 they were able to send an estimated 6–7 million Germans back to work, virtually eliminating unemployment. To most Germans this appeared to be a vast improvement upon the economic chaos of the 1920s.

Finally, in the liberal states themselves, governments were pushed towards taking a greater role in the economy and responsibility for the economic welfare of their citizens. Both the United States and Britain experimented with what would later be called Keynesian policies. These were policies advocated by the British economist John Maynard Keynes (1936). Keynes suggested that when businesses lost confidence in the economy and refused to invest, governments should spend money to ensure economic growth. After 1933 the United States took some steps in this direction by expanding credit, increasing payments to the unemployed and raising public investment through Roosevelt's New Deal policies. The British cheapened credit and protected their home market, but did not engage in large public works. The real success of the Keynesian policy would not come until the Allied countries inflated their economies by preparing for war in the late 1930s and early 1940s.

US role. The United States played a critical role in the establishment of the international financial system and its unravelling in the 1930s. Within the United States the financial community argued strongly for US financial leadership in international affairs, the reconstruction of Europe, free trade and the League of Nations (Frieden, 1987). They helped found professional schools such as Columbia's School of International Affairs and Princeton's Woodrow Wilson School. Bankers took the lead in institutions such as the Carnegie Endowment for International Peace and the Council on Foreign Relations, as well as the new journal *Foreign Affairs*. All of this was done to help spread the message that the United States needed an activist foreign policy.

Internationalist forces, led by the financial community, had some success in extending finance to Europe in the 1920s. However, they suffered a series of defeats on issues such as the League of Nations, freer trade and the cancelling of war debts. A coalition of manufacturers, some trade-sensitive agricultural interests and the isolationist Republican Party proved too strong. The internationalism of the banking community was out of step with most Americans, who were repelled by the European war and entanglement.

When the international financial crisis struck in the early 1930s the United States raised its trade barriers even further in the Smoot–Hawley Tariff of 1930. This worsened the economy within the United States and in other countries. Rather than showing leadership by leading coordinated action against the Depression, the United States retreated within its own borders. This economic isolationism was matched by political isolationism.

Some international relations theorists have been so influenced by the contrasting roles of Britain and the United States in the 19th and early 20th centuries that they developed a theory of international stability from these cases (Krasner, 1976). The theory is called hegemonic stability theory. It suggests that a superpower or hegemonic power is required for the maintenance of an international liberal economic system. Economic openness is most likely to occur when a hegemonic state is in the ascendancy and the system is likely to become less liberal as that state's power decreases relative to other states. Advocates of this view point to the fact that the liberal economic system of the mid-19th century was backed by British financial and military might. During the inter-war years, Britain no longer exercised the same degree of dominance and the United States was unwilling to commit itself to system maintenance. While the United States had the power, it lacked the will. The result was a slide to rival economic areas and eventually war. Following the Second World War, the United States took up the role of hegemonic power and created a liberal international economic system.

Surveying the wreckage of the inter-war years, Allied planners of the post-1945 era drew five lessons:

- International financial chaos played a key role in facilitating the rise of fascism in Germany, leading to a breakdown in the international system. Some mechanism would be needed to maintain a stable international monetary system and to facilitate the flow of liquidity. This view led to the creation of the International Monetary Fund (IMF), the World Bank and the Marshall Plan.
- An economic system divided into competing regions could prove dangerous. Some effort would need to be made to liberalize trade between states. After a failed attempt at creating an International Trade Organization (ITO) the response was the establishment of a multilateral trading system in the form of the General Agreement on Tariffs and Trade (GATT).
- The power of the masses and workers would need to be accommodated in some form or another. Leftist political forces could only be blunted if some of the concerns of their constituents were taken into account. The answer to this problem was the Keynesian state, which redistributed income to the broad population.

- These economic arrangements would require more robust security arrangements than had existed under the League of Nations. States would need to be prepared to fight at an early stage in order to prevent a larger war at a later date. The post-1945 period saw the emergence of the Cold War, a series of military alliances such as NATO and reliance upon nuclear weapons to prevent wars between the superpowers.
- The above four points could only be implemented if the United States played a more active international role than it had in the 1920s and 1930s. Contrary to the inter-war period, the internationalists won the battle within the United States and it assumed a role as major international power and leader of the Western bloc. Indeed, the period from the mid-20th until the mid-21st century may well be remembered as the American century.

The post-1945 order

This section outlines the post-1945 political economy. The main themes of this era are: the growth in US power and dominance of a Western liberal economic order; decolonization and the struggle for development; transformation of the role of the state; the rise of international organizations; and the information technology revolution. In addition to these themes another feature of the post-1945 order is historical change in key structures of the global political economy and we refer to these changes in the discussion which follows. Key historical developments in this period include the end of the post-war long boom of economic growth in the early 1970s; the end of the Keynesian approach to economic management and the rise of neoliberalism in the 1980s; changing forms of regional economic governance and the birth of the new regionalism in the 1990s; and the onset of contemporary globalization from the 1960s. Many of the issues we raise in this chapter will be examined in more detail when we move into an analysis of key frameworks of the global economy in Part III of the book.

It is common to refer to the Cold War system of 1945–89 as being composed of three worlds. The First World contained the United States and its allies in Western Europe, Canada, Australia, New Zealand and later Japan. The Second World was composed of the communist states of Eastern Europe and the Soviet Union. The Third World was the term used for the rest of the world's states which were occupied with the process of development. Some countries such as China might fall into two camps – the Second and Third Worlds. The next two sub-sections examine the relationship among these three worlds.

The United States and the Western economic system

In retrospect we can see the US transition from superpower to hyperpower or sole primary power as developing in a series of steps. The confrontation with the Soviet Union required a military shield to protect the United States and its allies. Western states were then bound together by a series of economic institutions which facilitated integration and cooperation. Finally, with the end of the Cold War, the United States and other states have been adjusting themselves to a new distribution of power.

Cold War confrontation.   The wartime alliance between the Western Allies and the Soviet Union was already under strain as Germany and Japan were in the process of being defeated. Indeed, it had always been a temporary alliance subject to rivalry and tension (Thorne, 1978). Following the war, Europe was divided between the two camps and a lukewarm alliance turned into a cold war. The Soviet Union placed friendly regimes in power in Eastern Europe and the United States led Western states in the creation of economic and military alliances against the Soviet Union.

The United States pledged both economic and military resources to the confrontation with the Soviet Union. In the economic realm, US funds helped with the reconstruction of Western Europe and Japan. In military affairs, the United States stationed troops in foreign countries and agreed to the creation of a Western military alliance – the North Atlantic Treaty Organization (NATO). At the heart of NATO was the threat that the United States would use nuclear weapons to deter Soviet aggression in Europe. Canada and the United States stationed troops in Europe so that any Soviet invasion would force a united defence. Once the Soviet Union also developed nuclear weapons, a balance of terror called MAD (Mutual Assured Destruction) froze confrontation in Europe and made the prospect of direct conflict between the USSR and the United States daunting (Freedman, 1985). Colonial powers France and Britain maintained the ability to intervene around the world and also developed nuclear weapons.

One of the effects of a relatively stable confrontation between the Soviet Union and the United States was that conflict between the superpowers was played out in other parts of the world. When the United States supplied arms to Israel, Saudi Arabia and Iran (before the revolution of 1979) the USSR supplied Syria, Iraq and Egypt. The Soviet Union supplied arms to the Vietnamese in their struggle against the United States and the Americans funded Afghan Islamic guerrillas against the Soviet Union. In southern Africa, the United States supported the racist government of South Africa which was engaged in fighting Cuban-backed forces in Angola. In Central America the United States backed right-wing governments against left-wing insurgent movements. The United States and the Soviet Union became involved in a series of national revolutions and wars of independence, greatly exacerbating local conflicts (Halliday, 1983).

The impact of this global competition varied across countries. Some East Asian states benefited from US attention and aid. For example, Japan, South Korea and Taiwan were able to use US investment and the security umbrella to develop their economies (Stubbs, 1999). However, in many other countries, Cold War rivalry fed the flames of local conflicts, contributing to escalating violence and increasing poverty. Southern Africa, Central America, and Indochina bore the brunt of Cold War conflict between the United States and the USSR. In addition, authoritarian regimes of the left and right were able to maintain power to the detriment of their population due to sponsorship of one or the other of the superpowers. These proxy wars and other violent conflict led to death, destruction, devastation and famine for millions of poor people while maintaining the semblance of a peaceful world in Western countries.

Post-Cold War security.   The demise of the Soviet Union and end of the Cold War in 1989 had a major impact upon the global political economy. In security terms the end of Soviet–US rivalry changed the face of global conflict. Some regional confrontations were moderated by the ending of superpower confrontation and UN peacekeeping was bolstered. Some parts of the world saw new conflicts emerge as Soviet power retreated (former Yugoslavia), while other parts of the world were ignored as their societies teetered on civil war (Rwanda). Conflict was much more likely to have an ethnic dimension and take place within or across states than between the professional armies of established states (Kaldor, 1997).

In economic terms new parts of the world were opened to capitalist activity as the post-Soviet states entered a period of transition to new economic and political systems. Along with China's opening to foreign investment that dated back to the late 1970s, this meant that nearly the whole world was once again actively seeking economic ties with foreigners. This offered considerable opportunities for investors, but raised some concern in developing states that badly needed investment and trade would be diverted from developing states to Eastern Europe and Russia.

In the realm of ideology it appeared for a time that the end of the Cold War had ended the battle of conflicting ideas about how society should be organized. Capitalism had triumphed over communism. Fukuyama (1992) suggested that history had ended in the sense that there would be no new models for society, only people converging upon the liberal democratic ideal. Such a view soon gave way to new debates and a resumption of ideological struggle. In the United States, some analysts (Huntington, 1993) raised the threat of conflict between civilizations as the successor to the Cold War. By the end of the decade, the triumph of liberal capitalism was also being resisted by citizen groups from environmental, feminist and labour fields advocating more equity-based arrangements.

Heading into the 21st century, some claimed that the era of two super-powers had been replaced by that of one hyperpower (Cohen, 2004). The United States was seen to be a military giant and economic powerhouse that dominated the world. It possessed the armed forces with the longest reach and most devastating arsenal on the planet. The United States was also home to the largest number of transnational corporations that exercised tremendous influence in manufacturing, financial, service and high-technology industries. In cultural terms the United States reached out through music, television, film and sporting events to spread a vision of its way of life around the world.

The view of the United States as a hyperpower overstates the American role just as talk of a Pax Britannica overstated Britain's role in the 19th century. In Europe, the European Union is busy tying itself into a more social-democratic political economy. In Asia, China is preparing for a world leadership role and Japan is attempting to regain its strength. The populous states of India and Brazil can be pressured by the United States, but American influence is limited. However, while the United States cannot force all other actors to follow its wishes, American participation is needed for effective global governance. As US President George Bush Jr demonstrated with his refusal to respect the Kyoto Protocol to reduce global warming, an agreement without the United States was not much of an agreement.

The simultaneous strength and weakness of US power was illustrated on 11 September 2001 when four US passenger aeroplanes were hijacked and aimed at centres of US power. Two planes destroyed the World Trade Center towers in New York, one hit the Pentagon and one crashed into a field. A transnational network of extremists was able to inflict thousands of civilian casualties on US centres of financial and military power for the first time in its history. The vulnerabilities brought about by sophisticated networks using public technologies against the world's greatest power were shocking to most observers.

US power following the attack was also evident as it mobilized an international coalition in a 'war against terror'. The United States was able to use its military forces to topple the Islamic fundamentalist government in Afghanistan which sheltered the al-Qaeda network accused of organizing the bombing. The United States also applied diplomatic pressure to numerous states to participate in the campaign or provide support for American efforts.

In March and April 2003 the United States and Britain launched an invasion of Iraq and toppled its government. They claimed the action was justified as self-defence, but were unable to convince the UN Security Council that Iraq posed an immediate danger. In addition to facing opposition from

France, Russia and Germany, the US government was unable to secure the support of trade-dependent allies in the Americas such as Chile, Mexico and Canada.

The Anglo-American invasion rekindled memories of 19th-century imperialism. The United States and Britain were able to harness their technological superiority to overwhelm a non-Western state and established an interim American-controlled administration. The US government used Iraqi oil revenues in a futile effort to rebuild infrastructure destroyed by the invasion. The occupying forces granted contracts for reconstruction to US and British companies. In addition, American evangelical Christians mobilized to provide aid and convert the locals in another echo of past imperialist practice. However, the resulting resistance to US occupation and ensuing violence imposed increasing financial costs and military casualties on the US forces. The loss of Iraqi life was substantial. During the second term of George Bush's presidency the United States was neither able to secure military victory nor propose a strategy for leaving Iraq. The price of US unilateralist initiatives had increased.

The Western economic system.   The United States used its unparalleled economic and military dominance to construct a set of institutions to manage the world economy. The international trade and payments order constructed as the Second World War drew to a close was in theory a negotiated order with the principal participants, the United States and the United Kingdom. However, in reality the order was largely shaped by US power and thus reflected US interests. Unlike the economic nationalism of the 1930s, this rejected bilateralism. The key features of the order were liberalism, legalism and multilateralism. The new order was based on liberal economic principles but not the laissez-faire liberalism that had characterized the 19th-century international economic order. In the wake of the political mobilization of the working class and the experiences of the depression, policy-makers attempted to balance social welfare concerns with a commitment to market principles. This multilateralism rested upon domestic political economies that were interventionist. There was no automatic adjustment as in the gold standard nor was free trade unrestricted. The goal was to create a system that had liberal attributes, but did not undermine domestic stability. Ruggie (1982) termed this order based on Keynesian principles one of 'embedded liberalism' to denote both the underlying liberal principles and the historic compromise with labour that permitted state intervention to secure domestic interests.

Western states participated in a number of economic institutions designed to free economic exchange. Three international organizations were created to oversee the liberal international economic order. While ostensibly committed to universal membership, the IMF, the International Bank for

Reconstruction and Development (IBRD, otherwise known as the World Bank) and the General Agreement on Tariffs and Trade (GATT) restricted membership to countries committed to following free-market principles in their domestic economic management. The IMF and World Bank were designed in 1944 to support a stable monetary system and fund post-war reconstruction. Additional funding to aid reconstruction was provided by the United States in the form of the Marshall Plan. The attempt to create the ITO failed, but the GATT served as a framework for gradually liberalizing trade. These three institutions were created to overcome the persistent economic problems that had arisen in the 1930s.

An important development in the post-war global political economy has been the creation of regional economic institutions. The most elaborate of these regional organizations arose and matured in Western Europe. Sheltering behind the security umbrella of the United States and NATO, European states created the European Economic Community (EEC) through the Treaty of Rome in 1957 to assist with economic integration. This was the continuation of a process of closer cooperation initiated by the European Coal and Steel Community (ECSC) in 1951. The EEC evolved into the European Union (EU) and in the process brought European states much closer to political union. The unprecedented levels of economic cooperation leading to monetary union have not translated into effective harmonization of foreign and security policies, but EU states collectively have emerged as rivals to US dominance in a number of issue areas.

Sheltered by the nuclear umbrella and supported by sympathetic economic institutions, the United States, Western Europe and Japan followed policies of economic growth in the post-war era. Government policy redistributed income, supported industry and maintained full employment. The provision of credit and a series of technical innovations facilitated a golden era of economic growth in Western states from the 1950s until the early 1970s. This system then came under strain as US spending on the Vietnam War and rising oil prices caused inflation and recession.

Beginning in the 1970s, northern states increasingly moved from providing welfare to preparing their citizens for global economic competition (see below). The United States and United Kingdom pushed for reforms to the trade, financial and monetary regimes which were designed to give greater play to market forces and reduce the ability of the state to intervene in the economy. These reforms undermined the balance of embedded liberalism, pushing the economic system in a more neoliberal direction. These neoliberal ideas were captured well by the term 'Washington Consensus'. This consensus in liberal economic policy was applied domestically and also exported to developing countries through international organizations and transnational policy networks.

The struggle for development

As the Soviet Union and the United States struggled for advantage in the Cold War, another historic process was taking place. This was the decolonization process and emergence of the 'Third World' as a political and economic actor. The states of the Third World embarked upon a struggle for development that has had, to this day, only limited success.

Decolonization.   The post-1945 period saw an impressive process of decolonization as the European empires discussed in Chapters 3–4 crumbled. In some cases, European states recognized the difficulty of continuing to rule foreign countries while in other cases local populations had to wage violent campaigns to force the colonialists to relinquish control.

The French were much more willing than the British to use force to maintain their empire (Chamberlain, 1985, pp. 55–72). France waged long, bloody and ultimately futile wars in Vietnam and Algeria. In Vietnam, nationalists defeated the French at Dien Bien Phu in 1954. The Algerians secured their independence in 1962 after years of fighting. French retreat in sub-Saharan Africa proceeded more peacefully as states were granted independence, but kept close economic and political ties with France.

The United States played a complex role in the process of decolonization. It granted the Philippines independence in 1946 and urged its European allies to abandon their empires. During the Suez crisis of 1956 it opposed the British/French/Israeli invasion of Egypt. However, as the Cold War intensified, the United States itself became involved in old colonial struggles, such as preventing the reunification of Vietnam.

There are a number of competing explanations for the onset of decolonization. The Second World War was a major factor (Abernethy, 2000, pp. 345–60). For the second time in 30 years European states inflicted damage on each other's productive and military capacities. France, Britain and the Netherlands emerged in a greatly weakened condition, much less able to hold on to territory by force. At the same time, Japanese success early in the war against the United States and Europeans in Asia revealed the vulnerability of their empires. The war itself had the effect of mobilizing and uprooting millions of people in the colonies. Similar to the European masses after the First World War, these people were not willing to return to the pre-war status quo.

Another important explanation is the growth of nationalist movements within the colonies and the increasing economic drain that colonies posed for European states (Darwin, 1988, pp. 17–24). Within countries such as India, Vietnam and Indonesia educated local leaderships mobilized local populations to change the calculus of empire. Through a variety of means they demonstrated to the European colonizers that the project of empire was

Box 5.1   Decolonization and violence

The effects of violence on the colonizer and the colonized were starkly illustrated by Frantz Fanon in the early 1960s. Writing in the shadow of Algeria's brutal struggle for independence from France, Fanon (1963, p. 94) argued that the use of violence against the colonizer served to cleanse the colonized from years of humiliation and oppression. What Fanon did not anticipate was that, once independence was won, it was often difficult for independence leaders to abandon the use of violence in ruling their new countries.

no longer sustainable. In the case of India, Gandhi's campaign of non-violent resistance highlighted the potential ungovernability of South Asia. In the cases of Vietnam, Indonesia and Algeria, wars of independence were required.

The impact of decolonization was dramatic. A large number of new states came into being, shifting the balance in international institutions such as the UN General Assembly. In some cases new organizations such as the United Nations Conference on Trade and Development (UNCTAD) were created to serve the interest of developing countries. In the 1970s, developing countries pushed for a change in the rules governing the global economy which was called the New International Economic Order. Many of the new states, although formally independent, were highly dependent on their former metropoles for economic ties. In the security field, many of the newly independent states tried to steer a third way in the Cold War between the USSR and the United States. This initiative was called the Non-Aligned Movement (NAM) and was led by India, Indonesia, Ghana and Yugoslavia in the 1960s and 1970s. Finally, decolonization pushed the question of development onto the international agenda, where it continues to be a significant issue.

Development success and failures.   The issue of development and growth will be examined in a separate chapter in the third part of the book, but a brief overview is required here. Some states have experienced success in their attempts to develop their economies in the post-1945 period. Japan was able to rebuild its economy after US occupation, while the four Asian Tigers of South Korea, Taiwan, Hong Kong and Singapore achieved incredible progress in terms of growth rates, education levels and advances in particular economic sectors. The rise of these centres of economic power and the oil-producing states in the 1970s was so dramatic that some analysts in the United States feared that American dominance or hegemony was in decline (Gilpin, 1987; Keohane, 1984). Some Asian leaders also began to believe that they had developed a political economy superior to the United States and began to advance the notion of a distinct and better set of Asian values as the explanation for their success (Zakaria, 1994). Both of these trends were diminished by renewed US growth in the 1990s and the Asian financial crisis of 1997.

In contrast to some Asian success stories, many of the world's most populous states such as China, India, Indonesia, Brazil and most of Africa have suffered a series of setbacks in their pursuit of development. In some cases, such as China, until the reform process embarked upon in the 1970s, disastrous central planning destroyed agricultural and industrial productivity. In other cases such as sub-Saharan Africa, countries were trapped into producing products that declined in value over time (coffee, tin, etc.). Insecurity within and between states led to resources being diverted to fighting other states or internal guerrilla movements. In many instances, the debt crisis of the 1980s halted development projects and forced states into a series of structural adjustment programmes that opened and undermined local economies.

State transformation

The function and nature of states at the beginning of the 21st century are different from their nature in the middle of the 20th century. In the 1950s, states in the First World were characterized by Keynesianism or Fordism. They were committed to fostering full employment and cushioning economic turbulence within their borders. In the Second World, Soviet command economies marshalled resources to feed industrialization and competition with the West. In much of the Third World, developmental states intervened in the economy to protect infant industries and begin the process of industrialization. By the year 2000 most of the centrally planned states had disappeared, while the welfare and developmental states had given way to different versions of the competition state.

From welfare to competition in the North. In advanced industrialized countries considerable concern has been expressed that the nature of the state has changed from providing welfare to its citizens to preparing both citizens and corporations for international competition. The idea of a 'competition state' captures this dynamic.

Cerny (2000) suggests that the transformation of the state's role includes several major policy changes. One change is that, rather than supporting particular industries or sectors, states are more likely to ensure that national economies provide a competitive environment. This involves initiatives at the macro- and micro-economic levels. At the macro level, states put a priority on low inflation to attract investment. At the micro or firm level, steps are taken to increase competition and flexibility. This might include deregulating or privatizing industries or changing labour legislation to permit more flexible (and less secure) employment practices. Finally, governments increasingly shift from maximizing general welfare through policies such as full employment and universal social programmes to target programmes designed to increase citizens' employability, such as training or reducing welfare benefits to encourage work at lower wage levels.

Liberal and authoritarian competition in the South.   States outside of the developed world have not been immune from the pressures of the global marketplace. Two developments dating back to the late 1970s and early 1980s have increased economic competition in developing states. One development was the unilateral decision by the government of China that it would begin opening to Western states by seeking trade and foreign direct investment. Although this was a slow process at the beginning, China grew to become the major recipient of foreign direct investment in the 1990s. This diverted investment from other developing countries and resulted in the growth of exports that competed with the products of other developing countries. For example, China, India and Indonesia might all be trying to sell the same product in the US market.

The second development was the debt crisis, which forced many states to abandon inward-looking development strategies in search of finding a niche in the global market. Biersteker (1992) refers to developing states turning towards liberal economic policies as 'The Triumph of Neoclassical Economics'. From a different perspective, McMichael (1996) describes the change as the abandonment of a national development project for a globalization project of fitting into the global economy. The crucial point is that this turn towards increased openness and economic competition is taking place under a variety of political frameworks. Communist China is aggressively courting foreign investment and trade, but retains an authoritarian state system which suppresses dissent and independent trade unions. In the 1970s Chile began its liberalization under the right-wing authoritarian rule of Augusto Pinochet. However, the 1990s also saw a number of southern states democratize (South Korea, South Africa, Brazil, Mexico) and continue the pursuit of a policy of insertion into the global economy.

The rise of offshore.   Another striking development in the state system was the growth of offshore regulation. The term 'offshore' refers to areas of the global economy where states create territorial or juridical enclaves characterized by a reduction in regulation (Palan, 1998, p. 626). One of the most significant developments in the offshore world has been the growth of tax havens. Tax havens are usually located in small states, such as the Cayman Islands. They allow companies and banks to move large sums of money through paper companies to avoid taxation and regulation. Some estimate that half of the world's money resides in or passes through tax havens (Palan, 2002, p. 151).

Similar offshore developments can be seen in other economic sectors. Different forms of regulation have been applied to specific territories within states to foster investment and economic growth. For example, China has created special economic zones to attract foreign direct investment. Many developing and developed states have created export processing zones (EPZs) or tax-free zones. In developed states these zones are likely to be in depressed areas desperate for economic growth such as inner cities. What all of these areas share is that a different type of economic regulation is applied to these geographic spaces than the rest of the economy. In some cases the zones may give companies tax holidays for a number of years in return for investment. In other cases, the main attraction may be the prohibition of independent trade unions from production in the zones.

The rise of offshore provides some business actors with greater economic flexibility to increase profits by reducing the costs of complying with regulation. Some states have benefited from offshore because it has allowed them to attract investment to their territory. However, other states have lost investment and the ability to tax or regulate in the public interest.

International organizations and governance

A striking feature of the global political economy has been the rise in international organizations in the second half of the 20th century. The number of international organizations has grown, and so has their importance in organizing the global economy. In this section we'll briefly examine three sets of organizations – the UN, international economic organizations and corporate and civic associations.

The UN.   The United Nations was created in 1945 as a successor to the League of Nations. There are two elements that have particular significance for the global political economy. The first is the Security Council and the second are the UN's specialized agencies. The UN Security Council is composed of five permanent members and ten rotating members who are elected for two-year terms. The Security Council can make international law, compelling states to respond to its wishes. The permanent members each have a veto over proposals before the Security Council. The Security Council does not usually address strictly economic affairs, but it does influence the security structure and can authorize the employment of economic sanctions against states. Since the end of the Cold War rivalry between the United States and the Soviet Union, the Security Council has taken a more active role in peacekeeping and monitoring elections (Weiss, Forsyth and Coates, 2001, pp. 65–110).

The United Nations contains a host of specialized agencies designed to promote cooperation and address particular issues. The World Health Organization (WHO) attempts to improve global public health; the United Nations Children's Fund (UNICEF) concentrates on improving the welfare of children; and the United Nations High Commissioner for Refugees (UNHCR) provides assistance to refugees. In general these agencies attempt to cope with the casualties of the global political economy. While doing excellent work they have relatively less power to influence overall economic structures than international economic institutions.

International economic organizations.   The multilateral framework created after the Second World War has proved remarkably resilient in the half-century plus since it was constructed. Because a number of chapters in Part III explore the role of these organizations in the context of trade, finance and development, we will only provide a brief review of the continued relevance of the multilateral framework at this point. Three themes have dominated the post-war multilateral framework – adaptation, challenge and expansion. International economic institutions have taken on increased significance in world affairs, especially since the 1980s. These institutions influence behaviour by providing advice on economic policy, demanding policy change in return for financing or settling economic disputes between actors.

In the wake of the debt crisis in the 1980s, the IMF and the World Bank have taken on enlarged roles in the global economy. Their financial assistance and policy advice have been critical in dealing with states in financial crisis. In return for assistance the institutions have demanded that states adopt structural adjustment policies by liberalizing their economies and opening up to trade and foreign investment.

In the trade area, the World Trade Organization (WTO) was created in 1995. The WTO is a significant change from the GATT because it provides the trade regime with a permanent institution, opens up new areas of economic activity (e.g., services) to liberalization, and provides a strong dispute settlement mechanism. This last feature means that states are much more likely to be bound by trade rules after the creation of the WTO than before.

How do we explain the longevity of these institutions? For most of this period these organizations have enjoyed the support of the leading states within the global economy. Successive US administrations, EU countries and Japan may at times push specific agendas that weaken one or other of these regimes, but they have consistently provided support for a renewed and reinvigorated multilateralism. In other words, the post-war consensus concerning the necessity for an open, multilateral economic system has not been eroded despite shifts in economic policy. The increased influence of these institutions has sparked a debate concerning their relevance and legitimacy with many civil society groups claiming that they are too powerful.

The IMF, World Bank and WTO are the most visible international economic institutions, but there are many others. The G-8 brings together the seven most advanced industrialized economies and Russia to discuss economic management of the global economy. The Group of 20 (G-20) focuses on financial issues such as financial stability. It includes the G-8 plus a number of prominent developing countries. The Bank for International Settlements (BIS), located in Geneva, is the forum for central bankers. The Organisation for Economic Co-operation and Development (OECD) is an advisory organization that brings together the industrialized countries of the world. Alongside these organizations can be added the numerous regional groupings and economic integration treaties such as the North American Free Trade Agreement (NAFTA), Common Market of the South (MERCOSUR), European Union, Asia-Pacific Economic Cooperation (APEC), Economic Community of West Africa (ECOWAS), South Asian Association for Regional Cooperation (SAARC) and Association of Southeast Asian Nations (ASEAN).

The multiplication of inter-state organizations means that states, corporations and citizens are increasingly governed through international organizations. In some cases the impact is slight. For example, the OECD might publish a report urging a particular economy to spend more money on training. In other cases the impact is greater. For example, the IMF may demand that a country cuts the amount it spends in its budget before giving desperately needed loans. Alternatively, the WTO might rule that a domestic environmental regulation violates trade law and must be modified.

Corporate and civic associations.   Both the for-profit and not-for-profit sectors have also been busy expanding their international contacts and forming international or transnational organizations. Boli and Thomas estimate that almost 60 per cent of international non-governmental organizations (NGOs) are concentrated in the economic or scientific fields (Boli and Thomas, 1999, p. 41). NGOs have been particularly active in international development. Although most publicity is given to the advocacy role of many of these organizations as they lobby governments and international organizations, NGOs have become increasingly important in the implementation of development projects (Sklias, 1999). In the 1980s Western governments increasingly used development NGOs as a channel for the provision of economic aid (Gordenker and Weiss, 1999, p. 25). Not-for-profit citizens' organizations have also increased their international presence, and have created transnational advocacy networks to lobby transnational corporations, multilateral economic institutions and the governments of nation-states (Keck and Sikkink, 1998). This activity has been enhanced by the revolution in communications which enables activists to build networks at relatively low cost. The anti-globalization protests at meetings of the WTO, World Bank, IMF and G-8 summits provide evidence of non-state actors attempting to influence international economic policy-making. NGOs and citizen groups have thus become important as actors in the normative and material structures of the global political economy.

In some areas where states have not set up appropriate regulatory frameworks, industries have formed their own associations and brought in rules or norms. For example, in the area of environmental standards, leading transnational companies have established the ISO 14000 set of regulations (Clapp, 1998). The role of industry associations in the construction and maintenance of global governance structures is becoming increasingly visible. While industry associations have long played a part at the domestic level in influencing national legislation, as the appropriate levels of decision-making move beyond the state so national and transnational industry bodies have sought to influence global policy-making (Sell, 2000; Smythe, 2000).

The information revolution

In Chapter 4 we examined the advent of the industrial revolution and how this changed the course of history. The last decades of the 20th century witnessed another dramatic technological revolution. This time it is based upon information rather than machine power. Some have suggested that we are experiencing the third great wave of human progress (Toffler, 1980). The first wave was the agricultural revolution and the second was the industrial revolution. We are too close to the beginning of the information revolution to determine its final form and implications, but some initial points can be developed.

Technological. Most readers of this text will be familiar with the information revolution because it has become an everyday part of their lives. Western university students may not be able to imagine a world without personal computers, mobile phones and the internet. Yet, these communication and information technologies only began their diffusion in the 1970s with the invention of the microprocessor (computer chip). In 1977 the first personal computer was introduced by Apple and user-friendly software was soon marketed by Microsoft.

Since the mid-1970s the application of information and knowledge to innovation and production has accelerated technological change. Computers have become smaller and more powerful. The internet has broadened the number of people exchanging information, products and entertainment. Digital technology has allowed for improved communications through voice (phones, radio) and visual devices (television, film).

Economic.   The economic impacts of the information revolution are still working their way through the global political economy. Information technology has certainly facilitated the globalization of economic activity. For example, financial transactions such as foreign exchange or the purchase or sale of stocks and bonds can take place 24 hours a day almost instantaneously. Improved communication between different parts of corporations allows for production to be dispersed across a wide geographical area.

The information revolution offers the prospects of increasing productivity as information and computers are applied to the production process. New economic sectors are being created with the advent of new forms of consumer electronics, medicine and agriculture. The ability to map and track genes holds out the possibility of new medical cures for diseases. Genetic manipulation has led to the creation of genetically modified crops which are more productive and more resistant to disease and insects. However, the advent of these technologies has also brought about ethical and political controversies. Concerns have been raised about the ethical implications of human cloning or using genetic tests to select designer babies. In food production, popular fears have been expressed at the dangers of genetic modification of foods and plants.

In some cases new technology may allow some countries to leapfrog development stages. For example, mobile phones allow developing countries to create a telephone network without the cost of laying cables. Despite such optimism, concerns have been expressed about the digital divide (Norris, 2001). Advanced industrialized societies are rapidly diffusing the technology among their citizens, but many developing countries face the prospect of being left even further behind. While a country such as Canada may be worrying about how they can bring the internet to rural populations, some countries in Africa are still struggling to provide electricity or safe drinking water. The danger is that, rather than allowing disadvantaged groups to catch up with developed countries, the gaps grow wider.

The enthusiasm for the information revolution created a bubble in the stock market in the late 1990s. Investors poured money into a wide range of information technology firms, inflating the stock market and creating instant paper fortunes for some entrepreneurs. Like all bubbles, this one burst leaving a wreckage of sour investors and broken companies (Table 5.1). The revolution continues, but with a more realistic appraisal of the time it will take for changes to work their way through the economy.

Table 5.1   Decline in value of selective high-technology stocks, 2000–3

	10 March 2000	**7 March 2003**
Yahoo!	$178.06	$19.62
Intel	$120.19	$16.01
Nortel Networks	$180.5*	$ 3.20
724 Solutions	$304.90*	$ 0.55

* Canadian dollars

Source: Data from *Globe and Mail,* 10 March 2003, B10.

Social.   Manuel Castells (1996) has suggested that the advent of the information revolution is having profound effects on social life. He argues that new forms of communication allow people to organize themselves through networks rather than hierarchies. In the network society, people build direct links with each other rather than working through institutions that have layers of authority. For example, people concerned about the environment may form a small environmental group rather than work through a political party. Companies may opt for flexible work teams rather than a workforce divided into rigid roles and tasks. Universities might turn to distance learning rather than gather students in a classroom.

The advent of the internet and e-mail has certainly provided the tools for groups of people to form networks around the world in order to advance their views about how society should be ordered. Citizen associations in the fields of the environment and women's issues, as well as peace campaigners, development advocates and labour groups, have used the new technology to share information and mobilize support.

Military.   The information age is also thought to be creating a revolution in warfare (Cohen, 1996). The United States has harnessed information technology to bolster its surveillance and attack capabilities. The American military is better able to identify targets and strike them from a distance than any of its opponents. The advantage might be compared to European use of cannon or repeating rifles against locals in the wars of empire in the 19th century. US success in the Persian Gulf wars of 1991 and 2003, as well as Afghanistan in 2001–2, indicates that a combination of new technologies and new tactics has made American military power much more effective. It is not invulnerable, but the United States certainly has an edge over any possible contender.

Conclusion

The key frameworks of the global political economy in the 21st century will be explored in Part III of this book. This conclusion provides an overview of their evolution in the 20th century and contrasts them with the historical eras examined in Chapters 3 and 4.

The post-1945 era saw an increase in both the volume and type of *trade*. Trade liberalization took place under a series of negotiating rounds of the GATT. Tariffs were gradually reduced and in the 1970s an effort was made to address non-tariff barriers to trade. In 1995 the creation of the WTO marked the next step in trade as countries began to liberalize trade in services and agriculture, as well as agreeing to submit their disputes to a binding dispute settlement mechanism. Alongside these multilateral trade initiatives a series of regional agreements were created to facilitate the movement of goods and services among neighbouring countries. The most significant of these were in Europe (European Union), North America (NAFTA), South America (MERCOSUR) and South-east Asia (ASEAN). As trade agreements intruded more directly upon national political economies, trade initiatives became the subject of extensive national and international debate. Concern has been expressed about their economic, environmental and social impacts. Unlike earlier eras, trade and investment take place under an elaborate system of rules and formal international organizations.

The most visible development in the area of *production* has been the growth of transnational corporations. TNCs account for the majority of the global production structure and 50 per cent of world trade. In 1998, 53,000 TNCs with 450,000 foreign subsidiaries had total sales of $9.5 trillion. The largest TNCs have annual sales greater than the GDP of most countries. This results in the investment decisions of TNCs having great impacts upon the economic fortunes of particular states. The influence of these corporations has led to suggestions that the state is losing power to economic actors and that democracy is threatened by their growing power. Since most large TNCs originate in and invest in developed states, the problem of development continues to plague many countries.

Another significant trend has been the increasing importance of East and South-east Asia as a site for international production. The development of the four tigers has been followed by the industrialization of the coastal Chinese mainland. China's government created special economic zones to lure foreign investment and build its export base. If it can maintain its political integrity and manage the inequalities brought about by industrialization, China has the potential to become a leading international power. Indeed, some analysts suggest that after a 200-year interlude the centre of economic gravity is once again returning to China (Frank, 1998).

The *financial* field has witnessed a transition from the immediate post-war period where markets were restricted and government actors played a large role to today's global system where capital is extremely mobile and private firms take the lead role. The international monetary system has moved from a system of fixed exchange rates to a system of fluctuating rates. Thus, we have a system of capital mobility and floating exchange rates, but the currencies are not tied to an accepted commodity such as gold. The 1970s is the transition decade from a system of national Keynesianism or embedded liberalism to a more open, neoliberal state and global economy. The openness of the global financial field is not unprecedented, but its particular form has not been seen before. Information technologies allow for a much more rapid movement of funds across state boundaries while the flow of news sends markets moving on the latest current events. Financial crisis in one country can spill over into neighbouring countries and around the globe in a matter of days.

The years since the Second World War have seen a shift from an international to a more global division of *labour*. The concept of a global division of labour captures a form of organization which reaches around the planet, but where work is not confined to particular states. In a global division of labour you find activities that in the past might have been thought of as being confined to particular states existing in very different types of states. Labour that one might associate with a developing country flourishes in a developed state and jobs thought to be the preserve of advanced industrialized countries exist alongside very labour-intensive jobs in developing states. For example, an expanding computer software industry develops in India alongside the majority of the population that lives in subsistence agriculture. The distinctive feature of these jobs is that they are plugged into a transnational production process and that they are not confined to particular parts of the globe, although they may be more concentrated in some areas rather than others.

The *gendered* nature of the post-1945 global political economy has become more clear with increasing research into the subject. Economies of all states relied upon women to provide free labour to care for family members so that men could participate in the paid workforce. In addition, economic restructuring in response to financial crisis demands that women provide even more services as states cut back upon social provision. At the same time, the increasing globalization of the economy is bringing more women into the global workforce in particular roles – as domestics or nannies, entertainment or sex workers, or workers in labour-intensive factories in the developing world. While some women pursue desirable career opportunities in the global economy, most struggle to make ends meet.

Development has become a significant issue in the post-1945 era with the process of decolonization. Although a large number of countries gained their independence in the post-war period, the struggle for development has been much more difficult. With the exception of some countries in East and South-east Asia, much of the world continues to lose ground relative to advanced industrialized countries. After a period of state-led development in the 1950s, 1960s and 1970s, developing countries are much more dependent upon private capital flows for investment. Some countries still struggle to industrialize while others attempt to make the jump from newly industrializing countries to advanced industrialized countries.

Environmental degradation became a large issue in the latter part of the 20th century. One of the consequences of European, North American, Japanese and Soviet industrialization programmes has been the poisoning of the natural environment. Issues such as global warming have become prominent. The proposed solutions, such as the Kyoto Protocol, have sparked heated debate within developed states and between developed and developing states. In the developing world poverty has led to economic practices which contribute to deforestation and pollution.

In the realm of *ideas*, the post-1945 era has seen a prolonged struggle over the superior method of organizing domestic political economies. In Western states Keynesian welfare policies dominated. Central planning in the Soviet model offered an alternative vision of society until the end of the Cold War in 1989. Although the capitalist system emerged triumphant in 1989, vigorous debates continue about what form of capitalism is appropriate for any particular economy. Usually the liberal Anglo-American systems are contrasted against more welfare-centred European arrangements or Asian corporatist practices which integrate business, government and subordinate labour organizations. Another significant development in thinking has been the rise of the concept of globalization. Over the last quarter of the 20th century the term 'global' was increasingly used to describe a range of activities in the cultural, economic and political realms. Globalization concerns the growth of supraterritorial relations between people (Scholte, 2000a). These relations can be found in engagement with and response to mass media (for example, pressure for humanitarian intervention following a CNN broadcast), developed through economic structures (global production and finance) or aroused in response to shifting centres of authority.

On the *security* front, most of the post-1945 era was dominated by the Cold War between the United States and the USSR. This competition structured political and economic relations around the world. Conflicts between the superpowers were often channelled to developing countries which resulted in losses and gains for those states. With the end of the Cold War in 1989 security issues of terrorism, nuclear proliferation and conflict within states took on increased prominence. The United States continued to build its military advantage by applying technological innovation to its armed forces. Increasingly, the developed world was characterized as a zone of peace (with the exception of occasional terror attacks), while much of the developing world faced with the prospect of inter-state or civil war. For most of the world's citizens premature death was much more likely to come from poverty, disease or malnutrition rather than war.

There are two *governance* developments that set this era apart from its predecessors. One element has been the proliferation of formal international organizations dedicated to coordinating policy on a wide range of issues. Institutions such as the IMF, World Bank and WTO exercise considerable influence over policy formation in the areas of trade, finance and development, especially in weaker and poorer states. A second feature has been the democratization of state institutions. Greater public influence over decision-makers (compared to previous eras) complicates foreign economic and diplomatic policies. Economic issues such as NAFTA and the operation of the WTO have become issues for debate in many states. This indicates that global structures of governance increasingly need to be rooted in the politics of democratic states. The automatic adjustment of the gold standard era's governance is no longer possible.

Part III

Dynamics

Chapter 6

International Trade

Trade across borders inflames passions and creates controversies that are absent in discussions of trade within countries. Early chapters of this book demonstrated the importance of trade in the evolution of the contemporary global economic system, and this chapter will not repeat those arguments. Instead it will provide an introduction to understanding the political economy of the global trading system. One striking feature of the contemporary international trading system arises from the conflict between the continuing political importance of the national border and its declining economic relevance. Political conflicts over trade exist simultaneously with the growth of transnational production (see Chapter 7) wherein production by firms is less restricted by national frontiers than at any time in history.

This chapter provides an introduction to international trade through an examination of the material and normative structures that constitute the international trading system. It begins with a brief definition of certain key terms, and an introduction to the importance of the means of exchange. In the theoretical perspectives section we discuss some of the more important theoretical disputes and examine empirical claims made by various proponents in key debates concerning the evolution and impact of free trade. The third section examines the major developments in the post-war international trading system. These include the tremendous expansion in trade, the development of new forms of protectionism, and the emergence and development of the regulation of trade through, first, the General Agreement on Tariffs and Trade (GATT) and, latterly, the World Trade Organization (WTO). The key issues considered in this chapter are the special needs of developing countries, the growth of regionalism and the debate over the legitimacy of the trading system.

Definitions

Simply speaking, trade refers to the exchange of one commodity for another. Whenever two or more individuals exchange goods and services they are engaged in trade. We can thus see that trade has been a feature of all civilizations. Trade as an activity takes place domestically when two or more individuals exchange goods and services. International trade arises when the exchange is conducted across national borders. In any discussion of international trade, two issues are of importance. These issues are the existence of barriers or restrictions to trade, and the medium of exchange in which trade is conducted. There are a number of different kinds of barriers to trade and we will be concerned here with political barriers rather than technical barriers such as travel and distance. Political barriers to trade are erected wherever different political authorities decide to prohibit or restrict their citizens' access to foreign goods and services. In other words, for a variety of reasons the goods and services from one political region may be prohibited from entering, or leaving for, another region; or they may be made more costly for citizens of a country in comparison with similar domestic goods and services. Within the global political economy, therefore, the national border has added significance in so far as different national authorities may attempt to control the activities of their citizens in making transactions across borders. Protectionism refers to policies designed to restrict the import of goods and services. In recent history discussions of protectionism have referred to national forms of protection, but this need not be the case. For example, until Federation in 1901, the Australian colonies had systems of protection against imports from each other. Protection can take many forms, the most common of which are tariffs, quotas, subsidies, currency controls, administrative regulations and voluntary export restraints.

A tariff refers to the application of a duty (denominated in monetary terms) against goods and services from a foreign supplier; in other words, a tax on the price of imports which raises their price to consumers (see Table 6.1 for selected industrial tariffs). The effect of a tariff is to reduce profits in the export market, but this loss can be outweighed by gains in the domestic market. Quotas refer to the application of a quantitative restriction against goods and services from another country or region, as well as health and safety requirements. That is, quotas are specific limits on the quantity of imports or on their value. Subsidies are made to particular industries to help them to be competitive on the international market. Examples of subsidies include depreciation allowances, cash grants and tax holidays. Currency controls limit the availability of foreign currency for the purchase of foreign goods. Administrative regulations include bureaucratic procedures, systems of advance payment, minimal domestic content rules, special marketing standards and health and safety provisions. Voluntary export restraints refer to the situation whereby one country agrees to limit its exports to a third country (or countries). This agreement is usually made because the importing country (countries) threatens to place barriers against the goods of the exporting country.

When two or more parties decide to engage in trade they have to agree on a medium of exchange. There are essentially two means of facilitating exchange – barter and money. As described in Chapter 3, under a barter

Table 6.1   Tariff rates on industrial products for selected WTO members (average applied rate)

Import markets	Level (%)	Year
North America		
Canada	3.7	2007
United States	3.2	2007
Mexico	11.2	2007
Latin America		
Argentina	12.2	2007
Brazil	12.5	2007
Chile	6.0	2007
Colombia	11.8	2007
Costa Rica	4.5	2007
Haiti	2.4	2007
Western Europe		
European Union (27)	3.8	2007
Switzerland	2.1	2007
Turkey	4.8	2007
Asia		
Bangladesh	14.2	2007
India	11.5	2007
Japan	2.6	2007
Korea, Republic of	6.6	2007
Malaysia	7.9	2007
Pakistan	13.8	2007
Oceania		
Australia	3.8	2007
Africa		
Mauritania	12.1	2007
Mauritius	2.9	2007
South Africa	7.6	2007

Source: Data from WTO (2008a), Part A.1 Tariffs and Imports: Summary and Duty Ranges.

system a direct exchange of commodities takes place. For example, person A swaps cows for goats with person B. When trade becomes more complex, either through the number of traders involved or because of the range of commodities traded, money tends to replace barter as the most efficient means of exchange. Money need not take the form we know today: historically many commodities, including cowrie shells and gold, have played the role of money, that is, a store of value and a means of exchange. In Chapter 8 we will consider how different international monetary systems facilitate or hinder international economic activity such as trade.

Theoretical perspectives: free trade and protectionism

Is trade beneficial or harmful? Should traders be free to move goods and services across national frontiers? And if trade is to be subject to restrictions, what kinds of barriers should be imposed and for what reasons? These questions have confronted policy-makers, citizens, business people and scholars for centuries. And in the era of globalization these questions take on an increased relevance.

Within the contemporary global economy international trade touches many societies and communities through direct and indirect effects. It reaches into our homes, places of work and recreational venues. Depending on where we live and how deeply our society is integrated into the global economy we can find daily reminders of the importance of international trade through the consumption patterns of our families and friends. At its simplest level, the food we eat and the clothes we wear provide evidence of the tremendous importance of trade across national frontiers. But despite the importance of international trade there is no consensus concerning the costs and benefits to countries from engaging in the pursuit of trade. Perhaps we should say that conflicting views exist because of the salience of trade! Given the conflicting values and interests in this structure of the global political economy it is not surprising to discover the absence of agreement on the answers to these questions.

We will now explore contrasting perspectives on the costs and benefits of international trade, beginning with arguments that emphasize the benefits of free trade before moving on to examine critical perspectives. Liberal political economy emphasizes the benefits of trade. For liberals, free trade benefits everyone, increases efficiency and raises productivity. In sharp contrast, nationalist and radical critics argue that free trade can undermine national economies, create uneven development and damage the environment.

Within academic and policy contexts, liberal trade theory provides the framework for the analysis of international trade. This is a sophisticated and substantial body of work which has emerged since its tentative origins in the

19th century. Liberal trade theory appears counter-intuitive since it propounds a positive-sum view of something that most people perceive as being zero-sum. A common sense view of transactions sees one side as gaining while the other one loses. Many people are sceptical of the notion that both sides to a transaction can make a profit. The liberal case for free trade, that is, a situation in which all can gain, is based on the theory of comparative advantage. According to the theory of comparative advantage, countries should specialize and produce goods and services for which they possess a comparative advantage.

The theory of comparative advantage thus lies at the centre of neoclassical trade theory. Prior to the development of the theory of comparative advantage (or comparative costs, as it is sometimes known) by the British political economist David Ricardo in the 19th century, the dominant approach to trade focused on absolute advantage. Mercantilist theories argued that the aim of a country was to increase its trade relative to that of its rivals thus increasing its wealth. For mercantilists, trade was a zero-sum game with one country's gain equivalent to a loss sustained by its trading partner. Since mercantilists believed there was a fixed amount of gold in the world it therefore followed that a country with a trade surplus received more gold and hence an increase in its wealth. Adam Smith had provided an answer to mercantilist theorists with his concept of absolute advantage. Smith argued that two countries could benefit from trade if they specialized in the goods they produced best and traded with each other. Smith's theory of absolute advantage was an advance on mercantilist thought but Ricardo's singular achievement was to demonstrate that trade was a positive-sum game in which all parties benefited even if one party had an absolute advantage in the production of all goods and services. Stated simply, the theory of comparative advantage shows that if a country specializes in the production of those goods and services in which it is relatively efficient (or alternatively, relatively less inefficient) compared to its competitors it will be better off. As illustrated in Chapter 4, Ricardo's model discussed two countries and two products and showed how, given different cost structures of production, trade was beneficial for both countries since it enabled them to consume more than they would be able to without trade.

Under a liberal trading order, trade would be undertaken by countries according to their comparative advantage. Countries would improve their economic growth, become more stable, powerful and efficient since they would be specializing in the production of goods and services in which they were the most efficient producers and enabling their consumers to buy foreign goods at the lowest prices. Specialization in accordance with comparative advantage promotes efficiency since by definition a small market is an obstacle to growth. Ricardo's theory provides the basic principles underlying modern trade theory. However, its assumption that differences in labour productivity were the sole determinant of comparative advantage is too limiting and modern trade theory focuses on factor endowments (capital, land and labour). Developed by Eli Heckscher (1919) and Bertil Ohlin (1933), the factor endowment theory states that comparative advantage arises from the different relative factor endowments of countries. In other words, a country will have a comparative advantage in the production of those goods that use intensively the factor it has most in abundance. Thus a country will export those goods which are relatively intensive in their most abundant factor. For example, if sheep farming is relatively intensive in land compared with textile production, which is labour-intensive, and Australia is land-abundant compared with Bangladesh, which is labour-abundant, the Heckscher–Ohlin theorem predicts that Australia will export sheep to Bangladesh in exchange for textiles.

Liberal trade theory has been further refined to take account of the growth of intra-firm and intra-industry trade, but these refinements do not challenge the basic underlying assumptions of the liberal paradigm. Liberal trade theory does not enquire into the origin of comparative advantage, that is, it does not ask how the different cost structures were established initially. It is also prescriptive since it suggests that the welfare of an individual country and that of the world as a whole will be improved if countries specialize according to their comparative advantage. This theory therefore prescribes free trade and warns of the dangers of protection (see Box 6.1). From a liberal perspective, protectionism is inefficient since it reduces competition, and increases the monopoly power and thus the profits of the industries (or companies) which benefit from protection. On the other hand, free trade increases the degree of products available to consumers, although ultimately it will reduce the degree of product differentiation in each country. The gains from trade come partly from the greater degree of product variety and partly from the lower price per product.

Free-trade theory emphasizes the gains or benefits from trade for a nation. There are two aspects to the gains from trade: the static benefits deriving from specialization according to comparative advantage and those deriving from and contributing to the process of economic growth and development over time. Trade in this view is an engine of growth and generates a number of dynamic, educative effects. These include the diffusion of knowledge of production and organizational techniques, and changed patterns of demand. Specialization leads to an increase in productivity and economic growth. The theory of comparative advantage, it is argued, is relevant for all countries and, indeed, provides hope for low-income countries. Liberal trade theorists argue that specialization brings the likelihood of an improvement in skills and an increase in the productivity of the workforce. They contend that since the export sector can act as a stimulus to the economy as a whole, and foreign investment accompanies increased trade, developing countries will

Box 6.1   The costs of protectionism: a liberal perspective

Many opponents of liberal trade argue that further liberalization damages the interests of people in poor countries. However, the liberal theories examined above suggest the reverse. That is, it is protectionism rather than free trade that hurts the global poor in both developing and developed states. Protectionism may be in the interests of some producers but overall it has a negative impact on consumers in rich and poor countries.

Concerning the impact of rich-country protectionism on the developing world, it has been estimated that such policies costs developing countries around $1,000 billion a year. Protectionism or unfair trade practices hit precisely those sectors where poor countries have the greatest potential to reap gains from trade. An IFPRI study has calculated that rich-country agricultural protectionism costs developing countries around US$24 billion in lost income (Diao, Diaz-Bonilla and Robinson, 2003, p. 2). The authors note that trade-distorting measures account for another US$40 billion of lost agricultural exports from the developing world. A recent study has concluded that although reform of the European Union's Common Agricultural Policy has reduced its trade-distorting impact on world markets, nevertheless, heavy subsidies to European farmers result in significant losses for some developing-country producers (Matthews, 2008).

Moreover, protectionism in OECD countries also has a detrimental effect on the host country. For example, it has been estimated that American protectionist policies cost consumers in the United States $70 billion in 1990, more than 1 per cent of GNP (Hufbauer and Elliott, 1994). A parallel study estimated that Japanese protectionist policies cost Japanese consumers $105 billion, about 3.6 per cent of GNP in 1989 (Sazanami, Urata and Kawai, 1995).

be better off under a free-trade regime. Liberal economists argue that the evidence shows that technological progress has been faster, all other things being equal, for countries that have been increasing their openness to the international flow of goods, services, capital, labour, technology and ideas. Low-income, developing countries can import technologies and information at virtually zero cost, whether explicitly (the actual process or plan), or implicitly (through the goods themselves). They insist that the process of innovation and the diffusion of knowledge is linked to international trade and is crucial for growth.

Despite its theoretical elegance, the theory of comparative advantage has consistently been attacked by critics, but has been sufficiently robust to withstand these various critiques. We will now discuss two schools of thought critical of the liberal arguments in support of free trade. First, we will examine the approaches of writers who can, broadly speaking, be grouped together under the umbrella of mercantilism and neomercantilism.

Mercantilist and neomercantilist writers advocate the regulation of economic life in order to enhance state power or to protect a variety of national groups from competition. Support for protection comes from groups who argue that protection of local production increases national economic welfare. Many people are willing to forgo absolute gain for relative gain. That is, in an anarchical international system states in pursuit of power may give primacy to the relative gains from trade and adopt protectionist measures in order to stabilize their economies even though it diminishes their absolute gains from trade.

Some state-based critiques of liberal trade theory have focused on the prescriptive power of the theory and others on the accuracy of its empirical claims. Two arguments have been made consistently since the 19th century concerning the desirability of free trade. The first argument is the so-called infant industry case. Supporters of industrialization argue that predominantly agricultural countries will experience obstacles in their attempts to industrialize since comparative advantage dictates that they continue to import industrial products whereas they may well have a future comparative advantage in the production of industrial products. The infant industry argument makes the case for temporary protection for industries likely to become competitive on the world stage. This perspective is not simply about individual industries but is tied to a wider societal vision. The process of industrialization, in this view, will be hindered in the absence of effective protection of fledgling local industries, thus providing support for a policy of tariff and other protection for new domestic industries. In other words, protection should be given to these industries until they become competitive and can reap the benefits of comparative advantage. Historically, protectionist policies, by providing the opportunity to develop economies of scale and domestic market stability, have been important and perhaps necessary components of government-led strategies of economic growth and restructuring in countries such as Germany and the United States. According to advocates of this form of protection, governments should intervene to protect those industries that have the potential to develop efficient production but which at the moment would be destroyed by fierce international competition. Some liberal theorists are willing to accept the infant industry argument as an exception to standard comparative advantage theory. However, while providing support for temporary forms of protection they, nevertheless, recognize that there is an inherent problem with the infant industry argument. Domestic producers are unlikely to willingly renounce the protection from which they benefit, and therefore the agreement on the point at which protection is to be discontinued may prove politically difficult even though the economic arguments are compelling.

The second historical argument against free trade claims that the dictates of national security take precedence over trade. In other words, countries need to be self-sufficient in the production of certain strategic industries. These may be related directly to the waging of war or they may refer to food-stuffs. Whether items are necessary for the direct defence of the nation or food security, dependence on external markets can threaten a nation's security. In the interests of national security countries are urged to temper support for free trade with policies protective of national security. It is widely accepted that if free trade jeopardizes other non-economic objectives such as national security it is necessary for governments to impose restrictions in order to protect society. From this perspective the real income gains that motivate free trade cannot be separated from the security externalities that can either impede or facilitate it. Trade with an adversary can be harmful to a nation's security; trade with an ally can support a nation's security. Although states resort to economic warfare and use economic sanctions in cases of conflict, it can be argued that the security dimension of trade is always present.

The infant industry argument and the national security argument have a long historical pedigree. Recently, two further arguments for protection have emerged to lend support to the state-based critique of free trade. First, strategic trade theory (Krugman, 1986, 1987) argues that countries should pursue competitive advantage in those industries of future economic benefit to the nation where the economic and social costs of falling behind competitors are huge. Second, a number of governments and domestic groups concerned about the impact of globalization on their culture have argued that protectionist measures should be implemented to protect the national culture. In the face of globalization many analysts warn that distinctive cultural practices will be swamped by the import of goods and ideas from abroad. Cultural protection in relation to film, media and communications technologies is therefore supported by those who want to resist what they see as undesirable consequences of globalization.

We can identify three different strands of the radical critique of free trade. The one with the longest historical legacy we call the unequal exchange perspective. Writers in this perspective have a Marxist heritage and they provide a powerful social justice critique of liberal trade principles. Although a single unequal exchange perspective does not exist, broadly speaking, we can discern three main parts to this critique. First, these writers stress the importance of historical power relations in the creation of comparative advantage (Frank, 1967). Unlike liberal analysts who take comparative advantage as a given, unequal exchange theorists enquire into the construction of different cost structures across national borders and argue that many have been determined by imperialist plunder. The second aspect of the unequal exchange perspective is an emphasis on the redistributional benefits of free trade. They emphasize the unequal gains to participants in international exchange, which they argue freeze the status quo and make it difficult for poorer countries to develop, and also the concentration of economic power in the hands of the wealthy (Coote, 1992; Oxfam International, 2002). Within the current world order trade from this perspective sustains the activities of transnational corporations and large bureaucracies (government departments or regional organizations) at the expense of peasants and workers (Madeley, 1992). A third variant of this perspective was developed by Arghiri Emmanuel (1972), an Italian Marxist, in his unequal exchange theory in which he argued that trade systematically discriminated against developing countries because of the lower wage rates in developing countries. Emmanuel assumed that labour productivity did not vary between rich and poor countries and therefore the product of labour was equal in rich and poor countries. But since the prices of goods produced by rich countries reflected their high wages and those produced by poor countries reflected their low wages the exchange was inherently unequal since goods produced by rich countries commanded a higher price internationally.

Another radical argument in favour of protection is made by environmental activists (Ekins, 1989; Morris, 1989) who claim that free trade contributes to environmental degradation. They argue that the externalities of trade are omitted from standard trade theory (Clapp and Dauvergne, 2005, pp. 129–30). Environmentalists contend that current trading practices are unsustainable and they campaign for a return to local trade (Shrybman, 1990). This is discussed in more detail later in Chapter 12. Feminist scholars have recently turned their attention to the gendered nature of trade, arguing that trade is not gender-neutral. In common with human rights and environmental activists, feminists argue that trade theory has ignored the social costs of trade (Fontana, Joekes and Masika, 1998). Similarly, scholars and activists wanting the incorporation of labour rights (Verma, 2003) and human rights issues into trade (see Abbott, Breining-Kaufmann and Cottier, 2006; Dommen, 2002) have also explored ways of incorporating these concerns into the traditional paradigm.

In this section we have examined competing perspectives on the relationship between free trade and national and/or world welfare. We have argued that modern international trade theory provides a normative framework for the conduct of international trade. It furnishes both an explanation of, and justification for, trade. Trade theory is thus, despite the claims of standard neoclassical economics, ideological and political. This does not mean that its analytical tools, prescriptions and conclusions are to be rejected as biased and unscientific. Rather, this recognition brings to the fore the fact that trade theory is not only socially constructed but is the subject and object of its own analysis. Actors in the trading system are influenced by the writings of trade theorists. While this captures part of the argument being made here it fails to fully extend its implications. The crucial point is that the 'reality' examined by trade theory is itself partly constructed by trade theory.

Moreover, it is arguable that even if the principle of comparative advantage is applied on a global basis the gains from trade will not be evenly distributed. In the short term it is likely that free trade will result in an unequal distribution of costs and benefits, thus undermining the basis for adherence to free-trade policies since those countries losing out will resort to protectionist measures such as tariffs or subsidies.

Major developments

There have been two notable developments in the world trading system since the end of the Second World War. One development has been a large increase in the volume of world trade. This has been accompanied by changing forms of protectionism as states struggle to cushion the dislocations caused by trade liberalization. The second development has been the transformation of the institutional arrangements governing world trade. The failure of states to create an International Trade Organization (ITO) after the Second World War left the General Agreement on Tariffs and Trade as the primary international framework governing trade relations. In 1995 the GATT gave way to the new World Trade Organization, an indication of a further institutionalization of trade rules.

Growth and protectionism

Since the end of the Second World War, trade has increased more rapidly than production, which is a clear indicator of the increased internationalization of economic activities and of the greater interconnectedness which has come to characterize the world economy. Between 1945 and 2007, growth in world trade consistently outstripped growth in world production (see Table 6.2). In this period world production doubled but international trade grew more than fourfold.

The onset of the global economic recession in 2008 led to the largest contraction in world trade since the Great Depression of the 1930s; forecasts predict a slow recovery (WTO, 2009a, p. 5). The long-term impact of the recession on trade and trade policies is unknown at the moment. In this section we will therefore review developments in international trade between 1945 and 2007 before concluding with an assessment of more

Table 6.2   Growth in the volume of world trade and production by major product groups, 2000–7 (annual percentage change)

	2000–7	2005	2006	2007
World merchandise exports	5.5	6.5	8.5	6.0
Agricultural products	4.0	6.0	6.0	4.5
Fuels and mining products	3.5	3.5	3.5	3.0
Manufactures	6.5	7.5	7.5	10.0
World merchandise production	3.0	3.0	3.0	4.0
Agriculture	2.5	2.0	1.5	2.5
Mining	1.5	1.5	1.0	0.0
Manufacturing	3.0	4.0	4.0	5.0
World GDP	3.0	3.0	3.5	3.5

Note: World merchandise production differs from world GDP in that it excludes services and construction.

Source: Data from WTO (2008b), p. 7.

recent developments. There are certain noticeable features of world trade growth in the post-war period and these will be discussed below. We will focus on the magnitude of trade, its geographical concentration, the commodity composition of trade and the growth in intra-industry and intra-firm trade.

The growth in trade has been uneven and there have been periods of recession when trade growth slowed, but overall the trend has been positive. For example, the WTO calculates that merchandise exports grew on average 6 per cent per annum between 1947 and 1997, and that total trade in 1997 was 14 times the level of 1950 (WTO, 1998). These trends continued in the early 21st century until the onset of the global financial crisis in 2008. Between 2000 and 2005 world merchandise trade grew approximately 10 per cent (WTO, 2006, p. 11); although there was some slowdown in 2006 and 2007 with annual increases of 8 per cent and 5.5 per cent, respectively (WTO, 2007, p. 2, 2008c, p. 2). These figures indicate that trade has been an important sector in the contemporary global economy and a main agent of economic growth. The relationship between trade and growth has been intensely debated during this period, especially since it is an important consideration for countries trying to promote economic development. The consensus among economists is that trade promotes growth. Countries with an open economy engaging in international trade have performed better than those countries where policy has restricted domestic markets to foreign products. The relation between trade and economic growth is twofold. First, trade acts as a stimulus to the local economy providing it with resources cheaper than it would cost to produce domestically. Trade thus raises the production-possibility frontier, enabling countries to consume more than they would have done in the absence of trade. The relationship between consumption and growth will be discussed below where we will show the importance of consumption to contemporary economic growth. Second, trade forces domestic producers to manufacture goods to world market standards, thus increasing productivity and product quality. This leads to a more efficient use of resources. In the light of these arguments it is possible to see one of the reasons for the failure of Soviet-style communism. Instead of embracing trade, communist authorities approached trade with suspicion, viewing it as a source of economic leakage rather than, as it turned out, a source of economic strength. Trade remained a residual element in national economic plans where the drive was for self-sufficiency. Even the attempt at integration through the Soviet-dominated trading organization, the Council for Mutual Economic Assistance (COMECON), was predicated less on exploring dynamic comparative advantage through the benefits of specialization than on protecting what were perceived to be national interests.

Not only has overall trade growth been uneven, it has also been so in respect of different countries and regions (see Table 6.3). The majority of transactions in world trade are restricted to the advanced industrial countries, and the fastest growth in trade occurred among these countries. On the other hand, least-developed countries (LDCs) account for less than 1 per cent of world trade (WTO, 2006, p. iii). Whereas the theory of comparative advantage predicts that trade will grow fastest between unlike economies, post-war trade growth has seen the reverse of this proposition.

In the 1950s and 1960s trade grew fastest in manufactured products. In 1945 the commodity composition of international trade reflected the sectoral composition of output in the leading economies and was therefore mainly composed of merchandise trade. But as services became the dominant sector in industrialized economies, so the trade in services has expanded with the result that one of the major developments in the international trading system has been the rise of trade in services. While trade in services is not the largest sector in world trade it has been the fastest-growing sector.

The term 'intra-industry trade' refers to the situation where trade occurs within the same industry rather than between industries. One of the main features of post-war trade growth has been the phenomenon of intra-industry trade. Countries have exchanged like products where price and product differentiation have played important parts. In consumer goods we have seen

Table 6.3   Value of world merchandise trade by region, 2007
(billion dollars)

Exports	Region	Imports
13,570	World	13,940
1,854	North America*	2,704
496	South and Central America	455
5,769	Europe	6,055
422	Africa	355
721	Middle East	462
3,798	Asia	3,528

*includes Mexico

Source: Data from WTO (2008b), p. 18.

the exchange of consumer durables so that although the United Kingdom, for example, produces motor vehicles and washing machines, it has also imported these items from other OECD member countries. International trade has supported both horizontal and vertical integration. The growth of intra-industry trade has also been matched by the growth of intra-firm trade. The rise of the transnational corporation and a global production system (see Chapter 7) has stimulated intra-firm trade. An increasing percentage of world trade takes place within firms rather than between separate, individual firms. One of the crucial implications for trade theory and for national governments is that if trade takes place within a transnational corporation pricing policies will not reflect real costs. In such cases trade is driven not by comparative costs but by the management decisions of the firm.

The period from 1947 to 1973 was one of unprecedented expansion for the world economy, with output and trade growing faster than in any previously recorded period. Global output expanded at an annual average of 5 per cent, while exports grew at 7 per cent per annum. This provided an economic climate conducive to trade liberalization, and it was against this background that protectionism was reduced on manufactured products. A number of significant structural changes took place between 1947 and 1973. The most important change in the context of the trading system was the shift away from a traditional dependence on the export of primary commodities to the increasing specialization in labour-intensive, low-technology manufactured products by a number of developing countries such as India, Brazil and the

East Asian NICs. These developing country exporters took advantage of expanding markets in the developed economies and the contraction of productive capacity in some sectors in the OECD countries as the dynamic comparative advantage of developing countries became evident. Industries such as textiles and footwear were initially developed in the industrialized countries but during this period the technological know-how associated with these activities was diffused to some developing countries.

During the long boom (1947–73) it was relatively easy for developed countries to make the necessary adjustments to imports of manufactures from the developing world because the employment-creating effects of international trade were outweighing the employment-displacing effects. The outcome of these developments was that the benefits of trade were obvious and, by and large, consumers and producers willingly acquiesced in the trade liberalization process. Thus protectionist pressures were specific rather than general.

With the downturn in the world economy following the first oil crisis in 1973–4 unemployment grew and became a critical political issue in the industrialized world. The importance of the recession of 1973–7 was to focus the attention of various pressure groups on the perceived connection between foreign trade and domestic employment – that is, on the link between employment displacement and import penetration. Employment preservation through the restriction of imports became an acceptable means of preventing unemployment from rising to unacceptable levels. What characterized this period was the resort to non-tariff instruments of policy. Countries abandoned the use of old protectionism in the form of tariffs for new protectionism using non-tariff barriers (NTBs). Because they were the most vulnerable, discrimination against developing countries grew at an alarming rate. As an OECD report declared, 'developing countries have in practice been most exposed to discriminatory export restraint agreements and other trade distorting measures, with the incidence of this discrimination being greatest in those sectors in which they have a comparative advantage' (Goldin, Knudsen and van der Mensbrugghe, 1993, p. 22).

If structural change accounted for the onset of protectionism, it was the existence of the GATT that shaped the forms the new protectionism would take. The GATT Articles provide for the introduction of restraints under certain designated circumstances. For example, Article XIX condones the use of import controls for the emergency protection of domestic industry. Recourse to these escape clauses became increasingly prevalent in the 1970s, as the major developed countries made more frequent usage of the protectionist option. However, recourse to Article XIX was rather limited since many countries taking protectionist action preferred to evade GATT stipulations on non-discrimination and reciprocity and therefore turned to extra-legal alternatives which suited their purposes better than Article XIX. These provisions are central to the explanation of a reluctance to use Article XIX and a willingness to look for alternatives outside the GATT framework. The most widely used NTBs were voluntary export restraints, import quotas, product standards, including regulations pertaining to health and technical safeguards, and anti-dumping measures and countervailing duties, which are still drawn upon today. An example of the use of health standards to discriminate against imports is given in Box 6.2. The negotiation of a voluntary

Box 6.2   Health risks and hormone-treated beef

The European Union first banned the importation of hormone-treated meat in 1989, arguing that injecting livestock with bovine somatropin (BST) posed a health risk to humans. BST, a growth hormone produced by beef cattle, was in use by major meat-producing countries including Canada and the United States. Scientists from meat-exporting countries that used BST argued that it was safe, but consumer groups in the EU and the European farm lobby protested that hormonal irregularities or cancer would result from its consumption. Was this a genuine health issue or a form of disguised protectionism? The EU claimed it was a health issue, but producers affected by the ban argued that it reflected an attempt to protect the inefficient EU meat industry. At the centre of the dispute is whether the EU's ban is in compliance with the WTO Agreement on Sanitary and Phytosanitary Measures (SPS).

In 1997 the WTO's Dispute Settlement Panel found the EU ban to be incompatible with its obligations under the SPS Agreement; and in 1998 the WTO's Appellate Body confirmed that the European ban on hormone fed beef violated its rules but noted that the EU ban would be justified if convincing scientific proof could be provided concerning the health risks of hormone-treated beef. The outcome from the WTO process supported the contention of meat exporters to the EU who had lost revenue as a result of the EU ban. For example, US red meat exports to the EU fell from $231 million in 1988 (a year before the ban) to $98 million in 1994. Despite this ruling, deep scepticism remains among EU consumers. The EU has, since 2003, cited new scientific evidence as the basis for their import restrictions in an attempt to make the EU ban consistent with the WTO's ruling; and to evade trade sanctions which had been imposed since July 1999. In October 2008 the Appellate Body permitted the EU to maintain their restrictions but also granted Canada and the US the authority to impose trade sanctions totalling in excess of US$125 million annually.

Source: Bridges TradeBioRes (2009).

export restraint allowed action to be taken on a discriminatory basis, a facility unavailable under Article XIX. In order to appease pressure groups at home while at the same time doing little to impair export prospects, governments followed the path of least resistance. This period also saw the mushrooming of administrative controls such as the use of health, safety and environmental standards. Protectionism also took the form of subsidies and government procurement policies. This move from GATT's rule of law brought with it a heightened absence of transparency, given that non-transparency is a property of NTBs.

The rise of new protectionism and the failure of the GATT to remedy these developments contributed to dissatisfaction with the organization's performance. This issue will be addressed in the next section. While the new protectionism is no longer a major issue since the creation of the WTO gave a boost to liberalizing forces, the confrontation between advocates of trade liberalization and those of protection remains an important issue in the contemporary global economy.

The growth in world trade in the 1990s and the early years of the 21st century has been uneven, reflecting the global economic cycle. This is evident in the context of the current crisis. With the onset of the global recession, world trade growth slowed significantly, recording a modest increase of 2 per cent in 2008 (WTO, 2009a, p. 4). The impact of the recession on the trends discussed above is dependent on the depth of the economic downturn and the policies taken by the leading economies.

Changing institutional arrangements

The origins of the post-World War II international trade regime are to be found in Anglo-American cooperation during the Second World War. The liberal trade regime that was created reflected primarily American interests. American preference for open-market arrangements and for the imposition of a multilateral rule-based system to limit national action is at the centre of the regime. Two particular issues were of concern to American policy-makers – British Imperial preferences and the system of protection that had developed in Latin America during the war. The United States therefore proposed a non-discriminatory, multilateral system of trade and payments. This meant in practice provision for reciprocity, international supervision of tariff and exchange rates, outlawing of quantitative restrictions, freely convertible currencies and the generalization of tariff reductions to all members of the regime. The trade regime is, to use a term coined by Ruggie (1982), one of 'embedded liberalism'. That is, its main features subscribe to liberal trade principles, but nevertheless recognition is made of deviations from the standard principles. The international trade regime is not a laissez-faire system but rather one of managed trade. The trading regime is based on four key principles: non-discrimination, reciprocity, transparency and multi-lateralism. These have been the guiding principles for a series of international institutions designed to govern post-war international trade.

Non-discrimination is enshrined in the Most Favoured Nation (MFN) clause. The MFN principle ensures that any concession granted to one member must be extended to all other members. Under MFN provisions all members of the GATT/WTO are treated in a non-discriminatory manner. A tariff on an import from a GATT/WTO member had to be placed on all other GATT/WTO members in a similar manner, with the exception of customs unions or free-trade areas. This principle is therefore at the centre of the multilateral trading system. Reciprocity is intended to ensure that when one country lowers its tariffs against the exports of another country it will in turn be granted equal trade concessions. The principle of reciprocity applied through multilateral bargaining means that, in theory, one country's concessions are paid for by a third country, which then passes it on to another country and the process repeats itself. Transparency refers to the fact that any discrimination must be clearly visible. The system is based on the principle that tariffs are the only permissible form of discrimination. Non-tariff barriers such as import quotas are banned and countries are urged to replace non-tariff barriers with tariffs. Finally, the system is based on multilateralism which implies and reflects the commitment to the creation of a multilateral trade regime, multilateral cooperation in maintaining a rule-based system and engaging in periodic rounds of tariff-cutting.

The Conference on Trade and Employment held in Havana, Cuba, in 1948 created the International Trade Organization (ITO) as the institutional framework of the post-war international trading system. However, opposition to the proposed ITO, especially in the United States, resulted in non-ratification of the treaty creating the ITO. Given the preponderant position of the United States in the world economy at this time, most governments delayed ratification until the US Congress gave its assent, but in 1951 President Truman, aware of widespread hostility to the ITO, decided not to seek Congressional assent, thus consigning the ITO to history. With the failure of the ITO, the General Agreement on Tariffs and Trade (GATT) became the institutional focus of the world trading system. GATT was the result of a tariff-cutting exercise by 23 nations prior to the Havana Conference. Meeting in Geneva in March 1947, the delegates decided on a series of tariff reductions, and a temporary mechanism to oversee these cuts. Instead of withering away as initially envisaged, the GATT was given permanence. GATT provided a code of rules, a dispute settlement mechanism and a forum for trade negotiations. Its main importance lay in its role as a forum for trade negotiations. In eight rounds (see Table 6.4) of multilateral trade negotiations (MTNs) between 1947 and 1994 it presided over a period of unprecedented growth in world trade.

Table 6.4 GATT negotiating rounds

Name	Dates	Number of countries participating
Geneva	1947	23
Annecy	1949	13
Torquay	1951	38
Geneva	1956	26
Dillon	1960–1	26
Kennedy	1964–7	62
Tokyo	1973–9	102
Uruguay	1986–93	123

Until the Kennedy Round, negotiations were conducted on an item-by-item basis, but in this round the negotiators moved to an across-the-board approach. The GATT enjoyed uneven success in its quest to reduce trade barriers. It was most successful in tackling barriers to manufactured goods but less so in preventing agricultural protectionism. Three main features of trade liberalization are visible in the GATT period.

First, the GATT achieved considerable success in reducing tariffs on manufactured goods. Beginning with the Geneva Conference in 1947, significant tariff reductions were negotiated in successive multilateral trade reductions on some 45,000 products, constituting approximately half of world trade at that stage (Williams, 1994, p. 150). Progress slowed somewhat between this first conference and the Kennedy Round, but substantial tariff reductions were achieved. The new approach used in the Kennedy Round yielded average tariff reductions of 36–9 per cent and, despite the unfavourable economic circumstances, tariff cuts in the Tokyo Round averaged between 33 and 38 per cent.

Second, the process of trade liberalization under GATT was uneven. Trade liberalization was almost solely confined to manufactured products – the most dominant growth sector. In 1947 at the first round of GATT negotiations, the average tariff on manufactured goods was around 40 per cent. By the end of the Kennedy Round, these tariffs had been lowered to an average of 10 per cent. The tariffs of the industrial countries were reduced by a further 35 per cent as a result of the Tokyo Round (Winham, 1986, p. 17). To illustrate the significance of tariff reductions to the industrial countries, we note that tariffs on industrial products in the United States declined from around 50 per cent in 1947 to about 4 per cent in 1979, and those in the United Kingdom moved from around 40 per cent to about 4 per cent in the same period (Greenaway and Hine, 1991). Industrial countries were willing to liberalize in sectors that were expanding but reluctant to do so in those in which they had lost or were losing comparative advantage and felt most under threat. Agricultural protection continued unchecked until the Uruguay Round, where a start was made on phasing out the protection afforded to farmers in the developed world. But reform of agricultural trade has proved difficult and will continue to be a sensitive political issue in future trade talks. Developed countries also devised a series of restrictive measures in relation to textiles and clothing. Under the guise of ensuring orderly market behaviour the GATT sanctioned the Multi-Fibre Agreement (MFA) to regulate trade in textiles and clothing. This was in effect a protectionist device which was not phased out until 2005 as a result of decisions made during the Uruguay Round negotiations.

Third, whereas trade liberalization was initially limited solely to trade in merchandise goods, beginning with the Tokyo Round, additional issues have been placed on the agenda. The Tokyo Round negotiations were conducted during the period known as the new protectionism, where states prohibited from a recourse to tariff barriers through their GATT commitments began to impose significant non-tariff barriers. At the conclusion of the Tokyo Round negotiators agreed six voluntary codes to prohibit the use of NTBs, but implementation was poor. They also attempted to develop a framework to regulate anti-dumping measures. During the Uruguay Round, the agenda of the world trading system was further expanded to include services, intellectual property rights, investment, environment, labour standards and domestic (non-trade) policies.

GATT also provided a normative framework and a dispute settlement mechanism. Assessment of GATT's impact as a normative framework is difficult but two issues can be examined. It is undeniable that GATT made a major contribution to the development of international economic law (Jackson, 1969; Kock, 1969). The GATT treaty is a legal document, and it provided a code of rules that set the framework for international commercial transactions. Additionally, governments used the existence of GATT disciplines as a mechanism to resist domestic demands for protection. One of GATT's major failures was its dispute settlement mechanism. Because the recommendations of the dispute panel required unanimous consent, contracting parties could block the decisions of GATT panels.

At the end of the Uruguay Round of negotiations a new trade organization, the WTO, was created. The WTO is the successor to the GATT and owes its existence to perceived deficiencies of GATT. Dissatisfaction with GATT grew because of the organization's failure to reverse the growth of protectionism, the weakness of its dispute settlement procedures and the uneven nature of its trade liberalization process. In an effort to reverse protectionism and bolster trade liberalization, the WTO was created as a permanent international organization with greater scope than the GATT. The WTO is the legal and institutional foundation of the world trading system. It is a legal agreement specifying the rights and obligations of its members. The WTO consists of a series of interlocking legal agreements and membership requires acceptance of these agreements as a single undertaking. On accession to the WTO, a state must adhere to the following agreements:

- the Agreement establishing the WTO;
- GATT 1994 and other multilateral trade agreements for goods including Sanitary and Phytosanitary Measures (SPS), the agreement on technical barriers to trade (TBT) and the agreement on Trade-Related Investment Measures (TRIMS);
- the General Agreement on Trade in Services (GATS);
- the agreement on Trade-Related Intellectual Property Rights measures (TRIPS);
- the Understanding on Rules and Procedures Governing the Settlement of Disputes;
- the Trade Policy Review Mechanism (TPRM).

The WTO also consists of Plurilateral Agreements governing civil aircraft, government procurement, and dairy and bovine products, but the acceptance of these agreements is not mandatory for membership.

While the GATT was essentially a contractual agreement among its member states, the WTO is an international organization with a legal personality akin to other intergovernmental organizations such as the IMF and World Bank. The sole formal actors in the WTO are the member states and the principal decision-making body is the Ministerial Conference, which meets every two years. To date, seven Ministerial Conferences have been held (see Table 6.5). The Ministerial Conference is empowered to make decisions on any issues covered by the WTO agreements. Since it only meets every two years it has delegated its competence to the General Council. The General Council, consisting of all WTO members, is the highest decision-making body in the interval between Ministerial Conferences. The General Council also acts as the Dispute Settlement Body and the Trade Policy Review Body. The organizational structure of the WTO is completed by three councils each with a functional area of specialization: the Council for Trade in Goods, the Council for Trade in Services and the Council for Trade-Related Intellectual Property Rights; and by various committees and a number of working groups and working parties.

In an attempt to improve the functioning of the world trading system

Table 6.5   WTO Ministerial Conferences

Place	Date
Singapore	9–13 December 1996
Geneva	18–20 May 1998
Seattle	30 November–3 December 1999
Doha	9–14 November 2001
Cancun	10–14 September 2003
Hong Kong	13–18 December 2005
Geneva	30 November–2 December 2009

under the WTO the procedure for settling trade disputes was considerably strengthened. The Dispute Settlement Understanding (DSU) provides the machinery for settling members' differences on their rights and obligations. It consists of a first-stage panel adjudication followed by an appeals process (the Appellate Body), and a clear schedule for the processing of disputes. Moreover, decisions from the dispute settlement process are based on a negative consensus. That is, they can only be overturned by the General Council if all members are in agreement. As a centre for the settlement of disputes, the WTO contributes to the stability and further evolution of the world trading system, since liberalization will not take place in the absence of effective dispute settlement procedures.

Furthermore, compared with the GATT, the WTO has transformed the management of world trade in three crucial respects. It engineered a shift from trade liberalization based on tariff concessions (shallow or negative integration) to discussions of domestic policies, institutional practices and regulations (deep or positive integration). It also constructed a new agenda expanding the scope (through the inclusion of services, trade-related intellectual property rights and domestic [non-trade] policies), and changing the character of negotiations from a focus on bargaining over products to negotiations over policies that shape the conditions of competition. Finally, it initiated a movement towards policy harmonization, for example in the areas of subsidies, trade-related investment measures and services. The WTO's extensive powers have given it a much higher profile than its predecessor.

Trade liberalization since 1947 has been accompanied by a rise in international trade (see Table 6.6) which supporters of further liberalization claim is a result of the process of removing restrictions to trade. They argue

Table 6.6   World merchandise trade, 1948–2007 (billions of US dollars)

	1948	1953	1963	1973	1983	1993	2003	2007
Exports World	58	84	157	579	1,838	3,670	7,342	13,619
Imports World	66	84	163	589	1,881	3,678	7,623	13,968

Source: Data from WTO (2008b), p. 32.

that the institutional framework creates liberalization and this in turn enhances increased trade (Finlayson and Zacher, 1981). Structuralist critics, on the contrary, claim that trade expansion would have taken place without these governing arrangements since the growth of trade has principally been a response to structural change in the world economy (Strange, 1985).

The debate concerning trade expansion and the institutional structure of world trade can be illuminated through another examination of the rise of so-called new protectionism in the 1970s. Old protectionism refers to the use of tariffs and quotas by states to protect vulnerable sectors from foreign competition, to avoid unemployment and to stimulate their economies. However, GATT rounds and GATT discipline between 1947 and 1973 reduced the tariffs on industrial products to negligible levels. The success of GATT was not only in reducing barriers to trade but also through the practice of binding tariffs, ensuring that, once lowered, a tariff could not subsequently be raised again. Thus, the commitments entered into by states both secured increased trade liberalization and also constrained the recourse to traditional mechanisms of protection. The response to the recession and consequent rise in unemployment after the end of the long boom was the development of new forms of protectionism. After 1973 governments increasingly turned to the use of NTBs. These included voluntary export restraints (VERs), the recourse to anti-dumping and countervailing duties, health, technical and other product standards. The new protectionist measures possessed limited transparency, were generally sector-specific and were lacking in uniform application. In a retreat from multilateralism, governments used NTBs to target specific industries in major competitor nations.

Key issues

There are numerous trade issues on the contemporary international agenda. However, the future of the liberal trading system and the role of the WTO as the key institutional node of the trade regime lie at the centre of current discussions. The long delays in concluding the Doha Development Agenda is a pertinent reminder of the central crisis of multilateral trade system. In this section we will discuss three broad issues that are relevant to the failure of the Doha talks and to the future of world trade. One issue is the place of developing countries in the world trading system. A second issue concerns the significance of regional trading agreements. A third issue is the question of the legitimacy of liberal trade agreements which ignore the social and environmental dimensions to trade.

Developing country interests

Although the economic structures of developing countries are diverse, a set of interests specific to developing countries have emerged within the world trading system. Central to this development has been the self-identification of developing countries, and the limited political influence they exert in international trade negotiations. While no single developing country coalition exists in the context of the WTO, developing countries have identified common interests (Narlikar and Tussie, 2004) and have at times created formal negotiating groups (see Box 6.3).

Two issues have consistently emerged at the centre of the debate. The first concerns the benefits of a liberal trading order, and the second relates to the continuation of protectionist forces in the post-war trading system. In relation to the first issue, a debate exists between those who contend that trade promotes development and those who maintain that industrialization is best achieved behind protectionist barriers. A related debate exists between those who argue that reform of trading arrangements will benefit developing countries and those who contend that the trading system is inherently exploitative. We will not revisit these debates here. Instead we will examine the ways in which developing countries have articulated their interests and the response to the concerns of the developing countries.

In the debates on trade liberalization since the creation of the WTO the developing countries have attempted to define and promote specific sets of interests. In November 2001, the first major round of multilateral trade negotiations since the Uruguay Round was launched at the Doha Ministerial Meeting of the WTO. The Doha Development Agenda (DDA) was specifically targeted at the interests of developing countries. As the *Ministerial Declaration* stated, 'The majority of WTO members are developing countries. We seek to place their needs and interests at the heart of the Work Programme adopted in this Declaration' (WTO, 2001, para. 2). The hopes and aspirations enunciated in 2001 were frustrated through a tortuous negotiating process and on 24 July 2006 the negotiations on the Doha Development Agenda were indefinitely suspended. The failure to make

Box 6.3   Developing country coalitions in the WTO

Individually, many developing countries are too small and have limited bargaining power in international trade negotiations. Coalitions frequently arise on a specific issue or emerge at a particular conference. Some major developing countries seek to enhance their bargaining power through joining a coalition and other smaller countries join groups for defensive purposes. Examples of developing country coalitions include:

The Like-Minded Group of developing countries was formed in 1996. The LMG has been active in opposing progress on the so-called new issues (i.e., TRIPS and GATS) and insists on implementation of the Uruguay Round agreements. The main members of the LMG are African and Asian countries.

The G-20 emerged in response to the Cancun agenda and was initiated by Brazil and India. The core membership of the G-20 are influential developing countries such as Brazil, China, India, South Africa, Pakistan, Egypt and Nigeria. The G-20's membership spans the various regions of the developing world. The focus of the G-20 is agricultural negotiations.

The G-90 was created at the Cancun conference and brings together some of the poorest developing countries. Its membership is made up from the LDC group, the African Pacific and Caribbean (ACP) caucus, the Small-Island States Group and the African Group.

The Cotton-4 formed prior to the Cancun conference in 2003 brings together the main African cotton producers – Benin, Burkina Faso, Chad and Mali.

significant progress on the talks reflects both the continued weakness of developing countries and the veto power possessed by the EU and the United States in trade negotiations.

Agricultural trade liberalization was of central concern to the developing countries during the Doha negotiations. Many developing countries remain dependent on the export of agricultural commodities, and even in those countries in which agriculture is not the major export sector, agriculture remains a significant employer of labour (see Table 6.7).

Whereas the industrialized countries have embraced liberalization in manufactured products, they have been reluctant to fully liberalize agricultural trade. Indeed, until the Uruguay Round, agriculture was kept off the

Table 6.7 GDP composition by sector: agriculture, 2009 (%)

Country	Share of GDP in agriculture
Liberia	76.9
Somalia	65
Central African Republic	55
Congo, Democratic Republic	55
Sierra Leone	49
Ethiopia	47.6
Cameroon	43.5
Burma	40.9
Laos	39.2
Malawi	38.1
Rwanda	35
Burundi	32.9
Papua New Guinea	32.8
Guyana	31.9
Afghanistan	31
Burkina Faso	29.1
Uganda	29
Uzbekistan	28.2
Cote d'Ivoire	27.9
Tanzania	27
Madagascar	26
Mozambique	23.4
Paraguay	23.1
Syria	22.5
Guinea	22.4
Albania	20.6
Chad	20.5
Pakistan	20.4

Source: Data from CIA (2009).

negotiating agenda. Despite the progress made during the Uruguay Round agriculture in the industrialized countries continues to enjoy high levels of protection. The agricultural support policies of the developed countries have an overall negative impact on developing countries. This is an area in which the developed world abandons its support of comparative advantage and for a number of economic, political and social reasons implements discriminatory policies. When protection leads to excess domestic production this results in lower world prices, thus reducing the incomes of producers in the developing world. Protection in the form of import levies and quotas in removing a large part of agricultural trade from the world market increases the volatility of international prices. The persistence of impediments to market access in agriculture therefore remains a major policy concern of developing countries. The persistence of subsidies on major agricultural exports from the developed countries, continued domestic support to agriculture and high tariffs resulting from tariffication (the process whereby NTBs are converted to tariffs) have conspired to restrict the gains made by developing countries. The issue of agricultural protection is also of interest to some developed-country exporters and has given rise to a grouping of developed- and developing-country producers. The Cairns Group (see Box 6.4) is an intergovernmental pressure group for agricultural reform linking developing countries and developed countries.

Although agriculture was prioritized as a key issue in the Doha talks and WTO members were committed to a significant reduction in trade-distorting subsidies and other forms of agricultural protection, the negotiations were

---

Box 6.4   The Cairns Group

Largely an Australian invention under the Hawke Government, the Cairns Group comprises 19 agricultural exporting countries. Formed in 1986, the Cairns Group has effectively put agriculture on the multilateral trade agenda after decades of stalemate over reduction in the protection received by agricultural products. It was largely as a result of the group's efforts that a framework for reform in farm products trade was established in the Uruguay Round and agriculture was, for the first time, subject to trade liberalization rules. These are set out in the WTO Agreement on Agriculture.

Membership: Argentina, Australia, Bolivia, Brazil, Canada, Chile, Colombia, Costa Rica, Guatemala, Indonesia, Malaysia, New Zealand, Pakistan, Paraguay, Peru, Philippines, South Africa, Thailand and Uruguay.

Box 6.5   The cotton initiative

The slow progress of the agricultural negotiations frustrated many least-developed countries who were aware that failure further weakened their fragile trading positions. In June 2003, prior to the WTO Ministerial Meeting in Cancun, four West African countries – Benin, Burkina Faso, Chad and Mali – submitted a paper to the WTO's Trade Negotiations Committee calling for the abolition of developed-country cotton subsidies, and financial compensation to be paid to the four countries while the subsidies remained. The proposal was submitted to the Cancun conference in September 2003 but no agreement was reached. There were objections by various states to both parts of the draft document – treating cotton as a separate issue, and the provision of financial compensation. These disagreements were overshadowed by the disdainful attitude of the US delegation to the proposal. In the charged atmosphere of Cancun the cotton initiative became a key symbol of developing countries' anger and disappointment. In the discussion post-Cancun to get the multilateral trade negotiations back on track after the 'failure' of two successive Ministerial Meetings the cotton initiative was placed on a separate negotiating track. A cotton sub-committee was created in November 2004 under the framework of the agricultural negotiations.

characterized by countless disagreements, shifting deadlines and eventually a failure to reach compromise. The slow pace of the agricultural negotiations prompted the development of solidarity among developing countries (Clapp, 2006). It also led to an unprecedented move by four West African cotton producers and the reshaping of the DDA to meet their specific interests (see Box 6.5).

The varying interest of developing countries was visible in the scramble for export markets following the end of the Multi-Fibre Arrangement (MFA) on 1 January 2005. The phasing out of the MFA has had a differential impact on developing-country exporters. The limited research available on the post-MFA textile industry has produced inconclusive findings. An analysis of the export performance of Asian countries post-MFA argues that the short-term impact of the end of restrictions has been small (Whalley, 2006). Another study argued that while a small number of countries will benefit a large number of (smaller) developing countries will be significantly worse off (Heron, 2006). Inevitably, a number of other developing countries have expressed concern that the textile industries in their area might close as production is concentrated in China. Several sub-Saharan African countries are particularly vulnerable (Dinesh and Little, 2004). With the ending of MFA protection, Taiwanese or Hong Kong businesses that invested in Africa to find a way around import quotas are now able to close down their African plants and locate production in the Chinese mainland.

The expansion of the multilateral trade agenda during the Uruguay Round to include new issues has remained controversial and has created difficulties for WTO trade governance. It has been argued that three issues – trade in services, intellectual property rights and investment measures – separately and together limit the policy autonomy of developing country governments (Wade, 2003). The most frequently discussed services – tourism, business services and finance – provide greater returns for the developed world, but in some business services, for example, in publishing and data processing, developing countries have been able to build up exportable services. While developing countries were able to safeguard some of their interests by insisting that the General Agreement on Trade in Services (GATS) be based on a positive list (that is, countries must list services to be liberalized), the impact of the liberalization in services on developing countries remains a hotly debated topic (Wiener, 2005).

The issue of intellectual property rights is also of great importance to developing countries (also see Chapter 13). Until the Uruguay Round copyrights, patents and other forms of intellectual property were not treated as trade or even trade-related issues. They were brought into the Uruguay Round on the insistence of American transnational companies who insisted that exports of counterfeit goods, especially from South-east Asia, were responsible for large revenue and profit losses (Sell, 2000). Moreover, pharmaceutical companies had long complained that their profits and research and development were harmed by the local production of their products without payment of a licence, and usually justified under national health guidelines. The Trade-Related Intellectual Property Rights (TRIPs) agreement gives greater influence to foreign investors and provides increased international patent protection to a range of products and processes previously exempt from patent protection (Hoogvelt, 1997, p. 136). It requires countries to accept the substance of existing international conventions on copyright (Berne Convention) and on patents (Paris Convention). Bringing these agreements under the WTO subjects them to WTO dispute settlement procedures and enforcement mechanisms. The agreement forces two kinds of costs upon middle- and low-income countries: revenue losses due to the increased cost of drugs, and the administrative costs of introducing relevant legal frameworks to protect patents.

The likely detrimental impact of the TRIPs agreement has been most clearly visible in the area of public health, where drug companies holding the patents to medicines can dictate the price of essential drugs. Concerns of developing countries over the availability of generic (cheaper) drugs led to the Declaration on the TRIPs Agreement and Public Health at the Doha Ministerial Meeting. This concession was an attempt to meet the concern many developing countries felt about the price of medicines. However, it has been argued that the declaration has made no significant difference to either importing countries or those with the capacity to manufacture pharmaceuticals (May, 2005, p. 173). Moreover, pharmaceutical companies can take out patents and thus deprive developing-country producers of revenues. That is, local knowledge that is currently free will cease to be so if a foreign company takes out a patent on that knowledge. The costs of introducing the required legal and administrative mechanisms will be highest for least-developed countries. It has been claimed that 'the main beneficiaries will be the core group of less than a dozen seeds and pharmaceuticals companies which control over 70% of the world's seeds trade' (Hoogvelt, 1997, p. 136). The issue of drug patents and HIV/AIDS is discussed in greater detail in Chapter 13.

Some critics are worried that the move towards giving foreign investors unfettered access to global markets will undermine the sovereignty of host governments. The issue surfaced in the negotiations on Trade-Related Investment Measures (TRIMs). Although an agreement with the potential to override national law does not exist it is believed by many that it is only a matter of time before such an agreement is signed. The attempt to create a regulatory code for foreign investment in the OECD met vociferous opposition from critics in the developed world, and also from groups claiming to speak for the developing world. Opposition to the Multilateral Agreement on Investment (MAI) from social movement activists was instrumental in the failure by governments to agree on the MAI (Goodman and Ranald, 2000).

Another issue of interest to developing countries relates to their special status in trade negotiations. Developing countries have been concerned since the 1960s with ensuring that their participation in international trade meets with their development needs. The demand for special and differential treatment (S&D) was based on the claim that the demands of development are incompatible with the free operation of market forces. The demand for S&D was first formally accepted in 1965 with the addition of a new chapter to the GATT. Part IV of the GATT entitled 'Trade and Development' gave legal sanction to the principle of special and differential treatment and provided the developing countries with a specific focus from which to mount further campaigns for reform. While the Tokyo Round extended S&D, the creation of the WTO has seen a move away from treating developing countries as a special case. Within the WTO increased emphasis is given to the trade needs of the least-developed countries; and developing countries, while given some concessions, are expected to conform to the general rules. Special and differential treatment under the WTO can be classified into five main groups:

- provisions aimed at increasing trade opportunity through market access;
- provisions requiring WTO members to safeguard the interests of the developing countries;
- provisions allowing flexibility to developing countries in rules and disciplines governing trade measures;
- provisions allowing longer transitional periods to developing countries;
- provisions for technical assistance.

Within each of these groups additional provisions are made specifically for the least-developed countries. The aim of the WTO is to include developing countries as full participants in the system, that is, to move to a position where it will be possible to withdraw any special and differential status. The provisions noted above with regard to the special and differential treatment of developing countries have largely been ineffectual. For example, the developed countries are not taking the special needs of developing countries into account in preparing and applying sanitary and phytosanitary measures, technical regulations, standards and conformity assessment procedures. Moreover, the transitional periods do not always give sufficient time to deal with specific shortfalls in capacity that are faced by individual members or with precise development needs. And, finally, many developing countries emphasize the critical and continued need for technical assistance. They call for better coordination of technical assistance from all sources, and have asked for increased funding of technical assistance in the core WTO budget. Taking cases before the dispute settlement mechanism requires the payment usually of large fees for specialist legal advice.

The special emphasis of the DDA on development brought increased prominence to S&D. The *Doha Ministerial Declaration* reaffirmed 'that provisions for special and differential treatment are an integral part of the WTO Agreements' (WTO, 2001, para. 44). Moreover, it was agreed that that 'all special and differential treatment provisions shall be reviewed with a view to strengthening them and making them more precise, effective and operational' (WTO, 2001, para. 44). To date there has been limited progress in meeting these objectives.

Regional trade agreements

The past decade and a half has witnessed an avalanche in the creation of regional trade agreement (RTAs). There are currently over 230 RTAs in force with most of those created since the establishment of the WTO. Between 1948 and 1994 GATT received notification of 124 RTAs but the WTO has received notification of 297 RTAs in the period between January 1995 and December 2008 (WTO, 2009b). Box 6.6 below provides an example of the evolution of RTAs as part of the trade strategy of a middle power

---

Box 6.6   Australia and Regional Trade Agreements

Australia's Free Trade Agreements
ASEAN–Australia–New Zealand FTA (2009)
Singapore–Australia FTA (2003)
Thailand–Australia FTA (2005)
Australia–United States FTA (2005)
Australia–New Zealand Closer Economic Relations (1988)
Australia–Chile FTA (2009)

Free Trade Agreements under negotiation
Australia–China FTA negotiations
Australia–Gulf Cooperation Council (GCC) FTA negotiations
Australia–Japan FTA negotiations
Australia–Korea FTA negotiations
Australia–Malaysia FTA negotiations
Pacific Agreement on Closer Economic Relations (PACER) Plus
Trans-Pacific Partnership Agreement

Free Trade Agreements under consideration
Australia–India Feasibility Study
Indonesia–Australia Feasibility Study

---

with a strong commitment to multilateral trade. An acceleration in the creation of RTAs seems to be concurrent with the slow pace of multilateral negotiations. Regional economic organizations have multiple objectives of which the promotion of trade liberalization is frequently only one aim. Other aims can include investment liberalization, the managing of economic conflict, domestic economic restructuring and political integration. Nevertheless, whether trade liberalization is a central objective or the means towards an end, the development of regionalism is a crucial feature of the trading system. Central to discussions of RTAs is their likely impact (positive or negative) on global welfare. Since members of RTAs are also members of the WTO, implicitly national governments are indicating compatibility between the pursuit of regionalism and multilateralism.

Analysts tend to periodize the development of regionalism into two phases. It is widely agreed that the creation of the European Economic Community (EEC) in 1957 initiated the first phase. The second period is dated from the mid-1990s. The impact of the two phases of regionalism on world trade is different. In the first phase regionalism was relatively inward. In the developing world the aim of regional economic arrangements was to stimulate industrialization, which meant that such organizations were more concerned with trade diversion than trade creation. Trade diversion refers to the process where low-cost suppliers from outside the union are replaced by high-cost suppliers within the regional grouping. Trade creation refers to the situation where, as a result of dismantling barriers within the region, trade is stimulated. In Europe, the scene of the two most successful early attempts at regional integration (the European Free Trade Area (EFTA) and the EEC), regionalism was concerned with dismantling barriers among the participants. In the second phase of regionalism many of the new associations have adopted a policy of open regionalism, making the reductions to trade more compatible with multilateral commitments.

Although regionalism can be seen in most parts of the world, specific regional agreements vary greatly in their goals and terms. This has led to some debate about the internal nature of regions and the relationship between regions. Internally, political struggles have been waged over the degree to which specific regions should have strong or weak institutions and the scope of policy-making that should be considered at the regional level. These struggles have influenced the different nature of the regions. For example, the European Union has some supranational institutions which oversee common rules. It also has provisions for regional development funding and labour rights. Most of its members have gone even further and adopted a single currency. In contrast, the North American Free Trade Agreement (NAFTA) tends to enforce existing national legislation, has no development funding and very weak provisions for the respect of labour and environmental standards. Whereas in Europe there is discussion about eventual political union, this subject is of little interest in North America. Moving to the Asia-Pacific area, we encounter an even looser regional organization – APEC (Asia-Pacific Economic Cooperation). APEC is more of a coordinating body between countries on the Pacific Rim than an attempt to build strong regional ties with robust institutions. Asian fears that the United States would use the body to influence their domestic economies or political regimes have led to a minimalist structure and trade liberalization agenda.

Some economists have raised fears that increasing regionalization will undermine the multilateral trading system (Baldwin and Thornton, 2008). It is argued that these regional agreements are inherently inefficient and discriminatory. RTAs will erode the MFN principle, increase barriers to products from other regions and divert the natural flow of free trade. Such actions could cause economic damage and undermine political support for a multilateral system. For example, Europeans and Americans disagree about how much risk should be accepted in the production of food. This has led to conflicts at the WTO over the EU banning the imports of products such as cattle that the Americans have injected with growth hormones. Other observers have argued that RTAs can be compatible with the multilateral trading system (Griswold, 2003).

A final issue is the fate of those areas of the world that are left out of the prominent regional trading areas. Regional integration is proceeding with some speed in Europe, North America and in East Asia through the activity of governments and firms. This excludes large areas of the world such as Africa, Latin America and South Asia. There have been several responses. In Latin America, Chile has lobbied for admission to NAFTA. In contrast, Brazil has put its energy into building MERCOSUR, the common market of several South American countries. Sub-Saharan Africa and South Asia have a series of regional agreements, but these are underdeveloped because they lack a powerful motor economy such as Germany, the United States or Japan. Their efforts at successful regional integration face large obstacles.

Legitimacy

As trade agreements at the multilateral and regional level have proliferated and influenced domestic political economies, increasing concern has been voiced by various segments of civil society in many states (Williams, 2005a). There are a wide range of issues that have attracted attention. Some groups worry that regional and global institutions are insulated from democratic control. They contend that business and political elites have considerable input into the structure of such agreements, but citizens find it difficult to hold their governments accountable for the decision-making authority transferred to international institutions. It should be noted, however, that firms are also formally excluded from the WTO. The influence of the corporate sector comes from their influence at the national level (and inclusion on national delegations) rather than directly at the multilateral level. Nevertheless, the democratic credentials of the WTO and regional trade agreements have been a subject of considerable debate. It has become widely accepted that democracy is a universal norm and in the context of a debate on democratization a focus has arisen concerning the representative nature of multilateral trade agreements.

This issue has been raised most vociferously in relation to the WTO but it has also surfaced in the European Union and NAFTA. At the European level, support for further integration has been diminished in a number of member countries, and nationalist sentiments gathered around right-wing parties have made some electoral gains. The so-called democratic deficit in the European Union became a topical issue in the mid-1990s and has remained so ever since. The debate on the WTO has focused on issues related to transparency, accountability and participation (Williams, 1999, pp. 158–60). Essential features of this debate are summarized in Box 6.7. The WTO has been responsive to criticism but this has not silenced its critics. In efforts to bolster its legitimacy, the WTO has derestricted documents,

Box 6.7 Democracy and the WTO

Is the WTO an undemocratic organization? The scale and ferocity of protests against the international trading regime in general and the WTO in particular suggest that the organization is undemocratic and therefore illegitimate. What are we to make of such claims? First, we can observe that no consensus exists on the definition, meaning or practice of democracy.

It can be argued that the WTO is one of the most democratic international organizations. First, its large and diverse membership represents most of the trading nations in the world and a variety of economic and political systems. Second, the consensus method of decision-making in the WTO gives each country a voice, and goes some way towards providing small, poorer countries with some source of influence. Third, the WTO is relatively transparent in terms of making access to its documents easy to obtain. In so far as negotiations are conducted in secret, it should be recalled that trade negotiations do involve complex and often controversial trade-offs.

The critics of the WTO reject the points made above and argue that the organization fails to provide sufficient access for civil society groups in its deliberations. Increased participation of social movement representatives will, it is claimed, provide: high-quality information; balanced input into policy-making; public education; and increased public support for the organization. These steps are needed to counter the alleged influence of transnational capital.

At the centre of the debate is, therefore, the intergovernmental nature of the WTO. But the solution is not a simple one. On one hand, if we accept the intergovernmental character of the WTO, the representative nature of national governments can be questioned. On the other hand, if we agree that an intergovernmental organization fails to capture the range of stakeholders affected by developments in the global trade regime, it does not follow that increased representation of NGOs necessarily makes the WTO more democratic since it cannot be assumed that NGOs are more representative than national governments. Indeed, developing countries remain hostile to increased representation of (largely northern) NGOs from social movements.

held consultations with NGOs and accepted submissions from outside parties (amicae briefs). Nevertheless, critics maintain the WTO is undemocratic, claiming that decisions are frequently made in secret and that the visible part of proceedings is a mere masquerade with little relation to the real exercise of power that takes place outside the public gaze (Kwa, 2003). Moreover, they argue that access to information on which decisions are made should be more readily available. In response, supporters of the WTO point out that the organization is an intergovernmental forum in which decisions are based on consensus, and subject to ratification by national parliaments. In this sense the organization is fully representative of its membership. A report by an independent British NGO on the accountability practices of five intergovernmental organizations, six TNCs and seven NGOs investigated the decision-making practices of the WTO. Although the report placed the WTO second in its category, it argued that 'the reality is that some members lack the capacity to engage meaningfully in decision-making' (Kovach, Neligan and Burall, 2002/3, p. 14). In respect of access to information the report noted that 'Information on the WTO's trade activities is excellent' (Kovach, Neligan and Burall, 2002/3, p. 15).

Other groups concern themselves with the detrimental effects of these agreements on social policies, environmental degradation and labour standards (Wallach and Woodall, 2004). Attention to global and regional trade organizations has developed as citizen attention has turned to the increasingly influential role these organizations play in a globalized world economy. The opposition to international economic agreements (including trade agreements) grew in the late 1990s and the first two years of the 21st century. The 1997 APEC meeting in Vancouver was marked by Canadian police pepper-spraying protesters, while the 1999 Seattle WTO Ministerial Meeting was also disrupted by public protests. As one activist noted in the wake of the Seattle protests, 'What civil society, North and South, should be doing at this point is either pushing for the abolition of the WTO or overloading or jamming it so that it cannot function effectively' (Bello, 2000). In Europe, citizens expressed concern about the direction of integration through a number of referenda and in support given to nationalist, especially right-wing, political parties. In the United States, President Clinton and initially President Bush found it difficult to secure negotiating authority from the US Congress to continue the liberalization process.

Increasingly, publics are concerned about further economic integration and trade agreements. Multilateral and regional trade organizations face a legitimacy problem because they are seen to place the values of liberalizing economic activity or protecting private interests above other values and interests. Some critics perceive the projects sponsored by such bodies as promoting economic globalization and social injustice. We will return to such issues in Chapter 15, which examines governance in the global economy.

Conclusion

Experience with tariff negotiations has led to the observation that most countries favour trade liberalization in principle but are reluctant to undertake unilateral reduction of trade barriers because it would open their markets, leaving them vulnerable to international firms. Therefore protectionism remains a prominent issue in the world economy. Protectionism is an attractive policy to domestic markets, and it is here that pressing demands originate. The demands for protection reflect structural changes bound up with the growth of transnational capitalism. It can also be seen as part of a process of structural change in the global economy which may reinforce the strength of social forces favourable to the maintenance of open trade. The demand for protection comes from rational actors in the economic process that are concerned with the nations' interests, which would suffer from free trade. The most obvious reason why protectionism remains a central feature of the world economy is that all economies need some degree of protectionism in order to develop.

As the world struggled with the impact of the global economic recession in 2008–9, trade once again became a key issue in the search for the return to prosperity. World leaders at the G-20 discussions have pledged to resist protectionist pressures. The extent to which the stalled Doha negotiations will be concluded and development concerns addressed remains unclear. Past attempts to breathe life into the talks have not met with success.

Chapter 7

Transnational Production

Hundreds of books, theses, government reports and thousands of papers in academic and professional journals have been written on the subject of transnational production, on the causes of foreign direct investment and also on the costs and benefits of inbound foreign investment for a host country. Scarcely a day goes by without a newspaper or magazine article praising or blaming what is now often referred to as the globalization of business activity. Despite, or perhaps because of, the extensive literature on transnational production no consensus exists on either the causes or impact of this phenomenon, although the growth of transnational production, it is widely agreed, has profoundly shaped the evolution of the global economy. For example, the current rhetoric of globalization assigns a crucial role to changes in the global production structure. However, it should also be noted that attention to the role of large international firms first arose in the 1960s. Prior to the current obsession with globalization, students of the global political economy had developed an awareness of the impact of the changing production structure on international relations.

The global production system is a complex process with millions of workers and workplaces integrated into diverse local, national, regional and global systems. The relationship between discrete centres of production and the global economy cannot be captured through any simple model. The link between sites of production and wider patterns of social, political and economic integration forming part of the global economy raises problems of comprehension for the student of international political economy. One way of trying to provide an entry to understanding the global production structure is by focusing on the role of the principal agents of this process, namely the large international firm, hereinafter referred to as the transnational corporation (TNC). An alternative approach would be to examine global commodity chains (see Box 7.1). The literature on transnational production tends to focus on the role of the large international firm as the key agent in this process and this chapter will adopt this standard approach. The transnational corporation is one of the defining features of economic life in the contemporary global economy. TNCs account for the major part of the global production structure, and approximately 50 per cent of world trade. In 2008, total global inflow of foreign direct investment was estimated to be $1,697 billion (UNCTAD, 2009b). Over half of the world's 500 largest corporations are located in only four countries – 140 in the United States, 68

Table 7.1 The 25 largest corporations by revenues (millions of dollars)

Rank	Name	Country	Industry	Revenues	Profits
1	Royal Dutch Shell	Netherlands	Petroleum	458,361	26,277
2	Exxon Mobil	US	Petroleum	442,851	45,220
3	Wal-Mart Stores	US	Retailer	405,607	13,400
4	BP	UK	Petroleum	367,053	21,157
5	Chevron	US	Petroleum	263,159	23,931
6	Total	France	Petroleum	234,674	15,500
7	ConocoPhillips	US	Petroleum	230,764	−16,998
8	ING Group	Netherlands	Financial services	226,577	−1,067
9	Sinopec	China	Petroleum	207,814	1,961
10	Toyota Motor	Japan	Automobiles	204,352	−4,349
11	Japan Post Holdings	Japan	Postal and financial services	198,700	4,208
12	General Electric	US	Diversified financials	183,207	17,410
13	China National Petroleum	China	Petroleum	181,123	10,271
14	Volkswagen	Germany	Automobiles	166,579	6,957
15	State Grid	China	Electricity	164,136	664
16	Dexia Group	Belgium	Banking	161,269	−4,868
17	ENI	Italy	Petroleum	159,348	12,917
18	General Motors	US	Automobiles	148,979	−30,860
19	Ford Motor	US	Automobiles	146,277	−14,672
20	Allianz	Germany	Insurance	142,395	−3,577
21	HSBC Holdings	UK	Banking	142,049	5,728
22	Gazprom	Russia	Natural gas	141,455	29,864
23	Daimler	Germany	Automobiles	140,328	1,973
24	BNP Paribas	France	Banking	136,096	4,422
25	Carrefour	France	Retail	129,134	1,862

Source: Data from Fortune (2009).

Box 7.1   Global commodity chains

A global commodity chain (GCC) is a 'network of labor and production processes whose end result is a finished commodity' (Gereffi and Koreniewicz, 1994, p. 2). A GCC analysis follows the processes involved in the production of a single commodity from the original raw materials to its end use. Unlike an approach which examines a particular TNC, GCC studies move through a series of actors from producers, sub-contractors and small companies, through large TNCs, across state regulation, into shipping, distribution and retail systems. By following a chain or network of connections one can chart the fascinating and disturbing stories behind the global production of goods from tomatoes (Barndt, 2002) to T-shirts (Rivoli, 2005). With its emphasis on shifting geographic scales and processes, GCC analysis offers distinct insight into global production.

---

in Japan, 40 in France and 39 in Germany (Fortune, 2009; see also Table 7.1).

We begin this chapter with a discussion of the various terms, such as 'transnational' or 'multinational' corporation, that have been used to describe large international firms. In the theoretical perspectives section we consider competing explanations for the emergence and growth of transnational production, and the impact of TNCs on national societies. The developments section outlines the globalization and changing organizational forms of production. The final section examines three key issues addressed in the contemporary global production system: the benefits and costs of TNCs, especially for developing countries; the changing relationship between the state and the firm; and the international regulation of TNCs.

Definitions

Economists distinguish between two types of foreign investment – foreign direct investment (FDI) and indirect foreign investment, also termed 'portfolio investment'. The transformation of the global production system has been brought about by rising levels of FDI. Foreign direct investment refers to investment made outside the home country of the investing company in which control over the resources transferred remains with the investor. It consists of a package of assets and intermediate goods such as capital, technology, management skills, access to markets and entrepreneurship. Foreign indirect (portfolio) investment refers to specific assets and intermediate products (for example, capital, debt or equity, technology) which are separately transferred between two independent economic agents through the modality of the market. In this instance, control over the resources is relinquished by the seller to the buyer. Only financial resources are transferred.

Two examples will help to clarify the difference between FDI and portfolio investment. If French car-maker Renault bought a controlling interest in US car-maker General Motors by buying its shares in the US stock market, this would be FDI. Renault would control GM and could decide to shut down plants or introduce new models of cars in the United States. In the 19th century, when British financiers bought bonds to fund the construction of US railways, it was portfolio investment. Control over corporate decisions stayed with the railway-builders. The British financiers did not tell the Americans which cities the railroads would connect. FDI means control of business decisions while portfolio investment does not. In this chapter we will follow conventional usage and use FDI as an indicator of the growth of international production.

Before 1914, long-term portfolio investment was more important than FDI. In that period FDI was relatively short term. FDI began to grow extensively after the Second World War. In the 1950s and 1960s FDI was predominantly in the manufacturing sector, and the largest amount of FDI flowed from the United States (Vernon, 1977). As a consequence of post-war recovery and the attainment of high productivity, the growth of the Euro-currency market and improvements in transport and communications, FDI flows from Europe and Japan began to grow. FDI continued to grow rapidly in the 1980s and 1990s (Julius, 1990; UNCTAD, 1999). For example, in the early 1980s the annual growth rate of FDI was approximately 14 per cent and between 1986 and 1996 FDI rose 350 per cent. This growth in FDI, fuelled by investment in services as well as manufacturing, has recently been brought to a halt by the global financial crisis and economic recession. Global FDI inflow continued to grow between 2000 and 2007, when it reached an historic high of $1,979 billion. The global economic crisis led to a 14 per cent fall to $1,697 billion in 2008 (see Table 7.2) and it is predicted that the fall will accelerate in 2009 before a slow recovery in 2010 (UNCTAD, 2009b, p. 4).

Table 7.2 World FDI flows, 2005–8 (FDI, billions of US dollars)

World	2005	2006	2007	2008
Inflows	973.3	1461.1	1978.8	1697.4
Outflows	879.0	1396.9	2146.5	1857.7

Source: Data from UNCTAD (2009).

While the distinction between foreign direct investment and indirect foreign investment is relatively non-contentious, no agreement exists on the term to be applied to firms engaging in transnational production or FDI. These firms are variously called multinational, international, transnational or global. It is now common to speak of multinational corporations (MNCs) or multinational enterprises (MNEs), international firms, transnational corporations (TNCs) or transnational enterprises (TNEs) and global corporations. Most writers make no distinction between these terms and have settled for one terminology rather than another without any seeming reflection on the implications of these terms. The most commonly used term is MNC but this chapter will refer to these economic agents as TNCs for reasons that will be explained below.

Serious attention was first given to the rise of transnational production in the late 1960s and early 1970s. At this stage both political and popular interest (Servan Schreiber, 1968; Bannock, 1971) and academic attention (Kindleberger, 1969; Vernon, 1971) turned to describing and assessing the importance of what was perceived as a new international actor, although large international firms had existed for centuries. The term 'multinational enterprise' was first given prominence by the Harvard Multinational Project, which produced a number of important studies including Mira Wilkins's analyses of the growth of American business (1970). These studies did much to establish the term 'multinational' to describe this new phenomenon. At the same time others from various perspectives preferred to use the term 'international corporation'; for example, Edith Penrose (1968) in her magisterial study of the oil industry. Raymond Vernon, in his widely influential book *Sovereignty at Bay* (1971), although based at Harvard, followed Penrose in using the term 'international corporation', as did Hugo Radice (1975) in an influential collection of critical essays.

While the term 'multinational' first gained widespread usage to describe large international firms, it was challenged from the mid-1970s by the term 'transnational corporation' or 'transnational enterprise' (Lall and Streeten, 1977; Vaitsos, 1975). The term 'transnational' reflected UN usage, and proponents of its use argued that whereas 'multinational' suggested a merger of capital from more than one nation-state, with a few notable exceptions (for example, Royal Dutch Shell and Unilever), most large international firms are owned and controlled by nationals of one country and conduct activities across national borders. The term 'transnational corporation' (or 'transnational enterprise') more accurately reflects the fact that these firms are usually owned and controlled by the nationals of one country and enter into direct production activities abroad. The term 'multinational corporation' thus appears inappropriate, and that of 'transnational corporation' more accurate, since these firms operate trans (that is, across) borders, thus giving greater weight to that term than to 'international'.

Another term sometimes used to refer to these large firms is 'global corporation'. The term 'global corporation' was popularized in the 1970s by Richard Barnett (Barnett and Muller, 1975). His central concern was the global reach of these firms and he coined the term to reflect the impact of their activities.

These choices revealed no essential differences in the operation of the firms so described. The distinctions arise from those who want to emphasize the issue of ownership and those analysts who prefer to stress the reach of these actors. Despite the differences in nomenclature, most analysts would agree that the firm they are describing could be defined as one with production facilities in two or more countries. Thus, in reality a single definition can suffice whether these firms are called multinational, international, transnational or global. A TNC is a firm that owns and controls production (value-added) facilities in two or more countries. It follows that all TNCs are not huge, uncontrollable firms, and TNCs will vary in size, resources, organizational structure (see Box 7.2) and influence potential. Furthermore, the estimation of the size, resources and power wielded by a TNC will vary depending on the standpoint of the analyst.

Box 7.2   Vertical, horizontal and conglomerate TNCs

One way to differentiate amongst TNCs is by their structure: vertical, horizontal or conglomerate integration (Grimwade, 2000, pp. 124–33). Vertical integration occurs when different stages of the production process are incorporated into one firm. For example, an oil company such as British Petroleum might own oil wells in the Middle East and the gas or petrol stations in the United Kingdom which sell the final product. This form of investment may occur because a corporation wants to ensure security of supply or reduce transaction costs within the firm. Horizontal integration takes place when a company makes the same product in a number of different countries. For example, Toyota has plants in the United States and Europe to avoid protectionism and gain access to local markets. Finally, conglomerate investment occurs when a company produces a number of different product lines in a variety of countries. Proctor and Gamble produces beauty, home, health, baby and pet products. This allows the company to diversify risk and make profits in a number of different sectors. Thus, different organizational structures and activities can lead TNCs to adopt a variety of global strategies for different reasons.

Theoretical perspectives: explaining the growth of TNCs

Two issues have dominated discussions of transnational production, namely the growth of the TNC and its impact on sovereign states. In this section we begin by reviewing some of the most influential theories devised to explain the growth of transnational production. In the second part of this section we provide a brief introduction to competing perspectives on the impact of TNCs. The three perspectives on IPE discussed in Chapter 1 provide broad interpretations of the issues discussed below. Economic nationalist perspectives emphasize the importance of state behaviour in creating the conditions necessary for the emergence of global production and focus on the ability of states to control the activity of TNCs. Liberal theory gives greater weight to the relevance of the market both in terms of explaining the growth of transnational production and in assessing the impact of TNCs on the state. Critical or radical theorists emphasize the changing nature of capitalist relations and retain a scepticism concerning the impact of TNCs on host economies.

The growth of transnational production has attracted attention across the spectrum of the social sciences with contributions from economics, geography, political science, sociology and business studies. Within the array of studies emanating from this profusion of disciplinary, interdisciplinary and cross-disciplinary research, three approaches (economic, organizational and motivational) to the study of TNCs are discernible. Economic approaches tend to emphasize the market characteristics that have given rise to the decision to invest abroad. Organizational perspectives give more emphasis to the internal structure of the corporation and seek explanations in terms of the decision-making structure of the firm. Motivational perspectives provide explanations in terms of the individuals and the belief systems they hold. It is not our intention to examine the wide range of theories that have been developed. Instead we will briefly outline some of the theories that have been most influential in the study of international political economy. These can be classified as liberal, structuralist and radical.

Two of the most important liberal theories were proposed by Raymond Vernon and John Dunning. The first widely cited theory was the product-cycle model developed by Raymond Vernon, which provided an explanation for the expansion of American business overseas (Vernon, 1966). Vernon argued that companies through advances in technology are able to gain competitive advantages in the American domestic market. In the initial stage these firms are content to sell their products abroad. However, the importers of American products begin to acquire the appropriate technology and start producing these goods domestically, thus providing products at a cheaper rate than the imported goods since they do not face transport costs. In order to protect their markets American producers are forced to establish factories abroad. The third stage of the product cycle occurs when foreign firms begin producing the product cheaper than US companies and begin exporting to the United States. According to this model the main motivation for FDI arises from the desire to exploit technological comparative advantage and maintain market share. Critics of the product-cycle theory pointed to its inability to explain non-American FDI (Caves, 1974). Another liberal theory has been developed by John Dunning, one of the most prolific writers on the TNC. Dunning, drawing on economic and managerial factors, has developed a comprehensive theory (see, for example, Dunning, 1973, 1981, 1988). His ownership, location, internationalization (OLI) model focuses on the decision to invest abroad, with emphasis on ownership characteristics and the desirability of the foreign location.

Susan Strange has provided a structuralist alternative to the liberal theories which shifts the emphasis from the decisions of firms to major structural change in the global economy (Strange, 1991, 1994). Strange lists three key structural changes that have accelerated transnational production: falling real costs of transport and communication; development of new technologies; and the creation of new financial instruments. She argues that structural changes in technology, communications and finance created the conditions for the growth of TNCs. She claims that a rapid increase in technology spurred by the revolution in information technology has quickened the pace of globalized production; increased capital mobility has facilitated dispersion of industry; and changes in the knowledge structure have made transborder communication and transportation cheaper and faster.

Marxist writers, with their traditional focus on the centralization and concentration of capital, were well placed to provide explanations for the growth of transnational production. An interesting contribution to the radical literature was made by Stephen Hymer. In his seminal study *The International Operation of National Firms* (1976), he argued that the dominance of American business ventures abroad arose from the oligoplistic business structure. In later works such as *The Multinational Corporation: A Radical Approach* (1979), he drew on Lenin's theory of imperialism and gave more attention to systemic factors and emphasized the uneven development of capital.

The theoretical dispute over the causes of transnational production is mirrored in the conflict concerning the impact of this activity on the nation-state and on national societies. Two broad positions are discernible – the positive and the negative. Some analysts have developed arguments that emphasize the positive results of foreign direct investment but these findings are disputed by those who claim that on balance the net effect of TNC investment is negative for host countries. The positive case stresses the net positive benefits of FDI. For the most part it can recognize the possibility of costs but tends to put the emphasis on the favourable aspects of foreign investment. The negative case coming out of radical and dependency analyses places the focus on the negative impact of foreign firms. Although some analysts in this tradition are willing to admit some gains from FDI, others are unwilling to accept a positive role for transnational capital under any circumstances. These writers tend to stress the size of these firms vis-à-vis governments.

It is not surprising that it should be liberal economists and the business community who contend that the net impact of TNC activity is positive. These analysts argue that both the direct and indirect effects of FDI are on the whole beneficial for host countries. Five main positive direct effects are claimed in this literature. First, it is argued that FDI provides additional resources and capabilities – that is, capital, technology, access to markets and management skills. Furthermore, it provides additional tax revenues through the increase in economic activity in the host country. These analysts also contend that FDI increases GDP thus increasing the tax base. Moreover, by better linking the host economy with the global marketplace, TNCs help to advance economic growth by fostering a more efficient division of labour. And, finally, they assert that FDI improves the balance of payments through import substitution, export generation or efficiency-seeking investment.

It is claimed that FDI provides three positive indirect effects. First, TNCs inject entrepreneurship, new management styles, new work cultures and more dynamic competitive practices. Second, by bringing more efficient resource allocation, competitive stimulus and spillover effects on suppliers and/or consumers, TNCs can help upgrade the domestic resources and capabilities, and the productivity of local firms; and also foster clusters of related activities to the benefit of the participating firms. Third, TNCs enhance national welfare by more directly exposing the host economy to: the political and economic systems of other countries; the values and demand structures of foreign households; superior attitudes to work practices, incentives and industrial relations; and the many different customs and behavioural norms of foreign countries.

The critics document four main negative direct effects. They argue that TNCs transfer too few or the wrong kind of resources or assets. TNCs can cut off foreign markets (that is, those serviced by domestic firms); can fail to adjust to localized capabilities and needs; and may not provide an addition to capital at all. Second, TNCs use transfer pricing and other devices to lower taxes paid. Also by restricting growth there is an overall loss of tax revenue. Third, FDI promotes a division of labour likely to be in the company's interests and this can be detrimental to the country's comparative advantage. The division of labour is likely to be based on what the firm perceives to be in its global interests, which may be inconsistent with dynamic comparative advantage as perceived by the host country. Finally,

TNCs worsen the balance of payments through limiting exports and promoting imports and outcompeting local firms which export more and import less.

The critics claim that TNCs bring four negative indirect effects. First, foreign entrepreneurship, management styles and working practices fail to accommodate or, where appropriate, to change local business cultures. The introduction of foreign industrial relations procedures may lead to industrial unrest. By the pursuit of anti-competitive practices, TNCs may bring an unacceptable degree of market concentration. Second, foreign firms can limit the upgrading of local resources and capabilities by restricting local production to low-value activities and importing the major proportion of higher-value intermediate products. They may also reduce the opportunities for domestic economies of scale by confining their linkages to foreign suppliers and industrial concerns. Third, TNCs may cause unrest by introducing conflicting values through advertising, business customs, labour practices and environmental standards. Finally, TNCs may exercise direct interference in the political regime or electoral process of the host country.

Below we will argue that the rise and development of the TNC is to be understood as the result of a changing political, economic, technological and managerial context. We will also try to suggest a way not of reconciling competing views on the impact of TNCs but of going beyond them. Instead of adhering to either a positive or negative overview, this perspective recognizes that the costs and benefits of FDI will vary from case to case and also that what constitutes costs and benefits will vary depending on the values of the observer. Our intention in putting forward this perspective arises from what we see as key flaws in the competing approaches to state–firm relations. The pro-TNC approach fails to think about power in the market. In viewing TNCs as wholly beneficial these writers pay limited, if any, attention to non-economic factors, and minimize the role of market failure and market distortions. The anti-TNC perspective, in demonizing the firm, gives no credence to governments' ability to shape economic policy, and fails to appreciate fully the structural changes that have taken place in the world economy.

Major developments

There have been two major changes in the global production structure. The first has been the globalization of production. There has been a proliferation of corporate activity and business networks around the world. The second major development has been the change in the underlying principles of the organization of production and key features of the global production system.

The globalization of production

The globalization of production is aptly captured by phrases such as 'from national production to global production', and 'from local markets to global markets'. It refers to the proliferation and stretching of corporate activity and business networks across the globe. The globalization of production is a consequence of structural change in the global economy, changing organizational forms and strategies of TNCs, and the policies of national governments. While initially the spread of transnational production was viewed as a distinctly American phenomenon, the overseas expansion of European and Japanese firms followed by TNCs originating from developing countries has demonstrated that it is a truly global event. For many analysts the creation of American hegemony in the aftermath of the Second World War brought with it the beginnings of globalized production 'based on offshore low-wage assembly' (Bernard, 1994, p. 221). This was also partly the consequence of American foreign policy, which encouraged manufacturing firms to invest in anti-communist countries to support its position during the Cold War. In the past three decades, however, transnational production has escaped its early origins in US economic growth and policy choices and has become a driving force in the global economy. Major enterprises in industrialized countries have found that they have 'outgrown national markets, national laws and national financial markets' and in response have begun producing 'for a global market according to a global corporate strategy' (Strange, 1991, p. 246).

The spread of the capitalist mode of production and free trade following the Second World War has led to the development of a complex and highly integrated world economy in which international trade and investment flows occur on a massive scale at increasingly rapid rates. International economic structures based on finance and trade have led to increasing interdependence and closer ties between countries. An important part of this process is associated with the growth of transnational production, with the increasing ability of firms to locate parts of their production overseas, while still maintaining direct control over the activities of foreign subsidiaries. This move by many enterprises to spread their activities into other countries has bolstered the globalization process, broadening the links between countries. The organizational form of the transnational corporation has undergone extensive change leading to the development of deep integration (Dicken, 1992) and these developments will be discussed in the next sub-section. In this sub-section we will consider structural changes in technology, transport and communications, and finance, and the political conditions attendant on these developments.

Technological change.   The global production system is dominated by rapid developments in the technological environment. New technologies have placed innovation at the centre of profitability, and the creation, implementation and diffusion of new technology are now critical to economic efficiency and international competitiveness. The new production techniques are characterized by cutting-edge technological innovation, sophisticated coordination of operations and more efficient means of meeting the needs of customers. With these developments production has thus grown in scale and become more cost-effective.

The accelerating pace of technological change has enhanced the capacity of successful producers to supply the market with new products and/or make them with new materials or new processes. At the same time the accelerating rate of technological change in the production process has been central to creating the world market system. Technological change has prompted the emergence of global markets for goods and services by contributing to greater homogeneity in consumer tastes worldwide, by causing firms to seek wider markets and by making it easier for firms to produce and market products globally. Additionally, new technology contributes to the processes whereby product and process lifetimes have shortened, sometimes dramatically. As companies are required to satisfy consumer demands and win strategic alliances, new technologies are being applied across a wider range of goods and services, making them easily available at more affordable prices. Technologies have been at the forefront of the process whereby new products replace old ones at an alarming rate. This process can be illustrated through a brief overview of some of the developments in home entertainment for consumers around the globe, but especially in advanced industrial countries. At the beginning of the 20th century, musical entertainment at home was produced by manual means with the use of piano, wind and string instruments. At the beginning of the 21st century, we have access to electronic and digital technology to aid us in our production of music. The vinyl record and the cassette tape have been supplanted by the compact disc. The video tape, a development which came into widespread usage less than 20 years ago, is now rapidly being replaced by the DVD.

Meanwhile, the cost to the firm of investment in research and development, and therefore of innovation, has risen. The time it takes to recoup profits from national markets is too long to keep up with the costs of developing and installing new technology, products and processes. To keep products competitive, especially when other companies may already be transnational, firms are having to gain access to overseas markets to increase the volume of their sales. Despite the growth of liberal trade it can still be difficult to access foreign markets, and the risk that trade barriers may be raised is always a problem. To overcome this problem firms have directed their efforts towards producing locally in the markets they wish to sell in, and this has proved to be more cost-effective (Strange, 1991, pp. 247–8).

Communications and transport.   One of the major reasons for the growth of transnational production has been the accelerated reduction in international transport and communications costs. The decrease in communications and transport costs has benefited strategic planning from headquarters and also facilitated the growth of outsourcing in industrial production. Reduced communications costs allow new systems of global information management to become feasible. Information and transport technologies lower the real costs and risks of management at a distance. Better communications networks which are reliable, fast and efficient have meant that TNCs can be in constant contact with all their subsidiaries and allow information to flow relatively freely within the firm despite geographical distance. Transport systems are also faster and more reliable so resources and products can be moved cheaply and easily from primary extraction to processing plants to markets. In the mid-1980s, for example, Apple computers 'travelled' around 2 million miles before reaching the final customer (Kaplinsky, 1991). These global assembly lines are extremely fluid with the production organization being 'centrally coordinated' (McMichael, 1996, p. 89). Communications networks also give TNCs greater access to markets: television, radio, magazines, newspapers and the internet have allowed firms' advertising to reach millions of people around the world, tapping into global markets at relatively low cost to the firm. Telecommunications technology allows firms to organize along global lines, moving components and software among offshore sites and selling products in world markets. As digital and communications technology has become more accessible and integrated into daily life, it has become embedded in all areas of existence, thus pushing us further towards a global marketplace.

Finance.   Central to transnational investment is the acquisition and deployment of capital. Developments in international finance have created integrated financial markets which facilitate global production (Stopford and Strange, 1991). Firms have been able to finance their production operations overseas as a result of the internationalization of finance. This globalization in the financial market is the result of three factors. The first factor leading to an expansion in the availability of capital is technological innovation which has produced reductions in cross-border transaction costs and facilitated private international capital transactions. The second factor is the removal of governmental, legal and technical barriers to the movement of capital thus easing cross-border capital flows. There has been a widespread liberalization of capital markets around the world. This partial and incomplete transformation began with the creation of the Euro-currency market in the 1960s and continued with the deregulation initiated by the United States in the mid-1970s and early 1980s. As barriers went down, the mobility of capital went up (see Table 7.3 for developments between 1990 and 2009).

Table 7.3   Growth of global capital flows (billions of US dollars)

	Net private capital flows		
Region	1990	2000	2009
Emerging and developing economies	38.046	71.627	286.567
Africa	2.390	–3.090	62.251
Central and Eastern Europe	6.508	8.642	181.730
CIS and Mongolia	–1.520	–27.865	25.970
Developing Asia	12.269	6.311	22.025
Middle East	3.471	–5.212	–86.216
Western hemisphere	14.928	62.84	180.807

Sources: IMF (2008); World Bank (2000), p. 336.

The old difficulties of raising money for investment in offshore operations and moving it across the exchanges vanished.

The third factor is the growth of innovation in financial instruments. A variety of financial instruments and capital mobility support the globalization of production and cross-border transactions of TNCs in global financial markets. Not surprisingly these developments have been most widely exploited among the developed countries where the barriers to integration have been the least. But they have also been important for developing countries. These instruments include interest rates, currency and stock market index futures and over-the-counter instruments such as derivatives, swaps, options, futures, forward transactions, bond-lending and reinsurance. As a result capital moves across borders and boundaries in places where previously it was difficult for it to do so. The impact of these developments transcends capital markets, in that capital mobility has introduced major changes in international trade and the organization of the TNC. This sustained growth of commerce and international investment is a central element in the globalization of production because it has provided the financing for the expansion of TNC operations.

The expansion of international finance has radically reshaped the structural and institutional composition of the world economy. The integration of capital markets into one worldwide market for savings and credit means that TNCs can enjoy far greater possibilities by raising money wherever they operate without having to transfer funds across frontiers and exchanges. It is either unnecessary for the TNCs to find new funds, or they can do so locally.

Attendant on these changes is the impact of capital flight on host countries. Short-term capital flows have caused instability in the international financial market and have played a part in the Mexican crisis of 1994, Asian financial crisis of 1997 and Argentinian crisis of 2001. The relationship between national governments and foreign investors can move from one of accommodation and cooperation to a hostile and adversarial one. Crucially, capital does not operate in a vacuum and the determination of the impact of capital on nation-states is linked to government–business relations. See Box 7.3 for an exploration of one such relationship.

Box 7.3   Government regulation, international capital and financial instability: the case of South Korea

Until the late 1980s, government intervention in the economy, and in particular the financial sector, was important for Korea's development process. Interference in major financial activities including interest rates and credit allocations enabled the state to support growth in strategically chosen industries. Following partial deregulation of Korea's capital controls, the economy's exposure to unregulated international capital flows made it vulnerable to capital flight and the whims of foreign speculators. Direct financing includes issuing bonds and stocks, and it increased from 15 per cent of financing in 1970 to 45.2 per cent in 1990. The government's deregulation of the short-term-based commercial paper (CP) market moved faster than the long-term interest rates of the banks in the 1990s led to a large expansion of short-term borrowing. Between 1992 and 1996, these short-term liabilities accounted for a massive 84.4 per cent of total capital flows into Korea and by 1996 they amounted to one-third of its GDP. When economic growth is high this 'hot money' is useful for investments in capacity that gets used by buoyant demand. However, when demand becomes sluggish, the high level of investment becomes excess capacity and the loans, which require repayment in the short term, become harder and harder to service. The increase in non-performing loans causes foreign investors to loose confidence in the economy and massive capital outflow ensues. Thus, the Korean 'bubble economy', inflated by short-term investment, was at the mercy of world economic growth, in particular export demand, and the confidence of foreign investors. Short-term capital flows constituted a major destabilizing factor to the Korean economy in the mid-1990s.

Political.   The globalization of production has also been influenced by the policies of national governments. The policy decisions taken by states cannot be seen simply as automatic reactions to structural change or as arising solely from competitive pressures. There is a mix of motives and pressures acting on national governments. We will mention three aspects in which political factors contributed to the globalization of production. First, we see the influence of political factors in the construction and maintenance of the liberal system of trade and payments ushered in after the Second World War, which formed the background to the early development of transnational production. We mentioned at the outset of this chapter the importance of American interests and US foreign policy in the outward expansion of American business enterprises. Of central importance in the development of transnational production was US military and political power underpinning the Bretton Woods system of liberal trade and payments, and American foreign policy supportive of an expansive capitalist system in the Cold War conflict with the Soviet Union. Second, we note that the liberalization in financial markets that stimulated changes in the production structure after 1973 was the result of political decisions taken by states. The degree, content and timing of liberalization in the United States and Europe shows varying influences of competitive pressure rather than a necessary correspondence between structural change and governmental regulation.

Third, we note that the relocation of manufacturing production to Third World states during the 1960s and 1970s was in response to various nationalist projects. A major, and often overlooked, reason for the shift in industrial production was the policies of developing-country governments to attract foreign investment. As some East Asian states embarked on their model of export-oriented industrialization they sought massive foreign investment. One such incentive was through the creation of export processing zones (EPZs). An EPZ is an estate created especially for industrial export production in which prevailing labour regulations and taxation laws do not normally apply. For example, in Mexico one investment firm was offered 100 per cent tax exemption for the first ten years, and 50 per cent exemption for the following ten years as an incentive to locate an EPZ near the border with the United States (McMichael, 1996, p. 94). EPZs are attractive to TNCs since they offer low-wage labour with minimal external costs, while governments reap the benefits of capital investment and foreign currency earnings from exports. Of course, this was not the only determinant of these flows of investment. There were a number of other reasons. These included the desire of firms to break into growing markets. The best way to do this was to locate all or part of their production in these Third World countries. Moreover, at this point firms were also encountering market saturation and a reduction in profits in the industrialized world.

EPZs remain controversial, with supporters and critics engaged in dispute

Box 7.4   Export processing zones: an ILO perspective

The 1999 International Labour Organization study, 'Labour and Social Issues Relating to Export Processing Zones', reported exponential growth in EPZs in the 1980s and 1990s, and the geographic spread of EPZs. The largest numbers of EPZs are in North America (320) and Asia (225). But the concentration of EPZs is rising in developing regions such as the Caribbean (51), Central America (41) and the Middle East (39) and the figures are likely to increase throughout the world. The report noted that while traditionally EPZs are associated with manufactured products, variations to this pattern have arisen in a number of places. For example, in Islamabad a number of Agri-Export Zones (AEZs) specializing in the export of cut flowers and rose onions had been established. On the central issue of the impact of EPZs on overall economic growth, the report stated that, there is a 'pervasive absence of meaningful linkages between the EPZs and the domestic economies of most of the host countries'. Moreover, the principal author of the report, Mr Auret Van Heedren, noted 'the frequent absence of minimal standards and poor labour–management relations have predictable outcomes, such as high labour turnover, absenteeism, stress and fatigue, low rates of productivity, excessive wastage of materials and labour unrest which are still too common in EPZs' (ILO, 1998, n.p.). The report concluded that while some countries had capitalized on the presence of EPZs in their territory, others had not. Whether or not an EPZ had benefited its host country is related to the degree of sophistication of the goods produced in the zone. Malaysia and Singapore attracted quality investment in high-tech manufactures and have utilized the presence of such industries to qualify their own workforce in highly skilled sectors. Other states, including Bangladesh, Pakistan and Sri Lanka, that host the more labour-intensive zones are finding that rather than increasing the quality of the workforce, EPZs are perpetuating a stagnant skill level in their workers. In textiles, garment manufacturing and electronics assembly women account for 90 per cent or more of the workers and it is in these processing and assembly operations where companies see labour as a cost to contain rather than an asset to develop.

concerning their negative or positive impacts. For supporters they provide a link to global markets and contribute to employment and income generation. For critics they are exploitative enclaves that fail to produce the hoped-for benefits and increase dependency on external agents. The impact of EPZs has been studied by governments, independent researchers and international organizations. Box 7.4 presents the findings of the International Labour Organization.

Changing organizational principles

The globalization of international production is a response to structural change and governmental policies. It is also the consequence of changing organizational patterns within firms, and changes in the wider system of production.

In the past each phase of the production process was completed by a different firm. Over time firms came to realize that by merging, so that one firm controlled several steps, they could reduce costs and improve production efficiency. Between each step of production there are transaction costs between firms. If these firms merged they could internalize these costs, resulting in an overall saving on external costs. Vertical integration or internalizing production flows is one of the major economic incentives that has led to the growth in TNCs. When a firm decides to move part of its production process overseas it retains control and reduces its costs by keeping the flows of 'globally-applicable technology and marketing expertise' (Casson, 1991, p. 271) within the company, thus eliminating the necessity of licensing out to firms within the host country. This internal trade serves only to redistribute income between different divisions of the company, eliminating the possibility that one parent of the transaction may default. This provides added security and control to the central managing body and prevents external forces from interrupting the production process. Much of the world's trade is now internalized in TNCs with the movement of components between foreign subsidiaries and parent companies during the production process. The benefits of internalizing transaction costs are an incentive for firms to transnationalize their production. The decision by one firm in an industry puts pressure on other firms to go global in order to remain competitive.

Another development has been in the creation of an integrated trans-border production system. This arises when the entire production process is spread across widely dispersed locations within and between countries. Facilitated by supraterritorial coordination, which links components, machinery, finance and services of a company anywhere in the world, a global production operation emerges. The emphasis in this environment is on the transfer of production to points of optimum conditions. Additionally, electronic networks have facilitated global alliances of manufacturing companies to allow more efficient outsourcing of production of parts or products to suppliers throughout the world.

From Fordist to post-Fordist production. The expansion of TNC activity in the 1950s and 1960s was in accordance with what has come to be called the Fordist production system. Named after the American industrialist Henry Ford, production under a Fordist system conformed to two simple principles, namely, mass production and mass consumption. The standard system for production was the factory system based on semi-skilled labour using specialized equipment to mass produce standardized goods. Competitive advantage accrued from cutting costs and this was achieved through an assembly-line system. Firms achieved economies of scale through mass production and increased efficiency by training workers to perform routine tasks. Under this system workers earned sufficient wages to boost consumer demand, thus ensuring factory production maintained a high rate of turnover. However, from the late 1970s there was a change in the organization of manufacturing activities which shifted the priorities of TNCs from labour costs and mass production to product innovation. Changes in the nature of consumer demand have meant that product innovation quality is more important than price competitiveness, although price is still an important factor. Companies now tend to look for flexible specialization, competitive differentiation and quality control as the main features of their production process. This means that mass production of goods which are very similar to the products of other companies will not necessarily give the competitive advantage required in today's market.

In the 1980s the Japanese automobile company Toyota developed the just-in-time (JIT) system in which component parts are delivered by Toyota's suppliers two hours before assembly – just in time. JIT permits Toyota to hold no inventory and allows design and production to be changed quickly in response to consumer demand and changes in the consumer market (McMichael, 1996, p. 107). These new systems of production reduce the ability of companies to mass produce goods which can then be stored until they are required on the market and the workers often need to be more skilled so that design and managerial decisions can be made on the factory floor. Furthermore, with the need to produce goods speedily in response to demands in the market, suppliers and assembly plants need to be in close geographical proximity. The advantage of low wages is not now as important in the location choice for production as it was under Fordist manufacturing systems. Factors that now affect location choice include proximity to suppliers and markets, and the availability of skilled labour and specialized technology. Post-Fordist production also has greater infrastructure requirements which many countries specializing in cheap labour are unable to meet.

Under these new conditions, many TNCs need to have entire production chains occurring in one region. For example, this shift gives East Asia a competitive advantage over Africa. In East Asia tremendous efforts had been made to increase the skills of the labour force and much of the required infrastructure had been built during industrialization in the 1960s and 1970s, with large networks of firms established, mostly already within TNC production lines.

For much of Africa, however, these developments mean that it is unlikely that there will be a significant amount of investment by TNCs in the foreseeable future given the lack of infrastructure, geographical distance and poorly educated population. While under post-Fordism the demand for mass-produced goods is still a feature of markets, the need for more flexible and innovative products has changed the direction of foreign investment.

Mergers, strategic alliances and joint ventures.   If the shift from Fordist to post-Fordist production captures the key organizing principle of capitalist production in managerial terms, there have also been changes in the ways in which TNCs organize in the emerging world market. The attitudes, organizational structures and behaviour of business corporations have adapted to changes in the global economy and the policies of governments. One development from the 1980s onwards has been the increase in mergers and acquisitions, joint ventures and other strategic alliances. Table 7.4 provides evidence of significant cross-border mergers and alliances between 2000 and 2008. The creation of strategic alliances, joint ventures and the resort to

Table 7.4   Cross-border mergers and alliances, 2000–8*

Year	Number of Deals	Percentage of Total	Value	Percentage of total
2000	175	2.2	866.2	75.7
2001	113	1.9	378.1	63.7
2002	81	1.8	213.9	57.8
2003	56	1.2	141.1	47.5
2004	75	1.5	199.8	52.5
2005	182	2.1	569.4	61.3
2006	215	2.4	711.2	63.6
2007	300	3.0	1161.0	70.9
2008**	137	3.1	439.4	70.6

* with values over $1 billion
** first 6 months only

Sources: Data from UNCTAD (2005a), p. 9; UNCTAD (2008), p. 6.

increased incidence of mergers and acquisitions is partly a response to the impact of technological change on product life cycles (as discussed above), partly the result of the development of new markets and partly a consequence of the expansion in the services sector. A single firm may lack the combination of technological know-how, funds for research and development, local market knowledge, access to finance and market share necessary to remain competitive in this rapidly changing environment. Thus firms have adapted organizationally to these developments.

Another development has been the emergence of new attitudes and strategies towards foreign investment. In the past firms tended to either increase investment or reduce investment sequentially. In the past 15 years or so, firms have used both investment and disinvestment strategies at the same time. They have expanded in one sector or territory while simultaneously contracting in another sector or territory. This is also a response to the rapid shortening of product cycles and the segmentation of market structures.

A third change has been the requirement under conditions of post-Fordist production to pay more attention to the relationship between market integration on one hand and the specialized nature of local markets on the other. For example, the global burger chain McDonald's, while serving standard fare in most of its global outlets, also develops products specifically designed for the local market. Firms are aware that they possess certain advantages or core competencies that have given them a competitive advantage but that these general characteristics are likely to be of limited utility unless their production is sensitive to the demands of consumers, and the shifting cultural context in which they operate.

Key issues

This section examines three key issues surrounding TNCs. The first issue concerns the evaluation of the benefits of FDI and we argue that this needs to be done on a case-by-case basis. Second, we examine the continuing debate over state–firm interactions. Third, we consider capital regulation.

Re-evaluating the benefits of FDI

As we pointed out in the section exploring theoretical perspectives, there are competing views concerning the impact of TNCs on national societies. These debates between supporters and opponents of foreign direct investment erupted in the 1960s and continue today. During the 1970s when the Third World's demand for a New International Economic Order was at its peak, and dependency analyses were fashionable, the views of the critics were given greater prominence. But with the triumph of neoliberalism and the imposition of adjustment policies in the developing world it is the views of the proponents of FDI that have been in the ascendancy. It is difficult to reconcile these contrasting views, and analysts use selective statistics and case studies to support their respective arguments. An example of an ongoing and intense discussion is the debate swirling around the world's largest retail corporation, Wal-Mart (see Box 7.5).

The approach taken in this text rejects the over-generalization of both perspectives. Instead it begins from the observation that FDI can have

---

Box 7.5   Wal-Mart, the TNC

Most of the world's largest TNCs are oil companies, car manufacturers, telecommunications, computer or financial companies. However, the retailer Wal-Mart is the third largest corporation in the world in terms of revenues (2008) and is the largest corporation in terms of numbers of people employed (2,100,000). Wal-Mart's website indicates it operates 8,100 stores in 15 countries serving over 200 million customers each week (http://walmartstores.com/AboutUs/). The growth and controversy surrounding Wal-Mart illustrate the far-reaching effects of TNCs. Wal-Mart has transformed from a company that originally trumpeted its support of US producers to one that now sources up to 70 per cent of its product from China. If Wal-Mart was an independent country, it would be China's eight largest trading partner (Jingjing, 2004).

As the largest retailer in the world it exercises immense influence and generates considerable controversy in the markets of several countries. Because of its large size Wal-Mart's decisions about which suppliers to use or what wage and benefits it will pay can set the standards for local and global labour markets and industries. Wal-Mart has been criticized for a series of actions such as: preventing its workers from joining unions, paying low wages, restricting health and employment benefits, promoting part-time labour at the expense of full-time employment, contributing to poor working conditions by demanding suppliers continually reduce costs, contributing to environmental degradation, and destroying local communities and businesses (www.walmartwatch.com). It has also been the subject of negative activist documentaries such as 'The High Cost of Low Prices'. Wal-Mart counters that it helps workers and communities by providing them with employment and that it reduces poverty by supplying low-cost products. It also highlights a wide range of activities from disaster relief to supporting the US military (www.walmartfacts.com).

negative or beneficial impacts but that this is essentially an empirical question which can only be answered in relation to concrete circumstances. This requires analysis to focus on specific country and firm characteristics rather than assuming a general orientation of firms and countries. In this subsection we consider the ways in which governments may seek to increase the benefits for their societies from inward foreign direct investment. In other words, we raise some of the key issues that should be examined in the context of specific case studies through an exploration of the interactions between governments and TNCs.

It is not always apparent if many of the objections to TNCs stem from their size and control over economic resources or whether the main objections are made in respect of the foreign ownership of productive assets. The benefits and costs of FDI have been assessed through the use of economic, political and cultural criteria. Economic criteria include the balance of payments, economic growth and tax revenues; political issues include interference in domestic politics and the effect on sovereignty; crucial cultural issues focus on taste transfer and protecting traditional national culture. The evaluation of the costs and benefits of TNC investment in a host country will therefore vary depending on which of these criteria the analyst thinks is most important. Different conclusions will be reached depending on the starting point of the observer. For example, if the main objection is to foreign ownership then even if it can be shown that economic growth has been positive, the critique of TNC involvement still retains its force.

What determines the net benefits of FDI? What can governments do to ensure that such investment best contributes to economic growth and development? The answers to these questions depend on the policies followed by host governments, the economic and social context of investment, the type of firm and the sector in which the investment is located.

The impacts that TNCs have on their host countries will be strongly influenced by the host government's policies. While we recognize that the impact of FDI is also dependent on a range of economic and societal variables not necessarily subject to governmental control we will for illustrative purposes focus on governmental policies. In deciding to welcome FDI, unless states promote policies designed to achieve greater economic and social welfare for their citizens from the activities of TNCs, they will fail to reap sufficient benefits. This is not solely an issue of governments becoming more accommodating to the needs of foreign firms. States need to maintain a certain level of control and input into the activities of foreign investors to ensure that they maximize the benefits to the host country. The different results available from studies of the impact of FDI, especially in developing countries, reflect the success or failure of governments to direct foreign investment to productive activity (Stopford and Strange, 1991). While in some countries little attention has been paid to this issue, others have made consistent efforts to direct the activities of TNCs in fulfilment of their national development plans. In Singapore, for example, TNCs have been directed towards investing in 'higher than average value-added activities' and upgrading 'the quality of labour' (Dunning, 1985, p. 415). This has resulted in greater levels of development and economic growth in Singapore and has now allowed it to develop stronger national industries with a more skilled labour force to draw on. While some countries have actively promoted export processing zones (EPZs) to attract foreign investment, others are careful to avoid export enclaves by ensuring that at least a proportion of the sales are produced or sub-contracted locally (Dunning, 1985, p. 418). The nature of the host government's policies towards TNCs is thus a crucial factor in determining if a TNC enhances or inhibits the development of local industries.

One of the major points of contention over the net benefits of FDI for developing countries concerns the transfer of technology. Indeed, this is one of the main reasons why many governments allow greater foreign investment, as they realize that in the absence of the finance and knowledge provided by TNCs, it would be much harder, and in many cases almost impossible, for them to gain access to industrial technologies. While in some cases this transfer of technology by TNCs has led to much faster diffusion of technology than would otherwise have been the case, it is unlikely to achieve maximum impact unless governments upgrade human and technological capabilities. However, as will be discussed below, government policies are only one side of the picture. No amount of regulation by a government or national policies to enhance the technological capability of the population will help to provide value-added FDI if the technology transferred is less advanced compared to the technology which is being developed and used in home countries at any given time. Studies have shown that the technology frequently transferred from industrial countries to developing countries is designed to maintain low-level production activities in developing countries (Bernard, 1994, p. 251). On the other hand, in advanced countries, the transfer of technology tends to be more effective with their better capabilities allowing them to 'absorb leading edge technologies' from foreign investors (Lall, 1991, p. 251).

The overall economic impact of TNCs through provision of additional capital, a positive impact on the balance of payments, increased tax revenue, and diffusion of skills and technology is dependent on governmental policies. Governments can devise a broad macro-economic framework, and institute legal and administrative reforms that ensure positive linkages between local firms and foreign capital. Within the developing world there exists a vast array of governmental attitudes, skills and ability to design and implement the requisite changes. In these circumstances the impact of FDI is likely to vary depending on the country in question. We do not intend to imply that the implementation of effective policies is a simple matter and that governments that fail to do so are simply incompetent. On the contrary, the domestic political economy of reform is a complex and difficult process. We do not have the time or space to explore the economic, political, cultural and institutional dimensions of domestic policy reform. In the context of this chapter the important point is that the benefits of FDI will vary depending on the local context.

The evidence does seem to suggest that those developing countries that have been open to foreign investment and allowed TNCs to establish export-oriented plants have generally industrialized at much greater rates than their more restrictive counterparts (Lall, 1991, p. 251). This is supported by figures on international trade which show that between 1960 and 1979 Third World countries increased their share of world trade from 6 per cent to 10 per cent (McMichael, 1996, p. 86), most of which was due to the export of manufactured goods produced by TNCs; evidence from post-communist economies also supports these findings. As previously mentioned above, government policies also play an important role in this industrializing process. It is vital that the state promotes integration with global structures by creating the necessary infrastructure, thus ensuring that even if the TNCs were to withdraw from the country, domestic firms would have sufficiently developed the capabilities for continued participation in world trade and production.

While the above suggests that the net effects of TNCs' participation in the local economy can contribute positively to development with relevant government policies, the likelihood that governments will be in a position to maximize bargaining with the firm has also to be discussed. The structural power of TNCs can lead to situations where sound macro-economic policies followed by governments may not always produce positive net benefits. For example, while export levels and visible industrialization may take place, the actual development of the host country may be inhibited. There is concern in both developed and developing countries that the plants established by TNCs in host countries serve only as 'offshore satellites for the main activities' in home countries (Dunning, 1985, p. 415). The result is that few benefits accrue to the host country since the profits are, for the most part, returned to the parent company. Even more importantly, high value-added activities, research and development activities for example, tend to remain concentrated in home countries and few of the cutting-edge technologies are transferred to foreign subsidiaries, limiting the opportunities for host governments to establish industries capable of producing high-end exports, or in some cases moving beyond basic component manufacture. It has been argued, for example, that the export-oriented industrialization achieved by some Third World countries was more a result of the First World 'shedding the production of consumer goods' (McMichael, 1996,

p. 86) rather than a positive attempt to assist developing countries along the path of industrialization.

Research and development (R&D) within enterprises has also tended to remain in home countries. A study of TNCs from Japan, Germany and the United States, the three largest sources of foreign investment, showed that 'an overwhelming share of their R&D spending' is maintained at home (Pauly and Reich, 1997, p. 22). Any R&D that does occur overseas is generally directed towards studies of the local markets for the customization of products or to collect knowledge which is then sent back to the home country (Pauly and Reich, 1997, p. 12). The Nike Corporation, for example, produces most of its shoes in Asia but all product design and sales promotion are done at the company's headquarters in the United States (McMichael, 1996, p. 98). As Lall puts it, by receiving the know-how (operational procedures) but not the 'know-why' (research and innovation capabilities), combined with the internalization of technology markets within TNCs, developing countries are restricted from moving their own technological base 'beyond that needed for adaptive activity ... and research' (1991, p. 253). Lall further claims that evidence from Taiwan and Korea has shown that know-how has developed far more in industries in which TNC entry has been restricted. In short, there is compelling evidence to suggest that TNCs from the advanced industrial countries continue to exercise a tight rein over their technological knowledge (Mudzafar, 2001).

Moreover, from a nationalist perspective, if the entry of foreign firms into local markets results in local firms being squeezed out despite an improvement in efficiency, this will be seen as a negative development which will ultimately undermine the economic development of the country. During the industrialization of the West, infant industries were often given the benefit of protectionist government policies to allow them to establish themselves before they faced competition. With the involvement of TNCs and the liberalization of international trade, however, new local industries in developing countries are not provided with similar opportunities. By the early 1970s the amount of manufacturing exports that was controlled by TNCs ranged from 20 per cent in Taiwan to 43 per cent in Brazil to 90 per cent in Singapore (McMichael, 1996, p. 82). Without careful management and policies by the host government, the technological transfer and industrializing promises of TNCs do not actually help developing countries come any closer to catching up with industrialized states. While some benefits have accrued to developing countries from investment by TNCs it has been argued by many critics that this is only a by-product of the move away from manufacturing and unskilled production by the advanced industrial countries. The Third World thus became an inexpensive source of consumer goods that are no longer viable to produce in highly industrialized nations.

State–firm interactions

The issue of the net impact of FDI on host societies is intimately connected with the wider question of the changing relations between the state and the firm. The central issue often debated here concerns the relative power of the state and the TNC. A number of commentators and social groups are concerned that the globalization of production has created or is creating a situation in which the state is losing some of its authority and power and is being replaced by the TNC in many areas.

TNCs act as the producers of wealth within the international political economy and as such have increased their ability to influence political systems. When firms were generally confined within national borders they relied on the state to represent their interests at the international level. Now, however, TNCs are becoming important actors within the global political economy (Stopford and Strange, 1991) and it is arguable that at times their influence can be greater than that of states. States are increasingly involved in bargaining with TNCs in order to attract foreign investment (Strange, 1994). Increasingly in both developed and developing countries states need to cooperate with TNCs to achieve economic, political and social goals. Trying to control the activities of many large firms through regulatory policies can be difficult and risky considering that the opportunities offered by foreign investment can be an important part of economic planning and growth. States have therefore moved into a new policy environment in which they must try to find a balance between attracting and encouraging investment and still maintaining a range of social goals and promoting the so-called national interest. Within this new environment states still retain territorial control and firms require access to territory in order to conduct their business activities. As such, states enjoy a degree of legitimacy that is denied to firms. The changing context of state–firm interactions has raised a number of issues. In this sub-section we focus on four: changing attitudes of governments towards TNCs; decision-making and national autonomy; the transformation of state policies; and the impact on labour.

Changing attitudes.   An important factor in determining the evolution of state–firm interactions are the views and attitudes held by the political elite concerning the net benefits of FDI. The attitudes of governments to TNCs have changed considerably over the last 40 years. With the onset of the North–South dialogue in the 1960s many Third World governments were highly critical of, if not downright hostile to, foreign investment. Attitudes began to change in the 1980s, with most governments in the developing world acclaiming FDI as good news. In the earlier period it was generally believed that the economic power of TNCs and their affiliates had adverse effects on national economies through such practices as transfer pricing and restrictions on the sources of imported components (Dunning, 1991, p. 231). In response, government policies attempted to bolster domestic industries while restricting the activities of foreign firms. Governments also used planning to allocate resources rather than markets.

There are a number of reasons for this change of heart. The first is the triumph of neoliberal economic ideology and the resort to neoliberal economic policies by most governments. The renewed faith of most countries in the workings of the market economy is demonstrated, for example, in the wholesale privatization of state-owned assets and the deregulation and liberalization of markets since the mid-1980s. The move to remove structural market distortions has been played out all over the developing world, and was initiated in the United States and Western Europe. For some analysts this development arises from the proven superiority of the liberal order, while for others this is the result of the imposition of structural adjustment policies by international financial institutions and multilateral development banks following the debt crisis.

The second explanation is the increasing globalization of economic activity and the integration of international production and cross-border markets by TNCs. This has led many countries to re-evaluate the costs and benefits of FDI and the opportunities provided by TNCs for increased participation in international trade and labour markets. In the Third World, in particular, industrialization policies based on import substitution were replaced with export-oriented policies using TNC systems of production and distribution. The third reason is that the key ingredients of contemporary economic growth of created assets, such as technology, intellectual capital, learning experience and organizational competence, are not only becoming more mobile across national boundaries, but also becoming increasingly housed in TNC systems.

The fourth reason why governments have modified their attitudes towards FDI is the successful industrialization of a number of countries particularly in East Asia. As a result the competition for the world's scarce resources of capital, technology and organizational skills is becoming increasingly intensive. The fifth is that the economic structures of the major industrialized countries are converging, one result of which is that competition between firms from these nations is becoming more intra-industry and more pronounced.

The sixth explanation is that the criterion for judging the success of FDI by host governments has changed over the years, and changed in a way which has made for a less confrontational and more cooperative stance between themselves and foreign investors. More particularly the emphasis of evaluating inbound TNC activity over the past two decades has switched from the direct contributions of foreign affiliates to its wider impact on the upgrading of the competitiveness of a host country's dynamic comparative advantage. And, finally, the learning experience of countries about what TNCs can and cannot do for host countries has created a belief in many governments that they can take action to ensure they more efficiently promote their economic and social goals. This appears to be a belief that has limited application in reality and many governments in the developed world find it difficult to fulfil these goals. For example, in 2001 the British government was confronted with its abject failure to protect jobs after two TNCs – Corus and Motorola – decided to disinvest. This happened despite the fact that investment was in depressed regions of the United Kingdom and the government tried to persuade the companies to maintain production.

Decision-making and national autonomy.   The ability of TNCs to transfer resources abroad in response to changing national and international conditions affects the autonomy of state decision-making authorities. An inherent conflict exists between the political organization of authority based on national governmental structures and the economic organization of value based on growing economic interdependence. The limits to effective public policy are partly determined by the capacity of a state to promote a climate for investment favourable to transnational capital.

The globalization of production presents extraordinary challenges to the economic management of a country. Economic development is no longer restricted to the national territorial forms that prevailed for most of the past two centuries. Instead national production is now located within world production systems. Countries can no longer rely on natural comparative advantage to win them a place in the global economy. Corporate decisions are made on the basis of global production strategies and relative efficiency. The utilization of high levels of technology and policies that encourage efficiency and promote competition are the new imperatives to international competitiveness. Although most economic activity is not global in this sense, nevertheless, this is an emerging trend and governments increasingly have to adjust to international demands and pressures. The innovation of financial instruments and the development of multinational banks and other financial institutions have made regulation of the economy more difficult. The integration of national economies and communication systems thus creates a global system of interaction in which the state is but one player amongst others and state borders are losing their significance.

Moreover, firms themselves can sometimes disregard the domestic regulation of governments. Given their global production and distribution systems, firms are not dependent on governmental policy in a single state. They can, for example, evade restrictive credit policies by borrowing on international capital markets, and escape taxation of corporate profits through timely inter-firm transfers of resources. In so far as TNCs are no longer constrained by the regulation of particular states, they are effectively footloose.

This problem of diminished or diminishing national authority is particularly relevant in the developing world. The sheer size and resources of many TNCs in comparison to developing countries provides for an unequal relationship between the two. This predisposes developing states to modify the demands they make of TNCs. Additionally, the capacity of firms to locate anywhere in the world exerts an inordinate amount of pressure on countries to acquiesce to their demands, or suffer negative consequences in their macro-economic stability. The mobility of capital increases the alternatives available to firms while at the same time circumscribing those available to states. Thus, for many, the benefits developing countries derive from FDI will remain negligible given the structural imbalance between TNCs and Third World governments.

Transforming state policies. The globalization of production has altered the attitudes of governments, shifted the bargaining power between states and TNCs, and also transformed the nature of the state. This change is captured by the phrase 'the competition state' (Cerny, 1995). States have become increasingly compelled to liberalize because of competitive deregulation pressures resulting from the mobility of capital (Cerny, 1993). Boundaries are shifting as resources are linked with indistinct borders, while industries shift and react to changed circumstances and new technologies. The threat of shifting production from one country to another causes countries to compete against each other. This has produced the phenomenon of competitive deregulation between states as they attempt to maintain their attractiveness to investors and to sustain global competitiveness. The competitive processes between states can lead to a situation in which wages, working conditions and environmental standards become depressed. This is a consequence of increased liberalization as states seek TNC investment.

The globalization of production and internationalization of finance have enhanced the capacity of the holders of capital to evade the jurisdiction of what is often perceived as hostile economic management. States must therefore be increasingly sensitive to the regulatory policies of their neighbours, since they are now effectively competing for the right to regulate investment. Further, this new competitive dynamic is propelling states to accommodate the preferences of market actors, and to actively court international investors by introducing more liberal regulatory standards (Andrews, 1994, pp. 193–218). States will only be able to influence this process and to regulate foreign direct investment by assigning or delegating to supranational institutions some of their power and authority. The development of offshore markets is another instrument that has eroded national financial barriers. These changes provide investors with prospects for minimal levels of taxation and regulation, thereby allowing for the unconstrained movement of financial resources. These instruments have also been critical in providing a wider source of funding for TNCs engaged in the process of globalizing their businesses.

Labour.   The issue of the impact of transnational production on labour is examined in Chapter 9. However, we cannot leave the topic of state–firm interactions without a brief mention of the debate concerning the state's role in protecting workers. Critics point to the massive profits TNCs can make as a result of transferring production from high-wage industrial countries to low-wage developing economies. Henderson calculated that in 1975, if one hour of electronics work in the United States was valued at 1,000 then the equivalent work was worth 12 in Hong Kong, 7 in Taiwan and 5 in Indonesia and Thailand (1991, p. 54). Consequently, TNCs moved production processes using low-skilled and unskilled labour to developing countries to take advantage of these low wages. But they were not only escaping higher wage rates, they were also trying to circumvent minimum health and safety requirements and to reap the benefits of working with a largely non-unionized workforce. Instead of protecting their workers, many Third World governments colluded with transnational capital to maintain poor working conditions. In a popular study of the impact of transnational production, Klein argues that, 'When the actual manufacturing process is so devalued, it stands to reason that the people doing the work of production are likely to be treated like detritus – the stuff left behind' (2001, p. 217). She produces figures which show that while assembly-line workers in the United States and Germany were paid $18.50 per hour, the equivalent rate for the same work in China was $0.87. From the perspective of some workers in particular industries in advanced industrial countries, the shift of labour-intensive production overseas altered the economic structure causing economic and social decay in the wake of high levels of unemployment.

Regulating capital

The impact of TNCs on states and societies and the difficulty that individual governments face in controlling these firms have led to calls for greater international regulation of the activities of international business. While civil society actors call for the regulation of international business, both government and private sector interests have been increasingly resistant to such demands. Corporate interests are oriented to promoting forms of international regulation conducive to accumulation of profits.

There are two contentious issues, one on each side of the regulatory agenda, that encapsulate the current dilemmas. Those groups trying to subject the behaviour of TNCs to greater scrutiny and to impose state sovereignty on firms' taxation provide an interesting example of the failure of both domestic and international regulatory power. Through diverse accounting procedures, firms have devised strategies to evade taxation and as a result the corporate tax contribution to the finances of governments has been declining. There is an attempt to reduce the power of firms to evade taxation at the national level through the introduction of international surveillance and cooperation between national governments. This is not a radical proposal and is supported by many liberal and conservative governments in the OECD. However, the attempt in 2001 by the OECD to develop guidelines for international taxation policies was defeated through the lobbying efforts of TNCs. They were successful in persuading the US government to oppose the OECD guidelines. On the other hand, a contrasting OECD set of regulations favourable to the expansion of international business was defeated by a coalition of civil society groups who felt that it increased the power of firms relative to that of governments. The Multilateral Agreement on Investment (MAI) aimed to set standards that would further liberalize national investment regimes. Thus, while TNCs have influenced global regulation they are unable to dictate its content.

To some observers of the contemporary global economy, TNCs are increasingly exercising a parallel authority alongside governments in matters of economic management affecting the location of industry and investment, in the direction of technological innovation and in the extraction of surplus value. Corporations have actively sought through industry associations and individual contacts with governments to influence the architecture of national, regional and global regulation. Firms have, to date, argued successfully for minimal regulation, and for self-regulation rather than public authority control in situations where some direct form of regulation is required (Clapp, 1998). The TNC has become endowed with a greater political role as it uses more diverse means of achieving its objectives. Not only have TNCs resorted to using access to the highest levels of decision-making with national governments, but also access to the WTO and other multilateral institutions to ensure the corporate agenda is prioritized everywhere (Sell, 2000; Smythe, 2000).

To some extent TNCs have joined states as the authorities exercising power (whether or not affirmed by them) over the course of national and global economic development. Moreover, companies exert considerable influence over the global economy as they account for an increasingly larger proportion of international intercourse than do governments. This development, facilitated by technological change, has redefined state sovereignty by reducing the magnitude of authority claims asserted by the state. Despite this, governments remain the decisive holders of authority in regard to the territories over which other states recognize their supremacy, but are restrained in their capacity to affect economic decisions within their borders.

Conclusion

The spread of TNCs since the 1950s and the creation of a global production structure have had significant effects on international economic and trade structures, industrial development and government policies. The growth and nature of transnational production have changed over time, especially with the introduction of post-Fordist production systems, and TNCs have greatly affected national and regional developments around the world. Much of the uneven development and industrialization that occurred in the final years of the 20th century can at least partly be explained by differences in TNC involvement and government policies towards foreign investment. The shift towards transnationalization by many enterprises has also changed traditional state–firm relations, with policies of cooperation essential to the economic planning of both actors. The large amounts of capital owned and controlled by TNCs combined with their participation in virtually every national economy in the world have given them a great deal of strategic power in the global political economy and their role in influencing international trade negotiations and other international agreements is an important issue in the contemporary global political economy.

The role of TNCs in creating a new international division of labour will be examined in a subsequent chapter. It will discuss the ways in which transnational production has affected mature industrial economies and developing countries. TNCs have been the major actors organizing a shift of unskilled and semi-skilled manufacturing production from the advanced industrial countries to the semi-periphery. Many developing countries were integrated into global production systems because of their large pool of low-wage labour.

Chapter 8

The Global Financial System

This chapter considers the global financial framework by focusing on its two most significant parts. Although they will be treated separately for analytical purposes, they have evolved in tandem and influence each other. We will look at the system which governs how one national currency is exchanged for another (the international monetary system or IMS) and we will examine how credit is created and distributed across borders (the credit system).

Both of these systems have undergone dramatic changes since they were established in the mid-1940s. The IMS has evolved from a system of fixed exchange rates to one where many of the currencies float. Recently, a number of states have abandoned their national currencies in favour of regional currencies (for example, the euro). In the global credit system, the creation and supply of credit has moved from being the responsibility of public authorities (governments) to being provided by corporations. In addition, advances in information technology and deregulation of financial flows have resulted in much more rapid transfer of capital across state boundaries. The consequence of these developments is that many states, even the most powerful, are increasingly sensitive to market fluctuations.

We'll begin the analysis by providing some definitions and background about transformations in the global financial system. The theoretical perspectives section outlines a key theory concerning the relationship between capital flows, exchange rates and domestic policy (Mundell–Fleming model). This proposition is used to find our way through other parts of the chapter. The third section outlines three major developments in the global financial system since the Second World War. These are the move from fixed to floating exchange rates, financial innovation and the 1980s debt crisis. The final section provides readers with an overview of three key issues facing today's global financial system. These issues are the rise of regional currencies, regulatory mechanisms and global financial crisis.

Definitions and background

In this section we consider the nature of the international monetary and credit systems as they were created after the Second World War. We begin by focusing on the IMS as a set of arrangements that govern the exchange of one nation's currency for another. A sound IMS is necessary if economic activity across state borders is to proceed smoothly. Importers and exporters need to be able to conduct business in their clients' currencies and be able to take profit in their own. The post-1945 IMS has undergone two dramatic changes. The biggest alteration was a move from fixed rates to floating rates. The second major change has been the growth of regional currencies replacing some national currencies. We'll examine the major developments in the next section.

Reviewing the turmoil of the inter-war period, US and British post-war planners were convinced of the need for a stable international monetary system for international economic activity and peace. The attempt to fix countries' currencies to gold proved disastrous following the First World War, but so did the system of competitive devaluation that followed the breakdown of the gold standard. Planners wanted a system that would provide stability in exchange rates, but would allow for some adjustment from time to time. Their solution was the gold exchange system of Bretton Woods.

The post-war IMS was negotiated at Bretton Woods in the United States in 1944. The two most influential participants were the United States and Great Britain. In general, the British favoured a system that would restrict capital flows and provide for strong international monetary institutions whereas the United States pushed for a more liberal system with less regulation. Since the British were in debt to the United States because of borrowing to finance their participation in the Second World War, the United States was able to secure an agreement that fell closer to its desires (Block, 1977, pp. 32–69).

The core of the system was the US dollar, which was fixed to gold at a rate of $35 to one ounce of gold. Similar to the classic gold standard discussed in Chapter 4, this would encourage people to have faith in the unchanging value of the key currency. However, in contrast to the gold standard, other currencies were not fixed to gold. They were fixed to the US dollar, but provisions were made to allow for their rate to be occasionally adjusted. The thinking behind this was that if the underlying productivity of the other countries' economies changed, the value of their currency should also change. For example, if a country experienced a natural disaster, which destroyed their industrial base, they should be allowed to lower the value of their currency. This would encourage exports and help rebuild the economy.

The Bretton Woods conference created two international institutions to help oversee the operation of the international financial system: the International Monetary Fund (IMF) and the International Bank for Reconstruction and Development (IBRD). The monetary system was to be supported by the IMF. Its purpose was to help countries that had temporary balance-of-payments problems. If for some reason a country was unable to pay for its imports, the Fund could loan money to help them through a temporary cash shortage. This money would be repaid when the difficulty had been overcome.

The Bretton Woods system relied upon people having faith that the US currency would be exchanged for gold at the fixed rate if there was a demand to do so. There was no reason to doubt this assumption in the 1950s. The United States possessed large gold reserves as a result of its role as a safe haven and creditor during the First and Second world wars. Many people and states wanted to hold US dollars because they were backed by gold, but were more valuable since you could earn interest on the dollars.

An economist named Robert Triffin noticed that there was a problem at the heart of this system (Eichengreen, 1996, p. 116). The problem was that as US dollars flooded out into the world through the Marshall Plan, US defence spending and Americans buying foreign goods, the balance between dollars and gold was deteriorating. Eventually there would be more dollars outside the United States than gold inside. At some point the United States would be unable to honour its gold commitments. This was called the Triffin dilemma. The outflow of dollars was needed to provide money or liquidity to other parts of the world, but this would eventually undermine the United States' attempts at keeping their currency fixed to gold. Foreigners would begin to worry that the United States would run out of gold and would start to cash in dollars for gold to make sure that they secured full value for their currency. In 1960 US foreign monetary liabilities first exceeded US gold reserves. In 1971 the United States broke the link with gold. This subject is taken up in the major developments section.

Turning to the issue of credit, readers will recall from the first part of this book that the credit mechanism is vital for economic growth and bestows a certain degree of power upon those who issue it. In 1945, war-torn countries needed credit to rebuild, so US and British planners devised a system to funnel money to Europe. The centrepiece was the IBRD (later known as the World Bank), which was designed to lend states money for long-term rebuilding projects. Despite these plans, the Western economies faced a serious problem. There was a severe liquidity shortage. The IBRD did not have enough funds to enable European states to rebuild and purchase goods, especially American goods that required US dollars. Other mechanisms had to be found to transfer capital. The United States ended up transferring money through three mechanisms: the Marshall Plan, military spending and foreign investment. The Marshall Plan transferred about $13 billion in grants from the US government to Western Europe. These loans were used to assist reconstruction and to bolster investor confidence.

The Marshall Plan was far more than a financial transaction as it was deeply rooted in Cold War politics. The US Congress was only persuaded to release the money for Europe following the communist coup in Czechoslovakia in

1948. The threat of a communist takeover in Europe was required before American legislators came to Europe's financial assistance. The strings attached to the grants were also influenced by Cold War rivalry. On the surface the grants were available to any European state, including the Soviet Union and communist East European states. However, a condition of disbursement was that the accepting state had to commit itself to liberalizing its economy and engaging in freer trade. This was impossible for any East European state to accept because their policy of a planned economy could not be combined with an open economy. As a result, communist states were excluded from the inflow of liquidity that the United States provided to its European allies. The United States also insisted that recipients cooperate in

---

Box 8.1   Balance-of-payments confusion

The balance of payments is a record of the economic transactions between one country and the outside world. It is composed of two parts – the current account and the capital account. The current account records the sum of the flow of goods and services between one country and the rest of the world. The capital account records the movement of short- and long-term capital. Any transaction that will lead to a payment to another country is registered as a debit. This includes purchasing imports and investing abroad. Any transaction that will lead to payment from another country is registered as a credit. Exports, inflow of foreign direct investment and profits on foreign investments all lead to credits. The balance of payments should always balance or be equal to zero because outflows of money to foreigners must be matched or financed by inflows. However, there are two complicating factors. First, no state is able to record all its trans-border economic transactions so the national balance of payments accounts do not balance on paper – there is always an error factor.

Second, even though the payments balance, there is often reference to a balance-of-payments deficit when countries go through financial crisis. What does this mean? People are usually referring to a country being unable to pay for the goods and services it would like to import. In economic terms the current account (goods and services) is in deficit and can no longer be financed by the capital account. The country is using internal resources such as the money held at the central bank to finance its external activity. Since foreign activity cannot be financed solely from limited domestic resources, a long-term balance-of-payments 'deficit' requires some action to restore the balance, such as reducing imports, devaluing the currency or structural adjustment.

the administration and dispersal of funds. A new organization, the Organisation for European Economic Co-operation was created to manage Marshall funds. This was one of the first post-war organizations facilitating European cooperation and integration. It was later expanded to states outside of Europe and renamed the Organisation for Economic Co-operation and Development (OECD).

The immediate response to demands for reconstruction funds was met by public sources, primarily the US government. However, the trend until the end of the century would be for larger and larger percentages of international liquidity and credit to be distributed by private sources. A key element of this shift was the rise of the Euro-currency markets, which will be examined further below. Before tracing the major developments in the monetary and credit systems, we'll pause to consider a theoretical insight from the field of economics.

Theoretical perspectives: the Mundell–Fleming model

There are three primary approaches to understanding the global financial system. Many in the financial community subscribe to a liberal view of the way the system should operate. The liberal view is that the exchange of currencies and provision of credit should be determined by private actors in the marketplace. As described below, the liberal view has picked up the label of the 'Washington Consensus'. This consensus is sometimes challenged by a more social-democratic view which attempts to temper market mechanisms and build in safeguards for financial stability and redistribution. This might involve slowing down the rate at which financial transactions occur or regulating the behaviour of private firms. Outside the corridors of power, variations of neoMarxist thought are highly critical of the liberal financial system because of instability and promotion of inequality between and within states. Dependency analysts focus on how northern states are able to use the financial system to retain great influence in the economies of developing economies. For example, US companies made considerable progress in Asian markets following the 1997 Asian financial crisis.

These different understandings of how the financial system operates will be recalled in the following sections. However, for now, we will focus upon a theoretical proposition about the relationship between the ability of money to cross borders (capital mobility), the existence of fixed or floating currencies (stable exchange rates) and the ability of a country to set its own interest rates to influence domestic economic growth and employment (monetary policy). This relationship is important because it has implications for regional currencies, financial crises and national autonomy, which are all key issues of debate.

As far back as the 1960s it was theorized by two economists (Mundell and Fleming) that states could not simultaneously have an independent monetary policy (supply of money and interest rates), stable exchange rates (either fixed or with gradual movement) and free flows of capital in and out of the country. Two of these objectives might be pursued, but the third could not be achieved for any length of time because it would violate the other two. Governments have to choose their priorities. For example, if a government favours capital mobility to attract investment, then it must choose between a fixed exchange rate which will facilitate trade and investment and an autonomous monetary policy which will support domestic economic conditions. If it chooses a fixed exchange rate, interest rates must support that policy by providing investors with returns which will keep their money in the country. If interest rates do not support the currency and instead target domestic concerns, such as unemployment, investors may move money out of the country, putting pressure on the exchange rate. The exchange rate comes under pressure because investors sell the currency as they move their money into other currencies and assets. This creates an excess supply of the currency, lowering its value and cost. If enough investors sell the currency it will be devalued, as happened in Britain in 1992 and Thailand in 1997 (more on this below).

Alternatively, if a state chooses to control its own interest rates based on the domestic economy in an environment of capital mobility, the exchange rate will fluctuate. This fluctuation in exchange rates may influence trade flows as the country's exports rise or fall in cost with the currency fluctuations. Countries such as Australia, Canada, the United States and Great Britain have capital mobility, floating exchange rates and interest rates responding to the domestic economy. However, if a country wants an independent monetary policy and fixed exchange rate, it will have to reduce capital flows. After the 1997 Asian financial crisis Malaysia limited capital mobility by imposing capital controls so that it could pursue domestic monetary priorities and stabilize the exchange rate.

When we use the term 'monetary autonomy' we are referring to the ability of a country to control its own money supply and interest rates in response to domestic conditions. In the 1950s and 1960s the decision about interest rates and money supply was usually taken by central banks under the direction of national governments. In the 1980s and 1990s many states made their central banks independent of government instruction and directed them to achieve low inflation. In times of slow economic growth and low inflation, central banks would lower interest rates and raise them when inflation increased. Committing to a fixed exchange rate means abandoning this policy tool because interest rates must be high enough to prevent investors from selling the currency.

These theoretical observations have moved from the academic world into difficult policy decisions for state leaders. Many states welcome capital mobility because it allows them to access more funds for investment and economic growth. Some states (mainly developing countries) have pursued fixed or stable exchange rates in order to reassure investors that the value of their money will not be lost through a depreciating currency, while others have wanted to avoid the uncertainty of fluctuating currencies. States also like to be able to have interest rates that respond to their own economies so that rates will be lowered during recessions to fight unemployment. However, these policies cannot be pursued simultaneously. As capital mobility has increased, it has become much more difficult for states to stabilize exchange rates *and* pursue nationally focused monetary policies (Pauly, 2000). In practice, most governments have opted for freeing capital flows and then struggled to strike a balance between having some domestic autonomy and an exchange rate that is either fixed or does not fluctuate too greatly. The goal of capital mobility has been easier to achieve than either that of exchange rate stability or that of domestic autonomy. We'll see just how difficult it has been to manage this trinity of factors when we consider financial crises below. In some cases this has led to increasing turbulence in financial markets, in others it has contributed to deflationary national policies. The contradictions radiating from an increasingly liberal and global financial system have led to an intense search for new methods and institutions to govern an increasingly volatile system.

Major developments

There have been dramatic changes in both the international monetary system and the provision of credit on a global basis since the post-war system was created. In this section we will highlight three major changes. The first change has been the move from fixed to floating exchange rates. We'll also look at an example of how one region has tried to adapt to the change in the 1970s and 1980s by reviewing the history of the European Monetary System. The second significant development has been financial innovation and liberalization. We'll chart the rise of the Euro-currency markets, the liberalization of capital controls and innovation of financial instruments. The third development was the debt crisis of the 1980s which devastated many developing countries and encouraged policy changes in many states.

The move to floating exchange rates

The system of fixed exchange rates was eventually undermined by the Triffin dilemma and the failure of countries to voluntarily adjust their exchange rates. The excess of US dollars compared to gold made some states and investors nervous. The government of France insisted upon turning in its dollars for gold. Investors sold dollars for other currencies, fearing that the United States would be forced to break its link with gold. The United States increasingly relied upon foreign central banks to support the US currency by buying dollars and upon foreign governments to stimulate imports from the United States. One of the underlying problems was that even though European and Japanese economies were now much stronger they were unwilling to revalue their currency against the dollar. By keeping rates fixed their industries gained an advantage over US industries. The over-valued dollar meant that foreign products were cheap for US consumers and US products were expensive in other countries. This contributed to a deterioration in the US trade balance.

In the summer of 1971 the US President, Richard Nixon, decided to unilaterally change the monetary system by ending the link between the US dollar and gold. He also imposed a temporary 10 per cent tax on imports. This is sometimes called the 'Nixon Shock'. Cutting the link with gold resulted in a devaluation of the dollar as it began to float against other currencies. This was meant to restore the competitiveness of the US economy. Although there were attempts to re-establish a fixed system, it was clear by 1973 that currencies would float for the foreseeable future. Two lessons can be drawn from the ending of the system of fixed exchange rates (Eichengreen, 1996). The first is the difficulty of maintaining fixed or pegged exchange rates in the face of increasing capital mobility. The second is that a fixed system required considerable international cooperation, which had its limits.

No one was quite sure what the consequences of moving to floating rates might be. Some predicted that it would ease economic tensions because currencies would find their proper value in the market and adjustment would be automatic. Others feared chaos as fluctuating currencies made planning and trading more difficult. The result was somewhere in the middle. Exchange rates proved to be more volatile than advocates of floating rates suggested, but they did not result in immediate financial chaos. Governments intervened in the market by buying and selling currencies in an attempt to halt large swings.

Floating rates turned out to be more of a problem in the 1980s. In 1979 the US central bank (Federal Reserve) moved against rising domestic inflation by dramatically raising interest rates. The hope was that higher US interest rates would slow the economy and stop price rises (inflation). If credit was more expensive, people and industries would borrow less and spend less, reducing demand. This reduced demand would stop inflation because people would be less able and willing to pay higher prices.

The effects of this change on exchange rates was dramatic. The higher US interest rates attracted investors into the US dollar, causing its value to rise.

Between 1980 and 1982 it rose in value compared to other currencies by about 30 per cent. At the same time that the Federal Reserve tightened monetary policy through high interest rates, US President Ronald Reagan loosened fiscal (budgetary) policy by increasing military spending and cutting taxes. This gave Americans more money in their pockets to buy imports. President Reagan ignored the international consequences and pursued tight monetary and loose fiscal policy. The implications for US trade were dramatic. Other countries were able to increase their exports to the United States and the United States found it harder to sell its exports abroad. The result was a rising US trade deficit and calls for greater protectionism.

A system of ad hoc cooperation trying to coordinate the economies of Europe, North America and Japan emerged as a result of turbulence in the foreign exchange markets (Eichengreen, 1996, pp. 145–52). At the Plaza meeting in September 1985 the G-5 (United States, Japan, Germany, United Kingdom and France) agreed to take action to reduce the value of the dollar. All countries wanted to head off the threat of increasing protectionism in the United States. The markets responded to this initiative and the dollar fell rapidly, losing 40 per cent from its peak against European and Japanese currencies. Two years later at the Louvre meeting of the G-7 (add Canada and Italy), the Japanese agreed to stimulus measures, the Germans to tax cuts and the United States to stabilize the dollar through adjustments in domestic policy. In the second half of 1988, the dollar resumed its decline.

The Western European response to increasing exchange rate volatility was to try and create their own zone of currency stability called the European Monetary System. In general, European leaders were dissatisfied with floating rates because of the problem of overshooting. When investors moved out of the dollar they tended to rush to the German Deutsche mark (DM) knocking it out of line with European currencies. Appreciation made it difficult for Germany to export its goods while the depreciation of other currencies caused inflation in those states. The Germans wanted to take pressure off the DM. If there were fixed rates, an investor would be just as happy to hold French francs as German marks. It was also hoped that fixed rates would build confidence and investment, encouraging transnational European companies (Swann, 1992, pp. 181–220).

The response was to create the ECU and the exchange rate mechanism (ERM). The ECU was a composite currency for bookkeeping purposes. States committed themselves to limiting the fluctuation of their exchange rate to the ECU by no more or less than a given percentage below the central rates. Once a currency reached its bilateral limit, the central banks of each country intervened in the foreign exchange markets by buying or selling currencies to support the one in difficulty. For example, if the Irish punt was about to fall out of the band, the Irish and other central banks would sell their foreign reserves to buy punts. In some cases, such as the United

Kingdom, countries were unable to maintain the required level. Nevertheless the ERM laid the groundwork for the eventual introduction of a single currency, the euro.

Originally the United Kingdom decided to stay out of the ERM. When it did join in 1990, its currency was fixed at a relatively high level compared to the other ERM countries. This hurt British exports to Europe and had a depressing effect on the British economy. In an environment of capital mobility Britain was forced to keep interest rates high to attract investors into the pound in order to maintain its level in the ERM. In the late summer and early autumn of 1992, investors began to doubt that the British government would be able to continue to support a high pound in the face of deepening recession in the United Kingdom. Investor concern about the willingness of the British people to sacrifice economic growth for a fixed exchange rate began when the Danish people voted to abstain from the monetary union project. Investors began to sell the pound for other currencies, fearing that the UK government would eventually drop out of the ERM and their investments would decrease in value as the currency depreciated. Even though the government was committed to defending the pound and the British central bank depleted its reserves through buying pounds on the market, the currency was eventually forced out of the ECU band. So many investors were selling pounds that the British government was unable to buy them all.

The British government was committed to capital mobility and a fixed exchange rate. Recalling our trinity theory, this meant that it would have to let interest rates target the exchange rate rather than the domestic economy. In the end, the government was unable to do so because the political cost of having very high interest rates in the middle of a recession was unsustainable. Investors recognized this and sold the pound until the British government recognized the situation as well. To understand this we need to understand the link between exchange rates and capital mobility.

The move to floating exchange rates, the easing or eliminating of restrictions on exchanging currencies and the information revolution have all led to increased capital mobility and activity in foreign exchange markets. The existence of floating rates has introduced the possibility of selling currencies while information technology has allowed traders to do this in greater amounts, in more ways and at greater speeds. Although the variations can be complicated, the underlying principle is simple. Profit can be made by selling a currency that will decline in value and then buying it back at a later time. For example, imagine that Susan sells her $1.00 (US) for 1.00 euro. If by the next day the euro rises in value or appreciates 10 per cent (10 cents) against the dollar, Susan can sell her 1 euro for $1.10, making a profit of 10 cents. If Susan had bought 100,000 euros, her profit would be $10,000 for less than a day's work. If these numbers are multiplied many times, the time period is shortened from a day to minutes, and losses as well as gains are factored in, one begins to get an idea of the frenzy of activity on foreign exchange markets.

In the case of the 1992 attack on the British pound, speculators were betting that the pound would fall by selling pounds for other currencies. In this case it was a very safe bet. If the government succeeded in keeping the pound in a narrow band through the ERM, the investors would only lose the money that it cost them to exchange currencies. However, if the pound did fall out of the ERM it could decline significantly and vast fortunes might be made. The most famous speculator in this event was George Soros who was rumoured to have made $1 billion by selling the pound.

This type of activity is interpreted in several different ways. For some it is damaging speculation. Wealth is created without anything actually being produced. Even more serious is the claim that flows of money in and out of countries can weaken otherwise healthy currencies and economies, creating economic hardship. An opposite, more liberal, view is that foreign exchange fluctuations serve a positive role by signalling when economies are pursuing harmful policies. This encourages governments to adopt corrective measures. A third position might hold that currencies react to real problems, but that because of the volume and speed at which they operate a herd mentality amongst investors can cause unnecessary economic damage.

In the first decade of the 21st century currency misalignment was once again a major issue, but this time between the United States and China. The United States ran a record trade deficit with China and argued that China should allow its currency to float freely against the dollar. A floating currency would rise in value against the dollar, making American products cheaper in China and Chinese products more expensive in the United States. However, the issue of the 'proper' value of the Chinese and US currencies is a complicated issue. The United States relies upon China to fund its budget deficits and China relies on the United States to buy its exports. A deterioration in their financial relationship could hurt both countries (See Box 8.2).

Financial innovation

A remarkable feature of the global financial system has been the degree of innovation in the past 50 years. Advances in telecommunications such as fax, high-speed telephone lines, satellite connections and the internet have allowed financial transactions to take place at a much faster pace and greater volume. In addition, new types of financial products have been introduced to provide investors with more options. This sub-section begins its consideration of financial innovations with the Euro-currency (or Eurodollar) markets.

Box 8.2   The United States–China financial relationship

In the early 21st century the financial relationship between the United States and China became complicated and volatile (Krugman, 2005). China attracted large amounts of capital in the form of foreign investment as US, European and Asian companies invested in Chinese production. Money also flowed into China because it was running trade surpluses with many countries, especially the United States. This should usually take care of itself because an inflow of money should raise the value of the Chinese currency, which would make China's trade surpluses shrink.

However, the Chinese government did not allow its currency to rise in value. It took the money flowing into China and sent it right back to the United States by buying dollar assets such as US government bonds. The easy inflow of Chinese money into the United States has meant that the United States can keep its interest rates low and easily fund large budget deficits. Budget deficits allowed the government to pursue war in Iraq and cut taxes. At the same time low interest rates encouraged American consumers to spend and facilitated a housing boom.

This arrangement benefited both China and the United States. China was able to base its economic development on exporting to the United States and the Americans were allowed to enjoy high rates of consumption. However, the model is unsustainable and faces major problems (Samuelson, 2009). Americans used borrowed money to consume

→

Actually the term Euro-currency markets is a bit misleading. It does not refer to European currencies. It refers to a wide series of financial transactions that take place in currencies other than the currency of the state in which the business is being conducted. For example, the Euro-currency market was initially composed of the exchange of US dollars in London. The Euro-currency market in New York operates in funds other than US dollars. The market in the Cayman Islands operates in any currency other than the local one. The primary reason why financial operators do not use the local currency is because state authorities do not regulate their activity if they are working with foreign currencies.

The Euro-currency market began in London after the Second World War and met several needs. The British state supported its expansion because it brought financial business back to London and helped the city re-establish its role as an important financial centre. The Soviet Union made use of the market as a place where it could store and exchange US dollars beyond the reach of its Cold War rival, the United States. US corporations investing in

→

rather than invest in new productive capacity. This raised questions about how the money would be paid back. The Chinese government became heavily dependent on export growth to provide employment and prevent social unrest. The relationship became more strained in the wake of the 2008 US financial crisis. The US government needs continued Chinese investment to finance its spending and budget deficits, which are designed to save financial institutions and reflate the US economy. However, the weakness of the US economy threatens the value of Chinese investments. If the Chinese start to shift their money away from the United States, the Federal Reserve will be forced to raise interest rates to attract investors. This in turn will slow the US economy and reduce growth. At this point Americans will have to pay the true cost of their budget deficits. If the adjustment happens slowly the economy will be able to adapt, but a rapid change in money flows could cause considerable economic turmoil in the US and the global economy. There are risks for China, as well. They are heavily dependent on the United States for an export market. A severe downturn in the US economy threatens Chinese exports and employment levels. This, in turn, could increase social instability in China. China is trying to avoid these dangers by increasing consumer spending in its domestic market. This is being done by spending on infrastructure programmes and reducing the need of citizens to save for health expenses by introducing a wider safety net and social programmes.

Europe increasingly used the market to escape restrictive US laws on banking activity. However, the big jump in the Euro-market's size came with the 1973 oil crisis and the increase in revenues flowing to OPEC states (Organization of Petroleum Exporting Countries). Many of these states turned to the Euro-markets to conduct their banking. Estimates of the money put into the markets show it rising from $3 billion in 1960 to $75 billion in 1970 to $1,000 billion by 1984 (Strange, 1988, p. 105).

Alongside the rise of currency markets, the 1970s and 1980s saw a global financial revolution. Capital was increasingly flowing between countries in larger volumes and at faster speeds. Technological advances allowed for cheap, instantaneous, constant communication. In the late 1970s and early 1980s a number of key states eliminated capital controls, allowing individuals and corporations to move their money freely in or out of their country. The United States took this step in 1974 and the United Kingdom followed in 1979. In 1986 the United Kingdom increased liberalization in its financial industry through what was called the 'Big Bang'. This was the name given to financial deregulation in Britain. It involved two major elements. The first was allowing any foreign company to enter into the United Kingdom's stock market and foreign exchanges. The second step was to allow banks, stockbroking firms and insurance companies to compete in each other's industries. This broke down the barriers which had formerly stipulated that only banks engaged in banking, insurance companies in insurance and stockbrokers in selling stocks. The advantage of this deregulation was that it increased competition in the financial industry. The disadvantage was that this competition might push some firms into more risky behaviour, possibly leading to financial crises.

The liberalization of financial activity did result both in increased competition and in a series of financial crises. Financial products proliferated, with a range of new instruments coming onto the market. These included currency swaps, futures, options and derivatives. However, financial problems also arose. In Great Britain an economic boom followed upon the creation of new wealth from the enlivened financial markets. However, the boom turned to bust in 1988 following the 1987 stock-market crash and the collapse in the housing market. Fuelled by the expansion in credit, many people bought houses at over-inflated prices and suffered the consequences when the economy slowed.

The financial liberalization and innovation of the 1980s accelerated in the 1990s. Large sums of money were expended to manage and profit from the increasing risks of the volatile financial markets. An increasingly popular method of coping with the risks (the possibility that exchange rates, the rate of inflation or the price of commodities might change) was the use of *derivatives*. The term 'derivatives' is used for an array of financial instruments that are derived from more basic financial instruments. The two most common forms are futures and options. These are derived or spun off from stocks or bonds. A future commits someone to buying a stock or a commodity at a specified time in the future for a price set today. Futures have been very common in the agricultural field where someone would agree to buy a farmer's product six months before it was available. This gave the farmer a guaranteed price and some security against the risk of planting a crop and then receiving a low price during the harvest period. One might also buy oil futures if there was fear that oil prices would rise in the future. Futures can be bought on margin, which means that the purchaser only has to put down a percentage of the purchase price when committing to the deal and the rest when the future comes due. An option requires someone to pay a small fee for the opportunity to buy a stock or bond at a specified price at a specified time. If the price of the commodity goes down, the trader can back out of the purchase, but loses their fee. If the price goes up they can buy the commodity and sell it for a profit.

Used wisely, derivatives can insure businesses and individuals against the risks of falling or rising prices. However, they are also used to make money in themselves. Traders and investors use them to make money by betting on the value of a product at some time in the future. If they are correct about the price movement, they can sell at a profit. If they are incorrect, they suffer a financial loss. Since these products can be bought on margin, large sums of money can be pledged without having the ability to pay at the time of purchase. This kind of a system encourages investors to take risks for potentially large pay-offs.

Box 8.3 Microcredit: financial innovation for the poor

Not all financial innovation is for rich people. Microcredit was created to improve poor people's access to credit. Poor people are often not able to access credit or if they do get credit it is usually on very poor terms and at extremely high interest rates. Women find it particularly difficult to secure credit because they often do not have assets to secure loans or are seen as poor lending risks by bankers. In the 1970s an innovative credit programme which distributed small loans directly to poor people (often women) began in Bangladesh. The Grameen Bank (www.grameen.com) pioneered small loans (about $100) to poor people so that they could generate income from self-employment. These loans were usually distributed to groups of borrowers and given without asking for collateral. The philosophy was that poor people could improve their circumstances with a small amount of credit to jump-start economic activity.

The Grameen model enjoyed considerable success in channelling credit to poor people. By the 1990s it was taken up as a model form of finance by the United Nations and World Bank. In February 1997 in Washington DC a Microcredit Summit was held which brought together microcredit participants from around the world. Their goal was to launch a campaign to bring microcredit to 100 million of the poorest people through financing self-employed poor women (www.microcreditsummit.org). In October 2006 the Grameen Bank and its founder Muhammad Yunus were awarded the Nobel Peace Prize for their development work.

While microcredit has attracted considerable positive publicity, concerns have also been raised about its role in the global economy. Some critics have argued that while microcredit might make poverty slightly more bearable it does nothing to tackle the larger political and economic structures which foster poverty (Elahi, 2004). Others see microcredit as an attempt to suppress political opposition to poverty by improving the welfare of a few people while discouraging attempts at broader-based social change (Weber, 2004).

We'll consider some of the dangers of rapid innovation in the key issues section.

The 1990s and early 21st century also saw the rise of two other large financial players – sovereign wealth funds and hedge funds. Sovereign wealth funds are investment companies created and controlled by national governments. They are economic nationalist instruments which allow governments to gather revenues and direct them into strategic foreign investments. Sovereign wealth funds are dominated by countries that have large surpluses of cash (oil exporters or countries with large trade surpluses) and favour state intervention in the economy. The biggest sovereign wealth funds are controlled by the United Arab Emirates, Singapore, Norway, Kuwait, Russia and China. In 2007 it was estimated that these funds held $2.5 trillion to $3 trillion in assets (Weissman, 2007). In some countries the rise of such funds have sparked concern because they do not behave in the same manner as private companies, may threaten other states' national interests and are accused of engaging in transnational 'nationalization' rather than transnational investment.

Hedge funds are financial companies that engage in complicated financial transactions in which combinations of assets are bought and sold over short and long time-frames (Krugman, 2008, pp. 120–2). Buying 'short' positions involves borrowing a stock from its owner for a period of time. The stock is initially sold and then bought at a future date and returned to the owner. If the value of the stock falls during this period, the hedge fund makes money because it sold the stock when it was high and bought it back when it dropped in value. A 'short' position is taken when one believes the value of the asset (oil, currencies) will fall over time. The profit is usually invested in a long position or an asset whose value will increase over time. Hedge funds have three characteristics which led them to play an important role in financial crises. First, the hedging is done with very little capital, allowing the funds to take very large positions in the markets. Second, hedge funds offer large financial returns when they do well, but imprudent bets can result in financial disaster since the funds are so heavily leveraged. Third, hedge funds largely operate beyond government regulation so that government officials have been largely unaware of their massive size and extensive holdings.

The 1980s debt crisis

For developing states the liberalization of capital markets had far more serious consequences – the debt crisis of the 1980s. A combination of supply and demand factors help us understand why developing countries became exposed to large debt (Lever and Huhne, 1986), but decisions about interest rates in developed states led to the onset of the crisis.

On the supply side, vast sums of money became available for lending purposes in the 1970s. The rise in oil prices had a dramatic effect on the international credit market. It caused a shift in wealth from oil consumers to oil producers. The producers, primarily members of OPEC, invested some of their money in the Eurodollar markets. This money then had to be lent out if the banks were to turn a profit. Bankers were flooded with cash and eagerly looked around for potential customers.

Fortunately for the banks, there was a great demand for credit. Developing countries were desperate for funds to help them industrialize their economies. In some cases, developing countries were oil consumers and required loans to help pay for rising oil prices. In other cases, a decision had been made to follow a strategy of indebted industrialization (Frieden, 1981). This meant that states borrowed money to invest in industrialization and would pay off the loans from the profits of their new industries. Loans were an attractive option because they did not come with the influence of foreign transnational corporations that accompanied foreign direct investment and most states had few funds of their own to invest.

In the late 1960s and early 1970s developing states appeared to be a sound investment because many had indeed enjoyed high growth rates up to that point. The market appeared to be working well by bringing together the capital-rich and the capital-poor to the benefit of both. However, events at the end of the 1970s took a turn for the worse and the debt crisis erupted in 1982.

In 1979 the Ayatollah Khomeini was able to overthrow the Shah of Iran in the Iranian revolution. Not long afterwards war erupted as Iraq invaded Iran in a misjudged attempt to take advantage of political turmoil. The result was a second oil shock. The US response to this oil shock was considerably different from that in 1973. Rather than let the higher prices move through the US economy via inflation, a decision was taken by the chairman of the US Federal Reserve to fight inflation by raising interest rates. Interest rates would reduce the rise in prices because credit would be more expensive and people would have less money to spend or invest. This would reduce the amount of money chasing goods and services, reducing demand, leading to a slowdown in price rises (deflation).

The effect of this policy in the United States was the onset of recession. The effects in other parts of the world were much more serious. The cost of international money went up, following the increase in US interest rates. Whereas interest rates on international loans were about 2 per cent in the early 1970s they rose to over 18 per cent in the early 1980s. This greatly increased the interest charges to developing states on their international loans. At the same time that developing states were facing higher interest charges it became more difficult for them to sell their products to developed states. The recession that swept the developed world reduced imports in two ways. Recession meant that demand for imports went down in general. In addition, recession fed protectionist forces in developed states, resulting in the restriction of imports to support domestic jobs.

The consequence for many developing countries was disastrous. Those states that were oil importers were faced with massive bills to cover their debts. Those developing states that were oil exporters (such as Mexico and Venezuela) were hurt because they had borrowed heavily to industrialize and were then caught as oil prices fell in response to lower demand during the recession.

In August 1982 Mexico announced that it could no longer service its debt. This meant that they could no longer cover the cost of interest payments, much less hope to repay the debt. Mexico's announcement burst the bubble and ushered in the debt crisis as banks recognized their exposure to a series of bad loans. Private funds flowing into Mexico and some other states halted. Before long it was evident that states such as Brazil, Venezuela, Argentina and many sub-Saharan African countries were in equally difficult financial positions.

It was in these circumstances that the IMF began to play a more prominent role. The Fund negotiated standby loans with debtors offering temporary assistance to states in need. In return for the loans states agreed to undertake structural adjustment programmes (SAPs). These programmes entailed the liberalization of economies to trade and foreign investment as well as the reduction of state subsidies and bureaucracies to balance national budgets.

The phrase 'Washington Consensus' was coined to capture the agreement upon economic policy that was shared between the two major international financial institutions in Washington (IMF and World Bank) and the US government itself. This consensus stipulated that the best path to economic development was through financial and trade liberalization and that international institutions should persuade countries to adopt such measures as quickly as possible. Although the Washington Consensus referred to conventional wisdom, critics of the IMF and World Bank associate the term with all that is wrong with rapid economic liberalization. In their eyes it stands for harmful and arrogant policies determined by financial and Western elites and imposed upon developing states. The rise and stall of the Washington Consensus is developed in more detail in Chapter 13.

The effects of these policies on the population in developing countries was devastating. The 1980s is known as the 'lost decade' of development. Many developing countries' economies were smaller and poorer in 1990 than in 1980. Over the 1980s and 1990s, debt in many developing countries was so great that governments had few resources to spend on social services and development (see Table 8.1).

The debt crisis sealed the 'triumph of neoclassical economics' in most

Table 8.1   National expenditure on social services vs debt

Region/ Country	Year(s)	Percentage of central government expenditure on	
		Basic social services	Debt service
Africa			
Tanzania	1994–5	15	46
Kenya	1995	13	40
Uganda	1994–5	21	9
South Africa	1996–7	14	8
Asia			
Philippines	1992	8	31
Sri Lanka	1996	13	22
Nepal	1997	14	15
Thailand	1997	15	1
Latin America and Caribbean			
Jamaica	1996	10	31
Brazil	1995	9	20
Costa Rica	1996	13	13
Chile	1996	11	3

Source: Data from UNICEF (1999), p. 32.

developing countries (Biersteker, 1992). Starved of international finance, states had little choice but to open their economies to foreign investors and trade. Mexico is the most dramatic example. Following its revolution in the early part of the 20th century, Mexico had tried to follow a development strategy which stressed the building of a national economy. It was a leading advocate of import substitution industrialization. Mexico erected tariff

Box 8.4   Debt and AIDS

The effects of the debt crisis go well beyond financial indicators. In sub-Saharan Africa, debt burdens have greatly complicated responses to the AIDS crisis. Approximately 5,000 people die every day from AIDS in Africa and the disease has rolled back previous gains in life expectancy and development. Structural adjustment programmes designed to address debt problems have led to the downsizing or privatization of health and educational services (Cheru, 2002). This has weakened the ability of governments to provide healthcare and information about AIDS to their populations. Money that might go into public health campaigns has been diverted to pay off external debt. Efforts by the World Bank and IMF to reduce the debt loads of heavily indebted poor countries (HIPC initiative) have freed up some money for some countries. However, given the extreme health emergency, broader and more rapid cancellation of external debt is required.

barriers against imports and tried to produce its own goods behind these barriers. However, following the debt crisis, Mexican policy concentrated upon integrating itself into the international market. As the 1980s and 1990s progressed, more and more developing countries followed a similar path. McMichael (1996) has described this as a transition from a development model of national economic growth to a globalization model of searching for a 'niche' in the world market. The Mexican liberalization process was capped and solidified by its pursuit and achievement of the 1993 North American Free Trade Agreement. NAFTA locked in Mexico's liberal reforms because it acted as an economic constitution for North America. However, despite the policy changes in many developing states the burden of debt compared to domestic national product continued to grow in the 1980s and 1990s (see Figures 8.1 and 8.2).

Key issues

This section focuses on three key issues that have dominated the global financial system in the last decade of the 20th century and the early years of the 21st. The three key issues are: the rise of regional currencies; financial crises and international regulatory mechanisms; and the global financial crisis which erupted in late 2008.

Figure 8.1 Developing-country external debt as a percentage of GNP

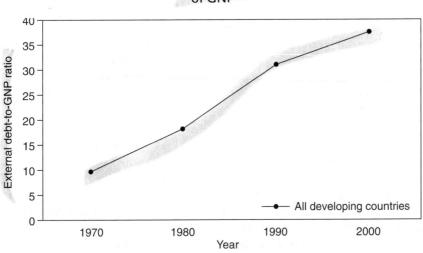

Source: Data from World Bank (2001), p. 246.

Figure 8.2 Regional averages: external debt as a percentage of GNP

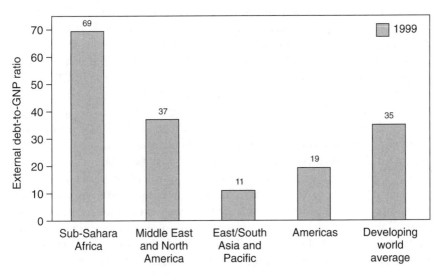

Source: Data from UNICEF (1999), pp. 30–1.

Changes in regional and reserve currencies

As was pointed out in Chapter 3, many different objects have served as money (tobacco, shells, gold), but it is essential that people have confidence that the chosen object reflects a particular value. When doubt begins to arise about the value of the money object or if its value fluctuates wildly people will seek another object to serve as the store of value. In this section we examine how doubts about the value and utility of particular currencies have led to a rise in regional currencies and speculation about the international role of the US dollar.

Regional currencies.   One of the most striking changes in the IMS has been the growth of regional currencies. In Europe many states have given up their own national currencies and adopted the euro. In other parts of the world weak local currencies have been, at times, abandoned for stronger currencies (dollarization). Both of these trends indicate a drift to a smaller number of large powerful currencies and the demise of some weaker national currencies. We will first examine the euro and then turn to dollarization.

On 1 January 2002, 12 European countries (Austria, Belgium, Finland, France, Germany, Greece, Ireland, Luxembourg, the Netherlands, Italy, Portugal, Spain) introduced the euro and began the phase-out of their national currencies. The euro was adopted by Slovenia in 2007, Cyprus and Malta in 2008 and Slovakia in 2009. Sixteen of the 27 members of the European Union now use the euro rather than national currencies. States joining the euro sacrificed national monetary autonomy in return for currency stability. The operation of the euro is overseen by a European Central Bank (ECB). After consultation with representatives from the national central banks, the ECB sets a single interest rate for all member states. It also manages the exchange rate between the euro and other currencies. The primary goal of the ECB is price stability, which means low inflation. In response to fears that some countries might not respect low inflation levels and might be tempted to run budget deficits, EU members agreed to a stability pact in June 1997. This stipulated that national governments must not run an annual budget deficit of more than 3 per cent of GDP. Fines can be applied to states that do not comply.

The drive to adopt the euro prompted considerable public debate. A number of objections were raised. One issue was that countries would lose the ability to devalue their currencies if there was an economic shock that hit their country. For example, a country reliant on oil exports such as Britain or Norway might be hit by low oil prices. With their own currency Britain would probably devalue, letting exports in other industries make up for employment losses in the oil industry. Under a single currency this would not be possible. The result might be that particular areas of the European Union could stagnate as they lost the ability to adjust their currencies.

A single monetary policy and interest rate may not suit such a diverse economy. For example, the Irish economy might expand while the German economy is stagnant. Because of the large size of the German economy, it is likely that in such a situation European interest rates would be lowered to boost German economic growth. This would help Germany, but hurt Ireland. The low interest rates in Ireland would fuel consumer and business spending and cause inflation.

Opponents argued that the mechanisms which allowed federal states such as the United States to overcome these problems were absent in Europe (Feldstein, 1992). The lack of labour mobility and absence of transfer payments were striking. Because of language and cultural barriers, Europeans were much less likely to migrate to jobs in another part of Europe. Many would stay in a stagnant area rather than move. Another difference with federal states is that there was little transfer of funds from richer to poorer areas for development or equalization payments. In the end, although there were economic arguments in favour of and against the euro, the decision to push forward was taken by those wishing to form a closer political union. The single currency was seen as a way of increasing the bonds between European citizens in preparation for closer political ties.

The creation of the euro was undertaken as much for its contribution to political union as its alleged economic benefits. In other parts of the world there is not the same desire for political union. Nevertheless, there have been moves by some states to reduce or eliminate their national currency in favour of a foreign currency. The general name for this trend is dollarization, although it can occur with a number of different currencies, not just the US dollar. In this sub-section we will look at dollarization in the Americas, where it does in fact occur through use of the US dollar.

Dollarization can take place in two ways and for two reasons (Dean and Globerman, 2001). The two ways it can take place are de facto and de jure. De facto dollarization means that national currencies still exist, but a large number of people use the dollar in practice. It is dollarization in fact. De jure dollarization means dollarization in law. This occurs when the national currency is legally replaced with the US dollar. Since the 1980s, de facto dollarization has occurred in many countries of the Americas while de jure dollarization has occurred in Panama, Ecuador and El Salvador.

Why would a country give up or reduce the use of its own currency? One reason is that individuals and businesses may lose faith in their own currency. High inflation or repeated devaluations may encourage people to hold their money in foreign currency as a preferred store of wealth. This is known as asset substitution. Fearing that their money may lose its value they choose to hold a safer currency, in this case the US dollar. A particularly severe case of this occurred in Zimbabwe in 2009 (see Box 8.5).

A second reason for adopting another currency is to facilitate trade relations

---

Box 8.5   Dollarization, randization and pulaization in Zimbabwe

One reason why countries may be tempted to accept foreign currencies rather than produce their own is to combat runaway inflation. In early 2009 the country of Zimbabwe experienced an upsurge in its rate of hyper-inflation. Its inflation rate was approximately 89 sextillion per cent (89 followed by 21 zeros). Prices in stores doubled every day. The central bank printed so much money that the Zimbabwean dollar lost almost all of its value. The central bank actually printed a note whose face value was a hundred trillion dollars (i.e., $100,000,000,000,000). Faced with hyperinflation and a collapse in the value of its currency a new Zimbabwean government essentially abandoned its own currency by announcing that all domestic purchases could be made in foreign currencies. Retailers and shops instantly began to accept US dollars, South African rand and Botswana pulas. The sudden appearance of viable currencies led to reopening of shops and a sudden increase in economic activity (York, 2009).

---

with a dominant economic partner. For example, Canada's economy is heavily reliant upon trade with the United States. If Canada adopted the US dollar it would increase economic exchange and eliminate problems of fluctuating currencies. In this case, Canadians (especially businesses) might favour the US dollar as the best medium of exchange. This is known as currency substitution.

In the case of Latin American countries, dollarization would bring some economic benefits. Foreign investors would no longer fear that they would lose money when a currency declined. It would be less risky to invest in Latin America. This should lead to more foreign investment and growth. Money would also become cheaper in dollarized countries. At the moment, Latin American states must pay an interest premium when lending domestically. This means that they must pay higher interest rates than the United States to encourage investors to buy government bonds and securities. This is necessary because their currency is a riskier investment. By adopting the US dollar this risk premium would disappear.

Despite obvious advantages, there are serious disadvantages to the dollarization process. Unlike the European example, there is no effort to make US monetary policy sensitive to the needs of other countries. There would be no central bank of the Americas similar to the ECB in Europe. Countries that enter into dollarization will have their money supply and interest rates controlled by the United States. This may reduce economic growth if the United States pursues a monetary policy that is contrary to the needs of the dollarized country. If a dollarized economy experiences some form of economic shock it will be unable to devalue its currency to restore competitiveness. Adjustment will have to take place by further depressing real wages and reducing incomes.

In a dollar bloc it is likely that most of the financial institutions will be from the United States. These institutions may not have much interest in lending money to local small businesses, poorer individuals, farmers and local governments. Clients of the formerly national institutions could well be starved of credit, hampering economic growth. On the other hand, dollarization may feed speculative bubbles as funds flow into particular sectors and flow out again with similar ease.

In short, dollarization offers some advantages, but creates more restraints on state policies. It reduces their flexibility and policy levers. If there are no funds to help with the process of adjustment (none are proposed) the economic costs of dollarization could prove to be very high. This in turn would likely lead to increased domestic political conflict as the costs of adjustment are distributed unequally through the national economy.

The advent of the euro and the dollarization process indicates several things about the international monetary system. First, many states are willing to consider the benefits of abandoning their national currency in favour of joining a currency bloc. In the European case, this is part of a deep process of economic and political integration. In the Americas, the motivation is primarily economic gain. Second, the existing international monetary system is not serving the interests of many of its members. Many developing countries cannot trade or borrow unless they do so in a major currency such as the US dollar. They must pay for goods in dollars and loans are denominated in dollars. Countries must continually earn more dollars to engage in international economic transactions. This means that they are very vulnerable to any shock that upsets their economic relationship with the outside world.

The status of the US dollar as a reserve currency.   The financial crisis that swept the United States in 2008 and spread to other countries has raised the issue of confidence in the world's major reserve currency – the US dollar. The world's reserve currency is the currency that is most used by central banks as a reserve asset and is the currency that is often used in the provision of loans or purchase of products. Many countries in the world hold a large share of their reserves in US dollars. Many products are priced in US dollars – the most important of these is oil. Many international loans are also denominated in dollars.

The US dollar has been the world's primary reserve currency since the end of the Second World War because investors and states have had more faith in the US economy than any other country. This has been of substantial benefit to the United States. Because of the high demand for the US dollar the United States has had to pay relatively low interest rates when it sells its government bonds to foreigners. Investors will take less in interest payments because of the security of their investment. This has allowed the United

States to fund large budget deficits relatively cheaply. Low interest rates have meant that the US government and US consumers have been able to live beyond their means and consume more than otherwise would have been possible. Since US borrowing is done in dollars, there is no risk of the US debt increasing if the value of the dollar falls. In such a situation the creditors would lose money as they saw the value of their loans fall in relation to their own country. This is the opposite situation that many developing countries face when they borrow in dollars and then have to make ever-larger payments if their currency weakens. The pricing of other key assets (such as oil) in dollars has also insulated the United States from other price fluctuations. For example, if the euro declines in value against the US dollar, Europeans must pay more for oil which is sold in US dollars. However, if the US currency loses value, it does not pay more for oil since oil remains priced in US dollars.

In the wake of the near collapse of the US financial system in 2008 a number of voices have been raised questioning the future role of the US dollar. The most significant one was that of the head of China's central bank who suggested in March 2009 that the dollar be replaced as the world's reserve currency. The proposal made clear that China was unhappy with the role of the dollar and the possibility that it might lose money on its investments in US debt if the dollar entered a decline (see Box 8.6). However, there is no clear successor to the dollar in sight. The Chinese have huge surpluses, but their restrictions on the use of their currency prevent it from being widely held. The euro is a possible challenger, but still does not command as much respect as the US dollar.

Box 8.6   Key facts about Chinese funding of US debt

- In 2008 China held over $2 trillion in foreign reserves; 80 per cent was in US dollars.
- In 2009 China owned approximately $1 trillion of US debt (about 14 per cent of total US public debt).
- In the first half of 2009 China bought more Treasury Bonds than in the same period in 2008. However, China's overall share of US Treasury Bond purchases decreased because US debt was rising even faster.
- Because of global financial uncertainty there were many buyers other than China for US Treasury Bonds in 2008.
- In 2009 China began to get out of longer-term Treasury debt in favour of short-term debt, fearing that US inflation might reduce the value of its long-term holdings.

Sources: Bradsher (2009a, 2009b).

The dollar is increasingly under pressure and could be eclipsed by one or a combination of other currencies. If that were to happen, Americans would have to pay more for imported goods as the value of the dollar declined. The United States would also have to raise interest rates on government and private debt to support the value of the dollar. A weaker dollar would challenge the United States to reduce consumption, restore fiscal balance, invest in infrastructure and human capital (Roubini, 2009). Simultaneously, it would shift the power and privileges of the reserve currency to other states and populations.

Financial crises and international regulatory mechanisms

Even though the 1980s debt crisis was managed in such a way that financial collapse was prevented, many people are still worried about the stability of the financial system. In the late 1980s one leading observer of the operation of the global financial markets termed it 'casino capitalism' (Strange, 1986). Strange argued that the increased volatility in most markets and the lack of sensible regulation over transactions had turned the financial markets into one large casino. Investors placed bets on the future of company profits, commodity prices, exchange rates, interest rates and many other economic indicators. The large sums involved and the rapidity with which money travelled encouraged investors to take risks and increased the possibility that crises would occur. Crucially, this casino has many involuntary players. People not placing the bets suffer the consequences when the financial wheel of fortune takes a bad turn. The citizens of developed states bear the cost of financial bail-outs through their taxes and the population of developing states pay through reduced living standards and in some cases malnutrition and death. This sub-section reviews several of the financial crises of the 1990s that reinforce concern about the stability of the international financial system and considers the arrangements put in place to deal with them.

Two financial collapses of the 1990s illustrate that the proliferation of financial instruments is difficult to regulate through market mechanisms and are also risky to employ even for the most brilliant financial and mathematical minds. The case of the collapse of Barings Bank in 1995 demonstrates the difficulties that financial firms have in keeping track of the activity of their employees. Over the summer of 1995, Nick Leeson, an employee of Barings Bank in Singapore, used derivatives to place a series of bets that the Japanese economy would prosper in the following years. Unfortunately for Japan and Barings Bank, economic recession continued and Japan was struck by a large earthquake. When the dust had settled and the margins were called, Barings could not cover its losses. The bank collapsed and Mr Leeson spent time in prison in Singapore. Criminals can be found in any organization, but what is striking is that the bank was unable to monitor its employee's actions and that it gave so much financial power to individual traders.

Perhaps an even more cautionary tale is that of Long Term Capital Management. This was an investment firm set up by leaders in the financial field, including two economics Nobel Prize winners, numerous mathematics PhDs and people with backgrounds in Wall Street firms and the Federal Reserve. They created a hedge fund which used derivatives to make large sums of money for their wealthy clients and banks. All their mathematical models proved of no assistance when Russia experienced economic difficulty in 1998 and the fund's assets disappeared. The US financial system teetered on the brink of collapse before a number of private financial institutions stepped in to pick up the pieces at the urging of the US government (Blustein, 2001, pp. 305–36). A system that encourages financial risk led a group of talented financial minds to financial ruin and almost caused a national and international financial crisis.

Development groups and social democratic critics of the liberal global financial system have suggested that capital mobility needs to be slowed down to provide greater stability. One proposal to do this has been the Tobin Tax. The Tobin Tax would levy a charge on foreign exchange dealings. The idea is that the tax would discourage those people trading currencies just to make money, but would not deter foreign exchange transactions for purposes such as medium- to long-term investment, buying imports or tourism.

Although there are technical objections to the Tobin Tax and other measures to slow the flow of capital, the primary obstacles are political. Vast fortunes are generated by the free flow of capital. Those who benefit from the system are adept at using their influence to prevent measures which might reduce their potential for increased wealth. The beneficiaries of capital mobility are those who have money to invest. This includes wealthy individuals, the financial industry itself and corporations with a need for investment or which are investing in financial instruments or the stock market.

Corporations and wealthy individuals have recently been joined by a large number of less wealthy individuals who have interests in the stock market. Over the past 20 years, large numbers of people from modest economic backgrounds in the developed world have had their pensions and savings invested in the stock market. As governments increasingly privatized the provision of pensions in the 1990s by scaling back state pensions, more people relied upon their own investments for retirement earnings. This has meant a large growth of individual investment in the stock market through mutual funds or unit trusts. In addition, employer pension funds of civil servants or teachers have become major stock market participants as they search for the best return for their customers. These organizations are called institutional investors and their investment decisions can move markets. The number of people in advanced industrialized countries committed to open financial markets has grown, making attempts to curb such openness much more politically difficult (Harmes, 1998). At the same time, the number of people vulnerable to a stock market slump has also grown. This opens the possibility of an anti-liberal backlash if a prolonged recession destroys millions of investors' retirement funds.

Turning to financial crises in states, we should consider the case of Mexico, a country which had undergone massive restructuring as a result of the 1980s debt crisis. Mexico plunged into another crisis in the mid-1990s. The decade had started well enough for Mexico. Its negotiation and signing of NAFTA had convinced investors that the government was committed to liberalization. Between 1990 and 1993, $91 billion flowed into Mexico, a fifth of all capital going to developing states (Strange, 1998, p. 103). Money flowed into the stock market, boosting share prices and creating a sense of increasing wealth. However, a series of events, including higher interest rates in the United States, rebellion in the state of Chiapas and the assassination of a presidential candidate, caused investors to doubt whether Mexico could maintain its fixed exchange rate with the US dollar. In December 1994, investors sold the Mexican peso in quantities so large that the government ran down its foreign currency reserves and was forced to abandon the link with the dollar. Although Mexico was committed to capital mobility (to attract investment) and exchange rate stability (to keep the investment), it was unable to withstand the destruction caused by rapid capital flows. When it was over, the Mexican government owed over $55 billion, mostly to private foreign investors such as pension funds. The US government, over the objection of the Congress, committed $20 billion dollars to a rescue package and pressed the IMF and BIS to contribute another $32 billion. The effects of the crisis on Mexicans were disastrous as living standards were cut in half. The poor suffered enormously and the middle class faced huge debts because of skyrocketing interest rates and diminishing of their savings when the peso devalued.

The Mexican crisis was notable for several reasons. First, it spilt over into other countries such as Brazil and Argentina, forcing them to take defensive measures such as raising their interest rates to stop capital flight. This became known as the 'Tequila effect'. Second, Mexico suffered a severe financial crisis despite having undergone over a decade of liberalization and economic restructuring after the first debt crisis. Third, the dangers of the flow of short-term capital into and out of a developing country were highlighted by the Mexican events. Finally, the players on the creditor side had changed. In the 1982 crisis, it was banks that were involved and eventually had to accept some losses on their loans. In 1994 it was non-bank actors such as pension funds, mutual funds and stock market investors that pulled the money out. Thanks to the US/IMF/BIS loan investors escaped with relatively little financial loss. The Mexican people were not as fortunate.

Two-and-a-half years later an even more remarkable financial crisis occurred. It was remarkable because it hit a group of countries which had formerly been held out as success stories – the newly industrializing countries of East and South-east Asia. In 1997 South Korea, Malaysia, Thailand and Indonesia suffered serious financial crisis. Hong Kong, Taiwan and even China were threatened by turmoil as well. Yet, only a few years earlier the World Bank (1993) had issued a report praising the 'development miracles' of East Asia. How could this have come about?

In July 1997, investors started to have doubts about whether the government of Thailand would be able to maintain the value of its currency against the US dollar. Similarly to events in Mexico in 1994 and Britain in 1992, they began to sell the local currency, betting that the government would eventually have to devalue. After defeating the Thai peg, attention turned to other countries in Asia. Successful speculative attacks were mounted against Indonesia, Malaysia, South Korea and unsuccessful attacks took place against China and Hong Kong. States formerly thought to be in good shape were forced to turn to the IMF for financial assistance.

There are several interesting aspects of the Asian crisis. One is that it revealed the degree to which almost any developing state could be subject to a financial crisis in a very short period of time. A second point is that the states affected by capital outflows adopted very different policies. Thailand closely followed advice from the IMF, as did Indonesia and South Korea later. In contrast, the government of Malaysia blamed foreigners for provoking the crisis and instituted capital controls to prevent rapid inflows and outflows of funds. A third point is that although many in the United States saw the reforms requested of states in crisis as natural and advisable, many in Asia saw them as an opportunity for US business and state elites to take advantage of Asian weakness (Higgott, 1998).

The series of financial crises at the end of the 20th century, which included East Asia and Russia, led many people to question the stability of the global financial system. Investors alarmed by crisis in one part of the world had the tendency to remove money from other parts of the world, spreading panic beyond the initial problem cases. This is known as contagion and is a considerable source of worry for money managers and state elites. The official response to these fears was to begin a discussion about new forms of governance in international finance. Hundreds of studies and many hours of meetings were devoted to the topic of a 'new financial architecture'. The two substantial institutional innovations that emerged out of this process were the Financial Stability Forum (FSF) and the Group of Twenty (G-20).

The Financial Stability Forum brings together officials from the most industrialized countries (G-7) with representatives of a wide range of international

financial institutions and regulators. Representatives from the International Monetary Fund and World Bank are joined by those from the Organization for Economic Cooperation and Development, the Bank for International Settlements, the Basle Committee on Banking Supervision, the International Organization of Securities Commissions, the International Association of Insurance Supervisors, the Committee on the Global Financial System and the Committee on Payments and Settlements. The FSF has concentrated its work on three issues: offshore financial centres, cross-border capital flows and highly leveraged institutions (hedge funds). Its investigation of offshore financial centres confirmed the view that these areas contributed to systemic instability. They proposed that more information about offshore centres should be gathered and that they be pressured to comply with international standards.

A more politically oriented body was created with the founding of the G-20 in September 1999. The G-20 is composed of the finance ministers and central bank governors of the G-7 states plus Argentina, Australia, Brazil, China, India, Indonesia, South Korea, Mexico, Russia, Saudi Arabia, South Africa and Turkey. It also includes representatives of the European Union, IMF and World Bank. As a group they account for over 85 per cent of the world's GDP and 65 per cent of the world's population. Whereas the FSF is essentially a gathering of the most economically developed states, the G-20 includes several of the largest developing states (Brazil, China, India and Indonesia). This is an attempt to bolster the legitimacy of financial reforms by having a broader base of countries participate in decision-making. The G-7 countries suffered from the accusation that they were a rich man's club.

Initially the G-20 concentrated on reviewing codes and standards for financial transactions and exchange rates. It was thought that the institution could serve as an arena where policy could be formulated and implementation followed up. The larger multilateral institutions of the IMF and World Bank could take formal decisions after the G-20 reached a consensus. At its second annual meeting in Montreal in October 2000, the G-20 broadened its future agenda to include issues of social safety nets, infectious diseases, the environment and debt relief (G-20, 2000). It is doubtful whether the G-20 framework has the resources to handle these issues, but public concern about the consequences of financial liberalization has forced them to take up a broader agenda. In the wake of the 2008 financial crisis in the United States, which spread to many other countries, the G-20 was given an expanded role.

A crucial aspect of the debate around the Asian financial crisis and the stability of the international financial system was whether the primary problem was with the units or the structure of the system. A problem with the units would mean that there was something wrong with the policies that individual states were following. They might be spending their money in a wasteful manner, following inefficient economic policies, borrowing excessively or have a financial system that lacked transparency. A system fault would mean that there was something wrong in how international finance was organized. This could stem from markets that moved too rapidly, or incentives to firms to engage in unwise lending, or a trading system that made it difficult for countries to earn sufficient resources. If the problem was at the unit level, the solution would be found in domestic reform. If the problem was at the systemic level, the solution would require changes to the rules governing the exchange and flow of money.

It is often the case that creditors and advanced industrialized countries believe that the problems of financial stability arise because of poor policies at the unit level. Efforts to increase stability are therefore aimed at reforming developing countries (again!). During the 1980s, Latin American countries were faulted because their economies were not sufficiently export-oriented. In the late 1990s, formerly successful Asian states were blamed for practising a corrupt form of capitalism – crony capitalism. In contrast, many developing countries and non-governmental organizations believe that the fault lies in a global financial system which rewards speculation and the rapid flow of capital.

Another shift in the distribution of costs from an international financial crisis occurred between 2001 and 2005. In December 2001 the government of Argentina declared that it could not pay its debts, causing the largest government default in history. Half of the debt that the government owed was to foreign bondholders. In previous cases of this sort the IMF would have negotiated a stringent structural adjustment programme with Argentina and forced the government to begin paying back money to the bondholders. However, a number of factors led to a different outcome. First, within Argentina the financial crisis created widespread chaos and a political mood that was hostile to paying back debt. A left-wing government came to power which was unwilling to give in quickly to the IMF or private bondholders. Second, the IMF had lent so much money to Argentina that it was vulnerable if Argentina refused to pay. This weakened the bargaining position of the IMF.

A third important difference lay with a change in US foreign economic policy. The George W. Bush administration was heavily influenced by right-wing economic views which were not in favour of using government money to bail out private investors. They believed that IMF support for governments in crisis created a moral hazard problem. The hazard was that private investors could recklessly invest in risky countries because they knew that the IMF would get their money back if things went wrong. The Bush administration wanted to force private investors to bear some of the economic loss of poor investment decisions. As a result, a right-wing US government supported a left-wing government in Argentina as it resisted IMF demands for immediate repayment of foreign bondholders at favourable rates (Helleiner, 2005). When Argentina finally did settle with the bondholders, they received only 30 cents for each dollar they had invested in Argentina's government debt.

Argentina's refusal to give into IMF demands and the change in US government policy raised questions about how future financial crises will be handled. IMF assistance cannot be automatically assumed and private bondholders may now have to bear more financial losses. Some tentative answers to these questions have been provided by the approach taken by the US authorities to the global financial crisis, which is discussed below.

Global financial crisis

In 2008 and into 2009 the world was buffeted by yet another financial crisis. The systemic consequence of this crisis has been so severe that it merits discussion as a key issue in its own right. However, unlike the financial crises of the 1980s and 1990s this one did not begin in developing countries. The origins, and indeed causes, lay in the United States. This section highlights the causes of that crisis, reviews its global consequences and considers the issues it poses. In the broadest sense, the financial crisis of 2008 came about because loans were extended to people who could not carry the debt load and the risk for these loans extended deep into the US financial system (O'Brien, 2009). A market fundamentalist philosophy and powerful political interests ensured that there was minimal regulation as a series of financial institutions took on greater and greater risk in a search for increased returns (see Chapter 13).

After the bursting of the technology bubble in 2001 the US Federal Reserve kept interest rates low to stimulate growth. Low interest rates encouraged people to buy houses. As demand for loans grew, the financial industry responded by creating new instruments which extended loans to people previously excluded from borrowing. Wall Street investment banks took home mortgages, divided them up into smaller slices, bundled them up as mortgage securities and then sold them off to other investors. The advantage of this system was that the risk of the original mortgage could be spread amongst a large number of investors. If a few mortgages went bad the large number of investors would easily be able to absorb the small fragments of financial loss.

These financial instruments and many others were popularized by 'parallel' or 'shadow banks' (Krugman, 2008, pp. 158–62). Shadow banks are financial institutions that engage in banking activity – taking deposits and lending out money – but are not classified as banks. Because they are not classified as banks, these institutions are not regulated like banks. They do not have to keep a similar percentage of their capital on reserve to pay out to borrowers and they do not have to pay into the deposit insurance system like banks do. Since they do not bear the regulatory costs of banks, they can make more profit, but they are exposed to more risk than deposit banks. Key shadow banks include investment banks, hedge funds and even insurance companies.

As the housing boom took off (house values doubled between 2000 and 2006), a number of worrying trends developed. Because the financial units which originally dispersed the mortgages (mortgage originators) sold the risk on to other parties, they became more willing to take on riskier and riskier customers. For example, the term 'Ninja loans' stood for 'no income, no job, no assets' and referred to mortgages that did not require customers to demonstrate that they were creditworthy (Dodd and Mills, 2008). Mortgages were offered to customers with little or no money for down payments and without due regard to their financial health. The link between the lender and borrower was broken because risk was passed on to other investors in the financial system. Those making the loans would not be held accountable for their actions because the loans were sold off to others.

By the end of 2006 the housing market had reached its peak and prices started to decline. Unfortunately, a very large number of individuals and financial institutions had structured their economic activity around inflated house prices and were now financially vulnerable. The emerging crisis was first seen in the sub-prime market. Sub-prime mortgages are given to customers who do not qualify for a mortgage on standard terms. As house prices declined sub-prime lenders lost money as clients defaulted on their mortgages. Over the next year more and more financial firms faced financial collapse from exposure both to bad mortgages and to the mortgage derivatives that had become so common (see Box 8.7). Credit markets tightened up and the crunch hit banks in other countries. Banks and investment vehicles such as hedge funds declared large losses over the year.

The use of derivatives had not only spread the risk associated with bad mortgages, it had hidden the extent and scope of the risks. No one knew how bad the financial mess was or could be. In September and October 2008 the crisis intensified, causing the Republican and allegedly conservative US President to embark upon one of the largest government interventions in US history. In October the US Treasury Secretary and Chairman of the Federal Reserve lobbied Congress for $700 billion to buy up toxic mortgages. After initially losing a vote in Congress, the administration was given the authority to put in place a rescue package. However, this initial plan was overtaken by events and the government soon changed course to follow the initiative of the UK government. Rather than focusing on buying up bad mortgages, the government directly infused $250 billion of capital into banks by taking shares in the largest US banks (Citigroup, Wells Fargo, JPMorgan Chase, Bank of America and Morgan Stanley). Further bail-outs followed, with the

Box 8.7 Spread of turmoil in the US financial industry

April 2007	Sub-prime mortgage lender New Century Financial seeks bankruptcy protection.
November 2007	US-based Citigroup seeks investment from Abu Dhabi sovereign wealth fund to maintain financial health.
March 2008	Investment bank Bear Sterns taken over by JP Morgan with government backing.
September 2008	US government takes over (nationalizes) two of the largest US mortgage companies (Fannie Mae and Freddie Mac). Investment bank Merrill Lynch sells itself to Bank of America. Investment bank Lehman Brothers goes bankrupt. US government provides $85 billion bail-out for insurance giant American International Group.

Federal Reserve eventually creating a 'bad bank' to buy up the toxic loans of financial industries in 2009.

The financial crisis spilled over into the 'real economy' as the United States plunged into recession. Turbulence in the financial markets reduced credit to consumers and businesses. As economic activity slowed, lay-offs began and unemployment rates rose. Pensioners also suffered devastating losses as their stock market funds dropped by a third. Consumers who funded their activity through credit or based on the inflated value of their homes or real estate values were being forced to cut back drastically on consumption. Attempts to reduce poverty by broadening home ownership suffered a serious reversal as the credit crisis forced economically vulnerable people from their homes. Economic conservatives (neoliberals) in the United States were outraged over the massive government intervention in the markets and drift to 'socialism' evident in the government's stake in banks, mortgage and insurance companies. Commentators on the left and right asked, 'Is this the end of American capitalism?' (Faiola, 2008).

The US financial crisis rapidly spread to other countries. With its large international financial services industry, Britain was especially hard hit. Many British financial institutions teetered on the brink of insolvency and the government was forced to mount massive bail-out packages. Several small states which had nurtured oversized financial industries were plunged into economic turmoil. The state of Iceland went bankrupt and Ireland's economy was hard hit. In Eastern Europe governments, companies and individuals that had taken out loans with West European banks in euros or Swiss francs suffered when their currencies weakened. Both Hungary and Ukraine turned to the IMF for emergency loans. Countries heavily reliant on exports for economic growth such as China suffered from the reduction of economic activity in major export markets such as the United States. Developing countries faced the prospect of reduced exports, as well as more difficult access to credit, investment and development assistance.

While the international impacts of the US financial crisis unfolded at an accelerating rate, a coherent international response did not. Initially, many states viewed the financial problem as a US concern and left it up to the United States to devise a solution. As the impact spread, some momentum built for global coordination, but agreement was difficult. The United States and China embarked upon large domestic spending initiatives to stimulate their economies, but continental Europe did not. A G-20 meeting in London in April 2009 signalled the increasing importance of that institution, but failed to adopt new rules for global financial regulations. The G-20 did announce the provision of more funding to developing countries, but was unable to secure from its members common programmes to stimulate economies, deal with toxic loans or provide a new framework for regulation. In the United Kingdom the greatest impact of the meeting was the fall-out from heavy-handed policing of demonstrators, including the death of one individual. In September 2009 G-20 leaders decided that the G-20 would take over from the G-8 as the major forum to guide the global economy.

One result of the crisis has been increased attention to the IMF. As was the case with the 1980s debt crisis, world leaders have turned to the Fund as a key instrument in combating the crisis. At the G-20 summit in April 2009 world leaders pledged to boost IMF lending resources to $750 billion to support lending to emerging markets, and provide assistance to low-income countries. But a renewed role for the IMF is linked to reform of the institution. This will be a slow and difficult process but one step in this direction was the decision to ratify the Fourth Amendment of the IMF's Charter, thus making the allocation of Special Drawing Rights more equitable. Special Drawing Rights allow countries to borrow more money than would otherwise be available.

The failure to develop a common response to financial crisis opens a number of difficult questions. If new regulations are not put in place, what is to prevent a similar crisis developing at another time and another place? If countries do not coordinate their responses, is it possible that they will adopt policies which are temporarily attractive, but damage the interests of other nations? Is it possible that countries will become more protectionist as a response to economic slowdown? Could this undermine global growth and recovery?

Conclusion

Underlying many of the technical debates about the global financial system are the issues of autonomy, convergence and democracy. The openness of financial markets has sparked a debate about whether all states are being forced to pursue similar policies (convergence) or whether there is still room for different economic strategies (autonomy). Following on from this is the question of the tension between the demands for financial restructuring and policy preferences articulated through the democratic process. We'll briefly outline these positions before concluding the chapter.

The idea that governments and populations have lost power to the market and business leaders is captured by the phrase 'increased structural power of capital' (Gill and Law, 1993). This means that the organization, or the structure, of the financial system gives more power to those who possess wealth and those who can move their money around the global system. Because financial markets operate around the clock and transactions can take place almost instantaneously, investors can move their money out of countries that adopt policies which might threaten their profits. For example, a government that runs budget deficits to fund welfare policies may threaten the profits of investors. Investors may then transfer money out of that country, hurting businesses and the government's finances. Financial interests are not able to dictate state policies, but they increase the cost of following policies that are seen to be against investors' profits. This reduces the autonomy of states and societies that have different priorities from investors. Although this line of argument started before discussion of globalization became fashionable, many people see globalization increasing the influence of financial markets.

One of the interesting kinds of organization which has received more attention in this time of financial globalization is the bond-rating agency, such as Moody's and Standard & Poor's (Sinclair, 1994, 2005). These private firms rate the debtworthiness of governments and corporations. If your rating goes down, the price of money goes up. A government or firm with a low bond rating must pay investors higher interest to compensate them for risk. Governments need to pay attention to the judgement of these agencies because a poor rating will influence the terms upon which they can access money. They raise or lower the cost of certain policy options.

The notion that state policy has been restricted by mobile capital has been challenged by scholars who maintain that states may still make significant choices. They argue that policies are not converging upon a particular liberal financial model. Sturdy domestic institutions and the power of organized labour and leftist political parties are factors which blunt the power of investors (Garrett, 2000). Liberal financial policies are implemented by particular governments who must be held responsible for those policies. For these analysts, power still resides at the state level and the attempt to find the cause of changing state policies at the global level is mistaken.

The debate about convergence and the structural power of capital has important implications for the practice of democracy. If the structural power of capital perspective is correct, democracy can be undermined because financial interests are having an increasingly large say over public policies. Voters may elect a government on a programme of economic growth and lowering unemployment, but the government may not follow these policies because of the financial implications. The will of the people is undermined by the power of the dollar. On the other hand, if analysts who discount the power of global financial markets are correct, then talk of globalization and structural power only serves to shift responsibility from governments to shadows beyond the state. Democracy can suffer because people give up trying to hold governments accountable for their actions. We will return to issues of governance and accountability in the final chapter of this book.

As governments moved to reassert control over their financial institutions in the wake of the US 2008 financial crisis it appears that those arguing that states have not been weakened by financial globalization seem to have been vindicated. Yet, the financial crisis also highlighted the tremendous inequality generated by neoliberal regulations. Government moved quickly to shore up institutions which had generated the problem, but the costs were often born by those who had little voice in designing the rules. In the United States and other developed countries citizens lost homes, retirement savings and jobs. In many developing countries the shortage of capital and development aid threatened development strategies and social policies. Whereas the debate about state power may have been resolved, the issue of inequality and democratic control of financial regulation is more pressing than ever.

Chapter 9

Global Division of Labour

When studying international economics or global political economy it is easy to concentrate attention on the activity of corporations or states and lose sight of the fate of particular people or groups of people. This chapter focuses on how people are caught up in a division of labour created by the global political economy. Where a person fits in in this division of labour has a significant role in determining how long they will live and what their quality of life will be. The focus on the division of labour reveals gross inequalities and great injustices that may not be as visible when examining other aspects of the global political economy.

The chapter begins by outlining some of the variations in terms surrounding the division of labour such as the international, global, gendered and racial division of labour. In the theoretical perspectives section we consider the liberal theory of division of labour and objections to this from economic nationalist and critical perspectives. Under major developments we consider changes in the production process (how things are made) and the move from an international to a global division of labour. The key issues considered in the chapter are: the integration of Chinese and Indian workers into the global economy; the global struggle for workers' rights; and the relationship between workers' rights and global stability.

Definitions

The division of labour refers to how people fit into the production process. Different societies and economic systems have different ways of organizing who does which particular job. Some societies have relatively simple divisions of labour where many people do similar tasks while other societies may have a detailed division of labour where people specialize in doing only one or two tasks. Take the example of the difference between people who live on farms and those who live in cities. Most farmers must take on a number of different jobs in order to survive. In addition to planting crops, they may have to be able to fix their machinery, preserve their own vegetables, bake their own bread and even take a second job in the city. Most city dwellers specialize in a particular job and then pay others to do tasks such as baking bread, growing crops, fixing machinery or even caring for children. In this case the city dwellers have a more specialized division of labour than the farmer.

There can also be different approaches to allocating tasks to particular individuals or groups. In some cases a division of labour may be based on race, such as in the apartheid era in South Africa or in the pre-civil war era in the southern United States. In both of these examples violence was used to enforce the allocation of tasks. In other cases unofficial discrimination or lack of skills may maintain a racial division of labour. Many Western societies aspire to a division of labour based upon merit and operating in response to impartial market forces, but ethnic, racial, class and gender divisions continue.

Moving beyond local communities one can speak of an international division of labour. This refers to a process whereby people in particular countries build or make particular things for export. Your geographic location has a great influence upon what type of job you do in the international economy. For example, if you are participating in the global economy and happen to live in Honduras you would probably be involved in the export of bananas; if you lived in Bangladesh it would likely be textiles, in China it could be toys, in California it could be aerospace or the entertainment industry.

The concept of a global division of labour captures a form of organization which reaches around the planet, but where work is not confined to particular states. In a global division of labour you find activities that in the past might have been thought of as being confined to particular states now existing in very different types of states. Labour one might associate with a developing country flourishes in a developed state and jobs thought to be the preserve of advanced industrialized countries exist alongside very labour-intensive jobs in developing states. For example, an expanding computer software industry is developing in India alongside the majority of the population that lives in subsistence agriculture. Alternatively, textile sweatshops thrive in Los Angeles and New York. The distinctive feature of these jobs is that they are plugged into a transnational production process and they are not confined to particular parts of the globe, although they may be more concentrated in some areas rather than others. To return to the example, most computer software jobs are in advanced industrialized countries and the textile industry is a much greater presence in developing states. Yet, some developing countries have information technology jobs and developed countries have immigrants working in the textile industry.

There is another important aspect of the division of labour and that is its gendered character. Men tend to be grouped in different jobs from women. Gender refers to the ideas societies have about what social roles and forms of employment are most appropriate for men and women. For example, if you look around a university, it appears that most professors are men and most secretaries are women. In the global economy, women are the majority of workers in export processing zones and men are the majority of the managers. In the finance industry, men are a majority of the stockbrokers, women the majority of bank tellers.

The interesting thing about the gendered division of labour is that it is not preordained or 'natural' but changes over time depending upon social and economic circumstances. For example, in Canada and the United States before the Second World War, women were largely confined to domestic tasks. However, with the shortage of male workers during the war, many women were called upon to work in factories where they were more than capable of doing 'male' work. Once the war ended, women were encouraged to return to the domestic role so that men could resume their 'natural' employment patterns.

A major issue in the global division of labour is the fate of the gendered division of labour. In some states, considerable progress has been made to break down the barriers between 'women's' work and 'men's' work. However, progress has been uneven and falls short in even the most progressive countries. On the global level, women occupy particular places in the division of labour and they are affected in particular ways.

Every society has a particular pattern of gendered work. The tendency is for women's work to be less well paid than work dominated by men. Women are often concentrated in particular types of employment. Women are overrepresented in the 'caring' and support professions such as clerical, teaching, nursing, counselling and childcare. Women usually combine this paid work with the unpaid work of maintaining the family home and childcare (see Figure 9.1). Finally, the vast majority of people engaged in prostitution are women or children. Being a woman in the global economy entails a much greater chance of being poorer, working harder and under worse conditions

Figure 9.1 Gender inequality in economic activity

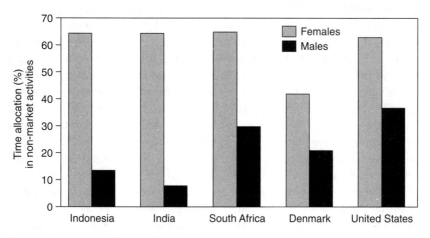

Source: Data from UNDP (2002), p. 238.

than a man. Further discussion of the gendered division of labour and its implications will be the subject of Chapter 10.

There can also be a racial and ethnic division of labour. In these cases groups of people from particular ethnic backgrounds or with visible physical differences are confined or corralled into specific forms of labour. The racial division is used to justify the different legal status and economic exploitation of these groups of workers (Persaud, 2001). The practice of slavery in the Americas was a brutal example of a racial division of labour. However, racial divisions have also been crucial to the employment relations of Koreans in Japan, Indonesians in Malaysia, Mexicans and Central Americans in the United States, Turks in Germany, Algerians in France, West Indians in Britain and Indians and Chinese in many countries.

Theoretical perspectives: Adam Smith and his critics

The economic benefits of an advanced division of labour both nationally and internationally are at the heart of liberal economic theory. The 'naturalness' of the existing division of labour has been criticized by those who highlight the role of power in creating and maintaining particular divisions of labour. Theorists and practitioners interested in the welfare of a particular state or nation have tried to influence the division of labour by supporting the development of particular forms of industry such as manufacturing or high technology. Feminist theorists have tried to undermine the gendered division of labour by revealing its manufactured nature.

We'll spend some time considering the liberal theory in detail before turning to alternative views. The liberal philosopher Adam Smith chose to begin his famous work *The Wealth of Nations* by explaining the benefits of an increasing division of labour: 'The greatest improvement in the productive powers of labour and the greater part of skill, dexterity, and judgement with which it is anywhere directed or applied, seem to have been the effects of the division of labour' (1776/1983, p. 109). Smith illustrated his point by contrasting a system of production where individuals made pins versus a system where the various tasks of making pins were broken down between a group of people. He suggested that a single person may only be able to make one pin in a day. If they were especially skilled they might be able to make as many as twenty in a day. However, if the job was to be broken down into tasks and assigned to individuals, many more pins could be made. One person could draw out the wire, another could cut it, and yet another could make the points. Smith divided the task of pin-making into 18 distinct operations. Under his system ten people could make 48,000 pins – the equivalent of one person making 4,800. One can certainly doubt the various numbers that Smith used, but the point is significant. The division of labour increases productivity.

Smith attributed this increase in productivity to three factors. First, practice at a particular task increases dexterity, which increases speed. The more someone does a task, the better and faster they can do it. Second, time is saved by eliminating the need to move from one job to another. Finally, by simplifying the production process through task specialization, machinery can be applied to the tasks. They can then be performed more quickly.

Smith also believed that the causes of the division of labour had three sources. The first was that brought about by what he saw as people's natural propensity to 'truck, barter and exchange'. He believed that it was part of people's nature to want new products and things that they could not provide for themselves. The second factor was 'self love'. People's interests in furthering their own position encouraged them to trade and engage in the division of labour. Finally, people were engaged in different activities due to 'habit, custom and education'. Some people were more skilled in particular trades, others had better education and still others were raised in particular tasks.

Recognizing the benefits that could be derived from a division of labour, Smith and other liberals moved on to some other points. In general, they believed that the more advanced a society, the greater the division of labour. Thus, states should take steps to support the division of labour. One thing they could do was to enlarge the size of the market. The larger the market, the more different types of products would be created and the greater the division of labour. Local markets could be expanded to national markets which could then be expanded by engaging in an international market through international trade.

Central to Smith, and liberal ideology, is the idea that the benefits of the division of labour and liberal policies flowed down to the lowest members of society. Smith argued that the difference between a prince and a peasant in Europe is not as great as between a peasant and an African king. The debatable point he wanted to make was that the worst off in the most advanced society fared better than the best off in a less advanced society. While this is clearly untrue, one can see the link between Smith's view of the benefits of an international division of labour and David Ricardo's theories of comparative advantage discussed in Chapters 4 and 6. Ricardo's view was that if each country specialized in the product that it could produce best, all countries could benefit from international trade. These benefits flowed from shifting national resources into the most competitive industries, increasing the degree of specialization in the international division of labour.

Modern liberal economic theory and many international institutions propagate these views by suggesting that countries and peoples will prosper by engaging in free trade and tasks that the market rewards. Thus, one sees that structural adjustment programmes of the IMF encourage developing states to open their economies and produce for the export market. The WTO was established to encourage states to reduce barriers to trade and facilitate an increasingly specialized division of labour.

Critiques of the liberal approach come from those who suggest that the division of labour is not natural and is shaped by power relations. There are three slightly different versions of this critique. Scholars working out of the dependency tradition note that countries are locked into particular forms of labour because their economies were the victims of imperialist expansion. A second set of theorists focusing primarily on advanced industrialized states argue that particular economic sectors are strategic and vital to state interests. States must shape the division of labour to ensure that they remain active in these areas. This second group shares some of the assumptions of the first about power relations shaping economic activity to the benefit of some states rather than others, but focuses on the struggle between advanced industrialized states rather than the gap between northern and southern states. Feminist scholars are the third group and they argue that the gendered division of labour is caused by patriarchy and the unequal distribution of power between men and women.

Looking back at history one finds considerable support for the claims of dependency theorists that the division of labour is not 'natural' but is based upon historical conflict which locks countries into particular roles (Dos Santos, 1970). An examination of the international system in the 19th and early 20th centuries reveals that there was a limited form of a division on an international basis with areas, countries or even continents specializing in particular tasks. In general, countries which had gone through the industrial revolution made manufactured goods and other states supplied raw materials or food. A crucial question is: when did the division of tasks begin and why? Was it, as Smith might have suggested, something natural? Or did force and conquest play a large role in establishing an international division of labour? Unlike liberal theory, which suggests that the division is an outcome of some natural process, French historian Braudel (1979, p. 50) argues that the 'past always counts'.

Let us review the fate of the triangular trade across the Atlantic and the resulting division of labour. Europeans exchanged manufactured textiles and guns for African slaves. These slaves were then forcibly transported to plantations in the Caribbean and the United States. The products from the Caribbean and the southern United States were then sold at immense profit in Europe and farther East. In the case of cotton, the raw material was transformed into textiles and sold on. This division of labour increased productivity and helped to feed the industrial revolution, but how did it come about? It is clear that the process which resulted in the African continent 'specializing' in slaves, the Americas specializing in raw materials and Europe in manufactures was not simply a product of different skills.

America's resources were exploited through the use of force and slave labour. Many of the products in which the Caribbean and Latin America 'specialize' (for example, sugar) were transplanted by European colonists from other parts of the world.

Another good example of force of arms shifting the division of labour is the textile industry in Britain and India in the 18th and 19th centuries. When Britain had the superior navy and inferior textiles, it managed to keep Indian textiles out of Britain. Both countries were able to produce textiles because British textiles could not compete in India and the Indian product was kept out of the British market. However, in later years when British textiles were superior (because of the industrial revolution) and India was held by force, Britain was able to destroy the Indian textile industry by selling its cheaper products in the Indian market.

One can conclude from such examples that the international division of labour was not an agreement between equal parties open to review. Economic patterns and power relations sometimes date back to an ancient state of affairs. The significance of this point is that political authorities in the form of states have a role in shaping where their population 'fits' in the division of labour.

Palan and Abbott (2000) have examined the various strategies that states have pursued in order to shape comparative advantage and their place in the division of labour. Depending upon their existing place in the global political economy and domestic political coalitions, some options are more feasible than others. Small to medium-sized states bordering economic powerhouses might try a strategy of regional integration. Poor, small states could opt to fit into the division of labour by acting as tax havens or selling their flags to shipping lines that use them as flags of convenience. Some states can exploit their knowledge base and use social programmes to shield their workers, while others attempt to gain a cost advantage by suppressing the cost of labour.

Feminists note that employment in the labour market is segregated by gender. Particular tasks are assigned to men and other tasks are assigned to women. Women are clustered in poorly paid, unpaid and insecure forms of work. They are rarely able to reach positions of power. An example of this glaring inequality can be seen in photographs of G-7 finance ministers, heads of state or business leaders. A woman's face rarely appears among the pictures of men in dark suits. Women are noticeable by their absence. Women are excluded from many occupations by a variety of obstacles and tools. These tools include the law, tradition, unequal educational opportunities, lack of public services and violence. From a gender perspective the division of labour is created by unequal power relations and is reproduced on a worldwide basis (Peterson and Runyan, 1993).

Major developments

There have been two major developments in the division of labour. The first has been the change and spread of different production processes. The way that things are produced has gone through a number of changes and this influences how people fit into the work process. One major change was the introduction of Fordism in the early 20th century, while the second change occurred at the end of the century with the introduction of more flexible work organizations. The second major development has been the move from an international division of labour to a global division of labour. This has reduced, but not eliminated, the connection between type of work and geographical location.

Changes in the production process

Although the benefits of a division of labour were known before the 1800s it was the industrial revolution and the application of modern factory manage- ment techniques which greatly boosted productivity. One man, Fredrick Taylor, had so much influence that a form of production was named after him – Taylorism. Taylorism refers to the practice of scientific management (Braverman, 1974, pp. 85–137). Similar to Smith, Taylor advocated the breaking down of production into individual tasks. He conducted detailed studies on the factory process and then recommended particular changes. In a famous case Taylor used a stopwatch to time the shovelling of iron and made changes to improve the amount that could be shovelled by one person in a day from 12 to 47 tons.

Key to Taylorism was management control over worker time. Managers concentrated knowledge and power in their hands. Workers were viewed as beasts of burden who had to be instructed in particular tasks and closely supervised. The result was that workers were increasingly deskilled as they fitted into the factory system. Workers could be substituted into a series of simplified tasks.

The person most famous for successfully applying and elaborating upon Taylorism was the car-maker Henry Ford. Ford engaged in the mass produc- tion of automobiles on factory lines. He standardized car models so that they could be made more quickly and cheaply. Advertisements for the Model T car promised customers they could have cars in any colour as long as it was black! The working conditions in Ford's factories were very difficult. He would often put the strongest workers at the beginning of the assembly line forcing all others to keep up to the fastest pace. On a more positive note, Ford introduced the $5 a day wage, which was higher than what his competi- tors paid. The wage was designed to attract workers and also offered the possibility that workers might one day be able to afford the products they were producing. It opened the door to mass consumption to go along with mass production.

Some approaches to political economy, such as the Regulation School, label the post-1945 economic system in the advanced industrialized countries 'Fordism' (Dunford, 2000). Fordism combined the model of mass production (the factory system) with mass consumption. Mass consumption was achieved by redistributing income from the wealthy to a broader base of citizens through programmes such as progressive taxation, old-age benefits, public healthcare and education, and unemployment insurance. Organized labour played a role in the system as it negotiated wage increases for its members as productivity in the economy increased.

The Fordist system contributed to a boom in Western economies in the 1950s and 1960s as the volume of consumer products exploded. However, by the 1970s, Fordism came under increasing pressure from inflation and the emergence of a new international division of labour. Competition from new producers in industrializing countries put pressure upon national Fordist arrangements. In the 1980s the Fordist method of production was increasingly challenged by what was variously called flexible specialization, lean production or Toyotaism (after the Japanese car company). These new methods emphasized a form of production that was more flexible than Fordism. For example, just-in-time inventory systems meant that companies would not stockpile parts; they would order them and receive them just-in-time for production. Workers were encouraged to work in teams, learn a variety of skills and abandon traditional union structures in favour of work teams or company unions.

Today we have a mixture of production methods in the global economy. Many automobile manufacturers have moved to Japanese production methods and more flexible specialization. However, the mass-production factory system is alive and well in many old industries such as textiles and some newer service industries. For example, call centres where workers are closely monitored and follow particular scripts operate on a rigid Fordist factory model.

From the new international to the global division of labour

Beginning in the 1970s, a number of people noticed a new international division of labour (Frobel, Heinrichs and Kreye, 1980). This observation reflected the development of manufacturing in the newly industrializing countries (NICs) such as Brazil, Mexico and the 'Four Tigers' – Hong Kong, Singapore, Taiwan and South Korea. It seemed to be reversing the historical trend where non-Western states supplied raw materials for Western states.

As discussed in Chapter 7, a combination of factors helps to explain the geographical dispersal of corporate activity to other parts of the world (Dicken, 1998). Technological change made it possible to split up the manufacturing process and locate different operations in different countries. Improved transport and communication systems allowed for better control of this diffusion of manufacturing. Another factor was the combination of growing costs in developed states and low-cost production sited in developing states. The Fordist system in industrialized countries resulted in rising wage rates for labour. In industrializing states, labour costs were low and efforts were made to keep them low through labour suppression or the creation of export processing zones. Many states in the developing world pursued an active policy of supporting industrialization and exporting to the developed world.

In advanced industrialized states, the growth of manufacturing in developing states caused some concern. The Fordist compromise of distributing benefits to workers came under increasing pressure. Locked in cost competition, some workers were forced to accept wage reductions and some manufacturing operations closed down. Workers were urged to be more flexible in terms of working longer or more varied hours. Factories closed in many industrial areas such as the north-east of the United States and a vigorous debate was launched about whether countries were 'deindustrializing'.

By the beginning of the 21st century the process of globalization was facilitating the creation of a global division of labour. As outlined earlier in the chapter, geographic space was coming to be less and less a factor in determining the location of production. Patterns of inequality were still massive and growing, but pockets of different types of activity could be found in most parts of the world. To be clear, the concept of a global division of labour does not suggest that all the people of the world are involved in the same labour market. Indeed, even those sympathetic to the notion of global labour estimate that only 15 per cent of the world's population is actively engaged in such activity (Harrod and O'Brien, 2002, p. 13). Yet, this is a significant and growing group. More and more people are influenced by the global economy and must adjust their behaviour to take account of forces beyond national borders. Some specific groups benefit greatly from this trend and push for more rapid liberal globalization (see Box 9.1).

Another interesting dimension of the global division of labour is migration. People have migrated for thousands of years, but new forms of transportation and communication make it easier to travel long distances and allow migrants to maintain contact with their home community. There are about 150 million people (3 per cent of the world's population) living in countries other than the one of their birth (Stalker, 2001, p. 8). This includes people who have settled permanently in new countries, contract workers on limited stays, professionals working for TNCs, undocumented workers (illegal immigrants), refugees and asylum seekers. Although migrants are a small percentage of the world's population, they play a vital role in the global economy (see Table 9.1 for the rise in remittances globally).

Box 9.1 Globalizing elites

A division of labour has implications for those people at the top of the income scale as well as the majority of people who live in poverty. Groups which benefit from a more liberal economic system and increasing capital mobility press for further liberalization and integration. A set of globalizing elites agitate for public policy which will allow them to continue to accumulate wealth at a rapid rate. They have political, economic and cultural orientations which favour global rather than national economic activity and lifestyles. Sklair (2001) has argued that groups of TNC executives, state and international bureaucrats, technical professionals, merchants and media officials form a transnational capitalist class. A major concern of these elites is to balance the continued opening of the global economy with the need for social stability (Gill, 2003). Globalization processes highlight and reinforce inequality, but they also provide marginalized groups with the opportunities to build alliances and challenge their subordinate position. Thus, the World Economic Forum, which serves as a meeting place for globalizing elites, is now challenged by the presence of a World Social Forum inhabited by non-elites seeking different forms of globalization.

Table 9.1 Remittances from migrants (billion dollars)

Year	Total	Developing countries	Developed countries
2002	62	50	12
2004	232	167	65
2007	327	251	76

Sources: Data from Ratha and Xu (2008); Ratha, Mohapatra and Silwal (2009).

In many developing states, the money that migrants send home from their employment in developed countries plays a significant economic role. Remittances are now larger than FDI and foreign aid in many countries. Major surges have flowed to the emerging economies like China, India and Mexico. For example, India received $27 billion in 2000, China received 25.7 billion and Mexican migrants sent home $25 billion (Ratha and Mohapatra, 2007). See Table 9.2 for statistics on significance of the remittance flows to developing countries.

Table 9.2   Remittance flows to developing countries, 2002–7
(billion dollars)

INFLOWS	2002	2003	2004	2005	2006	2007
Developing countries	116	143	163	194	226	251
East Asia and Pacific	29	35	39	47	53	59
Europe and central Asia	14	16	23	32	39	47
Latin America and Caribbean	28	35	42	48	57	61
Middle East and North Africa	15	20	23	24	27	29
South Asia	24	30	29	33	40	44
Sub-Saharan Africa	5	6	8	10	11	12
World	170	206	234	266	303	337

Sources: Data from Ratha and Xu (2008); Ratha, Mohapatra and Silwal (2009).

There are a number of positive economic benefits associated with remittances sent by migrants to their home country. Remittances increase a country's foreign exchange and have a positive impact on savings and investment, leading to higher human capital accumulation, investment and entrepreneurship. Furthermore, remittances can be better targeted to the needs of the poor than official aid or foreign direct investment; and is positively correlated with reducing the level and severity of poverty.

Developed countries are becoming more and more dependent upon migrant labour and immigration to fulfil their labour needs. Foreign workers are in demand because of two developments. First, the birth rate is so low in developed states that their population is shrinking. Second, the population is rapidly ageing, which means that there will not be enough workers to pay for the pensions and healthcare demanded by the older generation. It is estimated that if Europe wants to retain a healthy ratio of workers to retired people it will need to allow almost 159 million new immigrants into its territory by 2025 (*World Guide 2001/2002*, 2001, p. 21). Without increased immigration almost 47 per cent of Europeans would be retired in 2025.

The increasing importance of migrant workers and immigration has raised a number of significant issues in the global political economy (Stalker, 2001). Migrant workers often have poor employment conditions and are subject to abuse or exploitation. Social tensions can arise in receiving states because native workers or citizens may feel themselves under economic or cultural threat from foreign workers. Since migrants play a crucial economic role in the states that they leave and the states that they work in, it is essential that mechanisms are developed to deal with such issues.

Key issues

Migration is just one of many pressing issues surrounding the global division of labour. In this section we will focus on three others: the ways in which two huge, populous countries are becoming increasingly integrated into the global division of labour; the struggle over workers' rights in the global economy; and the relationship between workers' rights and global stability.

Global restructuring: the rise of China and India

A significant development in the global division of labour is the increasing integration of the world's two most populous countries, China and India, into the global economy. The adjustments required of workers in these countries and other countries as production and service provision move across state boundaries are substantial. They cause friction within and between countries.

China is the subject of immense attention because of the large share of foreign direct investment it attracts and the value of goods it exports to Western states. The label 'made in China' is found on an ever-increasing number of products. However, the rise of China as a centre of production is a complicated affair with a variety of implications.

Beginning in 1978 the Chinese communist government began a policy of selectively integrating some parts of its economy into the global economy. Special economic zones were created in several coastal areas to attract foreign investment and spur economic growth. The government later began a process of reducing the size of state-owned enterprises and forcing them to run on a more efficient basis. Although millions of jobs have been created in the special economic zones, millions of jobs have also been lost in the state sector and other parts of the economy. The majority of the people who lived in the countryside were excluded from the benefits of economic reforms. Foreign investment poured into the special economic zones and generated considerable growth. Indeed, China became the leading destination for FDI in the developing world in the 1990s.

The potential wealth and market share that China represents gives leverage to the Chinese government in its negotiations with foreign TNCs. For example, in return for the privilege of locating its search engine within China, Google agreed to censor websites objectionable to the Chinese government. Admitting that this censorship ran counter to its corporate ethics, Google claimed it would be worse not to offer Chinese users any information (Watts, 2006). Google joined Yahoo! and Microsoft in helping the government create the 'great firewall of China' by preventing Chinese citizens' access to sites dealing critically with Tibet, Taiwan and the Tiananmen Square massacre. Another example of Chinese state influence over TNCs was the ability of the Chinese government to extract a promise that European-based Airbus would set up production factories in China as part of a deal to sell planes to Chinese airlines.

China's ability to attract large amounts of foreign investment has increased employment and earned foreign exchange, but generates its own sets of problems. One issue is the impact on its own internal division of labour. The growth of special economic zones has created a growing gap between urban dwellers and those in the countryside. This in turn has caused the largest mass migration of people in history. Since economic reforms were introduced it is estimated that over 150 million people migrated from rural to urban areas. This figure may rise to 500 million by 2020. One city in China, Shanghai, has two-thirds as many migrants from the countryside (3 million) as there were Irish immigrants to the United States over the 100 years from 1820 to 1830 (4.5 million) (Yardley, 2004). The mass movement of Chinese workers poses large problems for government authorities. Many migrants are exploited by employers who fail to pay wages. Many do not have access to adequate housing or healthcare services. In the countryside economic conditions continue to stagnate generating resentment against the growing inequality of economic development.

Although it is not possible to gather accurate statistics, unrest amongst peasants and workers in China appears to be increasing in the early 21st century (Cody, 2004, 2005). Peasants often confront local Communist Party officials that are unsympathetic to their plight. Workers are unable to form independent trade unions and must rely upon the communist-controlled All China Federation of Trade Unions. In many cases union officials represent the Party's interest in pleasing foreign investors or they may even work for the company in question. Because of a lack of legitimate means to express dissent and articulate alternative working and living arrangements, worker and peasant frustration often explodes into violent and spontaneous demonstrations.

Another aspect of China's rapid integration into the global economy is the fact that the control of much of this production rests in the hands of foreign-controlled TNCs. Indeed, the increase of Chinese production is often simply the result of shifting economic activity from other parts of Asia. Asian, and to a lesser degree Western, investors have moved production out of East and South-east Asian states into China. Computers formerly manufactured in Taiwan, textiles sewn in Hong Kong and electronics made in Japan are now made in mainland China. Whereas it is true that the US trade deficit with

China has increased greatly, its trade deficit with Asia as a whole has not. This indicates that Asian manufacturers are using China as their assembly plant. The majority of exports out of China (60–70 per cent) are controlled by non-Chinese corporations or Chinese corporations sub-contracting for foreign corporations. While Chinese corporations make profits and millions of Chinese workers have secured jobs, China has not yet been able to develop global brands as the Japanese did in the 1970s. It has primarily been other Asian (Taiwanese, Japanese, Hong Kong, Korean) and Western TNCs that have reaped the profits of low Chinese production costs.

This has implications for the debate over whether or not Chinese manufacturing is undermining global labour standards. While Chinese suppression of independent labour unions does undermine labour standards in export industries, foreign TNCs must also accept some responsibility. Some foreign TNCs sign contracts with Chinese-based companies demanding they supply constantly cheaper products. The demand to 'roll back prices' leaves Chinese producers with very thin profit margins and an incentive to limit or reduce the amount of money paid to workers. The dilemma for Chinese companies is that raising prices to give more money to workers may well result in losing contracts from large Western retailers, such as Wal-Mart. Thus, consumer demand in Western countries for cheaper and cheaper products gives an incentive for Western TNCs to demand less costly products, which squeezes the wage levels and working conditions of Chinese workers.

The rise of Chinese manufacturing also puts tremendous pressure on all those countries and workers producing labour-intensive products similar to China (Breslin, 2005). Western workers have felt the pinch of Chinese competition, but it is an even greater challenge to workers in developing states. Mexico's strategy of using low wages to attract investment and become the assembly plant for North America is undermined by even lower-cost Chinese labour. Attempts by Indonesia and the Philippines to attract foreign investment face an uphill battle against mainland China. The elimination of the Multi-Fibre Agreement on textiles means that many developing countries that had invested in textiles as a development strategy risk losing their economic activity to China. An emerging power like India must also pay attention to Chinese competition.

The story of global competition for wages does not end there, however, because even China is not immune to the threat of capital leaving for cheaper labour. In 2005 and 2006 foreign investors in the Pearl Delta region of China began to complain of a labour shortage for their factories. There were plenty of workers available; the problem was that there were not enough workers of the preferred type. Factory owners wanted young women with high school education willing to work for low wages in very poor working conditions. Increasing resistance to this type of work from Chinese women threatened the profits of some China-based businesses, raising the spectre that capital might move on to Vietnam or Cambodia (Yardley and Barboza, 2005).

The world's second most populous country, India, has also become more integrated into the global economy since its government began a liberalization programme in the early 1990s (Jenkins, 2003). Whereas China has excelled as an assembly plant, India has enjoyed international success in the business services sector. Drawing upon the skills of Indians who are well educated and proficient in English, TNCs have established businesses located in India which provide a wide range of services for Western companies. Call centres handle all manner of customer services such as dealing with customer complaints or booking airfares for Western airlines. Data-processing activity for North American law or insurance companies can be shipped overnight to India and the completed work returned the next morning. Printing and proof-reading services for academic books can be done by Indians and shipped back to Britain.

The sub-contracting of these types of services to India (and many other countries) has been termed 'outsourcing'. While Chinese production threatens to undermine blue collar employment in industrialized countries, Indian outsourcing competes with white and pink collar employment. Service jobs can be shipped 'offshore' to cheaper Indian workers. In addition, the US government approved changes to its immigration laws in the 1990s which permitted work visas for information technology specialists to work within the United States itself. The increased competition to US workers from Indian service sector workers led to the invention of a new English verb: 'Bangalored'. Bangalore is a city in India which has served as a centre of the growth in information technology industry. To be 'Bangalored' means to lose one's job due to outsourcing.

The insertion of parts of India's economy into the global services market has generated political conflict both in the United States and India. In the United States, proponents of outsourcing stress the competitive advantages US companies can gain from cheaper global services. Workers who have lost their jobs or feel threatened by increased economic security attack outsourcing. During the 2004 US Presidential election the Democratic Party raised outsourcing as an issue of concern to workers and attacked the Republican Party for supporting corporate outsourcing strategies. In India, Hindu nationalist parties trumpeted high-technology successes as evidence of a rejuvenated and competitive country (Chakravartty, 2006). Other Indians worried that the government's emphasis on supporting high-technology and service industries came at the expense of helping the majority of India's population, which relies on small-scale agricultural production. These people highlight issues such as the large number of farmer suicides caused by rural desperation and the poor working conditions which requires mainly female call centre operators to work nights so that they can answer calls in the North American daytime. Thus, outsourcing became an election issue in India as well as in the United States. In India, however, the concern was with the balance of the new economy with other areas of the economy.

The ongoing integration of up to 2 billion people into the global workforce generates immense challenges and opportunities. A deepening global division of labour simultaneously increases productivity and offers the possibility of people in developing and developed world gaining from that increase. China's entry into the global economy has lifted millions of Chinese out of poverty and allowed Western workers to purchase many products at cheaper prices. However, these transformations also threaten social stability as inequality grows within countries and shifting manufacturing production reduces employment in some countries and regions. Workers from many different countries are pitted against each other in a competition for investment and wages. The challenge is whether states can develop mechanisms to redistribute wealth and manage social dislocation fast enough to maintain social order and harmony.

The integration of China and India into the global division of labour also raises questions from a power politics perspective. As China and India upgrade their economic capacity they accumulate wealth and power. This change in absolute and relative capabilities may cause insecurity among their neighbours, leading to conflict. For example, South Korea and Japan may feel threatened by growing Chinese military power. The United States might also see China as a potential military and economic rival. India and China might also have conflicts as they compete for investment and leadership of developing countries. Whether one takes a perspective that focuses upon social inequalities or on state power, the absorption of China and India into the global division of labour is significant.

The struggle for workers' rights in a global economy

Over the past two decades most international economic agreements such as the revitalization of European integration through the Single Market project and monetary union, the North American Free Trade Agreement (NAFTA), the creation of the WTO and the attempt to negotiate a Multilateral Agreement on Investment at the OECD have been designed to liberalize economic activity. In each of these cases non-business social interests have attempted to influence the content of the agreements. However, the attempt to bolster labour rights in a globalizing and liberalizing economic world is extremely difficult. Although a wide range of groups have joined the struggle, they face two difficult questions (O'Brien, 2002). The first question is: 'How do you regulate transnational capital?' The second question is: 'What is the appropriate relationship between equity groups located in different areas of the world?'

The first question of regulating capital concerns how people can create rules to place the activity of businesses that operate across state borders in a broader social context. How can they be prevented from undermining labour and environmental conditions? Corporate behaviour can be influenced through two different mechanisms. Firms can be regulated by states or by pressure in the market. With regard to state regulation, this can take place through the extraterritorial regulation of powerful states or the application of rules in multilateral institutions. Extraterritorial regulation involves a state demanding that corporations which have headquarters in their state or are engaged in economic activity in their state conduct global business according to the home state's rules. It sets the preferences of a particular state as the benchmark for corporate behaviour in other countries. In practice this means that corporate activity must conform to the desires of particular interests in advanced industrialized states.

Depending upon one's position on a particular issue, extraterritorial jurisdiction can have negative or positive effects. Most people would agree that developed states which prosecuted their corporations for using slave labour in foreign countries were doing a good thing. However, other prohibitions are viewed more negatively. Numerous states have objected to such activity in measures such as the US Helms–Burton legislation forbidding trade with Cuba. Since the United States is engaged in economic warfare with Cuba, it threatens corporations that do business in the United States with penalties if they trade with Cuba. Some Canadian executives of Canadian companies cannot enter the United States because they would be arrested for the economic activity of their companies in Cuba.

Extraterritorial rules reflect the balance of power within a particular state rather than a consensus of the international community. Since the rules are set nationally and not negotiated between a group of states they are idiosyncratic. The United States' single-minded pursuit of economic warfare against Cuba is incomprehensible to most other states. However, because the United States is such a powerful actor, its particular views have considerable impact. This is not a recipe for a global system with common rules.

It is because of the negative implications in unilateral extraterritorial regulation that multilateral arrangements involving a negotiated standard between numerous states are often viewed as preferable. However, multilateral agreements are difficult to negotiate and suffer from the accusation that they also benefit the strongest powers. This is illustrated in the debate about linking labour standards to the operation of the WTO.

Following the creation of the WTO many elements of the international labour movement, such as the International Confederation of Free Trade Unions (ICFTU), sought to have their concerns addressed in the organization. The international labour movement's goal (as represented by the main international confederations of trade unions) for the WTO is to have core labour standards (or a social clause) brought into its purview (O'Brien *et al.*, 2000, pp. 67–108). The social clause would commit states to respect seven crucial conventions of the ILO (Conventions 87, 98, 29, 105, 100, 111, 138). These conventions provide for: freedom of association, the right to collective bargaining, abolition of forced labour, prevention of discrimination in employment and a minimum age for employment. The key to having the conventions as part of the WTO is that for the first time they would become enforceable and not depend upon the whims of individual states. In contrast to the ILO's reliance on moral argument, the WTO has the ability to enforce compliance. In order to achieve this goal, groups such as the ICFTU and affiliates including the AFL-CIO have pressured the United States and the European Union into raising the issue of core labour standards at the WTO. They argued that continued support for trade liberalization in developed states required a minimum floor for workers' rights.

The labour movement has been unable to secure enforceable labour rights in international institutions mainly because of the opposition of a combination of liberal states, developing countries and business associations. Leaders in many liberal states argue that economic growth raises labour standards and any interference in trade for labour reasons would lower the gains from trade. Many leaders in developing states have expressed a fear that labour standards would only be used as a form of protection by developed states against developing countries. Finally, businesses remain opposed, fearing both a rise in protectionism and a reduction in their profits.

In addition to resistance from state and corporate elites, there are elements of the labour movement which oppose both the idea that core labour standards should be part of the WTO and the existence of the WTO itself. For example, the linkage between labour standards and the WTO was rejected in two national conferences of Indian unions in March and October 1995. Delegates expressed fears that the social clause initiative was driven by protectionist desires in northern countries. The Indian union suggestion was that, rather than working through the WTO, workers should push for a United Nations Labour Rights Convention and the establishment of National Labour Rights Commissions (ALU, 1995).

The difficulty in achieving state regulation of corporations has led to attempts to influence corporate behaviour by introducing, monitoring and enforcing codes of conduct. In Western countries in recent years, there has been an increased consumer awareness and concern about the methods used in production. This has spawned a series of campaigns against particular corporations by consumer and union groups. Such activity is part of a civil society campaign to 'Think Globally and Punish Locally' (Rodman, 1998). In college campuses across the United States, the largest student activist movement since the anti-apartheid campaign has formed around the issue of sweatshop labour. A national movement, 'Students Against Sweatshops', has lobbied for improved working conditions and labour rights in companies that supply products to universities. It has also put the question of ethics and the possibility of profiting from an ethical policy on the agenda of many corporations and in business publications.

Codes of conduct are meant to set basic principles for the behaviour of TNCs (and their sub-contractors) with respect to their labour practices and environmental policies. In some cases firms are willing partners in implementing such codes. For example, the Levi-Strauss Jean company's code of conduct is reproduced in union literature as an illustration of a TNC working with the union movement (ICFTU, 1996a, p. 59). Levi-Strauss is notable not just for its code of conduct banning labour exploitation, but also for its withdrawal from states operating extreme forms of authoritarian industrial relations, such as Burma and China in 1992.

One prominent union strategy is to select a particularly serious abuse of workers' rights, highlight the abuses in the media and attempt to pressure governments to legislate, consumers to boycott and corporations to change behaviour. Good examples are the campaigns against child labour and labour conditions in Far Eastern toy factories (ICFTU, 1995a). Another example is the campaign against child labour in the manufacture of footballs (ICFTU, 1996b). Prior to the start of the 1996 European Football Championships, the ICFTU revealed that footballs endorsed by the governing football association, FIFA, were made in Pakistan using child labour. This involved cooperation between the ICFTU, Norwegian unions who supplied the camera crew, British unions in the country of the championships and Pakistani unions on site in the targeted country. The adverse publicity resulted in FIFA adopting a new code of practice and more attention being given to labour issues around a key social/sporting event.

The pressure from organized labour and consumer groups in developed countries has forced the hands of government and international organizations as well as TNCs. For example, in April 1995, US President Bill Clinton announced a voluntary code of conduct covering business ethics and workers' rights for US companies working abroad. In an attempt to reinvigorate its role in the labour standards issue, the ILO has announced its intention to push for a global social label. The proposal is in response to the numerous private initiatives in social labelling. The Secretary General of the United Nations has also become involved by bringing together selected corporations, NGOs and trade unions to agree to labour and environmental standards. His initiative is called the Global Compact.

Market-based solutions have recently been favoured because of the hurdles in establishing agreement between states. The proliferation of codes and the ensuing debate have focused a spotlight on the plight of workers in many countries (Pearson and Seyfang, 2001). Although one can point to achievements of such activity, the fact is that it is a second-best strategy: it occurs because state regulation has failed (Kearney, 1999). Market activity is not seen as sufficient in national societies because of the inefficiency of effort required to launch continuing citizen campaigns. There are problems with collecting and distributing information, mobilizing citizens and the need for constant vigilance. A legal process and institution is needed to regularize activity and enforce general rules. If market-based activity is seen as inadequate for domestic purposes, why would it prove sufficient on a global scale?

In practice, there are a multitude of strategies from market to state-based initiatives seeking to address the labour standards issue. Some civil society actors have been successful in raising awareness, while the threat of state action (either unilaterally or multilaterally) has been useful to focus the minds of corporate and state elites. The challenge is to work out a suitable combination of these strategies (O'Brien, 2002).

The division of labour and global stability

It may seem strange to people living in the present era, but there was a time when the state of people's working conditions was thought to have an influence on international peace and security. Following the Russian Revolution and the end of the First World War, Western leaders were so worried about labour unrest contributing to conflict between states that they created an international organization to deal with labour issues – the ILO. The goal of the ILO was to ameliorate working conditions so that labour unrest would subside and communist agitation would fall on infertile ground.

It is time to once again consider the relationship between labour unrest and global order. This can be done in both liberal and critical theoretical traditions. From a liberal perspective, labour can be viewed as one of many domestic interest groups that make international cooperation very difficult (Milner, 1997). From a critical perspective, labour is part of a broad social force that seeks to challenge the existing basis of international order (Cox, 1986). Numerous labour-oriented groups are offering a challenge to the basic liberal principles that make up the global order. Here we'll consider just three groups of workers mobilizing to challenge the basis of global order: workers in the United States, those in newly industrializing countries and peasant farmers (O'Brien, 2000).

In the past 30 years, US labour has moved from being an unquestioning ally in the spread of US hegemony to being a growing obstacle to further liberalization and internationalization. US labour has not abandoned the state for worker internationalism, but it is rethinking its position. This raises doubts about the social base in the United States for maintaining leadership in the liberalization process.

In the immediate post-war era, US labour was firmly engaged in the politics of productivity (Maier, 1977). The politics of productivity involved subsuming class conflict by ensuring that growth and productivity gains were distributed across the economy. It reflected a belief that proper technical management of the economy would create the conditions for prosperity which would eliminate the need for harmful distributional battles. It was a method of neutralizing labour opposition by integrating unionized workers into a division of economic spoils. Internationally, organized labour played a crucial part in laying the groundwork for today's process of neoliberal globalization. US labour took a leading role in marginalizing radical workers' organizations in Latin America, Asia and Western Europe (Cox, 1977; Radosh, 1969). This ground-clearing work facilitated the expansion of US business and resulted in labour becoming an actor in the globalization process (Herod, 1997).

However, the rise of neoliberal governments in the United States and Britain, accompanied by a business offensive against workers, led to the ejection of labour from the governing coalition (Rupert, 1995a, pp. 167–207). This marginalization of moderate worker organizations corresponded with a movement by US elites to separate their destiny from the rest of the nation (Lasch, 1995; Reich, 1992). As the polarization of US society continues and the revolt of the elites is clearer, it becomes more practical for workers to look to the international realm for solidarity and assistance. In the US context, Rupert (1995b) has argued that the NAFTA debate may be a watershed in organized labour's acceptance of the dominant brand of liberalism. Not only did labour break with US corporations over the issue of linking workers' rights to regional trade agreements, but it also openly opposed a Democratic Party leadership and a sitting Democratic President. A second notable change in the policies of organized labour was the attempt to work with environmental and consumer groups to forge a common position on this element of economic policy. Finally, the AFL-CIO was forced to cultivate relations with the emerging independent Mexican unions rather than rely on the Mexican government-sponsored CTM union. The CTM proved adequate for US workers' interest in the Cold War when the fight was against communism, but allies in the fight against transnational exploitation would have to be found in unions controlled by their members.

In what ways might a more oppositional US labour movement influence the global political economy? One method is by changing the agenda for international institution-building. At the multilateral level, labour organizations have complicated the WTO's plan to extend liberalization into new sectors and regions as they press for inclusion of core labour standards (O'Brien, 1998). Labour organizations are pushing the IMF and the World Bank to revise the neoliberal content of their structural adjustment lending (ICFTU, 1995b). In the case of the World Bank lending to South Korea, this has resulted in provisions aimed at offering unprecedented (if limited) protection for workers (World Bank, 1998). At the regional level, an alliance of convenience between labour and right-wing populism stalled US approval for the expansion of NAFTA. A second method is shaping the international economic environment through corporate policy. In concert with other social groups labour has increased pressure on multinationals to change their investment locations or method of conducting business. This is particularly evident in the campaigns for company codes of conduct to temper poor labour and environmental practices mentioned above.

The recent, hesitant transformation of US labour may be part of a new internationalism for a broad spectrum of groups concerned with labour issues. A number of authors (Moody, 1997; Waterman, 1998) have raised the possibility of a new internationalism based upon transnational networks of labour activists inside and outside unions. These networks form alliances with other social movements in the North and South to offer an alternative prescription for economic, political and social order.

In newly industrializing countries, the 1997 financial crisis in East and South-east Asia placed the issue of workers' rights and activities firmly on the analytical agenda. The Asian development model, sometimes sympathetically described as paternalistic authoritarianism (Pye, 1988), was thought to prosper because, in contrast to Latin American authoritarian models, development was more egalitarian. Workers were often coerced, but they shared in the benefits of growth (in this view). Stability was ensured by growth. Suddenly, economic growth vanished, at least temporarily. Workers in South Korea faced the prospect of unemployment in a non-welfare state. The Korean state was forced to create new welfare provisions in order to deal with potential unrest in the new democracy (Huck-Ju, 2001). In Indonesia the economic collapse was more serious and eventually led to a transformation of the political system.

The social chaos arising from the financial meltdown in Asia and the reaction of workers to that chaos is a factor in determining regional and global stability. The World Bank recognized the danger of social disintegration when Bank President James Wolfensohn announced that approximately 60 per cent of the $16 billion it had promised in financial assistance would be directed to 'protecting the poor and providing a social safety net' (IHT, 1998). Social unrest was viewed as an imminent danger to internationally backed plans for financial restructuring. The threat to the IMF's and World Bank's rescue packages did not come from the political and economic elites of the target states, but from those who bear the costs of such restructuring – the working population.

As important as the role of workers in Asian states may be, there is another significant labour issue confronting the global political economy. To use McMichael's (1997) terms, it is the 'agrarian question'. The agrarian question concerns the implications of replacing peasant-based agriculture with capitalist agriculture. Although this was a subject of grave concern in Western states in the 19th century and attention to peasant affairs was also raised during social revolutions in China, Cuba and Vietnam in the middle of the 20th century, the agrarian question has not been posed again until very recently. It has re-emerged in response to the threat that liberalization of agriculture poses to billions of peasants around the world.

Slowly, but surely, a global peasant alliance is emerging to challenge the dominant notions of liberalization, consumption and environmental destruction. The most dramatic event has been the peasant and aboriginal rebellion in the southern Mexican state of Chiapas (Reding, 1994). Although the rebellion draws upon a historical legacy of oppression, it was clearly linked to steps taken by the Mexican government to liberalize agricultural landholdings in the run-up to the NAFTA. Local concerns were linked to broader developments in IPE. The Zapatistas have been quick to exploit modern technology to broadcast their cause worldwide and have begun the task of forging links with similarly minded groups in other parts of the world.

The Peoples' Global Action (PGA) against 'Free' Trade and the World Trade Organization is another example of a peasant-based anti-imperialist grouping. The PGA is an instrument for coordination which brings together peoples' movements to oppose trade liberalization (PGA, 1997). The PGA organizes conferences approximately three months before the biannual Ministerial Meetings of the World Trade Organization. Conferences are used to update the PGA manifesto and to coordinate global and local action against free trade. The conference committee for the February 1998 event included groups such as the Frente Zapatista de Liberación Nacional (FZLN) from Mexico, Karnataka State Farmers' Association (KRRS) from India, Movemento sem Terra (MST) from Brazil and the Peasant Movement of the Philippines (KMP). The PGA is committed to non-violent civil disobedience and a confrontational attitude in pursuit of its opposition to free trade. It represents a constituency firmly in opposition to dominant trends in the global political economy.

This analysis is not arguing that workers or peasants in the developing world will serve as the basis for a revolutionary movement to overthrow capitalism. There are certainly many peasants in the world, but the power they face in economic and military terms is immense. It is possible, however, to identify these groups as offering potentially significant resistance to the liberalization project. They represent a key force in world politics, but it is one usually hidden from view because of the standard IPE analytical categories. Analysis of the international order that ignores them would be incomplete and flawed.

Conclusion

The political fall-out from the financial and economic crisis of 2008–9 may once again raise the issue of worker welfare and political action onto the agenda. A person's place in the global division of labour has a great impact upon how long they will live, how much they consume and what kind of health they can enjoy. The existence and growth of massive inequalities around the world is literally a question of life and death to millions of people. At the same time that such problems proliferate, people are active in forming themselves into trade unions, community associations, political parties and non-governmental organizations to combat the negative effects of a growing global division of labour. They seek to increase equality and influence the division of labour to the benefit of the world's populations. Readers of this book are part of that process in their activity as citizens and consumers.

Chapter 10

Gender

This book has already alluded to the gendered nature of the global political economy. Distinctions between men and women have played an important role in the history of the development of the global political economy (Part II) and in all of the key structures already examined in Part III, namely, trade, production, finance and labour. Gender considerations are also relevant to the succeeding chapters, particularly those on development, the environment and security. The aim of this chapter is to take a systematic look at the gender dimension of the global political economy.

We begin by providing some definitions and background about gender and feminist approaches to International Relations and IPE. The theoretical perspectives section outlines how and why attention to the relationship between men, women and the global economy is important for the study of political economy. The third section of the chapter examines the integration of women into the world economy through a discussion of female employment trends. It follows this survey with an exploration of the internationalization of global gender policy through a focus on the evolution of global concern with the role of women in the world economy. The final section discusses three key issues facing women in the contemporary economy. These issues are the feminization of poverty, the globalization of reproductive work and the impact of restructuring and globalization.

Definitions and background

In everyday speech there is often a tendency to use the terms 'gender' and 'sex' interchangeably. This merging of the terms creates confusion between biology and social roles. It is now widely accepted that gender is a social construction and not a natural state. In the words of Jill Steans, 'gender refers not to what men and women are biologically, but to the ideological and material relations which exist between them' (1998, p. 10). This distinction is repeated by Peterson and Runyan when they state, 'Unlike sex (the biological distinction between males and females) gender refers to socially learned behaviours that distinguish between masculinity and femininity' (1993, p. 5). The central point made in these definitions is that women and men are different biologically but that this biological sex difference is not the same as the social distinctions made between men and women (see Box

Box 10.1   Feminization as devalorization

Among the insights of a gender analysis are the extensive implications of feminization as devalorization. This means that the characteristics often associated with femininity are valued less than those associated with masculinity. Femininity is associated with caring rather than controlling, submissiveness rather than aggression, feeling rather than thinking, weakness rather than strength, home life rather than public life. With feminine attributes valued less than masculine attributes anything that is feminized is then devalued. For example, labour markets are said to be increasingly feminized. This means more than just an increased number of women working in the labour market. It means that working conditions for the whole labour market are taking on the attributes of what was thought to be appropriate for female work – casual, informal, insecure, part-time and low-waged employment. The implications of devaluing the feminine are widespread because a whole series of groups, not just particular women can be feminized. The characteristics of femininity can be applied to whole races, groups of men, immigrants, refugees or other groups that are kept in a subordinate position. Thus feminists argue that denigrating the feminine can serve to support a whole series of hierarchies, not just those between men and women (Peterson, 2003).

10.1). To underscore this point consider the various ways in which the meanings attributed to masculinity and femininity vary across cultures and across historical time. The innate biological make-up of men and women does not change but the social expectations concerning appropriate behaviour, rights, responsibilities and resources are not static. While the roles ascribed to men and women vary across cultures and over time this does not mean that they are arbitrary or random. There are some features (e.g., assigning women the primary role in childcare), that seem to be common in many societies. Moreover, the construction of masculinity as superior to femininity in terms of power and access to resources also appears constant throughout history (Peterson and Runyan, 1993, pp. 5–6). Following from the above we will define gender as the socially constructed roles, behaviours, attitudes and values which communities and societies consider appropriate for men and women.

A focus on gender is important because it makes us aware of a key axis of power in society. Gender roles fundamentally shape production, distribution and consumption activities within states and across national borders. Gender thus plays a role in determining access to work, income, wealth, leisure, education, health, political power and decision-making (see Box 10.2). Comparative economic analysis reveals widespread discrimination on the basis of gender in education, health, economic opportunities and political participation (see Box 10.3). It has been established that gender bias may reduce economic growth (Dreze and Sen, 1989) thus providing an economic incentive and political rationale for targeting gender inequality. Many national governments and international organizations are currently focused on addressing problems stemming from gender inequality. Current

---

Box 10.2   Gender inequality facts

- About two-thirds of the 872 million illiterate people in developing countries are women.
- Adult illiteracy is almost exclusively a developing-country phenomenon.
- Of the 200 million women who become pregnant every year: 20 million pregnancies end in unsafe abortions; 585,000 women die from pregnancy-related causes; and a further 20 million women suffer severe or long-term disability.
- In the dry season women in Africa and Asia can spend between three and 28 hours per week collecting water for household use.
- Women's share of seats in national parliaments has increased worldwide since the early 1990s but women still only account for 16 per cent of legislators in national parliaments.

Sources: Wach and Reeves (2000); UNESCO (2004); UNFPA (2008).

Box 10.3   Measuring the global gender gap

The World Economic Forum's *Global Gender Gap Report 2008* (2008) provides a cross-country comparison of the gender gap in 130 countries. Using five indices – economic participation, educational attainment, political empowerment, and health and survival – the study used a scale of 0–1 to measure gender inequality where 0 = inequality, 1 = equality. Countries were then ranked using this scale. The top six countries were Norway (0.8239); Finland (0.8195); Sweden (0.8139), Iceland (0.804); Finland (0.7999); and New Zealand (0.7859). The bottom five countries were Benin (0.5582); Pakistan (0.5549); Saudi Arabia (0.5537); Chad (0.5290); and Yemen (0.4664).

Source: World Economic Forum (2008).

approaches to poverty and inequality focus on quantitative and qualitative measures (UNDP, 1995, pp. 72–86). A commitment to gender equality is necessary in order to transform the lives of women. It is the normative framework behind social and economic policies designed to reduce women's exclusion, invisibility and disempowerment.

A new wave of feminism originating in Western societies in the 1960s had far-reaching impacts culturally, politically and intellectually. One of its legacies was a revival of feminist scholarship concerned to explore the bases of gender inequality. The study of gender entered the discipline of International Relations and the sub-field of IPE through the work of feminist scholars. Unlike gender, which has a fairly settled meaning, no consensus exists on the definition of feminism. The absence of consensus on the definition of feminism is apparent in attempts to classify feminist theories. One classificatory scheme lists liberal feminism, Marxist feminism, radical feminism, socialist feminism, psychoanalytical and existential feminist thought, post-modern feminism and feminist critical theory (Steans, 1998, p. 16). Whitworth (1997, pp. 11–38), in her study of the application of feminist theory to International Relations, surveys a field comprising liberal feminism, radical feminism, feminist post-modernism and critical/feminist International Relations.

While recognizing the plurality of feminist discourses it is possible to discern two zones of agreement relevant to analysis of the global political economy. First, feminist scholars recognize that gender differences are also differences of power, and these differences permeate all aspects of social life. A focus on the gender dimension of the global political economy allows us to examine the roles women play in productive and reproductive relationships. Second, feminist research is committed to 'making a difference'. The goal of some feminists is meliorative change (i.e., change within the prevailing power structures), while others seek more revolutionary change and are interested in challenging the established order. At the heart of feminism is an agency of change. Whether committed to incremental change or emancipatory politics, feminist scholars recognize the close connections between activism, policy-making and academic research.

It has been argued that the feminist contribution to International Relations has been to highlight the ways in which the state and market are 'gendered by masculinist assumptions' (Youngs, 2004, p. 76). Feminists also show how the dominant approach 'ignores both women's realities and their active contributions to political and economic life' (Youngs, 2004, p. 76). Feminists have also demonstrated how a failure to examine gender 'obscures the interrelated social construction of male and female identities and roles' (Youngs, 2004, p. 76). These are important contributions and in the next section we review some of the major theoretical issues that have arisen in the context of explanations of the gendered nature of the global political economy.

Theoretical perspectives: GPE as if gender mattered

International Relations theorists are only one group of scholars seeking to explain the gendered nature of the global political economy. Economists, anthropologists, sociologists, political scientists and development specialists among others have all made relevant contributions. Indeed, it is arguable that these scholars have made more important and sustained analyses of global gender relations than IPE specialists. Research on gender and IPE thus has developed in two broad streams. On the one hand, it has evolved within the context of the conversation between IR theory and feminist scholars and in the internal debates in IPE as it strives to develop its identity. A second focus of research on gender and the global political economy emanates from feminist scholarship in the social sciences, particularly in economics and development studies. When feminist concerns first emerged in International Relations they encountered a discipline that was gender blind. The three paradigms (realism, liberalism and Marxism) excluded consideration of women and gender issues. Gender issues were rendered invisible and illegitimate by central assumptions contained in all three perspectives. Realism with its focus on the activities of states and its separation of the political and economic is incapable of theorizing social relations of power. Liberalism, which admitted the existence of actors other than the state, was also dominated by a focus on the realm of state interaction and a separation between state and market. The traditional Marxist approach to class conflict did not distinguish between male and female workers – that is, it did not develop gender as an analytical category. One notable exception was the development of Marxist feminist analyses. For example, Maria Mies (1998) explored the connection between capitalism and patriarchy in her analysis of the international division of labour.

The emergence of IPE as a distinct sub-field of International Relations held out the promise that the limited agenda of conventional IR scholarship would be extended (Allen, 1999). As we have noted in Chapter 1, when IPE emerged as a distinct sub-field of International Relations it was constructed as a debate between the three IR paradigms. Although IPE promised to break out of the straightjacket of IR assumptions, many of these were carried into its own framework. Conventional IPE has limited (if any) engagement with feminist scholarship and gender issues. IPE directs attention to economic structures and processes and is open to investigating the importance of firms, social movements, civil society and international organizations, but usually not gender. While it would be correct to acknowledge that IPE scholars have extended the scope of IR, most significantly in giving serious consideration to the behaviour of non-state actors, it has nevertheless constructed a new and limited orthodoxy. The lament of Tooze and Murphy (1991) concerning the restrictions of orthodox IPE still resonates a decade and a half later. If conventional IPE was too restricted on the one hand, on the other critical IPE held promise as a site from which to engage in exploration of gender in the global political economy. A number of studies in the 1990s noted the gender-blind nature of critical IPE but also thought that potentially favourable connections between critical IPE and feminist analyses could be developed. For example, Sandra Whitworth argued that 'The most useful point of departure for a feminist IR theory is one which relies on socialist-feminist insights and critical theory more generally and takes into account gender relations' (1997, p. 31). And while recognizing the limitations of critical IPE another feminist scholar claimed that critical global political economy was a 'useful but not a sufficient starting point for thinking about gender relations and feminist politics' (Steans, 1999, p. 113). However, two recent reviews of critical scholarship in IPE have argued that most critical IPE fails to engage in any significant manner with gender (Griffin, 2007; Waylen, 2006). Despite the relative neglect by IPE scholars of gender relations a vast and important literature examining the gender implications of international economic processes has developed.

There are a number of controversies and disputes in the political economy literature on the interrelationship between gender and global economic structures and processes. Instead of focusing on these various conflicts we instead explore how attention to gender assists in providing compelling explanations of global economic processes. In this discussion we take heed of the distinction between women as an empirical category and gender as an analytical category (Peterson, 2005). It should also be emphasized that we do not assume that there is a single feminist position or that this summary of the important theoretical issues will cover all the themes that various schools of thought consider vital.

In this exploration of the significance of the gendered nature of the global political economy we argue that a focus on gender is important for four reasons: (1) it enables analysts to focus on a more holistic political economy; (2) it uncovers important subjects and brings these new topics to attention; (3) it brings concern with development and poverty alleviation from the margins to a more central position; (4) it re-maps the conceptual landscape. These are all significant gains for a subject that seeks to fully explain global economic change.

In the first place, an assumption that the subject identities of men and women are identical is simply false. As we noted above, gender uncovers deep-rooted and systematic differences in power between men and women. A focus on gender uncovers the various ways in which power relations are constructed and maintained in the international economy. A political economy analysis that is attempting to explain the real world cannot be based on concepts that are gender-blind. It cannot be taken for granted that activities are gender-neutral. This point can be illustrated through an examination of the relationship between gender and trade. Research has shown that trade and trade policy affect men and women differently. A recent survey of the evidence claimed that 'trade policies continue to affect men and women differently due to gender inequalities in access to land, information, economic resources and decision-making' (Randriamaro, 2006, p. 11). The relationship between trade and gender is not a simple one; there are sector-specific differences and the results are influenced by geographic, cultural and other factors. Nevertheless, trade and trade liberalization have different impacts on women and men. For example, research has demonstrated the differential impact in agriculture and low-skilled labour-intensive manufac-tured products (Korinek, 2005). Trade liberalization has been shown to have a positive impact on women's employment in manufacturing industries (Seguino, 2000). Another study of the relationship between trade liberaliza-tion and women's employment and earnings confirmed these results and concluded that trade liberalization is likely to be advantageous for women through job creation (Nordås, 2003). The results of these studies can be explained with reference to the price competitiveness of the relevant export sectors. These export sectors have higher rates of female employment since women's wages are lower than men's wages. It should be noted that the differential wage rates between men and women are built on existing gender inequalities. However, women are less likely to reap the benefits of agricul-tural trade liberalization due to persistent gender inequalities in access to land and limited property rights (Korinek, 2005, pp. 13–15; Randriamaro, 2006, pp. 20–3).

Another important consequence of exploring the political economy of gender is that it uncovers issues ignored in conventional (masculinist) politi-cal economy. As a consequence it shifts attention away from a preoccupation with a limited range of questions and opens up space to consider issues marginalized, trivialized or simply ignored. From Cynthia Enloe's *Bananas, Beaches and Bases* (1989) onwards, feminist scholars in IPE have engaged with subject identities and the constructions of masculinity and femininity in the global political economy. Among Enloe's subjects were women invisible to IPE scholarship, including flight attendants, chambermaids and nannies. Feminist scholars have investigated the 'problem of the missing body' (Youngs, 2000, p. 1). Attention to women's bodies and the construction of identities has influenced research on, for example, nationalism, security, sex, reproductive technologies and the environment.

Feminist scholars with their focus on gender have given development a higher profile in IR and IPE. It is arguable that development is a core struc-ture of the global political economy and yet both conventional and hetero-dox IPE accounts tend to marginalize issues central to understanding development. Development is not only constituted through a range of competing discourses, it is linked in diverse ways to the operation of power internationally. A gendered lens on development has demonstrated that, prior to the invention and popularization of the concept of human security, analysis of development theory and practice brought to the fore key aspects of the contemporary human security paradigm. Furthermore, gendered analyses of the political economy of debt, environmental degradation, financial crises, poverty and structural adjustment programmes have provided salient insights into globalization.

Feminist scholars have not only made women visible, they have reshaped the conceptual landscape. They have interrogated existing concepts and demonstrated their implicit masculinist assumptions and they have developed new ways of thinking about political economy (Bakker, 1994; Young, Wolkowitz and McCullagh, 1984). Feminist economics has challenged many of the prevailing assumptions of neoclassical economics. First, feminist economists have argued that societal institutions are not neutral. In other words, the rationalist logic of 'economic man' is false and mistaken. Economic analysis cannot assume that all economic agents react in exactly the same fashion to price signals. This is because societal institutions are not neutral, and therefore do not provide the same starting point or incentive structures for men and women. For example, institutions such as property rights may restrict and shape the decisions of women (Deere and Doss, 2006).

Second, conventional economic analysis, with its focus on the market, disregards the full value of women's labour and economic contribution. Conventional economics takes unpaid reproductive labour as a given. This assumption masks the real cost of reproducing and maintaining the labour force. Thus, feminist economists have been engaged in strategies to make unpaid work visible and redefine what we mean by work so that it includes unpaid reproductive labour (Hoskyns and Rai, 2007). The invisibility of women's labour is exemplified by national account statistics which are based solely on monetized values arising from market-based transactions. Feminist scholars have suggested a different classification of work – 'formal market work, informal market work, subsistence production, unpaid care work, and volunteer work' (UNIFEM, 2005, p. 23).

In empirical terms it is safe to conclude that attention to gender is not only important, it is vital if a full account is to be given of transformation in the global political economy. Such analysis demonstrates how women and men enter into the global division of labour as gendered identities. And conceptual innovations are important in showing why gender analyses are crucial to explaining stability and change in the global political economy. A failure to examine gender relations in the international economy is a recipe for partial, inaccurate and irrelevant analysis. Policy conclusions following from such partial analyses will do little to address prevailing inequalities in the global economy.

Major developments

Women enter the economy in a diverse variety of roles, for example, as workers, consumers, and entrepreneurs. Women are active economic agents in all of the major sectors of economic activity – agriculture, industry and services. Chapter 9 introduced the concept of a gendered division of labour and discussed some of the specific consequences of this social arrangement. It highlighted the role that masculinist assumptions play in creating and maintaining inequalities. This section discusses two major developments relating to gender issues in the global economy. The first trend we discuss is the increasing integration of women into the workforce, particularly in the last quarter of a century. We then turn our attention to the emergence of women as a distinct constituency in the global economy, and examine the evolution of concern about gender issues at the level of global public policy.

Women in the world economy: employment trends and prospects

Women have been active participants in economic activity in all human societies. However, women have not always been engaged in productive activity which is remunerated in monetary terms. Thus, while women's contribution to economic growth and development has been invaluable it has not always been acknowledged and granted recognition by official agencies. The increasing participation by women in the paid workforce has increased the visibility of women's contribution to economic growth. As *The Economist* stated, 'Arguably, women are the most powerful engine of global growth' (2006). The post-1945 period has witnessed an increasing integration of women into the workforce. This is not an even process, and women's labour participation rates reflect differing geographic patterns dictated by specific cultural and societal values and mores. A focus on women's income-earning capacities is frequently linked with the prospects for increasing women's economic security. Nevertheless, it has become apparent that indicators showing increasing female participation in waged activity do not necessarily show decreases in gender inequality. In other words, while the level of participation is important it is also necessary to examine the quality of employment. Therefore, in this survey of female participation in the labour force, apart from employment participation rates, we also examine employment by sector, the nature and status of employment, and wages.

Statistics reveal that more women are in paid employment than at any previous period in history. In 2008, of a total global labour force of 3 billion people, 1.2 billion were women (ILO, 2009). However, women's share of the total employed labour force has not changed significantly in the past decade. In 1998, women made up 39.9 per cent of the global workforce and this rose

Table 10.1   Male and female labour force participation rates (LFPR), 2007

Region	Male LFPR (%)	Female LFPR (%)
World	77.6	52.6
Developed economies and the European Union	68.2	52.7
Central and Eastern Europe (non-EU) and CIS	69.8	49.7
East Asia	81.4	67.1
South-east Asia	82.8	59.1
South Asia	82.0	36.2
Latin America and the Caribbean	79.1	52.9
Middle East	78.3	33.3
Sub-Saharan Africa	86.1	62.6
North Africa	75.9	26.1

Sources: Adapted from ILO (2008), Table 2.1; ILO (2009), Table A.4.

slightly to 40.5 per cent per cent in 1998 (ILO, 2009, p. 9). While the gap between men and women as part of the labour force (i.e., those in work and those actively seeking work) has been decreasing there are also stark regional variations (see Table 10.1). Global employment statistics reveal that in 2007 for every 100 men there were 67 women in the labour force. But this average conceals the vast difference between the developed economies (inclusive of the European Union), where 82 women per 100 men were active, and the Middle East and North Africa, where the ratio was 35 economically active women per 100 men. Differentials in labour force participation rates are also evident in unemployment rates. Female unemployment rates are higher than those for men in all regions apart from Central and South-eastern Europe (non-EU) and CIS, and East Asia (ILO, 2008, pp. 24–5).

Employment trends are the result of short-term and long-term factors. This includes general economic growth, sectoral employment shifts and wage differentials. One determinant of female participation in the labour force is the demand for female labour. A number of sector specific factors account for the increase in female participation in the labour force. The service sector has replaced agriculture as the main employer for women. In 2007 46.3 per cent of women were employed in the service sector compared with 36 per cent in agriculture. These global figures conceal important regional variations. Agriculture remains the main form of employment for women in Africa (67.9 per cent) and South Asia (60.5 per cent), but in all other regions the service sector is the main source of employment for women (ILO, 2008). Developments in the industrial sector have impacted differently on women in the developed and the developing world. One consequence of global restructuring in the 1980s (see Chapter 7) was the rise in labour-intensive manufacturing industries in East Asia. These export industries (see below) are heavily reliant on female labour and consequently provided increased employment opportunities for women in East Asia. Increased employment opportunities in East Asia were accompanied by a decline in women's employment in manufacturing industries in the advanced industrial countries (Joekes, 1987, p. 135). But despite the rise in EPZs and consequent increase in female employment, in the developing world women's share in employment in manufacturing is below that of men. While it has been argued that the increased integration of women in the developed world into the paid economy has been a consequence of the rise in services in these countries (*The Economist*, 2006), it has also been pointed out that 'women are still concentrated in sectors that are traditionally associated with their gender roles, particularly in community, social and personal services, whereas men dominate better-paid sector jobs in financial and business services and real estate' (ILO, 2006).

The status of women's work cannot be inferred from the statistics on labour force participation and depend on the nature of employment and cultural factors in specific societies. Analysts have been concerned with the security of employment and the conditions of work (see the 'Key issues' section below for further discussion). It has been argued that women's employment is frequently temporary, part time and less secure than men's work (Mitter, 1986). In this context a recent study noted that 'The attractiveness of women as workers in labour-intensive export industries, whether they be domestically or foreign-owned, is related to the ease of shedding these workers, based in part on gender norms that relegate women's paid work to secondary importance after their domestic and care responsibilities' (UNRISD, 2005, p. 38). This casualization of work may lead to increased employment but frequently this employment is characterized by deteriorating working conditions. For example, enhanced employment in some industries comes at the cost of adequate occupational and health standards, and workers can be prevented from access to union representation and the opportunity to engage in collective bargaining. Furthermore, while in most cases women are entering the labour market voluntarily in response to the economic opportunities offered through paid work, and as an avenue to enhance income and status, this is not always the case. For some women entry to the labour market is the result of poverty and increased insecurity. The nature and conditions of work in occupations such as the sex industry and domestic service do not necessarily assist in enhancing women's empow-erment. We therefore cannot conclude that all labour force participation is necessarily positive and beneficial.

One persistent issue regarding women's employment relates to wages and earnings. In all societies women earn less than men on average. A UN report noted, 'Closing the gap between women's and men's pay continues to be a major challenge in most parts of the world' (UN, 2006, p. 54). Various expla-nations have been given for the gender pay gap. It has been argued that women's income potential is stifled by the barriers limiting their progress up the career ladder at the same rate as men. Women thus do not reach the higher-paid managerial positions (López-Claros and Zahidi, 2005, p. 3). Another possible explanation lies in women's poor bargaining power and negotiating capacity (ILO, 2006). Other studies have focused on the relative influence of gender-specific factors (e.g., women's educational attainment and employ-ment discrimination) versus overall labour market characteristics (Blau and Kahn, 2003). We can distinguish broadly between factors related to the employment profile of women and others related to wider social factors. On one hand, many women are clustered in low-wage occupations. Often these jobs are low-waged because they are traditionally designated as women's jobs. And even in so-called female occupations gender wage inequality is still preva-lent, with men earning more than women (ILO, 2009). On the other hand, we can observe the impact of social provisions such as maternity leave and child-care facilities on the economic opportunities open to women and their relative earning capacities. But even where women are in high-wage professions they do not earn the same as their male counterparts (see Box 10.4).

Box 10.4 The glass ceiling

The term the 'glass ceiling' refers to the situation where senior manage-ment positions are predominantly occupied by men and wage differen-tials between men and women remain wide at the top of the pay scale. Studies of the glass ceiling tend to focus on the failure of women to progress to top managerial positions. Obstacles to the recruitment and promotion of women are varied. Some are firm- and industry-specific (e.g., old boys' networks, male workplace cultures); others are societal (e.g., segregation in education, childcare provisions, parental leave and welfare provisions), which make it difficult for women to combine family life and career paths. Recent research confirms the existence of the glass ceiling. One study of employment in Sweden identified 'gender differences in reward as a primary factor responsible for the glass ceil-ing effect' (Albrecht, Bjorkland and Vroman, 2003, p. 172).

Gender and global public policy

In the past three decades gender issues have moved from the margins to a more central position in the policy statements issued by governments, regional organizations and multilateral agencies. Women did not just emerge onto the international agenda. Women's issues were 'brought into' the global public sphere as the result of conscious action. Specific human agency was behind the project designed to move women from a position of invisibility to one where their presence nationally and internationally was recognized. The project to 'bring women into the global political economy' was in part in recognition of their unacknowledged existence in economic activity and in part an effort to improve women's position. In the context of development policy Naila Kabeer notes that 'One way of charting the emergence of women as a distinctive category in development discourse is to monitor their changing significance within the policy declarations and institutional structures of the major development agencies' (1994, p. 1). In this subsection we briefly discuss the roles played by international organizations in shaping the development of global policy on gender equity. We focus on the role of these organizations in the creation of global norms. This entails examining the ways in which shared expectations about appropriate behaviour were developed through the generation and dissemination of ideas, and the rule-making and standard-setting of these bodies.

Historical developments.   From the perspective of the early 21st century it is relatively easy to accept attention to gender as a 'natural' feature of global policy. However, the development of international policy should not be taken for granted. Although the United Nations created a Commission on the Status of Women in 1946 it had made limited progress by the 1970s. The progressive evolution of global gender policy can be traced to December 1972 when the UN General Assembly (UNGA) adopted Resolution 3010 (XXVII) proclaiming 1975 as International Women's Year. The impetus for International Women's Year came from civil society, and not from a national government. It arose from the Women's International Democratic Federation (WIDF), a Finnish NGO (Pietilä and Vickers, 1990, p. 73). The president of the WIDF in 1972 was Herta Kuusinen, who as a Finnish parliamentarian was also an observer to the annual session of the UN Commission on the Status of Women, and in that capacity was instrumental in getting the call for an International Women's Year onto the agenda. The resolution was later unanimously adopted by the UNGA. The period between 1974 and 1995 is especially significant in the development of global policy on gender issues and the evolution of a new normative framework.

At the centre of these changes were four international conferences convened by the United Nations, as well as the International Decade for

Women. In December 1975 the United Nations General Assembly proclaimed the period 1976–85 as the United Nations Decade for the Advancement of Women. The Decade for Women provided a focal point for activities within the UN system and raised the profile of women's issues at the international level.

The four key conferences were: the World Conference on International Women's Year held in Mexico City in June–July 1975, the Second World Conference on Women held in Copenhagen in July 1980 to review progress since 1975, the Third World Conference on Women (World Conference to Review and Appraise the Achievements of the United Nations Decade for Women) held in Nairobi in July 1985 and the Fourth World Conference for Women held in September 1995 in Beijing.

The first three conferences were at times fractious affairs, with divisions more apparent than common purpose (Newland, 1988). Nevertheless, these events were important in raising the profile of women's issues and in making gender concerns of utmost importance for development policy. The conferences had an enormous symbolic impact (Tinker, 1990, p. 31). They made women's concerns legitimate and forced national governments to take note of the impacts of their policies on women. The preparatory phases of the conferences and their outcomes were crucial in agenda-setting because they produced detailed research and voluminous literature. As part of the preparatory process for these conferences governments were required for the first time to collect data which particularly revealed the gender-specific nature of economic, social and welfare policies. More accurate data enables more effective policies to be formulated in areas ranging from employment and income distribution to social security provision and welfare. Redefining work in the global economy effectively means recognizing both waged and unwaged work as essential to the social and economic well-being of countries. Moreover, the preparatory process of the conferences and the conference documentation were crucial in helping to identify and clarify women's needs and translate them into demands.

Each conference produced a report which set the normative and policy framework for subsequent action. The Mexico City Conference created the 'World Plan of Action for the Implementation of the Objectives of the International Women's Year'; the Copenhagen Conference led to the programme of 'Action for the Second Half of the Decade'; and at Nairobi the delegates adopted the 'Forward-looking Strategies for the Advancement of Women to the Year 2000' (FLS). These three documents were important in setting clear objectives and defined targets. For example the mid-decade review in 1985 was convened to review and appraise the degree to which the targets established in the 'World Plan of Action' (adopted at the Mexico City Conference) had been attained, and to prepare a precise plan of action for the remainder of the decade. The review of action taken was not particularly encouraging since it revealed that there had been, for example, limited improvement in the conditions of rural women. A redefined 'Plan of Action' was adopted in Copenhagen to oversee efforts in the second part of the decade. Of the three documents the FLS is the most important in terms of serving as a blueprint for the advancement of women. The key objectives set out in the document concern women's interests in health, employment, family life, political life and human rights.

It has been argued that 'Perhaps the most far reaching impact of the conferences was the mobilization of women which they engendered' (Tinker, 1990, p. 32). Given the limited participation in UN conferences, their direct impact was therefore also going to be limited. But parallel civil society meetings alongside the official ones provided an open market of ideas and increased the networking of women's organizations globally. The development of the UN Decade for Women and these conferences ensured that women in development became synonymous with the processes of change that were affecting women in the world.

The full incorporation of gender equality into all stages and at all levels of planning was a slow and evolutionary process. While it is difficult to establish a precise moment at which gender issues became an integral part of the policy process it is arguable that the Fourth World Conference for Women held in September 1995 in Beijing marked the widespread acceptance of gender mainstreaming (Hafner-Burton and Pollack, 2002). The *Beijing Declaration and Platform for Action* set impressive commitments for governments and international organizations. The *Beijing Declaration* (UN, 1995), in establishing a set of underlying principles, explicitly invoked the mainstreaming of gender policies. It stated, 'It is essential to design, implement and monitor, with the full participation of women, effective, efficient and mutually reinforcing gender-sensitive policies and programmes, including development policies and programmes, at all levels that will foster the empowerment and advancement of women' (para. 19); and governments committed 'to implement the following Platform for Action, ensuring that a gender perspective is reflected in all our policies and programmes' (para. 38).

Normative and institutional change.   While feminist critiques have shifted official policy at national, regional and global levels to consider the distinct interests of women, it is not, of course, the case that the mainstreaming of gender issues has automatically led to the end of discrimination or to policies that are always pro-women. The concept of mainstreaming as used here refers simply to the diverse ways in which gender issues are now firmly on the agenda, and automatically included as part of the policy process (planning, implementation and monitoring), rather than placed as an afterthought. Gender mainstreaming thus refers to the integration of gender perspectives with the goal of reducing gender inequality in all phases of decision-making

(UN, 2001). There are three main features that characterize the current mainstreaming of gender in policy and practice.

The first feature is the normative commitment to gender equality. Since the adoption of the Beijing *Platform for Action* in 1995, five documents have reinforced the commitment to gender mainstreaming at the international level: the ECOSOC Agreed Conclusions, 1997/2 (July 1997); the UN Secretary General's communication in October 1997 to heads of all major UN units on gender mainstreaming; Resolution A/S/23-10/Rev1, 'Further actions and initiatives to implement the Beijing Declaration and Platform for Action (Outcome Document)' adopted at the conclusion of the 23rd Special Session of the NGA; 'Women 2000: Gender Equality, Development and Peace for the Twenty-First Century' on 10 June 2000; and the Economic and Social Council's resolution 2001/41 of July 2001. These documents are crucial in establishing a framework of gender equality for the work of the UN system. They build on previous important initiatives such as the Convention on the Elimination of All Forms of Discrimination Against Women (CEDAW) adopted by the UNGA in 1979. These developments are not solely the result of activities by nation-states. They have been shaped by the activities of the international women's movement to shape global norms. A key strategy has been to frame women's issues in terms of the human rights discourse (Brown Thompson, 2002; Joachim, 2003).

The emergence and advancement of a norm of gender equality can be perceived in the ways in which international development policy is framed. In December 1961, UN General Assembly Resolution 1710 (XVI) inaugurated the (First) Development Decade. While it was a landmark event in bringing economic development to the forefront of world concern it made no mention of gender issues. By the time the International Development Strategy (IDS) for the Third United Nations Development Decade was agreed in 1980 it was no longer possible to ignore the gender dimension of development policy. The IDS endorsed the programmes of the Mexico City and Copenhagen Conferences and committed the UN to a substantial improvement in the status of women during the decade. The current consensus on global development policy is framed in the Millennium Development Goals (MDGs). The MDGs present an excellent example of the way in which global policy now integrates gender concerns. While all eight MDGs have implications for gender equality, three are explicitly focused on gender concerns. It is inconceivable that the MDGs devised in 2000 would not explicitly address the subordination of women, yet had they been promulgated in 1960 it is very unlikely that attention to gender would have gained any recognition. But this recognition of a gender dimension may still appear to be too limited (see Box 10.5).

The second feature concerns the way that the normative developments detailed above have been reinforced by the increasing institutionalization of gender issues within the UN system. Gender analysis is now common in the

Box 10.5   Gender and the Millennium Development Goals

Goal 3 of the MDG goals (see Box 11.1) is to 'Promote gender equality and empower women'. The formal target for achieving this goal is to 'eliminate gender disparity in primary and secondary education preferably by 2005 and to all levels of education no later than 2015'. Feminists would argue that gender equality initiatives must go beyond this one measure to address all the MDGs (www.mdgender.net). For example, MDG Goal 1 is to 'Eradicate extreme poverty and hunger'. More women than men are among the extreme poor and women also have responsibility for managing the welfare of children who are also living in extreme poverty. Thus, if they are to succeed, initiatives to alleviate extreme poverty should be gender-sensitive and adopt specific measures to improve the welfare of women and children.

specialized agencies of the United Nations. The Inter-Agency Network on Women and Gender Equality (IANWGE), established in 1996 and chaired by the Secretary General's Special Adviser on Gender Issues and Advancement of Women, is a focal point for gender mainstreaming activities in all branches of the UN system. The position of Special Adviser on Gender Issues and Advancement of Women and the Office of the Special Adviser on Gender Issues and Advancement of Women (OSAGI) were established post-Beijing and complement developments in the UN during the Decade for Women. The Committee on the Elimination of Discrimination Against Women was established in 1982 and charged with the responsibility for supervising the implementation of CEDAW. Apart from this committee other organizations have been created devoted to pursuing gender equality and ensuring that women play an active role in the development process. In 1976 a Voluntary Fund for the UN Decade for Women was established by the General Assembly of the United Nations. This Fund was transformed into the United Nations Development Fund for Women (UNIFEM) in 1984. Currently UNIFEM identifies four strategic areas to guide its work programme – reducing feminized poverty; ending violence against women; reversing the spread of HIV/AIDS among women and girls; and achieving democratic governance in societies. Another institutional innovation was the creation of the United Nations International Research and Training Institute for the Advancement of Women (INSTRAW) in 1985. Within the UN a Division for the Advancement of Women (part of the Division for Social and Economic Affairs) was created in 1988 as the central unit within the organization for all issues pertaining to women.

The third feature is that gender has been mainstreamed within many international organizations. The establishment of gender departments or sections in many international organizations reflects not only the degree of institutionalization of gender issues but also the normalization of gender as a framework of analysis. Since the Beijing Conference many international organizations have raised the profile of gender issues in their research, analysis and operational activities. For example, although the ILO's mandate on gender equality is grounded in ILO conventions from the 1950s, including the Equal Remuneration Convention 1951 and the Discrimination (Employment and Occupation) Convention 1958, in the wake of the Beijing Conference the Director General announced a policy on gender mainstreaming in 1999, and in 2001 the organization adopted an Action Plan on Gender Equality and Gender Mainstreaming. Another example is the World Health Organization (WHO). The WHO adopted a gender mainstreaming policy in 2002 (WHO, 2002), and has a specialist unit, the Department of Women, Gender and Health, to oversee WHO gender policy.

These changes are both a response to internal bureaucratic design and the result of external pressure. The normative shift has created a space for nonstate actors to pressure intergovernmental organizations. For example, women's groups in alliance with trade unions have been able to bring women's issues onto the agenda of the ILO. In 1996 the ILO adopted guidelines for employment in home work (Prugl, 1999). Home work is not housework, but work that companies have labourers do in their home. It is usually performed by women working for very low pay. The fact that the ILO examined home work is a sign that feminist views and women's issues are making inroads into mainstream institutions.

In this context the shift in policies at the World Bank presents an instructive case of the progress made in mainstreaming gender issues. The Bank was slow in integrating gender issues into its policies, and while other aid donors had by the end of the Nairobi Conference made provision to give attention to gender issues it did not issue its first policy paper ('Enhancing Women's Involvement in Economic Development') until 1994. Although a sole adviser on Women in Development had been appointed in 1977, and a Women in Development Office established in 1986, it was not until after the Beijing Conference in 1995 that a concerted attempt was made to engage with feminist analyses of development. It should be noted that the World Bank's engagement with gender issues is also partly a response to pressure from civic associations. For example, women's groups have been in an extended dialogue with the World Bank (O'Brien *et al.*, 2000, pp. 24–66). They have had some success in convincing Bank staff that development policies that ignore women are flawed. A recent innovation in Bank policy occurred following the September 2006 Annual Meeting of the IMF and World Bank, at which Paul Wolfowitz, the Bank's president, announced a new four-year

$25 million plan called *Gender Equality as Smart Economics* (World Bank, 2006d). The objective of this Gender Action Plan is to advance women's economic empowerment.

Transformations in the World Bank's policies, funding priorities and institutional arrangements have not automatically convinced its critics that it has effectively mainstreamed gender in its operations (Griffin, 2009). The record of the World Bank on gender mainstreaming is a topic for debate and the Bank's legitimacy in this area is questioned by groups that are yet to be convinced that the organization has a real, rather than a shallow, commitment to gender issues (Bessis, 2001). Critics contend that the World Bank's cognitive universe is neoclassical economics and as such its concern is with market efficiency. This contrasts with the gender justice objective of feminist economics (O'Brien *et al.*, 2000, p. 47). The criticisms of the World Bank and its response are, of course, important but from the perspective of the argument here the fundamental point is that the World Bank has not only had to respond to pressure to integrate gender concerns into its framework, but it is also sensitive to criticism concerning the ways in which it is mainstreaming gender.

Key issues

A gender perspective on the global economy reveals that men and women are impacted in different ways by changes in production, trade and financial flows. A gendered division of labour ensures that crises in the world economy are in great measure absorbed by poor and working-class women. In the first sub-section we present evidence related to the ways in which the global political economy impacts on poverty and women's capabilities. The discussion in the second sub-section analyses the globalization of reproductive work and highlights the various ways in which women's bodies are traded internationally. Finally, we explore three connections between gender, restructuring and globalization.

The feminization of poverty

The United Nations *Millennium Declaration* states that a key objective is 'to promote gender equality and the empowerment of women as effective ways to combat poverty, hunger, disease, and to stimulate development that is truly sustainable' (UN, 2000a). This statement represents the prevailing global consensus linking poverty and gender inequality. While it is directed specifically at the developing world, the feminization of poverty is a phenomenon applicable to women in all parts of the world. There are various alternative explanations to account for the apparent fact that women are more likely to be part of the very poor than men. Of the various factors accounting for female poverty three have been given prominence in the literature: an increase in female-headed households; the continued existence of intra-household inequalities and systematic bias against women and girls; and the impact of neoliberal economic policies (Moghadam, 2005).

The term 'feminization of poverty' originated in the United States in the late 1970s when researchers discovered an increase in female-headed households and a higher incidence of poverty among single mothers. US data since that period has continued to reveal a link between poverty and female-headed households. However, the universal applicability of the thesis that female-headed households are more likely to be poor than male-headed households has been the subject of some controversy and contention. While research indicates a rising trend in female-headed households around the world, evidence on the impact of family structure on poverty is less conclusive. Some studies in the developing world have found that female-headed households are more vulnerable than other groups and have less access to income-generating opportunities. However, the contention that there is a link between female-headed households and poverty has been dismissed as 'impressionistic and anecdotal' (Quisumbing, Haddad and Peña, 1995, p. 1). They argue that there is no strong evidence to support the claim that female-headed households are on average disproportionately represented among the poor. A recent review of the evidence suggests that there are cross-regional variations in the economic status of female-headed households (Moghadam, 2005). The importance of family structure on poverty is mediated by macro-social and political factors and by women's access to employment.

Research on the relationship between intra-household inequality and female poverty is more conclusive (Moghadam, 2005). Various studies have shown that in many societies (especially in South Asia) women are systematically discriminated against in the household. Women have unequal access to education, healthcare and nutrition and this unequal resource allocation impacts negatively their employment and income-generating opportunities. This intra-household inequality, when combined with existing social and economic structures of patriarchal dominance, exacerbates women's vulnerability and increases female poverty.

There has been a considerable amount of research on the human and social costs of neoliberal adjustment policies. This research also has demonstrated the gender dimension of neoliberal restructuring. While many men have suffered from structural adjustment, women have been systematically and more dramatically impoverished. The costs of economic restructuring under structural adjustment programmes (SAPs) are disproportionately borne by women. As governments attempt to balance budgets and engage in structural adjustment programmes to make their economies more internationally competitive, women are often forced to pay the price by taking up tasks hitherto performed by the state or giving up their existing sources of income in order to concentrate on caring for their families' immediate needs (Chang, 2000, pp. 124–9). In other words, structural adjustment programmes are dependent on unpaid women's labour (Nagar *et al.*, 2002). Furthermore, when food subsidies are reduced, women often cut back on their own nutrition in order to feed their children. As health and education are reduced, women often take on the additional burden of nursing family members, or girls are kept at home to help in domestic tasks rather than sent to school. The move to export agriculture for foreign currency can cause peasant women to lose their land or force them into becoming seasonal workers. In desperation, many women export their labour through migration. It is widely accepted that women's lives are negatively impacted by loss of food security, additional burdens of work, application of user fees in healthcare and education, and increasing domestic violence resulting from the imposition of neoliberal policies. However, a study of the impact of structural adjustment in Niger and Senegal concluded that 'It is a mistake (however) to assign a blanket impact for the SAPs where none existed' (Creevey, 2002, p. 110). Creevey argues that while adjustment policies in Niger and Senegal had a negative impact some women were empowered as their businesses flourished in response to market liberalization measures.

Globalization of reproductive work

The reproductive economy is the 'economy of families and the private sphere – where human life is generated, daily life maintained and socialization reproduced' (Peterson, 2003, p. 79). This private sphere is increasingly being globalized and marketized. Activities that formerly took place within the household can now be bought for money and provided through transnational structures. Three significant aspects are sex work, domestic services and the purchase of brides.

The concept of an international political economy of sex (Pettman, 1996a, 1996b, 2003) is useful when exploring the connections between women, sex and the global political economy. Women's bodies in this international political economy of sex are tradable commodities. Women are exported from one country to another in much the same way as one would export a commodity such as wheat. Much of this export is designed to alleviate poverty in the sending country as the worker sends part of her pay cheque home to support her family. But this trade is based on implicit (and at times explicit) male violence. Central to the international politics of sex is the domestication of women and the sexualization of women's labour. Women are treated as sexed beings on the basis of a heterosexual conception of sex. Women are assumed to be readily available for the gratification of heterosexual men's desires. The international political economy of sex and the attendant control over women's bodies is the context for domestic service, sex tourism, militarized prostitution and mail-order brides. A large number of women from developing countries are engaging in providing personal services to men and families in wealthier states. This can range from prostitution for a male clientele to providing cleaning, childcare and health-care services in homes and institutions.

The global sex trade has expanded to include many women and children since the 1970s. Some are employed in their own countries servicing local and foreign men while others are exported to foreign countries. Figures are difficult to come by since much of the industry is illegal but it is estimated to be worth billions of dollars per annum (Jeffreys, 2009). In 1998 one estimate of the significance of the sex sector in Malaysia, the Philippines and Thailand placed it at between 2 per cent and 14 per cent of GDP (Lim, 1998, p.7). It has been argued that 'much of the "foreign sex" trade is not so much indi-vidual or group sex tourism as militarised prostitution, grown up especially around huge foreign bases' (Pettman, 1996a, p. 201). Historical studies and social science research have established a close connection between milita-rization and prostitution. Occupying powers have traditionally expected local women to fulfil the 'needs' of their troops. This phenomenon is not solely a transnational one. Studies have documented the militarization of ethnic minority areas within national boundaries. Race plays a major role in the sexualization of local women, especially in border areas or areas that have histories of secessionist violence and large numbers of troops serving far from their homes (Chenoy, 2002; Moser and Clark, 2001).

The large sex trade in South-east Asia has its origins in the Korean and Vietnamese wars. US and allied soldiers taking time off from the conflicts sought out sex workers in countries such as Thailand and the Philippines (Barry, 1996, p. 132). Demand for prostitutes in these 'recreation' zones led to an upsurge in the sex trade. Once the Vietnam War ended in the mid-1970s, foreign tourists took the place of soldiers. These tourists tend to be Western and Japanese males who take advantage of the benefits of modern transportation to travel to other countries for sexual pleasure. The drawing power of prostitution for the tourist trade can be immense in some countries. For example, it is estimated that up to 73 per cent of tourists to Thailand are single males (not with a female partner) and that up to 3 per cent of all Thai women are engaged in some form of prostitution (Peterson and Runyan, 1993, p. 98).

This is a global business overlaid with racial stereotypes and designed to benefit men in developing and developed countries. Men purchase the services and keep the vast majority of the profits. Western men engage in activities that would be unacceptable or certainly much less available in their home states. Some local men prosper as they secure revenues from pimping, through bribes to police, or from hotels and bars. For Western men visiting sex tourist countries, native women combine exotic cultural traits that make them the desired sexual partners. Asian women are stereotyped as being more submissive and responsive to Western men's needs than the women of their own cultures.

This trade exacts a devastating price on the women and children who are involved. One cost has been the spread of sexually transmitted diseases such as AIDS. This in turn drives a demand for younger and younger prostitutes in the mistaken view that customers will avoid the disease if they turn to younger victims. Physical and psychological damage to people engaged in the trade is also high. Those exported to other countries often live in conditions of slavery.

As noted above, one particularly egregious practice is child sex tourism. There are efforts to address this problem in several sectors. The global NGO network End Child Prostitution, Child Pornography and Trafficking of Children for Sexual Purposes (ECPAT) campaigns to eliminate child prostitution, child pornography and the trafficking of children for sexual purposes. A number of Western states (e.g., Australia, Canada, the United States and the United Kingdom) have introduced legislation to enable domestic courts to prosecute residents who have engaged in child sex tourism. For example, an American citizen or resident who engages in sexual activity abroad with a child under 18 can face 30 years in a US prison.

In recent years domestic work has also developed as a major international business (Pettman, 2003, p. 163). Women from developing countries are imported into Western Europe, Canada, the United States and the Middle East to help provide childcare, do housework or to assist in nursing elderly people at home or in hospitals. The numbers of women engaged in this activity are large and the amount of money they contribute to their home economies through remittances is significant. Reliable figures are difficult to find and often dated, but here are some estimates. In 1984, over 18,000 Sri Lankan women were working as domestic servants abroad. In 1988, 81,000 Filipino women serving as servants abroad earned an estimated US$60–100 million in foreign exchange (Peterson and Runyan, 1993, p. 99). In the case of the Philippines, women make up almost half of the migrant labour force; men usually work abroad in the construction industry. By 1994 it was estimated that Filipino workers sent home up to US$7 billion annually. This exceeded income from sugar or minerals and was close to 3.5 per cent of the value of all goods and services produced in the country (Chang, 2000, p. 130). It was also an amount large enough to cover the interest payments on the Philippines' massive foreign debt.

This form of activity creates contradictory links between women in developing and developed states. Many women in developed states have been able to pursue careers similar to those of men in recent decades. The ability of First World women to attain professional success often depends on Third

World women taking over some of their household responsibilities as maids and nannies. Young, educated women are more likely to obtain career benefits from globalization than others (Gottfried, 2004). However, in countries where there has been a reduction in welfare services or an absence of affordable daycare (as in the United States), these women must seek out a private solution to the task of domestic work and childcare. One solution has been to hire foreign women to work as domestics. This can be done legally through employment agencies or illegally through less-established channels.

The degree to which labour from developing countries facilitates the lifestyles of the middle and upper middle professional classes in some developed states was very publicly illustrated in 1993. US President Clinton was eager to bring women into his cabinet to show that he was reaching out to a wide group of Americans. However, his plans for diversity were upset by the fact that two of the professional women he approached (a corporate lawyer and a federal judge) had used 'illegal' immigrants for childcare (Marcus, 1993). Clinton's third woman candidate and eventual Attorney-General, Janet Reno, was childless and did not face similar problems. Recently Baroness Scotland, the Attorney-General of the United Kingdom, was fined £5,000 for employing a Tongan housekeeper who did not have a legal work permit (*The Times*, 2009).

Another example of the transnational provision of domestic services is the exporting of wives. The mail-order bride has played a role in popular culture as amusing and humorous, in movies about the Wild West, and recently in the film *Birthday Girl* starring Nicole Kidman as a Russian mail-order bride. However, the reality of the mail-order bride is far removed from fiction and fantasy. The international trade in mail-order brides is lucrative and reflects power differentials in the global political economy, with some countries cast in the role of suppliers and others as buyers (Pettman, 1996a, p. 194). In the contemporary transnational trade mail-order brides usually originate from the developing world or economies in transition. However, the contention that mail-order brides are necessarily 'victims' has been countered by Constable (2006). She prefers the term 'correspondence brides' and argues persuasively that attention has to be given to 'variations in the circumstances, forms of introduction, and actual experiences of couples who have met through correspondence and eventually married' (2006, p. 2). When the specificity of these relationships is taken into account it becomes apparent that correspondence brides need not be viewed as victims of exploitation.

Gender and global restructuring

One of the earliest issues to gain the attention of feminist scholars was the subject of the gender implications of global restructuring. From pioneering studies of the impact of the New International Division of Labour on women

(Mitter, 1986) to current concerns with globalization, political economists have examined the impact of changes in the international division of labour (Busse and Spielmann, 2003; Mies, 1998); international trade (Korinek, 2005; Randriamaro, 2006); global finance (Aslanbeigui and Summerfield, 2000; Porter, 2005); and global production structures on women's labour (Barrientos, Kabeer and Hossain, 2004; Pyle and Ward, 2003). Here we briefly review some connections between globalization and women's economic activity.

Women have increasingly been integrated into global production through labour in TNCs, especially in EPZs – designated areas within a country which are designed to attract foreign investment by providing financial incentives or regulatory relief from national laws. On average, 80 per cent of the workforce in these zones are female. In China about 20 million people, of whom 70–80 per cent are female, work in export processing zones or special economic zones (David, 1996, pp. 22–3). Why is female labour so favoured in these zones? Factory managers might suggest that women are chosen because they have smaller fingers and can do more intricate work at a faster pace. Many women may be more skilled at dextrous work because of having developed skills such as sewing, but this is interpreted as a biological difference rather than a skill difference. Since it is not seen as a skill it does not need to be rewarded by higher pay.

Another reason why women make up a large percentage of the workers in EPZs is because they are thought (often incorrectly) to be more compliant with manager's demands. Women have less of a history of unionization and are often willing to put up with very poor working conditions to support families. It has been argued that the image of the compliant, docile female worker is a specific construction designed to serve the interests of states and TNCs. For example, a case study of a British TNC's operations in Malaysia in the 1990s argues that the pressures from global corporations and state authority structures within Malaysia have combined to produce the image of the low-waged, docile, diligent factory girl (Elias, 2005). Low-waged sewing jobs have been constructed in Malaysia as particularly suited to women, due to their manual dexterity, and particularly for Malay women whose traditions involved a great deal of sewing. Having many family members working in the same facility helps ensure that women comply with the behaviour and control methods already in place. This division of labour is based on a dominant structure of 'masculinist managerialism', a rationalized management system that depends on the creation of low-waged, pliable, female employment. Many women factory workers do not fit the docile and compliant stereotype and have been active in lobbying for better working conditions and the formation of independent trade unions. But since states attract TNCs by limiting space for labour organization, efforts at unionization are not encouraged. In Malaysia, highly feminized production sectors central to the government's export development strategy are also the sectors with the most restrictive anti-union policies (Elias, 2005, p. 207).

It can be argued that gender is a resource for globalizing capital. Women provide a source of low-cost labour for global capital, and are often exploited by it. This is the case with the Mexican maquiladora (Kopinak, 1995), as well as in traditional EPZs. The corporate desire to avoid demands of greater accountability for reproduction helps shape decisions for moving production facilities from richer to poorer, low-wage countries, outsourcing work and thus avoiding responsibility (Acker, 2004, pp. 27–8). TNCs continue to use the social construction of gender-role ideology and 'cultural sensitivities' to restrict choices and access to certain jobs and to provide unequal pay for women relative to men (Chow, 2003).

The incorporation of women into export-oriented work has had a number of contradictory outcomes. On the negative side, working conditions are often very difficult. Unions are often prohibited, working conditions and wages poor. Many workers are exposed to dangerous and unhealthy conditions as well as the threat of physical and sexual abuse (ICFTU, 1996a). In response to these issues, women have organized amongst themselves and participated in international campaigns to secure fair treatment from the multinational corporations that benefit from their labour.

However, working conditions vary widely in TNCs and can often be better than in local firms, providing opportunity to local women. These forms of employment have sometimes challenged local gender roles and provided women with better alternatives than pre-existing work options. Some women are able to leave restrictive home environments and secure increased status and independence thanks to the incomes that they earn in the factories. This has allowed many women to break free of patriarchal structures and gain some independence. The work available to women is, however, often less secure, less well paid and more demeaning than that available to men (Moghadam, 1999).

There are, in fact, a number of different patterns of work relations between women and TNCs in developing countries and one needs to be sensitive to this variety. In some cases work may be relatively well paid, providing young women an opportunity to accumulate some wealth and education. In other cases working conditions are brutal and abuse is widespread. The challenge is to expand the first type of employment and battle the second form through greater worker rights and economic development.

In response to the problems faced by many women in the global political economy some academic analysis has called for the 'ungendering' of labour (Peterson and Runyan, 1993, p. 160). This would involve creating an environment where gender did not play a role in the form of work one chose to do. Such a scenario would involve women increasing their presence in male-dominated areas and men their presence in female-dominated areas such as nursing and teaching. Such a transformation would require a shift in the balance of power between men and women and an acknowledgement of the value of the vast amount of work conducted by women that goes unpaid. One way of approaching this goal is for proper value to be attached to women's reproductive labour in systems of national accounts. The true cost of policies needs to be made visible. Another step would be for countries to support equal pay for equal or comparable work, national childcare policies and full reproductive rights.

The obstacles to change are great. Women must struggle against patriarchy in their own society, the strength of transnational corporations and the inequalities generated by capitalism and with the difficulties of reforming a global system. However, the struggle for greater gender equality is one of the central issues in the development of a global political economy.

Conclusion

The global political economy is gendered. That is, macro-economic policies have differential impacts on men and women. Persistent and pervasive female poverty is one consequence of the power relations between women and men. While the relevant measures may be open to dispute there is widespread agreement on the existence and consequences of gender inequality. How gender inequality is manifested and the impact this has on the lived experience of women and girls vary because gender inequality is constructed and maintained in a specific social context. Differences in political systems, cultural traditions and economic institutions all have an impact on gender inequality

Although there is no single feminist perspective, feminist scholarship in the social sciences has explored the diverse ways in which gender is important in the global economy. Feminists have provided detailed empirical evidence showing the gendered nature of political and economic processes. They have also produced important critiques of the masculinist biases of conventional political economy.

Chapter 11

Economic Development

Attention to economic growth and development springs from a number of different motives. These include the eradication of global poverty, a reduction in inequalities in living standards and a lessening in global disparities of power and influence. A commitment to the pursuit of economic development as a means to eliminate poverty signals an aspiration that has been widely accepted by peoples and their governments around the globe. The World Bank's *Voices of the Poor* (Narayan *et al.*, 2000) provides an excellent introduction to the reality of poverty in its various manifestations as experienced by poor people from many countries. Although some agreement exists on these objectives, there is no consensus on the methods and strategies necessary for the achievement of these goals.

This chapter is centrally concerned with the global pursuit of economic development in the period since the end of the Second World War. It provides an introduction to a central issue in the contemporary global political economy through an assessment of the ways in which states and other actors have engaged with the challenge of aspirations for material improvement in the context of persistent global inequality. Despite universal acceptance of, and support for, economic development, it nevertheless remains a profoundly controversial concept. Proponents differ concerning its definition and the policies likely to bring it about. Many of these debates concerning development are themselves linked to other debates surrounding capitalism and modernity. In this chapter we analyse development both as an aspiration or goal, and as a concrete set of practices.

The late 20th century's obsession with economic development (a fixation carried over to the 21st century) finds its roots in an earlier period. The origins of the quest for economic development are to be found in the onset of the era of modern economic growth begun in Western Europe with the industrial revolution in Britain in the 18th century. Since Britain's successful industrialization, modernizing elites around the globe have attempted to emulate this feat (Kemp, 1983, pp. 1–17). The linkages between industrialization and military power further fuelled the drive for modernization (Sen, 1981). Until the Second World War, a country's industrialization was perceived almost solely as a national objective. This does not mean that there were no international implications but rather that economic growth, understood principally in terms of industrialization, proceeded without appeals for international assistance. This phase came to an end when, in the post-war era, the promotion of economic growth in poorer countries became an international issue. The quest for economic development, as it was now called, has been a significant feature of the post-World War II international system. A proclaimed objective of Third World elites, international organizations and Western governments, economic development has become an indisputable and undeniable right of peoples living in poverty. It has been claimed that, 'The development project brought all nations into line with the idea of national economic growth, even across the Cold War divide' (McMichael, 1996, p. 243). This global consensus on development as a fundamental goal of nation-states and recognition of the inescapable international dimension of this process are currently articulated in the context of the Millennium Development Goals (MDGs). At the 2000 United Nations Millennium Summit world leaders adopted the Millennium Declaration which established eight goals to be achieved by 2015 (see Box 11.1). These eight goals are supplemented by eighteen measurable targets in order to identify progress made (see Box 11.2). In March 2002 the UN convened an International Conference on Financing for Development in Monterrey, Mexico. At the conclusion of the conference governments adopted the Monterrey Consensus. Together with the MDGs, the Monterrey Consensus provides the key normative underpinning of contemporary development strategy. It is noteworthy for its emphasis on the importance of enabling domestic environments in generating and supporting productive investment; and its recognition of a supportive international environment in the struggle to eradicate poverty, achieve sustained economic growth and promote sustainable development.

This chapter begins by exploring the debates over several of the key terms encountered in discussions of international development. In the theoretical perspectives section we explore two major debates – internal vs external causation and the role of the state. Under major developments we discuss

---

Box 11.1   The Millennium Development Goals

Goal 1: Eradicate extreme poverty and hunger
Goal 2: Achieve universal primary education
Goal 3: Promote gender equality and empower women
Goal 4: Reduce child mortality
Goal 5: Improve maternal health
Goal 6: Combat HIV/AIDS, malaria and other diseases
Goal 7: Ensure environmental sustainability
Goal 8: Develop a Global Partnership for Development

Source: Reproduced from http://www.un.org/millenniumgoals/goals.html

Box 11.2 Implementing the MDGs: targets to be achieved by 2015

Target 1: Halve the proportion of people whose income is less than one dollar a day

Target 2: Halve the proportion of people who suffer from hunger

Target 3: Ensure that all boys and girls complete a full course of primary education

Target 4: Eliminate gender disparity in primary and secondary education, preferably by 2005, and in all levels of education by 2015

Target 5: Reduce by two-thirds the mortality rate of children under five

Target 6: Reduce by three-quarters the maternal mortality ratio

Target 7: Halt and begin to reverse the spread of HIV/AIDS

Target 8: Halt and begin to reverse the incidence of malaria and other major diseases

Target 9: Integrate the principles of sustainable development into country policies and programmes; reverse the loss of environmental resources

Target 10: Reduce by half the proportion of people without sustainable access to safe drinking water

Target 11: Achieve a significant improvement in the lives of at least 100 million slum dwellers by 2020

Target 12: Develop further an open, rule-based, predictable, nondiscriminatory trading and financial system that includes a commitment to good governance, development and poverty reduction both nationally and internationally

Target 13: Address the special needs of the least developed countries

Target 14: Address the special needs of landlocked developing countries and small island developing states

Target 15: Deal comprehensively with the debt problems of developing countries

Target 16: In cooperation with developing countries develop decent and productive work for youth

Target 17: In cooperation with pharmaceutical companies, provide access to affordable essential drugs in developing countries

Target 18: In cooperation with the private sector, make available the benefits of new technologies, especially information and communications

Source: Summarized from http://www.un.org/millenniumgoals/goals.html

changes in approaches to development and development planning. The key issues considered in this chapter are: the organization of development; debt and debt relief; and North–South conflict.

Definitions

Like many concepts in the social sciences the concept of development remains ill-defined and contested. As Cherry Gertzl asserts, 'There is no consensus as to what development means or requires' (1995, p. 1). In this section we discuss how people have interpreted the concept of development, and also controversies surrounding the terminology to be applied to countries that are in the process of overcoming mass poverty. Development, as used in the literature, suggests both a process and a condition. It is a process, in so far as attention is given to the means whereby a society may transform itself so that it achieves self-sustaining economic growth. In the words of Anna Dickson, development is 'an on-going process of qualitatively ameliorated social, political and economic change' (1997, p. 16). The term is also used to denote the condition reached by those societies that have made the successful transition to self-sustaining growth. It has also been seen as the condition in which 'individuals are more aware of, and have greater access to (such) new technologies, and are induced to take advantage of their possibilities through the working of market forces' (Sundrum, 1983, p. 15). The definition given by Thomas and Reader captures development seen as both process and condition. They define development as a 'multidimensional process involving change from a less to a more socially desirable state' (1997, p. 91).

As the result of an historical accident, modern economic growth developed in Western Europe and has been successfully exported almost exclusively to territories settled by Europeans. One unfortunate result of this historical accident has been a tendency to examine development as a process taking place almost exclusively in non-European areas of the globe. Thus, although in 1948 the gap in living standards between some European societies (for example, Ireland, Portugal and Spain) and parts of the so-called developing world was fairly narrow, economic growth in Europe was never seen in terms of development. And when, after the fall of communism in Eastern Europe, attention turned to economic growth in the post-Soviet empire, these countries were categorized as transitional economies (or sometimes emerging markets) rather than as developing countries. Development then is, or shall we say became, the province of Africa, Asia, Latin America and the Caribbean, and the Pacific. For some writers, this geographical limitation is part of Western control of colonial and post-colonial peoples and territories (Escobar, 1995). The concept of development in this view was created as a means of taming and controlling the Third World. This is an influential thesis but whether one is convinced by its claims rests on its further assertion that the development discourse is incapable of meeting its stated objective (that is, economic progress) since it is an instrument of control. We return to this issue later.

In the immediate post-war period, development was defined in terms of economic growth, where the standard measure was the gross national product (GNP) of a country. This approach emphasized economic variables and gave little if any attention to social and cultural aspects of development. Moreover, because of its focus on aggregate growth, internal redistribution (that is, the different rates of growth of different regions) and the impact of growth on various social classes were not taken into account. Underlying this perspective was a naive faith in the so-called trickle-down effect. Redistributive issues were perceived as second-order concerns. In other words, overall economic growth was necessary before attention could be given to dealing with inequality. This view was given scientific support by the Kuznets curve, which plotted the relationship between economic growth and equality (Kuznets, 1966). According to the Kuznets curve an inverse relationship existed between growth and equity at early levels of development, with a more positive link developing as economic growth increased. This perspective which equated economic growth with development came increasingly under fire in the 1960s. When Dudley Seers (1969) published his 'The Meaning of Development' article in 1969, it provided the first comprehensive alternative to the traditional definition. Seers contended that the development as growth model was too restrictive, and failed to address the multifaceted nature of development. He was particularly concerned with equity, and insisted that the definition of development should include social objectives such as employment, health and shelter. Development in this perspective was concerned with decreasing poverty and improving welfare indicators. Not only has the definition of development changed but the scope of traditional concerns has widened over time. Initially development policies failed to recognize the gender dimension, but since the publication of Ester Boserup's pioneering study *Woman's Role in Economic Development* in 1970 (Boserup, 1989) increasing attention has been given to women's role in development. This is partly the result of academic research and writing and partly a response to grass-roots activism.

Many economists continue to measure development in terms of gross national product. This should not be seen as a refusal to update their methods but rather reflects the advantages in using a single measure. Despite the various deficiencies that have been raised concerning GNP as an indicator, it is a standard, well-known measure that allows cross-national comparisons to be made. But critics of an economic definition have also developed criteria with which to measure development. Perhaps the best-known such

Table 11.1 Social indicators of development for selected countries, 2005

HDI rank	Life expectancy at birth (years)	Adult literacy rate (%)	GDP/capita (PPP $US)	Human Development Index value
High human development				
1 Iceland	81.5	a	35,510	0.968
2 Norway	79.8	a	41,420	0.968
3 Australia	80.9	a	31,794	0.962
4 Canada	80.35	a	33,375	0.961
5 Ireland	78.4	a	38,505	0.959
Medium human development				
71 Dominica	79.6	88.0	6,393	0.796
72 Saint Lucia	79.5	94.8	6,707	0.795
73 Kazakhstan	79.4	99.5	7,877	0.794
74 Venezuela	79.2	93.0	6,632	0.792
75 Colombia	79.1	92.8	7,304	0.791
Low human development				
173 Mali	53.1	24.0	1,033	0.380
174 Niger	55.8	28.7	781	0.374
175 Guinea-Bissau	45.8	...	827	0.374
176 Burkina Faso	51.4	23.6	1,213	0.370
177 Sierra Leone	49.8	34.8	806	0.336

a – a value of 99.0 was applied for purposes of calculating the HDI

Source: Data from UNDP (2007/8), pp. 229–32.

measure is the Human Development Index (HDI) pioneered by the United Nations Development Programme (UNDP). The HDI is based on a definition of development that takes account of social factors (see Table 11.1).

In 1990 the UNDP published its first Human Development Report. It argued that 'the real wealth of a nation is its people. And the purpose of development is to create an enabling environment for people to enjoy long, healthy creative lives' (UNDP, 1990, p. 9). This focus on human development goes beyond income. The UNDP invented the Human Development Index as a basis for classifying countries. It is based on life expectancy, education (adult literacy and mean years of schooling) and income. The report ranks countries according to HDI and is published annually. The HDI then looks at data to find the current minimum value (for example, life expectancy of 40.5 in Zambia) and the current maximum value (a life expectancy of 82.3 in Japan). Each country is then ranked according to the distance travelled from the minimum towards the maximum (expressed as a percentage). Concentrating on the classification of countries, the *Human Development Report* divides countries into three groups. The first group comprises those with high human development, with a HDI of 0.8000 and above. Its membership is currently 70 and it includes all developed countries and some developing countries such as Argentina, Barbados and Cuba. The category of medium human development, with a HDI of between 0.5000 and 0.799 is the second group. Currently comprising 85 countries, it includes many middle-income developing countries, emerging economies and traditional developing states. For example, the category currently includes Armenia, China and South Africa. The third group, with a HDI of below 0.500 currently comprises 22 countries. This groups together many of the poorest countries in the world and is heavily concentrated in sub-Saharan Africa (for example, Burkina Faso, Niger and Sierra Leone) (UNDP, 2007/8).

The use of GNP per capita vs the HDI is not just a statistical exercise. Because the HDI measures social factors it will give higher rankings to societies that have a more equal distribution of wealth and invest in social services. In contrast, GNP per capita can rank societies that have a large amount of wealth highly no matter what its distribution amongst the population. Thus, HDI will favour countries with a social democratic or socialist leaning compared to GNP per capita. A country can do well on one index and poorly on the other (see Table 11.2). A country's relative ranking allows a government to claim it is doing well or the opposition to attack a government for poor performance.

It is now widely agreed that development cannot be confined solely to economic growth. While there is agreement that development refers to economic, social and cultural variables, no consensus exists on either how we measure development or how it might be attained. To some extent the

Table 11.2   HDI vs GNP ranking

HDI rank	Country	Change from GDP rank
3	Australia	+13
12	United States	−10
51	Cuba	+43
61	Saudi Arabia	−19
121	South Africa	−65

Source: UNDP (2007/8).

search for a consensual meaning is a fruitless one and we will conclude this discussion with two observations. First, development is more than mere economic growth and involves structural change and attitudinal change in a given society. It requires a structural transformation of the economy and a movement from a 'traditional' value system to a 'modern' one. Second, development consists of a set of material practices and a collection of ideas and statements. This controversy concerning the term 'development' is mirrored in debates concerning the terminology and classification of countries seeking to make the transition to the ranks of the advanced industrial countries.

Immediately after the Second World War these countries were variously called underdeveloped, poor or backward. As more and more of these countries gained their independence these terms came to be seen as derogatory and offensive. By the early 1960s these terms were replaced by the term 'less developed country' but by the mid-1960s this term itself was held to be offensive and was replaced by the now ubiquitous term 'developing country'. Another term to describe a group of developing countries was coined in the 1950s and has also come under critical scrutiny. The term 'Third World' reflected more a political than an economic division in the world but came to be used interchangeably with that of developing country. Various critics have argued that the term Third World implies inferiority since third comes after first and second. However, such criticism is misplaced and signally fails to acknowledge the origin of the term. When Alfred Sauvy first used the term in 1952, he was making an analogy with the Third Estate in French civil society and emphasizing the revolutionary potential of the countries so classified. Thus, governments and many civil society organizations in the developing world have retained the use of this term since they do not attach a negative connotation to it. In the 1970s it became fashionable to refer to the Third World as the South since most of these countries were in the southern hemisphere. In the 1990s this terminology was replaced by that of 'Global South', partly to indicate the fact that conditions of poverty and marginalization occurred in advanced industrial societies; thus, the term referred to people regardless of their geographical location. However, the term has become popularized in a manner that makes its usage no different from the term it replaced. It thus appears to be useful for the geographically illiterate in that it reminds them that South does not mean the south of whatever country they find themselves in! But whether one uses developing, Third World, South or Global South, the grouping is invariably the same.

While debate about terminology is not substantive, a further debate concerning divisions within this group of countries has greater political significance. The group defined as developing is large and heterogeneous, as we discuss below. The heterogeneity of the group has given rise to a debate on the criteria to be used in making divisions within the grouping, and the names to be given to these various sub-groups. Indeed, at various times it has been argued that instead of a singular category we should recognize a number of different types of countries that are not developed. Division into groups is an inherently subjective and political exercise. For example, following the first oil price rise in 1973 it became fashionable to talk about a Third World, a Fourth World and a Fifth World, ostensibly on the basis of their access to petroleum resources, but this was an ideological intervention at a time when the solidarity of the developing world threatened Western interests. In a similar vein, when in the 1990s financial analysts began to refer to developing countries that offered the opportunity for profitable investment as 'emerging markets', this signified a positive evaluation and was designed to speed the transfer of funds to these countries.

Theoretical perspectives on growth and development

The political economy of development has initiated a number of theoretical debates and controversies. Instead of detailing these various debates and issues that have engendered such conflict, this section examines two of the enduring schisms discernible in discussions on development and links them with historical debates. Theorists and practitioners interested in the economic development of a particular state or region can be divided according to their views on two issues. The first concerns the relative importance of internal or external factors for the failure of a society to achieve development. The second issue is related to the comparative roles of the state and the market in promoting development. As will become apparent, these debates reflect and replay the inter-paradigm debate in IPE. Liberal theorists have tended to emphasize the role of internal factors in the success or failure of a

state to achieve development. Writers influenced by the economic nationalist tradition have no consistent approach to this issue with some agreeing
with the liberal perspective and others agreeing with radical writers, who
give greater weight to the role of external factors in inhibiting national development. It is not surprising that in the arguments concerning the relative
importance of the state and market as agents of economic development, that
economic nationalist writers will emphasize the role of the state and liberal
theorists will give more credence to market-related factors. Critical perspective writers, while focusing on the role of global capitalism, have tended to
support state initiatives in this debate.

We spend some time exploring the first of these two issues before turning
to the second. Proponents of what we term the 'internal causation theory'
begin from the assumption that the absence of development in a particular
society results from that society's failure to harness its resources in a way
relevant to the demands of modern economic growth. The causes of underdevelopment are to be found in the underdeveloped society and the solution
to underdevelopment is therefore to be found at the domestic level. This view
was first and most systematically articulated in modernization theory.

Modernization theory originated in American sociology and economics,
and adopted an evolutionary perspective on social change, taking the view
that the currently underdeveloped societies were at an earlier stage of development than the advanced industrial countries. These poor countries could
develop if they adopted similar attitudes and social structures to the developed world. W. W. Rostow's *Stages of Economic Growth* (1960) presented
the definitive statement of modernization theory's approach. He argued that
there were five phases or stages of development which a country had to pass
through. The movement from one stage to the next depended on raising standards of living and adopting modern values.

In contrast to this focus on internal causes of and solutions to underdevelopment, a different approach, which can be termed the 'external causation theory', is adopted by many practitioners and scholars. From this
perspective underdevelopment is the result of external forces that constrain
a society's efforts to develop. The most widely influential example of external causation theory is dependency theory, which arose in the mid-1960s as
a direct challenge to modernization theory. The dependency school began
with analyses of Latin America (Dos Santos, 1970; Frank, 1967, 1969), but
was extended to cover Africa (Amin, 1976) and the Caribbean (Beckford,
1972; Thomas, 1974). Dependency theorists argued that lack of development was not the result of poverty and the absence of modern values but
instead was the direct consequence of economic exploitation. Whereas for
modernization theorists development depended essentially on national
efforts, for dependency theorists underdevelopment was the other side of
development. Underdevelopment was a condition historically created by

development. Dependency theory argues that the development of some countries has resulted in the underdevelopment of others. Current advanced industrial societies only achieved this status through the expropriation of economic surplus from the currently underdeveloped societies. Moreover, whereas modernization theory predicted a successful transition to development for the underdeveloped world through the adaptation of specified practices, dependency theory argued that development was an impossibility within a capitalist international economic system. It was only by delinking or opting out that the poor would be able to prosper. Dependency theory contends that the developing countries do not have any meaningful choices since they are controlled directly or indirectly by external influences.

From the perspective taken in this book, both internal causation and external causation theories are flawed. A complex phenomenon such as development is not attributable to forces arising from a single level of analysis. National societies are, as we have demonstrated in Part II of this book, integrally linked to an emerging global political economy. This observation severely weakens the internal causation perspective which relegates external causes to an, at best, secondary role. Similarly we have presented evidence to show that external structures are mediated through internal processes in ways that are not automatic, thus raising serious questions about the external causation approach. Moreover, the relationship between external and internal variables is not fixed and their relative importance will vary according to national society and historical period.

Turning to the two variants of the approaches discussed, it should be clear that modernization theory in its failure to address external structural constraints omitted a crucial set of considerations. Dependency theory was not only over-pessimistic but it overstated the impact of external conditions on domestic development, and could not account for differential rates of economic progress of countries faced with a similar external environment. While there are many cases in which developing countries have limited choice and are satellites or appendages of foreign companies or countries, one does not have to accept the simple dependency hypothesis since it overstates the constraints facing decision-makers.

In short, development is neither solely an internal affair nor driven relentlessly by external pressures. Furthermore, the distinction between domestic and external policy is an analytical convenience that cannot be sustained when examining policy-making and economic development in poor, weak states with open economies. For many governments in the Third World, blaming the external environment is an easy option when domestic reform proves difficult. For most developing countries, efforts to improve the external environment will not bring the hoped-for rewards unless at the same time efforts are made to change internal policy-making. The stress on external change can be misguided and is frequently employed in an effort to avoid dealing with domestic problems. A thoroughly benign external environment cannot assist a dysfunctional domestic system. And it is arguable that a malign external environment can do less damage to a country that has a degree of flexibility and efficiency in its decision-making.

On the other hand, attention to internal issues should not blind us to the fact that not all problems are domestic in origin. There have been and continue to be external forces over which poor countries have limited control. All developing countries can be injured or overwhelmed by external events and forces for which they bear no responsibility such as the oil crisis or global inflation. The international system imposes a hierarchy of hindrances and dangers that affect different countries in different ways but nevertheless do create barriers of injustice. However, there are many cases where the choices for Third World nations are not completely determined by outside forces, and these choices are neither trivial nor meaningless. The available choices may be sharply circumscribed by the weakness and poverty of the Third World and the options available may be heavily conditioned by the attitudes and assumptions of the advanced industrial countries, but even within these boundaries the possibility of better or worse decisions for each country has frequently remained open. Moreover, the persistent impact of nationalism, the growth of indigenous capacities and the impact of international organizations have increased the desire and ability of developing countries' elites to make their own decisions.

As enduring as the debate on the relative impact of external and internal variables is the debate between proponents of the market and those of the state as the critical actors in promoting development. While the debate concerning the relative merits of the state and the market continues to engage adversaries concerned with promoting development, we illustrate the key issues involved in the debate through an examination of a specific moment.

The success of the Asian newly industrializing countries (NICs) – Singapore, Taiwan, South Korea and Hong Kong, collectively known as the Four Tigers – spurred a debate concerning the reasons for their success. Between 1965 and 1980 these countries achieved impressive levels of economic performance characterized by fast growth, low inflation, macroeconomic stability and a strong fiscal position, high savings rates, open economies and thriving export sectors allied with improvement in welfare indicators such as life expectancy and literacy (see Table 11.3). In the 1980s and early 1990s a second tier of East Asian countries – Indonesia, Malaysia, the Philippines and Thailand – appeared poised to repeat this success.

Two competing schools of thought developed – the neoliberal school, which emphasized the export-oriented industrialization policies adopted by these states, and the developmental state school, which put most stress on the ability of the state to intervene successfully in the economy. Neoliberal scholars argued that the success of the NICs derived from their adherence to

Table 11.3 Economic and welfare indicators for Asian NICs

Economic indicators

	GNP/ capita	Average annual CPI (%)	Export of goods and services % of GDP		Gross domestic saving % of GDP	
	1960–78	1970–8	1960	1978	1960	1978
Korea	6.9	19.3	3	34	1	28
Rep. of Taiwan	6.6	10.3	11	59	13	33
Hong Kong	6.5	7.7	79	98	1	15
Singapore	7.4	6.1	163	164	3	27

Welfare indicators

	Adult literacy (%)		Life expectancy	
	1975	1998	1978	1998
Korea	93	97.5	63	72.6
Rep. of Taiwan	82	...	72	...
Hong Kong	90	92.9	72	78.6
Singapore	75	91.8	70	77.3

Sources: Data from World Bank (1980), p. 11; UNDP (2000), p. 157.

market discipline, and promotion of export-led growth. Unlike the majority of developing countries, which developed highly interventionist policies, the NICs, in pursuing growth, had chosen to deregulate their economies. Success was the result of the pursuit of liberal economic policies, a climate conducive to foreign investment and a minimal role for the state (Hughes, 1988, 1989; World Bank, 1993). For successful industrialization the government's role should be limited to the promotion of free trade, the provision of free labour markets, high interest rates to encourage savings and conservative budgets. Neoliberals criticized the suspicious and at times hostile attitude to the international economy taken by most developing countries. These countries tried to limit interaction with external actors and promoted industrialization through a process of import substitution. Import substitution industrialization (ISI) denotes a high-tariff policy in which the aim is to keep foreign products out, develop domestic infant industries, and industrialize behind these high protectionist barriers. ISI policies tended to run into bottlenecks unless the developing country had a sufficiently large market. The costs of industrialization were immense, and the costs of imported technology and intermediate goods meant that, far from saving foreign exchange, the country was still running a large import bill. Neoliberal theorists argued that successful industrialization in the NICs was based on a diametrically opposed strategy to ISI (see Table 11.4 for statistical support of the superiority of the NICs' export-led growth compared to Latin America's ISI growth). Instead of protecting the domestic market these countries had taken an open view towards foreign capital and had promoted industrialization through exports rather than import substitution.

Proponents of the developmental state perspective (Amsden, 1989; Wade, 1990; White, 1988) did not dispute the export orientation of the NICs but argued that the state had played a crucial and determining role in East Asian industrialization. In the first place these countries did not begin with a process of export-oriented industrialization (EOI) but had undergone an ISI phase first. The crucial issue was not ISI versus EOI but rather the point at which governments switched from ISI to EOI. Moreover, EOI was not, as was claimed by neoliberal apologists, a recipe for laissez-faire economics; on the contrary governments had been active in promoting EOI. In this perspective the quality of government intervention and the choice of industrial policies and strategies were critical to economic success. With the exception of Hong Kong, governmental intervention was extensive in East Asia. Successful government intervention was based on a powerful set of policy instruments, a corporatist/authoritarian model of the state and the ability to restructure the economy towards high-technology production. The success of the NICs was the result of strong states governing the market. In other words, government intervention was vital in promoting economic development.

The strength of the neoliberal approach lies in its critique of ISI, and its weakness arises from its failure to give sufficient attention to historical factors. The strength of the developmental state model arises from its comparative analysis of political factors in the success or failure of economic policy, and its weakness lies in the difficulty of assessing the effectiveness of government intervention in development policy. It is worth noting a third approach to explaining East Asian development. This is the cultural approach, which emphasizes the role of Asian values. According to this perspective, the NICs succeeded because of the impact of Confucianism on their societies (see Box 11.3). What this argument fails to confront is the many centuries in which Confucianism appeared to be an obstacle to economic progress. It isn't clear how or why centuries of stagnation were suddenly transformed into economic success when the cultural component remained the same.

Table 11.4 Comparison of Latin American and East Asian economies, 1965–80 (per cent)

	Annual rate of growth of real GDP		Annual rate of growth of manufacturing		Annual rate of growth of exports	
	1965–80	**1980–9**	**1965–80**	**1980–9**	**1965–80**	**1980–9**
Latin American countries						
Argentina	3.5	–0.3	2.7	–0.6	4.7	0.6
Brazil	8.8	3	9.8	2.2	9.3	5.6
Chile	1.9	2.7	0.6	2.9	7.9	4.9
Colombia	5.8	3.5	6.4	3.1	1.4	9.8
Mexico	6.5	0.7	7.4	0.7	7.6	3.7
Peru	3.9	0.4	3.8	0.4	1.6	0.4
Venezuela	3.7	1	5.8	4.9	–9.5	11.3
Latin America and Caribbean (average)	6	1.6	7	1.5	–1	3.6
East Asian countries						
Hong Kong	8.6	7.1	n.a.	n.a.	9.5	6.3
Indonesia	8	5.3	12	12.7	9.6	2.4
Korea	9.6	9.7	18.7	13.1	27.2	13.8
Malaysia	7.3	4.9	–	8	4.4	9.8
Singapore	10.1	6.1	13.2	5.9	4.7	8.1
Thailand	7.2	7	11.2	8.1	8.5	12.8
East Asian (average)	7.2	7.9	10.6	12.6	10	10

Sources: Data from World Bank (1989, 1990).

This debate between competing schools of thought was of profound importance to other developing countries since the various perspectives had implicit or, indeed, explicit assumptions concerning the relevance or lessons of East Asian success for their economies. The liberal laissez-faire model was the easiest to follow and partly accounts for its success/emulation for/by

Box 11.3   Confucianism and economic development

The core values of Confucianism are derived from the concept of *ren*. *Ren* (goodness, humanity) describes the highest human achievement reached through moral self-cultivation. The implications for the individual include a collective orientation, reciprocity and knowledge through intuition. One result of the high priority given to these values in the business environment is a focus on the social and relational aspects of the business transaction. Trust developed through interaction in the public and private lives of partners is built to ensure the long-term nature of business relationships. Decision-making is less confrontational and involves consensus and cooperation, with mutual benefits being a high priority of all business deals. The importance of the family to Confucianism permeates into business life with companies becoming the second family of individuals. Paternalistic leadership encourages respect and long-term commitment on the part of employees.

many developing countries. This required countries to deregulate, privatize and dismantle governmental controls. Although this was not easy to do in societies where vested interests supported protectionism, and governments depended on these vested interests, theoretically, it was the easiest of the options. The second option required changes in governance structures and more fundamental societal change. The conditions for the creation of a developmental state were far from obvious. The third approach was the most pessimistic since Asian cultural values could not easily be transferred to Africa, Latin America, the Caribbean or the Pacific.

Major developments

From the foregoing it should be obvious that the pursuit of economic development has excited passions, aroused debate and affected billions of people in the post-war era. While each society will have its own periodization based on political and economic indicators, we outline two broad historical periods in the evolution of development as an issue in the global political economy. Undoubtedly, views about development and development practices have altered many times in the past five decades in response to the experiences of developing countries and a changing global economy. Arguably, however, a major change occurred at the beginning of the 1980s when, in McMichael's (1996) terminology, the development project was discarded in favour of the globalization project. The first period we discuss is one in which the nation-state was perceived as a key instrument in the search for economic growth and development, and development was conceived principally in national terms. In the second period far greater emphasis has been given to the importance of market forces, and development has been conceived primarily in terms of the world market.

Development and national capitalism, 1947–81

Development in this period was conceived principally as a project of a strong and active government. States were expected in the Keynesian post-war compromise to establish a balance between supply and demand for goods; to encourage consumption; to promote growth of domestic industries; and to provide a safety net for their citizens in the form of social welfare. Keynesian economic theory sought a balance between non-intervention in the market by the state and guided control.

The political conditions for the nationalist development project were laid by the post-independence modernizing elites who were intent on securing economic growth as a mechanism to bolster their legitimacy. At the same time many of these regimes were weak or corrupt or both. They thus pursued policies that supported their continued hold on power rather than those most likely to lift the majority of their population from poverty. In a bid to protect both the regime and sovereignty many governments devised measures to increase the power of the state. A belief that the external environment was not conducive to development led, on one hand, to criticism of the international economy and the major international economic organizations and, on the other, to domestic policies of import substitution.

The quest for economic development was shaped and moulded by developments in the world economy and by the attitudes and actions of governments and international organizations. A number of changes in the international economy were to have a profound impact on the prospects for development in this first period. A striking characteristic of the international economy for most of this period was economic recovery and strong growth trends, especially among the advanced industrial countries. Between 1947 and 1971 the world economy experienced a period of unprecedented growth. This growth began to falter in 1971 with the collapse of the Bretton Woods system of monetary management and came to an end after the first oil crisis of 1973–4. During this period, although many developing countries experienced high growth rates, most of this increase was consumed by high population growth. Moreover, the benefits from the post-war long boom of economic growth were limited for the developing countries. The post-war boom was based on the growth of manufactured exports and since most developing countries relied on primary commodities the dynamism of the world economy was irrelevant to their prospects. But if their gains from post-war growth were meagre, the downturn in the world economy in the mid-1970s created an unfavourable economic climate. The first oil shock triggered, but was not solely responsible for, the onset of global recession in 1974. Non-oil-exporting developing countries were faced with a severely deteriorating balance of payments. It was in this period that Third World debt began to grow as governments borrowed to meet their obligations. The second oil shock of 1979 plunged many countries into severe balance-of-payments problems, and heralded the difficult times ahead. These events exposed the vulnerability of Third World economies and opened up divisions among them as the gap in the pace of growth between the middle-income and low-income countries widened.

The practice of development was also shaped by changing ideas about development. Early theories of economic development were concerned with establishing the characteristics of underdevelopment. Studies such as Gunnar Myrdal's *Asian Drama* (1968) helped to demonstrate the differences between the industrial world and the underdeveloped one. Without resorting to caricature, the standard view of an underdeveloped country saw it as one with a predominantly large population characterized by the absence of modern values. The theory of economic dualism developed in the 1950s asserted that developing countries were characterized both by a modern, dynamic and a traditional, stagnant sector. The task was to expand the small modern sector through investment. To the early development economists it seemed that development was a relatively simple matter of the application of certain techniques. At the beginning of this period there was also a naive belief in trickle-down economics. It was believed that economic growth would trickle down from the rich to the poor within societies. Over time it became increasingly apparent that this optimism was ill founded. During the 1960s these views were increasingly challenged as some analysts shifted the focus from the internal problems of developing countries to the negative impact of the external environment.

The orthodox position held at the beginning of this period came under sustained attack from a number of sources. Although there was agreement with the dominant position that industrialization provided the path to development, the view that underdevelopment arose from domestic failings was challenged by dependency theory. However, from the perspective of policy-making it was the terms of trade argument that made most impression. Simply put, the terms of trade thesis alleges that there is a persistent tendency for the terms of trade of primary commodities to fall vis-à-vis manufactured exports. This thesis was propounded by Raul Prebisch, the first Secretary General of UNCTAD, and was influential with policy-makers in the developing world. The terms of trade thesis led to export pessimism and supported ISI policies, but it also led to two specific campaigns. First, it provided the economic rationale for preferential access for the manufactured exports of developing countries. If dependence on primary commodities condemned developing countries to a foreign exchange gap it was logical to support their diversification into manufactured exports. Similarly, the terms of trade thesis provided the rationale for international commodity agreements as a mechanism to halt the decline in export earnings.

The downturn in the world economy in the mid-1970s and the failure of industrialization and trickle-down policies led to a new approach. The 'basic needs' approach, which gained support from the ILO and World Bank in the mid-1970s, rejected trickle-down policies and argued for redistribution with growth, and also replaced the focus on industrialization with one giving greater attention to agriculture and the rural sector. Furthermore, gender considerations had been absent from orthodox development theory. During this period, research on gender and development began to show the necessity to bring such considerations to the forefront.

Another crucial feature of this period was the development of a Third World coalition to campaign for change in the international economic order. Modernizing Third World elites began to articulate a distinctive set of interests within the global economy. Although divided by levels of economic development, ideology, political systems, culture and amazing diversity of domestic economic policies, the governing elites of developing countries were united in their demand for additional resources and reform of the international economic order. In the post-independence world, Third World elites were willing to assert their own vision of development. They did so through two main organizations. The Non-Aligned Movement (NAM) created in 1960, although mainly concerned with political issues, progressively addressed what it saw as the failures of the post-war liberal international economic order, and was instrumental in making reform of this order a key diplomatic issue in the 1970s. The second organization, the Group of 77 (G-77) became the chief vehicle through which Third World demands were aggregated and articulated (see Box 11.4 for membership). The developing countries, grouped together as the G-77, lobbied UN organizations and, as the Group of 24, brought a collective Third World voice to the World Bank and IMF. During this period the most intense and politically significant campaign occurred over proposals for a New International Economic Order (NIEO), which is discussed below.

The international political environment, and specifically the Cold War context, was also significant for most of this period. Western and communist states competed for the allegiance of Third World states and this competition was not solely political or strategic. It was also an engagement over economic ideology, markets and access to resources. Was capitalism superior to communism as the economic system likely to bring prosperity? Which side would have access to the strategic minerals in the developing world?

Box 11.4   Group of 77 membership, 2009

Afghanistan, Algeria, Angola, Antigua and Barbuda, Argentina, Bahamas, Bahrain, Bangladesh, Barbados, Belize, Benin, Bhutan, Bolivia (Plurinational State of), Bosnia and Herzegovina, Botswana, Brazil, Brunei Darussalam, Burkina Faso, Burundi, Cambodia, Cameroon, Cape Verde, Central African Republic, Chad, Chile, China, Colombia, Comoros, Congo, Costa Rica, Cote d'Ivoire, Cuba, Democratic People's Republic of Korea, Democratic Republic of the Congo, Djibouti, Dominica, Dominican Republic, Ecuador, Egypt, El Salvador, Equatorial Guinea, Eritrea, Ethiopia, Fiji, Gabon, Gambia, Ghana, Grenada, Guatemala, Guinea, Guinea-Bissau, Guyana, Haiti, Honduras, India, Indonesia, Iran (Islamic Republic of), Iraq, Jamaica, Jordan, Kenya, Kuwait, Lao People's Democratic Republic, Lebanon, Lesotho, Liberia, Libyan Arab Jamahiriya, Madagascar, Malawi, Malaysia, Maldives, Mali, Marshall Islands, Mauritania, Mauritius, Micronesia (Federated States of), Mongolia, Morocco, Mozambique, Myanmar, Namibia, Nepal, Nicaragua, Niger, Nigeria, Oman, Pakistan, Palestine, Panama, Papua New Guinea, Paraguay, Peru, Philippines, Qatar, Rwanda, St. Kitts and Nevis, St. Lucia, St. Vincent and the Grenadines, Samoa, São Tomé and Principe, Saudi Arabia, Senegal, Seychelles, Sierra Leone, Singapore, Solomon Islands, Somalia, South Africa, Sri Lanka, Sudan, Suriname, Swaziland, Syrian Arab Republic, Thailand, Timor-Leste, Togo, Tonga, Trinidad and Tobago, Tunisia, Turkmenistan, Uganda, United Arab Emirates, United Republic of Tanzania, Uruguay, Vanuatu, Venezuela (Bolivarian Republic of), Viet Nam, Yemen, Zambia, Zimbabwe.

Source: Group of 77 at the United Nations, http://www.g77.org/doc/members.html

---

Which side would find a lucrative market for its products? These questions framed the pursuit of development. Moreover, the Sino-Soviet split brought competition between Moscow and Beijing for Third World support. The West responded to the perceived threat of communism with reform of the World Bank and the GATT, and, in Latin America, the United States sponsored the Alliance for Progress. But at the same time that limited reform efforts were underway, and support was given for land reform, Western policy supported anti-communist governments rather than those committed to development. That is, the containment of communism was more important than the eradication of poverty. This support for the security state apparatus resulted in the squandering of economic resources.

Development, neoliberalism and beyond, 1982–2009

The eruption of the Mexican debt crisis in 1982 signalled a shift in the development project. Importantly, it changed relations between developing countries and industrial countries, between developing countries and international organizations, and among developing countries. At the end of the 1970s the second oil crisis and consequent recession hit many developing countries hard. It was apparent to astute commentators that development strategies at the end of the second Development Decade had failed. The World Bank began the process of structural adjustment lending in 1980 but it was the conditions created by the debt crisis that brought adjustment lending to the fore since it strengthened the conditionality imposed by the Bank and the IMF.

In August 1982 the Mexican government announced that it was unable to service its debt, thus bringing into the spotlight the severely indebted nature of many developing economies. The debt crisis was not only a problem for the international economy, it had fundamental implications for the distribution of power and for ways of thinking about development. The debt crisis initially challenged not only developing economies but also the Western banking system. During this period the debt crisis was the main issue in the international economy of importance to the development prospects of the developing countries. The economic consequences of the debt crisis were disastrous for most of the developing world. The 1980s have become known as the lost decade because of the overall decline in living standards, and the increased numbers of people living in poverty. The debt crisis also led to a fall of investment in the developing world and a sharper concentration of investment in a limited number of countries. It contributed to widening income gaps domestically and internationally, increased differentiation among the developing countries and reversed many of the gains made in the previous decade. Politically the debt crisis put the Third World coalition under severe strain partly because of the different levels of indebtedness, partly because of the uneven development which arose and partly because the response of Western creditors favoured the more politically and strategically important states. The debt crisis was also politically important since it increased the leverage of the multilateral financial institutions. The World Bank and IMF were given prominent roles in finding solutions to the crisis, and as lenders of the last resort were able to impose stringent disciplines on Third World debtors.

The debt crisis also heralded a major shift in the development paradigm. It swept away the basic needs and poverty alleviation approaches and replaced them with the neoliberal policy of structural adjustment (see Box 11.5). Although no single template exists for structural adjustment programmes they do have certain features in common. These include a

Box 11.5   Structural adjustment: the case of Mexico

Following the financial crisis in 1994 the Mexican government and the IMF agreed a structural adjustment programme. This was the second time in just over a decade that Mexico had sought the assistance of the IMF. The Mexican debt crisis in 1982 had ushered in an adjustment package.

On 1 February 1995, the International Monetary Fund approved an 18-month standby credit for Mexico of up to the equivalent of SDR 12070.2 million (about US$17.8 billion) in support of the government's 1995–6 economic and financial programme. The SAP attached to this loan has short- and long-term conditions. Structural adjustment is the long-term condition. In relation to its Mexican programme, the IMF stated: 'The domestic adjustment package, combining prudent fiscal and strong monetary and credit policies, a disciplined incomes policy, and further structural reforms, provides an appropriate policy response to current circumstances.'

Adjustment programmes have a number of common features. These include trade liberalization, privatization, deregulation, credit reduction and wage suppression. Critics of the programme argue that growing poverty, unemployment, depression of wages, the undermining of rural livelihoods and the disintegration of societies are also common to the programmes. The 1995 agreement consolidated and extended progress made in the area of IMF-imposed structural reform since 1982. It provided a reinforcement of the government's strategy for privatization, including privatization of basic infrastructure (rail, ports, airports, electricity generation and radio and telecommunications). Critics point to the adverse social effects that the programmes had on Mexico, including over 50 per cent of all Mexicans living in poverty, more than a quarter of a million people losing their jobs by May 1995, a sharp decline in real wages and the government's banning of free wage negotiation. Some even claim that economic policies are the cause of the Chiapas uprising.

curtailment of the role of the state in the economy, a bias towards the export sector and a penchant for free markets. Adjustment programmes sought to shift developing countries from a reliance on ISI to one on export-oriented industrialization (EOI). This shift in policy is frequently referred to as the Washington Consensus (Williamson, 1993), although the accuracy of this term to refer to a specific consensus that guided policy-making is disputed

(Naim, 2000a, 2000b). An intense debate that remains unresolved arose concerning the impact of adjustment programmes on the economy, the poor and women. Critics allege that structural adjustment programmes hurt the poorest, increase women's burdens and provide no effective solution to debt (Bangura and Beckman, 1991; Pio, 1994; Sahn, 1994). Supporters have acknowledged negative impacts of structural adjustment programmes, but have argued that these can be addressed (Kahn and Knight, 1986; Sisson, 1986). Their main contention is that countries undergoing adjustment have performed better economically than those without adjustment programmes.

As a consequence of the emphasis on rolling back the state, NGOs were given a greater role in development. Increasingly NGOs have played roles as service providers, bringing welfare, development relief and social services to the poor. In those circumstances, where the state proved incapable of meeting basic needs, NGOs have been critical in supporting the material needs of people. This emphasis on the role of NGOs has been supported by national governments in the industrialized world and by multilateral development agencies. It has been estimated that in 1990 NGOs disbursed $1 billion in development aid but by 1997 this figure had risen to $7.2 billion (UNDP, 2002, p. 102). Increasingly bilateral funds have been channelled through NGOs (Pinter, 2001, p. 201). Multilateral agencies have also increased funding to NGOs. The extent to which this increasingly close engagement between NGOs and official agencies is a positive development has been questioned by some analysts (Hulme and Edwards, 1997).

The failure of the demand for the NIEO suggested the difficulty faced by the Third World coalition as a force for change, but the impact of the debt crisis challenged its very *raison d'être*. The coalition survived the fragmentation and forces of disintegration and has re-emerged, although not as powerfully as in the 1970s, as the instrument through which a collective voice can be heard. It continues to insist that global inequalities remain relevant, and to coordinate positions before major conferences. Instead of arguing against the liberal system, as it did in the 1970s, it now seeks to ensure that developing countries are not discriminated against.

Until the end of the Cold War in 1989, the international political system was marked by continuing East–West tension and Sino-Soviet rivalry, with development needs sacrificed to political ends. The end of the Cold War in 1990 brought East–West competition in the developing world to a close. The end of communism has resulted in competition for investment and aid between former communist countries and traditional Third World countries. The end of communism also brought with it the end of the Soviet-style model and, given that China had since the onset of the Four Modernizations programme in 1979 effectively abandoned socialism, development was now cast firmly in capitalist terms. However, the dangers of an open world market were all too visibly brought to the fore by the Asian financial crisis that erupted in mid-1997. It showed again how vulnerable developing countries were, and how shallow much economic growth can be. The core Asian Tigers were not as hard hit as the second-tier countries, especially Thailand and Indonesia.

This post-Cold War period has been noticeable for a modification in the neoliberal development paradigm. The Rio Conference in 1992 officially established sustainable development as the new approach to development. Although no agreed definition of sustainable development exists, that of the Brundtland Commission (World Commission on Environment and Development, 1987) is most widely used. The Brundtland Commission defined sustainable development as development that meets the needs of the present generation without jeopardizing the resources available to future generations. The end of the Cold War and the movement to sustainable development were important in the new focus given to governance issues. It is now widely accepted that governance is an important component of the search for development, and in this pursuit democracy and democratization have come to occupy centre stage. This is a view of development far removed from the simple economic input model with which we began in the 1940s. Views have changed as the complexity of the task has become more apparent. But these changing views also represent the triumph of certain interests. The integration of sustainable development into the development paradigm as a core feature, renewed interest in poverty alleviation and a focus on governance resulted in an amelioration of the neoliberal approach or Washington Consensus. For some writers the emergence of a post-Washington Consensus, while an improvement on the original model, remains too narrow and incapable of meeting the needs of the poor (Hayami, 2003; Önis and Şenses, 2005).

The extent to which the 2008–9 economic crisis has forced a radical rethink of economic policy and a final abandonment of neoliberalism remains unclear. It is also too early to provide definitive evidence on the impact of the global financial and economic crises on developing countries. There, is, however, a widespread view that 'developing countries are being severely hit through weaker trade, tighter global financing conditions and lower remittances' (UN, 2009b, p. 1). Global growth slowed in 2008 and did not recover in 2009 and while the slackening of demand in the developed world, fall in private capital flows and foreign direct investment have on the whole reduced the income of developing countries and their growth prospects, the impact of the crisis has not been uniform in the developing world. Whether the focus is on employment, social protection (te Velde, 2009), trade (Meyn and Kennan, 2009) or remittances (Callí and Dell'Erba, 2009) the evidence suggests that the impact is varied, depending on both external and internal factors. It is apparent, nevertheless, that the poorest countries will be unable to escape the negative consequences of the economic downturn. A recent report from the World Bank estimates that the crisis will increase the number of people living in extreme poverty, on less than $1.25 a day, by 89 million more people by the end of 2010. The report further documents the impact of the global recession on core spending in areas such as education, health, infrastructure and social protection in the most vulnerable countries in 43 low-income countries. It is a $11.6 billion decline in core spending in areas such as education, health, infrastructure and social protection in the most vulnerable countries (World Bank, 2009b).

Key issues

Developing countries continue to face a large number of issues in their quest for economic development. These issues are raised throughout the book: developing countries and the trade regime in Chapter 6, bargaining with TNCs in Chapter 7, the debt crisis in Chapter 8, the division of labour in Chapter 9, sustainable development in Chapter 12 and governance issues in Chapter 15. This section focuses on three key issues that have dominated the global debate on development at the beginning of the 21st century and will continue to do so in the immediate future. The three key issues are: the organization of development; debt relief; and the North–South conflict.

The organization of development

Although the dominant view is that development will largely arise from national efforts, it is evident, as the previous section has shown, that development is also a process that is organized internationally. That is to say, national development aspirations and efforts are shaped by international organizations, the policies of donor states and ideas concerning the meaning and practice of development. A major issue in the global political economy of development is the role of international organizations in this process. There are a number of controversies concerning the specific policies and general impact of multilateral development agencies and international financial institutions. In this sub-section we provide a brief introduction to the role of the World Bank in the international organization of development.

The World Bank.   The World Bank is the world's premier multilateral development agency. It consists of five organizations – the International Bank for Reconstruction and Development (IBRD), International Development Association (IDA), International Finance Corporation (IFC), Multilateral Investment Guarantee Agency (MIGA) and the International Centre for the Settlement of Investment Disputes (ICSID). The Bank fulfils three main roles: it provides loans to countries; develops international

Table 11.5   IBRD lending by region, fiscal years 2000 and 2008

Share of total lending of $11.5 billion (2000) and share of total lending of $24.7 billion (2008)		
Percentage share of lending	**2000**	**2008**
Region		
Europe and central Asia	42	17
Latin America and the Caribbean	37	19
East Asia and Pacific	9	18
South Asia	8	17
Middle East and North Africa	4	6
Africa	1	23

Sources: Data from World Bank (2002), p. 27; World Bank (2008), p. 55.

norms; and resolves disputes. The most visible of these functions is that of the provision of loans to its member states. The IBRD provides loans and development assistance to middle-income countries and creditworthy poorer countries (see Tables 11.5–11.7), while the IDA provides long-term loans at zero interest to the poorest countries. Through its research and development activities and the conditions it attaches to its loans the World Bank contributes to the normative framework of international development. The Bank also tries to resolve disputes between its members and between its members and private creditors.

While the Bank has attracted some form of critical scrutiny from the outset of its operations, it has been in the forefront of controversy since the early 1980s. This is the result of a number of factors of which the most important are the impact of its adjustment policies on poorer countries in the 1980s and the impact of its policies on the environment. When the World Bank abandoned its basic needs approach in the early 1980s and, in tandem with the IMF, began to focus on structural adjustment lending, it ignited a debate on its lending policies that has still not lessened even though the Bank's lending policies have shifted significantly since these policies were first instituted. Adjustment policies pushed recipient countries to liberalize their economies, and to reduce the role of state intervention in economic management. Whether these were necessary reforms to counter decades of poor economic policies or were irrelevant and misguided policies that made

Table 11.6   IBRD lending by theme, fiscal year 2008

Share of total lending of $24.7 billion	
Theme	**Percentage share of lending**
Financial and private sector development	25
Public sector governance	18
Urban development	12
Environmental and natural resource management	11
Human development	9
Rural development	9
Trade and integration	7
Social protection and risk management	4
Social development, gender and inclusion	4
Economic management	2
Rule of law	1

Source: Data from World Bank (2008), p. 55.

poor countries even more vulnerable to external shocks remains an issue of debate between supporters and critics of these policies. All sides are, however, agreed that the initial policies had consequences that were detrimental to the poorest and most marginalized sections of societies undergoing adjustment. Adjustment policies, for example, increased the burdens on women. By the mid-1990s the Bank had come to accept many of the criticisms of these policies, and began designing safety nets for the most vulnerable groups in society (World Bank, 1998). The Bank also began to shift its lending priorities away from adjustment and towards the new goal of sustainable development. Under adjustment lending, it was believed that macro-economic growth was the main target and that poverty reduction would follow from a general improvement in the economy. The move to sustainable development lending has seen a greater focus on poverty reduction strategies but this is also coupled with an increased emphasis on the role of the private sector in the promotion of development.

Table 11.7   IBRD lending by sector, fiscal 2008

Share of total lending of $24.7 billion	
Sector	**Percentage share of lending**
Law and justice and public administration	21
Transportation	19
Energy and mining	17
Water, sanitation and flood protection	10
Education	8
Health and social services	7
Agriculture, fishing and forestry	6
Finance	6
Industry and trade	6
Information and communication	<1

Source: Data from World Bank (2008), p. 55.

The role of World Bank lending remains controversial. Supporters of the Bank argue that it provides developing countries with much-needed capital and they maintain that the projects it supports are vital in the fight against world poverty. In their view these resources provide important supplementary assistance for the governments of developing countries and enhance the perceived stability of the economy to international investors. Supporters of World Bank policies think that the conditions it attaches to its loans provide a framework of sound financial management for the governments of its borrower nations (Picciotto, 2003). On the other hand, critics accuse the Bank of putting profits before people, and of distorting development (Caufield, 1996; Danaher, 1994). To the critics these resources are often insufficient, inadequate and ineffective. They contend that the specific conditionality imposed by the Bank privileges external interests over those of the recipients and is focused on repayment of the loan rather than improving welfare.

The World Bank espouses a liberal economic vision and it was conceived as an important instrument in the construction of a liberal economic order.

As such, the Bank's policy prescriptions support the maintenance of liberal economic values. Over time there has been a shift from a Keynesian liberalism to a neoliberal vision. It is this liberal ideology that remains contested today. The Bank's normative framework of market principles and economic growth is opposed by radical critics and environmentalists who believe that the market-based approaches cannot effectively contribute to development and/or promote sustainability. In the 1970s and 1980s, Bank lending received stringent criticism for the laxity of its environmental controls which resulted in its funding projects such as hydro-electric dams that were environmentally disastrous (Rich, 1994). Although the Bank has developed an environmental portfolio (World Bank, 1995) its policies continue to be criticized by a number of social movement groups.

Another critical issue in terms of the organization of development concerns the democratic nature of the process. This is an issue that can also be illustrated through reference to the World Bank. In the context of the Bank this issue is seen in two ways. First, democracy is discussed in relation to the formal decision-making provisions of the organization. The highest decision-making authority in the Bank is the Board of Governors, consisting of a representative from each member country. The Board of Governors meets annually and its functions are carried out by the Executive Board, consisting of 24 Executive Directors, that meets twice a week. Voting power on both the Board of Governors and the Executive Board is based on weighted voting, with each member's votes dependent on their economic contribution to the organization. Thus, decisions in the Bank are biased in favour of its major shareholders (the United States, Japan, Germany, France and the United Kingdom). Critics of this system argue that the weighted voting mechanism should be replaced by a 'one state, one vote' rule. Discussions at the G-20 meetings in April and September 2009 have addressed the issues of the governance of the Bank (and the IMF) and world leaders will consider proposals to increase the role of the emerging countries in these institutions.

An example of the controversy relating to the Bank's governance occurred with the appointment of Paul Wolfowitz, a neoconservative academic and politician with limited experience of development issues, as the Bank's President. During his short tenure in office (2005–7) Mr Wolfowitz was the subject of frequent criticism. The debate over his appointment reflects an assumption in much of the literature on the World Bank that the Executive Head effectively dictates the organization's policies. This popular and persistent view is an oversimplification of power and influence in the Bank. For example, although Mr Wolfowitz reorganized the bureaucracy, his main policy initiatives during his two years of office were concerned with devising an anti-corruption strategy.

A second aspect of the debate on the democratization of the Bank refers to the openness of the Bank to influence from civil society groups and the populations subject to its policies. In the 1980s, development, environmental and women's groups launched a series of campaigns to make the Bank's decision-making more transparent and more accountable for the policies it implemented. While the Bank has not responded in a manner that satisfies all its critics, it has become more open to scrutiny by external groups and has increasingly engaged in consultative processes to discuss its policies and proposed changes in its programmes. For example, the Bank has created an Inspection Panel to hear complaints and has engaged in wide-ranging dialogues with civil society groups concerning the content of its annual *World Development Report*. The *World Development Report* has an enormous impact in the field of development policy.

As the above has demonstrated, there are conflicting views on the World Bank's role as a development agency. While the Bank has been the target of criticism from the right of the political spectrum (Bauer, 1984), it has attracted most criticism from the left, as detailed above. Is it possible to adjudicate between the Bank and its critics? To a large extent the perspective one takes on the Bank is linked with the standpoint taken on economic aid (see below), capitalism and government intervention in the economy. Second, as the world's largest multilateral development agency, the Bank's profile means that it inevitably receives a significant amount of criticism. Thus, in assessing the importance to be given to any critique it is necessary to probe the existence of alternatives. That is, what are the feasible alternatives in organizing the specific aspect of development? Third, much criticism of the Bank is often out of date. Many critics appear unaware of the adaptability of the Bank and produce critiques of policies or programmes that are no longer current. Therefore in assessing any criticism of the Bank it is important to ascertain its current relevance to Bank operations. Fourth, it is important to distinguish between the Bank's bureaucracy and its members. Criticism should be sensitive to the relationship between the Bank staff and its more influential members. Finally, it is important to recognize that the World Bank is a financial institution and any effective criticism must recognize the financial constraints under which the Bank operates.

Debt and debt relief

Third World indebtedness has been a major problem since the debt crisis (see Chapter 8). Civil society organizations such as Make Poverty History and the Jubilee Debt Campaign have been important advocacy groups, campaigning for the cancellation of developing country debt. The severity and hence impact of debt on a country's economy can be measured either by the total external debt as a proportion of gross domestic product (see Table 11.8) or by the debt service ratio (i.e., the relationship between debt service

Table 11.8   Ratio of external debt to GDP, 2001–5

Region	2001	2002	2003	2004	2005
Sub-Saharan Africa	62.6	59.8	52.7	45.7	35.9
Asia	29.2	26.9	25.0	23.3	20.23
Middle East	47.7	48.7	45.1	41.2	22.4
Western hemisphere	41.6	47.1	47.4	41.4	31.0

Sources: IMF (2005), p. 80; IMF (2006b), p. 244.

payments and export earnings). In many developing countries total external debt is high compared with GDP and long-term debts outweigh the size of many countries annual exports and thus their ability to generate income to repay their debts. The impact of debt is a severe constraint on development. It reduces the spending power of the indebted country, and constrains their ability to fund education, health and other social programmes. Furthermore, it weakens incentives to invest in the debtor country, and reduces economic growth.

In response to the pressure from civil society actors Western governments and international financial agencies have embarked on debt relief programmes. The two most important multilateral debt relief mechanisms are the Heavily Indebted Poor Countries (HIPC) Initiative and the Multilateral Debt Relief Initiative (MDRI). Launched in 1996 the HIPC Initiative is a joint IMF–World Bank scheme which brings together multilateral, bilateral and commercial creditors in a scheme to provide debt relief to poor countries. It was the first attempt to create a comprehensive debt relief framework for the world's poorest countries. As such the introduction of the HIPC Initiative showed some recognition that some debt cancellation would be required in order to move the poorest countries out of the poverty trap. Under the HIPC Initiative countries that qualify for debt relief have their debt reduced in return for meeting certain performance criteria. The aim of the programme is to create a sustainable economic framework for heavily indebted countries. The operation of the HIPC Initiative has been criticized for an absence of transparency in its operations – for example, when Nigeria was removed from the HIPC list in 1998. It has also been argued that the programme is too focused on the repayment of debt and not sufficiently on reducing poverty or improving economic growth (Oxfam International, 2000). In 1999 in response to these criticisms the HIPC Initiative was reformed. The enhanced HIPC Initiative increased country coverage and is intended to provide faster, deeper and broader debt relief and to strengthen the links between debt relief, poverty reduction and social policies. While debt reduction is not sufficient for debt sustainability, the initiative had become a vehicle for the transfer of additional funds to the HIPC (World Bank, 2006c). This programme has made an impact on the indebtedness of the eligible countries. To date 35 countries have benefited from $75 billion in debt relief, and their average debt service payments relative to GDP has fallen from 3.2 per cent of GDP in 2001 to 1.4 per cent of GDP in 2008 (IDA/IMF, 2009).

The MDRI created in 2006 provides for 100 per cent relief on eligible debt from the IMF, World Bank, the Inter-American Bank (IADB) and the African Development Bank (AfDB) to a group of low-income countries. Eligible countries are those that have reached or will attain the completion point under the HIPC Initiative (see Box 11.6). The MDRI is the result of a decision reached at the G-8 Gleneagles Summit in July 2005. The MDRI is different from the HIPC Initiative in two respects. First, it is more comprehensive in that it provides 100 per cent debt relief. Thus it will free up more resources to be dedicated to the fight against poverty. Second, debt relief is restricted to the IMF, World Bank, the IADB and the AfDB. While the MDRI meets the goals of 100 per cent debt cancellation sought by many campaigners for debt relief its impact remains uncertain, and some analysts are sceptical about the hoped for benefits (Moss, 2006). The implementation of MDRI will vary among the institutions.

Box 11.6   Multilateral debt relief initiative: country coverage, 2009

As of July 2009, 26 countries have reached the completion point under the Enhanced HIPC Initiative:

Benin, Bolivia, Burkina Faso, Burundi, Cameroon, Central African Republic, Ethiopia, the Gambia, Ghana, Guyana, Haiti, Honduras, Madagascar, Malawi, Mali, Mauritania, Mozambique, Nicaragua, Niger, Rwanda, Sao Tomé and Príncipe, Senegal, Sierra Leone, Tanzania, Uganda, Zambia.

A further nine countries have reached the decision point under the Enhanced HIPC Initiative:

Afghanistan, Chad, Côte d'Ivoire, Democratic Republic of the Congo, Guinea, Guinea-Bissau, Liberia, Republic of Congo, Togo.

Source: IDA/IMF (2009).

Notwithstanding the success to date of these two initiatives, a number of challenges remain. These include continued successful domestic reform in the HIPC countries, full debt relief from bilateral and other creditors, and adequate financing of the HIPC initiative. As an official report recently noted, 'Notwithstanding debt relief, maintaining debt sustainability beyond the completion-point is a concern for many HIPCs, and the current global crisis has exacerbated such concerns (IDA/IMF, 2009).

North–South conflict

It should be apparent from the arguments in this chapter that the practice of international development is a distinctly political process in which consideration of power is central. In contrast to a liberal perspective that emphasizes the mutuality of interests between developed and developing countries, we perceive the simultaneous existence of common and competing interests. An integral feature of the international political economy of development, therefore, is constituted by what is termed the North–South conflict. This refers to the existence of political differences and a diplomatic conflict between the governments of advanced industrial countries and the governments of developing countries. We have alluded to this conflict above and in this subsection we explore certain aspects of the historical evolution and contemporary manifestation of this aspect of international development. Within the global political economy, issues of dominance and dependence remain important and the answers to questions concerning who gets what, when and why are linked to the different ways in which interests are articulated. The answers to fundamental questions such as 'What is development? What are the best methods for promoting development?' cannot be divorced from the issue of exactly who gets to frame the answers to such questions. In other words, the central problem concerns the matter of who speaks for whom. This is a complex issue in which it is possible to identify a number of potential stakeholders. Although civil society groups involved in the promotion of economic development cannot be left out of any comprehensive answer to these questions, we focus our discussion at the level of official policy-making. States remain the key instruments of legitimacy in the global political order and development policies are officially implemented through agencies of the state. In this sub-section we will focus on the North–South conflict as an integral part of the international political economy of development through a brief exploration of its historical evolution. The ability of developing countries to exercise influence over international negotiations depends on the degree of solidarity they can achieve and therefore we assess the extent to which divisions among developing countries mean that they will be incapable of presenting a united front to the holders of power in the world economy.

The North–South conflict in an historical perspective.   The dissatisfaction of developing countries with the liberal international economic order first surfaced in the 1950s with demands for reform of the international trading order and calls for increased economic aid. These demands were made with increasing stridency within the United Nations system after developing countries gained the majority in the United Nations General Assembly in 1960. A concerted demand for additional financial resources and increased market access for their exports followed the creation of the United Nations Conference on Trade and Development (UNCTAD) in 1964 in Geneva. As part of the UN system, it became the principal forum for North–South confrontation over economic issues and the instrument through which the developing countries hoped reform would be undertaken. Between 1964 and 1973, UNCTAD spearheaded campaigns for increased market access for Third World manufactured exports, stabilization of international commodity prices and additional development assistance. UNCTAD's record during this period was mixed, with very limited gains.

The North–South conflict was given increased prominence in the 1970s with debate over a New International Economic Order (NIEO). Between 1973 and 1979 the NIEO dominated North–South discussions. Indeed, it can be argued that this period saw development with its highest international political profile. At the centre of NIEO demands were those pertaining to international commodity markets. The NIEO also encompassed reform of the GATT, IMF and the World Bank. Developing countries argued that these organizations were controlled by the advanced industrial countries and failed to support developing country interests. A number of resolutions were passed by the UN General Assembly of which the most important were the Declaration on the Establishment of a New International Economic Order (1974), the Programme of Action on the Establishment of a New International Economic Order (1974) and the Charter of Economic Rights and Duties of States (1975), creating the framework for the NIEO. These UN resolutions were seen by some scholars as important legal documents. They set out the mutual responsibilities of states, established a framework of action and the justification for a new order. The negotiations leading to the creation of an NIEO ended in failure. No single event or factor was responsible for the failure of the NIEO. However, the refusal of Western states to enter into serious negotiation was the most important reason for the collapse of the North–South dialogue.

For some analysts the fragmentation of the Third World coalition in the 1980s led to the demise of the North–South conflict, but this is a limited and limiting view that fails to situate North–South conflict as a structure of the international political economy of development. The North–South conflict arises from a real disparity in power and resources between rich and poor states. The gap between the richest and poorest countries of the world has increased rather than diminished in the past three decades (Hoogvelt, 1997, p. xi). As Thomas and Reader state, 'almost a third of humanity still lives in conditions of dire poverty, and 14 million people die of hunger annually' (1997, p. 90). The International Commission on Peace and Food stated in 1990 that in a world population of 5.3 billion nearly 2 billion people lived in poverty; and in 1994 over 40,000 people died of malnutrition daily (1994, p. 106).

Third World solidarity and fragmentation.   The above discussion has not assumed commonality among developing countries but has noted the existence of a common bargaining platform. We have already noted the existence of significant differences among developing countries and the three main regions – Africa, Asia and Latin America. The concern of an international political economy of development is not with any organic unity but rather with the political expressions of unity and discord. Unity does not in itself lead to specific gains but it is an indicator of the extent to which the developing countries can articulate a distinct vision in the global political economy. The historical record shows that Third World solidarity responds to changes in the global political economy and is not static.

Third World solidarity began to fragment in the 1980s primarily as the result of two developments. The debt crisis had a twofold impact on the coalition. First, it created a range of special interests as countries sought to battle their specific debt burdens and were given differential treatment within the international financial system. For example, while some countries welcomed wholesale debt reduction, others were concerned that such a strategy would undermine their creditworthiness. Second, the structural adjustment policies imposed by the World Bank and IMF in promoting liberal economic thought severely curtailed the independence of developing countries. The severely indebted countries, as supplicants of Western economic assistance, were in no position to demand change in the international economic order. The second major development in the international system of the 1980s with an impact on the Third World coalition was the success of the NICs, since it exacerbated the differences among developing countries. But the scale of fragmentation is somewhat exaggerated and we still see and hear the collective voice of the developing world in many international negotiations. The important point is the degree to which they can articulate a different view.

The extent to which recent developments in international trade negotiations have revived the Third World coalition and given the developing countries a distinctive voice is currently an issue of some political importance, especially since the insistence of developing countries that issues of concern to their economies should be given prominence was influential in shaping the agenda of the Doha Round. While it remains too early to reach any firm conclusions about this development, two preliminary points can be highlighted. First, within the WTO a single developing group does not exist. Instead there are a number of different developing country coalitions (Draper and Sally, 2005; Narlikar and Odell, 2006; Narlikar and Tussie, 2004). Second, to date, these coalitions have largely been concerned with agenda-setting rather than with negotiations on substantive issues. It remains unclear whether defections from these coalitions can be prevented once bargaining moves to issues where the economic interests of countries are visibly at stake.

Third World solidarity refers solely to the joint efforts by countries that identify as developing countries (Williams, 2005b). In this sense we can make two observations. A Third World coalition remains a part of the international debate on development. At all major international conferences, developing countries continue to try to present a common position. Furthermore, recognition that the G-8 failed to include the voices of important developing countries was a key reason for the emergence of the G-20 in 2008/9 as the key forum responsible for coordinating a concerted response to the global economic crisis. Apart from the continuing existence of poverty and inequality, many countries identify with a collective Third World voice because of their lack of influence in international organizations. This inability to influence the international agenda is most starkly seen in the weighted voting decision-making process of the IMF and World Bank. But it is also perceived in institutions such as the G-8 leading industrial countries that meet periodically to make decisions concerning the future of the global economy. The G-8 is a constant reminder that Third World governments do not shape the international agenda.

Second, the historical record shows that as a counter-hegemonic force the Third World coalition has been most important in presenting an alternative vision of development and a critique of the liberal economic order. It has not achieved important gains in material terms. Thus we should not expect in the future that there will be any change in the ability of poor countries to wrest concessions from the richer nations.

Conclusion

In a powerful and influential critique of post-war development policy, Arturo Escobar (1995) argues that the development discourse began in 1949 with President Truman's inaugural Presidential address in which he enunciated large-scale support for development. This perspective usefully alerts us to the role of external powers in constructing development and the importance of the international political climate. Escobar's view is, however, a limited one since it removes autonomy from developing countries, and makes them solely passive recipients of Western policy.

As we have seen, development is centrally concerned with material and normative issues. Whether the focus is on absolute poverty or relative poverty it is apparent that poverty shapes the life chances of millions of individuals around the globe, constraining access to material and non-material goods and services. While development remains principally a national concern, it has from the outset of the development assistance regime at the end of the Second World War been inscribed on the international agenda. Organization, promotion and execution of national and international development policies are the result of structural change in the global political economy and the adaptation of state and non-state actors to these changes.

Chapter 12

Global Environmental Change

The study of international political economy has only recently incorporated the environment as one of its concerns (Helleiner, 1996). There are two principal aspects to the integration of environmental concerns into IPE. First, a number of environmental problems have an impact on the global political economy, and some form of international agreement is necessary to cope with these problems. As Hurrell and Kingsbury note, 'international cooperation is required both to manage global environmental problems and to deal with domestic environmental problems in ways that do not place individual states at a political or competitive disadvantage' (1992, p. 5). This intersection of environmental concerns and the international political economy can be termed the problem of international or global governance.

Second, global environmental change is intimately linked to national and international systems of production, distribution and consumption. 'The most important aspect of increased globalization derives from the complex but close relationship between the generation of environmental problems and the workings of the effectively globalized world economy' (Hurrell and Kingsbury, 1992, p. 3). This can be characterized as the problem of sustainability. The historical process of capital accumulation and the pursuit of economic growth has contributed to current environmental degradation. Key issues concerning growth and development strategies, industrialization, international trade and North–South relations, for example, all require re-examination in the current historical conjuncture. In this context, it can be argued that modern global environmental challenges are characterized by three main features: uncertainty, irreversibility and uniqueness or non-substitutability (Pearce, 1990, p. 366). Since the 1992 United Nations Conference on Environment and Development in Rio, local and national authorities as well as international organizations, firms and non-governmental organizations have all in their various ways pledged allegiance in various forms to the concept of sustainable development. They have made numerous commitments to preserving environmental quality and to combating environmental degradation. While it is not surprising that the rhetoric has surpassed the reality, this result nevertheless has to be explained rather than taken for granted.

This chapter explores the interface between environmental issues and the global political economy. It looks at the ways in which attention to environmental issues alters perceptions of and actions within the global political

344

economy. The chapter begins by discussing some of the terms used in analysing the political economy of the environment. In the theoretical perspectives section we consider IPE and environmental studies explanations of environmental degradation. Under major developments we trace the evolution of the environment as an important issue in discussions on the international economy. The key issues considered in this chapter are: sustainable development, trade and environmental degradation, and negotiations on climate change.

Definitions and background

Right at the outset we are faced with the far from simple issue concerning whether the focus should be on environment or ecology. Without seeking to prejudge the issue we will use the term 'environment' to discuss the issues with which we are concerned rather than 'ecology'. Within the literature these terms are sometimes used synonymously and at other times they are used in order to distinguish anthropocentric approaches from those that reject species hierarchy.

Although used in various ways by different writers the central difference between the terms appears to rest between an approach: environmentalism – that retains humans at the centre of its analysis; and another, ecologism – that focuses on the interrelationship between humans and nature in a non-hierarchical manner. Given the widespread usage of the term 'environmentalism' to refer to the interactions between humans and the natural environment, this chapter will adopt the terms 'environment' and 'environmental' to denote the subject under scrutiny. At its simplest, environment refers to the surroundings of a specific unit, that is, a unit or a system exists within a context and it is the context (that which surrounds the unit or system) to which the term 'environment' refers. In the context of the study of political economy, concern with the environment focuses on the impact of human activity on the natural environment. Attention is given to the use and misuse of natural resources and nature by humans. Environmental degradation therefore occurs when humans (ab)use nature in ways that both threaten the sustainability of the natural resource base and create unwanted problems such as pollution for human societies.

Defining environmentalism is difficult since it houses a variety of perspectives rather than a single approach. One attempt to combine diverse perspectives into identifiable schools of thought has been made by Clapp and Dauvergne (2005). They present a fourfold typology of world views of environment change: market liberals, institutionalists, bioenvironmentalists and social greens (Clapp and Dauvergne, 2005, pp. 3–17). A more conventional approach distinguishes between two broad strands (or ideologies) of environmentalism, although no agreement exists on the terminology to be used for this purpose. One useful and often cited distinction in the literature is that between 'light green' and 'dark green' perspectives, where the term 'green' refers to a positive and supportive attitude towards the protection and preservation of the environment. A light green approach is essentially reformist accepting the major institutions of capitalist society and seeking to engender respect for the environment and preservation of the environment through strategies that do not disrupt modern economic growth and industrial society. On the other hand, the dark green or radical environmental approach begins from the assumption that fundamental practices will have consequences for future generations.

Other writers maintain a distinction between two main strands of environmentalism but use different terms to convey the central distinction. One author distinguishes between technocentric and ecocentric positions (O'Riordan, 1976), where technocentric refers to approaches that attempt to accommodate sustainable development in the context of market incentives whereas ecocentric positions challenge conventional economic goals and models. Dobson (1990) distinguishes between environmentalism and ecologism. Environmentalism is characterized as 'a managerial approach to the environment within the context of present political and economic practices' (Dobson, 1990, p. 35). Ecologism on the other hand, 'presupposes radical changes' in humanity's relationship with the environment in order to care for it. Goodin makes a similar point when he distinguishes between an environmentalist posture which is concerned with making environmental choices serve human interests and a green approach which refuses to reduce nature to human or divine interests, and posits an independent role for nature in the creation of value (1992, pp. 7–8). For Eckersley, the key division is between anthropocentric and ecocentric approaches. Anthropocentric thinking 'offers opportunities for *human* emancipation and fulfilment in an ecologically sustainable society' (1992, p. 26). On the other hand, an ecocentric theory is one which 'pursues these goals in the context of a broader notion of emancipation that also recognizes the moral standing of the non human world' (1992, p. 26).

Moving beyond approaches to environmentalism, we can recognize the existence of different ways of classifying issues of environmental concern. There are different approaches to classifying environmental problem sets. We can distinguish between physical changes such as: atmospheric pollution, ozone depletion, climate change, marine pollution, loss of biodiversity; development activities such as energy production and use, tourism, agricultural production; and aspects of the human condition and well-being such as population growth, health and security. A different classification distinguishes between problems arising directly from human activity on the land (for example, deforestation, top-soil erosion, watershed failure), and those arising as the indirect result of waste (for example, greenhouse gases, ozone-depleting gases, nuclear contamination and toxic waste). The first set of problems are relatively localized in their consequences, whereas the latter have direct global reach.

Furthermore, we can also distinguish environmental problems in terms of the situations faced by actors as they pursue cooperative or conflictual strategies, for example, global commons, shared natural resources, transboundary externalities or linked issues (Young, 1994). Problems such as the depletion of the ozone layer, the potential for climate change as a result of the greenhouse effect, the loss of biodiversity and deforestation and desertification are well documented. It is important to recognize that the impact of these trends and events on the physical fabric of the planet cannot be limited to environmental or technical considerations but are to be seen as essentially political in character since 'the globality of environmental problems stems not merely from the replicated institutions which create them and the spread of environmental activism, but also from both the very transboundary nature of pollution and depletion problems and the reliance on co-operative mechanisms for problem solving' (Laferrière, 1994, p. 95).

There are five commonly accepted features of environmentalism:

- Environmental degradation is global in the sense that it affects everyone, and can only be managed effectively through global cooperation.
- Environmental degradation can exacerbate intra-state and inter-state tensions.
- There are complex linkages between the environment and the global economy.
- Environmental issues are distinguished by uncertainty, that is, there is no guarantee that sometime in the future a finite natural resource will be replaced by technology.
- Irreversibility is a key feature of environmental politics, for example, once a species is extinct it is impossible to make it appear again.

However, the environmental problematique is a complex and multifaceted one, with diverse political, social, economic and ethical dimensions, and these common features provide a starting point for analysis rather than settled conclusions. For example, while many environmental problems are indeed global in scope, it is an overstatement and a mistake to assume that all environmental problems possess this quality. To assume that all environmental problems are global can lead to the erroneous conclusion that environmental degradation translates into shared concerns, that we share a common future and that we have a common interest in combating environmental destruction. Such a conclusion is apolitical and abstracts from the power relations inherent in both the causation of ecological harm and the steps necessary to provide workable solutions.

Theoretical perspectives: IPE and environmental studies

The recent upsurge of interest in the environment has resulted in the publication of numerous studies as analysts have explored the causal relationship between human practices and environmental degradation. These studies draw upon differing understandings of the causes of environmental degradation and propose a range of appropriate responses to address the problems that have arisen. Theorists and practitioners interested in global environmental politics have conflicting views on the causes of and solutions to environmental degradation. In this section we will explore two theoretical debates: one that has arisen in International Relations and IPE, and a second that is more familiar to students of environmental economics and environmental studies. We spend some time examining the debate between rival schools of thought in IPE (economic nationalism/realism, liberalism and Marxism) before turning to look at a debate based on differing conceptions of the relationship between humans and the environment (anthropocentric, environmental and ecocentric perspectives).

IPE debates

The traditional approaches to IPE, that is, economic nationalism, liberalism and Marxism, historically paid little or no attention to environmental issues. However, the emergence of the environment as an international political issue and the evident linkages between global environmental change and national and international systems of production, distribution and consumption have seen scholars working within these paradigms turn their attention to the analysis of global environmental politics. Most attention has been paid to the creation and maintenance of international cooperation on the environment, and the relationship between the global economy and the causes of environmental degradation. We first review the debate on international environmental cooperation before turning our attention to the political economy of sustainability.

The economic nationalist or realist approach to international environmental cooperation is based on two main assumptions. Realists assume that states act in terms of their national interests and that international cooperation is difficult to achieve and sustain, given the existence of competing national interests in an anarchical international system. With each state attempting to maximize its military and economic power, international cooperation on the environment, like any form of international cooperation, is inherently difficult since environmental interests will be subsumed to traditional political power goals.

The realist assumption that states are rational, self-interested utility maximizers leads to the conclusion that international cooperation on the environment will only be possible in situations where states perceive such cooperation to be in their interests. Moreover, realists contend that in an anarchical international system, cooperation on the environment will only be feasible on those issues and in those specific situations that support and maintain the interests of dominant states. Realist approaches are therefore sceptical about the possibility of extensive cooperation on environmental issues (Barrett, 1993; Blackhurst and Subramanian, 1992). There are, of course, many examples in environmental politics where states have either failed to establish a basis for cooperation or where a cooperative arrangement has broken down that provide support for the realist perspective. For example, the refusal of the United States to ratify the Kyoto Protocol lends support to the realist argument. However, realist political economy is less well placed to explain why, in the absence of the dominant power in the world economy (the United States), so many other states have been willing to ratify the Kyoto Protocol.

The willingness of many states to ratify the Kyoto Protocol in the absence of the United States is better explained by liberal IPE theories. Liberal IPE theories, although using the state as a key unit of analysis, begin from a recognition of the demands of interdependence. For liberal theorists international environmental cooperation arises from the recognition of mutual or shared interests. A globalizing world economy creates networks of interdependencies and bonds of common interests among the various actors, thus facilitating international cooperation. Although states remain important actors they are enmeshed in a network of transactions and interdependencies which limit and constrain their authority. Furthermore, environmental cooperation is made more feasible through the activities of non-state actors such as intergovernmental organizations, NGOs, scientific networks and firms.

There are a number of diverse critical and radical approaches to international environmental cooperation. Some radical writers argue that the rivalry between capitalist states makes international environmental cooperation unlikely. Whereas realist writers emphasize the interests of states in maximizing power, and liberal theorists show how interdependence creates mutual bonds of interest, radical scholars focus on inequality and dominance in the international system. In this perspective international cooperation is subsumed to the economic interests of dominant states and the capitalist class. International environmental cooperation is likely, but the forms of cooperation and the institutions created, since they are based on capitalism, will be incapable of providing effective solutions to environmental degradation. Some radical writers argue that in a hierarchical international power structure, the developed countries of the North dominate international decision-making, thus maintaining the historically established pattern of exploitation of southern countries. Negotiations on international environmental issues will therefore reflect northern interests and southern concerns will be marginalized (Haas, 1990b, pp. 47–52).

While all three perspectives appear to have something useful to contribute to analyses of international environmental cooperation, each perspective on its own is incapable of providing satisfactory answers to the range of issues and cooperative arrangements that arise in global environmental politics. The realist approach, for example, is flawed because its focus on states and emphasis on power is empirically unsustainable. A focus on states seriously limits analysis and omits consideration of important actors in the global political economy. Many analyses of global environmental politics have documented the critical roles played by international organizations, firms and NGOs.

Moreover, a number of studies have clearly demonstrated that international cooperation is possible and regimes can be created and maintained in the absence of a hegemon (Axelrod and Keohane, 1986; Keohane, 1984; Young, 1989, 1994). While liberal analysis, in admitting the importance of non-state actors, provides a more realistic account of environmental politics, liberal theories have a tendency to neglect the role of power in shaping institutions in the first place. They fail to give sufficient attention to considerations of structural inequalities. While radical theories show awareness of the importance of structural patterns of dominance and dependence, they frequently underestimate the importance of international actors. For example, international organizations are not mere epiphenomena with negligible impact on international relations, and the forms of bargaining that take place within such organizations do not merely reflect the distribution of power in the global system.

The second area of contention between the perspectives concerns the relationship between the global economy and environmental degradation. Since the issue of sustainable development will be discussed further below, at this point we only highlight some important differences between the three approaches. From an economic nationalist perspective sustainable development will only arise if states perceive such policies to be in their interests. Since states exert control over national economies the pursuit of sustainable development is dependent on states identifying this as a key goal. However, efforts to promote sustainability are likely to founder if economic growth remains the primary goal of political elites. As long as the elements of power are constituted through practices that degrade the environment, sustainable development will remain an aspiration rather than a reality.

In a liberal perspective, environmental degradation arises because of market failure, specifically the absence of mechanisms to provide a proper valuation of natural resources. The extension of market principles to the environment through, for example, the allocation of property rights and the inclusion of environmental values in pricing policies will lead to a more efficient allocation of resources and environmental protection. Sustainable economic policies in this view are dependent on increased economic growth rather than its retardation. The problem is not growth per se but rather the forms that growth has taken to date. Indeed, economic growth and proper environmental assessments are crucial strategies for the promotion of sustainability.

Radical theorists locate the cause of environmental degradation in the development of capitalism. They argue that environmental degradation arises from capitalism and that current economic practices and value systems cannot promote sustainable policies since the capitalist system is inherently exploitative. As Michael Redclift has claimed, 'The concentration on "growth" has served to obscure the fact that resource depletion and unsustainable development are a direct consequence of growth itself' (1987, p. 56).

Once again we can see that none of the perspectives provides a convincing explanation of the political economy of sustainability. First, the ahistorical approach of realist IPE ignores the causes of environmental degradation since it fails to enquire into the ways in which historically constructed patterns of production and consumption have created current environmental problems. Such an approach is incapable of challenging the processes of accumulation, production and reproduction central to capitalism and responsible for creating the environmental problems in the first place. Liberal theories are deficient because they fail to deal adequately with power and power relations. Specifically, they are unable to represent structural forms of power. NeoMarxist analysis, with its emphasis on the structural relationship between labour and capital and its location of environmental degradation in the political and economic structures of capitalist societies, does appear to represent an advance. But the historical evidence clearly shows that both capitalist and socialist regimes failed to protect the environment. The failure to implicate socialist development strategies in environmental degradation arises from a continued attachment to economic growth, and a failure to recognize the ecological limits to growth. Another weakness of radical theories lies in the tendency to equate capitalism with industrialization.

This debate between the three traditional IPE paradigms serves to show the limitations of the traditional paradigms when applied to the study of the environment. While realists, liberals and Marxists do, as we have seen, have different foundations, they nevertheless all share a paradigmatic assumption of, and commitment to, the necessity and desirability of economic growth.

Environmental studies debates

At this stage it is necessary to move away from the established way of conceptualizing IPE as a contest between three perspectives to focus on a different set of values at the heart of environmentalism. The shared commitment to anthropocentrism of the three IPE paradigms results in their failure to engage with debates in environmental studies between proponents of technocentric solutions on one hand and supporters of ecocentric goals on the other. In this sub-section we will examine the contestation between environmentalism (technocentrism) and ecologism (ecocentrism) since it extends analysis of environmental degradation and sustainability.

The technocentric perspective is based on the assumption that the central objective of economic growth is to satisfy the needs of humans. This perspective is based on the superiority of Western cultural values, and the transformational capacity of capitalism. Two variants of technocentrism can be identified – conservative and reformist. From the viewpoint of conservative technocentrism, modern economic growth is the basis for personal liberation and capitalism is the driving force for change. In this perspective, ecological change is necessarily attendant on economic growth but this does not mean that such change is negative. Writers in this perspective tend to emphasize the positive impact of economic growth and to argue that humans have in the past found solutions to impending environmental problems. Capitalism, it is claimed, is an ingenious system that through the search for profit will naturally find market-based solutions to environmental problems. Indeed, some economists have argued that concern with environmental issues is misplaced, and any attempt to hold back progress in the name of environmentalism will result in economic catastrophe. Wilfred Beckerman, in a polemical text *Small is Stupid* (1995), has presented a fierce attack on controls on economic growth.

While the conservative technocentric position contests the claim that modern economic growth is responsible for environmental degradation, reformist technocentric writers have, principally through the development of the sub-field of environmental economics, tried to demonstrate the continued relevance of conventional economic theory to the study of environmental change. The reformist technocentric approach is rooted in environmental economics and begins from the assumption that environmental degradation is an accidental outcome of modern economic growth. It is thus a reformist rather than a radical position and argues that if the environment is fully priced, environmental degradation will be reduced.

From this perspective environmental degradation arises from market failure. In order to protect the environment it is essential to value the environment through determining the 'real costs' of resource use, and then proposing the most efficient solutions. A tension exists among environmental economists between those who prefer the use of incentives and market-based solutions and those who argue in support of regulation, and command and control measures. This tension can be perceived in discussions on global warming. Proponents of market-based solutions argue in support of tradable permits whereas those who prefer interventionist solutions propose legislation restricting emission levels. Current national and international solutions to environmental change are largely based on this reformist perspective, and the policy debate is usually constructed in terms of market versus interventionist solutions.

This policy approach has been termed managerial environmentalism (Levy, 1997). It recognizes the link between human activity and the environment but believes that an accommodation can be found between current economic activity and the long-term goal of sustainable development. Central to environmental managerialism are two features, the first being a commitment to business and the belief that capitalism and the environment are not antithetical, while the second includes a liberal internationalist belief in multilateral cooperation. This technocentric approach contrasts sharply with more radical ecocentric approaches (see Box 12.1).

Box 12.1   Technocentric and ecocentric approaches to sustainability

The ecocentric approach to sustainable development recognizes the environment as central to survival and progress. This can be compared to a technocentric approach, which is centred around humans and views nature merely as an instrument in sustaining human life. They can be compared in relation to a number of issues. These include:

Primary economic objectives – economic growth (technocentric) vs zero economic growth (ecocentric)
Economic organization – large scale (technocentric); small scale (ecocentric)
Market incentives – green consumerism; economic instruments to regulate production (technocentric); limited consumerism; strong regulation of the economy (ecocentric)
Attitude to resource management – conservationist (technocentric); preservationist (ecocentric)
Attitude to trade – reconciliation of trade and environmental standards (technocentric); anti-trade and promotion of self-sufficiency (ecocentric)
Political project – maintenance of nation-states and the status quo (technocentric); creation of small-scale communities as the basis of political authority (ecocentric)
Global governance – reform of the existing international economic order (technocentric); resistance to industrialism, capitalism and modernity (ecocentric)
Ethical standards – intergenerational and intragenerational equity (technocentric); ecological justice; equality for all life forms (ecocentric)

The reformist technocentric approach has become an important part of contemporary discourse through the development of environmental economics. This is not to claim that concern about ecological limits to growth arose in this period for the first time. In the 1960s a self-conscious sub-discipline of environmental economics began to emerge. At the centre of environmental economics is the idea that the economy is an open system. Environmental economics is based on a materials balance view of the economy which begins from the assumption that the economy is an open system with three basic processes – extraction, processing and consumption. Resources (renewable and non-renewable) are extracted from the environment and processed for consumption. All economic activities create waste which must either be recycled in the economic process or absorbed in the environment. The central issue therefore becomes that of maintaining economic growth without decreasing the assimilative capacity of the environment to absorb wastes. Environmental economics builds on the insights of neoclassical economics, and has successfully incorporated the environment into standard economic theory. It has moved from a position in which the economy is seen as closed to one which stresses the open nature of the system. But the overall assumptions are similar to those of its parent discipline. The objective of the economy is still to maximize the welfare of society. The fundamental economic problem remains the efficient organization of production and consumption.

In contrast, an ecological focus forces us to confront the changing relationships that have developed between human activity, natural systems and the built environment. Social systems and natural systems exist in a dynamic interactive context and interdependencies between the two systems mirror developments in both. From the work of anthropologists we have extensive evidence of the myriad ways in which cultural beliefs, cultural artefacts, social structure and type of technology are intimately connected.

Unlike the technocentric perspective, an ecocentric perspective is founded on a rejection of continued economic growth and a critique of global capitalism. Writers within this approach are questioning of modern industrial growth and modern institutions. They reject anthropocentrism and argue instead for an ecological approach in which human needs are balanced by concern for all living organisms. Ecocentric theorists contend that the current emphasis in the organization of society is on human wants rather than human needs (Pepper, 1996, pp. 69–70). Human wants are socially derived and reflect the materialistic values of society, whereas human needs combine spiritual and material values to arrive at a balance between humans and the environment.

Ecological critiques of conventional economic theory point to a number of omissions in neoclassical economics, which render it incapable of providing solutions to global environmental degradation. According to ecologists one key reason for the failure of neoclassical economics to provide a convincing analysis of environmental change stems from the omission of the fundamental laws of thermodynamics and ecology from its basic assumptions. Moreover, unlike conventional economics, the ecocentric perspective views the economy as a sub-system of the natural world and the environment rather than vice versa. Conventional economics tends to view the economy as an open system but ecologists see it as a closed system. Ecologists also object to what they perceive as the obsession with the short-term and marginal analysis of neoclassical economics. Instead of focusing on the short term, ecologists insist that we need to give more attention to the long run. This critique is related to the issue of discounting for the future, and ecologists argue that the future discounting assumptions of conventional economics are seriously flawed. Furthermore, in common with other radical critiques, the ecological perspective rejects the sterile, abstract reasoning of conventional economics and its embrace of arid mathematics. Conventional economic theory is based on constructing theorems based on questionable assumptions about human nature instead of integrating observed human or organizational behaviour into its analyses.

Although there are a number of strands of ecological economics, they all share two central ideas. These are a commitment to restricting or imposing limits on growth because of a belief that natural or ecological limitations to the earth's carrying capacity are real; and a rejection of anthropocentrism, that is, a belief in holism and an interactive relationship between all species. Three strands of ecological economics have made important contributions to the theorization of global environmental degradation. Steady-state approaches focus on the issue of scale and attempt to maintain a link between the size of the economy and the overall system. Central to steady-state theory is a determination to maintain the natural resource base for future generations. Radical ecology is indebted to Marxist insights and emphasizes the ways in which capitalism leads to overproduction and hence environmental degradation. Co-evolutionary approaches attempt to combine knowledge, values, social organization, technology and ecosystems. In this view environmental degradation arises from the failure to respect the equilibrium of natural ecosystems and the neglect of the human/nature equilibrium.

Major developments

This section focuses on the evolution of the environment as an issue in the global political economy and the forms it has since taken. Over the past four decades increased attention has been given to global environmental issues, and there has been a proliferation of initiatives in the global political economy to address environmental degradation. The modern concern for the environment has gone through two phases. The first phase corresponds to the emergence of a new wave of environmentalism beginning in the 1960s. The second phase is marked by the United Nations Conference on Environment and Development (UNCED) in 1992 and ushers in the mainstreaming of environmental issues on national and international agendas.

Bringing the environment in

Lynton Caldwell (1988) notes that there were three types of international environmental agreements in the first part of the 20th century. The first category relates to wilderness and wildlife conservation and included agreements such as the Pacific Fur Treaty (1911) and the International Convention for the Regulation of Whaling (1946). A second type of environmental agreement was developed to govern maritime pollution and included the International Convention for the Prevention of the Pollution of the Sea by Oil (1954) and the Convention on the High Seas (1958). Agreements limiting the spread of nuclear weapons such as the Antarctic Treaty (1959) and the Treaty Banning Nuclear Weapons Tests in the Atmosphere, Outer Space and Under Water (1963) formed a third category. These efforts are important but they were not seen as part of an integrated concern with the environment.

Global concern with environmental degradation is a relatively recent phenomenon and stems from three sources. The first lies in international conferences convened by the United Nations. These conferences were notable for their preparatory process, the resolutions passed and the follow-up process. The first significant conference was the United Nations Conference on the Human Environment (UNCHE) convened in Stockholm in 1972 (see Box 12.2). Called in response to lobbying by Scandinavian countries concerned by pollution, the agenda of the conference extended discussion beyond pollution. During the preparatory phase the developing countries emphasized the link between development and the environment, laying the basis for the process that culminated in the Rio Conference 20 years later. UNCHE recognized the environmental consequences of modern economic growth and these linkages were enshrined in the conference recommendations. Although these were subsequently ignored by governments, one notable impact of the conference was the creation of the United Nations Environment Programme (UNEP), a permanent bureaucracy in the UN system to champion environmental issues.

The process begun in Stockholm culminated in 1992 when the United Nations Conference on Environment and Development (UNCED) held in Rio legitimized the environment as a concern for international economic diplomacy (see Box 12.3). The preparatory phase of the Rio Conference

Box 12.2　Advancing environmentalism: the United Nations Conference on the Human Environment (UNCHE)

Preparatory phase
1971 – Founex meeting – 27 experts gathered by Maurice Strong, Secretary-General of UNCHE. Establishes, for the first time, a clear link between environment and development.

The Conference
First major conference to bring governments together to discuss a variety of environmental issues. Attended by 1,200 representatives from 114 states; parallel formal NGO conference and an informal People's Forum.

Outcomes
Stockholm Declaration of 26 principles;
Action Plan of 109 recommendations;
Creation of the United Nations Environment Programme (UNEP).

attracted significant attention from governmental and non-governmental actors. Also, the high political profile of the disputes during the preparatory phase ensured maximum visibility for the conference proceedings. This became the largest conference ever held, in terms of the number of delegates present, and it also attracted the largest number of world leaders ever to convene in one place. The wide-ranging agenda gave rise to heated debate and produced Agenda 21, a document designed to provide a framework for future actions to halt environmental degradation. Agenda 21 also included a monitoring and implementation process. At the centre of the deliberations and conclusions of the Rio Conference was the concept of sustainable development. The assembled delegates reached agreement that environmental degradation potentially could have profound ramifications for economic growth and prosperity.

Ten years after the Rio Conference, world leaders, civil society representatives, business leaders and journalists convened in 2002 in Johannesburg for the World Summit on Sustainable Development (popularly called Rio+10). The Johannesburg Summit (see Box 12.4) provided an opportunity for the global community to assess progress made in implementing the goals established at Rio. In the intervening decade, while the normative commitment to the environment remained strong, effective policy change was less evident. For example, a reduction in greenhouse gases had

---

Box 12.3   Advancing environmentalism: the United Nations Conference on Environment and Development (UNCED)

Preparatory phase
Preparatory committee – established as a committee of the United Nations General Assembly.

Three preparatory committee meetings – three working groups established a framework for negotiation and draft declaration of principles (representing 85 per cent of the conference programme).

Conference
Attended by governmental representatives from 178 countries; including 114 heads of state or government.
Global Forum – 7,892 NGO delegates from 167 countries.

Outcomes
Rio Declaration on Environment and Development;
Agenda 21;
Statement of Forest Principles;
UN Framework Convention on Climate Change;
Convention on Biological Diversity.

---

not been achieved despite the firm commitment made at Rio. Thus, instead of seeking binding treaties the approach adopted at the Johannesburg Summit was to set targets.

The second factor contributing to the emergence of the environment as an international issue was scientific knowledge. Probably the most significant advance here was the discovery of a hole in the ozone layer above Antarctica by a team of British scientists in 1985. The health implications of the ozone hole shocked populations and galvanized governments to act. In one sense the image of the ozone hole was stark and readily comprehensible, and in another sense the solution was reasonably straightforward. In saying this we do not imply that it was easy to agree to a treaty, but rather that it did not involve a series of complicated linkages. But if the discovery of the ozone hole was part of a process of the expansion of knowledge, not all of this process was consensual. Peter Haas developed the concept of epistemic community to describe a collection of scientists and decision-makers sharing a knowledge base. Epistemic communities have played a part in providing solutions to environmental problems (Haas, 1990a).

But of equal importance to epistemic communities are the seminal books

Box 12.4   Advancing environmentalism: the United Nations World Summit on Sustainable Development (WSSD)

Preparatory phase
The preparatory process took place at the national, regional and global levels. At the global level four international meetings of the Preparatory Committee were held under the auspices of the Commission on Sustainable Development (CSD), established at UNCED. The aim of these meetings was to identify the main issues for the conference.

Regional meetings to identify issues for the WSSD were held between June 2001 and January 2002. National-level governments conducted progress reviews of the implementation of Agenda 21 and devised implementation strategies.

Conference
Attended by governmental representatives from 191 countries, including 82 heads of state or government; Global People's Forum attended by over 8,000 civil society representatives.

Outcomes
Plan of Implementation of the World Summit on Sustainable Development – a framework for action designed to achieve the implementation of the agreements reached at UNCED.

The Political Declaration including (as Annex 1) the Johannesburg Declaration on Sustainable Development – a set of non-binding statements reflecting the challenges faced in the search for sustainable development.

and articles that challenge conventional wisdom and alert publics to the linkages between environmental degradation and society. The publication in 1972 of *The Limits to Growth* by Dennis and Donella Meadows (1972) is one such contribution. Its controversial thesis was that the earth's finite resources would soon run out unless steps were taken to conserve energy use. Even though the projections made by the Meadows were subject to exhaustive tests and refuted by a range of experts, *The Limits to Growth* controversy was important in placing ecology on the agenda. A later report (Meadows, Meadows and Randers, 1993), published after sustainable development had become a major feature of contemporary political debate, maintained a pessimistic vision of the earth's future.

A third factor contributing to awareness of the linkages between

---

Box 12.5   Bhopal

In December 1984 a gas leak occurred in one of three of Union Carbide's pesticide tanks in Bhopal, India. An investigation revealed that a large amount of water was introduced into the tank where methyl isocyanate (MIC) was stored. This caused a reaction that ultimately released a vapour cloud, which infiltrated homes overnight and, within days, killed 3,000 people. Over the next few years, 2,000 deaths were attributed to the 'irrespirable gases'. An estimated 150,000 people directly affected by the gas leak now live with chronic illnesses such as fibrosis, bronchial asthma, chronic obstructive airways disease, emphysema and recurrent chest infections. Pulmonary tuberculosis among the exposed population is notably higher than India's national average. Over 578,000 people have been affected and have received some form of compensation. Union Carbide paid $US470 million to the Indian government to settle the victims' claims. Yet, only about half of it has been distributed, in most cases at $550 per recipient.

---

environment and the economy was a series of environmental mishaps in the 1960s, 1970s and 1980s. These included the Torrey Canyon disaster, Seveso, Bhopal (see Box 12.5) and Chernobyl. These incidents served to underline the fragility of human and marine life in the face of modern industrialization. They showed that modern production methods, industrialization and transport systems threatened health and safety rather than providing a welcome release from poverty. These disasters did not lead, except among a small group of people, to calls for abandoning economic growth but to a desire to find ways to reconcile growth and environmental sustainability.

These developments were given impetus by two political developments. In chronological terms the first was the development of the second wave of environmentalism in the United States and Western Europe in the 1960s. Some have argued that growing affluence among the middle classes contributed to the growth of an environmental movement in the West. While this is part of the explanation, environmentalism was also spurred by the disasters described above, and increasing scientific knowledge. Affluence, however, played a central role in the ability of these groups to organize effectively. Possessing unprecedented material resources and high levels of education, the diverse environmental movement spawned effective advocacy and lobbying organizations and political parties that were in a position to influence the agenda of politics in Western Europe and the United States. The second development concerned the end of the Cold War, and the removal of the straightjacket of East–West tensions from international discussions of the environment. From the period of Gorbachev's glasnost it became progressively easier to address environmental issues in a mature manner in the international arena.

Mainstreaming environmentalism

Following the Rio Conference, environmental issues definitively moved from the margins to the centre of politics at domestic and international levels. This is not to say that politicians, the public and academics necessarily engaged with environmental issues in a manner likely to halt unsustainable practices. Rather it signals a salience given to environmental issues in the sense that the environment became normalized in political discourse. The concerns of green parties and environmental activists are no longer regarded as outlandish or silly but have instead been co-opted to the orthodox political agenda. This enables a form of environmental management to become the standard approach in which politicians, business groups and social movement activists are accorded the same legitimacy. More fundamental questions regarding the nature of economic growth in a world of finite resources are not addressed in this new approach to the environment. There are three main features that characterize the current mainstreaming of the environment.

The first feature of the mainstreaming of the environment lies in the development of environmental regulation at the domestic level. States in both the North and the South have established ministries wholly or partly responsible for the environment. These ministries have ushered in legislation (for an example, see Table 12.1) to define acceptable limits of pollution, manage resources in a sustainable manner, and prescribe penalties for activities that contribute to environmental legislation. There are, of course, disputes at the domestic level concerning the best mix of policies to be followed, and there are still groups that oppose environmental legislation. Nevertheless, it has become commonplace in many states to initiate environmental impact assessments as routine measures when planning new projects.

Second, environmental issues have been mainstreamed within many international organizations. To many critics the so-called greening of international institutions offers little if any real contribution to environmental sustainability (Horta, 1996; Rich, 1994). These are important criticisms but in this context the key issue is the change in the attitudes of international organizations from hostility, scepticism and in some cases apparently open cynicism (see Box 12.6) to an engagement with the arguments of environmentalists. For example, the World Bank's approach to the environment has undergone significant change (World Bank, 1995). Whereas once the Bank ignored environmental issues and made no attempt to assess the environmental consequences of its loans, the post-UNCED World Bank has

Table 12.1 Sample of environmental legislation in Australia

• Captains Flat (Abatement of Pollution) Agreement Act 1975
• The Environment Protection (Alligator Rivers Region) Act 1978
• Environment Protection (Sea Dumping) Act 1981
• Wildlife Protection (Regulation of Exports and Imports) Act 1982
• Wildlife Protection (Regulation of Exports and Imports) Act 1982
• Environment Protection (Sea Dumping Regulations) 1983
• Sea Installations Act 1987
• Sea Installations Levy Act 1987
• Ozone Protection and Synthetic Greenhouse Gas Management Act 1989
• Hazardous Waste (Regulation of Exports and Imports) Act 1989
• Ozone Protection Act 1989
• The Hazardous Waste Act 1989 (amended 1996)
• National Environment Protection Council Act 1994
• Wet Tropics of Queensland World Heritage Area Conservation Act 1994
• Ozone Protection (Licence Fees–Imports) Act 1995
• Ozone Protection (Licence Fees–Manufacture) Act 1995
• Natural Heritage Trust of Australia Act 1997
• National Environment Protection Measures (Implementation) Act 1998
• Environment Protection and Biodiversity Conservation Act 1999
• Environmental Reform (Consequential Provisions) Act 1999
• Fuel Quality Standards Act 2000
• Product Stewardship (Oil) Act 2000
• Renewable Energy (Electricity) Act 2000
• Renewable Energy (Electricity) Charge 2000
• Renewable Energy (Electricity) Regulations 2001
• Environment Protection and Biodiversity Conservation Amendment (Wildlife Protection) Act 2001
• Lake Eyre Basin Intergovernmental Agreement Act 2001
• Water Efficiency Labelling and Standards Act 2005
• Water Act 2007

Source: Environment Australia http://www.deh.gov.au/

Box 12.6   The Summers memo

Activists' suspicions that the upper reaches of the World Bank did not take environmental policy seriously seemed to be confirmed in December 1991 when an internal memo signed by the Bank's Chief Economist Lawrence Summers was leaked to the world's media (www.counterpunch.org/summers.html). The memo suggested that it would be economically more efficient if the Bank encouraged the migration of dirty industries to developing countries. Three reasons were advanced for this argument: health costs were lower in developing countries, many developing areas were underpopulated and could absorb more pollution and many residents had more pressing concerns than whether the environment was attractive or the possibility that they might get a disease in old age.

In 2001, Lant Pritchett, then a junior economist at the Bank, claimed authorship of the memo (*Harvard Magazine*, 2001). He suggested that the leaked memo was incomplete and only an 'ironical aside' on the beneficial impacts of trade liberalization on developing countries. However, for many in the environmental movement the memo was an example of an ethically deplorable and morally repugnant attitude to both environmental degradation and poor people. The memo and surrounding controversy highlighted how the logics of environmental protection and economic efficiency can clash.

consciously attempted to develop a green portfolio. It has adopted two different strategies to achieve its goal of sustainable development: instituted mandatory environmental assessments, and systematic and routine environmental monitoring; and now disburses environmental loans. Its lending practices include one set of policies aimed at urban renewal and pollution control and another set of policies designed to promote biodiversity and reforestation.

The third feature of a mainstreaming of the environment in the global political economy can be seen in the behaviour of major firms. In response to the actions of environmental activists and the policies of government departments, business has shifted its profile and adopted an approach that emphasizes the sustainability of resources (Schmidheiny, 1992). Even some firms engaged in practices that at face value appear to be far removed from sustainable practices, such as mining and oil exploration and production, have embraced the concept of sustainable development. However, not all corporations have adopted this approach and many continue to operate in ways that continue conventional practices and therefore contribute to environmental degradation (Clapp, 2001; Dauvergne, 2001). And some firms, in rejecting the sustainability thesis, find ways to oppose and denigrate the efforts of environmentalists (Beder, 1997).

Key issues

The extent to which the efforts of national governments, international organizations and firms seriously address the environmental crisis remains the subject of fierce debate. Within the contemporary global political economy the politics of sustainability generates discussion on various issues. Conflicts arising from international trade, pollution control, the preservation of biodiversity and sustainable development have all figured prominently on the international agenda. This section focuses on three significant environmental issues: sustainable development, the relationship between trade and the environment and climate change. All three issues are at the centre of the debate between proponents and critics of environmental management.

Sustainable development

The problem with the term 'sustainable development' is its vagueness. It has proved very difficult to formulate a definition that is comprehensible while retaining analytical precision. Sustainable development has been the subject of diverse definitions from a number of commentators (Pearce, Markandya and Barbier, 1989, pp. 173–85). As a result it has come to mean very different things to ecologists, economists, planners and politicians. In its favour is the positive connotation implicit in the term. It is unlikely that any sane person or organization would willingly endorse unsustainable development or sustainable impoverishment, if that is not an oxymoron. Sustainable development is not necessarily identified with increased consumption and production but with an improved quality of life where the state of the natural environment is taken into consideration.

Of the many issues debated in the political economy of global environmental change, sustainable development is perhaps the most urgent. Sustainable development has become within a very short time a term to which everyone can subscribe but also attach a different meaning. The concept of sustainable development, like that of globalization, is hotly contested, with views ranging from those who reject the term as meaningless to others for whom it expresses the current development paradigm.

For some, sustainable development implies a commitment to sustainability with a consequent reduction in economic growth while for others the concept of sustainable development is seen as integral to a new era of economic growth. While some analysts question the utility of a concept subject to multiple meanings it should be pointed out that contestation over its meaning is not unique to sustainable development. This is a normal state of affairs regarding important concepts in the social sciences. In looking at the concept of sustainable development it is vital that analysis moves beyond the clever but simplistic observation that sustainable development is a contradiction in terms. Without definitions of development or sustainability such a conclusion is facile and incapable of wrestling with the core issues raised by sustainable development. In its various conceptualizations, sustainable development is a serious attempt to reconcile what at first sight appear to be contradictory objectives, and to meet the urgent test of fulfilling the needs of developing countries in their drive to eradicate poverty, and reducing the damage caused to the planet by unsustainable modes of production and consumption.

Different conceptions of development contribute to contending perspectives on sustainable development. Radical approaches reject capitalist development and argue that capitalism is responsible for both the creation and perpetuation of poverty and environmental degradation (Saurin, 1996). From this perspective development requires rejection of the current international economic order, and a search for development models that emphasize small-scale, participatory development. In this view the pursuit of economic growth can be counter-productive since such growth frequently stimulates policies which degrade the environment.

On the other hand, the dominant conception of sustainable development accepts the prevailing global political-economic structure, and locates development within the capitalist political economy. Within the dominant approach, economic growth per se is not a problem but an inescapable starting point. The report by the Trilateral Commission, *Beyond Interdependence*, states: 'Given the growth imperative evident in the material poverty of much of human kind, the only reasonable alternative is sustainable development' (McNeil, Winsemius and Yakushiji, 1991, p. v). As this report suggests, economic growth is necessary in order to eradicate poverty. The World Bank, which has adopted sustainable development as its goal, has argued that it is poverty which is responsible for environmental degradation. In this view economic growth provides the instruments through which societies can address environmental degradation.

In this debate between different approaches to development, history has shown convincingly that it is not the economic system, as such, but the importance attached to environmental values that is central. The radical critique is on firm ground when it draws connections between capitalist development and unsustainable modes of production and consumption. But it is surely on shaky ground when it assumes that a socialist (or non-capitalist) economic system automatically provides the conditions for sustainable practices. The evidences of the environmental disasters created by the communist regimes in central and Eastern Europe are stark reminders of the fact that environmental pollution was in many cases far worse under these regimes than in the capitalist West. The objection that these were not true communist states is irrelevant. It is irrelevant because one can equally claim that Western states are not examples of true capitalism. But, more importantly, these regimes provide a counter to the claim that capitalism creates environmental degradation, since, whatever we call their economic systems, they were certainly not capitalist.

Differing conceptions of sustainable development also arise from contending views on the meaning of sustainability, and the measures by which sustainability is to be achieved. Crucial questions include the following. Should sustainability be conceived in terms of a renewal of resources? How do we measure sustainability in relation to the needs of future generations? Should we use market-based solutions or command and control measures?

One of the sources of conceptual confusion surrounding the term is that no agreement exists regarding exactly what is to be sustained. The goal of sustainability sometimes refers to the resource base itself, and sometimes to the livelihoods which are derived from it. Some commentators refer to sustaining levels of production while others emphasize sustaining levels of consumption. This difference is important since development at the global level has become unsustainable largely due to the patterns of overconsumption and irresponsible production in the major developed countries. However, policies for sustainable development that have been put forward to date are essentially production-oriented.

Despite the controversy surrounding the term, a dominant approach to sustainable development is discernible in national and international policy-making circles. That is, current solutions to the problems of environmental degradation and poverty are framed according to a consensual definition which ignores alternative conceptualizations. The dominant discourse has its origins in the Brundtland Commission. The Commission's Report, *Our Common Future*, defines sustainable development as 'development that meets the needs of the present without compromising the ability of future generations to meet their own needs', where 'needs' is defined as the essential needs particularly of the world's poor, and 'development' is vaguely defined as the 'progressive transformation of economy and society' (World Commission on Environment and Development, 1987, p. 43). The Brundtland Commission's definition of sustainable development has become, if not the standard definition, the one that is most widely used in policy-making circles. The evidence on critical thresholds (natural parameters) raised by reports such as *The Limits to Growth* is barely acknowledged, and the main limitations acknowledged are the 'present state of technology and social organization' (World Commission on Environment and Development, 1987, p. 43).

A number of common themes emerge in the debate on sustainable development. First, sustainable development appears to require an inescapable commitment to equity, specifically, intergenerational equity. There is general agreement on the principle of intergenerational equity. In other words, sustainable development policies should ensure that the welfare of future generations is no lower than our own. Second, sustainable development requires an entrenchment of environmental considerations in policy-making and proponents of sustainable development focus on efficiency in resource use. Efficiency in resource use entails the internalization of environmental costs in pricing decisions. Looking more closely at the use of natural resources, and the pollution created as a result of economic production, efficiency is defined so that the full social costs of goods and services are reflected in the price of production inputs and consumer goods. Third, the literature on sustainable development has been concerned with the inter-country and intra-country effects of changes in economic policies. In the context of the global political economy, equity is normally discussed in relation to North–South issues. The advanced industrial states achieved their current living standards through a process of industrialization, which resulted in untold environmental degradation. This option is now closed to the developing countries. However, the adoption of sustainable policies will be costly, and unless the advanced industrial countries are willing to provide major transfers of resources, the necessary policies are unlikely to be implemented. Finally, a focus on sustainable development shifts the narrow focus on growth and obsession with GNP per capita and replaces it with greater attention to social aspects of development.

Sustainable development is the current dominant solution to development. It seeks to combine the right to development with sustainability objectives. Politically, it is imperative that sustainable development is focused on economic growth, since to argue for a steady state in the developing world is unacceptable to the elites and masses in Africa, Asia and Latin America. The concept is a delicate balancing act and does not in itself suggest how one can reconcile these objectives should they come into conflict.

But progress has been made in the implementation of sustainable development. One major step has been in the mainstreaming of environmental assessments, especially in aid projects. It has become commonplace to give importance to the environmental consequences of new projects. But the rhetoric of sustainable development should not be confused with the reality of effective implementation. Independent assessments of lending by multilateral agencies counsel caution in the depth of commitment to meeting environmental objectives. Moreover, most private sector investment is exempt from such scrutiny since, although environmental ministries have mushroomed in the developing world, many of these agencies lack the resources and power to intervene effectively in support of environmental objectives.

A second major step has been increasing attention to participatory development. In the absence of genuine participation by stakeholders affected by development schemes and projects, it is highly likely that old-fashioned unsustainable development practices will remain and may even be reinforced. In situations where the population has a clear stake in the programme or project sustainability, concerns are more likely to be implemented. Sustainable development has provided a site of contention and major policy initiatives as governments have tried to address environmental issues in the global economy.

Trade and environmental degradation

The second key issue concerns the relationship between international trade and environmental degradation. Unsurprisingly, this is an issue of contention between various actors in the global political economy. In broad terms, some observers and participants contend that trade and environmental protection are perfectly compatible and that the pursuit of trade liberalization will enhance rather than destroy environmental sustainability, while others maintain that free trade promotes unsustainable patterns of production and consumption (Williams, 1993). These conflicting views have been evident in the search for regulatory policies linking trade and the environment. We discuss two issues that have arisen and continue to be controversial in this issue area.

Does trade liberalization promote a 'race to the bottom', and does it lead to the creation of pollution havens? Many critics of free trade assert that unfettered trade has a deleterious impact on the environment through these two outcomes. Stated simply, in a competitive world in which firms are seeking to cut costs, they will move production from those countries that have high environmental standards to those with lower environmental standards. Given the importance of transnational corporations in world trade and the transnationalization of production, countries are, it is claimed, reducing their environmental laws in attempts to lure foreign investment. Since some countries will reap a competitive advantage through lax environmental standards, this will force others to abandon stronger environmental protection laws in order to remain competitive.

Another related point is that concerning pollution havens. The claim here is that, as a result of these lax environmental standards, some countries will become major recipients of pollution while others can enjoy the benefits of the products produced in ways detrimental to the natural environment without suffering any of the costs. To date, international regulation has not been developed in response to these fears. Governments have tended to support the contention that no conflict exists between free trade and environmental regulation. In this view they are supported by mainstream economists who argue that the 'race to the bottom' is not a universal feature. Economists contend that environmental costs are not the major determinant of the location of investment (Van Beers and Van den Bergh, 1997). Given the low priority given to environmental costs in the cost structure of most transnational corporations, it is unlikely that production will be located in any massive way to take advantage of lower standards (Wheeler, 2002). Indeed, it has been claimed that countries may indeed reap competitive advantages through higher environmental standards (Nordstrom and Vaughan, 1999). The pollution haven hypothesis is also rejected since it is only relevant in situations where environmental costs outweigh other locational advantages (Letuchamanan, 2000).

A second policy issue concerns what are called process and production methods (PPMs). WTO rules oblige members to treat domestic and foreign goods alike, irrespective of the manner in which they have been produced. WTO regulations are based on product standards, which means that governments can legitimately restrict imports on the basis of a product's characteristics, but not on the basis of the process used to produce the product. For environmentalists this decision leads to unsustainable production, trade and consumption.

This issue can be illustrated through a specific example. Suppose you wanted to buy a car and you were trying to decide between two different makes of car produced in two separate countries. Suppose that you were provided with information which proved conclusively that the production methods in one country harmed the surrounding environment but this was not the case in the second country. You might decide to buy the car from the country whose car manufacturing operations were not harmful to the environment because you supported environmental sustainability. On the other hand, if your value system was different and if the car made with polluting technology cost considerably less than the other car, you would be tempted to buy that one irrespective of the production method. The dilemma is therefore whether we treat products on the basis of the finished article, that is, a car is a car, or whether we create policy to distinguish between how the cars were made so that the one made with polluting technology could be subject to some form of restriction in our domestic market.

From an environmentalist perspective the production process used is crucial to determining the environmental degradation arising from trade. Thus, environmentalists have been campaigning for the incorporation of PPMs into the trade rules, and supporters of the status quo are opposed because they believe that discriminating on the basis of process rather than product will foster discriminatory tendencies in the world trading system (Williams, 2001, p. 5).

This issue raises the possible inconsistency between implementing domestic environmental reform and international environmental policy based on the failure of the WTO to accept PPM-based environmental trade measures. But there are a number of problems inherent in a move to PPM-based environmental trade measures. One crucial issue concerns the fact that countries vary in their ability and willingness to absorb pollution. They possess different absorptive capacities and differing environmental values. If environmental regulations designed for more advanced industrialized countries are forced on developing nations, surely this is an example of eco-imperialism.

Furthermore, any imposition of global standards will erode the comparative advantage of some states. Another problem with enforcing PPMs resides in difficulties inherent in devising monitoring and compliance systems during production processes. Notwithstanding these difficulties, PPM measures cannot be easily dismissed, partly because they are vital for the development of sustainability and partly because it is becoming increasingly difficult to maintain a distinction between production processes and products. For example, if we are concerned about sustainable energy we have to focus on the ways that energy is produced rather than the final product. In other words, attention will be drawn not to the product but to the production process. Furthermore, life-cycle approaches to resource use have demonstrated the importance of assessing the production process as well as the product. As an approach to environmental sustainability life-cycle analysis focuses on the production, consumption and disposal of products.

Climate change negotiations

In mid- to late 2006 climate change became a major political issue, especially in the developed world. The release of the movie *An Inconvenient Truth* in May 2006, and the publication of the Stern Review on *The Economics of Climate Change* in October 2006 appear to have not only increased the visibility of climate change as an issue but also suggest an important turning point in post-Kyoto discussions of climate change. In some respects the international political economy of climate change provides an illustrative introduction to the ways in which environmentalism has been mainstreamed in contemporary political discourse. In the first place, the visible impact of global warming in terms of hurricanes, droughts and disruptions to weather patterns (as well as international commitments) have led many governments to initiate measures aimed at halting global warming. These include emissions reduction schemes and the search for renewable energy sources. Second, there have been considerable efforts to organize responses to climate change at the international level. The Intergovernmental Panel on Climate Change (IPCC) established in 1988 was the first major signal that climate change had become an important international political issue. The United Nations Framework Convention on Climate Change (1992) and the Kyoto Protocol (1997) established normative and policy frameworks. Finally, it has become increasingly apparent that solutions to climate change depend heavily on the role of private sector actors.

Under the terms of the UNFCC states were mandated to 'gather and share information on greenhouse gas emissions, national policies and best practices; launch national strategies for addressing greenhouse gas emissions and adapting to expected impacts, including the provision of financial and technological support to developing countries; and cooperate in preparing for adaptation to the impacts of climate change'. To fulfil these goals the signatory states have held regular meetings in order to develop global policy on climate change. To date there have been 14 such meetings called Conferences of the Parties (COP). At COP-1, held in Berlin in 1995, many of the subsequent difficulties in reaching a workable agreement were apparent. The most significant COP to date was held in Kyoto in 1997 and resulted in the Kyoto Protocol on Climate Change. The Kyoto Protocol sets binding greenhouse gas (GHG) reduction targets for industrialized countries. Under the 'common but differentiated responsibility' principle the Kyoto Protocol distinguishes between developed and developing countries with the former (Annex B countries) only subject to binding commitments. The Kyoto framework consists of three mechanisms: emissions trading (allows countries to sell their unused emissions to countries that have exceeded their targets); the Clean Development Mechanism (allows a country with a binding commitment under the Protocol to implement an emission-reduction project in developing countries); and Joint Implementation (allows an Annex B country to earn emission reduction units through a project in another Annex B country). Although adopted in December 1997 the Protocol did not enter into force until February 2005 following ratification by Russia in November 2004. The Kyoto Protocol could not enter into force until it was ratified by 55 countries accounting for 55 per cent of carbon dioxide emissions in 1990. While it is widely agreed that the Kyoto Protocol is an inadequate instrument to halt climate change, there has been a distinct lack of political will to negotiate an effective climate regime (Depledge, 2006). The COP-15, held in Copenhagen in December 2009, was unable to design a satisfactory post-Kyoto framework for climate governance.

There have been a number of obstacles to negotiating an effective agreement. Although the treaty has been ratified by over 150 countries the refusal of the United States to do so under the Clinton and Bush administrations put the treaty in jeopardy. Until the election of President Obama in 2008 the United States rejected the Kyoto Protocol and any solution to limiting GHG emissions that involved binding targets which did not also impose such commitments on developing countries. A more receptive American administration provides some positive indication that progress can be made post-Copenhagen. Another central obstacle to progress has been the division between developed and developing states over the issue of equity. As the industrialization of developing countries such as China and India have proceeded rapidly their contribution to GHG emission has consequently risen. The key problem concerns the inclusion of these countries into the climate regime as effective participants. Unless some form of compensatory financing is provided it is unlikely that major developing countries will accept binding targets. On the other hand, developed states have made no commitments beyond 2012 and politicians, industrialists and the general public in many developed states are reluctant to accept further binding commitments in the absence of a quid pro quo from leading developing country emitters. The domestic politics of climate change has been an effective stumbling block to further progress (Harrison and Sundstrom, 2007).

Another stumbling block to progress has been the continued debate over climate science (Dessler and Parsons, 2006). Although most credible experts accept the findings of the IPCC, there is nevertheless, a vociferous and at times politically influential minority who challenge the majority view. Climate 'sceptics' variously deny the existence of global warming, adverse human impact on climate change, the speed of change and the possibility of devising appropriate climate policy. And even in circumstances where there is agreement on the salience of climate change and the necessity to halt GHG emissions there is no agreed policy framework. For example, carbon emissions trading is not recognized as a feasible mechanism by some authorities.

Conclusion

Given the extensive nature of the social, economic and political impact of environmental degradation, ecological concerns form a central role in the study of the global political economy. The connections between economics and the environment, combined with the necessity of collective action to counter common resource problems, place contemporary environmental concerns at the centre of international relations. The causes of environmental degradation are complex and require careful understanding of the ways in which economic systems interact with the ecosystem.

This chapter has shown that no consensus exists on how we might best understand the processes of environmental degradation, and the solutions to the environmental crisis. At one end of the spectrum, neoclassical environmental economics requires the extension of market-based principles to areas of economic activity previously exempt. At the other end, radical ecological approaches to economic activity are based on the necessity for fundamental changes in economic structures, value systems and social behaviour.

The introduction of environmental issues to IPE poses questions concerning the adequacy of the three IPE approaches to explain environmental sustainability and environmental cooperation. In the absence of a specific green international political economy perspective (Dryzek, 1996), this chapter has examined the emergence of environmental problems, the different perspectives on the environment and various solutions to environmental problems. It has argued that the study of global environmental issues, which the existing IPE perspectives have failed to address adequately, should be supplemented through attention to debates in environmental economics and ecological economics.

The interaction of social systems, natural systems and the built environment are features of human history and it would be pointless to search for a position from which environmental degradation began. What we conceive as environmental degradation is essentially social, and one generation may accept something as natural that a subsequent generation may find unacceptable. A minor but pertinent example is that of cigarette smoke, which as little as 30 years ago in much of North America and Western Europe was not seen as harmful to non-smokers. However, today it is generally accepted that secondary or passive smoking is detrimental to those who suffer its effects.

Chapter 13

Ideas

This chapter focuses upon what Susan Strange called the 'knowledge structure'. She defined the knowledge structure as 'determining what knowledge is discovered, how it is stored, and who communicates it, by what means, to whom and on what terms' (Strange, 1988, p. 117). Our approach replaces the term 'knowledge' with that of 'ideas', which is a broader term that includes mental images about how the world operates. We are interested in the framework of ideas and knowledge that shape, and are shaped by, activity in the global political economy. Ideas and knowledge play a significant role in influencing actors' behaviour and in outlining the limits of the possible for states, corporations and individuals.

Previous chapters have highlighted the role of ideas in the global political economy. For example, in the 19th century the age of imperialism was justified by racist ideas concerning the superiority of Europeans over non-Europeans. The material power of Western states at this time was the result of ideas which took concrete form in the technology of the industrial revolution. Today ideas about free trade inspire and justify regional trade agreements and the WTO, while technological innovation drives the information revolution.

In this chapter the definitional section outlines how the terms 'ideas', 'knowledge', 'information' and 'technology' are used. The theoretical section examines a number of approaches which highlight the role of ideas in the global political economy. These range from liberal theories, which see ideas as an independent variable shaping behaviour, to post-structuralist approaches, which see language shaping all understanding of reality. The developments section examines the growth of the information revolution and society. It also considers how one particular idea – the Washington Consensus – came to dominate thinking about the global political economy and why it suffered some setbacks in the late 1990s. Key issues for this chapter are technological diffusion, patent protections for pharmaceuticals and financial deregulation.

Definitions

The ideas addressed in this chapter are thoughts about how the human, human-made and natural worlds do or should operate. By the human world we mean the interactions between people. Human-made refers to the physical creations of people, such as cities or machines. The natural world refers to the physical environment, including plant and animal life.

At their most general, ideas are thoughts or mental pictures about how the world works. The broad category of ideas includes a number of overlapping elements of thought. One variant is the 'world view'. People adopt world views which contain assumptions about the forces that drive human nature and what constitutes appropriate action. Such a world view can also be referred to as ideology, ideas inspired by a set of principles which then guide human action in diverse situations. Ideologies are usually associated with large-scale political projects such as communism, fascism, socialism, conservatism, libertarianism. However, world views are also embedded in what people accept as 'common sense'. Common sense refers to ideas accepted by the majority of the population which guide everyday behaviour. Common sense can vary widely over time and place and have a dramatic impact upon how people live their lives. For example, it was common sense among many white people in the southern United States in the early 19th century that the economy be based upon slave labour. Common sense today in the same place rejects slavery as inhuman.

The category of ideas includes a number of related words that signify mental images in different forms. The term 'information' refers to news, data, facts or intelligence material. Information is a stream of facts about particular things. One can think of information about a country's economic performance, for example. Knowledge is slightly different, referring to an understanding of information which leads to it being used in a proper way or for a particular purpose. A person can have access to a great deal of information, but may lack knowledge because they do not know how to order or interpret the information. The word 'wisdom' is less widely used in today's technical and scientific world, but it refers to a type of knowledge that is gained from experience and reflection upon life. It is often associated with the elders of a society and emerges from experience. A final way that ideas are used in this chapter (and the book) is in the form of concrete objects produced by knowledge. This is referred to as 'technology' and involves the technical know-how to produce or manufacture particular products or services.

Theoretical perspectives: ideas about ideas

The traditional approaches to IPE of economic nationalism, liberalism and Marxism did not give much weight to the independent role of ideas. They engaged in theoretical debate about how the world worked, but did not pay much attention to how ideas shaped the operation of the global political economy. However, since the early 1990s a number of approaches to international relations have stressed the importance of ideas for understanding global political economy. They all suggest that the way that people think about the world influences human action. However, they differ a great deal about the degree to which ideas are politicized and what kind of relationship they have to material interests. The field is also marked by some confusion because people use categories, concepts and labels in contradictory ways. This section outlines the basics of key approaches, moving from liberal and conservative-constructivist approaches, which see an independent, but limited role for ideas, to critical approaches, which link ideas to interests, to post-structural/interpretive-constructivist strategies, which begin with ideas and language as the basis for all understanding and action.

A rather modest liberal attempt at highlighting the significance of ideas is the literature on epistemic communities. An epistemic community is 'a network of professionals with recognised expertise and competence in a particular domain and an authoritative claim to policy-relevant knowledge' (Haas, 1992, p. 3). Members of an epistemic community articulate conceptions of a problem and propose solutions in keeping with science rather than the political interests of state and other actors. They facilitate policy coordination between states by providing leaders with crucial information in an environment of uncertainty. They act as knowledge-brokers who can make a significant difference to the formation of international regimes. Through their control over ideas, knowledge communities exercise power and influence in international bargaining. The epistemic communities concept has been particularly important in helping us understand how scientists and scientific knowledge have been able to contribute to building international environmental regimes (Haas, 1992; Young, 1999, p. 126).

The epistemic approach has a number of limitations. One criticism is that it is unable to theorize the relationship between these communities and other groups such as interest groups or social movements. This has led some critics to charge that it is normatively biased in favour of expert groups over other possessors of knowledge and understanding (Toke, 1999). Other critics (Dunlop, 2000) have suggested that the epistemic communities 'other groups' problem causes this approach to miss how expert knowledge groups must engage in coalition-building in order to influence policy. A related criticism is that the epistemic communities literature does not offer an account of the ways in which knowledge can be used to support or justify existing policy positions (Litfin, 1994, p. 12). Furthermore, it has been argued that 'scientific communities are not necessarily consensual or impartial. Tensions and conflicts occur within epistemic communities' (Hurrell and Kingsbury, 1992, p. 19). Moreover, others claim that while scientists may possess relevant information, it is politicians that shape and determine policy. Thus, the policy outcome reflects the nature of social institutions, values and power rather than the activities of an epistemic community. The impact of epistemic communities may not always depend on their possession of the most reliable knowledge since possessors of knowledge that is open to critique and contestation can also be influential in policy discussions.

Another shortcoming is that the notion of expert communities influencing state policy is confined to those areas where scientific consensus is widespread. This involves a limited number of cases, most of which are concentrated in the field where the term first emerged – the study of international environmental issues. In practice, expertise, even scientific expertise, is often divided or can be embedded in different social contexts in various countries. A good example is the disagreement between the WTO, the United States and the EU over the safety of hormone-fed beef. Scientists from each side of the Atlantic may be able to agree about some of the technical issues, but the standards for acceptable risk are set by wider social processes (Skogstad, 2001).

The focus on epistemic communities took inspiration from, and contributed to, the constructivist turn in international relations. Constructivists argue that knowledge and action are socially constructed and can be shaped to different purposes. Whereas rationalist approaches to IR and IPE examine actors' strategic interaction based upon a set of presumed preferences, constructivists examine how those preferences came about in the first place and what impact they have upon actors' perceptions and actions. For constructivists, the ideational aspect of social life is as important as the material world. That is, there is both a social construction of reality and a construction of social reality (Guzzini, 2000, p. 149). In constructivist research norms are central to explanation. While rationalist approaches to IPE tend to give primacy to material structures and to consider norms, rules and institutions as by-products that aid actors in their pursuit of their material interests, constructivist approaches argue that intersubjective meanings are necessary in order for actors to interpret material power. Ideas are central in constructivist thought because objects, events and actors are only given meaning through intersubjective knowledge and practice. Constructivists claim that 'meaningful behaviour is possible only within an inter-subjective social context' (Hopf, 1998, p. 173). Normative structures give material power meaning and affect actors' interests and identities. The leading variant of this thought in the United States has been labelled 'conventional constructivism'. It focuses upon how norms and identities shape international politics (Checkel, 2004).

Working from a historical materialist tradition, neo-Gramscian authors have linked ideas with class interests. This critical approach is illustrated in the quote by Robert Cox in the first chapter of the book that 'Theory is always for someone and for some purpose'. This means that theory and theorists are always linked to configurations of power and are not neutral.

Powerful actors will find some sets of theories to their liking while the weak or dispossessed are likely to find comfort in other theories. Developed states with advanced industries are more likely to advance the idea of free trade than states of weaker economies, which fear domestic businesses will disappear.

Thus, a contest over ideas is a key ingredient in establishing the hegemony of a state or social group. If group A can convince groups B and C that the self-interested proposals put forward by A will also benefit B and C, A will be able to further its interests by co-opting other groups. Hegemony comes about when one group convinces subordinate groups that their interests will be served by following the lead of the dominant actors. For example, US leadership of the Western world between 1945 and 1971 was accepted by other Western states as being in the common interest. This type of analysis leads scholars to focus upon the ongoing battle to determine what is or is not the 'common sense' that frames political action. Mark Rupert (1995b), for example, has examined how the 'common sense' that free trade is good for US workers came to be challenged in the NAFTA debate. When common sense breaks down or is challenged by another view of common sense, it is likely that politics will become more heated and fluid. The debate over ideas becomes crucial to wielding political power.

Another critical approach to using ideas in the study of IPE is post-structuralism. Post-structuralism comes to the social sciences from French philosophy and cultural studies. People adopting a post-structural perspective stress how 'reality' is interpreted in many different ways. It can also be labelled as 'interpretive constructivism' because it draws upon linguistic theories of interpretation (Checkel, 2004, p. 231). Rather than a single post-structuralist theory, there are a number of post-structural approaches which concentrate on understanding how the language we use shapes our understanding and actions in the world (Belsey, 2002; Sarup, 1993). We use language, whether it be the spoken word, writing or visual images, to communicate our thoughts and represent reality. Yet, there is never a perfect fit between our language and the thing we are trying to describe. As a result there must always be some doubt about the relationship between 'reality' and how we communicate reality. Some versions of post-structuralism suggest that we can never get close to reality or 'truth'.

How can these ideas apply to IPE? Marieke de Goede (2003) argues that applying post-structuralism to global finance politicizes formerly unquestioned or seemingly neutral financial structures and arrangements. For example, accounting standards which are a technical form of language trying to represent 'reality' build a particular picture of reality which hides important elements. Standard accounting procedures do not incorporate the environmentally damaging impacts of economic activity and thus paint a very different picture than a set of standards which operate from an ecological perspective. To take another example, debates about economic matters may be closed to the public because they require participants to master a particular language – neoclassical economics – before their views will be heard in elite forums. Thus, language is seen to both shape the conduct of global finance and privilege some voices over others. The contribution that this approach makes is that it 'denaturalizes' what is thought to be a natural state of affairs. Once this has been done orthodox approaches to a particular order are vulnerable to challenge from other perspectives and interests.

An insight shared by a number of perspectives is that ideas become embedded in institutions (Goldstein and Keohane, 1993). Patterns of behaviour, legal codes and international organizations are created in a specific historic context and reflect the dominant set of ideas at the time that they are created. The institutions embody the ideas that created them. The provisions of the ILO which allow for separate government, business and labour voting rights reflect the idea that these three social partners have different interests and require separate expression. US trade law is marked by elements of free trade and protectionism because it is composed of legislation that hails from the free-trading and protectionist eras. Yet, the story does not end there. Once institutions are created, they then become a site of conflict as new groups try to shape the institutions to reflect a different set of ideas and priorities (Cox, 1983).

In summary, there are a wide variety of approaches to examining ideas in the global political economy. Yet, they all stress the significant role that ideas and knowledge play in influencing and shaping all the other facets of GPE. This chapter draws upon some of the insights advanced by these perspectives, but will ground the discussion of ideas by connecting them to the interests which advance particular sets of ideas and benefit from their adoption.

Major developments

The post-war decades have witnessed two important long-term developments in the areas of knowledge production and dissemination. On the technological side there has been the explosion of the information revolution and the creation of an information society. In the realm of world views there have been equally dramatic developments with shifts from embedded liberalism and Keynesianism to neoliberalism and the Washington Consensus to post-Washington Consensus uncertainty.

The information revolution and the information society

It has been claimed that the impact of information technology is fundamentally reshaping the global political economy (Castells, 1996). In April 1997 a report to the European Commission noted that 'The Information Society is the society that is currently being put in place, where low-cost information and data storage and transmission technologies are in general use. The generalization of information and data use is being accompanied by organizational, commercial, social and legal innovations that will profoundly change life both in the world of work and in society generally' (European Commission, 1997, p. 16). The contention that the revolution in information technology has fundamentally transformed economic and social organization has not been accepted by all analysts and we examine the extent to which technological change is leading to the creation of a 'new economy'. Apart from the impact of technology on economic and political relations another important issue concerns access to technology. The Geneva *Declaration of Principles* adopted at the World Summit on the Information Society in December 2003 recognized the importance of access to information technology in the construction of the new economy. Para. 24 of the *Declaration of Principles* states, 'The ability for all to access and contribute information, ideas and knowledge is essential in an inclusive Information Society' (UN, 2003). We examine the problem of access in terms of the global digital divide below, but first we turn our attention to the impact of information on economic, social and political structures and processes.

The concept of a new economy has been central to debates concerning the political economy of the information revolution. The definition of the 'new economy' and related concepts such as 'knowledge economy', 'networked economy' or 'digital economy' are the subject of debate among social scientists. Given the different terminology and the absence of a consensus definition, we outline key features that appear in a number of definitions. A central element in the 'new economy' is the importance of knowledge and technology as key drivers of economic growth. It is argued that the role of science and technology applied to economic processes is unprecedented in human history. Closely allied with this emphasis on knowledge is the contention that services (and especially knowledge-based services) are the most important sources of value-added in economic accumulation. The source for this change is to be found in technological innovations such as the invention of the microprocessor, innovations in software development and the introduction of network technologies. The microprocessor has led to a fall in prices of computer equipment; software has made computers easier to use; and the internet has revolutionized communication through its ability to connect peoples and systems. These technological developments, it is claimed, have had an impact on the macro-economy in terms of low unemployment and low inflation.

The thesis of a 'new economy' has come under sustained criticism. It has been dismissed as an invention of Wall Street and the media or as a myth designed to explain the performance of the American economy in the 1990s. As such it is based on 'half truths, bad history and wishful thinking'

(Madrick, 2001, p. 1). Other critics have attacked the conservative philosophy and implications of the 'new economy' thesis. From this perspective it is seen as an attack on trade unions and working people (Kotz and Wolfson, 2004) since the 'new economy' thesis supports privatization, deregulation, de-unionization and flexible labour markets in order to create the required conditions for the innovation necessary for continued high-technology growth. The extent to which the changes in industrial practices are required by technology and whether or not they lead to economic growth and prosperity have also been questioned.

It is not necessary to subscribe to the 'new economy' thesis to recognize the impact of knowledge and technology on political economic structures and practices. And equally it is possible to note changes brought by technological development at the same time as one rejects the 'new economy' thesis. Instead of mediating in this debate (much of which has taken place in regard to the American economy), we briefly review some of the ways that information technology and knowledge can be said to be having a profound impact on the global political economy. At the centre of any analysis has to be an assessment of whether these changes are historically unprecedented. The authors of a comparative analysis of current changes with the innovations taking place during the industrial revolution conclude that the role of knowledge is not 'fundamentally' new. What is new 'is the type of technologies in which economy and society exist – digital technologies built around ICT' (Carlaw, Oxley and Walker, 2006, p. 651). Thus, the key issue concerns the ways in which this particular form of knowledge is transforming traditional practices.

There are three ways in which the current application of knowledge is transforming the global political economy. First, these technologies are transforming the ways in which we work. This is not solely a phenomenon of advanced capitalist states but refers to any society or segment of society that has access to information technology. For example, in India call centre operators work through the night so that they can respond to customers working during the day in North America. Second, digital technologies are having an effect on the way we spend our leisure time, and directly on consumption patterns. These changes are visible in the ways people shop online, watch television, or listen to music on iPods. Third, advances in knowledge are having important effects on food and health technologies. The advances in biotechnologies are not only affecting the material world but also creating new ethical dilemmas – for example, over stem cell research or genetically modified food.

The term 'digital divide' refers to unequal access to digital technology; that is, some people are able to enjoy the benefits of digital technology and others are not. The term can be used in the domestic context to refer to unequal access across households or it can be used to refer to unequal access across national borders. The digital divide has been defined as 'the strikingly differential extent to which various forms of information technology are being exploited by developed, as opposed to developing countries' (James, 2001, p. 211). While the definition of the digital divide is reasonably straightforward, no agreed measurement exists. There have been a number of studies on the quantification of the digital divide. The ITU claims that 'over the last 10 years the digital divide between the developing and developed countries has been narrowing in terms of fixed telephone lines, mobile subscribers and Internet users' (2006, p. 4). On the other hand, UNCTAD's statistics (2005b, pp. 10–11) reveal a continued high level of differentiation between countries. Differences in methodology account for these contrasting conclusions. The ITU's approach is to examine average per capita distribution of hardware (fixed lines, mobile lines) and number of internet users in developed and developing countries. The UNCTAD study challenged this approach by applying standard methods of inequality (Gini coefficients and Lorenz curves) to the cross-national data.

The significance of the digital divide lies in the benefits flowing from access to the goods and services produced by the information economy and conversely the costs of failing to keep pace with technological change. The importance of the digital divide therefore lies in its relationship to development. The salience of information and communications technology (ICT) for development has become an issue of interest to national governments and international organizations. An UNCTAD report recognizes that the digital divide has 'significant consequences for social, economic and political development' (2005b, p. 8). From an economic nationalist perspective it becomes evident that an increasing digital divide between groups of states will increase the relative gains of those states with access to the information resources. Given the value-added produced by information technologies this increases the gains of information-rich states. It has been argued that access to information technology is positively correlated with rates of economic growth (Becchetti and Adriani, 2003, p. 2).

The digital divide need not remain a permanent feature of the global political economy and emphasis on differential access to technological resources need not obscure the impact that ICT can have on development. For example, ICT has an important role to play in meeting the challenges established by the MDGs (World Bank, 2003). The World Bank concluded that ICT 'is a powerful tool when used appropriately as part of an overall development strategy' (World Bank, 2003, p. 8). But it also cautions that 'ICT will only be helpful to the extent that users are able to use the technology and take advantage of the opportunities it creates' (World Bank, 2003, p. 8). However, the impact of ICT on the MDGs requires the appropriate enabling environment (Gilhooly, 2005). Without favourable economic, political and regulatory environments the promise of ICT will remain unfulfilled. The challenge lies in finding the right mix of private and public capital, political structures that incorporate the wide range of stakeholders (government, business and civil society) and targeted investment and regulation that foster innovation without replacing public monopolies with private ones.

The rise and stall of the Washington Consensus

The post-1945 era has seen a number of changes in the ideas that have guided dominant countries and economic institutions. This sub-section focuses upon one prominent set of ideas – a bundle of liberal prescriptions for economic development labelled the Washington Consensus. Our discussion highlights a number of key themes when considering the role of ideas in the global political economy. These themes are: the relationship between ideas and interests, the relationship between ideas and practices, the multiple interpretation of ideas and the varied implementation of ideas.

The dominant approach of Western countries from the late 1940s until the early 1970s has been called 'embedded liberalism' (Ruggie, 1982). Domestically, states redistributed income through welfare policies and supported employment through government management of the economy. While there were wide variations between the Anglo-American forms of state, which supported minimal welfare provision, and the more social-democratic states of Northern Europe, with elaborate welfare provision (Esping-Anderson, 1990), there was a shared commitment to state intervention to aid economic development. Internationally, the United States and Britain led the development of international institutions which facilitated the liberalization of economic activity, but allowed for considerable domestic opportunity for states to pursue national development strategies.

In developing countries prevailing economic orthodoxy also favoured a strong role for the state. The state's proper role was seen as developing and nurturing national economic activity. Similar to developments in the West, there was a wide variety of developmental states from those inspired and supported by the centrally planned model of the Soviet Union to East Asian states linking their prosperity to an export model of capitalism. What these various arrangements shared was the idea that the state played a crucial organizing role in assisting the developmental process. The developmental state perspective saw the international system as posing large challenges for national improvement. As outlined in Chapter 11, some intellectuals and state leaders feared that the existing system fostered dependency and that state action was required to redress inequalities.

Between 1980 and 1997 the notion of state-led development was eclipsed by an agreement amongst many financial, corporate and state elites that the secret to development was to give the freest reign possible to market forces to guide economic activity. The term 'Washington Consensus' was used as a shorthand for this view of economic development. This sub-section examines what that consensus was, how that consensus came about, the impacts that it had and whether we are now in a transition to a new, not-yet-clear concept of development.

The 'Washington Consensus' is a term coined by John Williamson (1990) to capture a set of economic development policies that had broad support amongst officials and economists in the US government (especially the US Treasury), IMF and World Bank. He was writing specifically about policies with regard to Latin American development. These policies included fiscal discipline (balancing budgets), liberalizing trade, freeing exchange rates and interest rates, privatizing state industries, deregulation, tax reform to broaden the tax base, redirecting public expenditure to increase economic returns and redistribute income, and securing property rights.

The idea that economic growth would best be achieved by reducing state involvement in the economy was the hallmark of Conservative governments in Britain (Thatcher) and the United States (Reagan) in the early 1980s. The marrying of neoclassical economic propositions with the political project of implementing them is often referred to as neoliberalism. The move to globalize the ideology of neoliberalism was facilitated by a number of developments. First, the ideas of neoclassical economics were spread by an epistemic community of economists trained in neoclassical economics departments in the United States. Second, the debt crisis of the early 1980s forced many developing countries to adopt a new policy paradigm. The old developmental state model in countries such as Mexico and Brazil had drowned in debt and there was little alternative to neoliberal restructuring if these states wanted to attract foreign capital for investment. Third, the United States used the IMF to encourage states to adopt the main tenets of the Washington Consensus. Countries in debt that needed loans from the IMF were required to adopt structural adjustment packages that included many of the policies advocated in the Consensus such as trade liberalization, reducing the role of the state, privatization, deregulation and fostering foreign direct investment.

The prescription of the Washington Consensus proved very powerful. Part of its power came from the fact that the major international financial institutions and the US government promoted it with vigour. Countries that adopted these prescriptions would be favoured by the IMF, the World Bank and the United States; countries that did not adopt them could expect problems. Another element of its influence was that the Consensus provided policy-makers with a clear set of prescriptions for overcoming serious economic situations. State decision-makers were told that if they implemented the package they could cure their economies. Many of the reforms were implemented by executive decree rather than needing the approval of legislatures and parliaments, making the adoption of the Consensus politically easy. A third element of strength was that with the onset of the debt crisis the state developmental strategy appeared to be discredited. The collapse of the Soviet Union in 1989 further bolstered the sense that there was no alternative to accepting liberal economic policies.

Despite the influence of the concept of the Washington Consensus, it would be inaccurate to portray it as a universal set of principles that dominated the functioning of the global economy. One thing that curbed its influence was that the Consensus was actually implemented in a very different way in different countries. Some countries implemented the whole package, but most picked and chose from the original ten items. Countries subscribed to the general principle, but only implemented particular steps.

Another weakness of the Consensus is that even amongst its advocates there were disagreements about its details (Naim, 2000a, 2000b). Some argued that countries in financial difficulties should undergo shock therapy. That is, they should implement a radical liberal agenda immediately. Others suggested that such a strategy created economic damage and that reforms should be introduced at a gradual pace. Some argued that countries should also liberalize their capital markets by allowing foreigners to invest in stock markets and facilitating the movement of short-term capital into their countries. Others disagreed and did not include capital account liberalization in their view of the Washington Consensus.

A third brake on the domination of the Consensus was resistance from those groups that disagreed with its prescriptions. During its heyday in the late 1980s and early 1990s the Consensus did command the allegiance of state and economic elites, but failed to gain the support of key social groups and movements. Environmentalists protested the ecological damaged caused by unregulated liberalization, labour groups protested the effects on wages and livelihoods and development groups questioned its effectiveness. Their ongoing opposition often prevented the full implementation of reforms.

Opposition to the Washington Consensus caused protests in the streets, but also changed and challenged the very meaning of the term. Whereas advocates viewed the term as indicating sound economic policies, opponents used the term to describe a broad approach to economic management that embodied a 'market fundamentalism'. 'Washington Consensus' became shorthand for all the liberal economic policies that seemed to be increasing inequality and poverty around the world. Despite his best efforts at clarification, Williamson could not enforce his view of the meaning of the term he invented.

By the end of the 1990s the power of the Washington Consensus as a set of ideas had been eroded. Developments in Asia, Africa and the Americas posed a serious challenge to the Consensus (Broad, 2004; Önis and Şenses, 2005). While many neoliberals had claimed that the success of newly industrializing countries in Asia (Korea, Taiwan, etc.) could be attributed to the liberal market policies followed by these states, detailed research painted a different picture. These economies were market-oriented in the sense that they produced for a global market, but they had interventionist states which supported and guided national corporate activity. This undercut one element of the neoliberal case. A further blow came in 1997 when the East Asian financial crisis was seen to be caused by countries prematurely liberalizing their capital markets and exposing themselves to financial chaos. Although capital liberalization was not technically part of the original Washington Consensus, it was closely identified with a broad neoliberal policy stance. The actions of the IMF, which applied standard liberal prescriptions of belt-tightening, worsened the crisis and generated a great deal of criticism from both the left and the right. In Africa numerous states that had experienced structural adjustment for almost 20 years continued to stagnate and had very poor economic growth. In the Americas, two states which had whole-heartedly adopted the prescriptions of the Consensus suffered financial crisis (Mexico in 1994, Argentina in 2001), leading many to question the wisdom of the original prescriptions. Within the United States itself a series of corporate criminal scandals such as the collapse of Enron raised questions about the abuse of power by corporations in deregulated markets.

The response to these problems by the advocates of the Washington Consensus was to reply that its shortcomings were due to failure in policy implementation. The ideas were correct, but they had undesired effects because they were either partially or imperfectly put into practice. This led advocates of the original Consensus to broaden their focus to include the public institutions that are required to implement reforms. There is now a new 'second generation' of reforms urged on developing countries. These reforms include the creation of 'good governance' through the rule of law, transparency and eliminating corruption in the public service. The basic elements of the Consensus remain in place, but they must now be supplemented by a wide series of measures reforming the governments and bureaucracies of developing countries (Krueger, 2000).

There are many ironies here. First, the Washington Consensus was originally an attempt to curtail the role of the state, but it has now evolved into a concern about improving state structures. The new plan echoes the concerns of many of the pre-1980 developmental state theorists who placed emphasis on the role of the government in assisting development. Second, one of the results of the implementation of Consensus policies was to weaken the state, but that state is now required to be more active and efficient. The demand for state action is there, but the capacity has been reduced. Third, the prescriptions for development are now so extensive that they demand developing countries have all of the features of developed states in order to begin the process of developing (Naim, 2000a, p. 522)! Fourth, although there is now broad demand for state reforms, there does not seem to be any roadmap for meeting the demands being placed on developing countries (Naim, 2000a, 2000b; Santiso, 2004).

By 2005 there was agreement that a new 'post-Washington Consensus' might develop, but there was confusion about what it could entail. As suggested above, advocates of the original approach argued for a Consensus-plus model which focused upon state reforms. Further to the left, others suggested that a social-democratic model which put more emphasis on democratic practices, increased regulation of the global economy and gave more attention to an equitable distribution of life chances might supplant the Washington Consensus (Held, 2005). Even further to the left, others argued for abandoning the original Consensus and putting in place much more nationally oriented development strategies (Fine, Lapavitas and Pincus, 2001). The Washington Consensus was further undermined by the 2008 US financial crisis, which cast doubt both upon the wisdom emerging from Washington and the ability of unregulated markets to foster economic growth.

From embedded liberalism to post-Washington Consensus, ideas about the functioning of the global economy have influenced the behaviour of policy-makers and other key actors. These ideas and prescriptions have also benefited or hurt the interests of various social groups. Thus, the struggle over ideas is also a struggle over power and wealth.

Key issues

Three key issues in the area of ideas and knowledge are: the pace and extent of technological diffusion; the scope and enforcement of intellectual property rights; and the role of ideas and institutions in the origins of the global financial crisis.

Technological diffusion

A vital issue for many countries, corporations and people is the phenomenon of technological diffusion. As a series of technological waves wash over advanced industrialized states, other states, corporations and people struggle to keep pace. Just as the industrial revolution conferred power on states, corporations and people who were able to harness industrialization at the expense of those who could not, the fear is that the information revolution may create similar inequalities. Inequalities and power differentials may compound because the states leading the information revolution tend to be those that emerged strongest from the industrial revolution. There are two further issues here. One concerns the diffusion of technology for production, while the other is the diffusion of technology through society as a whole.

Firms and countries producing products for the world market need up-to-date technology to ensure that their enterprises are as efficient as possible.

However, corporations jealously guard their technology and demand financial compensation for sharing inventions. Accessing newer technologies became harder and more expensive following the insertion of intellectual property rights into the remit of the WTO. This limits the ability of developing countries or firms in developing countries to copy technology in their development process. Whereas rivals to Britain during the industrial revolution copied, stole and purchased technology in the race to catch up, today's legal environment makes the copying and stealing options much more difficult. Corporations possessing advanced technology tend to be based in advanced economies, as are many of the leading knowledge institutions (see Box 13.1). Countries already lagging behind in development face increasing technological barriers to catching up with wealthy countries.

Box 13.1   The uneven distribution of knowledge: patents and Nobel Prize winners

A cursory examination of the number of patents issued by country and the number of Nobel Prize winners per country illustrates how unbalanced the creation and control of knowledge are in the global economy. Patents are issued to protect the intellectual property of companies and individuals. Non-patent-holders are prohibited from using this knowledge or must pay a licensing fee to the patent-owner. As a rough measure, those countries with a large number of patents are accumulating more knowledge and inventions, while those with a low number will have to buy their knowledge and technology from others or wait until the patents expire. In 2005 over 82,000 patents were issued in the United States and 31,000 in Japan. Only 565 were issued in China and 403 in India (USPTO, 2006). Even if only a small percentage of patents leads to commercially viable products, China and India are likely to be at a severe technological disadvantage to the United States and Japan.

A similar concentration of knowledge can be seen when examining the country of residence of Nobel Prize winners. Nobel Prizes are awarded each year to individuals or groups deemed to have made outstanding contributions to their fields. Over 60 per cent of the Nobel Prizes awarded in the fields of Chemistry, Physics, Physiology and Medicine and Economics since 1950 have gone to people based in the United States. Just under a third of the US winners were also immigrants to the United States (Wasow, 2006). This indicates both that the United States is home to many of the world's top knowledge institutions and that these institutions and the country draw in many leading scientists from around the world.

On the other hand, there are some cases where technological advances can help states leapfrog the development gap. For example, the introduction of mobile phones in developing countries allows for the establishment of a communications infrastructure without the financial and resource investment required to lay the cables which provide the infrastructure for landline telephones.

Property rights and life (HIV/AIDS)

A second key issue in the field of ideas is the degree to which there should be private ownership over ideas that pertain to the necessities of life or life forms themselves. The issue is particularly pressing in the cases of patent protection for life-saving drugs and patent protection for micro-organisms.

As outlined in Chapter 6, the issue of ownership of intellectual property became significant in global political economy after 1995 when the WTO was mandated to protect intellectual property rights (IPRs). Article 27, section 1 of the WTO's Agreement on Trade-Related Intellectual Property Rights (TRIPs) states that 'patents shall be available for any inventions, whether products or processes, in all fields of technology, provided that they are new, involve an inventive step and are capable of industrial application' (GATT, 1994). The WTO's IPR provisions reflect a particular set of ideas about the relationship between private property and knowledge. In this view companies or individuals that invest time and energy to create new intellectual products should have the legal right to prevent others from using or enjoying that knowledge, unless those other people first pay the inventor an agreed price. This policy is said to be justified on two grounds. One is that if intellectual property producers are not compensated properly they will not produce the products people need. A second argument is that intellectual property is a work of labour and deserves to be rewarded just as the production of other products is rewarded. Patent protection for pharmaceuticals is usually for 20 years.

This approach to intellectual property rights serves the immediate interests of large corporations that dominate the fields of pharmaceuticals, computer software and entertainment. Indeed, the idea of having the WTO enforce intellectual property rights was originally put forward to the US government by the International Property Committee which in 1986 was composed of the following companies: Bristol-Myers, Squibb, Digital Equipment Corporation, FCM, General Electric, Hewlett-Packard, IBM, Johnson & Johnson, Merck, Pfizer, Procter and Gamble, Rockwell International and Time-Warner (Sell, 2006, p. 194). The Committee faced a dual task. First, the TNCs had to convince the US government that international protection of their property rights was a US priority. Second, the United States had to convince or coerce other nations into accepting the same logic. However, even though the idea of stringent intellectual property enforcement was institutionalized in the WTO, the controversy was only just beginning.

A major issue with the WTO's IPR provisions was that they extended the patent for brand-name drugs that can be used to treat infectious diseases. In particular, it solidified the grip of Western pharmaceutical producers over their production of anti-retroviral (ARVs) drugs, which are used to treat HIV/AIDS. Patent protection means that generic-drug producers are not allowed to make cheap copies. The difficulty arises because the majority of HIV/AIDS patients live in Africa where incomes are so low that they cannot afford life-prolonging brand-name drugs. The cost of brand-name ARV treatment per patient for one year, depending upon the drug cocktail, can range from US$2,738 to almost US$22,000, whereas the annual per capita income in sub-Saharan Africa is only US$601 (Floyd and Gilks, 1998; World Bank, 2006b). A strict interpretation of IPRs would imply that approximately 26 million Africans suffering from HIV/AIDS are unable to access brand-name drugs because they or their governments cannot afford the cost.

The clash between the notion of protecting private property rights and the human right to life and health sparked a large-scale intercontinental struggle over the WTO's IPR provisions and national legislation that implemented those provisions. The TRIPs agreement allowed countries to make generic copies of life-saving drugs on public health grounds, but there were two shortcomings. First, a debate took place as to what drugs would qualify for this measure. Second, countries were allowed to make generic copies, but would not be allowed to import generic copies from other countries. Thus countries with a pharmaceutical industry such as Brazil or India could make copies, but countries in sub-Saharan Africa, which did not have the domestic industry, were not allowed to import them from India or Brazil. On one side of the conflict were the institution of the WTO, northern pharmaceutical companies and the US government. On the other side were governments of many developing states, generic-drug producers, local and transnational NGOs. Campaigners in this second group were able to effectively contrast the desperate need of sick and dying people against the corporate profits of drug TNCs. The pressure to relax IPRs built until WTO member states amended the TRIPs agreement so that poor countries were allowed to import generic copies of ARVs under the Doha Declaration on the TRIPs Agreement and Public Health.

The debate over the balance between protecting corporate interests and health rights revealed the glaring inequalities of the global political economy of health. The patents were mostly held by northern corporate interests, while many of the victims were in poor developing countries. Northern states were able to exert pressure on developing countries to agree to WTO provisions which went against the public health interests of their citizens.

Box 13.2 Bioprospectors and biopiracy

Bioprospectors search the land, sea and sky to find natural ingredients for new drugs and industrial products. Examples of such ingredients are the venom of sea snails in the Philippines used for the pain killer Prialt and Easter Island soil used for the kidney transplant drug Rapamune (Elias, 2006). While many of these discoveries prove useful, the problem lies in the power relations and economic profits behind the bioprospecting sorties. The raw materials being exploited are usually found in developing countries. The research needed to turn them into marketable products is undertaken by northern corporations or universities. As a result, the patents are held by people in the developed world and the profits flow into northern multinationals or research universities. The benefits do not flow to the people living in the territory from which the natural ingredient originated. In addition, many of the indigenous people familiar with the local life forms do not have a Western sense of property rights and object to outsiders claiming rights to these life forms. From their perspective northern institutions, which exploit life forms in developing countries, are engaged in biopiracy.

Moving away from a focus on HIV/AIDS, one can see the glaring mismatch between pharmaceutical R&D and global health needs. TNCs conduct research primarily into diseases of the affluent West while placing little emphasis on diseases that kill millions in the developing world. For example, with the majority of people suffering from malaria living in developing countries, it is much more profitable for drug companies to fund research into impotence, baldness, toenail fungus, or wrinkles. Although millions die from malaria, it is extremely unlikely that a new malaria drug would match Viagra's first-year sales of US$1 billion (Silverstein, 2002).

The move to globally enforce patent protection over products such as drugs, plants, seeds and even new uses for existing forms of life generates intense debates and new questions. Should corporations be given protection for the ideas and information they discover or generate? If so, should any limits be placed upon their activity? Is it acceptable that TNCs patent life forms? Isn't this a form of biopiracy (see Box 13.2)?

Ideas, interests and the global financial crisis

The US-centred financial crisis of 2008 destroyed trillions of dollars of wealth and plunged the world into a global recession. The origins of the crisis lay in the failure of governments, especially the US government, to adequately regulate financial industries. The question is: how did ideas of financial deregulation become so persuasive and why did they lead to crisis?

During the 1990s a series of ideas took hold of the practioners in financial markets and among their regulators that the greatest amount of wealth would be created by financial markets subject to the least regulation. Left alone financial markets were seen to be highly efficient and self correcting. Market participants were capable of self-regulation with minimal interventions by the state. Sound and profitable financial practices would win out over those that were questionable. While there might be some cases of inappropriate activity, these would be resolved in the market place. A fine example of this sentiment is provided by the then Chairman of the US Federal Reserve, Alan Greenspan, when he argued against allowing the Commodity Futures Trading Commission to regulate derivatives before a US Congressional hearing: 'The primary source of regulatory effectiveness has always been private traders being knowledgeable of their counterparties. Government regulation can only act as a backup. It should be careful to create net benefits to markets' (Greenspan, 1998).

These were not new ideas, particular elements of liberal theory had preached the virtue of minimally regulated markets for centuries. Yet, the repeated financial collapse of these markets, as in the case of the stock market crash of 1929, raises the intriguing question of why policy makers return to policies which have had disastrous consequences in the past. John Kenneth Gailbraith (1975) suggested that the cycle of deregulation, financial crisis and reregulation is due primarily to the fading of memory. The consequences of financial disaster linger for a generation or two, but new generations repeatedly imagine that they have overcome the vices of previous eras. Some new technology (e.g., computers) or a new technical method (e.g., advanced mathematical formula) convinces a new set of financiers and regulators that they have discovered the secret of never-ending wealth creation. In reality, they have discovered nothing and simply repeat the mistakes of their predecessors, but in slightly different ways.

While such an explanation has some plausibility, one must look beyond the power of ideas themselves or the fading of memory of regulators to explain the shift in financial regulation. The financial community was (and is) actively engaged in politics, continuously attempting to shift the regulatory framework to facilitate profit maximization. Over a ten-year period from 1998 until 2008 financial firms such as banks (both investment and commercial), insurance companies, hedge funds and real estate companies spent over $5 billion to purchase regulator influence. This included $1.7 billion in political contributions and $3.4 billion to pay an army of 3,000 registered lobbyists (Weissman and Donahue, 2009, p. 6).

The financial industry gave money both to Democrats and Republicans to ensure that, whichever party was in power, its interests were well represented.

Although the Republican Party was ideologically more sympathetic to deregulation, key Democratic Party officials advanced a similar agenda or received large contributions from the financial industry. An example of the ability of financial firms to influence government activity was that the investment bank Goldman Sachs had its chief executive officer selected to be US Treasury Secretary under both Democratic (Robert Rubin, 1995–9) and Republican (Henry Paulson, 2006–8) administrations.

The combined efforts of the financial industry were tremendously successful in revolutionizing their regulatory structure. Over the period of a decade, financial regulations were modified so that firms took on higher levels of risk under less government supervision (see Box 13.3). One set of initiatives allowed banks to increase in size, engage in new activity and appear more profitable than they actually were. Actions that fell into this category were: dismantling the barrier between insurance and banking industries, allowing off-balance sheet accounting to hide debt, allowing investment banks to adopt voluntary measures for setting their debt loads, allowing commercial banks to set their own reserve requirements based on internal risk models, facilitating mergers by dropping anti-trust regulations. At the same time that banks were growing bigger and taking on more risk, the efforts to regulate non-bank financial institutions and instruments were blocked. Both the Democratic President Bill Clinton and then later the Republican-controlled Congress prevented the Commodity Futures Trading Commission from regulating risky derivatives. Federal regulators also refused to prevent predatory lending by financial institutions, objected to state-level governments taking such action and removed the possibility of clients suing financial institutions for such activities. Large mortgage institutions were encouraged to lend to more and more risky clients in the name of spreading home ownership. Federal regulators also refused to examine the conflict of interests ensnaring credit rating agencies who were being paid by the firms they were rating.

The notion that deregulated financial markets were positive and that the property boom was increasing the stock of the nation's wealth was reinforced by mass media. Financial institutions ran television commercials encouraging individuals to take out low rate mortgages or to remortgage their houses and use the money for consumption. Individual pensions based on market investments were sold as the guarantee of a good life in retirement. Dedicated financial channels, like CNBC, broadcast the glories of the financial markets on a 24-hour schedule and fed the need of market traders for instant information. Given its need to serve the financial community, it is not surprising that CNBC analysts and guests missed the story of the financial crisis until it overwhelmed them. The most devastating critique of the role of CNBC was not even presented in the mainstream media, but appeared as a commentary on the John Stewart comedy show (Stewart,

Box 13.3   Twelve financial deregulation policies, 1998–2008

1. In 1999, Congress repealed the Glass-Steagall Act, which had prohibited the merger of commercial banking and investment banking.
2. Regulatory rules permitted off-balance-sheet accounting, allowing banks to hide their liabilities.
3. The Clinton administration blocked the Commodity Futures Trading Commission from regulating financial derivatives – which became the basis for massive speculation.
4. Congress in 2000 prohibited regulation of financial derivatives through the Commodity Futures Modernization Act.
5. The Securities and Exchange Commission in 2004 adopted a voluntary regulation scheme for investment banks that enabled them to incur much higher levels of debt.
6. Rules adopted by global regulators at the behest of the financial industry would enable commercial banks to determine their own capital reserve requirements, based on their internal 'risk-assessment models'.
7. Federal regulators refused to block widespread predatory lending practices earlier in this decade, failing to either issue appropriate regulations or even enforce existing ones.
8. Federal bank regulators claimed the power to supersede state consumer protection laws that could have diminished predatory lending and other abusive practices.
9. Federal rules prevent victims of abusive loans from suing firms that bought their loans from the banks that issued the original loan.
10. Fannie Mae and Freddie Mac expanded beyond their traditional scope of business and entered the sub-prime market, ultimately costing taxpayers hundreds of billions of dollars.
11. The abandonment of anti-trust and related regulatory principles enabled the creation of too-big-to-fail megabanks, which engaged in much riskier practices than smaller banks.
12. Beset by conflicts of interest, private credit rating companies incorrectly assessed the quality of mortgage-backed securities; a 2006 law handcuffed the SEC from properly regulating the firms.

Source: Weissman and Donahue (2009).

2009). Stewart contrasted the rosy and wildly mistaken comments of financial experts on business television networks with the real-world stories of financial collapse and suffering.

Ideas in favour of financial deregulation and the explosion of credit/debt enjoyed considerable support from a wide variety of sources. The financial services sector grew from being 15 per cent of US GDP in 1980 to over 20 per cent in 2004. Even more striking was the fact that the financial services industry exploded as a source of corporate profits, leaping from 20 per cent in 1990 to 45 per cent in 2004 (Phillips, 2008, p. 31). While corporate profits soared, so did individual fortunes. The average pay of chief executive officers (led by the financial sector) ballooned from being 24 times that of the average worker's salary in 1965 to 71 times in 1989 to 262 times the average worker's salary in 2005 (Mishel, 2006). Stock options, shares and bonuses ensured that executive pay at financial firms skyrocketed, even if corporate performance was poor. Beyond highly paid executives, many ordinary people also benefited from credit easing. In an environment where real wages did not grow, individuals were able to use debt to fund consumption. Many individuals ran up credit card debt to purchase consumer goods, took on large mortgages in response to easy terms and borrowed against the value of their homes. In only seven years (2000–7) US households doubled their debt to $13.8 trillion (McKinsey & Co., 2009).

Because of the widespread reach of the financial and housing bubbles, there was widespread support for financial deregulation from the elite to the mass level. This helps to explain how those who benefited from a particular policy were eager to advance it in the public realm. However, the financial collapse was also facilitated by the flawed use of mathematical and technical models.

Wall Street financial firms employ an army of professionals to guide and execute their market strategies. Many of these firms use PhDs in mathematics or economics from prestigious universities to create and implement mathematical strategies for seeking out the best investment returns. In a market that is presumed to be rational, the application of formal mathematical models will reveal the most efficient strategies. The mathematical models contributed to financial chaos because of two factors. The first factor was that the models focused on probabilities, but were unable to adapt to random or unforeseen developments (Taleb, 2004). The models assumed that the future would be similar to the present, when the future always holds surprises. When those surprises came along, the financial strategies based on the models proved disastrous. A second problem was that the models assumed that market actors would act rationally. This assumption often holds in normal or good economic times, but once things began to deteriorate market players were more likely to be motivated by fear and panic.

The revelation that the financial markets were not as rational, stable,

predictable and self-policing as previously thought has led to an interroga-
tion of the rational neolclassical model of economics. In response to the
widespread failure of these markets several economists have been attempting
to merge psychological variables into economic theory (Akerlofand Shiller,
2009; Lo, 2004). It is a step back towards a more constructivist view of political economy.

Conclusion

Underling the clash of ideas is a competition between different knowledge
structures and world views amongst many actors in the global political economy. This contest over world views has intensified with the drift to the post-
Washington Consensus. Rather than a single alternative to neoliberal views,
there is a wide array of opposing views and philosophies. The common
elements they share are a view that a neoliberal market should not be the
only mechanism and ultimate decision-maker in distributing resources or
adjudicating between values, and that the power of transnational corporations needs to be curbed or regulated.

There are a number of alternative knowledge systems circulating in the
global political economy. One set of understandings centres around indigenous knowledge. These belief systems have developed over many generations and posit a different understanding of human relationships with the
natural world. Rather than being masters of information or abstract models,
these systems draw upon experience with nature and the wisdom embodied
by elders or passed down through generations. As outlined in Chapter 12,
many environmental movements also embody an alternative form of knowledge. Similar to indigenous perspectives they see humans as being a part of
nature rather than masters of nature. Chapter 10 highlighted the contributions of feminist knowledge, which challenges the model of atomistic rational actors. Feminists often advance an ethic of care rather than the pursuit of
self-interest.

We can see these alternative forms of knowledge in action at the local level
and on the global scale. Globally the meetings of activists at the World Social
Forum show a diversity of approaches. The slogan of the World Social
Forum – 'Another World Is Possible' – offers a challenge to neoliberal ideas
which claim exclusive knowledge of the path to development. These alternative forms of knowledge and the social forces and institutions which support
them are engaged with dominant knowledge structures in a battle for
common sense that would reorient the ways the global political economy
functions. Ideas and knowledge play a central role in the evolution of the
global political economy. World views and common sense guide how people
react to developments and influence the actions they take. Although some

world views dominate, as the Washington Consensus did in the 1980s and 1990s, there are many alternative world views struggling to establish themselves. These world views can have significant distributional consequences because they tend to favour some social groups over others. Access to ideas in the form of knowledge and technology also has a significant role in the global political economy because it heavily influences economic growth and the life chances of people. As a result, the struggle over world views, technology and knowledge is a crucial aspect of the global political economy.

Chapter 14

Security

International political economy and international security have developed as distinct sub-fields of International Relations and Political Science and are both taught as separate subjects in many colleges and universities. Nevertheless, the intersection of political economy and security has long been recognized in studies of both sub-fields. Indeed, in one of the pioneering texts on IPE, the security structure is identified as a key structure of power in the international political economy (Strange, 1998). This chapter examines the global political economy of security and develops in a more explicit sense some of the security aspects of topics addressed elsewhere in the book. The security dimensions of some of these topics – for example, development (Ballentine and Sherman, 2003), environment (Dalby, 2002) and gender (Hudson, 2009) – have recently been explored in the literature.

This chapter provides an introduction to the political economy of security through an examination of changing views on security, different approaches to the search for security in world politics and the links between economic structures and processes and security dynamics. It begins with a discussion of competing definitions and conceptions of security. In the theoretical perspectives section we consider the various ways in which the main approaches to IPE theorize the relationship between economics and security, and we discuss key linkages between the economy and security concerns. Under the major developments section we consider changes in the global security structure since the end of the Second World War. The key issues considered in this chapter are: economic statecraft, transnational crime and pandemics and disease.

Definitions: three views of security

At its simplest, security refers to the protection from threats. However, the concept of security is contested and no consensus exists on the definition of security. The major point of contention is over the referent object of security – that is, what or who is being secured. Below we outline three approaches to security – the traditional state-centric approach; new security studies; and human security – which define much of contemporary research and thinking on security.

In the traditional approach to International Relations, the answer to the question 'Security for whom?' is not of much concern since the key object of study is the state and it is taken for granted that security refers to the security of the state. It is easy to see why the concept of security has usually been associated with the security of the state. Writing in response to the carnage of the First and Second world wars, as well as the threat of the Cold War, key International Relations thinkers have viewed the core of the field as being the issue of war and peace between states (Morgenthau, 1973). The international system is viewed as anarchic – it has no overarching authority, such as a government in domestic politics. Because of this anarchic condition states are placed in competition with each other and must pursue power to achieve security. Security, thus, has three central features. First, security and security studies is concerned with the preservation of the state from external (and internal threats) to its physical integrity and core values. Second, in an anarchical international system state security is an issue of primary concern for policy-makers and citizens. Indeed, it becomes the central priority since in the absence of an effective security policy a state is likely to lose its sovereignty. The third feature of this definition is an emphasis on military might as the key determinant of security. In other words, security is defined almost exclusively in military terms.

It could be assumed that this traditional understanding of security, as state-based and concerned with military conflict, provides a simple and unambiguous basis on which states could pursue national security. This, however, is not the case and, as Arnold Wolfers (1952) argued, 'national security' is an ambiguous and pliable concept and goal. National security involves pursuing a policy which will reduce threats to a nation or the values that the nation embodies. However, it is difficult to say which precise policies will increase security in any given situation. One problem which arises is the 'security dilemma' in which the attempts of State A to increase its security pose a security threat to State B. From the perspective of State A its increased security (military) resources are simply for defensive purposes and therefore do not pose a threat to other states in the international system. However, from the perspective of State B the increase in State A's security resources may appear as a threat. State B then takes steps to respond to the threat, but this increases the insecurity of State A, which responds by taking measures which increases State B's insecurity, etc. For example, the Soviet Union was threatened by the US monopoly of nuclear weapons after the Second World War. The securing of nuclear weapons by the USSR initially made it feel more secure, but this increased US insecurity. The United States took steps to once again increase its security, causing the USSR to do the same and have the same impact on the United States. This led to an insecurity spiral and an arms race. Another difficulty with pursuing national security is that it can use up resources which might leave the nation more insecure. For example, a large military build-up might leave the nation economically vulnerable.

At the end of the Cold War this traditional concept of security was challenged by different perspectives which we will term 'new security studies'. Although they have different assumptions and methods they were all developed as an explicit critique of the traditional definition and were concerned with proffering a new approach to analysis and policy. The first attack on the traditional concept emerged from writers who urged an expanded definition of security (Buzan, 1991). These writers accepted some key assumptions of the traditional approach but also provided a less exclusive conception of security, with a focus on social issues (Buzan, Waever and de Wilde, 1997). The assumptions concerning the state as the referent object of security and the importance of anarchy in creating insecurity were maintained, but they were modified in important ways. First, it was recognized that, although the state is the primary referent object, the pursuit of national security does not always result in protecting individuals from threat. Second, it was acknowledged that the effect of international anarchy on security was not simple and straightforward. That is, the condition of anarchy is mediated by systemic changes leading to different types of anarchy with different implications for the pursuit of national security. The third innovation of new security studies was a shift in perception of the nature and type of threat. Instead of defining security in military terms it was now seen in relation to five sectors: military; economics; the environment; societal; and political. Thus, for example, while military security is concerned with violence between states, environmental security is concerned with threats arising from environmental issues such as conflict over resources or climate change.

The challenge provided by the conditions at the end of the Cold War served to undermine the settled consensus and led to a more radical approach. In their challenge to the traditional approach, proponents of critical security studies go further than those who seek to expand the concept of security. At the core of critical security approaches is a focus on the emancipation of the individual (Krause and Williams, 1997; Wyn Jones, 1999). Thus, critical security approaches replace the state as the referent object with the individual. They also reject the assumption of international anarchy as a pre-given feature of the international system. Finally, in promoting an alternative conception of security this approach recognizes that threats to individual freedom come from a number of sources. Indeed, in a move which is directly counter to that of traditional theorists, critical security writers often posit the state as the key source of threat to individual security.

The concept of human security represents another approach which seeks to shift the focus away from the state-centric concerns of traditional security discourse. The term 'human security' was developed to capture a concern with the large number of threats to human life that existed beyond death caused by inter-state warfare. There were two elements to this approach. First, the end of the Cold War had reduced the threat of large-scale inter-state

Box 14.1　Food security

Although there are many definitions of food security, the FAO's definition, which states that 'Food security exists when all people, at all times,
have physical and economic access to sufficient, safe and nutritious
food to meet their dietary needs and food preferences for an active and
healthy life' (FAO, 2002), is widely accepted.

The issue of food security came to prominence in 2008 when, as a
result of rising food prices, demonstrators took to the streets in over 40
countries to protest high prices and food shortages. Following the
collapse of Lehmann Brothers in September 2008 the attention of the
world shifted from the potential threat posed by the world food crisis to
the ramifications of the global financial crisis. However, although
world food prices declined in 2009 they nevertheless constitute a severe
strain for many consumers in developing countries. The combination of
the global financial crisis and the world food crisis has contributed to
increasing poverty levels in the developing world. A recent report
published by the Economic and Social Commission for Asia and the
Pacific (ESCAP) states that the financial crisis has become a food crisis
for 583 million people in the Asia-Pacific region (UNESCAP, 2009).

The human security implications of food insecurity are devastating.
Food insecurity increases world hunger, resulting in a higher incidence
of malnutrition, reduced spending on education and healthcare and
deepening poverty. The impact of food insecurity is felt most by the
poor, especially the landless and female-headed household. The most
recent estimates from FAO calculate the number of hungry people at
923 million (FAO, 2009).

conflicts, but the incidence of intra-state conflict had become more prominent. Death from physical violence was more likely to be caused by civil wars
or ethnic disputes within or across state boundaries than a formal war
between states. Second, the easing of superpower tensions helped people
recognize that death by starvation and disease was killing far more people
than warfare. Issues such as the provision of food were increasingly seen as
a security problem (see Box 14.1). Human security proponents thus seek to
expand the agenda in order to bring the perspective of the individual and
communities into focus and to address a range of threats to international
security beyond those posed by other states.

The concept of human security was first introduced in the *Human
Development Report, 1994* published by the United Nations Development
Programme (UNDP, 1994). This report set the tone for succeeding

approaches to human security by focusing on a wide definition that takes a preventive, 'people-centred' approach. The UNDP definition focuses both on 'freedom from fear and freedom from want', thus covering safety from threats of hunger, disease and repression as well as protection from sudden and hurtful disruptions in the patterns of daily life. The report lists seven different elements of human security: economic security, food security, health security, environmental security, personal security, community security and political security (UNDP, 1994, pp. 24–5). Human security conceived in these terms as the prerogative of the individual effectively links security to human rights and human dignity.

Although the concept of human security has received considerable attention from scholars and policy-makers there is no consensus on a precise definition. Since its inception the concept of human security has been defined and reinterpreted in numerous ways. While some groups have accepted the broad view of human security taken by the UNDP, others prefer a more narrow definition. A broad definition is provided by Mary Kaldor (2007, p. 182), who defines human security as 'the security of individuals and communities rather than states and it combines human rights and human development'. In a similar vein, the Commission on Human Security defines human security as the 'vital core of all human lives' without any specification regarding the content and context of this phrase on the grounds that 'different societies would interpret its meaning differently' (2003, p. 7).

On the other hand, the Human Security Centre's annual *Human Security Report* (2005, p. viii) takes the view that the concept should be confined to examining violent threats to individuals. In this approach attention is paid to civil wars, terrorism, false imprisonment, torture by state officials (police, intelligence services), but not issues such as famine or development. Another limited definition is provided by Axworthy (2001), a former Canadian foreign minister and key architect of a distinctly Canadian approach to human security. The focus in this approach is less on the threats associated with underdevelopment and more on the insecurity resulting from violent conflict while recognizing that such conflicts are not confined to inter-state conflict. Human security is thus defined in terms of freedom from fear.

Theoretical perspectives: integrating security and political economy

Readers will recall from Chapter 1 that the three traditional IPE perspectives had very different views of conflict and cooperation. These views have had consequences for how people have studied and thought about the relationship between security and political economy. The dominant approach to economics – liberalism – has stipulated that the economic and political worlds are separate arenas dominated by different methods of behaviour. The economic world operates according to a set of economic laws, while the political world deviates from these laws. In the economic world rational actors pursuing efficiency are rewarded, while the political world is marked by more emotional and irrational behaviour and rewards. As a result, economic liberals and liberals in IPE have tended to downplay or ignore the link between political economy and security. The one exception is that liberals have often argued that free trade and democratic politics are likely to increase peace between states. In contrast, power politics and critical approaches have tended to acknowledge the mutual influence of economics and security, but in different ways. Power politics approaches have viewed economic interests as subservient to security interests, while many critical approaches have viewed security issues as being heavily influenced if not dictated by economic interests.

Leading figures from the three traditional international political economy perspectives have all written on aspects of the relationship between security and political economy (Earle, 1986). Economic nationalists such as Alexander Hamilton and Fredrick List argued that financial and industrial strength were prerequisites for military strength. In their view it was the responsibility of the state to take action to protect national economic interests. Thus, Hamilton is often remembered for arguing that the United States must protect its manufacturing base to bolster national power. List alleged that free trade was only in the interest of the strongest economic powers.

Early liberal thought contained several approaches to the relationship between economics and security. Adam Smith usually criticized the overly protectionist policies of mercantilists, yet he acknowledged that there were circumstances where the interests of the state should trump commercial interests (Earle, 1986). For example, writing in the 1700s Smith supported the British Navigation Acts, which stipulated that trade to Britain or its colonies must be carried in British ships. The purpose of this act was to ensure a strong merchant marine and Royal Navy, as well as protecting British economic interests. These acts were eventually repealed in the mid-1800s. While Smith supported a professional army and military defence of British interests overseas, some later free traders such as Richard Cobden adopted a more pacifist stance and campaigned against foreign interventions (such as the Crimean War).

A series of Marxist theorists and practitioners saw an intimate relationship between organized violence and political economy. To Marx and Engels wars were both a ruse that ruling classes used to divert attention from domestic problems and an opportunity for workers to overthrow the ruling class should the war go badly (Neumann and von Hagen, 1986). States might engage in imperialism because of domestic economic needs and desires, but foreign adventures had the potential to weaken the security apparatus of the state and provide an opening for oppositional forces. Indeed, Vladimir Lenin capitalized on Russia's disastrous performance in the First World War to launch and prosecute the Russian Revolution. In the 20th century Marxists played a key role in launching revolutionary and nationalist wars in China, Vietnam, Africa and Cuba. Political power was seized and new economic systems were put in place following military defeat of their class opponents.

Scholarly interest in the relationship between economic activity and security has varied over time in response to the external environment. One issue of current concern to policy-makers and scholars relates to defence procurement (see Box 14.2).

The shifting balance between security concerns and economics can be illustrated through the history of the United States. Mastandumo (1998) argues that during those times when there has been no great external threat US economic and foreign policy have been pursued on different tracks. However, during times of high threat, foreign and economic policies were integrated with one serving the interests of the other. At some points during the Cold War US economic policy was used to further foreign policy goals, while at other times foreign policy was used to advance economic goals. For example, when the United States was concerned about Soviet expansionism there was a tendency to support Japan and Europe through the Marshall Plan and open US markets to the exports of their allies. In the 1970s and 1980s foreign economic policy became more prominent as international monetary and trade issues were viewed as increasingly significant. Former allies were increasingly pressured to change their economic policies as security ties were seen as being less significant.

One of the cornerstones of much realist analysis of international relations has been a belief that issues of high politics are more important than issues of low politics (Keohane and Nye, 1977, p. 23). High politics is seen as those issues that relate to the military security of the state and low politics refers to other international issues (e.g., economic, environmental). However, even from a realist perspective there is considerable justification for examining the relationship between security and political economy (Ripsman, 2005). As noted above, traditional mercantilist thought stressed that economic power is a prerequisite for military power. A state's military power is dependent on the economic resources at its disposal. Over time, the key economic resources relevant for the production of military forces and support for war-making efforts have changed but the connection between a strong domestic economy and national security has remained a key assumption of foreign and security policy. A state's economic strength can be defined in terms of 'the productive resources that its society possesses; labour, technology, natural resources, real capital (in the form of factories, power dams, railroads, inventories of materials and manufactures, and so on); and claims on

Box 14.2   Defence procurement

Defence procurement is an area where political economy and national security clearly overlap. It can be defined as the processes by which national governments procure military equipment and services. Defence procurement varies from state to state depending upon the state of civil–military relations, the level of industrialization and technological development, global and regional tension, levels of threat perception and the general organization of military forces.

Defence procurement is more than an exercise in commercial policy because the state plays a key role in the development of the defence sector and the complicated links between that sector and the rest of the economy. Distinctive elements of procuring military goods and services include: (a) the role of the government as the key buyer and regulator; (b) the high cost of arms; (c) the importance of research and development; (d) the inflationary spiral of weapons production; (e) uncertainties related to the production process and the changing nature of external threat; (f) information asymmetries between the buyer and the supplier; and (g) an oligopolistic market structure (De Fraja and Hartley, 1996; Rogerson, 1993).

Governance issues play a major role in the defence procurement industry since secrecy and lack of transparency, often justified on security grounds, can lead to corruption and waste. In March 2009, US President Obama estimated that changes in Defense Department procurement policies could save the country over $40 billion (Gilmore, 2009). The high cost of weapons also makes defence procurement a political issue. For example, given that the United Kingdom suffered an intense economic slowdown between 2008 and 2010, does it make sense to spend billions of pounds on nuclear-armed submarines? The industrial-economic interests mixed with the political-diplomatic issues involved in purchasing weapons makes defence procurement an especially contentious issue. Moreover, the relationship between defence procurement, military spending and economic growth is a subject of heated debate. In the context of developing countries some analysts argue that governments should pursue strategies of military modernization and self-reliance in defence procurement. Other analysts contend that the development of weapons systems is economically wasteful (Balakrishnan, 2008; Singh, 2005).

the output of other societies inherent in reserves of international liquidity (gold, foreign currencies) and foreign investments' (Knorr, 1975, p. 46).

The contribution of economic resources to military potential will, of course, depend on the ways in which they are mobilized and the alternative uses of national economic product. The linkages between economic resources and national military power gives rise to a number of dilemmas and policy problems. For example, to what extent should a state seek to organize production along nationalist lines or should it be open to foreign trade and investment? A nationalist policy may ensure the construction of domestic industries geared to national defence and ensure self-sufficiency in strategic goods. But such an economic nationalist policy may also be undertaken at a cost to efficiency and lead to a reduction in aggregate economic wealth. Such dilemmas form the centre of debates between neomercantilists and liberal theorists.

Just as some modern-day realists have examined the link between political economy and security, some liberals have suggested that peace is intimately connected to following liberal policies. Proponents of commercial liberalism who focus on the influence of the market on domestic and transnational actors contend that economic exchange reduces the likelihood of war among states (Moravscik, 1997). From a liberal perspective humans are rational, risk-averse actors who make decisions on the basis of personal gain and loss. On the basis of these assumptions trade and investment across national borders provide positive benefits to states and thus the resort to war is likely to diminish economic and social welfare. In such circumstances rational states will focus on the gains from economic intercourse rather than the costs of war. The contention that liberal economic policies and a liberal international order are positively related with peace has been a long been mainstay of liberal political theory (Howard, 2008). In the 1970s these arguments were given added relevance with the development of interdependence theory (Keohane and Nye, 1977). Interdependence theory argued that under conditions of complex interdependence there was an absence of issue hierarchy. Foreign policy was not simply reducible to a concern with national security; military force had limited utility and is ineffective in controlling outcomes; and that when economic interdependence between states is high it contributes to a search for peaceful solutions to conflicts and reduces the resort to violence.

There is an enormous body of theoretical and statistical literature which seeks to examine the commercial liberal proposition that peace is a product of economic interdependence. The results of these studies are mixed. On one hand, some studies provide statistical evidence in support of the claim (O'Neal, O'Neal and Maoz, 1996; O'Neal and Russett, 1997), while, on the other hand, other studies find no conclusive supportive evidence (Barbieri, 1996; Ripsman and Blanchard 1996/7). This literature suffers from a number of ambiguities, with the most import being the failure to agree on definition of economic interdependence.

A related liberal theory links the domestic political system with the possibility of international conflict. Going back to the thinking of Immanuel Kant in the 18th century, liberals argue that a peaceful international system requires the presence of a large number of democratic states. The extensive democratic peace literature debates the connection between democracy and peace. Proponents of the link argue that democratic states do not engage in warfare with each other while opponents dispute the data upon which these claims have been made. Proponents of the democratic peace thesis argue that democratic states tend to resolve conflict over the bargaining table because of the constraints built into democratic political structures and the cultural values of peaceful resolution typical of democratic decision-making structures. However, they also insist that democracies are not constrained from waging war against authoritarian and totalitarian states (Russett, 1993). Critics contend that there is no conclusive evidence to prove that democratic states are peaceful in their relations with each other because they are democratic. Indeed, it may be the case that peaceful conditions produce democratic states rather then the reverse as the democratic peace thesis holds. It has also been suggested that the mathematical probability that democratic states would fight each other is small because historically there have been few democracies (Brown, Lynn-Jones and Miller, 1996). It has also been argued that countries in the transition to democracy become more violent and war-prone (Mansfield and Snyder, 1996)

Critical approaches to international relations have argued both that capitalism can promote violence and that the existing structure of capitalism inflicts continuous violence upon some groups of people. The notion of 'structural violence' is that the operation of the system itself causes people to be injured or killed (Galtung, 1969). For example, the world has enough food for everyone, but the system of distribution and payment is flawed so that millions of people regularly die from lack of nourishment. No individual or groups is specifically targeted nor is it intended that people die from starvation. Nevertheless, we have organized food production and distribution in such a way that people die on a regular basis from starvation. This violence is structural and inherent in the system as it is presently organized.

Major developments

There have been dramatic changes in the global security structure since the end of the Second World War. We define a security structure as the overarching framework of material, institutional and ideational resources in response to perceptions of threat. A security structure thus comprises material and normative elements. In this section we will discuss two major changes in the global security structure. The first change was the creation after 1945 of a security structure dominated by a bipolar international system. This system featured the rise of the national security state and the military industrial complex. The collapse of bipolarity and the ending of the Cold War triggered a new security structure. This post-Cold War security structure was less state-centric and has seen the rise of new security challenges.

The Cold War security structure

During the Cold War (1948–89) the meaning of security in international relations literature almost exclusively referred to the military preservation of the nation-state. Threats to national security were seen as emanating from external sources. Fundamental threats to territorial integrity or value systems were held to emanate from either a real conflict of interests or from ideological motivations or from both. Given the dominant status of the United States and the Soviet Union, the interests of these two superpowers were inevitably on a collision course according to experts who emphasize the Cold War as a clash of interest. The bipolar distribution of power inevitably led to a struggle for power. On the other hand, it is possible to conceive of the rivalry as the outcome of an ideological conflict between capitalism on one hand and communism on the other. Whether the origins of the Cold War are rooted in a struggle for power, an ideological dispute or even the result of misperceptions, from the perspective of international political economy the key issues relate to the ways in which this global conflict shaped political and economic systems and patterns of international economic intercourse.

Two issues are of particular importance in this respect. First, the central goal of states was conceived as self-preservation and the discourse of security placed emphasis on military weapons as the primary requirement for defence and security. As a result there was increased military spending on both sides of the divide, and an arms race. In this scenario nuclear weapons became (and remain) the most important tool within a state's military arsenal. The existence of nuclear weapons gave rise to policies of deterrence (to avoid the use of these deadly weapons); non-proliferation (to halt the spread of this destructive tool); and the security dilemma. The cost of military armaments and the impact of defence spending on national economies was a contributory factor to the search for arms agreements.

The second issue related to the impact of the bipolar security structure on international economic relations. One result of the Cold War was the creation of effectively two separate systems of international trade and payments. The bipolar security structure with opposing alliance systems gave rise to a Western system of free-market economies on one hand, and a system of centrally planned economies on the other. These two systems devised separate international organizations to regulate economic inter-course. For example, the World Bank and the International Monetary Fund, among other institutions, played central roles in coordinating Western policy, while the Council of Mutual Economic Assistance (COMECON) was created to manage relations among centrally planned economies in the Soviet orbit. Another consequence of the Cold War security structure was the economic competition between the United States and its allies and the Soviet Union in the developing world. The rivals were in competition not only over access to resources and markets but also over economic systems, as each tried to win converts to its economic ideology. In this sense it was believed that national security was enhanced by 'capturing' states to the economic system preferred by the United States or the Soviet Union.

The close relationship between the pursuit of security and the national economy during the Cold War can be seen in the rise of the military-industrial complex. In his final speech to the nation in 1961, US President Dwight D. Eisenhower (1961) warned his citizens that 'In the councils of government, we must guard against the acquisition of unwarranted influ-ence, whether sought or unsought, by the military industrial complex.' He was referring to the political influence exercised by the existence of a large military establishment and a massive arms industry. The outgoing President feared the that combined power of a military desiring new and more weapons systems and an arms industry eager to sell those weapons would influence public policy in a direction that would be against the national inter-est and personal liberty. In many ways this was a shocking statement. Eisenhower was not a left-wing radical. He was a war hero who had commanded the D-Day invasion of Normandy and was the first commander of NATO forces in Europe. And yet, this person, who was schooled in the military and rose to be President, highlighted the dangers of an expansionist military and arms industry to American democracy.

The origins of the military-industrial complex lie in the changing nature of warfare. Over a number of centuries warfare transformed from an activ-ity waged by a small number of people (knights, mercenaries or small profes-sional armies) to one fought by nations and societies as a whole (Howard, 2009). The French Revolution mobilized a whole society that eventually served as the basis for Napoleon's conquest of Europe. The US Civil War was an early indication of the destruction to come from new weapons and the use of industrial strength and might to destroy an opponent. The First World War confirmed the trend of whole nations being mobilized for combat, while victory in the Second World War required the harnessing of large industries to produce tanks and ships in the United States and USSR, as well as the creation of new super-weapons such as radar and nuclear bombs. Cold War security for the USSR and United States rested upon large mili-taries based in numerous countries and the deployment of advanced military technology. Military technologies ranged from the latest innovation in fighter aircraft to nuclear-powered and -armed submarines to intercontinental ballistic missiles. The large corporations that supplied these technologies and the militaries that used them formed a relationship of mutual dependence as both sought to influence the procurement policies of their political leaders.

The post-Cold War security structure

The most significant change in the security structure since the end of the Second World War has been the end of the Cold War. It is not too dramatic to note that the world fundamentally changed with the collapse of the Berlin Wall and the demise of the Soviet Union. This change brought with it not only a rethinking of security relations but also changes in the dominant security discourse. The focus on the national security state was now challenged by considerations of a broader nature (discussed under new security, above). The end of the Cold War heralded an end to bipolarity and ushered in a unipolar world order with the United States as the sole superpower. Some analysts thought that the end of bipolarity signalled the opportunity to pursue a peace dividend. The peace dividend could arise by diverting finance that had previously been spent on armaments to peaceful purposes, and also by seizing the opportunity for international cooperation with the cessation of superpower rivalry.

In this new world order the hope of many experts that an era of multilateral cooperation for security purposes would develop initially appeared to be well founded. In 1992 Boutros-Ghali, the UN Secretary-General, proclaimed the Agenda for Peace. The Agenda for Peace committed the UN to identification of conflict at an early stage; peace-making efforts to bring parties to an agreement; peacekeeping and peace-building. However, the conditions required to sustain the new multilateralism proved elusive. The imperatives of national security remained of vital importance to most states and the economic and political resources necessary to underwrite the new order were not forthcoming. As the financial and human costs of the new interventionism became evident leading states were less inclined to support such policies. The casualties suffered by US forces in Somalia in 1993 proved an important turning point and paved the way for inaction in Rwanda, with its tragic consequences.

Another departure from Cold War politics was a growing willingness to address rather than ignore fundamental problems within the borders of war-torn states. This developed concurrently with a new focus on the security of the individual and on human rights. Recognition that the most direct threats to individuals frequently arise from their own governments ushered in the theory and practice of humanitarian intervention (Wheeler, 2000).

Commitment to non-intervention in the affairs of states sacrosanct in the previous four decades made way for a more subtle interpretation according to which, on occasions, the rights of individuals takes precedence over the rights of repressive governments and the sovereign states that they represent. Humanitarian intervention proved controversial in theory and practice and is no longer the dominant framing of attempts to protect individuals. The doctrine of the Responsibility to Protect (R2P) has effectively replaced humanitarian intervention as the appropriate policy response to situations of internal strife and human suffering. The R2P norm was brought to prominence in the report of the International Commission on Intervention and State Sovereignty (ICISS, 2001), and endorsed by world leaders at the United Nations World Summit in 2005 (UN, 2005).

External intervention in domestic conflict is a feature of the post-Cold War security structure because in this era wars within countries have exacted a heavy toll on humanity. Since 1945 three-quarters of all armed conflicts have been within countries and as many people have died in internal conflicts between 1980 and 2002 as in the First World War (Kahl, 2005, p. 77). These conflicts are supported by a particular global political economy which nurtures such chaos and makes them difficult to resolve. Mary Kaldor (1999) has labelled the wave of conflicts following the Cold War as 'New Wars'. These wars take place in states with weak or non-existent central authority. They are sometimes referred to as 'failed states'. The state is unable to retain its monopoly of violence, which leads to a proliferation of armed groups including renegade army units, paramilitaries, local self-defence units, mercenaries and foreign troops. The state is unable to raise sufficient revenues for taxation nor support the national economy. As a result a great deal of economic activity grinds to a halt or becomes dominated by criminal gangs and mafias. Local strongmen use fear, insecurity and hatred of other populations to maintain power and engage in a population displacement policy through murder, ethnic cleansing or making particular regions uninhabitable.

Since new wars cause such damage to existing state structures and economic activity, local military forces finance their activities by extracting resources from the local population and tapping external sources of finance. The population as a whole must also turn increasingly to external actors for survival. Local warlords use a variety of tactics to raise funds from the local populations. They can force locals to sell possessions at cut-rate prices, collect protection money from terrified inhabitants, tax the movement of goods, loot local resources, hold prominent individuals hostage, control criminal activity. Hard-pressed civilians may be forced to rely on humanitarian assistance from international organizations in the form of refugee camps, emergency shelter, food aid or development assistance in order to survive. Another source of external support comes in the form of remittances sent by family members working in more prosperous states.

External financial resources for local warlords come from a variety of sources. If these groups happen to control a valuable local resource they can sell those products on the international market. Examples include cocaine from Columbia, heroin from Afghanistan, diamonds from Sierra Leone and cassiterite (tin) from the Congo. In some cases large multinationals are crucial in facilitating the movement of these products to the global marketplace. Similar to civilian use of remittances, local ethnic militias can tap their diaspora communities for funds to purchase arms and supplies. Local warlords can also draw upon the services of foreign governments. In some cases this may involve explicit support from neighbouring states, such as Serbian and Croatian support for groups in Bosnia or Rwandan support for opposition groups in the Congo. In other cases local warlords will divert international humanitarian aid by taxing convoys or charging exorbitant customs duties to allow access to local populations.

The issue of groups financing themselves through the sale of precious natural resources raises the broader issue of the relationship between competition for scarce resources and organized violence. Conflict analysts have noted a relationship between civil wars and two resource conditions (Kahl, 2005). The first condition is characterized by growing populations, environmental degradation and increased competition for renewable resources. In this scenario ever-increasing numbers of people are caught in a downward spiral of destroying their local environment to meet survival needs, which increases political conflict and undermines long-term stability. A second condition occurs not when there is a shortage of natural resources, but when groups control highly valued resources such as diamonds, oil or minerals. In these cases there is an incentive for other groups to engage in violence to control these resources. In addition, groups which control precious resources are likely to overinvest in their development and neglect other aspects of economic and political development. In the longer run this leaves the economy and polity vulnerable to economic shocks.

A political economy approach to new wars suggests that while historical and identity issues are significant aspects of these engagements, the fuel sustaining them is to be found in the economic and political structures combatants have created (Griffiths, 1999). Nationalist and ethnic sentiments can be used to mobilize people, but localized acts of ethnic cleansing are often aimed at seizing the land and property of those being ejected. Local elites organize the confiscation of their former neighbours' property and create a new economic structure which serves their interests. Since the local economy collapses as a result of violent conflict, the general civilian population is often impoverished while criminal gangs control the import of products to satisfy local needs. The alleged solidarity within ethnic communities gives way to a reign of intimidation and corruption. Once the violence has begun local warlords actively scuttle peace accords and block reconciliation because a return to legitimate state structures threatens their economic profiteering. Resolving the conflict requires attention to the newly established criminal economic interests.

Perhaps the most visible feature of the post-Cold War security structure is the threat of global terrorism. International terrorism is, of course, not new but the events of September 11 2001, when al-Qaeda terrorists highjacked several US planes and used them as weapons against the World Trade Center in New York and the Pentagon in Washington DC, ushered in a heightened sense of insecurity and altered the security landscape in the advanced industrialized world. The terrorist atrocities of September 11 led to a shift in the determinants of international security. It raised three key issues.

First, it raised the issue of the extent to which the source of military threat had shifted from state actors to non-state actors. Suddenly a key threat was seen to emanate from non-state actors rather than states. The attacks of September 11 demonstrated that a relatively small non-state actor was capable of inflicting significant physical and emotional damage on even the strongest states. Non-state actors pose a particular problem for state strategists. They do not respond to conventional notions of deterrence because states have difficulty targeting small groups. Moreover, non-state actors make defence difficult because they use unconventional strategies, such as using civilian airliners as flying bombs. Questions were raised about whether the modern infrastructure of advanced economies was uniquely vulnerable to new forms of warfare. Could a cyber attack knock out a country's communications systems and seriously damage a nations' economy? Might whole systems be thrown into panic by the effective targeting of power plants? Was it possible that a small nuclear suitcase bomb could be detonated in a large urban centre? Furthermore, conventional military retaliation has proved unsuccessful in a campaign against terrorists who do not accept international legal principles. As Cronin argues, the threat of terrorism is a two-tiered challenge in which solutions are required that 'deal with the religious fanatics and the far more politically motivated states, entities, and peoples who would support them because they feel powerless and left behind in a globalized world' (2002/3, p. 38). At best a military response can be successful in the short term but is unlikely to be so in the longer term, where underlying problems related to poverty, poor governance and marginalization have to be solved in order to detach the terrorists from their support base. In short, only a human security approach can remove the enabling environment in which terrorists thrive. However, it can also be noted that because these actors do not control a state, it is very difficult for them to sustain a long-term extensive campaign against opposing states (Goldman and Blanken, 2005). They may be able to temporarily disrupt a state or an economy with an attack, but those states and economies are durable and able to absorb occasional shocks. The attacks do not threaten the viability of their opponents.

Second, global terrorism has heightened personal insecurity and increased psychological vulnerability. In one sense the fear that terrorists can strike anywhere and at any time has led to increased levels of security in many aspects of everyday life. International air travel has changed irrevocably. The bombs which brought down Air India Flight 182 over the Irish Sea in June 1985 and Pan Am Flight 103 in December 1988 over Lockerbie in Scotland did not lead to the type of surveillance and restrictions on cabin baggage which have followed in the wake of the September 11 attacks and the attempt by Richard Reid to detonate a shoe bomb on American Airlines Flight 63 in December 2001. A series of bombings such as the October 2002 Bali nightclub explosion; the March 2004 Madrid train bombings; and the coordinated attacks on London underground trains and buses in July 2005 intensified the (Western) sense of insecurity. Key features of this contemporary terrorism are the transnational terrorist networks, the failure of the terrorists to issue authorities with a warning, the resort to the use of suicide bombers and the random civilian targets chosen, raising fundamental questions concerning the ability of the state to protect its citizens.

Third, the onset of global terrorism has changed the political and security landscape of inter-state relations. Following the events of September 11, combating terrorism became a key American security goal. President Bush famously declared a war on terror and reshaped American strategic priorities. The pursuit of international terrorists and states harbouring terrorists became a key priority. Other states also swiftly declared terrorism as a key security threat and anti-terrorism legislation was enacted in many states to counter this new danger. Many states recognized a common enemy and developed joint counter-terrorism strategies. As the international political landscape was transformed, discussion turned to the so-called clash of civilizations and inherent conflict between militant Islam and Western values. Global terrorism has also changed military priorities and the deployment of resources. Following the September 11 attacks, the United States and its allies launched military action against the perpetrators of the attacks and states that were deemed to be harbouring and supporting terrorists. Actions against the Taliban in Afghanistan succeeded in ousting the Taliban from power, but coalition forces have failed to create a secure environment in that country. As the war has progressed the support of Western publics has begun to wane.

Key issues

Traditional threats to security such as terrorism and nuclear war remain important in contemporary global politics. For many people, instruments of violence threaten their physical security on a daily basis. In this section we examine three issues relevant to the political economy of security. Economic statecraft links economic security and foreign policy and thus raises fundamental questions concerning economic instruments of state policy. Both transnational crime and pandemics and disease are threats that can be viewed through conventional and human security perspectives and thus demonstrate the complex relationship between economics and security.

Economic statecraft and security

Economic statecraft can be defined as the use of economic resources to exert political influence. Two issues have been most prominent in recent studies of economic statecraft: economic aid and economic sanctions. Economic aid is generally seen in terms of 'carrots' (i.e., inducements, although nations may, at times, withdraw aid and thus use it as a 'stick') and economic sanctions in terms of 'sticks' or coercion. Both aid and sanctions have become controversial features of diplomatic practice.

Foreign aid can be categorized in a number of different ways. For example, a donor may classify the provision of aid in terms of bilateral development aid, economic assistance supporting political and security goals, humanitarian aid, multilateral economic assistance and military aid. In this section we will be specifically concerned with bilateral development aid and economic assistance supporting political and security goals. We will not be explicitly concerned with the economic effectiveness of bilateral aid, humanitarian aid, multilateral aid or military aid. Our focus is on the use of economic aid as an instrument of statecraft (i.e., with bilateral development assistance which nominally has the objective of promoting economic growth) and aid specifically targeted to meet political and security goals. Of course, various donor motives are not completely separate. The objectives of promoting economic growth and poverty reduction, mitigating conflict and expanding democratic governance are perfectly compatible. For example, aid which results in improved economic growth can create the conditions for political stability and thus fulfil a political objective. Analysis of the allocation of aid shows conclusively the importance of political concerns in donors' motives (Maizels and Nisanke, 1984). For some analysts key political goals are related to the preservation of order, stability and peace in the international system (Brandt Commission, 1983), while for others the main motive is more closely related to the national interests of donor states.

Changes in aid policy are the result of changing circumstances, changing norms governing the recipient–donor relationship and international development policy and changing views about the efficacy of aid. Aid as an instrument of statecraft is viewed by donors within the overall context of their foreign relations with recipient countries, other potentially affected countries and competitor nations. During the era of the Cold War, aid was an important instrument of foreign policy. Both the United States and its allies and the Soviet Union and its allies used economic aid as an instrument in the Cold War struggle, with Western countries' aid programmes targeted to supporting anti-communist regimes and aid from the communist bloc focused on supporting anti-Western sentiment in the Third World. Economic aid was deployed in the ideological conflict between the rival economic and political systems and to win votes in international organizations such as the United Nations. For the ex-colonial powers determined to maintain post-colonial spheres of influence, financial influence and, especially in the case of France, to promote its national culture, aid was geographically concentrated in their ex-colonies. For example, French foreign aid went almost exclusively to ex-French colonies and British aid was concentrated on its ex-colonies.

In the post-Cold War environment democracy promotion has emerged as a key goal of democratic states and foreign aid as a suitable instrument with which to pursue this objective. Sizable funds have been specifically allocated to democracy promotion by aid agencies. For example, USAID budgeted $1,051 million in 2004 for democracy and governance/conflict (Tarnoff and Nowells, 2004). The political economy of aid and democracy has focused on the usefulness of this tool of economic statecraft. The evidence suggests that the results have been disappointing (Brown, 2005; Crawford, 2005). One reason for the failure of economic aid to promote democracy rests with the internal obstacles in the recipient states. It has been argued that the absence of a receptive political culture, chronic poverty and non-existent institutions inhibit the efforts of donors to promote democracy in Africa (Brown, 2005, pp.183–4). Donor shortcomings are another reason for the failure of democracy promotion (Brown, 2005, pp. 185–9). A study of the European Union and democracy promotion in Ghana has failed because the EU states approach democracy promotion in a narrow manner and are more concerned with fostering their self-interests than developing the norms and principles of democratic governance (Crawford, 2005). In a different but related manner, Cohen and Küpçü (2009) contend that American democracy promotion efforts have been hampered by a failure to adequately distinguish democracy from other strategic objectives such as development, humanitarian and public health assistance. A third reason rests with the tool of political conditionality itself (Brown, 2005, pp. 184–5). Political conditionality can be limited by constraints on both the donor and recipient sides. Donors may have unclear objectives, and are limited by the sovereignty of the recipient states from imposing their goals. On the recipient side political conditionality is limited by the ability of local elites to evade demands for change, compliance by authoritarian rulers that appear on the surface to meet the demands for change while maintaining existing practices, and the capacity to shrug off demands for change if access to alternative sources of finance are available.

Economic sanctions, which were at one time a relatively non-contentious tool of foreign policy, have recently become a controversial issue in global politics. The political economy of economic sanctions has focused on the utility of sanctions as an instrument of foreign policy and the impact of sanctions on the target population. On both issues there are diverse opinions and competing research findings. On such a controversial issue it is not surprising to note that there is no agreed definition of economic sanctions. Some scholars concerned with the usefulness of sanctions as an instrument of statecraft tend to support definitions which make reference to the purpose of sanctions. From this perspective Margaret Doxey defined sanctions as 'penalties threatened or imposed as a declared consequence of the target's failure to observe international standards or international obligations' (1996, p. 9). Other writers have tried to develop definitions which omit reference to the intent of the sanctions. Thus, Hufbauer *et al.* (2007, p. 3) define economic sanctions simply as 'the deliberate, government-inspired withdrawal or threat of withdrawal of customary trade or financial relations'.

Although economic sanctions have been dated to 432 BC (Dadkhah, 2006, p. 1386; Hufbauer *et al.*, 2007, p. 9), they became prominent in the 20th century with the creation of the League of Nations. The Covenant of the League of Nations (and the UN Charter) allocates to collective economic sanctions an important role in the preservation of international peace and security. After the end of the Cold War states have increasingly turned to the use of economic sanctions. Between 1914 and 1989 there were 121 cases of economic sanctions but between 1990 and 2000 there were 53 cases (Hufbauer *et al.*, 2007, pp. 20–32). Sanctions have been utilized in relation to major contemporary issues such as ethnic cleansing, human rights abuses, nuclear proliferation and terrorism.

One of the main reasons why the evidence on the utility of sanctions is so inconclusive is because the motivations of the sender countries are not always clear. Governments impose sanctions for a variety of reasons. Some of these reasons are instrumental, that is, the sender seeks to impose costs on the target state such that the target will alter its behaviour and comply with the demands of the sender. However, sender states also impose sanctions for expressive or symbolic reasons. Sanctions imposed for expressive purposes serve to send a signal of disapproval to the target state but do not envisage compliance, or they have been imposed in order to meet the demands of a domestic interest group rather than to achieve their declared aims. Sanctions can also fail because the costs are too high. Costs incurred by domestic producers or allies weaken the resolve to maintain the economic measures. Furthermore, the success of sanctions is also dependent on the extent to which the target state can evade the coercive measures either through mobilizing domestic resources (political and economic) or by finding substitute suppliers of the embargoed goods. History is replete with examples of both domestic mobilization against external intervention in the form of sanctions and of sanctions busting.

Given these caveats, it is not surprising that there is no consensus on the impact of sanctions. The most authoritative study (Hufbauer *et al.*, 2007) rejects the claim that sanctions don't work. These authors argue that in the cases they examine between 1914 and 2000 sanctions were partially successful 34 per cent of the time (Hufbauer *et al.*, 2007, p. 158). The reasons for success and failure were related to the type of policy change sought; the costs of enforcing sanctions; the extent to which sanctions were instrumental or expressive; and conflicting aims among senders.

Prior to the upsurge in sanctions since 1990 there was limited interest in the potentially harmful consequences of economic sanctions on civilian populations. With the increased resort to sanctions in the post-Cold War period and a changing moral climate, debates concerning the legality and utility of sanctions have been complemented with concern over the possibly damaging impact of sanctions on target populations. A series of high-profile cases, most notably sanctions against the Saddam Hussein regime in Iraq, has spurred interest in the humanitarian consequences of sanctions. It has led to a change in perception concerning the destructive nature of sanctions. Interest in the humanitarian impact of economic sanctions poses a number of issues and has given rise to contending views. A central issue concerns the extent to which foreign policy goals should take precedence over the human rights of target populations; and the circumstances under which humanitarian actors will decide on the unacceptable consequences of sanctions. It has been argued, on one hand, that the unintended, harmful consequences of sanctions can be accepted as long as the desired political goal is achieved. On the other hand, it is contended that, given the close relationship between political goals and humanitarian objectives, the senders should cease their activities once it becomes apparent that the objectives cannot be attained (Weiss *et al.*, 1997, pp.18–19).

Transnational crime

In the past two decades organized crime has become a major security issue. In the post-Cold War security structure transnational organized crime has become recognized as a major threat to national security. It has been a major theme in US national security strategy since 1996 when President Clinton defined the fight against organized crime as a national security priority. There is no agreed definition of organized crime since a monolithic transnational criminal organization does not exist. The *United Nations Convention against Organized Crime* adopts a broad definition. It defines an organized criminal group as a 'structured group of three or more persons, existing for a period of time and acting in concert with the aim of committing one or more serious crimes or offences ... in order to obtain directly or indirectly a financial or other material benefit.' (UN, 2000b, Article 2a). Organized criminal activity covers a wide range of illegal activities including drug trafficking, trafficking in persons, trading in human organs, money laundering, illicit traffic in weapons, theft of art and cultural objects, corruption and bribery of officials, environmental crime and the use of legal networks for illegal business activities.

The expansion of transnational criminal activities has been linked to the end of the Cold War and the intensification of globalization. Criminal networks have taken advantage of weak central governments in the former communist world, and the increase in ethnic conflict in central and Eastern Europe to expand their activities. Economic globalization has provided the conditions for the massive expansion of transnational organized crime. Economic liberalization, technological change and the transformation of transport systems have facilitated the growth of transnational criminal activity (Serrano, 2002, p. 25). The liberalization of trade and finance has provided avenues for the operation of criminal gangs. Communication and information technology has not only provided the infrastructure to allow these groups to coordinate their activities, it also has opened up new avenues of illegal activity such as internet fraud. The expansion of transport networks has increased the flow of legal and illegal goods.

Transnational organized crime poses a security threat in traditional and human security terms. It poses a direct threat to the political stability of weak states, and an indirect one to stronger states. Transnational organized crime poses a direct threat to governance and state institutions through increasing corruption in government and subverting good governance. The ensuing lack of legitimacy can undermine governmental and state authority. Moreover, links between transnational criminal groups and terrorists pose a direct threat to all states. In areas where governmental control is weak transnational organized crime can inflame regional conflict and destabilize regional relations through illegal cross-border activity, which can lead to the creation of territorial zones outside the control of the central government; or through the supply of illegal weapons to combatants. The economic activities of transnational criminal groups also pose a traditional threat to the security of the state. An interdependent global economy provides opportunities for money laundering and tax evasion. Transnational organized criminal activities can threaten legal markets, destroy legitimate businesses and expand illegal markets, resulting in a negative impact on economic growth and development. Poor economic performance often results in situations where a large illegal economy has been allowed to flourish.

Transnational crime also has serious implications for human security. It can have a damaging impact on state capacity by limiting the government's revenue with a resultant decline of spending on infrastructural projects and social services. Thus, there is a direct impact on human security when services such as education and health are curtailed. Moreover, activities such as the supply of illegal drugs, trafficking in persons for sexual exploitation, forced labour or harvesting of body are obviously injurious to the persons subject to such activities. Furthermore, transnational crime is accompanied by increased violence, loss of individual autonomy and consequent increased insecurity.

Disease, pandemics and security

The detection and control of pandemics and infectious diseases that might lead to pandemics has emerged as an important security issue with implications for both traditional security and human security concerns. The link between health and security has been made by scholars from both the human security (Curley and Thomas, 2004) and traditional security paradigms (Peterson, 2002/3). Both sets of scholars have focused on the risks posed by new diseases such as HIV/AIDs; emerging infections like SARS; or re-emerging diseases such as drug-resistant tuberculosis (TB) or malaria.

Health is an intrinsic aspect of most definitions of human security because health is a critical component of well-being and poor health threatens the quality of life an individual may attain. Brower and Chalk (2003, pp. 7–10) discuss six ways in which the international transmission of disease poses a threat to human security. First, disease is a direct threat to human life. Second, disease can erode a state's legitimacy by undermining public confidence if the state authorities fail to respond adequately to outbreak of disease or pandemic. Third, disease can threaten a state's economic capacity though its impact on public health spending and the productivity of the workforce. Fourth, disease can negatively impact a state's 'social order, functioning and psyche' (Brower and Chalk, 2003, p. 9). Fifth, infectious disease can promote regional volatility and instability through mass population movements, economic dislocation and defence under-preparedness. Finally, through biowarfare or bioterrorism diseases can become a security threat.

Instead of viewing health as a human security problem some scholars have instead demonstrated the compatibility of health with traditional approaches to security. From this perspective infectious disease is a national security issue. Infectious diseases can affect national security either directly or indirectly. Since health is a key component of national power, infectious diseases may undermine national power and hence alter the balance of power or contribute to economic, social and political instability. Moreover, infectious diseases may contribute to or exacerbate inter-state conflicts. Infectious diseases can also play a direct role in military conflict through the release of biological warfare (Peterson, 2002/3). Price-Smith (2009) combines both human security and traditional perspectives in his approach to the security implications of infectious disease. He argues that there are three crucial linkages between disease and national security. Disease may present a direct threat to state security by undermining state capacity; it has the potential to foster economic and political discord; and he points out that warfare gives rise to the proliferation of infectious disease.

Whether a traditional or human security perspective is adopted, scholars locate the new-found interest in the security dimensions of health in the post-Cold War security structure. The end of the Cold War was pivotal in creating more open borders and enhancing the movement of people. But the forces of globalization – specifically trade and commerce and travel and tourism – have contributed to the rapid spread of infectious disease (Cecchine and Moore, 2006). For example, the rapid movement of SARS virus in 2003 from China and South-east Asia was facilitated by air travel. In a globalized world national borders are incapable of fully securing individuals within the state from the transnational spread of infectious disease. While it may be argued that state borders have never been an effective barrier against the spread of disease, increased interdependence and resultant mass movement of people has increased the risk of the spread of disease across national borders.

Much of the literature on the security implications of diseases focuses on infectious diseases rather than on non-contagious diseases since it is easier to present such diseases as a threat. Thus, variants of the influenza virus have been particularly susceptible to this treatment. Both H5N1 (avian flu) and H1N1 (swine flu) have captured media attention around the world and governments have been forced to respond to these diseases as security threats. Clearly not all infectious diseases pose a security concern but there is sufficient evidence concerning the security implications of diseases and epidemics to suggest their impact on national, regional and international security. Perhaps the disease that has been the subject of the greatest attention from academics and policy-makers is HIV/AIDS (see Box 14.3).

The security implications of disease and the problems created for international cooperation were highlighted by the SARS crisis of 2003. In late 2002 Severe Acute Respiratory Syndrome (SARS) broke out in China and created a national health emergency as well as a global health crisis. The Chinese government failed to deal adequately with the crisis. The disease was first notified to the Chinese Ministry of Health in January 2003 but the government failed to notify the World Health Organization. When cases were reported in late February and early March in Canada, Singapore, Thailand and Viet Nam, the Chinese government remained silent. China was finally forced to admit the scale of the crisis as the result of international pressure, especially the activities of the WHO. The spread of the virus not only threatened the health of individuals in South-east Asia; it also had detrimental impacts on the stability and prosperity of these countries. This episode

---

Box 14.3   The securitization of HIV/AIDS

In 2001 HIV/AIDS moved decisively from a health issue to a security issue when both the United Nations General Assembly and the United Nations Security Council held special sessions on the pandemic. It was the first time in history that a health issue had been placed on the agenda of the Security Council. The speech of James Wolfensohn, then World Bank President, to the UN Security Council encapsulates the securitization of HIV/AIDS. He informed delegates, 'Many of us used to think of AIDS as a health issue. We were wrong. AIDS can no longer be confined to the health or social sector portfolios. Across Africa, AIDS is turning back the clock on development. Nothing we have seen is a greater challenge to the peace and stabilities of African societies than the epidemic of AIDS. ... We face a major development crisis, and more than that a security crisis. For without economic and social hope we will not have peace, and AIDS surely undermines both' (cited in Brower and Chalk, 2003, p. 31).

Singer (2002) presents a conventional and alarming interpretation of HIV/AIDS as a security threat. He posits a number of security implications of AIDS. These include direct weakening of the military; increased state vulnerability as the result of declining state capacity; state failure; an upsurge in new combatants and renewed civil conflict; and a hollowing out of the capacity of international peacekeepers.

Sources: Brower and Chalk (2003); Singer (2002).

---

demonstrated the security implications of disease. As two commentators noted, 'the impact of SARS quickly moved beyond a health issue, to become a political and economic threat as well as a major foreign policy challenge' (Curley and Thomas, 2004, p. 23).

Conclusion

The first chapter of this book noted how various disciplines have tended to evolve without much reference to developments in other fields. Some approaches to security and to international political economy have been equally insular. Despite this, many theoretical approaches have noted the intersection of security and economic issues. At the broadest level the international security system limits the free exchange of goods and services because of inter- and intra-state conflict. Political economy developments also influence the relative security of various national and sub-national populations. The introduction of new concepts of security, such as human security, has encouraged analysts to think about the multiple threats to individuals. Issues of disease, hunger and environmental degradation (see Chapter 12) pose equally serious physical and psychological threats to human survival as direct physical violence. In these areas, political economy variables, which influence the distribution of food, the manufacture of vaccines and the exploitation of the environment, have a clear impact upon human security.

Chapter 15

Governing the Global Political Economy

The subject of this chapter is global governance. While previous parts of the book have given some attention to global governance, this chapter explores the concept in greater detail. Specific attention is given to current understandings of governance, multiple levels of governance, contemporary issues facing the global political economy and the attendant challenges ahead for global managers and citizens. The definitions section explores key terms such as 'globalization' and 'global governance'. The theoretical perspectives section is given over to the debate about the role of the state in global governance. The major developments we highlight are the proliferation of governance levels and actors. The key governance challenges facing the global political economy are: development and economic growth, equality and justice, and democracy and regulation. Overall we paint a picture of an increasingly globalized world with states, firms and citizens struggling to create, manage and distribute wealth and power (O'Brien, 2003).

Definitions

The term 'globalization' is used very widely, but people often mean different things when they use the term. For example, some people use the term to imply internationalization (an increase in the volume of economic flows across borders), while others use it to indicate liberalization (the removal of restrictions to cross-border flows, such as the elimination of trade or investment barriers). Both internationalization and liberalization are often used in the context of economic activity. The term 'globalization' can also be used in the realm of knowledge or ideational dissemination. For example, some analysts focus on universalization (particular ideas or principles being accepted by all people), while others emphasize Westernization (the increasing prevalence of ideas and practices originating in Europe or the United States). These terms are most often used when discussing the spread of principles such as human rights or culture, such as the expansion of the US movie industry. The term 'deterritorialization' highlights the changing nature of geography and creation of new relationships between different groups of people.

Only deterritorialization adequately captures what is new about globalization. Following Scholte (2000a), we understand globalization to mean a process of relative deterritorialization. Territory is not disappearing, but it is becoming less important to human affairs. Deterritorialization involves the shrinking of time and space, as well as the creation of new sets of social relations and new centres of authority. We can see that time and space have become less significant obstacles to human interaction as technologies make it easier to travel across large distances or communicate with people around the world. The lowering of time and distance barriers allows people to become involved in the lives of other people in other parts of the planet much more easily. However, such an approach is also fully aware that this compression is extremely uneven. Some areas of the globe are left behind as advanced areas exploit technology and upgrade communication and transport infrastructure. That is, globalization is not occurring at the same rate and same pace in all countries or regions.

The term 'global governance', like that of globalization, is also subject to a variety of meanings. It has been used in an analytical sense to refer to an approach to world politics distinct from traditional International Relations theorizing with its focus on the activities of states and also in a normative manner to refer to a positive political project in world politics (Dingwerth and Pattberg, 2006). Some writers contend that global governance constitutes a specific discourse of international politics whose function is to legitimize specific liberal solutions to practical problems (Brand, 2005).

By 'global governance', we mean the overarching system which regulates human affairs on a worldwide basis. Another term would be the system of 'world order' (Cox, 1996a). The mechanisms and rules of global governance are created by the actions and agreements of key actors in the global system. The primary political actor is the state, but other actors such as corporations and civic associations can also influence and participate in global governance. A striking feature of global governance in the past 50 years has been the increasing role played by international (that is inter-state) organizations in facilitating governance. More recent developments have been the growing role of corporations and the mobilization of citizens through civic associations.

Theoretical perspectives: whither the state?

The growth of the global political economy has sparked intense debate about the future of the state. Are global flows of finance and trade overwhelming the autonomy of states? Are states increasingly powerless or do they retain the ability to shape the world to benefit their citizens? In various chapters in this book we have suggested states vary in their nature over time and between places. For example, Chapter 5, on the 20th century, discussed the evolution of the welfare state into a competition state. It argued that states were increasingly positioning their citizens for global competition rather than ensuring their welfare on a universal basis. We also charted the role of offshore finance and regulation in transforming the state. In a similar manner Chapter 11, on development, noted the change from national capitalism to more neoliberal forms of state. In chapters on trade, production and finance we have highlighted the various constraints and policy options available to states in the South and North. We have stressed the different possibilities open to stronger and weaker states. Chapter 14, on security, highlighted the growth of the national security state and charted its transformations in the post-Cold War security structure.

Despite these varieties in state form, the state as an institution retains a pivotal role in creating and maintaining governance in the global system because of the centrality of the connection between law and political authority. The state is the central legal actor and primary representative of individuals in the international system. Agreements binding the population of a country can only be made by a state. While its representative function is often imperfect, the state is the only institution that can make a legitimate claim to represent all of the people within its territory. Attempts to reform global governance must work through the state system.

Not all states are equally important in the process of global governance. The most developed and wealthy states are the most significant because they can veto changes or coerce other states to follow particular sets of policies. Thus, the United States is a central actor because of its wealth and power. Changes in US domestic politics can have a significant influence on the processes of global governance. For example, the election of a Republican to the US presidency in 2000 made international agreement to slow climate change much more difficult. President George W. Bush had much closer ties to the oil industry than his Democratic predecessor and successor. Many suggestions for slowing global warming threatened the profits of US oil companies and were not welcomed by the Republican President. Since the United States is the world's largest producer of the pollutants which contribute to global warming, a treaty without US participation is not very effective. Bush's successor, Barack Obama has moved in a different direction and directly engaged the world on climate change issues. In a similar way, on different issues, the position of the European Union and its member states is crucial to securing or blocking changes in global regulation.

Other states in the system are important for different reasons. The early 21st century has seen the emergence of a number of developing countries taking on a leadership role (see Box 15.1). For example, China's views carry increasing weight because of the size of its population relative to other countries and its recent modernization. China's population is estimated to be 1.3

Box 15.1   The BRICs

BRIC is an acronym used to group together four large influential developing countries – Brazil, Russia, India and China. Although they do not share a common ideology or political platform, these emerging regional and global powers are straining to make their voices heard in international fora and global meetings. Together they represent more than half the world's population. Brazil, China and India have been particularly assertive in trade talks with developed states by insisting that OECD countries open up their markets. China's financing of the US debt gives it increasing voice in international financial affairs. China and Russia both possess nuclear weapons, making their views on global security particularly relevant. As a major energy exporter, Russia has gained power and influence since the turn of the century. The emergence of the BRICs as a significant group indicates a dilution of US and European power, perhaps foreshadowing the emergence of a more mutlipolar global political economy.

billion of the global total of 6.5 billion. In military terms it is a force to be considered because of its large army and nuclear weapons. In economic terms, the Chinese state controls access to what is potentially the largest market when it reaches a sufficient stage of development. Thus, corporations and states tread more lightly when they deal with China than with small, less powerful states. It is much easier to exert pressure on a small country such as Nicaragua to respect universal human rights than on China.

Another example of a developing state whose views can carry some weight is South Africa. The South African state has a great deal of legitimacy to speak on behalf of oppressed people in Africa and the developing world because of its struggle to overthrow apartheid. In addition, because South Africa is a democratic state, its views carry more weight in global discussions than the views of a similar-sized authoritarian state. An interesting example of the role that the South African state played in challenging the existing form of global governance was its campaign to challenge the patent protection afforded to multinational drug companies that produce anti-AIDS drugs. The South Africans made a moral argument for violating the patent protection that is enshrined in the WTO.

Despite the importance of the state to global governance, some groups have moved away from concentrating all of their effort on influencing state power. The major explanation for this is that the ability of the state to offer protection from the harmful aspects of globalization seems to have been reduced. The populations of the weakest states in the developing world have been at the mercy of Western states and large corporations for many years. Recently, however, it appears that even advanced industrialized states seem less able to protect their citizens from increasing global competition. This has been described by one observer as the state shifting its role from providing welfare for its citizens to preparing the population for increased competition (Cerny, 2000). The state does not shrink or disappear, but changes its role. The process of globalization is seen to have made it more difficult to support the traditional welfare state, which cushioned the effects of competition (Mishra, 1999).

The view that the state is losing power has been widely challenged. Some have suggested that globalization is exaggerated, by arguing that the degree of internationalization as measured by percentages of trade and investment flows has precedents in the early 1900s (Hirst and Thompson, 1996). Citing the persistent differences between North American, European and Asian models of capitalism, students of comparative politics dispute that there has been a movement to policy convergence (Garrett, 2000). These scholars deny that the state is weaker or is unable to protect its citizens. They suggest that if political forces advocating social protection gather the political will and organize themselves properly, the government can be pointed in the direction of social protection. From this perspective globalization has very little to do with increasing inequality or decreasing social protection.

Controversies about the relative importance of the state continue to rage and observable trends point in different directions. On one side it is possible to see that most states around the world, in stark contrast to the 1970s, actively seek multinational investment. This indicates that in relative terms corporations have become more important to states. Second, in contrast to earlier decades, states seem more intent upon furnishing those companies with an attractive environment than with regulating their activity. Some have referred to states engaging in 'beauty contests' in an effort to attract foreign investment (Palan and Abbott, 2000). Of course, the balance of power between any particular state and any particular firm will vary depending upon their position in the global economy. On the other side, the financial crisis of 2008–9 saw a resurgence in state regulation as governments bailed out the financial industry and considered imposing new regulations upon global finance. Suddenly, global finance looked very weak and states looked strong. Once again, however, it is important to note that only particular states were able to reassert authority, while many poor and weak states were not.

Major developments

One of the most important issues facing students of, and practitioners within, the global political economy is the management of change. That is, what determines changes in the rules under which a particular form of global governance operates? For example, how do actors with a commitment to environmentalism shift the system in a direction which puts a higher emphasis on environmental protection? The relatively brief history of world orders or global governance warns against expecting rapid change and highlights the link between crisis and changes in governance. Dramatic transformations in governing relations between states have tended to follow large-scale wars. For example, in the aftermath of the Napoleonic Wars at the beginning of the 19th century the European state system was managed by the Concert of Europe. The next large change in organizing the international system followed the terrible destruction of the First World War. The League of Nations and a number of other international organizations and treaties were created to try and improve governance and maintain peace. The Second World War marked the end of that system and ushered in a new world order in 1945. Many of today's international organizations such as the UN, the IMF, the World Bank and NATO date back to this era. The end of the Cold War between the United States and the Soviet Union in 1989 resulted in the strengthening of existing Western institutions rather than the creation of a new form of international organization.

Large-scale changes in reforming or replacing existing global governance structures are unlikely unless there is a devastating crisis in the international system. With the relatively peaceful end to the Cold War, the chances are low that a new world war will erupt in the near future to cause major change in global governance. It is more likely that wholesale change would come about as a result of a severe financial crisis which plunged the world into economic depression. Financial collapse would force decision-makers to change the existing system or replace it with a new set of rules. Since such a collapse would impoverish millions and probably lead to violent conflict within and between states, it is not a method of changing global governance that many people would choose. Such a scenario is only attractive to those who have nothing to gain from the existing system. Some feared that the financial crisis in the United States in 2008 might be just such an event. The crisis has not led to wholesale changes in the governance architecture. The G-20 has taken the lead in responding to the global economic crisis and its efforts to date signal piecemeal rather than radical reform of the international financial system. While there has been intense debate concerning the failure of regulation and the loopholes in financial management that triggered the crisis, proposed reforms do not indicate major changes to governance arrangements.

In the absence of change on a grand and destructive scale, we must look to particular developments in governance institutions and particular actors to foster innovations that might gradually guide the globalization process in a more positive direction. In this section we will highlight the proliferation of new governance arenas and actors that are shaping global governance.

Proliferation of governance levels

A striking feature of governance in the global political economy is the numerous levels upon which it takes place. While the state remains important, as outlined in the theoretical perspectives section, governance is taking place on a number of other levels. Foremost amongst these are governance at the sub-national, regional and global levels. Some elements of governance have also shifted away from the state into the private/corporate realm, but this will be dealt with in the following sub-section. The term 'multilevel governance' helps us to think about the vertical power relationships, while terms such as 'international regimes' get us to focus upon the relationships at the international level.

Multilevel governance is a term that emerged from studies of the European Union (Marks, Hooge and Blank, 1996). It posits that authority and policy-making in Europe is shared across sub-national, national and supranational levels. National governments must be mindful of EU treaties and the operations of EU institutions. For example, the European Commission has the power to roll back national subsidy or state aid programmes and members of the euro community must live with the monetary policy of the European Central Bank. National governments are also sensitive to the demands and interests of sub-federal governments or regions. In studies of urban politics, multilevel governance is taken even closer to the local level as studies can examine governing arrangements at the inter-urban, city and even neighbourhood levels (Kearns and Forrest, 2000).

The focus of multilevel governance is the vertical relationship of power and politics running up and down between different levels. Are national states losing power to regional integration projects such as the European Union or the North American Free Trade Agreement? Conversely, are national states losing influence in relationship to sub-national levels such as regional or provincial governments? Central to these studies is the notion that, even though governance is taking place across a number of levels, the people involved are bounded by some form of community. Thus, although there are many political differences in the EU and problems negotiating common policies, there is a sense of a common European community and a common set of institutions, whether that is the European parliament or the euro.

As regional trade and economic groupings have multiplied in most parts of the world, the issue of multilevel governance has become more pressing. How is it possible to coordinate policies across sub-national, state and regional levels? A related problem is: how do these regions relate to global governance? Are regions compatible with global rules? This issue is most visible in reconciling trade rules. An example of this was the beef hormone case cited in Chapter 6. A European view of appropriate risk clashed with an

American view of the supremacy of science. To take another example, the American desire for formal institutions in regional agreements runs counter to Asian preferences for informal arrangements and minimal institutions. Thus, the problems of multilevel governance can be extended up past the regional level to international institutions such as the WTO.

At the international level many approaches focus upon world or international organizations and their ability to address global problems (Hewson and Sinclair, 1999). International organizations are often best placed to address collective action problems at the global level. Greater international cooperation is vital to tackle the range of problems identified in this chapter. These organizations are significant because they provide both the forum for negotiating globalization rules and the mechanisms for monitoring and enforcing rules.

In the field of international relations, the governance arrangements put in place by states in particular issue areas are often referred to as regimes. Regimes are 'implicit or explicit principles, norms, rules and decision-making procedures around which actors' expectations converge in a given area of international relations' (Krasner, 1983, p. 2). Regimes are ideas and rules about how states should behave. A vast literature explains the conditions under which regimes are created, maintained and destroyed. Most approaches see regimes as being created through state-to-state negotiations with states acting as self-interested, goal-seeking actors pursuing the maximization of individual utility (Hasenclever, Mayer and Rittberger, 1997). In other words, states create regimes because they believe that a regular pattern of cooperation will bring them benefits. In many cases, states participate in regimes that are not ideal because the cost of conflict outside of the regime is greater than the bad deal they get inside the regime (Keohane, 1984). For example, developing states may object to many aspects of the trade regime, but they prefer to be members than to operate outside the main trading institution.

We can identify a number of ways through which regimes influence behaviour. Some regimes have a strong legal framework which compels states to obey rules by the threat of economic sanctions. The WTO is an excellent example. It has a strong dispute settlement mechanism which adjudicates trade conflicts based upon the rules contained in the agreements that created the WTO. Countries in violation of the rules must change their policies or face economic sanctions from the states they have injured. Even powerful states obey these rules because they have an interest in a predictable system of rules that fosters increased trade and economic activity. The WTO puts the value of free trade above other goals, leading to conflict with those people who feel that free trade undermines environmental standards. In this case liberal values and market mechanisms are privileged over other approaches. Environmental protection must take place in the context of free trade.

The distribution of money and provision of credit can also be used to foster compliance with particular rules. This is the approach used by the World Bank and the IMF. These organizations loan money to states that are in need of funds to weather an economic crisis or to assist in long-term development strategies. The loans are usually conditional upon the recipients undertaking certain policies. These policies have varied over time, but usually ask states to liberalize their economies so that they earn money to pay back the loans. Institutions which disperse money are influenced by their largest financial contributors. In the case of the World Bank and the IMF, voting rights are distributed in proportion to the financial contributions of member states. At the IMF the Group of Seven developed states, which represents 717 million people, controls 46 per cent of the votes. In contrast the five largest developing countries, with a population of 2.957 billion people, control only 8.06 per cent of IMF votes (see Table 15.1). Because the United States is the largest contributor to both the IMF and the World Bank, it has the largest share of votes and influence. Thus, policies that the United States advocates are the most likely to be spread through this channel of influence in the global governance process. For example, IMF loans to South Korea during the East Asian financial crisis stipulated that Korea open up its manufacturing and financial industries to foreign investors, many of whom were from the United States.

At other times, states' behaviour can be influenced by appeals to morality. This is the approach used by the International Labour Organization (ILO). The ILO conducts research on labour issues and highlights the abuse of workers' rights through reports and investigations. It facilitates negotiations between states to set minimum standards for countries to follow and publicizes failure to comply with the standards. The organization's work is based upon the belief that states may change their behaviour if they face international condemnation. Although the ILO has been operating for almost 100 years, its ability to influence states' behaviour is limited by its lack of enforcement measures. Many states ignore its reports and advice.

Expertise can also be used to convince actors that it is in their best interest to behave in a particular way. For example, organizations such as the OECD and the IMF issue reports on the economic policy of particular states and suggest how they should adapt to globalization. Reports do not order states to change their policies, but they advise that a particular change will help foster economic growth. These institutions tend to offer liberal approaches to economic restructuring and until very recently were unlikely to advocate policies that might protect society by reducing the influence of unregulated markets.

A final element that influences behaviour is the structure of the global system itself. This is known as structural power. Drawing upon theories of the privileged power position of business in a national context, Gill and Law

Table 15.1   IMF voting rights vs population

Country	% of IMF votes	Population in millions
United States	17.8	298
Japan	6.13	128
Germany	5.99	82
France	4.95	60
United Kingdom	4.95	59
Italy	3.25	58
Canada	2.94	32
G-7 total	**46.07**	**717**
China	2.94	1,315
India	1.92	1,103
Brazil	1.41	186
Indonesia	0.97	222
Nigeria	0.82	131
Five LDCs total	**8.06**	**2,957**

Sources: Data from IMF (2006a); UN (2004).

(1993) argue that the internationalization of economic activity has increased the direct and indirect power of business in relationship to the state. The nature of the system makes particular types of behaviour more likely and punishes some forms of behaviour more harshly than others. For example, states must pay attention to the desires of international investors if they want to attract capital for investment or keep national wealth and businesses from fleeing to other locations. This encourages state leaders to move their economies in a more liberal direction.

It is important to note that, in the system of global governance, the institutions that are tasked with liberalizing the global economy and increasing the role of the market are more influential than those seeking to protect society from economic failures. On the market liberalization side, the IMF and World Bank are able to use the provision of finance for influence and the

WTO has its important dispute settlement mechanism. However, the ILO, which protects labour standards, is confined to an advocacy role. Other institutions with social mandates, such as UNICEF which assists poor children, or the World Health Organization, must work within the economic policies advocated by the liberal institutions. The structure of governance seems to favour the increasing power of the market at the expense of social values. Returning to Polanyi's (1957) view of the dislocating effects of the liberal market, this is likely to lead to social turbulence and conflict over the rules of global governance.

Proliferation of actors

In addition to the state and inter-state agreements, two other actors and realms of activity have become prominent in discussion of global political economy governance: the corporation and global civil society.

In the early 1990s, some observers argued that the growing power of transnational corporations in relation to the state necessitated a revision of international relations and international business theory. Drawing upon a study of investment relations in Brazil, Malaysia and Kenya, Stopford and Strange (1991) argued that state–firm and even firm–firm bargaining was becoming more important to the international system. States are increasingly interested in attracting foreign investment and firms are increasingly capable of influencing governmental investment policy. Thus, a key feature of how rules are created and enforced in the global economy is the negotiation conducted between states and firms.

A good example of how corporations can influence global governance is provided by the insertion of intellectual property rights (IPRs) into the WTO. IPRs include things such as copyright protection for books and music, as well as patent protection for inventions and scientific discoveries. They do not really fall under the umbrella of free trade because their enforcement does not increase the flow of goods between states. However, in the 1980s many Western corporations in industries such as pharmaceuticals, computer software, movies and music became concerned that competitors were copying their products. An association of leading US transnational corporations, including Du Pont, General Electric, IBM and Monsanto, convinced the US government that IPRs should be protected in trade agreements. Eventually the corporations were able to have rules that they largely drafted inserted into the WTO (Sell, 1999; Sell and Prakash, 2004). These are some of the rules that the government of South Africa fought against in an attempt to provide affordable drugs to combat the large numbers of deaths from AIDS in southern Africa (Lanoszka, 2003; Thomas, 2002).

In addition to the trend of increasing corporate influence over state policy-makers, one can also point to the rise of private authority. Private authority exists where firms exercise decision-making power over a particular issue area and this activity is viewed as legitimate. Cutler, Haufler and Porter (1999) have identified six mechanisms for the exercise of private authority: industry norms; coordination service firms (for example, bond rating); production alliances; cartels; business associations; and private regimes. They argue that private firms are increasingly exercising authority in particular issue areas in the global economy. Studies of the telecommunications industry, insurance business, accountancy and cartels support the notion of private authority (Strange, 1996). A recent study of the relationship between private actors and the UN system has argued that increased private sector participation in the multilateral system is having varied but significant impacts on the ways these institutions function (Bull, Bøås and McNeill, 2004).

It is important to note that recognizing the role and significance of corporate activity does not imply that state power is unimportant or that all corporations behave the same way. One can acknowledge the role of corporate activity in global governance while at the same time agreeing with authors (Doremus *et al.*, 1998) who argue that there are differences in behaviour between corporations from different states and that states often support the behaviour of corporations headquartered in their territory. Corporations have an interest in influencing the terms of global governance, even if their particular interests are not identical.

In their pursuit of profits corporations will attempt to influence the structures of global governance. Not all corporations will have the same immediate goals, nor follow the same tactics. Indeed, business conflict theory (Skidmore-Hess, 1996) advises us to expect clashes of interest between corporations in international as well as domestic realms. Corporations from particular states or sectors may demonstrate distinctive characteristics. Firms that are internationally competitive will have different preferences from those that are not internationally competitive. Despite or because of these differences, corporations will attempt to shape governance structures by influencing state, international organization, corporate and civil society behaviour. The role of the corporation in international relations has grown to such an extent that attempts to understand or influence global governance must take the role of corporations into account.

In addition to resource-rich corporations, voluntary citizen organizations operating in global civil society are playing an increasing role in influencing the principles of global governance. Indeed, in the 1980s and 1990s, prominent civic actors played the role of unofficial opposition to global governance agencies and inter-state agreements. They stressed an agenda that puts citizen autonomy and security at the centre of governance questions. Peace groups have opposed particular weapons systems and military strategies. The campaign to ban the production and use of landmines is a prime example. Development, women's, environmental and labour groups have opposed the dominance of liberal policies emanating from international economic institutions. Citizen action across state borders to overcome the anti-democratic actions of their own states has been described as 'democratic internationalism' (Gilbert, 1999).

The global civil society sphere is the space where civic actors meet to engage in debate and political activity in an effort to shape the direction of global and national society (Scholte, 2000b). It is primarily composed of voluntary, non-profit associations. To differentiate them from profit-seeking non-governmental organizations such as corporations, this chapter uses the term 'civic associations'. The most visible organizations tend to be those working in high-profile areas, such as Greenpeace and Friends of the Earth in the environmental field or Amnesty International in the human rights area. However, there are many other forms of organization. For example, international trade union bodies such as the International Trade Union Confederation claim a representative (175 million members) as well as advocacy role. Religious organizations are also very active. In terms of numbers of formal organizations, the bulk of activity takes place in relatively uncontroversial forms such as industry associations and scientific knowledge organizations (medicine, sciences, communications) (Boli and Thomas, 1999, p. 41). Aggregating visible NGOs with less visible local activity, one can point to the emergence of fluid social movements around issues such as development, human rights, peace and women's issues.

The global civil society arena is occupied by several actors which do not share the characteristics of being non-profit voluntary equity-seeking civic associations. One prominent group is composed of business associations. These associations seek to create an environment where corporations can maximize profits. A prominent example is the International Chamber of Commerce. In addition to lobbying state and civil society actors, it attempts to foster an environment which encourages self-regulation (Schneider, 2000).

Although it goes against the grain of our understanding of domestic civil society, there are civic associations that lack civility. Civility, or the agreement to manage interaction according to a common set of rules and without recourse to violence, is a hallmark of domestic notions of civil society. Those who choose not to be bound by such rules are considered to be outside the bounds of civil society. An example would be a criminal organization such as the Mafia (see also Chapter 14 for a discussion of transnational organized crime). In the global system there is less agreement about common rules and much less enforcement than in most national societies. As a result, there is a greater space for uncivil groups to operate alongside peaceful civic associations. Examples include organized crime, violent ethnic nationalists and terror organizations. They are shunned by the majority of civic associations,

Box 15.2　The covert world

The covert world is an integral yet often neglected element of the global political economy (Cox, 2002b). It encompasses the illegitimate, illegal and barely visible actions of states, corporations and civic associations. Activities of prime importance include: the drug trade which funnels narcotics to customers in the United States and Europe; the sex trade which supplies vulnerable women and children to satisfy the desires of wealthy clients; the smuggling of people to supply undocumented workers to staff construction, health and domestic services at a low cost; the trade in human organs, providing new or better lives for those who can pay; the small-arms trade, which floods the world with hand guns, rifles and machine guns; and the service of mercenaries to provide state or corporate security.

The covert world responds to and complements the overt world of legal global political economy relations. Chaotic economic relations and the withdrawal of state regulation or service provision provide opportunities for covert activities. The economic collapse of regions such as the former Soviet Union or Mexico provides the people desperate enough to become caught up in human trafficking. The reduction in the welfare state, combined with an ageing population in Western states, creates a demand for the private provision of health and domestic services at low cost. The breakdown in state security provides the demand for corporations to hire private security firms and even for states such as the United States to privatize elements of warfare in countries such as Iraq. The globalization of finance and creation of offshore financial centres provide the opportunities for illegally obtained money to be transported and laundered. The Cold War, followed by the War on Terror provides the excuse for security services to engage in illegal activities to fund and run security operations. Actors in the covert world respond to the incentives of the overt world to provide illegal services, often through the use of violence against defenceless people.

but they exist in a similar space. They are a major influence in the illicit side of global political economy – the covert world (see Box 15.2).

While there are many different groups with specific agendas, most politically active groups would describe themselves as pursuing the objectives of equity or social justice. Equity and justice could be sought in respect to gender relations (women's groups), distribution of resources (development groups), quality of life (environmental groups), or human security (human rights). There are, of course, differences between members of civil society, just as there are conflicts between states or corporations. Organized labour is challenged by NGOs claiming to speak on behalf of the informal sector. Women's groups in the developing world have an ambivalent and sometimes conflictual relationship with northern feminist groups. Environmentalists seeking radical changes to the doctrine of economic growth are in conflict with more conservative conservationist groups. Various NGOs claim to speak on behalf of social movements or constituencies, but the plethora of groups and lack of transparency make it difficult to determine the legitimacy of their claims.

Although the precise nature of global civil society is debatable (Amoore and Langley, 2004; Lipschutz, 2005) it is less contentious that transnational civic actors have an influence on world politics and inter-state relations. Scholarly attention has tended to focus upon human rights, environmental and women's groups' attempts to influence norms and values in the global system (Keck and Sikkink, 1998). International NGOs seeking social transformation operate on a number of levels to influence global governance: they create and activate global networks, participate in multilateral arenas, facilitate inter-state cooperation, act within states to influence policy and enhance public participation (Alger, 1997). Even in areas often considered to be the sole domain of states, such as international security, civil society groups can play a role in shaping the agenda and contributing to policy change (Price, 1998).

At the minimum we can say that civic actors increasingly serve a role as disseminators of information, mobilizers of public opinion, articulators of dissent and protest. Ignoring their role, as the architects of the Multilateral Agreement on Investment did (Mayne and Picciotto, 1999), is likely to lead to governance breakdown. Civic associations can be instrumental in undermining the legitimacy of international organizations, even as states continue to support them.

The Global Compact

If global governance is to push ahead, one would imagine that some form of accommodation is required between the three different types of key actors (state, corporate and civic). For example, a trade regime would have to simultaneously be sensitive to the interests of developing states for increased equity, corporate interests for expansion and profit, and social interests for restricting human and environmental exploitation. This is an enormously complicated task. An example of such an approach is the Global Compact developed by the Secretary-General's office of the United Nations.

The Global Compact asks corporations to incorporate ten principles drawn from the Universal Declaration of Human Rights, the ILO's Fundamental Principles on Rights at Work, the Rio Principles on

Environment and Development, and the United Nations Convention against Corruption into their corporate practices. The Compact does not monitor corporate practice nor does it assess corporate performance. It is designed to identify and disseminate good practices. The Global Compact asks leaders of some of the world's most prominent corporations to publicly commit themselves to good labour and environmental practices.

The Global Compact simultaneously addresses the concerns of some corporate, state and civic associations. From a developing country point of view, the initiative is tolerable because it is aimed at influencing the policy of multinational corporations rather than restricting state policy or punishing developing states for poor labour conditions. This is preferable to the WTO enforcing standards because it removes the threat of northern protectionism. From the corporate viewpoint, it is tolerable because regulations are voluntary and allow continued expansion of the global economy and accumulation of profits. They can claim to be good corporate citizens without being bound by compulsory regulation. For some civic actors, it represents a limited advance in enshrining some principles of social protection. It is a small step that might lead to more binding forms of regulation.

To be sure, the Global Compact has severe shortcomings. Many of the companies participating in the venture are those which have been attacked as abusers of environmental and human rights or accused of engaging in super-exploitation of workers. The list includes Shell, Nike, Disney and Rio Tinto. Each of these companies has been or is subject to boycotts or anti-corporate campaigns by civic associations. One can question the degree to which such companies will actually change their behaviour. Domestically, reliance only upon voluntary regulation of corporate behaviour is unacceptable. Why would such activity at the global level prove any more satisfying? The ILO has hundreds of conventions but sees many abused because of a lack of enforcement powers. How would this initiative be any different? Another problem is that the selection of participating civic associations in the Compact was very narrow and not reflective of the wider community. The UN selected civic groups based on their judgement of who would be the most likely to cooperate. Reaction from many other groups has been very critical. The initiative has been condemned because it threatens the integrity of the UN, as corporations attempt to 'bluewash' their record by association with the UN (Transnational Resource and Action Center, 2000).

This example of the Global Compact is informative for our efforts to understand global governance reform for three reasons. First, it illustrates that the concerns of civic actors about the damaging aspects of globalization are being taken seriously by other actors in the system. The United Nations is responding to public unease about the costs of globalization. This initiative follows public demonstrations against institutions such as the WTO and the IMF. The UN Secretary-General is trying to put a more humane face on globalization so that the process will continue, but in a less brutal manner. The goal is to restrain competition that is based upon the abuse of labour and environmental standards so that the public will not fight the liberal rules under which globalization is taking place. Corporations are also being forced to respond to civic pressure by setting up codes of conduct and projecting the image of moral behaviour.

Second, it highlights the failure of existing global governance arrangements. We already have an institution that is designed to bolster labour standards – the ILO. However, the ineffectiveness of the ILO has forced labour activists to turn to the enforcement mechanisms found in the WTO to support labour standards. Many developing states oppose dealing with labour standards because they fear that developed states might increase their protectionism through the device of labour standards. Those groups in civil society trying to improve labour standards find themselves blocked at the WTO and faced with a weak ILO. Existing global governance mechanisms seem unable to improve social standards. Thus, new initiatives such as the Global Compact are being devised in an urgent attempt to resolve difficult dilemmas.

Finally, the Global Compact illustrates just how difficult it is to create new governance arrangements. The cost of freer markets is creating more public resistance, but many states and corporations resist instruments that would require better labour, environmental or social standards. Agreements which secure widespread corporate and state support are unlikely to satisfy the social interests which are pressing for protection. At the moment social interests may have to accept incremental steps towards reforming institutions and policies on the global level.

The point here is not to argue the merits or demerits of the Global Compact. It is to illustrate a recent response to the difficult problem of regulating the economic aspects of globalization. The Compact may be an inadequate response, but it is a leading example of state–corporate–civic association action that may increasingly guide the global political economy.

21st-century challenges

Inhabitants of the global political economy face numerous challenges in the 21st century. In this section we outline three pressing governance issues: economic development and growth, equality and justice, democracy and regulation.

Development and growth

World leaders have pledged to eradicate extreme global poverty by 2015. The *Millennium Declaration* (UN, 2000a, para. 11) states that 'we will spare no effort to free our fellow men, women and children from the abject and dehumanising conditions of extreme poverty'. Such an achievement would be truly staggering but no one seriously believes that this objective will be fulfilled. The fate of most of humanity remains desperate in a world of plenty. In the early 21st century modern economic growth has still not been dispersed to the majority of the world's 6.5 billion inhabitants. The challenge of economic development became an international issue in the years immediately following the Second World War and was driven by the leaders of newly independent states. In order to maintain their hold on power, political elites were obliged to respond to what in the 1960s was frequently referred to as the revolution of rising expectations. Some 40 years after the UN proclaimed the First Development Decade prospects remain bleak. One of the major challenges is therefore to meet the development needs of peoples living in Third World countries. What exactly does this entail at the current historical conjuncture? And what conditions are currently considered necessary to bring this change about?

In Chapter 11 we examined the changing meaning of the concept of development, and showed how the focus has shifted from a concentration on economic growth to a consideration of social factors. In the absence of an agreed definition of development, we can nevertheless suggest certain key features of the concept as it is currently understood. An improvement in material capabilities remains central to most conceptions of development. At the heart of national and international development efforts is the objective of raising material living standards. In effective terms this translates into the provision of basic necessities such as adequate foodstuffs, clean water, electricity, shelter, improved transportation and better sanitation. It will in time lead to the consumption of a wider range of products, but in essence development consists in satisfying basic needs. Of course, clean water, electricity and so on are meaningless outside the context of human beings. Directly linked to the provision of these needs are another set of equally basic services without which people will be unable to fulfil their life chances. These include education and healthcare. But development has increasingly come to mean the attainment of non-material values. In this respect we need to think about the ability of people to make their own decisions and to have greater control over their own lives. Amartya Sen (1981), the Indian Nobel laureate, developed his theory of entitlements to show that famine arose not because of the absence of food but in circumstances where those starving lacked the bundle of resources that enabled them to have access to food. Development clearly entails increased participation and the empowerment of marginalized groups.

Early efforts at promoting development were gender-blind, but we are aware that one of the main challenges of development in the 21st century will be to ensure that women are fully integrated into national development strategies. For a number of reasons this remains a daunting task. The problems facing women in developing countries remain the subject of analysis and policy prescriptions (Datta and Kornberg, 2002). In the light of the experience of women in the advanced industrial countries, the mainstreaming of gender will not in itself lead to equality. Although women in Western developed societies have achieved legal equality they continue to experience many forms of discrimination and structural exclusion. In terms of formal equality, women in the West have made the most significant gains but the concept of the glass ceiling is well understood, and is an actuality for many women. The glass ceiling refers to the existence of an invisible barrier that limits women from attaining the highest positions in many sectors and firms. Thus, the battle to produce development policies that will support women's livelihoods in the developing world remains a daunting task.

How are the mechanisms of global governance responding to the challenge of economic development? As will have been apparent from previous chapters, the answer to this question depends on the perspective of the observer. We have rehearsed many of these arguments already and so we will not repeat them here. There are a number of identifiable problems of governance which the various perspectives will have to address and it is to these that we now turn. The first problem we will discuss is that of coordination of various initiatives. There are a number of agencies – national, regional and international – attempting to promote development, but no means of coordinating the various activities that exist at present. Indeed, governmental, inter-governmental and non-governmental actors can pursue diverse and conflicting objectives within a single country or region. Moreover, no system of allocation exists to ensure that resources are delivered where they are most needed, and duplication of effort is avoided.

A second problem also relates to the overall framework in which economic development is promoted. In Chapter 8 we discussed the global financial system and raised problems of regulation. We have seen a number of financial crises, most notably in Mexico, East Asia and Argentina, that have reversed decades of progress. In the absence of reform of the international financial architecture, hard won gains can be lost within a matter of days.

Governance has been identified as a crucial issue in the promotion of development and it is now widely accepted that in the absence of effective governance mechanisms there will be limited achievement of development goals. However, at the moment there is an absence of consensus concerning how good governance is to be pursued. Lectures from developed countries on good governance ring hollow when political motives still play such a large part in the foreign aid policies of leading donor nations.

Equality and justice

Current discussions may lead one to conclude that global inequality is unique to globalization, which it is claimed is wreaking havoc on the development prospects of Third World countries, and creating an underclass in advanced industrial societies. As we have seen in this book, the global economy and international economic exchange have always created winners and losers. To point to the historical existence of a phenomenon is not, however, to claim that it is unimportant. It makes us aware that these issues have been of concern to people for a very long time. At the beginning of the 21st century the search for equality and justice is as pressing as ever. The 1994 *Human Development Report* noted 'a breathtaking globalization of prosperity side by side with a depressing globalization of poverty' (UNDP, 1994, p. 1), and it is the existence of such glaring disparities that drives part of the agenda for greater social equity.

Governments around the world and international institutions will have to give greater attention to social justice issues in the coming decades. To some extent, the dominance of neoliberal ideology masked issues of equity and justice in its naive faith in market solutions. At the end of the 20th century these issues began to be taken more seriously and there was evidence of a move away from the Washington Consensus as discussed in Chapter 12. The search for equality and justice is being driven by the impact of changes in the global economy and the reaction of various groups to these developments. The process of globalization is leading to increasing inequality within and between nations. In other words, the challenge of inequality is not to be seen simply in terms of differences between states but also in terms of internal inequality. Caroline Thomas reminds us that, 'two-thirds of the global population seem to have gained little or nothing from the economic growth that has occurred as a result of globalization to date' (2000, p. 11). Globalization is affecting income inequality within countries and it has the potential to adversely affect the standards of living of workers in developed countries (Kitching, 2001, p. 266).

If left unchecked this will give rise to greater tensions and instability within and between nations. One example of the response to increasing inequality within many advanced industrial societies has been the rise of ethno-nationalist parties blaming foreigners for loss of employment and a range of social ills. As governments have cut back on public spending, reduced social safety nets and increased privatization, the poor and disadvantaged in industrial countries have become even more marginalized. Centre-left and centre-right governments have increasingly lost the ability to appeal to large segments of those left behind by economic and technological change. The result has been an increase in support for right-wing, populist parties. Of course, while this phenomenon is occurring in a number of countries, there is nothing automatic about these developments and the success of these parties also depends on domestic circumstances. Moreover, the timing of increased support reflects developments in local politics.

The link between domestic politics, global processes and the search for international solutions is illustrated in the continuing debate over migration in advanced industrial societies. A crisis over asylum seekers erupted in Western Europe and Australia in 2000–2, and continues to make political headlines. One direct and visible effect of rising inequality between states is reflected in current debates on asylum seekers, and the debate is also a reflection of rising levels of inequality in affluent societies. Among the refugee flows are so-called economic migrants seeking a better life and responding to the lack of opportunity in their home countries. The existence of glaring disparities between rich and poor nations will continue to fuel a trade in people-smuggling and illegal migration. The uncharitable reception of asylum seekers also reflects the attitude of those who feel that they are currently losers in the process of globalization. They resent what they see as scarce resources being spent on foreigners. The solution to this problem does not lie in individual initiatives by single governments but requires international cooperation.

While it is important to remember that shifting patterns of equality are not to be seen in simple North–South terms, the impact of change in the global political economy is experienced differently and much more harshly within the South. While globalization has the potential to create significant benefits for developing countries, these countries will only gain if they institute effective management systems at the domestic level and attain support from international agencies. Unless states find ways to cope with the adjustment and social costs attendant on further integration into the global economy they will be unable to reap the benefits of globalization (Cook and Kirkpatrick, 1994, p. 64). We can see evidence of major variations among regions in the developing world: while Africa seems to be falling further behind, the countries of South-east Asia appear to have benefited from their incorporation into the global economy. This is obviously not a straightforward process as the Asian financial crisis demonstrated, but the economies in Asia hardest hit by the crisis are now returning to higher growth rates.

By influencing the location and distribution of wealth and productive power in the world economy, globalization defines and reshapes global patterns of hierarchy and inequality. The challenge for global governance in the 21st century is to devise structures to reverse persistent inequality and widening income disparities which lead to a more unstable and unruly world. The extent to which national and global leaders currently have the understanding and political will to respond creatively to these challenges remains open to doubt. One set of actors within the global political economy has prioritized issues of equality and justice. Many national and transnational civic associations are actively involved in seeking to promote a social justice agenda. We will illustrate this movement by reference to one campaign.

As noted in Chapters 8 and 11, the debt crisis has had a profound impact on the developing world. Efforts to reduce Third World debt provide an example of the struggle currently being waged to address social justice in the context of the global economy. One of the key actors in this struggle is a civic organization known as the Jubilee Debt Campaign (previously known as Jubilee 2000). Members of the Jubilee Debt Campaign base their strategy on the belief that total debt remission is both economically feasible and ethically defensible. As two of their proponents ask, 'How many more deaths are needed before [debt] unsustainability is recognized and treated?' (Dent and Peters, 1998, p. 15). The aim of the Jubilee Debt Campaign is to inject justice into an economic system given over to profit and stability. The coalition has used a diverse range of tactics to grab the attention of world leaders. These range from normal lobbying tactics to mass actions designed to hit the international headlines. For example, the Jubilee activists have engaged in street protests at G-7 summits, including forming a human chain around the meeting site of the 1997 G-7 Denver Summit (Michael, 2001, p. 11). The campaign has not succeeded in its aim of total debt cancellation for all poor countries, but the Heavily Indebted Poor Countries (HIPC) Initiative was a response by creditor governments to calls for debt cancellation. Subsequent G-7 decisions on debt, such as the decision at the Cologne Summit in 1999 to cancel $27 billion and the MDRI agreed at the G-8 Gleneagles Summit in July 2005, reflect the influence of the coalition. The Jubilee Debt Campaign is part of a larger movement of citizens seeking the promotion of global security, democracy and justice. The Jubilee Debt Campaign has been joined by another anti-poverty movement – the Global Call to Action Against Poverty (see Box 15.3).

Another component of this search for justice in the global economy is the fair trade movement. Advocates of fair trade argue that the current trading order is fundamentally biased against the developing world and seek to initiate a more just trading order. This position usually takes two forms. One central concern relates to the prices paid to producers in the developing world, and the campaign is for more equitable prices. In this scenario the market confines poor countries to export goods whose prices are vulnerable to fluctuations and also historically low. The other issue of concern relates to labour standards. In this view international trade is unfair because the internationalization of production leads to the exploitation of workers in the developing world (Sengenberger and Wilkinson, 1995, p. 112). Trade is an important part of this process since production is largely for export.

Box 15.3   The Global Call to Action Against Poverty

The Global Call to Action Against Poverty (www.whiteband.org) is a coalition of groups around the world that mounted an intense mobilization campaign to call attention to global poverty issues and solutions in 2005. In the United Kingdom and several other developed countries it took the form of the Make Poverty History Campaign. The Make Poverty History initiative ran stark television commercials featuring movie and music personalities marking the death of a person in poverty every few seconds. The campaign urged supporters to wear white armbands as a sign of their concern. Letter-writing campaigns and large-scale meetings were used to put pressure on political leaders in developed states to make global poverty alleviation a priority.

The Make Poverty History campaign advocated a number of changes to the operation of global governance (www.makepovertyhistory.org). On the trade front, they demanded increased access for developing countries to developed countries' markets and increased protection for developing countries. With regard to debt, the campaign called for cancellation of debt for all those countries unable to pay. On finance issues the demand is for more and better aid, while undemocratic conditionality on loans should be eliminated. Fighting corruption is a final element in the campaign. These campaigns had some success in raising poverty issues in 2005, but the struggle to implement this alternative global governance agenda continues.

Democracy and regulation

The increasing globalization of the world economy has been accompanied by increasing global regulation. For example, since the early 1990s international institutions such as the IMF, World Bank and WTO have taken on a more prominent role in governing the global economy. Rules and norms are needed to guide state, corporate and citizen activity in this environment. However, new forms of regulation raise difficult issues about democratic control over the regulators and the process of creating rules and norms. The impression that existing regulatory structures serve the needs of the rich and powerful has led to considerable public unease about global governance.

A good example of this unease can be found in the area of financial regulation. Following the East Asian financial crises, a wide range of actors called for a new form of financial architecture that would safeguard the public interest. During financial crises the regulations governing capital mobility and debt seemed to privilege the owners of capital and punish poor people in developing countries. During 2002 a series of financial scandals at a number of large US companies such as Enron raised serious questions about the degree to which accounting regulations and stock market practices hurt the public interest because they facilitated corporate theft and plunder. Public unease over the direction of the global economy was heightened by these regulation failures.

In April 2000 Joseph Stiglitz, a former Chief Economist and Senior Vice-President of the World Bank, wrote, 'Next week's meeting of the International Monetary Fund will bring to Washington DC many of the same demonstrators who thrashed the World Trade Organization in Seattle last fall. They'll say the IMF is arrogant. They'll say the IMF doesn't really listen to the developing countries it is supposed to help. They'll say the IMF is secretive and insulated from democratic accountability. They'll say the IMF's economic "remedies" often make things worse – turning slowdowns into recessions and recessions into depressions' (2000). Stiglitz concedes that the demonstrators do have a point – an opinion in sharp contrast with the views of most mainstream commentators. Stiglitz's comments go to the heart of a current challenge to institutions of global governance. A critical issue that we have touched on at various times in this book is the subject of the legitimacy of institutions of global governance, and this issue will remain important in the early part of the 21st century. There is currently official and popular dissatisfaction with many institutions of global governance and one of the challenges ahead will be to find ways to ensure that these institutions meet current tests of democratic control. The global financial crisis of 2008–9 once again raised the issue of democratic control over financial regulation, but the answers were no more clear.

Few theorists or practitioners would disagree with the claim of a former UN Secretary-General that 'Respect for democratic principles at all levels of social existence is crucial in communities, within states, and within the international community' (Boutros Ghali, 1995, p. 2). While consensus exists concerning the spread of democracy, none is forthcoming concerning the reasons for the upsurge of interest in global democracy. The final two decades of the 20th century witnessed a sharp increase in the number of democratic states giving rise to what has been termed the 'third wave' of democratization (Huntington, 1991). As a result of democratization processes in Asia, Africa, Latin America and Europe, democracy has become an unquestioned global norm. There has been a burgeoning literature on the causes of democratization, the theory and practice of democracy, and the global order and democracy. But democracy remains an aspiration for many of the world's peoples, a goal proclaimed by almost all politicians wherever they reside, and a crucial political value in the 21st century. It is difficult to envisage a serious political party or politician that did not claim attachment to the values embodied within democratic constitutions. The reality may well fall far short of the ideal and it may be that the date for a transition to democracy is postponed into the future, but across the globe democracy has triumphed as the preferred form of government. Democracy thus stands as a crucial test of the legitimacy of political arrangements in the contemporary world. In other words, institutions lacking in democratic features are held to be illegitimate and, by extension, unjust. The ramifications of the triumph of democracy are evident in sub-national, national and international politics. There has been a diffusion of democratic norms – at the core of recent protests against the international economic institutions the central issue is one of democratic governance.

The changing global economic order poses fundamental questions for the exercise of global democratic governance. Three disjunctures in the global system challenge the image of increasing global democracy presented above. First, a key aspect of globalization has been the creation of new non-state centres of authority (Cutler, Haufler and Porter, 1999; Hall and Biersteker, 2002). One feature of this is what can be termed the 'privatization of regulation' (Cutler, 1995; Sinclair, 1994). Policy decisions taken by, for example, financial institutions can have profound effects on the policies of governments and inter-governmental organizations. Second, there are limitations on state sovereignty in the sense that the authority and power of national authorities is undermined by the creation of regional and global organizations. In other words, international organizations are not to be conceived as solely the instruments of states. Another centre of authority is to be found in the increased influence of international organizations. Through the expanded mandate of organizations like the European Union and the WTO their member governments and their citizens are increasingly subject to new forms of regulation over which there is little direct control. Finally, the development of international economic law is creating a system in which political authority is migrating to regional and global centres without a proper system of checks and balances.

One response to these developments is to claim that these international economic organizations (IEOs) remain firmly inter-governmental, and therefore are democratic because they are accountable to their member states. It can be argued that this claim fails to recognize shifting authority patterns and structures in a changing world order. For example, both through the impact on state preferences and directly on the bureaucracy of such organizations, non-state actors influence the agendas and functioning of global institutions. Any assessment of the role of international economic institutions must therefore begin from a recognition of the transformation in multilateralism (O'Brien *et al.*, 2000). No longer can multilateralism be conceived solely in state-centric terms – that is, states are no longer the only salient actors in the construction of multilateral regimes. IEOs in this perspective are assessed not solely on their ability to fulfil the needs of states but rather on whether they meet the aspirations of social movement actors as well as states. It is within this context of change that the democratic credentials of IEOs have to be assessed. From this perspective representation can be conceived as concern for the interests of stakeholders. Institutions of global governance will fail to meet the test of democratic control in the absence of transparent procedures, access for non-governmental groups and mechanisms through which policy can be explained and justified to the range of stakeholders.

Some political theorists (Held, 1995) have attempted to project national democratic institutions onto the international stage to remedy the problem of democratic deficits in a globalizing era. Attempts to have international parliaments seem premature given the decentralization of the international system. An alternative approach has been developed by Coleman and Porter (2000), who have suggested the application of six criteria to judging the degree of democracy surrounding a particular institution or regime. The criteria are: transparency, openness to direct participation, quality of discourse, representation, effectiveness and fairness. They argue that international governance arrangements can be modified to improve performance on these measures without rebuilding domestic institutions such as legislatures at the international level. For example, transparency can be increased by providing clear and timely information about an institution's operations.

Participation in the policy process can be increased by greater consultation with a wide range of interests. The quality of discourse can be improved by launching education campaigns and fostering debate around key issues. Representation concerns can be mitigated by creating institutional linkages with concerned parties. Effectiveness may be increased by streamlining decision-making processes and developing institutional autonomy. Fairness would be bolstered by procedures deemed to be legitimate and policy outcomes that were sensitive to the distribution of costs and benefits.

Conclusion

This chapter focused attention on one of the themes running through the book, namely the issue of governance. In the second part of the book we examined governance structures (or the lack of them) in various historical periods. In the third part of the book, examining key frameworks in the contemporary global political economy, we noted the importance of governance institutions for the functioning of the global economy. In this chapter we outlined how governance is accomplished in the contemporary global political economy, and discussed the actors involved in this process. The second section of this chapter provided a brief introduction to three key challenges to institutions of governance. We have not suggested solutions to these challenges but have raised some of the difficulties in addressing these issues.

As globalization intensifies, the fate of peoples around the world is increasingly interconnected. Despite rapid advances in technology and production, the world faces daunting challenges of inequality, environmental degradation and democratic governance. Attention to, and action in, the global political economy is needed now more than ever.

Chapter 16

Conclusion: Issues in Contemporary GPE Theory

In providing an introduction to the study of the global political economy this book is itself a product of the material and ideational environment in which it was written. In a dynamic global economy, key concerns of policy-makers, citizens and other participants in this economy will evolve and priorities will change. The explanatory frameworks designed to explain transformations in the global political economy will also change as they reflect changing empirical realities and conceptual innovations. This chapter is centrally concerned with current theorizing in GPE. As the chapter title indicates, one of our starting points is a rejection of *international* political economy in favour of *global* political economy. Nevertheless, in discussing contemporary theoretical developments we will use both international political economy (IPE) and global political economy (GPE) to refer to the field, since IPE, the more established term, remains in frequent usage.

The chapter begins with a review of the framework used in the book and situates our approach in relation to competing explanations of change in the global political economy. In doing so, we restate the two central guiding principles of this attempt to understand GPE. First, we argue that in order to fully comprehend contemporary globalization it is necessary to understand the historical context of current institutions, ideas, policies and practices. Second, we contend that the eclectic framework presented in the book provides a method enabling the reader to transcend the conception of GPE as a field defined by the debate between three competing perspectives.

The second part of the chapter provides an introduction to key current issues and trends. There are many different ways of classifying and categorizing theory in GPE. Benjamin Cohen (2007) has sparked a lively debate about the relative merits of 'American' and 'British' approaches to IPE. His characterization of two independent traditions on each side of the Atlantic, and the respective merits of the schools of thought, has been challenged by Higgott and Watson (2008) and Ravenhill (2008), among others. This exchange underscores the points we make below concerning different strands in contemporary IPE. However, rather than divide the field in geographic terms, we prefer to classify approaches in terms of consolidation, integration and expansion.

Understanding GPE: the eclectic framework revisited

The earlier chapters of this book dealt with theory in several ways. First, we addressed theory directly in the two opening chapters. Chapter 1 began by positioning the field in relations to other bodies of social science knowledge, such as economics and political science. It then moved on to explicitly address theoretical issues in the section on contending perspectives on international political economy. The contending perspectives section outlined the three standard approaches to IPE – mercantilist or economic-nationalist approaches, a variety of liberal theories and a range of critical theories including Marxism. In practice, these approaches are very diverse and individual scholars combine or develop elements of the approaches in a number of different ways. To give readers a sense of these complexities, in Chapter 2 we reviewed the careers of four prominent IPE scholars – Susan Strange, Robert Keohane, Robert Cox and John Ruggie. Their work has ranged across a large number of issues and has been informed by a wide variety of perspectives. The issues that they have been concerned with have also evolved and we highlighted how key themes have become more prominent under the process of intensified globalization. These themes were: the transformation of the state, cooperation, regionalism and inequality. Chapter 2 also examined the question of methodology and the different tools that can be used in theoretical investigations.

A second method of approaching theory has been to deploy a varied mixture of approaches in the 'theoretical perspectives' sections of chapters in Part III. Rather than simply repeating the views of each perspective for each issue area, we highlighted some of the particularly common or useful approaches to global political economy. At the outset we argued that none of the three standard paradigms – economic nationalist, liberal or Marxist – provides sufficiently compelling explanations for the range of issues and actors in the global political economy. These existing approaches to GPE are partial, incomplete and too often inflexible. They thus fail to provide satisfactory explanations of developments in the global political economy. By highlighting a variety of theoretical approaches beyond the traditional core we are able to bring in insights from other perspectives and disciplines. Examples of this included: the Mundell–Fleming model from economics, used in the finance chapter; environmental studies approaches in the environment chapter; feminist theory in the gender chapter; and post-structural approaches in the ideas chapter. The result is a more interdisciplinary approach to GPE which still takes account of insights from traditional perspectives.

Our attempt to explain the evolution and contemporary functioning of the global economy begins from recognition of the complex and multilayered nature of political economy. While the assumption of rational human behaviour underlying rational choice models has something important to tell us about events in the global economy, and makes for parsimonious theory, it is nevertheless deficient in failing to take account of diverse cultural practices and variations in historical experience. Similarly, while structuralist approaches are useful in delineating the determinate social structure within which human action takes place they too often neglect or subsume the role of agency.

To recap, our eclectic approach begins from the assumption that analysis of the global political economy should be based on recognition of six key factors. First, we stress the inseparability of economics and politics. This, we argue, should be an essential characteristic of political economy. Approaches that separate economics from politics tend to reify and freeze economic or political structures and processes. Second, our approach is sensitive to historical change. Thus, not only is the second part of the book concerned with showing how the contemporary global economy came into being, it also demonstrates that concepts are not ahistorical, but arise in specific historical periods and do not have consistent meanings throughout history. The third feature of our approach is a structurationist perspective on the agency–structure debate. Agents and structures are co-determined in complex ways, and empirical analysis rather than abstract theorizing reveals the direction of causality. Fourth, we adopt elements of a constructivist position and detail the salience of ideas or cognitive structures as significant elements in the structuring of outcomes in the global political economy. Fifth, we highlight the importance of institutions and institutional change in analysis of the global political economy. And sixth, our approach to the global political economy is based on recognition of the close relationship between changes in domestic social orders and structures of international order and global political economy.

It should be apparent that our framework is not a random mix of existing theories, as can be seen from a comparison of its main features with those of the dominant paradigms within the academic study of IPE. In other words, it is not based on adopting the most fruitful aspects of each, and making a new synthesis. Liberal theories are based on the assumption of a potential harmony of interests among economic agents. Economic-nationalist and radical theories are based on an assumption of conflict among economic actors. The eclectic framework deployed in this text rejects both founding assumptions and instead posits the existence of both harmony and conflict within the system. Not only are the various issue areas or subsets of economic activity not necessarily subject to the same outcomes, different historical epochs also may give rise to differing results. Trading relations may be conflictual or harmonious depending on, for example, institutions, structures and actors. To assume they are either one or the other in the absence of concrete analysis is to construct a theoretical straightjacket into which the empirical material is placed. However, these comments do not imply support for some form of naked empiricism! As we have demonstrated above, analysis of the global political economy should not begin from a rejection of theoretical categories, and is not based on the assumption that data exists which can be analysed in a non-theoretical manner.

The structure and content of this book constructs an explicit argument concerning the key issues and themes in global political economy. The second section presents a historical introduction to the contemporary global political economy. Unlike most texts on GPE it recognizes the importance of non-European economies and social orders to the development of global economic activity. We show that while the long 16th century was a decisive period in shaping the contemporary world order, cross-border trade and economic activity pre-dating the rise of Europe is central to understanding the evolution of the world economy. Moreover, Part III of the text locates contemporary globalization firmly within an expanded context. It suggests that the debate over whether globalization is a recent phenomenon (i.e., a development of the 1970s) or is a long-term feature of the world economy is a rather sterile and unproductive one. Trans-border economic intercourse has existed for centuries and exhibits features of both fragmentation and integration. The integration of various economic, social, and political orders into a global economy has to take account of quantitative and qualitative features. In other words, it is not only the intensity and extensity (Held *et al.*, 1999) of transactions but also the ideational structures that determine the key aspects of an historical epoch. Thus, to dispute the novel nature of contemporary globalization because trade was more open in the late 19th century is to take a partial view of political economic structures and processes.

In Part III we explored the dynamics of trade, production, finance, labour, gender, development, environment, ideas, security and governance. This selection, we believe, provides a comprehensive introduction to the key structures in the global economy. Given the absence of consensus on the study of IPE this choice of topics is not self-evident. These structures and issue areas were derived from the key assumptions underlying our approach to the global political economy. The structures are fundamental to outcomes in the world economy and each is global in its scope and impact. While few would disagree that production and finance are key structures in the global economy, some may argue that environment and development are less important, while even more would skip over discussions of labour and gender. However, we argue that neither sustainability nor inequality can be dismissed as secondary concerns when studying the global political economy. It has certainly become apparent in the last 20 years that the future of humans and the planet is of immediate concern and the environment can no longer be taken for granted as a sink for waste or source of continuous resources. Similarly, the persistence of global inequality not only restricts the life chances of millions of men, women and children, it occupies the attention of many governmental, corporate and civic actors.

This review of the main features and approach of the text illustrates that GPE remains a contested field. There is no sign that this situation is likely to change in the near future. Below we identify three trends in the field and discuss how they are likely to shape our thinking about the global political economy.

Trends in contemporary GPE theory

The three trends we discern we have termed 'consolidation', 'integration' and 'expansion'. The consolidation of the field is undertaken by scholars who view the subject matter as being the politics of international economic relations. The task here is to build upon a presumed consensus concerning the key questions to be investigated and methods for pursuing that investigation. The second trend is an attempt to combine IPE with other broad political economy traditions such as those in comparative political economy or classical political economy. This group is not as certain as the first group that there is a consensus upon key questions and methodologies. The third trend is expansion of subject matter in terms of geographic scope (to developing countries), new subjects such as consumption and new theoretical approaches such as post-structuralism. This trend drifts even further from the consensus articulated by the first group.

Consolidation

One trend in the field is the attempt to consolidate a politics of international relations approach to IPE. In this approach the boundaries and subject matter of the field are relatively clearly identified. The suitable theoretical approaches and methodologies are generally agreed upon. Interventions seeking to contribute to theoretical reflection in this tradition emphasize similar methodologies rather than challenge the methodological and epistemological convictions of scholars in the field. A recent plea for greater engagement with behavioural economics (Elms, 2008) is a case in point. The task facing scholars and students is to build upon each other's work by solving a number of agreed-upon problems.

A good general statement of this position has been provided by two US specialists outlining the field of IPE in 2003. Jeffry Frieden and Lisa Martin (2003) argue that the subject matter of IPE is the politics of international economics. The issues areas of trade, monetary policy and international institutions have been the central focus of the field, but other areas such as international investment are ripe for investigation. Theoretically, the key challenge is specifying the relationship between domestic and international levels of analysis. To what degree and how does domestic politics influence state decisions and the international level? How does interaction between states impact upon the domestic politics of international economic issues?

This textbook has not adopted a consolidating approach to IPE. A consolidated approach is in evidence in texts such as Grieco and Ikenberry's (2003) *State Power and World Markets*. They focus upon the relationship between states and markets and ask a bounded set of questions such as: what accounts for openness and stability in the world economy, how do states shape the economic environment to promote national interests, how are states challenged by the international market and how do states manage openness?

A significant element of this consolidated approach is that, while it claims to reflect 'the principal focuses of North American scholarship ... it is not reflective of much European scholarship' (Frieden and Martin, 2003, p. 118). Indeed, the 'consolidation consensus' reflects the views of a rather small number of prominent US specialists. Many of these specialists work at elite US universities and publish their work in journals such as *International Organization*. This 'American' approach to IPE is contrasted to the work of a variety of other scholars (both in the United States and other countries) working on very different agendas with different methodologies (Murphy and Nelson, 2001). Contributors to a recent special issue of the journal *Review of International Political Economy* (RIPE, 2009) focused on the 'American School of IPE' support the thesis that consolidation around a narrow set of questions and restricted methodology characterizes dominant scholarship in the United States.

The consolidation of IPE has both rewards and costs. The acceptance of a narrow range of questions for investigation and agreement upon a shared method allows researchers to make progress on a number of specific issues. The problem is that a narrow vision shears IPE of its critical edge. The field becomes a tool for problem solving and ignores many crucial questions such as how the world should be transformed, what the good life would look like and we how might get there. This text has cast a wide net to catch a larger number of issues and perspectives than the consolidation approach. This may have come at the cost of some precision and focus, but two other trends in IPE suggest that it is a price worth paying.

Integration

Rather than consolidating the politics of international economics, a different approach has been to try and integrate IPE with other variants of political economy. One effort has been focused upon bringing comparative and international political economy together, while another effort has been made to connect IPE with classical political economy.

If it is perhaps an overstatement to claim that IPE developed in the shadow of comparative political economy, nevertheless IPE research, at least, has been heavily influenced by comparative political economy perspectives, even if this has not been explicitly acknowledged. In many ways IPE is a heterodox discipline willing to borrow liberally from other fields. The interchange between IPE and comparative political economy has to date largely been taken for granted. In other words, to a large extent this development has gone unnoticed. If the main focus of IPE is on global structures, comparative political economy places emphasis on national diversity and varieties of capitalism. However, the IPE literature has given attention to the salience of domestic structures and the changing nature of capitalism.

Concern with the impact of globalization and recognition of the differential impact of globalizing processes orient students of IPE to the importance of institutions and policy regimes in explaining outcomes. And globalization has impacted on studies of comparative political economy as analysts have become increasingly aware of the ways in which global processes affect competition and regulation in national political economies. Thus, IPE researchers and comparative politics specialists have increasingly been engaged in the study of similar issues (Graz, 2001). For example, the debate on the future of the state has engaged comparative political economy specialists (Weiss, 1998, 2003) and IPE scholars (Cerny, 2000).

There are two reasons why linkages between IPE and comparative political economy are likely to become more explicit in the near future. First, increased attention to regionalism and regional processes by students of IPE (Soderbaum and Shaw, 2003; Boas, Marchand and Shaw, 2005) brings to the fore the importance of regional and domestic structures. The complexity of the new regionalism necessitates comparative analysis as well as a focus on systemic structures. Second, renewed emphasis on the public–private interface directs attention to developments at national, regional and global levels. Thus, systemic-level IPE is unable to analyse issues relating to accountability, authority and governance in the absence of detailed assessment of national structures.

IPE developed as a distinct sub-field in the context of International Relations. As such debates in IPE have tended to reflect wider debates in IR, and the growth of IPE has influenced further research in IR. A tradition of classical political economy which can be traced back to the writings of liberal theorists such as Smith and Ricardo and a radical tradition dating from Marx remained open to IPE theorists and, while not part of the mainstream, has influenced scholarship in IPE. IPE shares with classical political economy a commitment to integrating politics and economics. While all perspectives in IPE make some claim to descent from classical political economy, there have been recent calls for a return to classical political economy. As the editors of *New Political Economy* declared, 'What is needed is a new political economy which combines the breadth of vision of the classical political economy of the 19th century with the analytical advances of twentieth-century social science' (Gamble *et al.*, 1996, p. 1). This insistence on a return to classical political economy has recently been heeded by Matthew Watson (2005), who seeks foundations for IPE in the works of Adam Smith, Thorstein Veblen and Karl Polyani.

There are two reasons for recent interest in classical political economy. First, some of the key questions in contemporary economic governance are the same as those preoccupying the classical economists. At the centre of contemporary concerns are the twin issues of relative national wealth and continuing inequality. The failure of both mainstream economic theory and traditional IPE to provide satisfactory answers to these questions has revived interest in classical political economy. Second, global capitalism as a system is under the microscope in a way that it has not been since the middle of the 20th century. It has become increasingly difficult to merely assume capitalism to be a standard and neutral feature in analyses of political economy. Thus, institutional and cultural variables are now to the forefront.

Expansion

A third trend has been the attempt to expand the subject matter of IPE. One strategy has been to take the adjective 'global' seriously and pursue a subject of *global* political economy. A second approach has been to expand by developing new issues of enquiry. Promising new issues include race and consumption in the global political economy.

Nicola Phillips has claimed that 'Despite its pretensions to "global" scope and relevance, the study of International Political Economy (IPE) remains entrenched in a highly specific and narrow set of theoretical, conceptual and empirical foundations' (Phillips, 2005, p. 1). She argues that this restrictive IPE arose from a concern with the economies of the advanced industrial countries and resulted in two kinds of limitation. First, IPE's empirical scope was too narrow (this is a theme we will return to below but in a different manner from Phillips) since it focused on the problems and concerns of these 'core' countries. Second, by privileging and universalizing the historical experiences of Western Europe, Japan and the United States, IPE scholars were transferring concepts of bounded utility to the rest of the world. The concerns raised by Phillips were shared by her co-authors in a volume dedicated to globalizing IPE. These sentiments have also been echoed by Ian Taylor (2005), who contends that the neglect of the developing world by IPE theory and analysis impoverishes IPE. He argues that IPE will only become fully global if it incorporates knowledge about the varied developing societies into its central concerns.

Both Phillips and Taylor acknowledge that, despite claims to the contrary, IPE has for the most part been limited in its concerns. In an age of globalization a discipline that strives to provide explanation for global processes can no longer be based on a narrow empirical and conceptual focus. The globalizing IPE project outlined by Phillips specifically rejects an approach that simply involves giving greater attention to other regions of the world. She contends that such a project should include 'not only an empirical broadening to widen the focus outside the "core" parts of the world and their experiences, but also, crucially, a serious reflection (then) on the theoretical implications of this broadening and the ways in which we might act on them in order to "globalize" the study of IPE' (Phillips, 2005, p. 7).

This project remains at an early stage and the ways in which this challenge will be developed remains unclear. Nevertheless, there are two reasons that suggest increased attention will be given to this aim in the near future. First, it has become increasingly obvious that globalizing processes are unequal and therefore affect different countries, regions and peoples in diverse ways. The failure of IPE to provide adequate explanations for global diversity exposes starkly not only its empirical but also its conceptual limitations. From the understanding of the state and sovereignty at the centre of much IPE analysis, to the conceptualization of market activity, the simple imposition of concepts developed in the advanced industrial countries is likely to prove unproductive. Moreover, the recognition in the discipline of International Relations that it has characterised much of the world as 'the people without history', to use Eric Wolfe's felicitous phrase, and has therefore neglected them has led to recent scholarship engaging with this marginalization of the developing world (Gruffydd Jones, 2005; Lavelle, 2005). Second, the developing world (or more broadly the non-core societies) is currently perceived to be the source of most instability and violence in the world. The traditional security paradigm and newer approaches to security such as human security perspectives both locate threat and danger whether from religious extremism, collapsed states, refugee flows or environmental collapse as stemming from the non-Western world. Thus IPE's focus is likely to be concerned with (in)stability in the developing world.

IPE scholarship emerged in International Relations at a time when traditional realist and liberal theories struggled to explain interdependence. IPE has expanded the IR agenda both theoretically and empirically and yet, as we have shown above, IPE remains constrained and limited. One of the many ways in which IPE remains bounded is in its narrow agenda. Initially this focused principally on trade and financial issues. Recently there has been some change in that, conceptually, IPE analysts have incorporated the role of corporate actors and civic groups, have shown awareness of social orders and have been sensitive to the interrelationship between domestic and international structures. Empirically IPE has embraced an expanded agenda which includes gender, the role of transnational issues and transnational actors.

However, IPE remains relatively silent concerning issues relating to culture, race or leisure. Unlike gender, which has been integrated into studies of the political, race remains under-theorized in IR and IPE. Studies of the leisure industry, whether sport or fashion, is neglected in IPE. In this respect critical scholarship is no different from conventional approaches. A survey of the two leading British journals of IPE – *New Political Economy* and the *Review of International Political Economy* – for the period 2000–8 finds one article on culture (Drache and Froese, 2006), similarly a single article on the leisure industry (Milanovic, 2005) and none on race.

There are three reasons why these non-traditional issues are likely to become more important for IPE in the near future. First, attention to globalizing processes has ensured that lawyers, economists, sociologists, anthropologists and other social scientists have been theorizing the global and have not been as restricted in their choice of subjects as IPE analysts. For example, a legal scholar has explored the racialized nature of the global economy (Gott, 2000) and an economist has recently written about fashion and style in the world economy (Brown, 2005). An expanded IPE that gives attention to culture, race and leisure is likely to result from conversations between IPE, development studies and comparative political economy. Second, material change in the global political economy is directly related to the three issues under discussion. Processes of global inequality are not only gendered, they are also inherently racialized; leisure consumption accounts for billions of dollars in production and exchange; and cultural issues pervade discussions in national polities. Third, advances of post-structuralist approaches into IPE highlight the degree to which language, culture and identity contribute to the creation and functioning of a global political economy (De Goede, 2006).

Conclusion

Three of the issues discussed above – globalizing IPE, IPE and classical political economy, and comparative political economy and IPE – reflect scholarly discontent with IR and IPE. The final topic discussed (i.e., the silence and marginalization of subjects such as culture, race and leisure) is only starting to spark similar theoretical reflection. Nevertheless, we identify these topics as important for the future development of IPE. We argue that theoretical debates in IPE are essentially the product of two forces. On one hand, they reflect the engagement of IPE scholars with real-world changes. In this respect, current debates are a reflection of the experience of globalization. On the other hand, developments in IPE theory are an outcome of theoretical debates among scholars concerning the precision and adequacy of theories and concepts. On both counts we see room for growth in the scope of IPE.

While one branch of IPE (the consolidation approach) is narrowing the field, other trends are opening up the field to new subject matter. This raises the question about the appropriate boundary for GPE. If the subject is continuously widening, will it expand to encompass all of the social sciences? Will this result in it trying to say so much that nothing of importance is uttered? Post-structuralist approaches in particular run this risk.

Our own view is that GPE does have a core – it revolves around issues of power and inequality in a global economy. Given the complex, multifaceted and protracted nature of the problems facing the world's population, the shift to integration and expansion of IPE theories is a welcome development.

Glossary

Absolute advantage – when a country can produce a product more efficiently than another country using the same amount of resources. Thought, before the theory of comparative advantage (q.v.), to be the basis for trade.

Absolute gain – an increase in volume or value of the total number of units produced or consumed. Often used in contrast to relative gain (q.v.).

Arbitrage – the simultaneous purchase of financial instruments in one market and resale in another market for a higher price.

Balance of payments – the summary of a country's international transactions with the rest of the world over a specified period.

Bretton Woods – the conference at which the International Monetary Fund and World Bank were created was held at Bretton Woods, New Hampshire (USA) in 1944. These two organizations are frequently referred to as the Bretton Woods institutions. The Bretton Woods system is the term given to the liberal economic order established after the Second World War.

Capital market – the market for medium- and long-term financial instruments. The capital market is different from the money market, which is for short-term investments.

Central bank – the official bank of a country which performs a number of key functions, including issuing currency, controlling the money supply and regulating the country's banking and financial institutions.

Common market – a common market exists when the members of a customs union (q.v.) also agree common policies on the freedom of movement of capital and labour.

Comparative advantage – theory of international trade which states that countries will gain from trade if they transfer resources between industries to specialize in the sectors in which they are the most efficient. They need not hold an absolute advantage (q.v.) to gain from trade.

Conditionality – the conditions attached to IMF and World Bank loans requiring the borrowing country to implement budgetary and policy changes as a condition of receiving the loan.

Currency appreciation – an increase in the value of a currency relative to other currencies.

Currency depreciation – a decrease in the value of a currency relative to other currencies.

Customs union – a customs union exists when a group of countries remove barriers to goods among themselves and also adopt a common external tariff regime.

Derivatives – financial instruments derived from securities; for example, futures, options, convertible bonds.

Devaluation – a reduction in the official rate at which one currency is traded for another; that is, a reduction in the value of a national currency in relation to other national currencies. A devaluation promotes exports by making the country's goods cheaper for foreigners and restricts imports by making foreign goods more expensive for domestic consumers.

Division of labour – the process of assigning different tasks to different people (in a society).

Dollarization – the replacement of a national currency with the US currency (or that of another nation).

Economies of scale – the reduction in the average cost of each unit resulting from efficiency gains achieved by an increased production output.

Effective rate of protection – the protection given to an industry by the entire structure of tariffs, taking into account inputs as well as outputs. That is, the effective rate of protection measures the percentage by which a country's trade barriers increase the value-added per unit of output.

Euro – the name given to the single currency used by the countries of the European Monetary Union (EMU).

Euro-currencies – national currencies held in a banking system outside the home country; that is, the country of origin of the currency. Originally, these were dollars held outside the United States in Europe.

Eurodollars – US dollars deposited in banks outside the United States.

Exchange control – government regulation of the purchase and sale of foreign currencies.

Exchange rate – the rate (price) at which national currencies can be bought and sold.

Export-oriented industrialization (EOI) – a strategy to achieve economic growth through the promotion of primarily manufactured exports.

Export processing zone (EPZ) – an industrial zone producing goods for export that has been designated free of all duties and taxes by the government.

Export quotas – non-tariff barriers to trade consisting of a limit on the export of a good, for example, voluntary export restraints (VERs) (q.v.).

Export subsidies – payments made by the government to encourage the export of specific products.

Fixed exchange rate – a system under which currencies are fixed (or pegged) at a set price (official rate) relative to each other. Under such a regime government intervention is necessary to ensure that market rates are close to the official rates.

Floating exchange rate – under a floating exchange rate regime the value of a currency is determined by the foreign exchange market.

Fordism – the term applied to the socio-economic system of mass production and mass consumption.

Foreign direct investment (FDI) – investment which brings control over physical assets by a firm (usually a TNC) into a foreign country.

Foreign exchange – the purchase and sale of national currencies.

Forward exchange rate – the exchange rate applicable in a forward trade that has been agreed on. The 'forward' rate is for a period of 30, 60, 90 or 180 days in the future.

Free trade agreement (FTA) – an agreement between two or more countries that significantly reduces tariffs and trade barriers.

Free trade area – a free trade area exists when a group of countries agree to reduce barriers (tariffs, NTBs, quotas) to trade with each other but maintain separate, independent tariff regimes for the external world; for example, the North American Free Trade Agreement (NAFTA) (q.v.).

General Agreement on Tariffs and Trade (GATT) – the main institutional focus of the international trade regime in the period 1947–94.

Gender – the socially constructed roles, behaviours, attitudes and values which communities and societies considers appropriate for men and women.

Gross Domestic Product (GDP) – the total value of goods and services produced within a country in a specified time period, usually one year.

Gross National Product (GNP) – GDP, plus income earned by domestic residents from overseas investments, minus the income earned by non-residents in the domestic market.

G-7 – a consultative group of the seven major industrialized countries: Canada, France, Germany, Italy, Japan, the United Kingdom and the United States.

G-8 – the G-7 plus Russia.

Group of 77 (G-77) – a coalition of developing countries currently comprising over 130 members.

Heavily Indebted Poor Countries (HIPC) Initiative – a debt relief scheme targeted at reducing the debt burdens of the poorest countries to a sustainable level.

Hedging – a strategy designed to protect against loss through the purchase of one investment to reduce the risk of holding another security.

Import quota – restriction on the import of (a) good(s) into a country specified either in terms of the monetary value or the physical amount of the imported item(s).

Import substitution industrialization (ISI) – a strategy to achieve economic growth through the promotion of domestic industry and the restriction of imports.

International Monetary Fund (IMF) – an international organization created at the Bretton Woods (q.v.) conference (1944) to promote international monetary cooperation. It provides loans to countries experiencing balance-of-payments problems.

Keynesianism – refers to the economic thought of John Maynard Keynes. Keynes argued that full employment and stable macro-economic policies required government intervention in the economy. Government intervention could be in the form of increased government expenditure, or through tax reductions (fiscal policies) or in the form of lowering the interest rate and increasing money supply (monetary policy).

Liquidity – the ease and speed with which a financial asset can be turned into cash.

Macro-economics – studies the behaviour of the economy as a whole. It focuses on phenomena such as inflation, national output and employment.

MERCOSUR – a common market (q.v.) agreement linking Argentina, Brazil, Paraguay, Uruguay and Venezuela.

Monopoly – occurs when one firm or country is the sole supplier of a product. This confers power upon the monopoly holder and may lead to abuse of power.

Most favoured nation (MFN) – the principle in GATT/WTO (q.v.) agreements that stipulates that countries extend to every other country the same degree of preferential treatment.

NAFTA – the North American Free Trade Agreement, comprising Canada, Mexico and the United States.

New International Economic Order (NIEO) – the name given to the coordinated demands made by developing countries (in the 1970s) for reform of the international economic order.

Nominal rate of protection – the protection afforded an industry directly by a tariff and/or a non-tariff barrier on its output; that is, the percentage tariff imposed on a good as it enters a country.

Non-tariff barrier – any non-tariff policy that interferes with exports or imports, for example, quotas and VERs (q.v.).

Official development assistance (ODA) – grants and loans made by developed countries to developing countries.

Portfolio investment – investment by firms in foreign assets which does not bring management and control over the investment.

Quantitative restrictions (QRs) – restrictions on trade, usually imports, limiting the quantity of the good or service that is traded, for example, quotas and VERs (q.v.).

Race – the socially constructed roles, behaviours, attitudes and values that a given society considers appropriate for people on the basis of biological, anthropological or genetic criteria.

Relative gain – refers to whether a country or unit is benefiting more or less than a country or unit with which it is competing. States may value relative gain over absolute gain (q.v.).

Rent-seeking – the expenditure of resources to influence public policy in order to bring about economic returns in excess of those that a competitive marketplace would allow. Rent-seeking typically consists of lobbying government for tax, spending or regulatory polices that will provide a comparative advantage to a particular individual, firm or industry.

Security – a financial asset such as bonds or shares.

Special drawing rights (SDRs) – a reserve asset created by the IMF for use among central banks. The value of an SDR is determined by the average of a weighted basket of currencies (the US dollar, the Japanese yen, the British pound and the euro).

Spot exchange rate – the exchange rate between two currencies for immediate delivery; that is, for trades on the spot.

Structural adjustment loans – finance provided by the IMF and World Bank to developing countries on the condition that the recipient government implement a series of market reforms designed to lessen government intervention in the economy.

Tariff – a tax on goods passing through a customs border. Tariffs are usually applied to the importation of particular goods but may also be applied to exports. Tariffs are used as a protectionist device to restrict imports and as a revenue-raising device.

Transnational corporation (TNC) – a firm that owns or controls production facilities in two or more countries.

Triffin dilemma – The United States could not indefinitely expand the world's dollar holdings and maintain convertibility of the dollar with gold at a fixed price. Since the US gold stock is finite, at some stage foreign holdings of dollars (US liabilities) will be greater than the gold held by the US Treasury.

Voluntary export restraints (VERs) – a self-imposed restriction on a country's exports, usually in response to threats of import restrictions by (a) trading partner(s).

World Bank Group – consists of five organizations. The central organization, the International Bank for Reconstruction and Development (IBRD), was created at the Bretton Woods (q.v.) conference.

World Trade Organization (WTO) – the main institutional framework of the international trade regime. The WTO succeeded the GATT (q.v.) on 1 January 1995.

References

Abbott, F. M., Breining-Kaufmann, C. and Cottier, T. (eds) (2006) *International Trade and Human Rights: Foundations and Conceptual Issues* (Ann Arbor: University of Michigan Press).

Abdelal, R. (2009) 'Constructivism as an Approach to International Political Economy', in M. Blyth (ed.) *Routledge Handbook of International Political Economy (IPE): IPE as a Global Conversation* (London: Routledge), pp. 62–76.

Abernethy, D. B. (2000) *The Dynamics of Global Dominance: European Overseas Empires 1415–1980* (New Haven, CT: Yale University Press).

Abu-Lughod, J. L. (1989) *Before European Hegemony: The World System A.D. 1250–1350* (New York: Oxford University Press).

Acker, J. (2004) 'Gender, Capitalism and Globalization', *Critical Sociology*, 30(1), pp. 17–41.

Afshar, H. and Barrientos, S. (1999) *Women, Globalization and Fragmentation in the Developing World* (Basingstoke: Palgrave (now Palgrave Macmillan)).

Akerlof, G. and Shiller, R. (2009) *Animal Spirits: How Human Psychology Drives the Economy, and Why It Matters for Global Capitalism* (Princeton, NJ: Princeton University Press).

Albrecht, J, Bjorkland, A. and Vroman, S. (2003) 'Is There a Glass Ceiling in Sweden?', *Journal of Labor Economics*, 21(1), pp. 145–77.

Alger, C. F. (1997) 'Transnational Social Movements, World Politics and Global Governance', in J. Smith, C. Chatfield and R. Pagnucco (eds) *Transnational Social Movements and Global Politics: Solidarity Beyond the State* (Syracuse, NY: Syracuse University Press).

Allen, M. (1999) 'Women, Bargaining and Change in Seven Structures of World Political Economy', *Review of International Studies,* 25(4), pp. 453–74.

ALU (1995) 'Towards a UN Labour Rights Convention, Conclusions of the National Consultation Concerning the Social Clause in World Trade Agreements', *Asian Labour Update*, 20, pp. 11–12, 17.

Amin, S. (1976) *Unequal Development* (New York: Monthly Review).

Amin, S. (1997) *Capitalism in the Age of Globalization* (London: Zed).

Amoore, L. and Langley, P. (2004) 'Ambiguities of Global Civil Society', *Review of International Studies*, 30(1), pp. 89–110.

Amsden, A. H. (1989) *Asia's Next Giant: South Korea and Late Industrialization* (New York: Oxford University Press).

Andrews, D. M. (1994) 'Capital Mobility and State Autonomy: Towards a Structural Theory of International Monetary Relations', *International Studies Quarterly*, 38, pp. 93–218.

Aslanbeigui, N. and Summerfield, G. (2000) 'The Asian Crisis, Gender, and the International Financial Architecture', *Feminist Economics*, 6(3), pp. 81–103.

Axelrod, R. and Keohane, R. (1986) 'Achieving Cooperation Under Anarchy: Strategies and Institutions', in K. Oye (ed.) *Cooperation Under Anarchy* (Princeton, NJ: Princeton University Press).

Axworthy, L. (2001) 'Human Security and Global Governance: Putting People First', *Global Governance*, 7(1), pp. 19–23.

Bakker, I. (ed.) (1994) *The Strategic Silence: Gender and Economic Policy* (London: Zed).

Bakrania, S. and Lucas, B. (2009) 'The Impact of the Financial Crisis on Conflict and State Fragility in Sub-Saharan Africa', *Governance and Social Development Resource Centre*, available at http://www.gsdrc.org/docs/open/EIRS6.pdf

Balakrishnan, K. (2008) 'Defence Industrialisation in Malaysia: Development Challenges and the Revolution in Military Affairs', *Security Challenges*, 4(4), pp. 135–55

Baldwin, D. A. (1985) *Economic Statecraft* (Princeton, NJ: Princeton University Press).

Baldwin, R. E. and Thornton, P. (2008) *Multilateralising Regionalism: Ideas for a WTO Action Plan on Regionalism* (London: Centre for Economic Policy Research).

Ballentine, K. and Sherman, J. (2003) *The Political Economy of Armed Conflict: Beyond Greed and Grievance* (Boulder, CO: Lynne Rienner).

Bangura, Y. and Beckman, B. (1991) 'African Workers and Structural Adjustment: The Nigerian Case', in D. Ghai (ed.) *The IMF and the South: The Social Impact of Crisis and Adjustment* (London: Zed).

Bannock, G. (1971) *The Juggernauts* (London: Weidenfeld and Nicolson).

Banuri, T., Khan, S. R. and Mahmood, M. (1997) *Just Development: Beyond Adjustment with a Human Face* (Karachi: Oxford University Press).

Baran, P. A and Sweezy, P. M. (1966) *Monopoly Capital* (New York: Monthly Review Press).

Barbieri, K. (1996) 'Economic Interdependence', *Journal of Peace Research*, 33(1), pp. 29–49.

Barndt, D. (2002) *Tangled Routes: Women, Work, and Globalization on the Tomato Trail* (Lanham, MD: Rowman & Littlefield).

Barnett, R. J. and Muller, R. E. (1975) *Global Reach* (London: Jonathan Cape).

Barraclough, G. (1967) *An Introduction to Contemporary History* (New York: Penguin).

Barrett, S. (1993) 'International Cooperation for Environmental Protection', in R. Dorfman and N. S. Dorfman (eds) *Economics of the Environment*, 3rd edition (New York: W. W. Norton).

Barrientos, S., Kabeer, N. and Hossain, N. (2004) 'The Gender Dimension of the Globalization of Production', *Policy Integration Department Working Papers*, 17, prepared for the World Commission on the Social Dimensions of Globalization (Geneva: International Labour Organization).

Barry, K. (1996) *The Prostitution of Sexuality* (New York: New York University Press).

Bauer, P. T. (1981) *Equality, the Third World and Economic Delusion* (London: Weidenfeld and Nicolson).

Bauer, P. T. (1984) *Reality and Rhetoric* (London: Weidenfeld and Nicolson).

Becchetti, F. and Adriani, F. (2003) *Does the Digital Divide Matter? The Role of Information and Communication Technology in Cross-Country Level and Growth Estimates* (Rome: Centre for International Studies on Economic Growth).

Beckerman, W. (1995) *Small is Stupid: Blowing the Whistle on the Greens* (London: Duckworth).

Beckford, G. (1972) *Persistent Poverty* (New York: Oxford University Press).

Beder, S. (1997) *Corporate Spin: The Global Assault on Environmentalism* (Melbourne: Scribe).

Bello, W. (2000) 'Why Reform of the WTO is NOT the Agenda', available at www.zmarg.org/CrisesCurEvts/Globalism/notreformbello. Last accessed 26 January 2007.

Belsey, C. (2002) *Poststructuralism: A Very Short Introduction* (Oxford: Oxford University Press).

Bennett, A. L. and Oliver, J. K. (2002) *International Organizations: Principles and Issues*, 7th edition (Upper Saddle River, NJ: Prentice-Hall).

Bernard, M. (1994) 'Post-Fordism, Transnational Production and the Changing Global Political Economy', in R. Stubbs and G. R. D. Underhill (eds) *Political Economy and the Changing Global Order*, 1st edition (London: Macmillan (now Palgrave Macmillan)).

Bessis, S. (2001) 'The World Bank and Women: "Instrumental Feminism"', in S. Perry and C. Schenk (eds) *Eye To Eye: Women Practising Development Across Cultures* (London and New York: Zed).

Biersteker, T. J. (1992) 'The Triumph of Neoclassical Economics in the Developing World', in J. N. Rosenau and E. O. Czempiel (eds) *Governance without Government: Order and Change in World Politics* (Cambridge: Cambridge University Press).

Blackhurst, R. and Subramanian, A. (1992) 'Promoting Multilateral Cooperation on the Environment', in K. Anderson and R. Blackhurst (eds) *The Greening of World Trade Issues* (London: Harvester Wheatsheaf).

Blau, F. and Kahn, L. (2003) 'Understanding International Differences in the Gender Pay Gap', *Journal of Labor Economics*, 21(1), pp. 106–44.

Block, F. L. (1977) *The Origins of International Economic Disorder* (Berkeley, CA: University of California Press).

Blustein, P. (2001) *The Chastening: Inside the Crisis that Rocked the Global Financial System and Humbled the IMF* (New York: Public Affairs).

Boas, M., Marchand, M. and Shaw, T. M. (eds) (2005) *Political Economy of Regions and Regionalisms* (Basingstoke: Palgrave Macmillan).

Boli, J. and Thomas, G. M. (1999) *Constructing World Culture: International Nongovernmental Organizations Since 1875* (Stanford, CA: Stanford University Press).

Boserup, E. (1989) *Woman's Role in Economic Development* (London: Earthscan).

Bouchon, G. and Lombard, D. (1987) 'The Indian Ocean in the Fifteenth Century', in A. Das Gupta and M. N. Pearson (eds) *India and the Indian Ocean 1500–1800* (Calcutta: Oxford University Press).

Bourgignon, E. and Morrison, C. (1992) *Adjustment and Equity in Developing Countries: A New Approach* (Paris: OECD).

Boutros Ghali, B. (1995) *An Agenda for Peace* (New York: United Nations).

Bradsher, K. (2009a). 'China Losing Taste for Debt From US', *New York Times*, 7 January.

Bradsher, K. (2009b). 'China Grows More Picky About Debt', *New York Times*, 21 May.

Brand, U. (2005) 'Order and Regulation: Global Governance as a Hegemonic Discourse of International Politics?', *Review of International Political Economy*, 12(1), pp. 155–76.

Brandt Commission (1983) *Common Crisis: North–South Cooperation for World Poverty* (London: Pan).

Braudel, F. (1979) *The Perspective of the World: Civilization and Capitalism 15th–18th Century, Volume 3* (New York: Harper and Row).

Braudel, F. (1994) *A History of Civilizations* (New York: Allen Lane).

Braverman, H. (1974) *Labor and Monopoly Capital: The Degradation of Work in the Twentieth Century* (New York: Monthly Review).

Breslin, S. (2005) 'Power and Production: Rethinking China's Global Economic Role', *Review of International Studies*, 31, pp. 735–53.

Bridges Trade BioRes (2009) 'Trans-Atlantic Beef Hormone Dispute Heats Up Once Again', 9 (1).

Broad, R. (2004) 'The Washington Consensus Meets the Global Backlash', *Globalization*, 1(2) (December), pp. 129–54.

Brower, J. and P. Chalk (2003) *The Global Threat of New and Reemerging Infectious Diseases: Reconciling US National Security and Public Health Policy* (Santa Monica, CA: Rand).

Brown, D. (2005) 'Conspicuous Consumption, Fashion and Style in the Global Marketplace', in P. A. O'Hara (ed.) *Global Political Economy and the Wealth of Nations: Performance, Institutions, Problems and Policies* (London: Routledge).

Brown, M. E., Lynn-Jones, M. and Miller, S. E. (eds) (1996) *Debating the Democratic Peace* (Cambridge, MA: MIT Press).

Brown, S. (2005) 'Foreign Aid and Democracy Promotion: Lessons from Africa', *The European Journal of Development Research*, 17(2), pp. 179–98.

Brown Thompson, K. (2002) 'Women's Rights Are Human Rights', in S. Khagram, J. V. Riker and K. Sikkink (eds) *Restructuring World Politics: Transnational Social Movements, Networks and Norms* (Minneapolis, MN: University of Minnesota Press).

Bull, B., Bøås, M. and McNeill, D. (2004) 'Private Sector Influence in the Multilateral System: A Changing Structure of World Governance?', *Global Governance*, 10(4), pp. 481–98.

Burtless, G., Lawrence, R. Z., Litan, R. E. and Shapiro, R. J. (1998) *Globaphobia: Confronting Fears about Open Trade* (Washington DC: Brookings Institution).

Busse, M. and Spielmann, C. (2003) 'Gender Discrimination and the International Division of Labour', HWWA *Discussion Papers*, 245 (Hamburg: Institute of International Economics), available at www.hwwa.de. Last accessed 25 October 2006.

Buzan, B. (1991) *Peoples, States and Fear*, 2nd edition (Hemel Hempstead: Harvester Wheatsheaf).

Buzan, B., Waever, O. and de Wilde, J. (1997) *Security: A New Framework for Analysis* (Boulder, CO: Lynne Rienner).

Caldwell, L. (1988) 'Beyond Environmental Diplomacy: The Changing Institutional Structure of International Cooperation', in J. E. Carroll (ed.) *International Environmental Diplomacy* (Cambridge: Cambridge University Press).

Callí M. with S. Dell'Erba (2009) 'The Global Financial Crisis and Remittances: What Past Evidence Suggests', *Working Paper 303* (London: ODI).

Carlaw, K., Oxley, L. and Walker, P. (2006) 'Beyond the Hype: Intellectual Property and the Knowledge Society/Knowledge Economy', *Journal of Economic Surveys*, 20(4), pp. 633–58.

Carlson, L. J. (2000) 'Game Theory: International Trade, Conflict and Cooperation', in R. Palan (ed.) *Global Political Economy: Contemporary Theories* (London: Routledge).

Carr, E. H. (1939) *The Twenty Years' Crisis 1919–1939: An Introduction to the Study of International Relations* (London: Macmillan (now Palgrave Macmillan)).

Casson, M. (1991) 'Modelling the Multinational Enterprise: A Research Agenda', *Millennium*, 20(2), pp. 271–85.

Castells, M. (1996) *The Rise of the Network Society* (Oxford: Blackwell).

Caufield, C. (1996) *Masters of Illusion: The World Bank and the Poverty of Nations* (New York: Henry Holt).

Caves, R. E. (1974) 'The Causes of Direct Investment: Foreign Firms' Share in Canadian and UK Manufacturing Industries', *Review of Economics and Statistics*, 56(3), pp. 279–93.

Cecchine, G. and Moore, M. (2006) *Infectious Disease and National Security: Strategic Information Needs* (Santa Monica, CA: Rand).

Cerny, P. G. (1993) 'The Deregulation and Re-regulation of Financial Markets in a More Open World', in P. G. Cerny (ed.) *Finance and World Politics: Markets, Regimes and States in the Post-Hegemonic Era* (Aldershot: Edward Elgar).

Cerny, P. G. (1995) 'Globalization and the Changing Logic of Collective Action', *International Organization*, 49(4), pp. 595–625.

Cerny, P. G. (2000) 'The Competition State', in R. Stubbs and G. R. D. Underhill (eds) *Political Economy and the Changing Global Order*, 2nd edition (Toronto: Oxford University Press).

Chakravartty, P. (2006) 'White-collar Nationalisms', *Social Semiotics*, 16(1) (April), pp. 39–55.

Chamberlain. M. E. (1985) *Decolonization: The Fall of European Empires* (London: Basil Blackwell).

Chang, G. (2000) *Disposable Domestics: Immigrant Women Workers in the Global Economy* (Boston, MA: South End).

Checkel, J. (2004) 'Social Constructivisms in Global and European Politics: A Review Essay', *Review of International Studies*, 30, pp. 229–44.

Chenoy, A. M. (2002) *Militarism and Women in South Asia* (New Delhi: Kali).

Cheru, F. (2002) 'Debt, Adjustment and the Politics of Effective Response to HIV/AIDS in Africa', *Third World Quarterly*, 23(2), pp. 299–312.

Chow, E. N. (2003) 'Gender Matters: Studying Globalization and Social Change in the 21st Century', *International Sociology*, 18(3), pp. 443–60.

CIA (2009) *World Factbook* (Washington DC: Brassey's), available at https://www.cia.gov/cia/publications/fields/2012.html

Clapp, J. (1998) 'The Privatization of Global Governance: ISO 1400 and the Developing World', *Global Governance*, 4(3), pp. 295–316.

Clapp, J. (2001) *Toxic Exports: The Transfer of Hazardous Wastes from Rich to Poor Countries* (Ithaca, NY: Cornell University Press).

Clapp, J. (2006) 'WTO Agricultural Negotiations: Implications for the Global South', *Third World Quarterly*, 27(4), pp. 563–77.

Clapp, J. and Dauvergne, P. (2005) *Paths to a Green World: the Political Economy of the Global Environment* (Cambridge, MA: MIT Press).

Cody, E. (2004) 'In China, Workers Turn Tough', *Washington Post*, 27 November.

Cody, E. (2005) 'For Chinese, Peasant Revolt is a Rare Victory', *Washington Post*, 13 June.

Cohen, B. J. (2007) 'The Transatlantic Divide: Why are American and British IPE so Different?', *Review of International Political Economy*, 14(2), pp. 197–219.

Cohen, E. A. (1996) 'A Revolution in Warfare', *Foreign Affairs*, 75(2), pp. 37–54.

Cohen, E. A. (2004) 'History and the Hyperpower', *Foreign Affairs*, 83(4) (July/August), pp. 49–63.

Cohen, M. A. and Küpçü, M. F. (2009) *Revitalizing US Democracy Promotion: A Comprehensive Plan for Reform* (Washington DC: New America Foundation) http://www.newamerica.net/files/Revitalizing_US_Democracy_Promotion.pdf, last accessed 24 November 2009.

Coleman, W. and Porter, T. (2000) 'International Institutions, Globalisation and Democracy: Assessing the Challenges', *Global Society*, 14(3), pp. 377–98.

Coleman, W. and Underhill, G. (eds) (1998) *Regionalism and Global Economic Integration* (London: Routledge).

Commission on Human Security (2003) *Human Security Now* (New York: Commission on Human Security).

Conrad, J. (1902/1999) *The Heart of Darkness* (New York: Penguin).

Constable, C. (2006) 'Brides, Maids, and Prostitutes: Reflections on the Study of "Trafficked" Women', *PORTAL Journal of Multidisciplinary International Studies*, 3(2).

Cook, P. and Kirkpatrick, C. (1994) 'Globalisation, Regionalization and Third World Development', *Regional Studies*, 31(1), pp. 55–66.

Cooper, R. N. (1987) *The International Monetary System: Essays in World Economics* (Cambridge, MA: MIT Press).

Coote, B. (1992) *The Trade Trap* (Oxford: Oxfam).

Cox, R. W. (1977) 'Labor and Hegemony', *International Organization*, 31, pp. 385–424.

Cox, R. W. (1979) 'Ideologies and the NIEO: Reflections on Some Recent Literature', *International Organisation*, 33, pp. 370–95.

Cox, R. W. (1983) 'Gramsci, Hegemony and International Relations: An Essay in Method', *Millennium*, 12(2), pp. 162–75.

Cox, R. W. (1986) 'Social Forces, States and World Order: Beyond International Relations Theory', in R. Keohane (ed.) *Neorealism and its Critics* (New York: Columbia University Press).

Cox, R. W. (1987) *Production, Power, and World Order: Social Forces in the Making of History* (New York: Columbia University Press).

Cox, R. W. (1996a) (with T. Sinclair) *Approaches to World Order* (Cambridge: Cambridge University Press).

Cox, R. W. (1996b) 'Civilisations in World Political Economy', *New Political Economy*, 1(2), pp. 141–56.

Cox, R. W. (2002a) 'Reflections and Transitions', in R. Cox (with M. Schechter) (ed.) *The Political Economy of a Plural World: Critical Reflections on Power, Morals and Civilization* (London: Routledge), pp. 26–43.

Cox, R. W. (2002b) 'The Covert World', in R. Cox (with M. Schechter) (ed.) *The Political Economy of a Plural World: Critical Reflections on Power, Morals and Civilization* (London: Routledge), pp. 118–38.

Cox, R. W. and Jacobson, H. K. (1974) *The Anatomy of Influence: Decision Making in International Organization* (New Haven, CT: Yale University Press).

Craig, G. A. and George, A. L. (1983) *Force and Statecraft: Diplomatic Problems of Our Time* (New York: Oxford University Press).

Crawford, G. (2005) 'The European Union and Democracy Promotion in Africa: The Case of Ghana', *European Journal of Development Research*, 17(4), pp. 571–600.

Creevey, L. (2002) 'Structural Adjustment and the Empowerment (or Disempowerment) of Women in Niger and Senegal', in R. Datta and J. Kornberg (eds) *Women in Developing Countries: Assessing Strategies For Empowerment* (Boulder, CO and London: Lynne Rienner).

Croce, B. (1941) *History as the Story of Liberty* (London: George Allen and Unwin).

Cronin, A. K. (2002/3) 'Behind the Curve: Globalization and International Terrorism', *International Security*, 55(1), pp. 30–58.

Crosby A. W. (1996) *Ecological Imperialism: The Biological Expansion of Europe, 900–1900* (Cambridge: Cambridge University Press).

Curley, M. and Thomas, N. (2004) 'Human Security and Public Health in Southeast Asia', *Australian Journal of International Affairs*, 55(1), pp.17–32.

Curtin, P. D. (2000) *The World and the West: The European Challenge and the Overseas Response in the Age of Empire* (Cambridge: Cambridge University Press).

Cutler, C. (1995) 'Global Capitalism and Liberal Myths: Dispute Settlement in Private International Trade Relations', *Millennium*, 24(3), pp. 377–97.

Cutler, C., Haufler, V. and Porter, T. (eds) (1999) *Private Authority and International Affairs* (Albany, NY: SUNY Press).

Dadkhah, K. M. (2006) 'Sanctions, Economic', in T.M Leonard (ed.) *Encyclopaedia of the Developing World*, Volume 3 (New York: Routledge), pp. 1386–7.

Dalby, S. (2002) *Environmental Security* (Minneapolis: University of Minnesota Press).

Danaher, K. (ed.) (1994) *50 Years Is Enough: The Case Against the World Bank and IMF* (Boston, MA: South End).

Darwin, J. (1988) *Britain and Decolonisation: The Retreat from Empire in the Post-War World* (Basingstoke: Macmillan (now Palgrave Macmillan)).

Datta, R. and Kornberg, J. (eds) (2002) *Women in Developing Countries: Assessing Strategies for Empowerment* (Boulder, CO: Lynne Rienner).

Dauvergne, P. (2001) *Loggers and Degradation in the Asia-Pacific: Corporations and Environmental Management* (Cambridge: Cambridge University Press).

David, N. (1996) *Worlds Apart: Women and the Global Economy* (Brussels: International Confederation of Free Trade Unions).

Davies, N. (1982) *The Ancient Kingdoms of Mexico* (London: Allen Lane).

Davis, M. (2001) *Late Victorian Holocausts: El Niño Famines and the Making of the Third World* (London: Verso).

De Fraja, G. and Hartley, K. (1996) 'Defence Procurement: Theory and UK Policy', *Oxford Review of Economic Policy*, 12(4), pp.70–88.

De Goede, M. (2003) 'Beyond Economism in International Political Economy', *Review of International Studies*, 29(1), pp. 79–97.

De Goede, M. (2006) *International Political Economy and Poststructural Politics* (Basingstoke: Palgrave Macmillan).

Dean, J. W. and Globerman, S. (eds) (2001) *Dollarization in the Americas?* (Boulder, CO: Westview).

Deere, C. D. and Doss, C. R. (2006) 'The Gender Asset Gap: What Do We Know and Why Does it Matter?', *Feminist Economics*, 12(1/2), pp. 1–50.

Denmark, R. and O'Brien, R. (1997) 'Contesting the Canon: International Political Economy at UK and US Universities', *Review of International Political Economy*, 4(1), pp. 214–38.

Dent, M. and Peters, B. (1998) 'Poverty and Debt in the Third World: Confronting a Global Crisis', *Conflict Studies*, 310, pp. 1–24.

Depledge, J. (2006) 'The Opposite of Learning: Ossification in the Climate Change Regime', *Global Environmental Politics*, 6(1), pp. 1–22.

Dessler, A. E. and Parson, E. A. (2006) *The Science and Politics of Global Climate Change: A Guide to the Debate* (Cambridge: Cambridge University Press).

Diamond, J. (1997) *Guns, Germs, and Steel: The Fates of Human Societies* (New York: W. W. Norton).

Diao, X., Diaz-Bonilla, E. and Robinson, S. (2003) *How Much Does it Hurt? The Impact of Agricultural Trade Policies on Developing Countries* (Washington DC: IFPRI).

Dicken, P. (1992) *Global Shift: The Internationalization of Economic Activity*, 2nd edition (London: Paul Chapman).

Dicken, P. (1998) *Global Shift: Transforming the World Economy*, 3rd edition (New York: Guilford).

Dicken, P. (2007) *Global Shift: Mapping the Changing Contours of the World Economy*, 5th edition (New York: Guilford).

Dickenson, T. and Schaeffer, R. (2001) *Fast Forward: Work, Gender and Protest in a Changing World* (Boston, MA: Rowman and Littlefield).

Dickson, A. K. (1997) *Development and International Relations* (Cambridge: Polity).

Dinesh, K. and Little, D. (2004) 'International Apparel Trade and Developing Economies in Africa', *International Journal of Social Economics*, 31(1–2), pp. 131–42.

Dingwerth, K. and Pattberg, P. (2006) 'Global Governance as a Perspective on World Politics', *Global Governance*, 12(2), pp. 185–203.

Dobson, A. (1990) *Green Political Thought* (London: Routledge).

Dodd, R. and Mills, P. (2008) 'Outbreak: US Subprime Contagion', *Finance and Development*, June, pp. 14–18.

Dommen, C. (2002) 'Raising Human Rights Concerns in the World Trade Organization: Actors, Processes and Possible Strategies', *Human Rights Quarterly*, 24(1), pp. 1–50.

Doremus, P., Keller, W. W., Pauly, L. W. and Reich, S. (1998) *The Myth of the Global Corporation* (Princeton, NJ: Princeton University Press).

Dos Santos, T. (1970) 'The Structure of Dependency', *American Economic Review*, 60(21), pp. 231–6.

Doxey, M. P. (1996) *International Sanctions in Contemporary Perspective*, 2nd edition (London: Palgrave Macmillan).

Doyle, M. W. (1996) *Empires* (Ithaca, NY: Cornell University Press).

Drache, D. and Froese, M. D. (2006) 'Globalisation, World Trade and the Cultural Commons: Identity, Citizenship and Pluralism', *New Political Economy*, 11(3), pp. 361–82.

Draper, P. and Sally, R. (2005) *Developing Country Coalitions in Multilateral Trade Negotiations: Aligning the Majors* (Johannesburg: South African Institute of International Affairs).

Dreze, J. and Sen, A. K. (1989) *Hunger and Public Action* (Oxford: Clarendon).

Dryzek, J. (1996) 'Foundations for Environmental Political Economy: The Search for *Homo Ecologicus*', *New Political Economy*, 1(1), pp. 27–40.

Dunford, M. (2000) 'Globalisation and Theories of Regulation', in R. Palan (ed.) *Global Political Economy: Contemporary Theories* (London: Routledge).

Dunlop, C. (2000) 'Epistemic Communities: A Reply to Toke', *Politics*, 20(3), pp. 135–44.

Dunning, J. (1973) 'The Determinants of International Production', *Oxford Economic Papers*, 25(3), pp. 289–336.

Dunning, J. (1981) *International Production and the Multinational Enterprise* (London: Allen and Unwin).

Dunning, J. (1985) *Multinational Enterprises, Economic Structure and International Competitiveness* (Chichester: John Wiley).

Dunning, J. (1988) *Explaining International Production* (London: Unwin Hyman).

Dunning, J. (1991) 'Governments and Multinational Enterprises: From Confrontation to Cooperation', *Millennium*, 20(2), pp. 225–39.

Earle, E. M. (1986) 'Alexander Hamilton, Fredrich List: The Economic Foundations of Military Power', in Peter Paret (ed.) *Makers of Modern Strategy: From Machiavelli to the Nuclear Age* (Princeton, NJ: Princeton University Press), pp. 215–61.

Eckersley, R. (1992) *Environmentalism and Political Theory* (London: UCL Press).

Eichengreen, B. (1996) *Globalizing Capital: A History of the International Monetary System* (Princeton, NJ: Princeton University Press).

Eisenhower, D. D. (1961) 'Farewell Address', 17 January, available at www.eisenhowermemorial.org. Last accessed 5 March 2009.

Ekins, P. (1989) 'Trade and Self-Reliance', *Ecologist*, 19(5), pp. 186–90.

Elahi, K. (2004) 'Microcredit and the Third World: Perspectives from Moral and Political Philosophy', *International Journal of Social Economics*, 31(7), pp. 643–54.

Elias, J. (2005) 'The Gendered Political Economy of Control and Resistance on the Shop Floor of the Multinational Firm: A Case-study from Malaysia', *New Political Economy*, 10(2), pp. 203–22.

Elias, P. (2006) 'Bioprospectors Raise Ire as They Patent More Life Forms', *Detroit News*, 21 January.

Elms, D. K. (2008) 'New Directions for IPE: Drawing from Behavioral Economics', *International Studies Review*, 10(2), pp. 239–65.

Elster, Jon (1985) *Making Sense of Marx* (Cambridge: Cambridge University Press).

Emmanuel, A. (1972) *Unequal Exchange* (London: New Left Books).

Enloe, C. (1989) *Bananas, Beaches and Bases: Making Feminist Sense of International Politics* (London: Pandora).

Escobar, A. (1995) *Encountering Development: The Making and Unmaking of the Third World* (Princeton, NJ: Princeton University Press).

Esping-Anderson, G. (1990) *The Three Worlds of Welfare Capitalism* (Princeton, NJ: Princeton University Press).

European Commission (1997) *Building the European Information Society for Us All: Final Policy Report of a High-Level Group* (Brussels: European Commission, Directorate-General for Employment, Industrial Relations and Social Affairs).

Faiola, A. (2008). 'The End of American Capitalism?', *The Washington Post*, 10 October.

Fanon, F. (1963) *The Wretched of the Earth* (New York: Grove).

FAO (2002) *The State of Food Insecurity in the World 2001* (Rome: FAO).

FAO (2009) *The State of Food Insecurity in the World 2008* (Rome: FAO).

Feldstein, M. (1992) 'The Case Against EMU', *The Economist*, 13 June, pp. 19–22.

Fine, B., Lapavitas, C. and Pincus, J. (eds) (2001) *Development Policy in the Twenty-First Century: Beyond the post-Washington Consensus* (London: Routledge).

Finlayson, J. A. and Zacher, M. W. (1981) 'The GATT and the Regulation of Trade Barriers: Regime Dynamics and Functions', *International Organization*, 35(3), pp. 561–602.

Finnemore, M. and Sikkink, K. (1998) 'International Norm Dynamics and Political Change', *International Organization*, 52(4) (Autumn), pp. 887–917.

Floyd, K. and Gilks, C. (1998) 'Cost and Financial Aspects of Providing Anti-Retroviral Therapy', background paper for the online conference 'Anti-Retroviral (ARV) Treatment in Developing Countries: Questions of Economics, Equity and Ethics', available at www.worldbank.org/aids-econ/arv/index.htm#Readings. Last accessed 30 May 2006.

Fontana, M., Joekes, S. and Masika, R. (1998) 'Global Trade Expansion and Liberalisation: Gender Issues and Impacts', *BRIDGE Report*, 42 (Brighton: Institute of Development Studies).

Fortune (2009) Fortune Global 500, available at www.money.cnn.com. Last accessed 26 September 2009.

Frank, A. G. (1967) *Capitalism and Underdevelopment in Latin America* (New York: Monthly Review).

Frank, A. G. (1969) *Latin America: Underdevelopment or Revolution* (New York: Monthly Review).

Frank, A. G. (1998) *ReOrient: Global Economy in the Asian Age* (Berkeley, CA: University of California Press).

Freedman, L. (1985) *The Evolution of Nuclear Strategy* (London: Macmillan (now Palgrave Macmillan)).

Frieden, J. (1981) 'Third World Indebted Industrialization: International Finance and State Capitalism in Mexico, Brazil, Algeria and South Korea', *International Organization*, 35(1), pp. 407–31.

Frieden, J. (1987) *Banking on the World* (New York: Harper and Row).

Frieden, J. and Martin, L. (2003) 'International Political Economy: Global and Domestic Interactions', in I. Katznelson and H. V. Milner (eds) *Political Science: The State of the Discipline* (New York: W. W. Norton).

Frobel, F., Heinrichs, J. and Kreye, O. (1980) *New International Division of Labour* (Cambridge: Cambridge University Press).

Fukuyama, F. (1992) *The End of History and the Last Man* (New York: Free Press).

G-20 (2000) News release: 'Meeting of the G-20 Finance Ministers and Central Bank Governors, Montreal', 25 October.

Galbraith, J. K. (1975) *The Great Crash 1929* (London: Penguin).

Galbraith, J. K. (1996) *Money: Whence It Came and Where It Went* (Boston, MA: Houghton Mifflin).

Galtung, Johan (1969) 'Violence, Peace and Peace Research', *Journal of Peace Research*, 6(3), pp. 167–91.

Gamble, A. and Payne, A. (eds) (1996) *Regionalism and World Order* (Basingstoke: Macmillan (now Palgrave Macmillan)).

Gamble, A., Payne, A., Dietrich, M., Hoogvelt, A. and Kenny, M. (1996) 'Editorial Statement', *New Political Economy*, 1(1).

Gamier, D. (2005) *Ayutthaya – Venice of the East* (Bangkok: River).

Garrett, G. (2000) 'Shrinking States? Globalization and National Autonomy', in N. Woods (ed.) *The Political Economy of Globalization* (London: Macmillan (now Palgrave Macmillan)).

GATT (1994) 'Annex 1 C (Trade-Related Aspects of Intellectual Property Rights)', to *Marrakesh Agreement Establishing the World Trade Organization* (Geneva: World Trade Organisation), available at www.wto.org/english/docs_e/legal_e/27-trips_01_e.htm. Last accessed 29 May 2006.

Geddes, B. (2003) *Paradigms and Sand Castles: Theory Building and Research Design in Comparative Politics* (Ann Arbor: University of Michigan Press).

Gereffi, G. and Korzeniewicz, M. (eds) (1994) *Commodity Chains and Global Capitalism* (London: Praeger).

Germain, R. (1997) *The International Organization of Credit: States and Global Finance in the World-Economy* (Cambridge: Cambridge University Press).

Gerth, H. H. and Mills, C. W. (eds) (1958) *From Max Weber: Essays in Sociology* (New York: Oxford University Press).

Gertzl, C. (1995) 'The New World Order: Implications for Development', *Briefing Papers*, 35 (Canberra: Development Bulletin).

Gilbert, A. (1999) *Must Global Politics Constrain Democracy? Great Power Realism, Democratic Peace, and Democratic Internationalism* (Princeton, NJ: Princeton University Press).

Gilhooly, D. (ed.) (2005) *Creating an Enabling Environment: Toward the Millennium Development Goals. Proceedings of the Berlin Global Forum of the United Nations ICT Task Force* (New York: United Nations).

Gill, S. (ed.) (1993) *Gramsci, Historical Materialism and International Relations* (Cambridge: Cambridge University Press).

Gill, S. (2003) 'Globalizing Elites in the Emerging World Order', *Power and Resistance in the New World Order* (New York: Palgrave Macmillan).

Gill, S. and Law, D. (1988) *The Global Political Economy* (Baltimore, MD: Johns Hopkins University Press).

Gill, S. and Law, D. (1993) 'Global Hegemony and the Structural Power of Capital', in S. Gill (ed.) *Gramsci, Historical Materialism and International Relations* (Cambridge: Cambridge University Press).

Gilmore, G. (2009) 'Obama Cites $40 Billion in Defense Procurement Budget', American Forces Press Service, available at www.defenselink.mil/news

Gilpin, R. (1981) *Change and War in World Politics* (Cambridge: Cambridge University Press).

Gilpin, R. (1987) *The Political Economy of International Relations* (Princeton, NJ: Princeton University Press).

Goldin I., Knudsen, O. and van der Mensbrugghe, D. (1993) *Trade Liberalisation: Global Economic Implications* (Paris: OECD).

Goldman, Emily O. and Leo J. Blanken (2005) 'The Economic Foundations of Military Power', in P. Dombrowski (ed.) *Guns and Butter: The Political Economy of International Security* (Boulder: Lynne Rienner), pp. 35–54,

Goldstein, J. and Keohane, R. (eds) (1993) *Ideas and Foreign Policy: Beliefs, Institutions and Political Change* (Ithaca, NY: Cornell University Press).

Goldstein, J., Kahler, M., Keohane, R. O. and Slaughter, A. (2000) 'Introduction: Legalization and World Politics', *International Organization*, 54(3), pp. 385–99.

Goodin, R. E. (1992) *Green Political Theory* (Cambridge: Polity).

Goodman, J. and Ranald, P. (eds) (2000) *Stopping the Juggernaut: Public Interest Versus the Multilateral Agreement on Investment* (Annandale, NSW: Pluto).

Gordender, L. and Weiss, L. (1999) 'Pluralizing Global Governance: Analytical Approaches and Dimensions', in L. Weiss and L. Gordender (eds) *NGOs, the UN and Global Governance* (Boulder, CO: Lynne Rienner).

Gott, G. (2000) 'Critical Race Globalism? Global Political Economy and the Intersections of Race, Nation and Class', *University of California Davis Law Review*, 33, pp. 1503–18.

Gottfried, H. (2004) 'Gendering Globalization Discourses', *Critical Sociology*, 30(1), pp. 9–15.

Graz, J. C. (2001) 'Beyond States and Markets: Comparative and Global Political Economy in the Age of Hybrids', *Review of International Political Economy*, 8(4), pp. 739–48.

Greenaway, D. and Hine, R. C. (1991) 'Introduction: Trends in World Trade and Protection', in D. Greenaway, R. Hine, A. O'Brien and R. Thornton (eds) *Global Protectionism* (London: Macmillan (now Palgrave Macmillan)).

Greenspan, A. (1998) 'The Regulation of OTC Derivatives', Testimony of Chairman Alan Greenspan Before the Committee on Banking and Financial Services, US House of Representatives, 24 July, available at www.federalreserve.gov/

Grieco, J. M. and Ikenberry, G. J. (2003) *State Power and World Markets: The International Political Economy* (New York: W.W. Norton).

Griffin, P. (2007) 'Refashioning IPE: What and How Gender Analysis Teaches International (Global) Political Economy', *Review of International Political Economy*, 14(4), pp. 719–36.

Griffin, P. (2009) *Gendering the World Bank: Neoliberalism and the Gendered Foundations of Global Governance* (Basingstoke: Palgrave Macmillan).

Griffiths, H. (1999) 'A Political Economy of Ethnic Conflict and Ethno-nationalism and Organized Crime', *Civil Wars*, 2(2), pp. 56–73.

Grimwade, N. (2000) *International Trade: New Patterns of Trade, Production and Investment* (London: Routledge).

Griswold, D. (2003) 'Free-Trade Agreements: Stepping Stones to a More Open World', Trade Briefing Paper No. 18 (Cato Institute Centre for Trade Policy Studies), available at http://www.freetrade.org/pubs/briefs/tbp-018.pdf

Gritsch, M. (2005) 'The Nation-state and Economic Globalization: Soft Geo-politics and Increased State Autonomy', *Review of International Political Economy*, 12(1), pp. 1–25.

Gruffydd Jones, B. (2005) 'Africa and the Poverty of International Relations', *Third World Quarterly*, 26(6), pp. 987–1003.

Guardian (2008) 'EU Countries May Use Economic Crisis to Ditch Climate Change Commitments', 9 October.

Guzzini, S. (2000) 'A Reconstruction of Constructivism in International Relations', *European Journal of International Relations*, 6(2), pp. 147–82.

Haas, P. (1990a) 'Obtaining International Environmental Protection Through Epistemic Consensus', *Millennium*, 19(3), pp. 347–63.

Haas, P. (1990b) *Saving the Mediterranean* (New York: Columbia University Press).

Haas, P. (1992) 'Introduction: Epistemic Communities and International Policy Coordination', *International Organization*, 46(1), pp. 1–35.

Hafner-Burton, E. and Pollack, M. A. (2002) 'Mainstreaming Gender in Global Governance', *European Journal of International Relations*, 8(3), pp. 339–73.

Hall, P. and Soskice, D. (eds) (2001) *Varieties of Capitalism: The Institutional Foundations of Comparative Advantage* (Oxford: Oxford University Press).

Hall, R. and Biersteker, T. (eds) (2002) *The Emergence of Private Authority in Global Governance* (Cambridge: Cambridge University Press).

Halliday, F. (1983) *The Making of the Second Cold War* (London: Verso).

Hamilton, A. (1791/1991) 'Report on Manufactures', in G. T. Crane and A. Amawi (eds) *The Theoretical Evolution of International Political Economy: A Reader* (Oxford: Oxford University Press).

Harrison, K. and Sundstrom, L. M. (2007) 'The Comparative Politics of Climate Change', *Global Environmental Politics*, 7(4), pp. 1–18.

Harmes, A. (1998) 'Institutional Investors and the Reproduction of Neoliberalism', *Review of International Political Economy*, 5(1), pp. 92–121.

Harrod, J. and O'Brien, R. (eds) (2002) *Global Unions? Theory and Strategy of Organised Labour in the Global Political Economy* (London: Routledge).

Harvard Magazine (2001) 'A Worldly Professor: Toxic Memo (May–June), available at www.harvardmagazine.com/on-line/050171.html. Last accessed 12 November 2006.

Harvey, David (2009) 'Is this Really the End of Neoliberalism?', *Counterpunch*, 15 March, available at http://www.counterpunch.org/harvey03132009.html#

Hasenclever, A., Mayer, P. and Rittberger, V. (1997) *Theories of International Regimes* (Cambridge: Cambridge University Press).

Hayami, J. (2003) 'From the Washington Consensus to the post-Washington Consensus: Retrospect and Prospect', *Asian Development Review*, 20(2), pp. 40–65.

Heckscher, E. (1919) 'The Effect of Foreign Trade on the Distribution of Income', *Ekonomisk Tidskrift*, 21, pp. 497–512. Reprinted in H. S. Ellis and L. A. Metzler (eds) (1949) *Readings in the Theory of International Trade* (Homewood, IL: Irwin).

Held, D. (1995) *Democracy and the Global Order: From the Modern State to Cosmopolitan Governance* (Cambridge: Polity).

Held, D. (2005) 'At the Global Crossroads: The End of the Washington Consensus and the Rise of Global Social Democracy?', *Globalization*, 52(1) (May), pp. 95–113.

Held, D., McGrew, A., Goldblatt, D. and Perraton, J. (1999) *Global Transformations: Politics, Economics and Culture* (Cambridge: Polity).

Helleiner, E. (1996) 'International Political Economy and the Greens', *New Political Economy*, 1(1), pp. 59–77.

Helleiner, E. (2005) 'The Strange Story of Bush and the Argentine Debt Crisis', *Third World Quarterly*, 26(6), pp. 951–69.

Helleiner, E. and Pagliari, S. (2009) 'Towards a New Bretton Woods? The First G20 Leaders Summit and the Regulation of Global Finance', *New Political Economy*, 14(2), pp. 275–87.

Henderson, J. (1991) *The Globalization of High Technology Production* (London: Routledge).

Herod, A. (1997) 'Labor as an Agent of Globalization and as a Global Agent', in K. Cox (ed.) *Spaces of Globalization* (New York: Guilford).

Herod, A. (2001). *Labor Geographies: Workers and the Landscapes of Capitalism* (New York: Guilford).

Heron, T. (2006) 'The Ending of the Multifibre Arrangement: A Development Boon for the South?', *The European Journal of Development Research*, 18(1), pp.1–21.

Hewson, M. and Sinclair, T. J. (1999) 'The Emergence of Global Governance Theory', in M. Hewson and T. J. Sinclair (eds) *Approaches to Global Governance Theory* (Albany, NY: SUNY Press).

Higgott, R. (1998) 'The Asian Economic Crisis: A Study in the Politics of Resentment', *New Political Economy*, 4(1), pp. 333–56.

Higgott, R. and Watson, M. (2008) 'All at Sea in a Barbed Wire Canoe: Professor Cohen's Transatlantic Voyage in IPE', *Review of International Political Economy*, 15(1), pp. 1–17.

Hines, C. (2000) *Localization: A Global Manifesto* (London: Earthscan).

Hirst, P. and Thompson, G. (1996) *Globalization in Question* (Cambridge: Polity).

Hobsbawm, E. J. (1987) *Industry and Empire: From 1750 to the Present Day* (Harmondsworth: Penguin).

Hobson, J. (1902) *Imperialism: A Study* (London: George Allen and Unwin).

Hobson, J. M. (2004) *The Eastern Origins of Western Civilization* (Cambridge: Cambridge University Press).

Hochschild, A. (1999) *King Leopold's Ghost: A Story of Greed, Terror and Heroism in Colonial Africa* (New York: First Mariner).

Hoogvelt, A. (1997) *Globalization and the Postcolonial World* (London: Macmillan (now Palgrave Macmillan)).

Hopf, T. (1998) 'The Promise of Constructivism in International Relations', *International Security*, 23(1), pp. 171–200.

Horta, K. (1996) 'The World Bank and the International Monetary Fund', in J. Werksman (ed.) *Greening International Institutions* (London: Earthscan), pp. 131–47.

Hoskyns, C. and Rai, S. M. (2007) 'Recasting the Global Political Economy: Counting Women's Unpaid Work', *New Political Economy*, 12(3), pp. 297–317.

Howard, M. E. (2008) *War and the Liberal Conscience* (New York: Columbia University Press).

Howard, M. E. (2009) *War in European History* (New York: Oxford University Press).

Huck-Ju, K. (2001) 'Globalization, Unemployment and Policy Responses in Korea: Repositioning the State?', *Global Social Policy*, 1(2), pp. 213–34.

Hudson, N. F. (2009) *Gender, Human Security and the United Nations: Security Language as a Political Framework for Women* (London: Routledge).

Hufbauer, G. C. and Elliott, K. (1994) *Measuring the Costs of Protection in the United States* (Washington DC: Institute for International Economics).

Hufbauer, G. C., Schott, J. J., Elliott, K. A. and Oegg, B. . (2007) *Economic Sanctions Reconsidered*, 3rd edition (Washington DC: Peterson Institute of International Economics).

Hughes, H. (ed.) (1988) *Achieving Industrialization in Asia* (Cambridge: Cambridge University Press).

Hughes, H. (1989) 'Catching Up: The Asian Newly Industrializing Economies in the 1990s', *Asian Development Review*, 7(2), pp. 128–44.

Hulme, D. and Edwards, M. (eds) (1997) *NGOs, States and Donors: Too Close For Comfort?* (Basingstoke: Macmillan (now Palgrave Macmillan)).

Human Security Centre (2005) *Human Security Report* (Oxford: Oxford University Press).

Huntington, S. P. (1991) *The Third Wave of Democratization in the Late Twentieth Century* (Norman, OK: University of Oklahoma Press).

Huntington, S. P. (1993) 'The Clash of Civilizations?', *Foreign Affairs*, 72(3), pp. 2–49.

Hurrell, A. (1995) 'Explaining the Resurgence of Regionalism in World Politics', *Review of International Studies*, 21(4), pp. 331–58.

Hurrell, A. and Kingsbury, B. (1992) 'The International Politics of the Environment: An Introduction', in A. Hurrell and B. Kingsbury (eds) *The International Politics of the Environment* (Oxford: Clarendon).

Hurrell, A. and Woods, N. (1995) 'Globalization and Inequality', *Millennium*, 24(3), pp. 447–70.

Hymer, S. (1976) *The International Operation of National Firms* (Cambridge, MA: MIT Press).

Hymer, S. (1979) *The Multinational Corporation: A Radical Approach* (Cambridge: Cambridge University Press).

ICFTU (1995a) *From the Ashes: A Toy Factory Fire in Thailand* (Brussels: International Confederation of Free Trade Unions).

ICFTU (1995b) 'Rethinking the Role of the IMF and World Bank: ICFTU Proposals to the Annual Meetings of the Board of Governors of the IMF and World Bank', Washington DC, 10–12 October.

ICFTU (1996a) *Behind the Wire: Anti-union Repression in the Export Processing Zones* (Brussels: International Confederation of Free Trade Unions).

ICFTU (1996b) *No Time to Play: Child Workers in the Global Economy* (Brussels: International Confederation of Free Trade Unions).

IDA/IMF (2009) 'Heavily Indebted Poor Countries (HIPC) Initiative and Multilateral Debt Relief Initiative (MDRI) – Status of Implementation', available at http://web.worldbank.org/WBSITE/EXTERNAL/TOPICS/EXTDEBTDEPT/0,,contentMDK:22326067~menuPK:64166739~pagePK:64166689~piPK:64166646~theSitePK:469043~isCURL:Y,00.html

IHT (1998) 'World Bank Targets the Next Asian Danger: Growing Social Unrest', *International Herald Tribune*, 2 February, p. 4.

Iliffe, J. (1995) *Africans: The History of a Continent* (Cambridge: Cambridge University Press).

ILO (1998) *World of Work*, No. 278 (December), available at http://www.ilo.org/public/english/bureau/inf/magazine/27/news.htm

ILO (2006) *Global Employment Trends: BRIEF, January 2006*, available at www.ilo.org/public/english/employment/strat/download/getb06en.Pdf. Last accessed 26 January 2007.

ILO (2008) *Global Employment Trends For Women* (Geneva: ILO).

ILO (2009) *Global Employment Trends For Women* (Geneva: ILO).

IMF (2005) *World Economic Outlook 2005: Building Institutions* (Washington DC: International Monetary Fund).

IMF (2006a) *IMF Members' Quotas and Voting Power, and IMF Board of Governors* (Washington DC: International Monetary Fund), available at www.imf.org. Last accessed 3 June 2006.

IMF (2006b) *World Economic Outlook 2006: Globalization and Inflation* (Washington DC: International Monetary Fund).

IMF (2008) *World Economic Outlook Database October* (Washington DC: International Monetary Fund)

International Commission on Intervention and State Sovereignty (ICISS) (2001) *The Responsibility to Protect* (Ottawa: International Development Centre), available at http://www.humansecurity-chs.org/finalreport/English/FinalReport.pdf

International Commission on Peace and Food (1994) *Uncommon Opportunities: An Agenda for Peace and Equitable Development: Report of the International Commission on Peace and Food* (London: Zed).

ITU (2006) *World Telecommunication/ICT Development Report 2006: Measuring ICT for Social and Economic Development* (Geneva: International Telecommunications Union).

Jackson, J. H. (1969) *World Trade Law and the GATT: A Legal Analysis of the General Agreement on Tariffs and Trade* (Indianapolis, IN: Bobbs-Merrill).

Jackson, J. H. (2006) *Sovereignty, the WTO, and Changing Fundamentals of International Law* (Cambridge: Cambridge University Press).

James, J. (2001) 'Bridging the Digital Divide with Low-Cost Information Technologies', *Journal of Information Science*, 27(4), pp. 211–17.

Jeffreys, S. (2009) *The Industrial Vagina: The Political Economy of the Global Sex Trade* (Abingdon and New York: Routledge).

Jenkins, R. (2003) 'International Development Institutions and National Economic Contexts: Neoliberalism Encounters India's Indigenous Political Traditions', *Economy and Society*, 32(4) (November), pp. 584–610.

Jingjing, J. (2004) 'Wal-Mart's China Inventory to Hit US$ 18b This Year', *China Daily*, 19 November, available at www.chinadaily.com. Last accessed 17 October 2006.

Joachim, J. (2003) 'Framing Issues and Seizing Opportunities: The UN, NGOs, and Women's Rights', *International Studies Quarterly*, 47(2), pp. 247–74.

Joekes, S. P. (1987) *Women in the World Economy: An INSTRAW Study* (New York and Oxford: Oxford University Press).

Julius, D. (1990) *Global Companies and Public Policy: The Growing Challenge of Foreign Direct Investment* (London: Royal Institute of International Affairs/ Pinter).

Kabeer, N. (1994) *Reversed Realities: Gender Hierarchies in Development Thought* (London: Verso).

Kahl, C. H. (2005) 'Plight or Plunder? Natural Resources and Civil War', in P. Dombrowski (ed.) *Guns and Butter: The Political Economy of International Security* (Boulder, CO: Lynne Rienner), pp. 77–98.

Kahn, M. S. and Knight, M. D. (1986) 'Fund-Supported Adjustment Programs', *Occasional Papers*, 42 (Washington DC: International Monetary Fund).

Kaldor, M. (1997) *Restructuring the Global Military Sector: New Wars* (London: Pinter).

Kaldor, M. (1999). *New and Old Wars: Organized Violence in a Global Era* (Stanford: Standford University Press).

Kaldor, M. (2007) *Human Security: Reflections on Globalizaiton and Intervention* (Cambridge: Polity).

Kant, I. (1795/1991) 'Perpetual Peace: A Philosophical Sketch', in H. Reis (ed.) *Kant: Political Writings* (Cambridge: Cambridge University Press).

Kaplinsky, R. (1991) 'TNCs in the Third World: Stability or Discontinuity?', *Millennium*, 20(2), pp. 257–68.

Kearney, N. (1999) 'Corporate Codes of Conduct: the Privatized Application of Labour Standards', in R. Mayne and S. Picciotto (eds) *Regulating International Business – Beyond Liberalization* (Basingstoke: Macmillan (now Palgrave Macmillan)/Oxfam).

Kearns, A. and Forrest, R. (2000) 'Social Cohesion and Multilevel Urban Governance', *Urban Studies*, 37(5–6), pp. 995–1017.

Keck, M. and Sikkink, K. (1998) *Activists Beyond Borders: Advocacy Networks in International Politics* (Ithaca, NY: Cornell University Press).

Kemp, T. (1983) *Industrialization in the Non-Western World* (London: Longman).

Kennedy, P. (1987) *The Rise and Fall of the Great Powers: Economic Change and Military Conflict from 1500 to 2000* (New York: Random House).

Keohane, R. O. (1984) *After Hegemony* (Princeton, NJ: Princeton University Press).

Keohane, R. O. (1989a) 'A Personal Intellectual History', in *International Institutions and State Power: Essays in International Relations Theory* (Boulder, CO: Westview).

Keohane, R. O. (1989b) *International Institutions and State Power: Essays in International Relations Theory* (Boulder, CO: Westview).

Keohane, R. O. (2002) 'Introduction: From Interdependence and Institutions to Globalization and Governance', in *Power and Governance in a Partially Globalizing World* (London: Routledge).

Keohane, R. O. and Nye, J. (1977) *Power and Interdependence: World Politics in Transition* (Boston, MA: Little, Brown).

Keynes, J. M. (1936) *The General Theory of Employment, Interest and Money* (London: Macmillan (now Palgrave Macmillan)).

Khagram, S., Riker, J. V. and Sikkink, K. (2002) 'From Santiago to Seattle: Transnational Advocacy Groups Restructuring World Politics', in S. Khagram, J. V. Riker and K. Sikkink (eds) *Restructuring World Politics: Transnational Movements, Networks and Norms* (Minneapolis, MN: University of Minnesota Press).

Kindleberger, C. P. (1969) *American Business Abroad* (New Haven, CT: Yale University Press).

Kindleberger, C. P. (1986) *The World Depression 1929–1939* (Berkeley, CA: University of California Press).

Kindleberger, C. P. (1993) *A Financial History of Western Europe*, 2nd edition (Oxford: Oxford University Press).

Kitching, G. (2001) *Seeking Social Justice Through Globalization* (University Park, PA: Pennsylvania State University Press).

Klein, N. (2001) *No Logo: Taking Aim at the Brand Bullies* (New York: St Martin's).

Knorr, K. (1975) *The Power of Nations* (New York: Basic Books).

Kock, K. (1969) *International Trade Policy and the GATT, 1947–1967* (Stockholm: Almqvist and Wiksell).

Kopinak, K. (1995) 'Gender as a Vehicle for the Subordination of Women Maquiladora Workers in Mexico', *Latin American Perspectives*, 22(1), pp. 30–48.

Korinek, J. (2005) 'Trade and Gender: Issues and Interactions', *Trade Policy Working Papers*, 24 (Paris: OECD).

Kotz, D. M. and Wolfson, M. H. (2004) 'Déjà Vu All Over Again: The "New" Economy in Historical Perspective', *Labor Studies Journal*, 28(4), pp. 25–44.

Kovach, H., Neligan, C. and Burall, S. (2002/3) *Power Without Accountability?* (London: One World Trust).

Krasner, S. D. (1976) 'State Power and the Structure of International Trade', *World Politics*, 28(3), pp. 317–48.

Krasner, S. D. (ed.) (1983) *International Regimes* (Ithaca, NY: Cornell University Press).

Krause, K. and Williams, M. C. (eds) (1997)*Critical Security Studies: Concepts and Cases* (London: UCL Press).

Krueger, A. (ed.) (2000) *Economic Policy Reform: The Second Stage* (Chicago: University of Chicago Press).

Krugman, P. (ed.) (1986) *Strategic Trade Policy and the New International Economics* (Cambridge, MA: MIT Press).

Krugman, P. (1987) 'Is Free Trade Passé?', *Journal of Economic Perspectives*, 1(2), pp. 131–44.

Krugman, P. (2005) 'The Chinese Connection', *New York Times*, 20 May.

Krugman, P. (2008) *Depression Economics* (New York: W. W. Norton).

Krugman, P. and Venables, A. J. (1995) 'Globalization and the Inequality of Nations', *Quarterly Journal of Economics*, 110(4), pp. 857–80.

Kuznets, S. (1966) *Modern Economic Growth* (New Haven, CT: Yale University Press).

Kwa, Aileen (2003) *Power Politics in the WTO* (Bangkok: Focus on the Global South).

Laferrière, E. (1994) 'Environmentalism and the Global Divide', *Environmental Politics*, 3(1), pp. 91–113.

Lall, S. (1991) 'Multinational Enterprises and Developing Countries: Some Issues for Research in the 1990s', *Millennium*, 20(2), pp. 251–6.

Lall, S. and Streeten, P. (1977) *Foreign Investment, Transnationals and Developing Countries* (London: Macmillan (now Palgrave Macmillan)).

Landes, D. S. (1998) *The Wealth and Poverty of Nations* (New York: W. W. Norton).

Lanoszka, A. (2003) 'The Global Politics of Intellectual Property Rights and Pharmaceutical Drug Policies in Developing Countries', *International Political Science Review*, 24(2), pp. 181–97.

Lasch, C. (1995) *The Revolt of the Elites and the Betrayal of Democracy* (New York: W. W. Norton).

Lavelle, K. C. (2005) 'Moving in from the Periphery: Africa and the Study of International Political Economy', *Review of International Political Economy*, 12(2), pp. 364–79.

Lenin, V. I. (1917/1969) *Imperialism, the Highest Stage of Capitalism* (New York: International).

Letuchamanan, R. (2000) 'Testing the Pollution Haven Hypothesis', in P. Könz, C. Bellmann, L. Assuncao and R. Melendez-Ortiz (eds) *Trade, Environment and Sustainable Development: Views from SubSaharan Africa and Latin America* (Geneva: International Center for Trade and Sustainable Development; Tokyo: Institute of Advanced Studies, United Nations University).

Lever, H. and Huhne, C. (1986) 'The Demand for Credit and the Supply of Credit', in *Debt and Danger* (Boston, MA: Atlantic Monthly).

Levy, D. (1997) 'Environmental Management as Political Sustainability', *Organization and Environment*, 10(2), pp. 126–47.

Lim, L. L. (ed.) (1998) *The Sex Sector: The Economic and Social Bases of Prostitution in Southeast Asia* (Geneva: ILO).

Lipschutz, R. D. (2005) 'Power, Politics and Global Civil Society', *Millennium*, 33(3), pp. 747–70.

List, F. (1885/1991) 'Political and Cosmopolitical Economy', in G. T. Crane and A. Amawi (eds) *The Theoretical Evolution of International Political Economy: A Reader* (Oxford: Oxford University Press).

Litfin, K. T. (1994) *Ozone Discourses: Science and Politics in Global Environmental Cooperation* (New York: Columbia University Press).

Lo, A. (2004) 'The Adaptive Market Hypothesis: Market Efficiency from an Evolutionary Perspective', *Journal of Portfolio Management*, 30th Anniversary Issue, pp. 15–29.

López-Claros, A. and Zahidi, S. (2005) *Women's Empowerment: Measuring the Global Gender Gap* (Geneva: World Economic Forum).

Madeley, J. (1992) *Trade and the Poor* (London: Intermediate Technology).

Madrick, J. (2001) 'The Business Media and the New Economy', *Research Papers*, R-24 (Joan Shorenstein Center on the Press, Politics and Public Policy, John F. Kennedy School of Government, Harvard University).

Maier, C. S. (1977) 'The Politics of Productivity: Foundations of American International Economic Policy after World War II', *International Organization*, 31, pp. 607–33.

Maizels, A. and Nisanke, M. K. (1984) 'Motivations for Aid to Developing Countries', *World Development*, 12(9), pp. 879–900.

Mansfield, E. S. and Snyder, J. (1995) 'Democratization and War', *Foreign Affairs*, 74(3), pp. 79–97.

Marchand, M. and Runyan, A. (2000) *Gender and Global Restructuring* (London: Routledge).

Marcus, R. (1993) 'Woman Chosen as Attorney General', *Washington Post*, 12 February, p. 2.

Marks, G., Hooge, L. and Blank, K. (1996) 'European Integration from the 1980s: State-Centric vs Multi-level Governance,' *Journal of Common Market Studies*, 34(3) (September), pp. 341–78.

Marx, K. and Engels, F. (1848/1977) 'The Communist Manifesto', in D. McLellan (ed.) *Karl Marx: Selected Writings* (Oxford: Oxford University Press).

Mastandumo, M. (1998) 'Economics and Security in Statecraft and Scholarship', *International Organization*, 52(4), pp. 825–54.

Matthews, A. (2008) 'The European Union's Common Agricultural Policy and Developing Countries: the Struggle for Coherence', *Journal of European Integration*, 30(3), pp. 381–99.

May, C. (2005) 'Intellectual Property Rights', in D. Kelly and W. Grant (eds) *The Politics of International Trade: Actors, Issues, and Regional Dynamics* (London: Palgrave Macmillan), pp. 164–82.

Mayne, R. and Picciotto, S. (eds) (1999) *Regulating International Business: Beyond Liberalization* (Basingstoke: Macmillan (now Palgrave Macmillan)/Oxfam).

McKinsey & Co. (2009) 'Will Consumer Debt Reduction Cripple the Economy?', available at http://www.mckinsey.com/mgi/publications/us_consumers/

McLeod, R. H. and Garnaut, R. (1998) *East Asia in Crisis: From Being a Miracle to Needing One?* (London: Routledge).

McMichael, P. (1996) *Development and Social Change: A Global Perspective* (Thousand Oaks, CA: Pine Forge).

McMichael, P. (1997) 'Rethinking Globalization: The Agrarian Question Revisited', *Review of International Political Economy*, 4(4), pp. 630–62.

McNeill, J., Winsemius, P. and Yakushiji, T. (1991) *Beyond Interdependence: The Meshing of the World's Economy and the Earth's Ecology* (New York: Oxford University Press).

McNeill, W. (1982) *The Pursuit of Power: Technology, Armed Force, and Society since AD 1000* (Chicago: University of Chicago Press).

Meadows, D. and Meadows, D. (1972) *The Limits to Growth* (London: Earth Island).

Meadows, D., Meadows, D. and Randers, J. (1993) *Beyond the Limits: Global Collapse or a Sustainable Future* (London: Earthscan).

Meyn, M. and Kennan, J. (2009) 'The Implications of the Global Financial Crisis for Developing Countries' Export Volumes and Values', *Working Paper 305* (London: ODI).

Michael, M. (2001) 'Jubilee 2000: Drop the Debt, Not the Campaign', *Dollars and Sense*, 11, p. 11.

Mies, M. (1998) *Patriarchy and Accumulation on a World Scale: Women in the International Division of Labour* (London: Zed).

Mihevc, J. (1995) *The Market Tells Them So: The World Bank and Economic Fundamentalism in Africa* (London: Zed).

Milanovic, B. (2005) 'Globalization and Goals: Does Soccer Show the Way?', *Review of International Political Economy*, 12(5), pp. 829–50.

Mill, J. S. (1859/1980) *On Liberty* (Harmondsworth: Penguin).

Milner, H. (1997) *Interests, Institutions and Information: Domestic Politics and International Relations* (Princeton, NJ: Princeton University Press).

Mishel, L. (2006) 'CEO-to-Worker Pay Imbalance Grows', *Snapshot*, Washington: Economic Policy Institute, 21 June, available at www.epi.org

Mishra, R. (1999) *Globalization and the Welfare State* (Cheltenham: Edward Elgar).

Miskimin, H. A. (1975) *The Economy of Early Renaissance Europe 1300–1460* (Cambridge: Cambridge University Press).

Mitter, S. (1986) *Common Fate, Common Bond: Women in the Global Economy* (London: Pluto).

Moghadam, V. M. (1999) 'Gender and Globalization: Female Labour and Women's Mobilization', *Journal of World-Systems Research*, 5(2), pp. 367–88.

Moghadam, V. M. (2005) 'The "Feminization of Poverty" and Women's Human Rights', *SHS Papers in Women's Studies/Gender Research*, 2 (Paris: UNESCO).

Moody, K. (1997) *Workers in a Lean World: Unions in the International Economy* (London: Verso).

Moravcsik, A. (1997) 'Taking Preferences Seriously: A Liberal Theory of International Politics', *International Organization*, 51(4), pp. 513–53.

Morgenthau, H. J. (1973) *Politics Among Nations: The Struggle for Power and Peace*, 5th edition (New York: Alfred A. Knopf).

Morris, D. (1989) 'Free Trade: The Great Destroyer', *Ecologist*, 19(5), pp. 190–5.

Moser, C. O. and Clark, F. C. (eds) (2001) *Victims, Perpetrators or Actors? Gender, Armed Conflict and Political Violence* (New York: Zed).

Moss, T. (2006) 'The G-8's Multilateral Debt Relief Initiative and Poverty Reduction in Sub-Saharan Africa', *African Affairs*, 105(419), pp. 285–93.

Mote, F. W. (1999) *Imperial China: 900–1800* (Cambridge, MA: Harvard University Press).

Mudzafar, J. (2001) 'Transfer of Technology in Marketing', available at www.sibelink.com.my/g15magazine

Murphy, C, and Nelson, D. (2001) 'International Political Economy: A Tale of Two Heterodoxies', *British Journal of Politics and International Relations*, 3(3) (October), pp. 393–412.

Myrdal, G. (1968) *Asian Drama: An Enquiry into the Poverty of Nations* (London: Penguin).

Nagar, R., Lawson, V., McDowell, L. and Hanson, S. (2002) 'Locating Globalization: Feminist (Re)Readings of the Subject and Spaces of Globalization', *Economic Geography*, 78(3), pp. 57–84.

Naim, M. (2000a) 'Fads and Fashion in Economic Reforms: Washington Consensus or Washington Confusion?', *Third World Quarterly*, 21(3), pp. 505–28.

Naim, M. (2000b) 'Washington Consensus or Washington Confusion?', *Foreign Policy*, 118, pp. 87–103.

Narayan, D., Patel, R., Schafft, K., Rademacher, A. and Koch-Schulte, S. (2000) *Can Anyone Hear Us? Voices of the Poor, Volume 1* (New York: Oxford University Press).

Narlikar, A and Odell, J. S. (2006) 'The Strict Distributive Strategy for a Bargaining Coalition: The Like Minded Group and the World Trade Organization, 1998–2001', in J. S. Odell (ed.) *Negotiating Trade: Developing Countries in the WTO and NAFTA* (Cambridge: Cambridge University Press), pp. 115–44.

Narlikar, A. and Tussie, D. (2004) 'The G-20 at the Cancun Ministerial: Developing Countries and their Evolving Coalitions in the WTO', *World Economy*, 27(7), pp. 947–66.

Neumann, S and von Hagen, M. (1986) 'Engels and Marx on Revolution, War and the Army in Society', in P. Paret (ed.) *Makers of Modern Strategy: From Machiavelli to the Nuclear Age* (Princeton, NJ: Princeton University Press), pp. 262–80.

Newland, K. (1988) 'From Transnational Relationships to International Relations: Women in Development and the International Decade for Women', *Millennium*, 17(3), pp. 507–16.

Nikiforuk, A. (1996) *The Fourth Horseman: A Short History of Plagues, Scourges and Emerging Viruses* (Toronto: Penguin).

Nordås, H. K. (2003) 'The Impact of Trade Liberalization on Women's Job Opportunities and Earnings in Developing Countries', *World Trade Review*, 2(2), pp. 221–31.

Nordstrom, H. and Vaughan, S. (1999) *Trade and Environment* (Geneva: WTO).

Norris, P. (2001) *Digital Divide: Civic Engagement, Information Poverty, and the Internet Worldwide* (New York: Cambridge University Press).

Nye, J. S. and Donahue, J. D. (eds) (2000) 'Introduction', in *Governance in a Globalizing World* (Washington DC: Brookings Institution).

O'Brien, R. (1995) 'North American Integration and International Relations Theory', *Canadian Journal of Political Science*, 28(4), pp. 693–724.

O'Brien, R. (1998) 'Shallow Foundations: Labour and the Selective Regulation of Free Trade', in G. Cook (ed.) *The Economics and Politics of International Trade* (London: Routledge).

O'Brien, R. (2000) 'Labour and IPE: Rediscovering Human Agency', in R. Palan (ed.) *Global Political Economy: Contemporary Theories* (New York: Routledge).

O'Brien, R. (2002) 'The Varied Paths to Minimum Global Labour Standards', in J. Harrod and R. O'Brien (eds) *Global Unions? Theory and Strategy of Organised Labour in the Global Political Economy* (London: Routledge).

O'Brien, R. (2003) 'Paths to Reforming Global Governance', in R. Sandbrook (ed.) *Civilizing Globalisation* (Albany, NY: SUNY Press), pp. 123–37.

O'Brien, R. (2009) 'North American Regional Report: Neoliberalism Wounded', *Global Social Policy*, 9(1), pp. 127–33.

O'Brien, R., Goetz, A. M., Scholte, J. A. and Williams, M. (2000) *Contesting Global Governance: Multilateral Economic Institutions and Global Social Movements* (Cambridge: Cambridge University Press).

O'Neal, J. R. and Russett, B. M. (1997) 'The Classical Liberals Were Right: Democracy, Interdependence, and Conflict, 1950–1985', *International Studies Quarterly*, 41(2), pp. 267–93.

O'Neal, J. R., O'Neal, F. H. and Maoz, Z. (1996) 'The Liberal Peace: Interdependence, Democracy, and International Conflict, 1950–1985', *Journal of Peace Research*, 33(1), pp.11–28.

Odell, J. (2001) 'Case Study Methods in International Political Economy', *International Studies Perspectives*, 2, pp. 161–76.

Ohlin, B. (1933) *Interregional and International Trade* (Cambridge, MA: Harvard University Press).

Ohmae, K. (1990) *The Borderless World* (London: Fontana).

Önis, Z and Şenses, F. (2005) 'Rethinking the Emerging post-Washington Consensus', *Development and Change*, 36(2), pp. 263–90.

O'Riordan, T. (1976) *Environmentalism* (London: Pion).

Oxfam International (2000) *Debt Relief and Poverty Reduction: Failing to Deliver* (Oxford: Oxfam), available at: www.oxfam.org.uk. Last accessed 26 January 2007.

Oxfam International (2002) *Rigged Rules and Double Standards: Trade, Globalisation, and the Fight against Poverty* (Oxford: Oxfam).

Pakenham, T. (1991) *The Scramble for Africa 1876–1912* (London: Abacus).

Palan, R. (1998) 'Trying to Have Your Cake and Eating It: How and Why the State System Has Created Offshore', *International Studies Quarterly*, 41, pp. 625–44.

Palan, R. (2000) 'The Constructivist Underpinnings of the New International Political Economy', in R. Palan (ed.) *Global Political Economy: Contemporary Theories* (London: Routledge).

Palan, R. (2002) 'Tax Havens and the Commercialization of State Sovereignty', *International Organization*, 56(1), pp. 151–76.

Palan, R. and Abbott, J. (with Deans, P.) (2000) *State Strategies in the Global Political Economy* (London: Pinter).

Parker, G. (1996) *The Military Revolution and the Rise of the West 1500–1800* (Cambridge: Cambridge University Press).

Pauly, L. W. (2000) 'Capital Mobility and the New Global Order', in R. Stubbs and G. R. D. Underhill (eds) *Political Economy and the Changing Global Order*, 2nd edition (Toronto: Oxford University Press).

Pauly, L. W. and Reich, S. (1997) 'National Structures and Multinational Corporate Behaviour: Enduring Differences in the Age of Globalization', *International Organization*, 51(1), pp. 1–30.

Pearce, D. (1990) 'Economics and the Global Environmental Challenge', *Millennium*, 19(3), pp. 365–87.

Pearce, D., Markandya, A. and Barbier, E. (1989) *Blueprint for a Green Economy* (London: Earthscan).

Pearson, R. and Seyfang, G. (2001) 'New Hope or False Dawn? Voluntary Codes of Conduct, Labour Regulation and Social Policy in a Globalizing World', *Global Social Policy*, 1(1), pp. 49–78.

Penrose, E. T. (1968) *The Large International Firm in Developing Countries: The International Petroleum Industry* (Cambridge, MA: MIT Press).

Pepper, D. (1996) *Modern Environmentalism: An Introduction* (London: Routledge).

Persaud, R. B. (2001) 'Racial Assumptions in Global Labor Recruitment and Supply', *Alternatives*, 26(4), pp. 377–99.

Peterson, S. (2002/3) 'Epidemic Disease and National Security', *Security Studies*, 12(2), pp. 43–81.

Peterson, V. S. (2003) *A Critical Rewriting of Global Political Economy: Integrating Reproductive, Productive and Virtual Economies* (London: Routledge).

Peterson, V. S. (2005) 'How (the Meaning of) Gender Matters in Political Economy', *New Political Economy*, 10(4), pp. 499–521.

Peterson, S. V. and Runyan, A. S. (1993) *Global Gender Issues* (Boulder, CO: Westview).

Pettman, J. J. (1996a) *Worlding Women: A Feminist International Politics* (London: Routledge).

Pettman, J. J. (1996b) 'An International Political Economy of Sex', in E. Kofman and G. Youngs (eds) *Globalization: Theory and Practice* (London: Pinter).

Pettman, J. J. (2003) 'International Sex and Service', in E. Kofman and G. Youngs (eds) *Globalization: Theory and Practice*, 2nd edition (London and New York: Continuum).

PGA (1997) *First Conference of the Peoples' Global Action against 'Free' Trade and the World Trade Organisation* (Manila: Peoples' Global Action Secretariat).

Phillips, K. (2008) *Bad Money: Reckless Finance, Failed Politics, and the Global Crisis of American Capitalism* (New York: Viking).

Phillips, N. (2005) ' "Globalizing" the Study of International Political Economy', in N. Phillips (ed.) *Globalizing International Political Economy* (Basingstoke: Palgrave Macmillan).

Picciotto, R. (2003) 'A New World Bank for a New Century', in C. Roe Goddard, P. Cronin and K. C. Dash (eds) *International Political Economy: State-Market Relations in a Changing Global Order*, 2nd edition (Boulder, CO: Lynne Rienner), pp. 341–51.

Pietilä, H. and Vickers, J. (1990) *Making Women Matter: The Role of the United Nations* (London: Zed).

Pinter, F. (2001) 'Funding of Global Civil Society Organisations', in H. Anheier, M. Glasius and M. Kaldor (eds) *Global Civil Society 2001* (Oxford: Oxford University Press), pp. 195–217.

Pio, A. (1994) 'The Social Impact of Adjustment in Africa', in G. A. Cornia and G. K. Helleiner (eds) *From Adjustment to Development in Africa: Conflict, Controversy, Convergence, Consensus?* (New York: St Martin's).

Pisani-Ferry, J. and Santos, I. (2009) 'Reshaping the Global Economy', *Finance and Development*, 46(1), pp. 8–12.

Polanyi, K. (1957) *The Great Transformation* (Boston, MA: Beacon Hill).

Pomeranz, K. and Topik, S. (1999) *The World that Trade Created: Society, Culture and the World Economy, 1400 – the Present* (London: M. E. Sharpe).

Porter, T. (2005) *Globalization and Finance* (Cambridge: Polity).

Price, R. (1998) 'Reversing the Gun Sights: Transnational Civil Society Targets Land Mines', *International Organization*, 52(3), pp. 613–44.

Price-Smith, A. T. (2009) *Contagion and Chaos: Disease, Ecology, and National Security in the Era of Globalization* (Cambridge, MA: MIT Press).

Prugl, E. (1999) *The Global Construction of Gender: Home Based Work in the Political Economy of the 20th Century* (New York: Columbia University Press).

Pyle, J. L. and Ward, K. B. (2003) 'Recasting our Understanding of Gender and Work during Global Restructuring', *International Sociology*, 18(3), pp. 461–89.

Pye, L. W. (1988) 'The New Asian Capitalism: A Political Portrait', in P. L. Berger and H. M. Hsia (eds) *In Search of an East Asian Development Model* (Oxford: Transaction).

Quisumbing, A. R., Haddad, L. and Peña, C. (1995) 'Gender and Poverty: New Evidence from 10 Developing Countries', *Food and Nutrition Division Discussion Papers*, 9 (Washington DC: International Food Policy Research Institute).

Radice, H. (ed.) (1975) *International Firms and Modern Imperialism* (London: Penguin).

Radosh, R. (1969) *American Labour and United States Foreign Policy* (New York: Random House).

Randriamaro, Z. (2006) 'Gender and Trade', *BRIDGE Report* (Brighton: Institute of Development Studies), available at www.bridge.ids.ac.uk/reports/CEP-Trade-OR.pdf. Last accessed 25 October 2006.

Ratha, D. and Mohapatra, S. (2007) 'Increasing the Macroeconomic Impact of Remittances on Development', available at: http://siteresources.worldbank.org/INTPROSPECTS/Resources/334934-1110315015165/Increasing_the_Macro_Impact_of_Remittances_on_Development.pdf

Ratha, D. and Xu, Z. (2008) Migration and Development Factbook 2008, available at: http://econ.worldbank.org/WBSITE/EXTERNAL/EXTDEC/EXTRESEARCH/EXTPROGRAMS/EXINTERNATIONAL/0,,contentMDK:21352016~pagePK:641654016~piPK:64165026~theSitePK:1572893,00

Ratha, D., Mohapatra, S. and Silwal, A. (2009) *Migration and Development Brief 10*, available at: http://siteresources.worldbank.org/INTPROSPECTS/Resources/334934-1110315015165/Migration&Development

Ravenhill, J. (2008) 'In Search of the Missing Middle', *Review of International Political Economy*, 15(1), p. 18.

Redclift, M. (1987) *Sustainable Development* (London: Routledge).

Reding, A. (1994) 'Chiapas is Mexico', *World Policy Journal*, 11(1), pp. 11–25.

Reich, R. (1992) *The Work of Nations* (New York: Vintage).

Ricardo, D. (1817/1992) *The Principles of Political Economy and Taxation* (London: J. M. Dent, Everyman's Library).

Rich, B. (1994) *Mortgaging the Earth: The World Bank, Environmental Impoverishment and the Crisis of Development* (London: Earthscan).

RIPE (2009) Special Issue – 'Not So Quiet on the Western Front: The American School of IPE', *Review of International Political Economy*, 16(1).

Ripsman, N. M. (2005) 'False Dichotomies: Why Economics Is High Politics', in Peter Dombrowski (ed.) *Guns and Butter: The Political Economy of International Security* (Boulder, CO: Lynne Rienner), pp. 15–31.

Ripsman, N. M. and Blanchard, J.-M. F. (1996/7) 'Commercial Liberalism under Fire: Evidence from 1914 and 1936', *Security Studies*, 6(2), pp. 4–50.

Risso, P. (1995) *Merchants and Faith: Muslim Commerce and Culture in the Indian Ocean* (Boulder, CO: Westview).

Rivoli, P. (2005) *The Travels of a T-Shirt in the Global Economy: An Economist Examines the Markets, Power, and Politics of World Trade* (Hoboken, NJ: John Wiley).

Robinson, R. (1972) 'Non-European Foundations of European Imperialism: Sketch for a Theory of Collaboration', in R. Owen and B. Sutcliffe (eds) *Studies in the Theory of Imperialism* (Bristol: Longman).

Rodman, K. A. (1998) 'Think Globally, Punish Locally: Nonstate Actors, Multinational Corporations and Human Rights Sanctions', *Ethics and International Affairs*, 12, pp. 19–41.

Rogerson, W. P. (1993) 'Economic Incentives and the Defense Procurement Process', Discussion Paper No.1078 Northwestern University: Center for Mathematical Studies in Economics and Management Science.

Rostow, W. W. (1960) *The Stages of Economic Growth* (Cambridge: Cambridge University Press).

Roubini, N. (2009) 'The Almighty Renminbi?', *New York Times*, 14 May.

Rubinstein, A. (2006) 'A Sceptic's Comment on the Study of Economics', *The Economic Journal*, 116 (March), c1–c9.

Ruggie, J. G. (1982) 'International Regimes, Transactions and Change: Embedded Liberalism in the Postwar Economic Order', *International Organization*, 36(2), pp. 379–415.

Ruggie, J. G. (1998) *Constructing the World Polity: Essays on International Institutionalization* (New York: Routledge).

Rupert, M. (1995a) *Producing Hegemony: The Politics of Mass Production and American Global Power* (Cambridge: Cambridge University Press).

Rupert, M. (1995b) '(Re)Politicizing the Global Economy: Liberal Common Sense and Ideological Struggle in the US NAFTA Debate', *Review of International Political Economy*, 2, pp. 658–92.

Russett, B. M. (1993) *Grasping the Democratic Peace: Principles for a Post-Cold War World* (Princeton, NJ: Princeton University Press).

Sahn, D. E. (1994) 'The Impact of Macroeconomic Adjustment on Incomes, Health and Nutrition: Sub-Saharan Africa in the 1980s', in G. A. Cornia and G. K. Helleiner (eds) *From Adjustment to Development in Africa: Conflict, Controversy, Convergence, Consensus?* (New York: St Martin's).

Samuelson, R. (2009) 'Chinas Dollar Deception', *The Washington Post*, 6 April.

Santiso, C. (2004) 'The Contentious Washington Consensus: Reforming the Reforms in Emerging Markets', *Review of International Political Economy*, 11(4) (October), pp. 828–44.

Sarup, M. (1993) *An Introductory Guide to Post-structuralism and Postmodernism*, 2nd edition (Athens, GA: University of Georgia Press).

Saurin, J. (1996) 'International Relations, Social Ecology, and the Globalisation of Environmental Change', in J. Vogler and M. F. Imber (eds) *The Environment and International Relations* (London: Routledge).

Sazanami, Y., Urata, S. and Kawai, H. (1995) *Measuring the Costs of Protection in Japan* (Washington DC: Institute for International Economics).

Schechter, M. G. (2002) 'Critiques of Coxian Theory: Background to a Conversation', in R. W. Cox (with M. G. Schechter) *The Political Economy of a Plural World: Reflection on Power, Morals and Civilization* (London: Routledge).

Schmidheiny, S. (1992) *Changing Course: A Global Business Perspective on Development and the Environment* (Cambridge, MA: MIT Press).

Schneider, V. (2000) 'Global Economic Governance by Private Actors: The International Chamber of Commerce', in J. Greenwood and H. Jacek (eds) *Organized Business and the New Global Order* (New York: St Martin's).

Scholte, J. A. (2000a) *Globalization: A Critical Introduction* (New York: St Martin's).

Scholte, J. A. (2000b) 'Global Civil Society', in N. Woods (ed.) *The Political Economy of Globalization* (London: Macmillan (now Palgrave Macmillan)).

Schwartz, H. (1994) *States Versus Markets* (New York: St Martin's).

Seers, D. (1969) 'The Meaning of Development', *International Development Review*, 11(4), pp. 2–6.

Seguino, S. (2000) 'Gender Inequality and Economic Growth: A Cross-Country Analysis', *World Development*, 28(7), pp. 1211–30.

Sell, S. (1999) 'Multinational Corporations as Agents of Change: The Globalization of Intellectual Property Rights', in C. Cutler, V. Haufler and T. Porter (eds) *Private Authority and International Affairs* (Albany, NY: SUNY Press).

Sell, S. (2000) 'Structures, Agents and Institutions: Private Corporate Power and the Globalisation of Intellectual Property Rights', in R. A. Higgott, G. R. D. Underhill and A. Bieler (eds) *Non-state Actors and Authority in the Global System* (London: Routledge).

Sell, S. (2006) 'Big Business, the WTO and Development', in R. Stubbs and G. R. D. Underhill (eds) *Political Economy and the Changing Global Order*, 3rd edition (Oxford: Oxford University Press), pp. 183–96.

Sell, S. and Prakash, A. (2004) 'Using Ideas Strategically: The Contest Between Business and NGO Networks in Intellectual Property Rights', *International Studies Quarterly*, 48(1), pp. 143–75.

Sen, A. K. (1981) *Poverty and Famines: An Essay on Entitlement and Deprivation* (Oxford: Clarendon).

Sengenberger, W. and Wilkinson, F. (1995) 'Globalisation and Labor Standards', in J. Michie and J. G. Smith (eds) *Managing the Global Economy* (Oxford: Oxford University Press).

Serrano, M. (2002) 'Transnational Organized Crime and International Security: Business as Usual?', in M. Berdal and M. Serrano (eds) *Transnational Organized Crime and International Security: Business as Usual?* (Boulder, CO: Lynne Rienner).

Servan Schreiber, J. J. (1968) *The American Challenge*, trans. R. Steel (New York: Athenaeum).

Shillington, K. (1995) *History of Africa* (New York: St Martin's).

Shrybman, S. (1990) 'International Trade and the Environment: An Environmental Assessment of the General Agreement on Tariffs and Trade', *Ecologist*, 20(1), pp. 30–4.

Silverstein, K. (2002) 'Millions for Viagra, Pennies for Diseases of the Poor', available at www.planetaportoalegre.net/publique. Last accessed 30 May 2006.

Sinclair, T. (1994) 'Passing Judgement: Credit Rating Processes as Regulating Mechanisms of Governance', *Review of International Political Economy*, 1(1), pp. 133–60.

Sinclair, T. (2005) *The New Masters of Capital: American Bond Rating Agencies and the Politics of Creditworthiness* (Ithaca, NY: Cornell University Press).

Singer, P. W. (2002) 'AIDS and International Security', *Survival*, 44(1), pp. 145–58.

Singh, B. K. (2005) 'The Political Economy of China's Defence Modernisation', *Strategic Analysis*, 29(4), pp. 680–705.

Sisson, C. A. (1986) 'Fund-supported Programs and Income Distribution in LDCs', *Finance and Development*, 231, pp. 33–8.

Skidmore, D. (1997) *Contested Social Orders and International Politics* (Nashville, TN: Vanderbilt University Press).

Skidmore-Hess, D. (1996) 'Business Conflict and Theories of the State', in R. W. Cox (ed.) *Business and the State in International Relations* (Boulder, CO: Westview).

Sklair, L. (2001) *The Transnational Capitalist Class* (Oxford: Blackwell).

Sklias, P. (1999) *Non-Governmental Organisations and the International Political Economy, with Special Reference to the European Union's Development Policy* (Athens: Nubis).

Skogstad, G. (2001) 'The WTO and Food Safety Regulatory Policy in the EU', *Journal of Common Market Studies*, 39(3), pp. 485–505.

Smith, A. (1776/1983) *The Wealth of Nations* (New York: Penguin).

Smythe, E. (2000) 'State Authority and Investment Security: Non-state Actors and the Negotiation of the Multilateral Agreement on Investment at the OECD', in R. A. Higgott, G. R. D. Underhill and A. Bieler (eds) *Non-state Actors and Authority in the Global System* (London: Routledge).

Soderbaum, F. and Shaw, T. M. (eds) (2003) *Theories of the New Regionalism* (Basingstoke: Palgrave Macmillan).

Spero, J. (1981) *Politics of International Economic Relations* (London: Unwin Hyman).

Spruyt, H. (1994) *The Sovereign State and its Competitors* (Princeton, NJ: Princeton University Press).

Spruyt, H. (2000) 'New Institutionalism and International Relations', in R. Palan (ed.) *Global Political Economy: Contemporary Theories* (London: Routledge).

Stalker, P. (2001) *The No-Nonsense Guide to International Migration* (Oxford: New Internationalist).

Steans, J. (1998) *Gender and International Relations* (Cambridge: Polity).

Steans, J. (1999) 'The Private Is Global: Feminist Politics and Global Political Economy', *New Political Economy*, 4(1), pp. 113–28.

Stearns, P. N. (1993) *The Industrial Revolution in World History* (Boulder, CO: Westview).

Stephen, R. (2007) 'Sovereign Wealth Funds', *New York Times*, 3 December, available at www.nytimes/topics.com

Stern Review (2006) *The Economics of Climate Change* (London: HM Treasury), available at www.hm-treasury.gov.uk/independent_reviews/stern_review_ economics_climate_ change/sternreview_index.cfm. Last accessed 12 November 2006.

Stewart, F. (1995) *Adjustment and Poverty: Options and Choices* (London: Routledge).

Stewart, F. and Berry, A. (1999) 'Globalization, Liberalization and Inequality: Expectations and Experience', in A. Hurrell and N. Woods (eds) *Inequality, Globalization and World Politics* (Oxford: Oxford University Press).

Stewart, J. (2009) 'CNBC Financial Advice', available at www.thedailyshow.com. Last accessed 4 March.

Stiglitz, J. (2000) 'The Insider: What I Learned at the World Economic Crisis', *New Republic*, 17 April, available at www.tnr.com/041700/stiglitz041700.html

Stiglitz, J. (2002) *Globalization and Its Discontents* (London: Penguin).

Stilwell, F. (2002) *Political Economy: the Contest of Economic Ideas* (Oxford: Oxford University Press).

Stopford, J. M. and Strange, S. (1991) *Rival States, Rival Firms: Competition for World Market Shares* (Cambridge: Cambridge University Press).

Strange, S. (1982) 'Cave Hic Dragones: A Critique of Regime Analysis', *International Organization*, 36(2), pp. 337–54.

Strange, S. (1985) 'Protectionism and World Politics', *International Organization*, 39(2), pp. 233–59.

Strange, S. (1986) *Casino Capitalism* (Oxford: Blackwell).

Strange, S. (1987) 'The Persistent Myth of Lost Hegemony', *International Organization*, 41, pp. 551–74.

Strange, S. (1988) *States and Markets* (London: Pinter).

Strange, S. (1991) 'Big Business and the State', *Millennium*, 20(2), pp. 245–50.

Strange, S. (1994) 'Rethinking Structural Change in the International Political Economy: States, Firms and Diplomacy', in R. Stubbs and G. R. D. Underhill (eds) *Political Economy and the Changing Global Order*, 2nd edition (Toronto: Oxford University Press).

Strange, S. (1996) *The Retreat of the State: The Diffusion of Power in the World Economy* (Cambridge: Cambridge University Press).

Strange, S. (1998) *Mad Money: When Markets Outgrow Governments* (Manchester: Manchester University Press).

Strange, S. (2002) 'I Never Meant to Be an Academic', in R. Tooze and C. May (eds) *Authority and Markets: Susan Strange's Writings on International Political Economy* (New York: Palgrave Macmillan).

Stubbs, R. (1999) 'War and Economic Development: Export-Oriented Industrialization in East and Southeast Asia', *Comparative Politics*, 31(3), pp. 337–55.

Stubbs, R. and Underhill, G. R. D. (eds) (1996) *Political Economy and the Changing Global Order*, 1st edition (London: Macmillan (now Palgrave Macmillan)).

Stubbs, R. and Underhill, G. R. D. (eds) (2000) *Political Economy and the Changing Global Order*, 2nd edition (Toronto: Oxford University Press).

Stubbs, R. and Underhill, G. R. D. (eds) (2006) *Political Economy and the Changing Global Order*, 3rd edition (Oxford: Oxford University Press).

Sundrum, R. M. (1983) *Development Economics: A Framework of Analysis and Policy* (Chichester: John Wiley).

Swann, D. (1992) *The Economics of the Common Market*, 7th edition (London: Penguin).

Taleb, N. (2004) *Fooled by Randomness* (New York: Random House).

Tarnoff, C. and L. Nowells (2004) 'Foreign Aid: An Introductory Overview of US Programs and Policy', *CRS Report for Congress*, available at: http://pdf.dec.org/pdf_docs/PCAAB191.pdf

Taylor, I. (2005) 'Globalization Studies and the Developing World: Making International Political Economy Truly Global', *Third World Quarterly*, 26(7), pp. 1025–42.

te Velde, D. W. (2009) 'The Global Financial Crisis and Developing Countries: Synthesis of the Findings of 10 Country Case Studies', *Working Paper 306* (London: ODI).

The Economist (2006) 'A Guide to Womenomics: The Future of the World Lies Increasingly in Female Hands', 12 April, available at www.economist.com/finance/displaystory.cfm?story_id=6802551. Last accessed 26 January 2007.

The Times (2009) 'Brown Spares Baroness Scotland, But Tells Her to Apologise "Profusely"', 22 September.

Thomas, C. (2000) *Global Governance, Development and Human Security* (London: Pluto).

Thomas, C. (2002) 'Trade Policy and the Politics of Access to Drugs', *Third World Quarterly*, 23(2), pp. 251–64.

Thomas, C. and Reader, M. (1997) 'Development and Inequality', in B. White, R. Little and M. Smith (eds) *Issues in World Politics* (London: Macmillan (now Palgrave Macmillan)).

Thomas, C. Y. (1974) *Dependence and Transformation* (New York: Monthly Review).

Thompson, W. R. (2000) *The Emergence of the Global Political Economy* (New York: Routledge).

Thorne, C. (1978) *Allies of a Kind: The United States, Britain, and the War against Japan, 1941–1945* (London: Hamish Hamilton).

Tilly, C. (1999) *Coercion, Capital, and European States AD 990–1992* (Oxford: Blackwell).

Tinker, I. (1990) 'The Making of a Field: Advocates, Practitioners, and Scholars', in I. Tinker (ed.) *Persistent Inequalities: Women and World Development* (Oxford: Oxford University Press).

Toffler, A. (1980) *The Third Wave* (New York: Morrow).

Toke, D. (1999) 'Epistemic Communities and Environmental Groups', *Politics*, 19(2), pp. 97–102.

Tooze, R. and May, C. (2002) 'Authority and Markets: Interpreting the Work of Susan Strange', in R. Tooze and C. May (eds) *Authority and Markets: Susan Strange's Writings on International Political Economy* (New York: Palgrave Macmillan).

Tooze, R. and Murphy, C. (eds) (1991) *The New International Political Economy* (Boulder, CO: Lynne Rienner).

Transnational Resource and Action Center (2000) *Tangled up in Blue: Corporate Partnerships at the United Nations*, available at www.corpwatch.org

UN (1995) *Beijing Declaration and Platform for Action*, Fourth World Conference on Women, 15 September 1995, A/CONF.177/20 (1995) and A/CONF.177/20/Add.1 (1995).

UN (2000a) *The Millennium Declaration*, UN General Assembly Resolution 55/2, adopted 18 September 2000.

UN (2000b) *United Nations Convention against Organized Crime and the Protocols Thereto*, available at http://www.unodc.org/documents/treaties/UNTOC/Publications/TOC%20Convention/TOCebook-e.pdf

UN (2001) *Gender Mainstreaming: An Overview* (New York: United Nations, Office of the Special Adviser on Gender Issuers and Advancement of Women).

UN (2003) *Declaration of Principles; World Summit on the Information Society*, UN Doc: WSIS-03/GENEVA/DOC/4-E.

UN (2004) *World Population Prospects: The 2004 Revision* (New York: United Nations, Population Division), available at http://esa.un.org/unpp. Last accessed 3 June 2006.

UN (2005) 'World Summit Outcome 2005', UN General Assembly Resolution A/RES/60/1, 24 October, paras 138, 139, available at: www.un.org/summit2005/documents.html

UN (2006) *The World's Women 2005: Progress in Statistics* (New York: United Nations, Department of Economic and Social Affairs, Statistics Division).

UN (2009a) *The Millennium Development Goals Report 2008* (New York: United Nations), available at http://www.undp.org/publications/MDG_Report_2009_ENG.pdf

UN (2009b) *The World Financial and Economic Crisis and its Impact on Development. Report of the Secretary-General* (New York: United Nations).

UNCTAD (1999) *World Investment Report 1999: Foreign Direct Investment and the Challenge of Development* (New York: United Nations).

UNCTAD (2005a) *World Investment Report 2005* (Geneva: UNCTAD).

UNCTAD (2005b) *The Digital Divide: ICT Development Indices 2004* (New York and Geneva: United Nations).

UNCTAD (2008) *World Investment Report 2008* (Geneva: UNCTAD).

UNCTAD (2009a) *The Global Economic Crisis: Systemic Failures and Multilateral Remedies* (Geneva: UNCTAD).

UNCTAD (2009b) *World Investment Report 2009* (Geneva: UNCTAD).

UNDP (1990) *Human Development Report* (Geneva: UNDP).

UNDP (1994) *Human Development Report* (Geneva: UNDP).

UNDP (1995) *Human Development Report* (Geneva: UNDP).

UNDP (2000) *Human Development Report* (Geneva: UNDP).

UNDP (2002) *Human Development Report* (Geneva: UNDP).

UNDP (2003) *Human Development Report* (Geneva: UNDP).

UNDP (2005) *Human Development Report* (Geneva: UNDP).

UNDP (2007/8) *Human Development Report* (Geneva: UNDP).

UNESCAP (2009) *Sustainable Agriculture and Food Security in Asia and the Pacific* (Bangkok: Escap).

UNESCO (2004) *EFA Global Monitoring Report 2005* (Paris: UNESCO).

UNFPA (2008) *State of World Population 2008. Reaching Common Ground: Culture, Gender and Human Rights*, http://www.unfpa.org/swp/

UNICEF (1999) *The Progress of Nations 1999* (New York: UNICEF),available at www.unicef.org/pon99/pon99_5.pdf. Last accessed 5 May 2003.

UNIFEM (2005) *The Progress of the World's Women 2005: Women, Work and Poverty* (New York: United Nations Development Fund for Women).

UNRISD (2005) *Gender Equality: Striving for Justice in an Unequal World* (New York: United Nations Research Institute for Social Development).

USPTO (2006) *Patent by Country, State and Year – All Patent Types* (Alexandria, VA: United States Patent Office), available at www.uspto.gov/go/taficst_all.htm. Last accessed 28 September 2006.

Vaitsos, C. (1975) 'Power, Knowledge and Development Policy: Relations Between Transnational Enterprises and Developing Countries', in G. K. Helleiner (ed.) *A World Divided: The Less Developed Countries in the International Economy* (Cambridge: Cambridge University Press).

Van Beers, C. and Van den Bergh, J. C. J. M. (1997) 'An Empirical Multi-Country Analysis of the Impact of Environmental Regulations on Trade Flows', *Kyklos*, 50(1), pp. 29–46.

Verma, A. (2003) 'Global Labour Standards: Can We Get from Here to There?', *The International Journal of Comparative Labour Law and Industrial Relations*, 19(4), pp. 515–34.

Vernon, R. (1966) 'International Investment and International Trade in the Product Cycle', *Quarterly Journal of Economics*, 80(2), pp. 190–207.

Vernon, R. (1971) *Sovereignty at Bay* (London: Penguin).

Vernon, R. (1977) *Storm Over the Multinationals: The Real Issues* (London: Macmillan (now Palgrave Macmillan)).

Wach, H. and Reeves, H. (2000) 'Gender and Development: Facts and Figures', *BRIDGE Reports*, 54 (Brighton: Institute for Development Studies), available at www.bridge.ids.ac.uk/reports. Last accessed 27 October 2006.

Wade, R. (1990) *Governing the Market: Economic Theory and the Role of Government in East Asian Industrialization* (Princeton, NJ: Princeton University Press).

Wade, R. H. (2003) 'What Strategies Are Viable for Developing Countries Today? The World Trade Organization and the Shrinking Of "Development Space"', *Review of International Political Economy*, 10(4), pp. 621–44.

Wade, R. and Veneroso, F. (1998) 'The Asian Crisis: The High Debt Model vs the Wall Street–Treasury–IMF Complex', *New Left Review*, 228, pp. 3–22.

Waley-Cohen, J. (1999) *The Sextants of Beijing: Global Currents in Chinese History* (New York: W. W. Norton).

Wallach, L. and Woodall, P. (2004) *Whose Trade Organization? A Comprehensive Guide to the WTO* (New York and London: New Press).

Walton, S. (2002) 'The Danger of Global Finance: A Reassessment of the Asian Crisis', *Journal of Asia-Pacific Affairs*, 4(1), pp. 107–21.

Wasow, B. (2006) *Losing the Genius for Openness* (Washington DC: Century Foundation), available at www.immigrationline.org/commentary.asp?opedid= 1217. Last accessed 28 September 2006.

Waterman, P. (1998) *Globalization, Social Movements and the New International-isms* (London: Mansell).

Watson, M. (2005) *Foundations of International Political Economy* (Basingstoke: Palgrave Macmillan).

Watts, J. (2006) 'Backlash as Google Shores up Great Firewall of China', *Guardian*, 25 January.

Waylen, G. (2006) 'You Still Don't Understand: Why Troubled Engagements Continue Between Feminists and (Critical) IPE', *Review of International Studies*, 32(1), pp. 145–64.

Weber, H. (2004) 'The "New Economy" and Social Risk: Banking on the Poor?', *Review of International Political Economy*, 11(2) (May), pp. 356–86.

Weingast B and Wittman, D. (2006) 'The Reach of Political Economy', in B. Weingast and D. Wittman (eds) *The Oxford Handbook of Political Economy* (Oxford: Oxford University Press), pp. 3–25.

Weissman, R. (2007) 'Sovereign Wealth Funds', *New York Times*, 3 December.

Weissman, R. and Donahue, J. (2009) *Sold Out: How Washington and Wall Street Betrayed America* (Washington: Essential Information and Consumer Education Fund).

Weiss, L. (1998) *The Myth of the Powerless State* (Ithaca, NY: Cornell University Press).

Weiss, L. (1999) 'State Power and the Asian Crisis', *New Political Economy*, 4(3), pp. 317–42.

Weiss, L. (ed.) (2003) *States in the Global Economy: Bringing Domestic Institutions Back In* (Cambridge: Cambridge University Press).

Weiss, T. G. (2009) 'Moving Beyond North–South Theatre', *Third World Quarterly*, 30(2) pp. 271–84.

Weiss, T. G., Forsyth, D. P. and Coates, R. A. (2001) *The United Nations and Changing World Politics* (Boulder, CO: Westview).

Weiss, T. G., Cortright, D., Lopez, G. A. and Minear, L. (1997) 'Economic Sanctions and their Humanitarian Impacts: An Overview', in T. G. Weiss, D. Cortright, G. A. Lopez and L. Minear (eds) *Political Gain and Civilian Pain: Humanitarian Impacts of Economic Sanctions* (Lanham, MD: Rowman and Littlefield), pp. 15–34.

Wendt, A. (1987) 'The Agent-Structure Problem in International Relations Theory', *International Organization*, 41, pp. 335–70.

Whalley, J. (2006) 'The Post-MFA Performance of Developing Asia', *NBER Working Papers*, 12178 (Washington DC: National Bureau of Economic Research).

Wheeler, D. (2002) 'Beyond Pollution Havens', *Global Environmental Politics*, 2(2), pp. 1–10.

Wheeler, N. J. (2000) *Saving Strangers: Humanitarian Intervention in International Society* (Oxford: Oxford University Press).

White, G. (ed.) (1988) *Developmental States in East Asia* (London: Macmillan (now Palgrave Macmillan)).

Whitworth, S. (1997) *Feminism and International Relations* (Basingstoke: Macmillan (now Palgrave Macmillan)).

WHO (2002) *Integrating Gender Perspectives in the Work of WHO: WHO Gender Policy* (Geneva: World Health Organization).

Wiener, J. (2005) 'GATS and the Politics of "Trade in Services"', in D. Kelly and W. Grant (eds) *The Politics of International Trade: Actors, Issues, and Regional Dynamics* (Basingstoke: Palgrave Macmillan), pp. 144–63.

Wilkins, M. (1970) *The Emergence of the Multinational Enterprise* (Cambridge, MA: Harvard University Press).

Williams, E. (1944) *Capitalism and Slavery* (Chapel Hill, NC: University of North Carolina Press).

Williams, M. (1993) 'International Trade and the Environment: Issues, Perspectives and Challenges', *Environmental Politics*, 2(4), pp. 80–97.

Williams, M. (1994) *International Economic Organisations and the Third World* (London: Harvester Wheatsheaf).

Williams, M. (1999) 'The World Trade Organisation, Social Movements and "Democracy"', in A. Taylor and C. Thomas (eds) *Global Trade and Global Social Issues* (London: Routledge).

Williams, M. (2001) 'Trade and Environment in the World Trading System: A Decade of Stalemate?', *Global Environmental Politics*, 1(4), pp. 1–9.

Williams, M. (2005a) 'Civil Society and the World Trading System', in D. Kelly and W. Grant (eds) *The Politics of International Trade: Actors, Issues, and Regional Dynamics* (Basingstoke: Palgrave Macmillan), pp. 30–46.

Williams, M. (2005b) 'The Third World and Global Environmental Negotiations: Interests, Institutions and Ideas', *Global Environmental Politics*, 5(3), pp. 48–69.

Williamson, J. (1990) 'What Washington Means by Policy Reform', in *Latin American Adjustment: How Much Has Happened?* (Washington DC: Institute of International Economics), pp. 5–20.

Williamson, J. (1993) 'Democracy and the Washington Consensus', *World Development*, 11(8), pp. 1329–36.

Wilson, W. (1918/1986) 'The Fourteen Points', in J. A. Vasquez (ed.) *Classics of International Relations* (London: Prentice-Hall).

Winham, G. R. (1986) *International Trade and the Tokyo Round Negotiations* (Princeton, NJ: Princeton University Press).

Wolf, E. R. (1982) *Europe and the People without History* (Berkeley, CA: University of California Press).

Wolfers, Arnold. 1952. '"National Security" as an Ambiguous Symbol', *Political Science Quarterly*, 67 (December), pp. 481–502.

Wollstonecraft, M. (1792/1992) *A Vindication of the Rights of Woman* (London: Penguin).

World Bank (1980) *World Development Report* (New York: Oxford University Press).

World Bank (1989) *World Development Report* (New York: Oxford University Press).

World Bank (1990) *World Development Report* (New York: Oxford University Press).

World Bank (1993) *The East Asian Miracle: Economic Growth and Public Policy* (Oxford: Oxford University Press; Washington DC: World Bank).

World Bank (1995) *Mainstreaming the Environment* (Washington DC: World Bank).

World Bank (1996) *World Development Report* (New York: Oxford University Press).

World Bank (1998) *Partnerships for Development: A New World Bank Approach* (Washington DC: World Bank).

World Bank (2000) *World Development Indicators* (Washington DC: World Bank).

World Bank (2001) *Global Development Finance 2001* (Washington DC: World Bank), available at www.worldbank.orglprospects/gdf2001/vol1-pdf/pdf. Last accessed 5 May 2003.

World Bank (2002) *The World Bank Annual Report 2002* (Washington DC: World Bank).

World Bank (2003) *ICT and MDGs: A World Bank Group Perspective* (Washington DC: World Bank, Global ICT Department).

World Bank (2006a) *The World Bank Annual Report 2006* (Washington DC: World Bank).

World Bank (2006b) *Key Development Data and Statistics: Sub-Saharan Africa*, available at http://devdata.worldbank.org. Last accessed 30 May 2006.

World Bank (2006c) *Debt Relief for the Poorest: An Evaluation Update of the HIPC Initiative* (Washington DC: World Bank, Independent Evaluations Group).

World Bank (2006d) *Gender Equality as Smart Economics: A World Bank Group Gender Action Plan (Fiscal Years 2007–10)* (Washington DC: World Bank).

World Bank (2006e) *World Development Indicators* (Washington DC: World Bank).

World Bank (2008) *Annual Report 2008* (Washington DC: World Bank).

World Bank (2009a) 'The Global Financial Crisis: Assessing Vulnerability for Women and Children', available at http://www.worldbank.org/financialcrisis/pdf/Women-Children-Vulnerability-March09.pdf

World Bank (2009b) Protecting Progress: The Challenge Facing Low-income Countries in the Global Recession (Washington DC: World Bank).

World Commission on Environment and Development (1987) *Our Common Future* (The Brundtland Report) (Oxford: Oxford University Press).

World Economic Forum (2008) *Global Gender Gap Report* (Geneva: World Economic Forum).

World Guide 2001/2002 (2001) (Oxford: New Internationalist).

WTO (1998) *International Trade Statistics 1998* (Geneva: WTO).

WTO (2001) *Doha Ministerial Declaration* (Geneva: WTO).

WTO (2006) *World Trade Report 2006* (Geneva: WTO).

WTO (2007) *World Trade Report 2007* (Geneva: World Trade Organization).

WTO (2008a) *World Tariff Profiles 2008* (Geneva: World Trade Organization and International Trade Centre) UNCTAD/WTO 2008.

WTO (2008b) *International Trade Statistics 2008* (Geneva: World Trade Organization).

WTO (2008c) *Annual Report 2008* (Geneva: World Trade Organization).

WTO (2009a) *World Trade Report 2009* (Geneva: World Trade Organization).

WTO (2009b) Regional Trade Agreements, available at: http://www.wto.org/english/tratop_e/region_e/region_e.htm

Wyn Jones, R. (1999) *Security, Strategy, and Critical Theory* (Boulder, CO: Lynne Reinner).

Yardley, J. (2004) 'In a Tidal Wave, China's Masses Pour From Farm to City', *New York Times*, 12 September.

Yardley, J. and Barboza, D. (2005) 'Help Wanted: China Finds Itself with a Labor Shortage', *New York Times*, 3 April.

York, G. (2009) 'How Zimbabwe Slew the Dragon of Hyperinflation', *Globe and Mail*, 23 March B1.

Young, K., Wolkowitz, C. and McCullagh, R. (eds) (1984) *Of Marriage and the Market: Women's Subordination Internationally and Its Lessons*, 2nd edition (London: Routledge and Kegan Paul).

Young, O. (1989) 'The Politics of Regime Formation: Managing Global Resources and the Environment', *International Organization*, 43(3), pp. 349–77.

Young, O. (1994) *International Governance: Protecting the Environment in a Stateless Society* (Ithaca, NY, and London: Cornell University Press).

Young, R. (ed.) (1999) *The Effectiveness of International Economic Regimes: Causal Connections and Behavioral Mechanisms* (Cambridge, MA: MIT Press).

Youngs, G. (2000) 'Introduction', in G. Youngs (ed.) *Political Economy, Power and the Body* (Basingstoke: Macmillan (now Palgrave Macmillan)).

Youngs, G. (2004) 'Feminist International Relations: A Contradiction in Terms? Or: How Women and Gender are Essential to Understanding the World "We" Live In', *International Affairs*, 80(1), pp. 75–87.

Zakaria, F. (1994) 'Culture Is Destiny: A Conversation with Lee Kuan Yew', *Foreign Affairs*, 73(2), pp. 109–26.

Index

Abu-Lughod, Janet 14, 55, 56, 57, 58, 61
absolute advantage 101, 151, 462
absolute vs relative gain 154, 462, 465
Afghanistan 128, 140, 172, 326, 338, 412, 414
AFL–CIO 273, 276
Africa 57, 62, 86, 149, 160, 171, 172, 173, 175, 180, 197, 202, 203
  15th century 61
  scramble for 70, 107–8
  slave trade 74–8, 82, 83, 84
  see also individual countries, Congo, debt crisis, development, slavery
agency
  and change 283, 292, 453
  and structure 48, 49, 453
Agenda 21 357, 358, 359
agrarian question 277–8
agriculture 71, 73, 79, 83, 139, 141, 142, 158, 171–3, 256, 278, 288, 289–290, 300, 325, 334
agri-export zones 200
aid *see* economic aid
Al-Qaida 128, 413118
Alexandria 58, 63
Algeria 106, 131, 132, 258, 326
Alliance for Progress 326
Americas
  15th century 51–2
  conquest of 71–4
  dollarization 239–41
  see also MERCOSUR, NAFTA
Amnesty International 436
Angola 105, 126, 326
Antarctic Treaty 356
anthropocentric 345, 346, 348
anti-dumping 162, 166, 169
anti-globalization movement 138, 278, 436, 439
Antigua and Barbuda 326

Apocalypse Now 105
Apple 138, 196
Argentina 91, 149, 173, 234, 245, 247, 313, 321, 326, 386, 442, 465
  2001 crisis 248–9
Asia
  relations with Europe 1400–1800 78–81
  see also individual countries, Asian financial crisis, Asian values
Asian financial crisis 133, 198, 221, 222, 247–8, 329–30, 386, 432, 444
  rival interpretations 14–16
Asia-Pacific Economic Cooperation 46, 137, 179, 182
Asian values 133, 320
  see also Confucianism
asset substitution 239
Association of South East Asian Nations 46, 137, 141, 178
Australia 70, 149, 152, 247, 302, 312, 314
  and asylum seekers 444
  environmental legislation 362
  trade 148, 173, 178
Austria 43, 104, 118, 121, 238
autonomy 45, 50, 60, 238, 253, 420, 435, 449
  national 212–13, 222–223, 425–8
Ayutthaya 80
Aztec empire 57, 61–2, 85

Bahamas 326
Bahrain 326
balance of payments 218, 324
  and TNCs 192–3, 206, 207
  defined 96–7, 220, 462
  illustration 97–8
balance of power 88, 102–4, 114, 117, 272, 306, 420, 428
Baltic Sea 62, 63
Bananas, Beaches and Bases 286

'Bangalored'   270
Bangladesh   149, 152, 200, 231, 256, 326
Bank for International Settlements 137, 245, 246, 247
banks
   and financial instability   67
   types   66
   see also finance
Baran, Paul   13
Barbados   313, 326
Barings Bank   243–4
Barnett, Richard   189
Barraclough, Geoffrey   111
barter   65, 96, 148, 150, 259
basic needs approach   44, 325, 327, 329, 332, 341
Basle Committee on Banking Supervision   247
beaver   74
Beckerman, Wilfred   352
Beijing   59, 326
   World Conference for Women   293, 294, 295, 297
Belgium   185, 238
   15th century   62, 64
   and the Congo   70, 104–5, 106, 107, 108
Bhopal   360
Biersteker, Thomas   134
'big bang'   229
biodiversity   346, 347, 362, 363, 364
biopiracy   391
bioprospectors   391
Birthday Girl   303
'bluewash'   439
Boli, John   137
Bolivia   61, 173, 326, 338
bond-rating agencies   47, 253, 435
Boserup, Ester   311
Bosnia   326, 412
Botswana   240, 326
bovine somatropin   162
Brandeis University   39
Braudel, Fernand   260
Brazil   128, 133, 134, 180, 209, 278, 321, 326, 384, 390
   pre-1900   70, 74, 75, 110
   finance issues   234, 236, 245

global governance   247, 427, 433
   trade   149, 160, 171, 173 180
   TNCs   229, 263, 434
Bretton Woods system   199, 218–9, 323, 463
Britain 17, 18, 21, 38, 39, 42, 87, 88 , 123, 126, 128, 129, 258, 276, 383, 384
   and India   70, 79, 106, 261
   and slave trade   77
   balance of power   103–4
   Bretton Woods   218
   ERM   226–7
   Euro   238
   financial crisis   248, 251
   financial deregulation   229–30
   free trade   100–2, 111–2, 403
   gold standard   97, 98
   industrial revolution   88–94, 307, 388
   inter-war period   117, 120, 121
   see also Pax Britannica, imperialism
British East India Company   79, 80, 89
Bruges   63, 64
Brundtland Commission   330, 366
business associations   39, 273, 435, 436
   see also transnational corporations
business conflict theory   435
Bush, George W.   128, 129, 248, 371, 414, 426

Cairns Group   173
Cairo   58, 63
Caldwell, Lynton   356
California   43, 256
call centres   263, 270
Canada   43, 125, 126, 129, 139, 149, 162, 173, 222, 225, 257, 302, 312, 421, 433, 464, 465
   dollarization   239–40
   pre-1900   73, 74, 80, 83, 88
canals   66
   Grand   59
   Panama   91
   Suez   79, 91
capital
   controls   121, 198, 222, 223, 229, 246

mobility   142, 191, 197, 221–3, 224, 226, 227–8, 244–5, 265, 446
capital account   220, 385
capitalism
  and environment   350–5
  and imperialism   104, 105, 108
  and peace   13, 23, 99, 403
  'casino'   39, 243
  'crony'   15, 16, 248
  exploitation   25, 26, 27, 112, 113, 258, 266, 274, 376, 303, 439, 445
  gender   248, 303–6
  rival models   15, 34–5 143, 323–5, 336–31, 457
  triumph of 24, 127, 134, 143, 211
  uneven development of   25–6, 191, 216, 327
Caribbean   70, 74, 83, 84, 90, 171, 200, 235, 260, 261, 266, 289, 310, 316, 321, 322, 332
Carnegie Endowment for International Peace   123
Carr, E. H.   118
Castells, Manuel   140
Cayman Islands   134, 229
Central America   70, 71, 91, 126, 127, 160, 200, 258
central bank independence   222
Cerny, Phil   133
Chatham House   38
Chernobyl   360
Chiapas   45, 278, 328
children   74, 79, 136, 309, 434, 437
  and work   87, 90, 113, 257, 301
  care for   255
  poverty of   296, 300, 441, 455
Chile   61, 129, 134, 173, 178, 180, 235, 321, 326
China   110, 122, 185, 246, 265, 278, 313, 326, 325, 388, 404
  15th century   55, 57, 58–9, 60, 61, 62, 64, 69, 71, 73, 78
  and foreign investment   127, 134, 135, 140, 232
  and global division of labour   214, 256, 267–70, 271, 274, 304
  and global governance   128, 171, 247, 426, 427, 433
  and Japan   118

and US   226–7, 228, 242
  development   125, 133
  environment   372
  financial crisis   252
  health   412
  opium wars   70, 81, 86, 114
  Taiping rebellion   106
  trade   174, 178, 205
Christianity   69, 73, 107
civic associations   47, 53
  and global governance   137–8, 297, 425, 436, 437, 438, 438, 445
  see also civil society, NGOs
civil society   43, 284, 292, 294, 383, 436–8, 440
  and debt relief and development   336, 337, 339
  and environment   43, 47, 357, 359
  and international institutions   47, 137, 189, 181, 182, 336
  and TNCs   214, 215, 273, 274, 435
civilizations   42, 53, 54, 55, 58, 60, 61, 69, 71, 82, 84, 92, 127, 147, 414
class   14, 24, 25–6, 28, 29, 41, 50, 74, 83, 92, 93, 97, 98, 112, 115, 245, 256, 276, 284, 311, 349, 360, 377, 404, 443
  transnational   14, 265
  see also division of labour
Clinton, Bill   274, 393
cloning   139
codes of conduct   274–4, 277, 440
Cold War   125, 194, 199, 228, 276, 308, 325, 360
  characteristics   126–7, 143, 291–20, 404, 408–10, 415–16, 437
  decolonization   131–2
  end of   24, 127, 329, 400
  see also security structure
Coleman, William   449
Cologne   445
Columbia University   41
  School of International Affairs   43, 123
Columbus, Christopher   57, 68
Committee on Payments and Settlements   247

Committee on the Global Financial System   247
Common Agricultural Policy   153
common pool resources
  see public goods
common sense   151, 375, 378, 396
communication   103, 111, 138–9, 155, 187, 191, 194, 196, 212, 229, 264, 309, 380, 382, 389, 413, 419, 425, 435, 436
  see also information technology
communism   93, 122, 127, 159, 276, 325, 326, 329, 375, 408
Communist Manifesto   93
comparative advantage   11, 23, 102, 159, 161, 166, 173
  and division of labour   259, 261, 370
  and TNCs   152, 191, 192, 212
  criticisms of   145–7
  defined   462
  explained   100–1, 151
compliance   41, 162, 273, 370, 416, 417, 432
Concert of Europe   103, 429
Conference on Trade and Employment
  see International Trade Organization
Confucianism   7, 320, 322
  see also Asian values
Congo   70, 78, 104–5, 106, 107, 172, 326, 338, 412
Congo Reform Association   105
Conrad, Joseph   105
constructivism   36–7, 44, 45, 377, 378, 396
consumers   10, 148, 151, 152, 153, 161, 162, 192, 195, 204, 224, 226, 233, 242, 251, 274, 279, 288, 401
consumption   20, 22, 32, 150, 159, 162, 243, 251, 278, 281, 323, 381, 393, 395, 441, 455, 458, 460
  and environment   348, 351, 354, 354–6, 368, 369, 370
  mass consumption   202, 226, 263
  pre-1900   61, 73, 80, 82, 98
  underconsumption   26, 28, 108
Convention on the High Seas   356
convergence   253–4, 428

cooperation   13, 33, 40, 82, 85, 103, 130, 136, 163, 164, 198, 215, 224, 225, 275, 322, 431, 438, 444, 452
  conflict and   20–1, 23–4, 26, 402, 410, 421
  environmental   348–51, 353, 373
  see also regimes, regionalism
Corn Laws   99, 100
corporations
  and global governance   434–5
  origins   6, 81, 91
  see also transnational corporations
Corus   212
Costa Rica   149, 173, 235, 326
cotton   42, 58, 70, 75, 76, 79, 84, 87–91, 92, 94, 260
  and WTO   171, 174
Council on Foreign Relations   123
Council for Mutual Economic Assistance (Comecon)   159, 409
Cox, Robert W.   3, 26, 27, 28, 41–3, 45, 377, 452
credit
  credit crisis   1, 249–52
  origins   66
  post-1945 system   219–20
  see also finance
crime   398, 415, 418–20, 436
critical theory   42–3, 283, 285
  see also dependency, environmentalism, feminism, Marxism
Croce, Benedetto   53
Crusades   57, 63, 75
CTM   276
Cuba   107, 122, 126, 164, 272, 278, 313, 314, 326, 404
culture   9, 11, 69, 79, 83, 86, 192, 193, 281, 291, 302, 303, 325, 460
  and economic growth   53, 92, 416
  approaches   14
  protection of   155, 206
currency
  controls   148
  substitution   240
current account   220
  see also balance of payments
Cutler, Claire   435
Czechoslovakia   118, 119

De Goede, Marieke 378
debt crisis
  and AIDS 236
  causes 232–4
  consequences 234–7, 327–31
debt relief 336–9
decolonization 111, 125, 131–2, 142
democracy 32, 253, 254, 277, 330,
    409, 416
  and free trade 13
  and global governance 446–9
  and IMF 446
  and peace 407
  and TNCs 141
  and World Bank 335
  and WTO 180, 181
  criteria 449
  third wave of 447
democratic internationalism 436
deflation 97, 98, 223, 233
Denmark 257
Denver 445
dependency 26, 192, 200, 204, 221,
    260, 316–7, 324, 383
depression 11, 13, 328, 429, 447
  Great 119, 121, 124, 129, 157
deregulation 196, 198, 211, 213, 217,
    229, 230, 328, 384, 392, 393, 394,
    395
derivatives 197, 230, 243, 244, 250,
    392, 393, 394
  defined 463
developing countries
  and TNCs 204–9
  remittances 265–6
  trade 170–6
  see also debt crisis, development,
    G-20, Third World
development
  1400–1800 84
  19th century 113
  Cold War 126–7, 325–6
  definitions 310–5
  economic aid 137, 336, 340, 415–16
  external determinants 316–17
  financial crisis 232–7, 252
  gendered 295–8, 298–300, 304–6,
    333, 441–2
  global governance 440–2

internal causation 316
national capitalism 323–6
neoliberalism 327–31
participatory 365, 368
post-1945 142–3
success and failures 132–3
technology 382–3, 387–9
underdevelopment 26, 316–7, 324,
    402
  see also debt crisis, developing
    countries, sustainable development,
    trade, World Bank
Diamond, Jared 54
Dickson, Anna 310
digital divide 139, 380, 381–2
disease 71–2, 75, 76, 79, 82, 105,
    139, 144, 247, 298, 302, 308, 309,
    360, 363, 391, 401, 402
  pandemics 420–2
  see also HIV/AIDS
Disney 439
division of labour
  1400–1800 83
  19th century 112–3
  criticisms of 260–1
  defined 255–8
  Fordism 133, 233, 262–3, 464
  gendered 79, 256–7, 258, 260,
    288–91, 298–306
  global 142, 256–7, 263–7, 271
  global stability 275–8
  liberal theory 258–60
  migration 54, 71, 73, 86, 95, 102,
    264–7, 268, 270, 300, 363, 444
  new international 216, 263–4
  post-1945 142
  racial 74, 256, 258
  Taylorism 262
  see also elites, slavery
Dobson, Andrew 346
dollarization 239–41, 463
domestic politics see state–society
    relations, world order
domestic work 302–3
double movement 122
drugs 63, 70, 80–1, 82, 175, 309,
    389–91, 420, 427, 434
  see also intellectual property rights,
    opium

Du Pont   434
Duke University   39
Dunning, John   190, 191
Dutch East India Company   83, 91

East Asia   15–16, 180, 202, 211, 246,
    266, 289, 290, 332, 383, 432, 442
    explanation of success   318–22
Eastern Origins of Western Civilization
    53
Eckersley, Robyn   246
ecological imperialism   72
ecologism   *see* environment
economic aid   415–6
economic nationalist theory   17–21,
    38, 43, 348, 375
economics   10–11
    environmental   10, 352, 354, 372,
        373
    feminist   10, 287, 298
    institutional   11, 12, 34
    Keynsesian   10–11, 22, 27, 123,
        125, 129, 133, 143, 323, 334, 379,
        465
    neoclassical   10–11, 12, 134, 156,
        234, 287, 298, 354–5, 384
    see also comparative advantage, free
        trade, liberalism, Washington
        Consensus
Economist, The   238, 288
ECU   325
Ecuador   61, 239, 326
Egypt   55, 57, 58, 71, 91, 106, 126,
    131, 171, 326
Eisenhower, Dwight D.   409
elites   62, 87, 111, 112, 115, 120, 180,
    234, 276, 307, 308, 318, 323, 325,
    350, 367, 383
    economic   98, 273, 277, 385
    local   110, 412, 414
    globalizing   14, 28, 265
    state   246, 275, 384
    see also division of labour
emerging markets   252, 310, 315
embedded liberalism   *see* liberalism
Emmanuel, Arghiri   156
empire
    1500–1800   71–81
    19th century   106–11

see also global governance,
    imperialism
End Child Prostitution   302
Enlightenment   92, 114
Enloe, Cynthia   286
Enron   386, 447
environment
    1400–1800   84
    19th century   113
    activism   347
    corporate behaviour   363–4
    definitions   345–7
    environmental studies debates
        351–5
    global warming   128, 143, 352,
        370–2, 426
    IPE debates   21, 348–51
    mainstreaming   361–4
    market solutions   350–1
    ozone layer   346, 347, 358, 362
    pollution havens   368
    post-1945   143
    protection   351, 363, 368, 429, 431
    trade   353, 368–70
    types of problems   346–7
    see also economics (environmental),
        environmental degradation,
        environmentalism, global
        environmental change
environmental degradation   143, 156,
    182, 205, 287, 344, 345, 347,
    349–72, 412, 423
    environmentalism   17, 27
    dark Green and light Green   346
    distinguishing features   345–7
    ecologism   345, 346, 352
    epistemic communities   358
    technocratic and ecocentric   346,
        352, 353–4, 355
    see also environment, environmental
        degradation
    epistemic communities   358, 376–7
equity   28, 54, 128, 187, 272, 292,
    311, 353, 367, 371, 436, 436, 438,
    443–6
Escobar, Arturo   342
Ethiopia   61, 70, 107, 108, 118, 172,
    326, 338
Euro   238–9, 242

Eurocurrency (Eurodollar) market
227–29, 233, 463
Europe
15th–18th centuries   67–9
19th century   102–4
Cold War   126–7
Eastern   125, 126, 127, 197, 252,
289, 310, 366, 419
expansionism   69–81, 106–11
inter-war   118–23
World Wars   117–19
see also individual countries
European Central Bank   238, 430
European Coal and Steel Community
130
European Economic Community   130,
178
European Free Trade Area   179
European Monetary System   225–8
European Union   46, 128, 130, 137,
141, 149, 143, 162, 179, 180, 238,
247, 273, 289, 416, 426, 430, 448
Exchange Rate Mechanism   225–7
exchange rates   *see* international
monetary system
export-oriented industrialization   199,
208, 211, 248, 305, 318, 320, 328
export processing zones   135, 199,
200, 207, 256, 264, 304
see also offshore

factory   113, 202, 262, 263, 269, 304
origins   89–90
fair trade   445
famine   110, 114, 127, 402, 441
Fanon, Frantz   132
Fascism   119, 122, 123, 124, 375
feminism   17, 27, 283
see also gender, women
feminization of poverty   298–300
FIFA   274
Fifth World   315
Fiji   80, 326
finance   217–54
1400–1800   64–7, 83
19th century   94, 97, 98, 99, 112
deregulation   229–30, 392–6
innovation   229–32
regulation   252, 54, 392–3, 446–7

TNCs   196–8
see also credit, financial crisis, gold
standard, international monetary
system
financial community internationalism
99, 123–4
financial crisis   1, 243–252
and global governance   446–9
Argentina   248–9
Asia   14–16, 246–8
human cost   243
inter-war   120–1
Mexico   234, 236–7, 245–6
UK   226–8
US/global   1, 249–52, 391–6
Financial Stability Forum   246
Finland   238, 282
First World   125, 133, 208, 302
fish   32, 61, 70, 74, 344
food   54, 61, 63, 72, 73, 101, 110,
131, 150, 179, 260, 381, 402, 407,
411, 423, 441
security   155, 300, 401
see also famine
Ford, Henry   202, 262
Fordism   133, 203, 262–3, 484
see also post-Fordism
Foreign Affairs   123
foreign direct investment   14, 134
defined   186–9
growth   190–3
see also transnational corporations
foreign exchange markets   225, 228
Fourth World   315
France   94, 95, 102, 104, 129, 335,
433
imperialism   70, 106, 108, 131,
152, 248
inter-war period   117, 120, 121,
126
international finance   224, 225, 238
pre-1800   57, 63, 67, 68
protectionism   20, 416
TNCs   185, 186
Frank, Andre Gunder   25, 27
free riders   33
free trade
19th century   100–2, 111–2
see also comparative advantage, trade

510   Index

Frieden, Jeffry   455
Friends of the Earth   436
Fukuyama, Francis   127
futures   197, 230, 392, 393, 394187, 221

game theory   33
  Prisoner's Dilemma   33–5
Gandhi, Mahatma   132
gender   14, 24, 27, 29, 42, 46, 142
  1400–1800   78–9, 83–4
  19th century   113
  and development   311, 325, 333, 442–3
  and trade   156, 144, 147, 271
  and security
  defined   280–1, 464
  devalorization   281
  division of labour   256–7, 260, 261
  employment trends   288–91
  glass ceiling   291
  global public policy   292–8
  inequality   282
  ILO   297
  IPE theory   283–7, 454, 460
  mainstreaming in international organizations   294–8
  MDGs   296, 308, 309
  poverty   298–300
  reproductive work   300–3
  structural adjustment   303–6
  World Bank   297–8
  see also division of labour, feminism, women
General Agreement on Tariffs and Trade   125, 130, 136, 141, 147, 163, 167, 189, 177, 326, 340, 389, 464
  Article XIX (escape clause)   161–2
  dispute settlement   164, 166, 167
  negotiating rounds   165–6
  normative framework   164
  origins   164
  special and differential treatment   176
General Agreement on Trade and Services   167, 171, 175
General Electric   185, 389, 434
genetically modified crops   139

Genoa   62, 63, 68
Germany   67, 88, 94, 97, 104, 129, 180, 185, 186, 209, 214, 258, 335, 433, 464
  Cold War   126
  Euro   238
  European monetary system   225
  imperialism   70, 107, 108
  inter-war period   117, 199, 120–1, 122, 124
  protectionism   18, 88, 95, 102, 154
  second industrial revolution   88, 103, 113
Gertzl, Cherry   310
Gill, Stephen   3, 26, 432
Gilpin, Robert   3, 19, 27
global civil society   434, 435–8
Global Compact   44, 274, 438–40
global commodity chains   184, 186
global corporations   see transnational corporations
global environmental change   344–73
  key issues   364–73
  see also environment
global financial system   1, 39, 217–54
  see also finance
global governance   21, 43, 47, 128, 138, 353, 424–50
  and democracy and regulation   446–8
  and development and growth   440–2
  and equality and justice   443–6
  and international organizations   135–6, 431–4
  civic associations   436–8
  corporations   434–6
  defined   425
  expertise   432
  governance levels   430–4
  large-scale change   429
  morality   432
  regimes   431–2
  states   425–8
  see also global compact
global political economy   passim
  eclectic framework   29, 452–5
  theoretical consolidation   455–6
  theoretical expansion   458–60

theoretical integration 456–8
use of the term 2, 10, 14
see also international political
economy
Global South 315
see also Third World, developing
countries
globalization 5–6
defined 143, 425
impact on IPE research 45–7
finance 223–9
production 194–200
project 134, 323
reproductive work 300–2
views of 19–20, 21, 26
gold exchange standard 218
gold standard 88, 96–9, 129, 144,
218
inter-war period 117, 121–2
Goldman Sachs 393
Google 267–8
governance
1400–1800 85–6
19th century 114–15
good 309, 386, 419, 442
post-1945 144
see also global governance, states
Grieco, Joseph 456
Gramsci, Antonio 2641
see also neo-Gramscian approaches
Greece 238
green parties 361
green theories *see* environmentalism
Greenpeace 436
Gresham, Thomas 66
Gresham's law 66
gross national product 311, 464
Group of 5 225
Group of 7 225, 246, 247, 261, 433,
445, 464
Group of 8 157, 137, 252, 338, 342,
454, 464
Group of 20 1, 137, 171, 183, 246,
247, 252, 335, 342, 429
Group of 24 325
Group of 77 325–464
growth 157–63, 190–3, 314–22,
440–2
see also development

Guatemala 61, 173, 326
Gujarat 60
Guns, Germs and Steel 54

Haas, Peter 358
Hamilton, Alexander 18, 27, 403
Hanseatic League 64, 67, 68
harmony of interest critique 24, 188
Harvard University 39, 43
Harvard Multinational Project 188
Haufler, Virginia 435
Hawaii 70, 80, 107
Hayek, Friedrich 22
health 205, 227, 236, 266, 282, 290,
294, 366, 360, 363, 381
and beef 162
and development 44, 311, 313,
331, 334, 337
and security 401, 402, 416, 420–2,
437
and safety 168, 214, 358
and trade 175–6, 390–1
public good 11, 263, 268
standards 169
women 299, 300, 301, 305, 308
see also disease, World Health
Organization
Heart of Darkness 105
Heavily Indebted Poor Countries
Initiative 236, 337–9, 445, 464
Heckscher, Eli 152
Heckscher–Ohlin theorem 152
hedge funds 232, 247, 250, 392
hegemony 26, 27, 38, 40, 42, 44, 132,
194, 378
hegemonic stability theory 124
Helms–Burton Act 272
Hereros 108
historical materialism 41
see also Marxism
historicism 48, 54, 453
HIV/AIDS 29
and debt 236
and development 296, 302, 308,
309
and propery rights 389–91, 427,
437
and security 420, 421, 422
Hobson, John 108

Hobson John M.   53, 94
Holland   70, 106
   see also Netherlands
Honduras   256, 326, 338
Hong Kong   132, 168, 175, 214, 246,
   263, 268, 269, 318, 319, 320, 321
home work   297
hormone-treated beef   162 377, 430
Human Development Index   312, 313,
   314
Human Development Report   313,
   401–2, 443
human rights   44, 105, 111, 156, 294,
   295, 402, 410, 417, 418, 424, 427,
   436, 438, 439
human security   *see* security
humanities   14
Hymer, Stephen   191
Hurrell, Andrew   344
hyperpower   *see* United States

IBM   389, 434
ideas   374–97
   1400–1800   84–5
   19th century   113–4
   competing knowledges   396–7
   defined   374–5
   post-1945   143
   theories about   375–9
   see also economic nationalism,
      liberalism, intellectual property
      rights, technology, Washington
      Consensus
ideology   12, 24, 26, 88, 93, 103, 112,
   114, 127, 211, 259, 305, 325, 335,
   375, 384, 409, 427, 443
   see also ideas
Ikenberry, G. John   456
imperial preferences   163
imperialism   4, 14, 20, 25, 26, 28,
   129, 118, 374, 403
   1400–1800   69–81
   19th century   104, 106–11
   ecological imperialism/eco-
      imperialism   72, 370
   theories of   2899, 108, 191
import-substitution industrialization
   192, 211, 235, 319, 320, 323, 424
Incas   57, 61, 73, 84

indebted industrialization   323
India   278, 326, 360, 372, 388, 390,
   414, 427, 433, 441
   1400–1800   60
   and British imperialism   70, 79–80,
      88–9
   and environment   360, 372
   and global division of labour
      270–1, 273
   technology industry   256, 381
   textile industry   90–1, 261
indigenous knowledge   391, 396
individual   10, 12, 16, 21–2, 25, 27,
   52–3, 34–5, 40, 49, 93, 177, 190,
   310, 322, 400, 402, 411, 411, 421,
   426
Indonesia   58, 70, 80, 83, 106, 131,
   132, 133, 134, 173, 178, 247, 257,
   258, 269, 277, 318, 321, 326, 330,
   433
   Asian financial crisis   14, 15, 246
industrial revolution
   described   88–91
   explanations of British origins   92–4
   international dimensions   90–1, 94
   outside Britain   94–5
inequality   45, 46, 111, 221, 254, 264,
   265, 268, 271, 311, 342, 349, 382,
   385, 428, 443–6, 452, 454, 455,
   458, 460, 461
   gender   257, 261, 282–3, 288–91,
      298–305
   see also poverty
infant industry protection   154–5
inflation   33, 36, 49, 66, 97, 120, 130,
   133, 222, 224, 225, 230, 233, 238,
   239, 240, 242, 318, 380, 405, 465
information revolution   87, 113,
   138–40, 227, 374, 379–83, 387–9
institutional investors   245
institutionalism   34–6
   liberal   28
intellectual property rights   166, 167,
   168, 175, 388, 389–91, 434
   see also Trade-Related Intellectual
      Property Rights
inter-war period
   economic failure   119–21
   lessons   124–5

popular mobilization   122–3
security failure   177–8
US role   123–4
interdependence   2, 21, 23, 24, 27, 40,
    45, 194, 349, 365, 406, 407, 421,
    457
interest rates   99, 197, 198, 226–7,
    231, 238, 239, 240, 241, 243, 245,
    249, 319, 384
and debt crisis   224–5, 232–4
and domestic monetary policy   221–3
International Association of Insurance
    Supervisors   247
International Bank for Reconstruction
    and Development   130, 218, 219,
    331–4, 466
see also World Bank
International Chamber of Commerce
    436
International Commission on Peace and
    Food   341
International Confederation of Free
    Trade Unions   272–3, 274
see also International Trade Union
    Confederation
International Convention for the
    Prevention of the Pollution of the
    Sea by Oil   356
International Convention for the
    Regulation of Whaling   356
international economic organizations
    23, 136–7, 436, 448
see also particular organizations
international environmental agreements
    356
International Labour Organization
    41, 42, 325, 379, 432, 434
and global compact   438–40
and women   297
core labour rights   273
EPZ study   200
peace   275
International Organization of
    Securities Commission   247
International Organization   456
international organizations   13, 23,
    40, 42, 47, 111, 117, 129–30,
    135–8, 141, 144, 431–4
see also particular organizations

International Monetary Fund   464
Argentina   248–9
Asian financial crisis   15–16, 446
conditionality   137, 234, 246,
    259–60, 332, 341, 384, 386
evolving role   136 234
debt relief   236, 337–9
global financial crisis   252
global governance   138, 144, 247,
    325, 335, 340, 342, 432, 433, 439
    447
Mexico   245–6, 328
origins   124, 129, 130, 219
protests   276, 277
see also debt relief, Structural
    Adjustment Programmes,
    Washington Consensus
international monetary system   3, 13,
    124
defined   96
dollarization   239–41
fixed to floating   223–5
inter-war era   120–1
key elements   96–7
post-1945   142, 218–9
regional currencies   237–9
relationship to capital mobility
    221–3
trade   225
see also Bretton Woods, gold
    standard
international political economy
and environmental studies   348–51
as a field of study   2
theories   14–28, 451–61
see also global political economy,
    methodology
International Relations   13–4
International Trade Organization
    124, 157, 164
International Trade Union
    Confederation 436
International Women's Year   292–3
internationalism   123, 275, 277, 436
internet   138, 139, 140, 196, 229,
    380, 382, 419
Iran   126, 233, 326
Iraq   55, 126, 233, 326, 418
war with US   128, 129, 226, 437

Ireland   238, 239, 251, 310, 312
Islam   55, 57, 58, 60, 61, 71, 126, 128, 414
Islamabad   200
ISO 14000   138
Israel   57, 126, 131
Italy   104, 185, 225, 238, 433, 464
   1400–1600   63, 64, 66, 68
   imperialism   70, 107, 118
   inter-war   119, 122
   see also Genoa, Venice

Jacobson, Harold   42
Japan   98, 149, 178, 243, 258, 301, 313, 388, 458
   Cold War   127, 130, 404
   economic model   35, 132, 202, 263
   global governance   128, 136, 225, 271, 335, 433
   imperialism   107, 111, 118
   industrial revolution   88, 95, 99, 112, 143
   protectionism   18, 153, 224
   Second World War   119, 125, 126, 131
   TNCs   185, 186, 187, 194, 202, 209, 268, 269
Jubilee 2000   445
just-in-time production   202, 263

Kabeer, Naila   292
Kaldor, Mary   402, 411
Kant, Immanuel   23, 27, 407
Karnataka State Farmers' Association   298
Kenya   235, 326
Keohane, Robert   3, 27, 39–41, 45, 452
Keynes, John Maynard   22, 27, 123, 465
Keynesianism   10–11, 23, 50, 123, 124, 129, 133, 142, 143, 323, 335, 379, 465
Khomeini, Ayatollah   233
Kidman, Nicole   303
Kindleberger, Charles   121
Kingsbury, Benedict   344
Klein, Naomi   214

knowledge   37, 92, 94, 138, 152, 176, 204, 207, 209, 261, 262, 322, 355, 358, 360, 376–7, 389, 392, 426, 459
   and global governance   396–7
   defined   374, 375
   distribution   388
   economy   379–83
   importance   4–5, 54
   in social sciences   29–30, 452
   structure   38, 191, 374
   see also ideas, technology
Krasner, Stephen   19, 27
Kuznets curve   311
Kyoto Protocol   113, 128, 143, 349, 370, 371

labour
   1400–1800   83
   19th century   112–3
   child   87, 90, 113, 257, 274, 301, 302, 437
   informal   281, 287, 438
   mobility   239
   organized   254, 263, 274, 276, 438
   post-1945   142
   rights   156, 179, 271–5
   standards   28, 166, 182, 269, 272, 273–5, 276, 434, 440, 445
   see also division of labour, migration, peasants, slavery, trade unions, work
Landes, David   4, 53, 92
landmines   435
Latin America   81, 149, 180, 235, 248, 261, 266, 276, 277, 289, 310, 326, 332, 341, 367, 384, 447
   compared with East Asia   320–2
   dollarization   240–1
   history   73, 83, 84, 104, 106, 163
   industrialization   117
Law, David   3, 432
League of Nations   118, 123, 125, 135, 417, 429
legalization   46
legitimacy   *see* democracy
Leeson, Nick   243
lender of last resort   67, 121, 327
Lenin, V. I.   27, 28, 99, 108, 191, 404

Leopold II of Belgium 104
Levi Strauss Jean company 274
liberalism 9, 13, 21–4, 25, 34, 37
  19th century 92–3
  actors 21–2
  conflict and cooperation 23–4
  division of labour 258–60
  dynamics 22–3
  embedded 43, 129, 130, 142, 163,
    379, 383, 387
  environment 336
  view of Asian financial crisis 15, 16
  see also free trade, neoliberalism,
    Washington Consensus
leisure 282, 381, 460
Limits to Growth 359, 366
List, Fredrick 18, 27, 95, 403
London 63, 91, 97, 98, 229, 252
London School of Economics and
  Political Science 38
Long Term Capital Management 244
Los Angeles 256
Libya 70, 107, 326
Louvre meeting 225
Luxembourg 238

Madagascar 106, 172, 326, 338
Mafia 35, 39. 411, 436
malaria 71, 74, 75, 91, 308, 309, 391,
  420
Malaysia 58, 149, 173, 178, 200,
  222, 246, 258, 301, 304, 318, 321,
  326, 434
malnutrition 144, 243, 341, 401
Mamlukes 57, 58
Manchester 90
Manchuria 107, 118
masculinity 280, 281, 283, 286, 287,
  288, 304, 306
Marco Polo 58
markets
  danger 122
  failure 22, 40, 41, 193, 350, 352
  forces 130, 176, 310, 323, 383
  importance 22–3, 82
  influence on states 133–5
  political origins 18–19, 425–8
Marshall Plan 124, 130, 219, 404
Martin, Lisa 455

Marx, Karl 12, 24, 25, 27, 42, 93,
  403, 407
Marxism 13, 24–8, 37, 69, 108, 284,
  348, 375, 452
  see also critical theory, dependency,
    Lenin, neo-Gramscian approaches
McDonald's 204
McMaster Univeristy 43
McMichael, Philip 134, 236, 277, 323
Meadows, Dennis and Donella 359
Mediterranean 55, 57, 58, 60, 62, 63,
  64, 75, 109
mercantilism 13, 17, 18, 27, 49, 154
  see also economic nationalism
MERCOSUR 137, 141, 180, 465
methodology 12, 30–7, 41, 45, 382,
  452, 456
Mexico 129, 134, 199, 236, 247, 263,
  269, 278, 293, 308, 321, 384, 437,
  442
  15th century 61–2, 71, 73, 86
  debt crisis 234–7
  financial crisis 245–6, 386
  structural adjustment 328
Microsoft 138, 268
Middle East 57–8, 60, 63, 64, 70,
  160, 197, 200, 237, 266, 289, 302,
  332, 337
Mies, Maria 284
migration 54, 71, 83, 86, 95, 102,
  264–7, 268, 270, 300, 444
military industrial complex 408, 409
Millennium Development Goals 44,
  295, 296, 308, 309, 382
Mill, John Stuart 93
Ming dynasty 59
modernization theory 316–7
monetary autonomy 222–3, 238
money
  debasement 65
  origins 64–8
  regional currencies 237–41
  reserve currency 241–3
  utility 65
  see also international monetary
    system
Mongols 55, 58
Monopoly Capital 13
Monsanto 434

Montreal   247
Moody's   253
most favoured nation   1164, 465
Motorola   212
Movemento sem Terra   278
Mozambique   106, 172, 326, 338
Multi-Fibre Agreement   166, 174, 269
Multilateral Agreement on Investment
    176, 215, 271, 438
multilateralism   129, 136, 164, 169,
    178, 410
multinational corporations   *see*
    transnational corporations
mutual assured destruction   126
Myrdal, Gunnar   324

Nanjing   59
nationalism   *see* economic nationalism
NATO   125, 126, 130, 409, 429
naval power   59, 69, 85, 93, 103, 261,
    403
Nazis   121, 123
Ndebele   107
neo-Gramscian approaches   3, 24, 47,
    377
neoliberalism   125, 205, 327–31, 384
Netherlands   62, 131, 238
    see also Holland
New Deal   123
New England   74
New International Economic Order 2 6,
    132, 204, 325, 329, 340, 485
New Political Economy   458, 460
new wars   411, 412
New York   41, 80, 97, 128, 229, 256,
    413
New Zealand   70, 80, 125, 173, 178,
    282
Newfoundland   74
newly industrializing countries   161,
    143, 246, 263, 275, 277, 318–20,
    341, 385
Nicaragua   326, 338
Nike   209, 439
nineteenth century   87–111
    compared with 21st   111
Nixon shock   224
Nobel Prize   231, 244, 388, 441
Non-Aligned Movement   132, 325

non-discrimination   161, 164
non-governmental organizations   27,
    47, 137–8, 294, 436, 438
    and development 329, 350
    and environment   349
    and WTO   181, 182, 390
    see also civic associations
non-tariff barriers   161, 162, 163,
    166, 169, 173, 464
North American Free Trade Agreement
    46, 137, 141, 144, 179, 180, 236,
    245, 276, 277, 278, 465
North–South conflict   2, 339–42
Nye, Joseph   27, 40

Observer   38
Ohlin, Bertil   152
oil   40, 129, 132, 188, 230, 232,
    238, 241, 242, 356, 362, 412,
    426
    crisis   13, 130, 161, 229, 233–4,
    315, 318, 322, 324, 327
Organization of Petroleum Exporting
    Countries   229, 233
official development assistance   465
    see also economic aid
offshore   134–5, 194, 196, 197, 208,
    213, 247, 270, 426, 437
    see also export processing zones
opium   79, 80, 81, 106, 114
Organisation for Economic Co-
    operation and Development
    (OECD)   137, 153, 160, 161,
    176, 221, 271, 427, 432
Organisation for European Economic
    Co-operation   221
Ottoman Empire   57–8, 60, 63, 69
outsourcing   196, 201, 270–1, 305
ownership location investment model
    191
*Oxford Handbook of Political
    Economy*   12
Oxford University   38

Pacific Fur Treaty   356
Pakistan   149, 171, 172, 173, 200,
    274, 282, 326
Palan, Ronen   261
Panama   91, 239, 326

pandemic 420–2
see also disease
Paraguay 172, 173, 326, 465
patents *see* intellectual property rights
patriarchy 49, 260, 284, 306
Paulson, Henry 393
Pax Britannica
balance of power 102, 492–4
free trade 100–02
gold standard 96–9
inaccuracy of term 104–6
see also imperialism, industrial
revolution
peace 13, 117, 127, 131, 136, 140,
251, 410, 412, 415, 417, 422, 429,
435–6
and labour 275–8
and liberalism 23, 46, 118, 144,
218, 403, 406–7
see also Pax Britanicca, security
peacekeeping 127, 136, 410
Peasant Movement of the Philippines
278
peasants 115, 122, 156, 259, 268,
275, 278, 300
Penrose, Edith 188
pensions 244, 245, 251, 266, 393
Peoples' Global Action 278
Persian Gulf 57, 60
wars 140
see also Iraq
personal services 290, 301
Peru 61, 71, 173, 321, 326
Peterson, Spike 280
pharmaceuticals 176, 374, 389, 391
companies 47, 175, 176, 309, 390,
434
Philippines 70, 73, 107, 131, 174, 235,
269, 278, 301, 302, 318, 326, 391
Phillips, Nicola 458, 459
Plaza meeting 225
Polanyi, Karl 41, 92, 98, 122, 434
Political Economy 12–13
Political Science 11–12
Poor Law reform 92
Porter, Tony 435, 449
portfolio investment 186–7, 465
Portugal 59, 63, 69, 70, 71, 73, 74,
75, 106, 108, 238, 310

positive-sum game 21, 151
post-colonial 14, 310, 416
post-Fordism 203
post-structuralism 17, 378–9, 455
poverty 15, 36, 76, 110, 143, 144,
206, 265, 266, 283, 285, 287, 290,
296, 307, 308, 309, 310, 315, 318,
334, 341, 342, 343, 360, 366, 385,
413, 416
and global governance 440–2
anti-poverty movement 336, 445–6
causes 26, 54, 127, 316–17, 322,
328, 401
extreme 1, 296, 308, 331, 341
gendered 298–300, 306
reduction 251, 271, 311, 326, 327,
330, 333, 336–9, 365, 415
see also economic development,
growth, inequality
power
and feminism 283, 285–6
state 15, 18, 19, 154, 254, 271,
427, 435, 456
structural 26, 38, 39, 208, 253,
254, 432
power politics *see* economic
nationalism
Prebisch, Raul 328
prediction 16–17
Princeton University 39
Woodrow Wilson School 123
private authority 434–5
privatization 211, 236, 328, 381,
384, 433, 448
process and production methods
369–70
product cycle 191, 204
production 184–216
1400–1800 82–3
19th century 112
globalization 194–201
post-1945 141
see also division of labour, industrial
revolution, transnational
corporations
prostitution *see* sex trade
protectionism 165, 189, 225, 273,
439, 440
agricultural 165, 173–4

protectionism (*cont.*)
  costs of   152, 153
  defined   148
  explanations for   32, 161, 322
  forms of   161–2, 163
  new   161, 163, 166, 169
  persistence   203
  textiles   174–5
  see also economic nationalism
public goods   10, 32
public policy   11, 32, 108, 212, 265,
    409
  and gender   292–8

quotas   105, 148, 162, 164, 169, 173,
    175, 483

race   256, 281, 301, 458, 460, 465
  racism   76, 110, 114
race to the bottom   368–9
Radice, Hugo   166
railroads   66, 88, 91, 95, 112, 187,
    404
rationalist approaches   44, 287, 377
rational choice   32–436–7, 41, 453
Reader, Melvin   310, 341
Reagan, Ronald   225, 384
realism   13, 20, 27, 118, 248
  see also economic nationalism
recession   11, 44, 121, 158, 223, 226,
    243, 245, 447
  inter-war   121
  1970s   130 , 161, 169, 233–4, 324,
    327
  2008   1, 157, 163, 183, 187, 251,
    331, 391
reciprocity   111, 161, 164, 322
Red Sea   57, 58, 60
Redclift, Michael   351
regional currencies   *see* money
regionalism   46, 125, 178–9, 452, 457
regimes   24, 38, 40–1, 43–4, 45, 102,
    130, 136, 179, 215, 323, 350,
    376
  and global governance   431–4, 448,
    457
regulation   148, 162, 168, 177, 199,
    215, 369, 439
  environmental   138, 362, 370

financial   252, 254, 393–4, 428,
    446–7
  see also global governance, regimes
Regulation School   263
religions   58, 113
  see also Christianity, Islam
remittances   264–6, 302, 330, 411,
    412
Reno, Janet   303
reproductive economy   300–3
research and development   *see*
    technology
Rhodes, Cecil   107
Ricardo, David   12, 21, 27, 101–2,
    151, 259, 457
Rio Principles on Environment and
    Development   438–9
Rio Tinto   439
Rise of the West   25, 53–4
Robinson, Ronald   110
Roosevelt, F. D. R.   123
Rostow, W.W.   316
Royal Dutch Shell   185, 188, 439
rubber   70, 104–5, 106
Rubin, Robert   393
Ruggie, John   3, 43–5, 129, 163, 452
Runyan, A.   280
Rupert, Mark   276, 378
Russia   102, 104, 127, 129, 137, 185,
    232, 246, 303
  and global governance   247, 371,
    427
  imperialism   107
  industrial revolution   88, 95, 98
  revolution   108, 122, 275, 404
  see also Soviet Union
Rwanda   127, 172, 326, 338, 410,
    412

sanctions   118, 135, 152, 417–18,
    431
Saudi Arabia   126, 247, 282, 314, 326
Sauvy, Alfred   314
Scholte, Jan Aart   425
scientific knowledge   94, 376, 436
  and environment   358–9
Scotland   75, 303, 414
Seattle   168, 182, 447
Second World   23, 117, 119, 124

security
  and political economy 402–8
  1400–1800 85
  19th century 102–6, 114
  Cold War 126–7, 408–10
  critical 400
  crime 419–20
  definitions 398–402
  dilemma 399, 408
  disease 420–2
  economic statecraft 415–8
  food 155, 300, 401, 402
  human 287, 400–2, 413, 415, 419,
    420, 421, 437, 459
  inter-war 117–9
  national 155, 399–400, 404,
    405–7, 408, 409, 410, 418, 430,
    421, 426
  post-Cold War 127–8, 410–14
Seers, Dudley 311
Sen, Amartya 441
Senegal 75, 300, 326, 338
September 11 (9/11) 128, 413, 414
services *see* General Agreement on
  Trade in Services
Seveso 360
sex trade 301, 437
Sicily 75
Sierra Leone 172, 312, 338, 326, 412
silver 63, 64, 65, 70, 73, 79, 76, 80,
  81, 84, 86
Singapore 132, 168, 178, 200, 207,
  209, 232, 243, 263, 318, 319, 321,
  422
Sklair, Leslie 265
slavery 4, 42, 55, 75–8, 82, 258, 260,
  301, 375
Smith, Adam 9, 12, 21, 27, 93, 151,
  258–9, 262, 403, 457, 458
smoking 373
Smoot–Hawley Tariff 124
social forces 26, 28, 42, 122, 183,
  396
social movements 28, 46, 47, 181,
  277, 304, 376, 436, 438
social science 9–10
Soros, George 228
South Africa 53, 126, 150, 173, 235,
  240, 256, 257, 314, 326

and global governance 171, 247,
  427, 434
South Korea 134, 247, 271, 277
  and Asian financial crisis 15, 198,
    246, 432
  industrialization 127, 132, 283,
    318
  sovereign wealth funds 232
sovereignty 21, 67, 79, 176, 188, 206,
  214, 215, 323, 206, 214, 216, 323,
  399, 411, 416, 448, 459
Soviet Union 109, 125, 220, 229,
  385, 416, 429
  and Cold War 126–7, 389, 408–10
Spain 68, 69, 70, 71, 73, 74, 106,
  110, 238, 310
special and differential treatment
  176–7
speculation 16, 228, 238, 248, 294
Spero, Joan 3
spices 58, 59, 62, 63, 70, 82
Sri Lanka 200, 235, 302, 326
Standard & Poor's 253
Stanford University 39
state
  and global governance 425–8
  and globalization 45–6
  authoritarian 127, 134, 277, 320,
    407, 416, 427
  communist 122, 125, 220, 366
  'competition' 133, 213
  defined 69
  developmental 50, 134, 318–20,
    322, 383, 384, 386
  Fascist 118, 122
  liberal 92–3, 94, 114, 115, 122,
    123, 142, 273
  offshore 134–5
  origins 66–9
  national capitalism 323–6
  national security 408, 410, 426
  neoliberalism 327–31
  transformation 133–5
  welfare 199, 277, 426, 428, 437
  see also embedded liberalism,
    neoliberalism, Washington
    Consensus
state–firm relations 39, 193, 210,
  214, 216, 434

iety relations   50, 453, 426
:ntury   115
/ar   122–3
see also embedded liberalism,
   neoliberalism, world order
State Power and World Markets   456
States and Markets   38
statist   *see* economic nationalism
steamships   91
Steans, Jill   280
Stiglitz, Joseph   447
stock market   35, 64, 139, 187, 197,
   230, 244, 245, 251, 385, 394, 447
Stockholm Conference   356, 357
Stopford, John   434
strategic trade theory   95, 155
Strange, Susan   3, 27, 29, 38–9, 65,
   191, 243, 374, 434, 452
structure and agency debate   49, 292,
   453
Students Against Sweatshops   273–4
Structural Adjustment Programmes
   (SAPs)   133, 136, 211, 220, 248,
   259, 327, 332, 384, 386
   content   234, 466
   gendered impact   299–300
   Mexico   328, 235
   resistance to   276, 329
   see also Washington Consensus
subsidy   148, 153, 157, 163, 168, 173,
   174, 234, 300, 430, 463
Suez Crisis   131
sugar   53, 62, 70, 74, 75, 76, 79, 84,
   261, 302
sustainable development   308, 309,
   344, 346, 350, 353, 357, 359, 363,
   364–8
   defined   330
sweatshops   256, 273
Sweden   282, 291
Sweezy, Paul   13
Syria   1126, 172, 326

Taiwan   107, 127, 132, 175, 209,
   214, 246, 263, 268, 269, 318, 319,
   385
tariffs   44, 148, 161 169
   defined   466
   rates of selected countries   149

reductions within GATT   141,
   165–6
   tariffication   173
Taylor, Fredrick   262
Taylor, Ian   458, 459
Taylorism   262
tax   74, 79, 93, 135, 148, 192, 199,
   206, 207, 214, 224, 243 263, 384,
   394, 411, 412
   avoidance   212, 213, 215, 419
   currency   16, 244
   cuts   225, 226
   havens   154, 261
tea   80
technocentrism   *see* environment
technology
   bubble   139, 249
   change   194–5, 204, 263–4, 380,
      382, 434
   defined   375
   diffusion   138, 152–3, 195, 207,
      207, 264, 387–9
   military   20, 75, 140
   see also industrial revolution,
      information revolution, naval
      power
'Tequila effect'   245
terror   105, 106, 437
terrorism   128, 143, 402, 413–14,
   417, 419, 420
textiles   161, 166, 200, 256, 260, 261,
   263, 269
   pre-1900   64, 73, 75, 95
Thailand   80, 173, 178, 214, 235,
   301, 318, 321, 326, 330, 421
   financial crisis   14, 222, 246
theory
   contemporary GPE   451–61
   explanation for diversity   28–9
   methods   30–7
   purpose   16–17
   traditional IPE   14–29
Tilly, Charles   68
Third World
   and Cold War   126–7
   coalition   325, 327, 329, 340–2
   use of term   314–5
   see also developing countries,
      development

Thomas, Caroline   310, 341, 443
Thomas, George   137
Trilateral Commission   365
Tobin Tax   244
Torrey Canyon disaster   360
Touré, Samori   108
Toyota   185, 189, 202, 173, 179, 192
Toyotaism   263
trade
   1400–1800   82
   19th-century free trade   100–2,
      111–12
   concentration in OECD   159
   defined   147
   developing countries   170–7
   environmental degradation   368–70
   gains from   20, 152, 153, 154, 157,
      273
   growth of   157–61, 168–9
   institutional arrangements   163–9
   intra-firm   152, 160
   intra-industry   152, 158, 159–60,
      211
   post-1945   141
   terms of trade   324–5
   see also comparative advantage,
      protectionism, regionalism, WTO
Trade-Related Intellectual Property
   Rights   167, 168, 175–6, 389–91
   see also intellectual property rights
Trade-Related Investment Measures
   167, 176
trade unions   90, 93, 134, 135, 268,
   272, 274, 279, 297, 304, 381, 436
transnational class   14, 24
   see also globalizing elites
transnational corporations
   communications   196
   costs and benefits   191–3, 204–9
   defined   186–9
   developing countries   189–90
   finance   196–8
   Fordism   201–3
   global governance   434–5, 438–40
   globalization of   194–201
   growth theories   190–3
   labour   214
   largest   185–6
   mergers   203–45

organizational principles   201–4
political factors   199–201
regulating   214–5
significance   184–5
structure   189
technological change   194–5
see also corporations, division of
   labour, state–firm relations
transnational networks   277
see also civil society, non-
   governmental organizations
transparency   16, 163, 164, 169, 180,
   248, 386, 405, 438, 439
transportation   62, 76, 94, 191, 264,
   301, 334, 441
Treaty Banning Nuclear Weapons Tests
   in the Atmosphere, Outer Space
   and Under Water   356
triangular trade   74–8, 280
Triffin, Robert   219
Triffin dilemma   223, 466
Truman, Harry S.   164, 342
Turkey   57, 80, 102, 149, 247

underdevelopment   26, 316, 317, 324,
   402
unemployment   1, 13, 36, 98, 120–1,
   123, 161, 169, 214, 222, 223, 251,
   254, 263, 277, 289, 328, 380
unequal exchange perspective   155–6
United Nations Development Fund for
   Women   296
Unilever   188
Union Carbide   360
United Kingdom   1, 39, 43, 110, 129,
   130, 160, 166, 212, 225, 226, 229,
   230, 252, 302, 303, 335, 405, 433,
   464
   see also Britain
United Nations   43, 44, 94, 136–6
   General Assembly   44, 132, 292,
      293, 295, 296, 340, 358, 422
   Millennium Declaration   298, 308,
      441
   Security Council   128, 135, 422
   see also global compact, *individual
      agencies*
United Nations Children's Fund   136,
   434

United Nations Conference on Environment and Development 344, 356, 357, 357
United Nations Conference on the Human Environment 356, 357
United Nations Conference on Trade and Development 132, 324, 340, 382
United Nations Development Programme 313, 402
United Nations Environment Programme 356, 357
United Nations High Commissioner for Refugees 136
United States
  and Argentina 248–9
  and Asian financial crisis 15–16, 221, 386, 432
  and Bretton Woods 218–19
  and China 242
  and Cold War 126–7, 132, 135–6, 408–9
  and Cuba 107, 126, 272
  and debt crisis 233–4
  and decolonization 131
  and dollar 240–3
  and global governance 390
  and Iraq 128–9, 226, 233
  and IMS 218–9
  and ITO 164
  and Kyoto 128, 349, 371
  and Mexican financial crisis 245–6
  and post-1945 credit system 218–20
  and spread of TNCs 199
  civil war 95, 104, 114, 409
  drug trade 80, 437
  Federal Reserve 224, 225, 233, 244, 249, 250, 251, 392
  financial crisis 249–52, 391–6
  hegemony 38, 40, 42, 44, 45, 132, 194, 275, 378
  hyperpower 126, 128
  imperialism 70, 107, 129
  industrialization 95
  inter-war period 123–4
  isolationism 124
  labour 275–6, 277
  oil crisis 233
  post-1945 order 126–30
  protectionism 18, 43, 102, 153–5, 225
  Second World War 124–5
  structural power 39
  reliance on foreign domestics 303
  Treasury 15, 242, 250, 384, 393
  see also Washington Consensus
Uruguay 165, 173, 326
Uruguay Round 166, 170, 171, 173, 175

Van Heedren, Auret 200
Vancouver 182
Vasco da Gama 78
Venezuela 234, 312, 321, 326
Venice 62, 63, 68, 80
Vernon, Raymond 188, 190
Viagra 411
Vienna 57, 58, 63
Vietnam 70, 106, 122, 126, 130, 131, 132, 270, 278, 301, 404
Voices of the Poor 307
voluntary export restraints 148, 162, 169

Wall Street 15, 244, 249, 380, 395
Wal-Mart 185, 205, 269
Washington Consensus 150, 221, 234, 328–9, 330, 383–7, 443
war and sex trade 301
  and state formation 68–9
  new wars 411–2
  see also security, World Wars
Warwick University 38
Wealth and Poverty of Nations 53
Weber, Max 41, 69
West
  advantages in warfare 74, 79, 85, 107, 108, 140
  economic system 108, 129–30
  rise of 25, 53, 54
Whitworth, Sandra 283, 285
Wilkins, Mira 188
Williams, Eric 77
Williamson, John 384, 385
Wilson, Woodrow 23, 27, 117, 123
wisdom 234, 359, 375, 386, 387, 396
Wolfe, Eric 459

Wolfensohn, James 277, 422
Wolfowitz, Paul 297, 335, 283, 320
Wollstonecraft, Mary 24, 93
women
  and colonialism 79
  Decade for 293, 294, 296
  employment trends 288–91
  in factories 87, 90, 113, 269, 290, 304–5
  world conferences 293, 294
  see also division of labour, feminism, gender, work
Women's International Democratic Federation 292
work
  domestic 302–3
  unpaid 257, 261, 287, 300, 306
  sex trade 301, 457
  see also division of labour, slavery
working class 25, 93, 98, 112, 115, 128, 298
  see also class, labour
World Bank 307, 326, 382, 409, 422, 466
  and basic needs 325
  and democracy 335–6
  and environment 361–2, 365
  and global governance 247, 326, 340, 342, 432, 433
  and women 231, 297–8, 283, 318
  criticism of 138, 332–4
  debt relief 236, 337–8
  inspection panel 336
  International Development Association 331–2
  liberal policies 276, 319
  origins 124, 130
  primary roles 331
  social safety net 277, 333
  structure 331
  structural adjustment lending 327, 332, 341
  see also Washington Consensus
World Conference for Women 293
World Development Report 336

World Economic Forum 265, 282
World Health Organization 136, 297, 421, 434
world order 26, 43–4, 50, 410, 425, 429, 454
  see also global governance
World Social Forum 265, 396
World Trade Organization
  agreements 167
  and democracy 181
  and environment 357–61
  compared with GATT 166–8
  Doha Declaration/Round 168, 170, 171, 173, 176, 177, 183, 341, 390
  developing countries 170–7
  deep integration 166
  dispute settlement 14, 136, 141, 162, 164, 166, 167, 168, 175, 177, 431, 434
  global governance 431, 434, 439, 440, 446, 448
  labour rights 273, 439
  legitimacy 180–2
  origins 166–7, 148, 157
  regionalism 177–80
  Seattle ministerial 168, 182, 447
  see also General Agreement on Trade in Services, process and production methods, Trade-Related Intellectual Property Rights, Trade-Related Investment Measures
world views 84, 114, 375, 379, 396–7
World Wars 68, 117–24
  lessons of 124–5

Yahoo! 140, 268
York University 41
Yugoslavia 127, 132

Zambia 313, 326, 328
Zanzibar 58
Zapatistas 278
Zheng He 59
zero-sum game 17, 21, 26, 72, 151
Zulus 108